Books by Victor Alexandrov

KHRUSHCHEV OF THE UKRAINE: A BIOGRAPHY
THE KREMLIN: NERVE-CENTRE OF RUSSIAN HISTORY
THE TUKHACHEVSKY AFFAIR
THE END OF THE ROMANOVS

Fiction

JOURNEY THROUGH CHAOS

THE END OF THE ROMANOVS

Victor Alexandrov

The End
of the
Romanovs

Translated by
WILLIAM SUTCLIFFE

LITTLE, BROWN AND COMPANY • BOSTON • TORONTO

CONTENTS

8 CONTENTS

FOREWORD

THIS work is the result of years of research which has involved checking and re-checking a whole mass of contradictory material.

In presenting it to the public the author has had two main preoccupations: firstly, to situate in its historical and psychological context an event which captured the imagination of the Western world and played a major part in the political evolution of one of the greatest countries; and, secondly, to make a vivid reconstruction of the tragedy of an illustrious family and provide a setting for an amazing series of photographs that were found by pure chance.

There is no need to labour the point that these pages, written more than forty-five years after the Ekaterinburg drama, are as removed as it is possible to be today from the venomous climate within which the first accounts were published. With the lapse of time the historian can keep aloof from political contamination and give the true (if not the probable) its rightful place between tearful hagiography and partisan pamphleteering.

The photographs illustrating this book are made up exclusively of prints and enlargements made from a collection of negatives now in the possession of the author. In the suitcases of the examining magistrate, Sokolov, were found two wooden boxes full of photostats . . . How they landed up on an auctioneer's table in the Salle Drouot in Paris is a mystery: and how Prince Orlov, a relation of the imperial family, kept them for more than thirty years in a strongbox on his Fontainebleau property is one of the secrets of the emigration. (Have we not good reason to think that Empress Alexandra Feodorovna's index finger—one of Sokolov's macabre finds in a mineshaft near Ekaterinburg—today reposes in a bottle of formol in the basement of a New York bank?)

Among the important people who made an inventory of the contents of the two boxes of documents and recognised their outstanding interest were the Grand Duke Andrew Vladimirovitch and W. Maklakov, a prominent politician under the old regime and then a historian.

The two last chapters of this book are based on revelations made by a former Soviet diplomat whose desire to remain anonymous the author must respect. These revelations corroborate information gathered from other sources and fill in the gaps in the puzzle of the Romanov affair—hitherto left with loose ends. For these reasons we have thought them worthy of our trust and capable of throwing final light on what has hitherto been called the mystery of Ekaterinburg.

V.A.

PART ONE
THE ROMANOV
DOSSIER

*

comprising family portraits taken
by Tsar Nicholas II and evidence
on the assassination collected by
Nicholas Sokolov

HISTORICAL OUTLINE

TSAR NICHOLAS II was an ardent photographer. Both before and after the Revolution, he took many family snap-shots, little realising that he was in fact making a valuable addition to the scanty documentary evidence of the last tragic chapter of his family's history.

The negatives of these photographs were lost for more than forty years. Then they were discovered, by the author of this book, along with photographs of other documents assembled shortly after the execution at Ekaterinburg by the White Army examining magistrate. Here, briefly, is the history of the documents contained in this 'dossier'.

July 17, 1918 The Romanovs are executed in the Ipatiev house at Ekaterinburg and the remains buried in a wood near Koptiaki.

July 30, 1918 The White Army arrives in Ekaterinburg. The Ipatiev house is searched and a number of relics found. Some Red Army men, minor participants in the crime, are arrested.

February 5, 1919 Admiral Kolchak, White Army Commander, hands over the files on the Romanov case to Nicholas Sokolov, the examining magistrate. Sokolov goes over the case from the very beginning, questioning all the witnesses and photographing hundreds of documents.

July 1919 to March 1920 Final victory of the Bolshevik troops. Sokolov flies towards the east, jealously guarding his treasure—particularly three small cases, two of which contain photographic plates, and the third some relics—among them a woman's finger, belonging almost certainly to the former Empress. He makes his way to Omsk and then on to Chita and Harbin.

March 19, 1920   Sokolov is aided by General Janin, Head of the French Military Mission. Janin agrees to look after the three small cases and these are placed on board his special train and accompany him back to France.

November 23, 1924   Nicholas Sokolov dies of a heart attack in the small French town of Salbris. He has published his memoirs and the results of his enquiry and has said that he was never able to recover his cases.

December 1930   Xavier de Hautecloque reveals in the *Petit Journal* that General Janin handed the cases, on the orders of the Grand Duke Nicholas Nicholaievitch, uncle of the murdered Tsar, to M. de Giers, former Tsarist Ambassador in Rome. But their whereabouts remain as mysterious as ever. M. de Giers asserts that the question is a State secret . . .

October 9, 1950   While examining various objects which are being auctioned at the Salle Drouot in Paris, M. I. Gurvich, a Russian antique dealer and bibliophile, finds on a table in Room 12 a number of Russian objects, paintings and mementoes. They belong to the Orlov estate. Prince N. Orlov, a descendant of one of the three Orlov brothers (favourites of Catherine the Great), has died in exile on his estate at Fontainebleau. The inscriptions on the articles are hardly readable, but appear to be personal belongings of the Prince of little value. Nevertheless, M. Gurvich buys them all and stores them in his attic. The cases are once more forgotten . . .

April 1962

Victor Alexandrov, while searching for manuscripts of Catherine the Great, pays a visit to M. Gurvich. In the Val-de-Grâce district of Paris he is taken to the attic and shown a mass of documents. In a corner is a large painting of a man in evening dress, with a black patch over one eye, who seems to stand guard over a pile of cases and paintings.

'That's His Excellency, Prince Orlov, and that's the treasure of the Orlovs,' M. Gurvich jokes. The two men begin to search about in a heap of old junk and suddenly they come across the cases, filled with photographic plates packed among heaps of broken glass. On the lid, inside the cases, written on an old yellow label in Russian Cyrillics is the name: 'N. Sokolov . . .'

FOOTNOTE

Since then Victor Alexandrov has ascertained that the third case, the one containing the relics of the Imperial Russian family, had been placed by Prince Orlov and M. de Giers, well before the war, in a Paris bank. In 1943, thinking that the valuables of the Russian Imperial family were in it, the German Gestapo, on the strength of information received, had the safe in the bank opened. At the end of hostilities, leading representatives of the Russian emigrant community—among them the

Grand Duke Andrew, the historian Maklakov and a number of Generals who had
formed a 'Committee for the safe-keeping
of the Imperial relics'—searched vainly
throughout Paris trying to trace this last
case. An unconfirmed rumour, circulating
among the old Russian *émigré* taxi-drivers in
Paris, has it that the relics are now securely
stored in the safe of a Manhattan Bank.

1 Nicholas Sokolov, the examining magistrate appointed by Admiral
Kolchak to investigate the assassination of the Romanovs. Before
he joined the White Army, he crossed the Urals into Siberia making a perilous journey on foot, disguised as a countryman. Having
arrived safely, he had this photograph taken against a suitably
rustic back-cloth.

2 Sokolov's two wooden boxes in which were stored the results of
his painstaking investigation. They passed out of his possession and
out of sight, until they were discovered by chance by the author.

THE EVIDENCE

3 Tsarevitch Alexis Nicholaievitch (aged 8) in 1912 with his sailor guard Derevenko. It was his guard's duty to make sure that he came to no harm at all; even a scratch could lead to the death of the haemophilic prince. Derevenko was to disown his masters at the time of the revolution, when he was succeeded by another sailor, Nagorny, who followed the Imperial family into captivity.

4 Grand Duchess Olga was 18 years old when the Tsar took this photograph of her in medieval Russian costume. She is wearing a *kokochnik*, a tiara encrusted with pearls. Signed by Olga, the photograph was found pinned to the wall of the Tsar's room in Ekaterinburg after the assassination.

5 On the eve of the outbreak of war in 1914, Rasputin writes to the Tsar, warning him that the war will be the end of Russia and the Romanovs. "Calamity, great sorrow, gloom, not the slightest ray of light, a sea of tears which cannot be measured, and blood", writes the monk. "There are no words to describe this terror . . . the punishment of God is terrible when He takes away the intelligence. It is the beginning of the end. You, O Tsar, Father of our people, do not allow the mad to triumph and lead you to your doom, you and your people . . . Russia? One can truly think that, throughout the centuries, there has never been such a sad martyr, completely drowned in blood. Great is her ruin, boundless her affliction".

The letter, wrongly spelt and unpunctuated, is headed by the bishop's cross which Rasputin used to put at the top of his letters.

6 A signed photograph of the Tsarina dated 1915 (not taken by the Tsar, but found at Ekaterinburg after the assassination). She is wearing the cross given her by Rasputin, and in the background is a bunch of the yellow roses which she had sent her every day from the Crimea.

7 Crowds greeted the royal train when the Tsar returned from a visit to general headquarters at Mokylev. The royal photographer took a picture of his still loyal subjects.

8 The first winter of the war. The Tsarevitch, in the park at Tsarskoye-Selo, wears the uniform of a sailor from the Imperial yacht "Standard".

10   Another photograph found at Ekaterinburg but dating from the
time at Tsarskoye-Selo. This is the Tsar's daughter Marie, most beautiful of the Grand Duchesses.

9   On the terrace at Tsarskoye-Selo, Grand Duchesses Tatiana and
Olga are photographed in the dress uniform of the Uhlans and of a
colonel of Hussars.

11 The Tsarina, a German educated in England, conducted her correspondence in English. This letter, written to her lady in waiting, the Countess Hendrikova, a week after the murder of Rasputin in 1916 is full of mystical foreboding. "She sees the bright lights wonder and the little shining tree is the reflection of the heavenly stars and light. Cannot write more, heart too heavy. God bless you and a loving kiss from an old, old woman." The footnote reads: "Besides everything, try for a moment to realise what it is to know a friend in *daily*, hourly danger of also being foully murdered. But God is all mercy."

12 A revealing photograph, probably taken by one of the Tsar's daughters. Seated in a familiar attitude on her husband's gold encrusted desk, the Tsarina appears to be dictating her wishes (and, therefore, those of Rasputin) to the weak-willed Tsar. The photograph was taken in 1916.

13 and 14 It is June 1917. The Tsar has abdicated, but the Imperial family still live in luxury at Tsarskoye-Selo. On a footbridge in the park, the Tsarevitch plays with his King Charles spaniel, Jimmy – or with a tame thrush.

15 The ex-Tsar maintained his passion for photography to the end. This photograph of his daughters Olga and Marie must have been one of the last he took at Tsarskoye-Selo.

16 The last day before the exile begins, as recorded in the schoolboy diary of the Tsarevitch. It was found by the White Army investigators at the home of the Red guard Letemin. The left-hand page dated July 31st (August 13th new style) says:

"During the day I bathed. The water was 18° C. I threw Olga fully clothed into the lake from the gang plank. We said goodbye to people who are not coming with us. We showed Isa, Nastinka (Anastasia), Trina (Catherine), papa's room. We have not slept all night and watched how the fusiliers loaded the baggage. We drank some tea with mama at midnight.

"Kerensky came and said we must leave at 6.10 in the morning. Have left Tsarskoyé-Selo by train. As soon as the train got under way, went to bed and slept until lunch. Had lunch, drank some tea and took the meal with mama in her compartment. Played at cards."

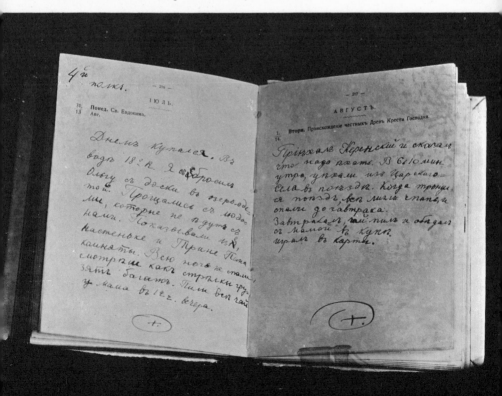

17 The heir to the throne is celebrating his thirteenth birthday. His father marks the occasion by taking a snap of him in front of the train which is taking them into exile.

The royal exiles left the train and transferred to a small steamboat which took them up the River Taura. It seems to have been an agreeable journey. General Kobylinsky, placed in charge of the operation by Kerensky, treated the prisoners with every consideration, and allowed them ashore for a picnic, the occasion on which the next four photographs were taken.

18 Nicholas and Alexandra.

21 Left to right: Anastasia, Colonel Kobylinsky, Jimmy the spaniel, Alexis, Nicholas, Tatiana, Olga, Marie.

19 Nicholas with his daughters Tatiana and Olga. Kobylinsky stands beside the camera with his back turned.

20 Alexandra. She took her jewels into exile with her – note the pearl necklace.

22 The house of exile. Here, in Government House in the newly named Liberty Street, the Imperial family stayed from August 1917 until they were removed to Ekaterinburg in April 1918. At first they lived in considerable comfort and, until the overthrow of the Kerensky government, were allowed full use of their fortune. Opposite their residence stood the large house of the merchant Kornilov where the forty members of the Imperial suite were lodged.

23 The ex-Tsarina's bedroom, with family photographs on the wall.

24 The ex-Tsar's study.

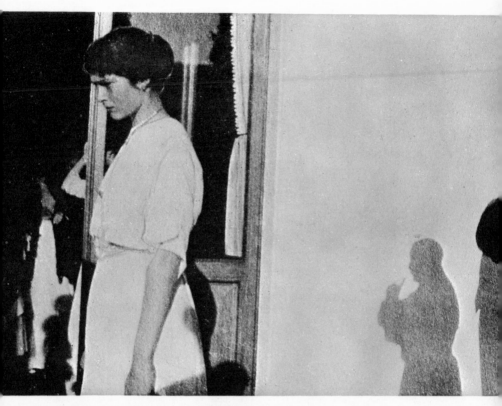

26 A remarkable photograph of Marie taken at Tobolsk. By a trick
of the lighting, the shadow of her father taking the photograph is
thrown on the wall.

25 The Imperial sisters still wear their fashionable summer dresses
from Paris. Tatiana and Olga pose for their father on the balcony at
Tobolsk.

27 When he was not taking photographs, the ex-Tsar spent a good deal of time at Tobolsk sawing wood.

28 Alexis passed the time at archery. With him in the courtyard at Tobolsk is Lieutenant Malichev, a pro-Monarchist officer in the Guards.

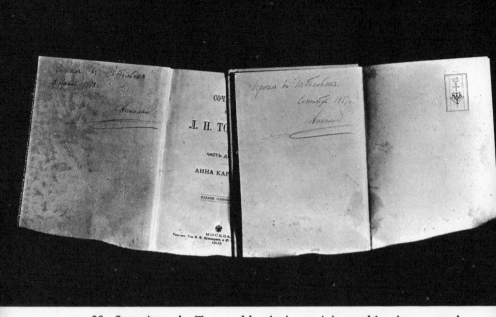

29 Sometimes the Tsar read books in captivity, and he always noted the date. "Read at Tobolsk February 1918", he noted on the fly-leaf of *Anna Karenina*, and in the book on the right (title unknown), "Read at Tobolsk September 1917".

30 For Christmas, the ex-Tsarina gave Olga a diary which she inscribed: "Wishing my darling Olga every blessing for Christmas 1917. With a kiss from your old Mama. Tobolsk." Photographed with it is a sheet headed "Prayer" which reads as follows:

Send us, oh Lord, patience
in these times of violence and gloom
that we may support the persecution of the people
and the tortures of our executioners.

Give us strength, oh just Lord
to forgive the next cruelty,
welcome with softness the
heavy blood-stained cross.

And in these days of seditious trouble
when the enemy assails us
help us to bear the disgrace and transgressions
(last line illegible).

31 The Siberian winter is setting in. Olga and Tatiana photographed in the courtyard of their prison-house.

32 This snap, taken by the ex-Tsar on the verandah, seems to typify the boredom of imprisonment. With the three royal sisters is the maid Anna Demidova, who was to share their fate at Ekaterinburg.

33 It is the Spring of 1918. The Kerensky regime has been over-thrown, and now that the Bolshevik grip is tightening over Siberia, the life of the prisoners has become harder. The new, harder conditions seem to be exemplified in this study of (left to right) Marie, Alexis, Tatiana and Olga.

34 The last day at Tobolsk. The ex-Tsar is sent to Ekaterinburg with his wife and one daughter. The other daughters stay behind to accompany Alexis, when he recovers from a severe attack of bronchitis. Before he left, the Tsar photographed his sick son.

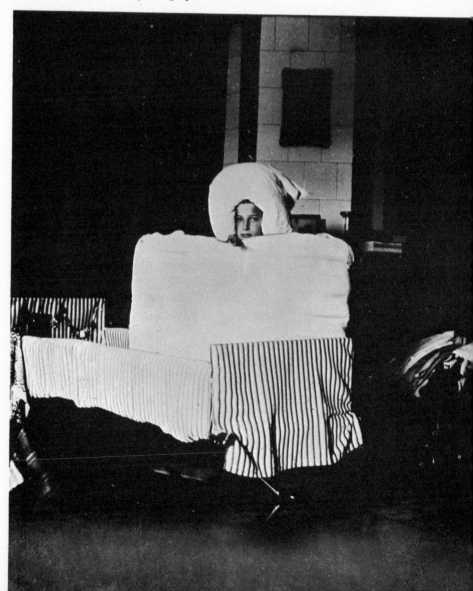

35 The Romanovs left Tobolsk in the custody of the mysterious Vassili Vassilievitch Yacovlev, whose role in the tragic story is examined at length in Part II. Whatever his intentions may have been, he was compelled to hand over the prisoners to the Ural Soviet at Ekaterinburg, and their doom was sealed. Yacovlev was given this receipt for the prisoners. It is on headed paper of the Workers' and Peasants' Soviet of the Ural Region, dated April 30, 1918, and signed Beloborodov, countersigned Didkovsky. It states:

"I the undersigned Chairman of the Executive Committee of the Workers' and Peasants' Soviet of the Ural Region, Alexander Georgevitch Beloborodov have received from Commissar Vassili Vassilievitch of the Central Executive of all the Russias delivery from Tobolsk of 1.) the ex-Tsar Nicolas Romanov, 2.) the ex-Tsarina Alexandra Feodorovna Romanov, 3.) the ex-Grand Duchess Marie Nicholaievna Romanov for detention under surveillance in the town of Ekaterinburg."

36 The Ipatiev house in Ekaterinburg where the prisoners spent their last months. The arched windows of the basement, where they were executed, can be seen.

...КРЕСТЬЯНСКОЕ
...ТЕЛЬСТВО
...ДЕРАТИВНОЙ РЕСПУБЛИКИ
...ОВЕТОВ.

...И ОБЛАСТНОЙ СОВЕТ
...АБОЧИХ,
...СКИХ и СОЛДАТСКИХ
...ПУТАТОВ.

...ЗИДИУМ
...1

Екатеринбургъ, 30 апреля 191...

Росписка

1918 года, апреля 30 дня, я нижеподписавшийся Председатель Уральского Областного Совета Раб., Кр. и солд. депутатов Александр Георгиевич Белобородов получил от комиссара Всероссийского Центрального Исполнительного Комитета Василия Васильевича Яковлева доставленных им из г. Тобольска 1) бывшаго царя Николая Александровича Романова, 2) бывшую царицу Александру Федоровну Романову и 3) дочь, вел. княжну Марию Николаевну Романову, для содержания их под стражей в г. Екатеринбурге.

А. Белобородов

Чл. Обл. Исполн. Комитета
Д. Дидковский

37 One end of the large bedroom on the first floor where the ex-Tsar, Tsarina and Tsarevitch slept.

40 This room in the Ipatiev house is believed to have been photographed by the Whites after the departure of the Reds, with the ashes of personal effects of the Romanovs still on the floor.

38 They had these pictures on the wall. A painting of the Tsar and a sketch of the Tsarevitch, both by the Russian painter Serov; photos of Alexis with his mother and with friends; and portraits of Marie and Tatiana.

39 For some reason, the Tsarina's calendar on the wall had stayed at June 23rd.

41 The last picture of Anastasia taken by her father only a few weeks before their death.

42 The last, simple bedroom of the Grand Duchesses. Here they are said to have read THE GOLOVIEV FAMILY, a novel of bitter realism by Saltykov.

46 The room in the basement where the shooting took place, with its damaged wall and floor.

43 A mysterious telegram signed "Boar". Addressed to the French Consul in Moscow a week before the execution of the Romanovs, it seems to indicate that the Allied governments were worried about their fate. It reads: "Arrived Ekaterinburg staying at present British Consulate. Rumours about Romanovs false."

44 Telegram 4640. This message dated July 8, from Beloborodov, Chairman of the Ural Soviet, was addressed to the Military Commander of the area among others. It asked for reliable men to replace the existing guard of a special train – presumably intended to take the Romanovs somewhere else. No such guard was provided.

45 Confirmation that the whole family have been executed goes to the Kremlin in code. Dated July 17, a few hours after the execution, it is signed by Beloborodov. Decoded after the war by the French at Sokolov's request, it reads: "Tell Sverdlov that the whole Romanov family met the same fate as Nicholas. Officially it should be pretended that they died during their evacuation."

47 After the execution, at 2 a.m., a truck came through this doorway of the house bearing the bodies of the Romanovs.

48 A curious side-light. This quotation from Heine was scrawled on the wall of the Ipatiev house, probably within a few hours of the murder. There is reason to believe that it was done by an Austrian prisoner called Rudolf Lacher, who acted as orderly to Commissar Yurovsky. It reads: *"Belsatzar ward in selbiger Nacht/Von seiner Knechten umgebracht."* (On the same night Belshazzar was assassinated by his slaves).

49 The opening of the mine-shaft in the clearing called "Four Brothers" in the forest of Koptiaki, selected for the burial place of the Romanovs. Here the bodies were first burned and then thrown in.

50 Bullets dug out of the wall.

54 The investigation is under way. The Red Army has (temporarily) abandoned the area. The Whites have taken over. Soldiers, aided by peasants, start excavations at the mine-shaft.

51 Gold bracelets belonging to the Princesses and Dr. Botkin's pince-nez found in the mine.

52 Topazes and diamonds found in the ashes.

53 An embroidered handkerchief belonging to Anastasia, found in a copse.

55 Telegram 4852. Interesting confirmation that Molotov must have been in the know about the assassination is contained in this telegram sent on the same day to Zinoviev in Moscow from the committee of the Regional Soviet. It reads: "The Soviet of the Ural Region considers it absolutely necessary for comrade Khostina to carry out this work and to keep her in Ural region. Inform Molotov and also Bogolepov." Molotov was about to be appointed director of Ural and Siberian affairs.

56 An undelivered note for Anna Viroubova, found among the Tsarina's papers at Ekaterinburg. It could have been written there or in Tobolsk. It refers to "the solitude and heart-ache. But she taught you how to bear your troubles and trials and God won't forsake you". The fragment goes on to "recommend you not to wear the image as the ring is not firm – put it on a ribbon with another image on the other side and place it in your Bible."

57 Some of the property recovered by the White Army in the Ipatiev house. Note the Tsarina's big umbrella (top left), a bottle of verbena water just below it, and the Tsarevitch's toy soldiers.

58 Part of Nicholas II's collection of ikons which he took into exile.

59 Medals and pious souvenirs found among the effects, including the gold chain with a crucifix habitually worn by the Tsarina.

60 This group is said to contain the "executioners of the Grand Dukes" at Alapaievsk. Some of them were certainly concerned in the Ekaterinburg execution too—notably Piotr Voikov in the middle, with the paper on his knees. He later became USSR ambassador in Warsaw where he was assassinated. He left an unpublished account of the execution which is quoted in Part 2.

61 A group of important Bolsheviks of the Ural Soviet photographed in front of the Hotel Amerika in Ekaterinburg. Four of the mounted men in the back row have been identified – Mechtchiarin (on left), then Tchebriakov, Khlechtchov and Bambaiev. In the front row, Beloborodov is on the extreme left (marked with cross) and next to him are believed to be Voikov and Yurovsky.

62 The investigator. Nicholas Sokolov, in the forest of Koptiaki, where the Romanovs were buried. He was the first man to make a complete investigation, and to photograph the evidence.

PART TWO

THE END OF
THE ROMANOVS

*

Chapter I

THE KREMLIN CHIMES

*

MAY 23, 1918, had been a very lively day at the Kremlin. The chimes in the Spassky Tower had just been reorganised, following plans drawn up by the mathematician and organist, Gabrilovitch. Henceforward they were not to peal out the pompous rhythms of *Bozhe tsaria khrani* every quarter of an hour, but the throbbing notes of the *Internationale*.

But the clock was either reluctant to abandon its age-long habits or else had some mechanical fault, for at times it confused the battle-cry of the proletariat with the musty music of old feudal Russia. It would start off with 'Rise up, you prisoners of hunger' and then innocently proceed with *'Tsarstvui na strakh vragam'* ('Rule by inspiring your enemies with fear')—the favourite words of the 'perfect autocrat', Emperor Nicholas I, the man who hanged those first Russian revolutionaries, the Decembrists, from the walls of the Peter and Paul Fortress in 1825.

An amused group of listeners was enjoying the carillon's pranks. Standing near the main part of the building called after the Knights, and opposite the famous Potiechny Palace, they pointed to the Spassky Tower and laughed. Their hilarious outbursts, coupled with their self-confidence, marked them out as notabilities of the new regime recently installed behind the crenellated walls of the fortress.

The little man in the worker's cap was Lenin himself. The one wearing the *dachniki*[1] was Leo Trotsky. He had recently resigned his post as *narkom* at the Ministry of Foreign Affairs (March 13, 1918) so as to be appointed *narkom* for the Armies—*narkom* being short for *narodny komissar*, or People's Commissar, the title Lenin gave his Ministers.

Also with them were Sverdlov, chairman of the Republic of Soviets; Dzershinsky, head of the Cheka; Zinoviev, hot from

1. The white cap worn in summer by people at their country villas or *dachas*.

his fief in Petrograd; Kamenev, leader of the Moscow Soviet; and a handful of other dignitaries of the New Russia.

Lunatcharsky, *narkom* of Public Instruction and well known for his passion for music, produced explosions of hilarity at each false note. But Lenin's laughter was the loudest of all. This 'born statesman' (as Wells called him), now at the outset of his career as leader of the Russia of the Soviets—a Russia dismembered by the treaty of Brest-Litovsk and almost reduced to the old frontiers of Muscovy under Ivan III—could seem almost childish on occasion. Trotsky, his companion of the time, wrote later in his autobiography:

> It was very easy to make Lenin laugh, especially when he was tired. He laughed like a child. This man, the most virile of them all, had a childish side. It was a delight to see him assuming comical postures as he tried in vain to repress a laughing fit while presiding over the *Sovnarkom* [the Council of the People's Commissars]. On his convulsed face his Mongol cheekbones seemed to become more and more prominent. . . .

When the crowd of Soviet dignitaries dispersed, Lenin and Trotsky could be seen entering the walls of the Kremlin together. On such walks they talked over important problems that had to be solved that same evening at the meeting of the *Sovnarkom*. Lenin was well aware that if Trotsky's views were not in accord with his own there would be deadlock for lack of the necessary majority.[1]

On that particular day Trotsky, the 'Carnot of the Russian Revolution', made no effort to conciliate the head of the Government. It was obvious that the two men were already thinking of the battle of words in which they would soon indulge. The night session of May 23 was to be marked in Kremlin annals by an exhausting political discussion concerning the fate of citizen Nicholas Romanov, the ex-Tsar, and his family.

Leo Trotsky's normally expressive face seemed to be covered by a mask of fatigue. Stamping his feet on the wooden paving, Lenin cast an ironical glance at two massive bronzes squatting

---

1. When Trotsky was in disagreement with Lenin on important questions discussed at the *Sovnarkom* these were resolved by vote. Often the majority of the *narkoms* voted with Trotsky against Lenin.

on their pediments—the famous Tsar-Cannon and the no less famous Tsar-Bell.

'Leo Davidovitch, just look at those two survivals of the barbarism of the past. It would need superhuman strength to shake up this apathetic country and rid it of dead weights such as these.'[1]

To which Trotsky answered, in the stirring voice that he had cultivated in the course of innumerable harangues:

'In this place and at this moment others besides ourselves might murmur Hamlet's words: "The time is out of joint, O cursed spite / That ever I was born to set it right!"[2] We are the soldiers and leaders of the world revolution, Vladimir Ilytch.[3] It is the great tragedy of history that this revolution should have been born in the most backward country of Europe!'

Lenin nodded.

'I agree, Leo Davidovitch. Our revolution is a mere sketch, a mere embryo of world revolution. Russia will serve as its spring-board. But if this spring-board disappeared before other countries had launched their own revolutions, then the continuity would be broken. Our task is precisely to adapt the Russian Revolution to world revolution. It was with this in view that we signed the objectionable treaty of Brest-Litovsk. And that is why I put the question of the Romanovs' fate before the *Sovnarkom* this morning—as well as at the request of the Wilhelmstrasse. I shall bring it up again this evening at the meeting of the Central Committee. . . . I hope you will give me your support.'

Trotsky answered sharply:

'No, Vladimir Ilytch, never. As chairman of the first Workers' Soviet in the 1905 revolution, I signed the manifesto of the "permanent revolution". We must respect that manifesto. I shall stand by my signature, and shan't embark on a fraudulent bankruptcy under the eyes of the foreign proletariat. . . . We swore in 1905 that we would disavow the Tsar's loans. Today the Soviet Government has issued an official communiqué, through me, that those loans are annulled. We swore that the

1. Tsar-Cannon and Tsar-Bell were popular nicknames for two striking curiosities of the Kremlin: an enormous cannon which had never fired a shot, and a gigantic but cracked bell that had never emitted a sound.
2. Quoted by Trotsky in the chapter of his autobiography devoted to his talks with Lenin.
3. Lenin called himself by his real name, Vladimir Ilytch Ulianov.

crowned criminal who ordered the terrible shootings of January 9, 1905, would be judged and led to the scaffold. My signature stands on that historic document. The "Bloody Sunday" of the first revolution shall be avenged.'

Lenin's lip curled in sarcasm.

'There were other signatures besides yours on that manifesto,' he said. 'The priest Gapon's, and Krustalev-Nossar's—the petty lawyer who was your co-chairman on the St Petersburg Soviet. What has happened to them?'

Trotsky stiffened under the affront, and Lenin went on:

'The priest, Gapon, was hanged by the revolutionary workers as an *agent provocateur* and spy of the *Okhrana* [Tsarist police]. Krustalev-Nossar became a *kadet*[1] and was shot by the Poltava Cheka in the March of that year.'

The two leaders of the Russian Revolution paused. Lenin took hold of Trotsky's arm and tried to convince him:

'I would like to dispose of the Romanov dossier without raising a huge cloud of dust. If you persist in your romantic attitude I shall submit to the majority decision. Our Marxist comrades are being dangerously seduced by romanticism. Only, I tell you again, you are making a mistake. It would be more diplomatic, I mean more realistic, to accept my proposal, which is also the one put forward by your friend, Adolf Abramovitch.[2] I propose that we meet at your house this evening, Leo Davidovitch, and discuss this question yet again. Comrades Sverdlov, Zinoviev, Tziuriupa, Dzershinsky, Kamenev, Pokrovsky, Kalinin, Krassin, Kollontaï, Muralov, Ivan Smirnov, Bukharin, Krestinsky and Serebriakov will be there.'

Trotsky seemed satisfied and agreed. All he asked was that three other Bolshevik dignitaries, Petrovsky, Rykov and Lomov, should also attend the meeting.

On May 23, 1918, it was already being whispered around Moscow that very grave events were about to take place.

It was known that Joffé had recently been summoned to the

1. Member of Miliukov's *konstitutional-demokrat* party (hence the abbreviation K.D., or *kadet*).

2. A. A. Joffé, at that time a member of the central committee of the Party, and Soviet Ambassador in Berlin. He committed suicide in 1927, leaving a letter for Trotsky in which, while maintaining his friendship, he reproached him for lack of realism and excessive political romanticism.

Wilhelmstrasse by Minister von Kühlmann. This leading German dipomat had told the Soviet Ambassador that his Government was keeping a wary eye on the revolt of Czechoslovak contingents in Siberia which were breaking their way through towards Europe. These troops, under the command of Generals Syrovy and Gaïda and composed of deserters and prisoners of war still wearing Austrian uniform and with an odd assortment of arms, refused to submit to the 'shameful' peace of Brest-Litovsk. Lending support to the detachments of the White Cossack General Dutov in the Urals, and to those of the 'Ufa Constituent Assembly', these Czech legionaries were showing every intention of marching on Moscow in the company of the Whites. Their aim was to re-establish a second front on which the Germans would fight themselves out.

Kühlmann had warned Joffé that if the Czechs and White Guards succeeded in occupying the area between the Urals and the Volga the German High Command would order its troops to press on towards Orcha and Pskov and lay siege to Moscow. In addition the German High Command would give effective aid to Krassnov, the ataman of the Don Cossacks, in view of a push towards the Volga.

A few hours after the interview between Joffé and Kühlmann the German military attaché in Moscow had called on Trotsky to confirm Kühlmann's ultimatum. He had warned Trotsky that the German High Command would move its troops stationed in the Ukraine and at Rostov on the Don in the direction of Tsaritzin.[1] These troops would advance up the Volga so as to seal off the banks of the great river. Generals Ludendorff and Hoffmann[2] were terrified at the prospect of a re-establishment of an anti-German front in the east, and decided, at whatever cost, to

1. It is worth noting that the plan for this movement towards Tsaritzin (subsequently Stalingrad, and today Volgograd) was carefully preserved in the German archives and was to serve in 1941–2 when the Wehrmacht was working out 'Operation Stalingrad'. Knowledge of this plan as worked out by Generals Ludendorff and Hoffmann (known in the USSR thanks to the archives of the Supreme War Council presided over by Trotsky from 1918 to 1924) was, in August 1942, to assist Zhukov and the Soviet Generals to guess the strategic direction of the German offensive launched along the Don.

2. It was in fact General Hoffmann who led the German delegation at Brest-Litovsk. His *Diktat* imposed on the Soviet delegation was much harder than the *Diktat* of Versailles.

forestall the reconstitution of this front. On the eve of their decisive offensive in Champagne the Germans did not want to be hamstrung in Russia.

In his report to Lenin and Trotsky, Joffé added that the ex-Tsarina's brother, Prince of Hesse-Darmstadt, had called on him on two separate occasions. This aristocrat had courteously offered his services to the Soviet representative as mediator between Moscow and Berlin so as to save Soviet Russia from the burden of total occupation by the Germans. Moreover, the Prince had offered to negotiate a suspension of the Soviet war debt, amounting to three hundred million gold roubles, as fixed by the treaty of Brest-Litovsk, or at least to reduce it. Naturally the release of the Tsarina Alexandra and her family would be the ultimate proof of the Kremlin's 'goodwill'.

Behind this move there appeared the very clear intention of getting ex-Tsar Nicholas, once free of his jailors, to accept and endorse the peace of Brest-Litovsk. The Prince of Hesse-Darmstadt had let Joffé understand that this offer was unofficial and was to be kept secret.

Night had fallen on the domes and pointed towers of the Kremlin. Two sailors armed to the teeth were on duty at the entrance of the former state apartments.

In 1918 these apartments had been divided into a number of flats. Lenin and Trotsky had taken up residence there, protected by carefully selected members of the Cheka. A long corridor separated the flats of the two men, in the middle of which was a large room that served as communal refectory for the leaders of the Russian Revolution. The food was appalling. There was very little fresh meat, but a good deal of salted meat that stank of brine. The flour and semolina were mixed with sand. A disagreeable smell came from the kitchen where the famous *vobla* soup (dried fish broth) was prepared, the dish that was the mainstay of a starving people and its leaders.

'But', as Trotsky says in his memoirs, 'we had a great abundance of red caviar, as the export of this product had ceased as a result of the blockade imposed on us by the Allies. . . . I am not alone in recalling the early years of the Russian Revolution as being symbolically tinted by the red of salmon caviar.'

Towards nine in the evening, Trotsky's study, a large room

well over twenty feet long, filled up with members of the Central Committee: Lenin, Trotsky, Sverdlov, Krestinsky, Serebriakov and the rest. One of the refectory tables was placed in the middle of the room, and two uncomfortable oak benches bent under the weight of the revolutionary dignitaries. At the very moment when the historic session was about to begin, two other members of the Central Committee arrived, back from Stockholm: Krassin and Radek.

Trotsky, delegated by Lenin to take the chair, asked Lenin to speak. The head of the Government gave a brief account of the position and described what had been said about the Romanovs in the conversations between Joffé and the Prince of Hesse-Darmstadt. Those proposals, he concluded, could in due course serve as a basis for a compromise. Prudent and circumspect as ever, Lenin avoided making a long speech. His aim was to get *carte blanche* so that, when the opportune moment came, he could make a swift decision—as he had done with the signing of the Brest-Litovsk treaty. It was his well-known tactics of *peredychka* ('wait and see'). On being cross-questioned by a number of Central Committee members, Lenin added that his plan of campaign had so far proved just and realistic. And, throwing a sidelong glance at Trotsky, he added:

'Comrade Trotsky is in a position to tell you about the visit of the French General Lavergne who came to see me on behalf of Marshal Foch. The General told me that the French Government would from now onwards give due consideration to the *Diktat* of Brest-Litovsk which we were unable to avoid. He pointed out that his Government wanted above all to help us reorganise our army. Should we request it, officers of the French mission in Russia would be put at comrade Trotsky's disposal as experts and technical advisers. Comrade Trotsky could also tell you about the visit of another French officer, the Marquis de Lubersac. This officer, also speaking in the name of the French High Command, suggests that we should sign a secret agreement bearing on technical military collaboration.'[1]

Discussion broke out. Leonid Krassin was the only member to give whole-hearted support to Lenin's proposal. Zinoviev and Kamenev gave it doubtful support.

1. Trotsky mentions this visit in his autobiography, but refers to the Marquis de Lubersac as 'the one-eyed officer of the Deuxième Bureau'.

Suddenly up jumped a little man with a face framed in a frill beard. He was wearing a well-cut suit and had been sitting on Lenin's left like an old companion-in-arms (he had travelled across Germany with Lenin in the famous 'sealed coach'). His horn-rimmed spectacles jumped on his bony nose as he leapt to Vladimir Ilytch's defence.

Karl Bernardovitch Radek easily reduced the barrackers to silence. The news he had brought from Stockholm seemed important and contributed a new element to the general discussion.

'My Swedish informers have learned quite recently that close interest in the butcher Nicholas is being shown on the other side of the Atlantic. If the City of London is mainly concerned with hundreds of chests of gold buried in the cellars of Kazan, Wall Street is showing a . . . philanthropic interest in a thoroughly devalued personality—the head of the Romanovs. The National City Bank is financing the operation; the broker is Thomas Masaryk, a professor who is preparing to install himself as liberator in the Hradshin in Prague. He is the man who has remote control over the Czech legions in Siberia, and he it is who has promised his associates to free the ex-Tsar. All the deliveries made on credit to the Whites by "Remington Arms" and the "Metallic Cartridge Union" depend on the speed with which the Czechs approach Ekaterinburg and the prisoners in the Ipatiev house. Three million gold dollars, machine-guns and rifles in exchange for the puppet Nikolachka is how Masaryk sees the piece of business proposed to him by the American bankers.'

Careful to produce the desired effect, Radek paused for breath before continuing in a low voice:

'The American cargo boat *Thomas*, which is expected at Vladivostok in mid-July, is due to land fourteen thousand rifles, as well, doubtless, as embarking the Romanov family. . . .'

An uproar followed this announcement and cries of 'Action, action' broke out from all sides.

Then it was Bukharin's turn to speak. His stentorian tones exploded in Lenin's face:

'We covered ourselves with shame when we signed the treaty of Brest-Litovsk. Then it could at least be argued that we did it out of necessity to save the Revolution. But why should we be humiliated again over the Romanovs?'

'The same necessity could be argued again,' Lenin countered.

'What you want to do is follow the Russian proverb which says that the *muzhik* [peasant] never makes the sign of the cross until he hears the thunder. That is, when it's too late.'

Bukharin raged:

'I wouldn't make the sign of the cross either before thunder or after it, Vladimir Ilytch. . . . We can't hand Nicholas Romanov over to the Kaiser. We can't pardon the butcher of "Bloody Sunday" as the Kerenskyites wanted to do. We must carry through our duty to the end; the crowned butcher must be judged, condemned and executed.'

By the small hours Lenin's tactics of *peredychka* had not succeeded in rallying the votes. Nevertheless there was no longer any question in the Kremlin of giving Nicholas Romanov a resounding trial, as Bukharin proposed.[1]

And it was left to Karl Radek to make a positive resolution. 'In a word this business ought to be settled at the level of the local revolutionary tribunals. Let's leave our excellent comrade, Jacob Sverdlov, a true son of the Urals, to solve the problem, in collaboration with the Workers', Peasants' and Red Guards' Soviet at Ekaterinburg.'

And knocking out his pipe on the meeting-table before refilling and relighting it, Radek concluded:

'I propose that we interrupt the discussion and draw up the preliminary resolution.'

'What preliminary resolution?' Lenin put in. 'We can't waste precious time in verbiage. We're no longer at the Smolny Institute in Petrograd, but at the Kremlin. We're the Government of Proletarian Russia.'

'Good. I put comrade Lenin's suggestion to the vote,' said Trotsky.

The proposal obtained two votes only,[2] which were by way of abstention. The rest voted against Lenin.

'Your turn to speak, comrade Bukharin,' said Trotsky in an expressionless voice.

1. According to the Soviet archives the trial of the ex-Tsar was planned for July 1918. The Kremlin's special envoy to the Ekaterinburg Soviet, War Commissar F. I. Golochtchekin was instructed to prepare the files for this trial.
2. The minutes of this meeting are preserved in the archives of the Central Committee at the Kremlin, dossier 'The peace of Brest-Litovsk', series 75, folder 1, devoted to the liquidation of Nicholas II and his family.

Bukharin rose. He held in his hands a piece of paper covered with jerky handwriting.

'Here we are,' he said, and read rapidly without raising his voice. The phrases, such as 'solemn oath', 'crowned blood-drinker', 'dawn of world revolution rising on the Augean stables of the Russian Tsars', formed the basic theme for the eloquence of the author of *The ABC of Communism*. He was said to have the brain of a Netchaëv (the famous nihilist terrorist) and the soul of a Tolstoy.

'There, that's the end of what I have to read,' said Bukharin as he folded the paper and put it back in his pocket. Then he began to speak:

'As the outcome of all that, we consider it our duty to the Russian people and to world revolution, whose greatest enemy was Tsarism, to demand that Nicholas Romanov should be brought before a special tribunal in public session so that he may be punished for his crimes and errors.'

Bukharin's proposal was put to the vote. Lenin and Krassin voted against. Zinoviev, Krestinsky and Rykov abstained.

Chapter II

THE RED URALS

*

E VENTS did not permit the Kremlin to carry out Bukharin's proposal. The Czechoslovak revolt had rapidly and unexpectedly gained ground. Though the lands to the east of the Volga had not been wholly occupied by the Czechoslovaks and the forces of the Ufa Directory, the lines of communication with Ekaterinburg were almost entirely cut. The Tsar and his family were prisoners of the Ural Regional Soviet, but their jailors themselves were more often than not cut off from Moscow by the front line. Only telegraphic communication remained relatively practicable, thanks to the lines running north-east and along the Tiumen–Perm–Kotlas railway.

It was early July 1918. In the office of Alexander Georgievitch Beloborodov, president of the Ural Regional Soviet, a meeting of Soviet dignitaries had been sitting without interruption. Fifteen people were gathered round a table in a large room formerly used for receptions by the Tsarist authorities of the region. From the windows the winding line of the river Isseth could be seen, on which Ekaterinburg was situated. To the north-west the flames from the blast-furnaces of the Zlokazov factory were hidden in a black fog.

The gruff and taciturn A. G. Beloborodov was presiding over the meeting. A former clerk from Perm, and now the first 'Red Governor General' of the Ural industrial region, he listened inattentively to his comrades' speeches, for his thoughts were in Perm with his wife and children. His native town was threatened by the civil war.

On the smoky horizon a few hundred versts from Ekaterinburg could be heard the dull thunder of gunfire. Troops were moving up to the front day and night. From the whole of the Ural province and Siberia, trains were arriving with their cargoes of men, munitions and supplies. The noise of cannon had rocked the whole region. Both Reds and Whites were recruiting throughout the countryside, and anger and hatred clouded the recruits' eyes so that they saw nothing but blood. The hour of vengeance had come. All who could shoulder a gun left their women and piled into the goods trains—some with a white armband on their way to join up with Dutov and Kolchak, others with a red armband on their way to join General Tukhachevsky Frunze and his partisans.

Squatting in the goods trains, these thousands of ill-equipped *muzhiks*, drunk with battle and following in the wake of agitators from the great cities, whistled nostalgic tunes or bawled obscene songs. They slept, ate, and killed their fleas. NCOs marched the length of the convoys, giving contradictory orders and rousing soldiers heavy with sleep, stumbling, shouting, cursing one another. Men ran in disorder, then quickly got into formation and hurled themselves in pursuit of the enemy. One after another great fires broke out, lighting up the whole vast horizon of Siberia. Rockets cut their way through the sky; shells howled as they sought their objectives.

Red partisans, worn out, collapsed in the woods and slept, only to start again the next day, blood-soaked and urged on by hatred. During that summer of 1918 the fratricidal war spread from the plains of the Ukraine, invaded by the Kaiser's armies, to the frontiers of the Urals, where a new White army had formed and was sweeping like an avalanche westwards, capturing thousands of prisoners, huge stores of provisions, arms and equipment. This army was well organised and the Czechs were its spearhead.

It was an appalling war. Important prisoners were shot on the spot. Their families were shot. Women were raped. Dutov, ataman of the Cossacks, was the cruellest of the White Generals.

The civil war was also a secret war. In Kazan, Simbirsk and Perm, as in Ekaterinburg, Tsarist officers were living in hiding or in disguise. According to reports reaching the formidable Dzershinsky in the Kremlin, more than five thousand of these officers were awaiting the moment when they would emerge from their hiding places.[1]

1. During the early months of 1918 general officers from the Military Academy at Petrograd Headquarters were arriving in dozens at Ekaterinburg. The leaders of the counter revolution in the Ural region were grouped round the Tsarist officer Rostovzeff and Essaul Mamkin.

These White *Chouans* of the Russian Revolution had a twofold aim: to free the captive Tsar and his family, and to lay hands on the fabulous treasure of the Imperial Bank which had been evacuated in 1915 from Petrograd to Kazan. The Reds had a firm hold over the ten thousand boxes crammed with gold pieces and the hundreds of sacks filled with foreign bank-notes. The Cheka kept watch day and night over the cellars of the Bank of Kazan where the hoard was locked up.

As it happened, Kazan was also a centre of the monarchists and sworn enemies of Bolshevism. A Serbian battalion of deserters from the Austro-Hungarian army had been lying low there for months. Its leader, Major Blagotitch, had managed to obtain a slender subsidy from Allied military representatives. Like all southern Slavs he had a gift for intrigue, and he combined his conspiratorial abilities with a sincere devotion to Nicholas II as an orthodox monarch. It was the Serbs, the Montenegrins and the Moslems of the Caucasus who were the last-ditchers of the Romanov cause.

In early July 1918 Blagotitch sent an emissary to Simbirsk. He had been informed that a meeting had been arranged there for all representatives of clandestine opinion. The town was also Lenin's birthplace.

On July 6 a Serbian lieutenant disguised as a pedlar made his way at nightfall into the corridors of the Troitsko Spasski Hotel in Simbirsk. He knocked three times on a certain door and gave the password 'Kazan'. A voice answered with another agreed word, 'Moskva'. On the door was a poster: 'Join the Red Army.' It closed quickly behind the newcomer.

Eight men were sitting on divans. A military map, torn at the corners, was spread out on the carpet.

Colonel Kappel, wearing a former officer's uniform from which all insignia of rank had been removed, was presiding over the clandestine meeting. This energetic soldier was soon to become aide to Admiral Kolchak, and, after the latter's death, leader of the last White units in Siberia. On his right was a former local politician, the engineer Lebediev of the *kadet* party; on his left a man in civilian clothes which ill-concealed his military bearing —Captain Stepanov, sent to Simbirsk by a secret monarchist committee of the Ural province. Next to Stepanov was a former member of the Duma, Fortunatov, representing the middle classes of Simbirsk; while opposite Kappel a young captain in Red Army uniform, Grigoriev, was expressing sensational views:

'Moscow and the towns on the Volga will rise up as one man against the traitors who signed the peace of Brest-Litovsk. The left-wing of the Social-Revolutionaries will also fight against the Germans. We are ready to put the military delegates from Moscow, Vatsetis and Latzis, under arrest. In exchange for our good intentions regarding you, comrade Savinkov requests your neutrality.'

The two men looked one another in the eye and then shook hands with a certain embarrassment.

Hardly had Grigoriev left the room when Captain Stepanov burst out with joy:

'*Zametchatielno!* [Splendid!] The comrades are devouring each other like a pack of wolves. It is up to us to make good the occasion, and we must begin by getting the Tsar and his family out of the clutches of the Cheka.'

'Excellent programme,' said Colonel Kappel. 'We shall have to organise their escape in the ten days following the Social-Revolutionary revolt. But who have you in mind to carry it out?'

'In spite of various betrayals, we still hold the trumps: a squadron of determined young *fronteviki* (seasoned at the front) officers, and the emissary of the Czechoslovak forces, Captain Schveits of the first regiment of Hussars, who is in hiding with one of our people at Ekaterinburg.'

'Is that all?'

'Of course not. There is the man who gives us a weekly report of what is going on, and who has provided us with the plans of the Ipatiev house drawn up by the Emperor himself. I mean Dr Derevenko, the Tsarevitch's second official doctor, and the key man in the escape project.'

By dawn next morning, when Stepanov left Simbirsk for Ekaterinburg, he had finalised all the details of the operations with Kappel. The Ipatiev house would be stormed by night; the Red Guards would be distracted by uprisings at Perm and other centres near Ekaterinburg; a commando of officers would escort the fugitives to a secret refuge; and a big Czech offensive would take place around July 15.

Unfortunately for himself and the other conspirators, Stepanov was arrested on the station platform when he arrived at Ekaterinburg at dawn on July 13. At dawn a few weeks before, the 10th of June, a group of White officers under the command of Captain Rostovzeff had tried to sieze Ekaterinburg. Their aim was to overthrow the local Soviet government and set the Imperial family free. But, warned by the Ekaterinburg Cheka, a detachment of armed horse and Red Guards under the command of P. Ermakov reached Verkh-Issetsk. By the evening of June 10 the revolt had been checked and the town fell once more into the hands of the Red Guards. Rostovzeff was shot. Dozens of White officers were detained in the Cheka prison at Ekaterinburg. The Cheka and its spies had not been idle.

Beloborodov's colleague, Miasnikov, had just arrived from Perm. He was to leave for Moscow via Kotlas, Vologda and Yaroslavl with a personal report for Lenin, and had promised to take Beloborodov's wife and family with him. Beloborodov was awaiting his arrival so as to fix the arrangements once and for all.[1]

'Come, Sasha, are you asleep? Don't you want to join in the vote?' asked Miasnikov.

Beloborodov pulled himself together. He looked at all the well-known faces: F. I. Golochtchekin, Piotr Voïkov, Yakob Yurovsky, Tchutzkaev, Kabanov, Lepa, Didkovsky, Safarov, Gladunov, Ermakov and Talmatchev.

Safarov was reading the draft minutes of the meeting:

'The Regional Soviet of the Urals refuses categorically to take on the responsibility of transferring Nicholas Romanov in the direction of Moscow, as comrade Bukharin has suggested, and considers it absolutely necessary to liquidate him.

'There is considerable danger of citizen Romanov being used by the Czechoslovaks and the counter-revolutionaries of Ufa and Perm, and this cannot be disregarded. . . . As for the family of the former Tsar and all those who have chosen of their own free will to remain at his disposal, they have opted, by this choice, for their death. They must be liquidated at the same time.[2]

1. Beloborodov's family perished in the course of this journey; a ferry on the river Vytchegda was overloaded and sank.
2. Another person present at the reading of the indictment was Abulov, delegate from the front. His superior officer, R. I. Berzin, front-line commander, had just given the green light to the Ural Soviet for the liquidation of the Romanovs.

'The Regional Soviet also considers it indispensable to execute the former Grand Duke Michael Alexandrovitch and all other Grand Dukes of the former Imperial family who are within its administrative region and might eventually play the part of pretenders in the service of the counter-revolution.

'If, as the comrades of the All-Russian Central Executive Committee maintain, considerations of foreign policy demand absolute secrecy concerning the liquidation of the Grand Duchesses and the ex-Tsarina, who are claimed by their German family, the Regional Soviet of the Urals declares its readiness to organise the execution by the intermediary of its Executive Committee so that it may remain absolutely secret.

'The Regional Executive Committee nominates a *troika* composed of comrades Golochtchekin, Voïkov and Yurovsky charged with directing the operation, and asks for the approval of the Central Executive Committee of Soviets for all the measures above proposed. . . .'[1]

Beloborodov was only half listening. Safarov's voice—he was the son of a Bashkir of the old native nobility of the middle Urals—had a military ring. The Bashkir people had always been involved in the struggle against Tsarism. Their cavalry constituted the loyal core of Pugatchev's partisans, in contrast to the treachery of the Cossacks who handed over Lenin's precursor to Catherine II's executioners.

Safarov, nicknamed 'Georges' in the Bolshevik Party, was a descendant of the great Bashkir national hero, Prince Iulay-bey, Pugatchev's ally. Safarov the Bashkir was wreaking his revenge on the descendants of the German Holstein-Gottorp dynasty for the martyrdom of his dismembered ancestors. And he was avenging their blood in the very town named after the 'lewd Tsarina' (as the poet Pushkin called Catherine II) who, with her husband Peter III, had established the Holstein-Gottorp dynasty in Russia.

The time had come to vote. Standing erect and solemn,

---

1. Minutes published in 1923 in the periodical *Istoria borby uralskogo 'proletariata'*, Sverdlovsk (Ekaterinburg). We should add that on the orders of the Special Revolutionary Military Committee, set up by the All-Russian Central Executive Committee and composed of Podvoisky, Sverdlov, Dzershinsky, etc., the local Soviets had been duly authorised to take all initiatives, however important, in case of an immediate counter-revolutionary threat.

Voïkov asked for 'individual votes with the details of the ballot written into the minutes of the meeting'.

Beloborodov shrugged his shoulders and made a gesture of assent to the meeting's secretary, Nikulin. Safarov's draft was accepted unanimously. A secondary proposal, also made by Safarov, equally found favour. It recommended that the secretary of the Committee of the Ural Regional Communist Party and War Commissar, F. I. Golochtchekin, together with Miasnikov, should be dispatched post-haste to Moscow to obtain endorsement of the decision from the Central Executive Committee of the Soviets. The two envoys were to be back in Ekaterinburg 'not later than July 15'.[1]

When F. R. Golochtchekin got back to Ekaterinburg all the 'technical' measures had been taken for the liquidation of the Tsar, his family and his retainers.

Yurovsky, now in command of the 'house of special assignment', had dismissed the former commander, Avdeiev, and his aide, Moshkin. A platoon of Lithuanians and Magyars, commanded by the Lithuanian Adolf Karlovitch Lepa,[2] had received instructions as to its task.

Piotr Zakharovitch Ermakov,[3] now president of the Cheka and with twenty men at his disposal, had already selected the mineshaft at a place called 'The Four Brothers', and the two clearings nearby, which were to serve for the destruction of the bodies and for the secret stowing of their ashes—the pits contained traces of ice and snow even at the height of summer.

All that now remained was an administrative formality—the organisation of some semblance of a trial—after which Goloch-

---

1. This decision was also published in *Istoria borby uralskogo 'proletariata'*, No. 9 (1923). The number was withdrawn from circulation in 1925 by decision of the Politburo headed by Stalin. The same decision of the Politburo had forbidden Yakob Yurovsky to publish his 'Memoranda concerning the House of Special Assignment' at the State publishers of Sverdlovsk (Ekaterinburg).

2. Lepa had a brilliant subsequent career. He was secretary of the Party at Verny, chief of the staff section of the Central Committee under Molotov, and first secretary at the Soviet Embassy in Warsaw. He was shot during the Great Purge.

3. Ermakov's aides were: Viktor Vaganov, Puzanov (later chairman of the RSFSR) and Alexander Medvediev. The first two were victims of the Great Purge. Medvediev was shot by Kolchak's troops.

tchekin would communicate to Yurovsky and his men the hour of execution.

The scene of this formality was not to be the ancient building of the former Prefecture in which the Executive Committee of the Ural Soviet met, but a simple hotel bedroom, converted into a court-room for the occasion.

Chapter III

THE TRIBUNAL
OF THE HOTEL AMERIKA

*

AN ENORMOUS cloud, black as lead, held the town of
Ekaterinburg in its thrall. On the morning of July 15,
1918, a storm from Siberia had laid its hand on the big
township crouching at the foot of the Ural mountains on the
furthest frontiers of Europe. An east wind set the dust swirling
and enveloped in one and the same atmospheric upheaval the
workers' cottages and the rich homes of the merchants built in
the grandiose style of Alexander III.

On the banks of the river Isseth, rushing along in a yellow
tumultuous flood, the Zlokasov factory, with its cracked brick
walls, was spilling out its workers. A crowd of them, dressed in
rags and with their caps low over their eyes, hurried towards the
centre of the town. Pushing against the wind and the first drops
of rain, they made their way towards the great square of Ekaterinburg, that veritable forum of the Revolution to which each day
brought its crop of speeches and bad news. For the civil-war
front was now only a hundred versts away, and the Whites were
inching nearer and nearer with every hour that passed.

A platoon of Red Guards, carrying long guns and girt with
triple bandoliers of cartridges, guarded the entrance to the
former Prefecture. A great streamer, stretched across the façade
of the seat of the Ural Soviet, proclaimed the need for the workers
of the world to unite.

Young peasants and old women in shawls had already gathered
in front of a hoarding plastered with Bolshevik Party announce-
ments. A man in a loose, embroidered shirt and wearing a soldier's
cap was reading out the text of the latest poster.

'Comrades, it says: "The louse will conquer Socialism or
Socialism will conquer the louse. All into battle against the
louse!" And it's signed Vladimir Ilytch Lenin.'

No sooner had his deep voice died down than a dumpy little man—the blacksmith Kuzma Riabov—pushed his way through the crowd.

'Why are you all goggling in surprise, comrades? The lice are threatening us all. We're all agreed about that. But we in Ekaterinburg are threatened twice over. We have additional lice, giant lice, lice with crowns.'

Riabov pushed back his hair over his bald patch with blackened hands. His thick lips lengthened in a spasm of hatred.

'For centuries the workers of the Ural region have been groaning under the whip and stick wielded by the Tsar's favourites. The Tyrants of Petrograd have reduced us to the condition of beasts. And now the last of the Romanovs, the man responsible for the hell of prisons and factories, is there—only a few steps away. Just over there, on the Voznessensky Prospekt, they are fattening him on *balyk* [sturgeon] and good fresh butter from the convents of the neighbourhood. He is well fed by nuns and priests and couldn't care less about us, I can assure you.'

The blacksmith was a familiar orator and the little crowd pressed round him. He went on:

'Nikolachka is laughing in our faces, comrades. He knows better than anyone that the Whites and Czechs are approaching our town. He is waiting to be released and restored to the throne. And soon the *champala* [the cat o' nine tails] will be at work on our naked backs again. The Revolution is going to the devil. And here you are worrying about lice when the worst vermin of all is in hiding behind the walls of the bourgeois Ipatiev's house.'

And Kuzma Riabov pointed a bony finger towards an imposing piece of masonry standing squarely on an eminence at the corner of Ascension Street and Voznessensky Prospekt.

'The residence of the Romanovs,' clucked a *baba* (a toothless old woman).

From the main square one could see, beyond the Prospekt, the little streets descending towards the clear lake that occupied the centre of Ekaterinburg. The Ipatiev house had been built on an incline so that on one side the ground floor looked out on to the street and on the other dug into the hillside like a basement. The entry to the upper storey was on the Voznessensky Prospekt side. The flight of stone steps was connected with the street pavement by a ramp which the previous occupant, the rich merchant Ipatiev, had built for carriages. A double palisade, constructed a few weeks earlier by order of the Ural Soviet, surrounded the building and prevented it from being overlooked.

Suddenly an avalanche of hailstones broke over Ekaterinburg. Caught in the violence of the elements the knot of people scattered in all directions. The women took refuge in porches, the men set out for a nearby shelter. On finding himself alone the blacksmith left the square and walked boldly through the storm as far as a three-storeyed building in the Voznessensky Prospekt. An inscription in gold lettering, HOTEL AMERIKA, looked down over an improvised check-point where two sailors, armed with grenades and Nagan pistols stuck in their belts, were demanding entry permits from everyone going into the building. But Riabov merely hailed them with a gesture and disappeared inside the hotel—once a rendezvous for commercial travellers.

'Hullo, Kuzma's here earlier than usual,' observed one of the sailors.

'His boss, comrade Beloborodov, will certainly need him for the next meeting of the Zlokasov factories,' the other answered.

At the end of a corridor on the first floor Kuzma knocked on the door of room No. 3. An NCO appeared and said:

'Later, *tovaritch*. The comrade-commissars are discussing something very urgent.'

Beyond the door, under the eyes of an orderly, five people were sitting round an Empire-style table with gilt corners. Books and sheets of blank paper were scattered all over the cloth pitted with cigarette burns. But there was also room for a green-shaded lamp, a massive bronze inkstand and the remains of a cold meal.

The five men were wearing crumpled coats or worn military reefers. Their faces were lined with lack of sleep and their shoulders drooped with fatigue. Tobacco-stained fingers stubbed out cigarettes in an enormous ashtray decorated with a smooth, cold dragon's head. In front of each of them, all mixed up with breadcrumbs, lay freshly printed tracts and the rubber stamps of the Supreme Authority of the Bolshevik Government in the Ural region.

The room was sweltering in the heat. Everything stank of sweat and stale tobacco. Through the open window there was a square of grey sky. The pelting rain on nearby roof-tops slackened off a little, but the disagreeable summer storm had done nothing but make the atmosphere still more oppressive.

Now and again the door on to the corridor would open, revealing serried masses of soldiers under a weak electric light; a chambermaid[1] would then tiptoe into the room and place a large, rounded receptacle on the table—this was a Tula samovar full of boiling water for tea; or a Red guardsman rigged out in leather with a rifle at the sling would bring in rolls of telegrams or documents to be signed.

The man who was plainly presiding over this little meeting was sitting on a stool too low for him. Of medium size, he was huddled in a green tunic and his face was marked by the ravages of life. His wide, bulging forehead was resting on his delicate, intellectual's hand so that his eyes and his slightly curved nose were concealed. All that could be seen was his sensual mouth and his badly shaven cheeks afflicted with a nervous tic. The three other participants in this strange conference never took their eyes off him. A fifth man was buried in an armchair by the window breathing in the damp air in little gasps. He, too, had his eyes on the leader, but more furtively.

If comrade Golochtchekin appeared to be dozing or day-dreaming this was mere seeming. The man whose nickname was 'the eye of the Kremlin', the supreme political and military commissar of the Ural region, was in fact watching his subordinates and colleagues with the patience of a cat. 'Philippe', as he had been called in the clandestine days before the Revolution, had been a professional revolutionary ever since he had left the St. Petersburg school of dentistry in 1903. A man of trust in the Bolshevik Party and with personal contacts with Lenin and Sverdlov, he had experienced the rigours of Siberian prisons and the fiery discussions of revolutionary groups in exile. After the revolt of the Kronstadt sailors he had been arrested in 1906 by the *Okhrana* (the Tsarist political police) and had spent two years in a cellar in the sinister Schlüsselburg Fortress. No sooner was he freed than he became the clandestine leader of the Bolshevik

---

1. Several weeks later the four chambermaids of the Hotel Amerika—Morozova, Chveikina, Piankova and Dediuchina—told examining magistrate Sergeiev of the White Army the details of what they had seen, and their evidence plays a crucial part in the reconstruction of this scene.

organisation in the Moscow area, only to be arrested again and banished to the eternal snows of the Narym prison on the Arctic circle, where he first met Sverdlov. From here he escaped and took refuge abroad, and 1912 saw him as a representative of the clandestine movements at the great conference of exiles in Prague. Very satisfied with him, Lenin dispatched him to the Ural region, where he soon showed matchless qualities as an organiser. After the October Revolution Golochtchekin was put in charge of the Red militia in the region and became leader of the revolutionary units opposing Ataman Dutov's Cossacks.

The man sitting on Golochtchekin's right was thin, blond and blue-eyed, with the clear forehead of an intellectual. His name was Piotr Voïkov. With a gesture that seemed almost automatic he was for ever scribbling over the sheets of blank paper. His studies in chemistry and economics had given the new Commissar for Supplies for the Ural Region a mania for taking notes. Eight years later, as Ambassador of the USSR in Warsaw, he was to write up his memories of Ekaterinburg in his diary.

On the other side of the table, perched on a broken chair, was Beloborodov, the chairman of the Ural Soviet. Oddly enough in view of the heat in the Hotel Amerika, he was muffled in a military cloak. His face was streaming with sweat and at times he was seen to be shivering with fever. His determined chin was covered in a thick growth and his left arm was in a sling. He was ill and utterly worn-out after an exhausting tour of the front, and his only part in the discussion took the form of short exclamations of agreement in a hoarse voice.

'Comrades,' Golochtchekin concluded, 'the Central Committee is deeply worried. The Czechs are advancing by forced marches and we have no hope of stopping them.'

'Agreed. Any further delay on our part would be criminal and we would be held responsible to the nation and to the march of the Revolution.' The man seated by the window had got up to give his resounding approval to the military commander of the Ural Region. Yakob Yurovsky now held a key post in the Ural Soviet: he was the man responsible for the military surveillance of the 'house of special assignment' where the Imperial family was interned.

While speaking the massive Yurovsky kept taking off and replacing his spectacles which left red marks on his nose. He looked sombrely at the other participants in the conference and extended a pale hairy hand towards them. His gleaming, black—almost blue—hair, scattered with threads of silver, was carefully combed. His frock-coat, though worn, still retained something of its elegance.

Yurovsky was a cosmopolitan, self-educated man born into a family of small Jewish tradespeople at Tomsk. During a stay in Berlin he had been converted to Lutheranism. First a watchmaker, then a photographer, he soon joined up with extreme left-wing movements. He was called up in the ambulance corps and experienced the hell of the front in the ranks of the 698th (Perm) Regiment. He was in the Carpathian retreat and had played an eloquent part in the meetings of the mutinous soldiers. His activity as a militant Bolshevik was noticed by the leaders at Smolny and they dispatched him on mission to the Ural region where he had lived in his youth. His travel orders had come directly from the Kremlin and were signed by Sverdlov.

The sailor with the herculean shoulders, Viktor Vaganov, entered room No. 3 yet again. This time he brought a file in green ink and gave it to the fifth member of the Extraordinary Commission assembled in the Hotel Amerika.

'Comrade Commissar, here are the last reports on the inquiry into the five White bandits arrested at Verkh-Issetsk.'

Even against the somewhat striking décor of the Hotel Amerika, comrade Commissar Piotr Zakharovitch Ermakov stood out as a colourful, not to say exotic, personality. He was the head of the local Cheka and Golochtchekin's right-hand man. Poised precariously on a rickety stool, he had one of his hands buried in his greasy hair which fell down to his shoulders. Each time the chairman paused in his reading so as to take a sip of tea, Ermakov's back stiffened as if in approval. Beneath the strong arches of his eyebrows his dark and glaring eyes were fixed on Commissar Golochtchekin with the devotion of a faithful dog. When he raised his head he revealed a yellowish face pitted with small-pox, and cheeks as beardless as those of an Eastern eunuch. Ermakov was a revolutionary by vocation, a sort of anarchist, long trained in all the strategic violence of clandestine activity. Ever since 1906 he had been known as the specialist of the 'ex'—meaning the 'ex-propriations'—that came in so useful for Party funds. He rifled the stores or residences of the rich boyars, stole horses, held tradesmen up to ransom and robbed travellers. His most ambitious raid—on the Treasury of Verkh-Issetsk—was his undoing. Denounced by a spy, he was found guilty of the murder of a watchman and sent to eastern Siberia. He emerged after ten years, in the spring of 1917, thanks to the general amnesty granted by Prince Lvov's Government. When he returned to Verkh-Issetsk he was treated as a workers' hero and soon rose to positions of importance in the political police of the new regime. He was appointed chief of the Ekaterinburg security service after his intrepid behaviour when, at the head of a hundred-odd Red cavalry, he had checked the White officers' revolt there on June 10. Previously he had held that position at Verkh-Issetsk.

Ermakov had recruited a squad of nineteen Chekists from amongst the toughest militiamen and ex-jailbirds of his acquaintance, those inured to the hardest and most repulsive tasks. By sifting these he would be able to select the men to help him on the bloody night in the basement of the Ipatiev house.

Meanwhile Golochtchekin, in a baritone voice accustomed to dealing with the most turbulent meetings, was reaching the end of his report to the Workers', Peasants' and Red Guards' Soviet of the Ural region. With nervous hand he turned over page after page of the school exercise book[1] in which he had set down his ideas during the five long days of his journey from Moscow to Ekaterinburg in a goods train requisitioned by the military authorities.

'In Moscow there are endless plots. All the enemies of the Revolution have joined forces against us: monarchists, *kadets*, Social-Revolutionaries and anarchists. Attempts at assassination occur almost daily. An infernal machine has been discovered in a cellar at the Kremlin. On the eve of my departure from Moscow,

1. The ex-dentist Golochtchekin had a habit of making jottings for his speeches in schoolboy notebooks. He was an outstanding orator with wide popular appeal and he had made a big impression on the Ekaterinburg population when, during a meeting at the 'Lorange' cinema on January 5, 1918, he faced a hostile crowd with a red armband and standing between two Red Guards in long cloaks and resting on their rifles. There he announced with a martial air that he was going to take energetic measures against some citizens in the town—'those who supported the White rabble displaying its poisoned fangs'. Three days earlier, in the same cinema, Golochtchekin had announced an important piece of news: the formation of a proletarian army. . . .

the Cheka happily foiled an attempt to poison the Kremlin water supply. But the worst traitors of all are the Social-Revolutionaries. While they are hypocrites enough to form part of comrade Lenin's Government, they are sabotaging our struggle against the Whites. There is no need for me to remind you of the machination by which the Social-Revolutionary Blumkin tried to overthrow the revolutionary regime by assassinating the German Ambassador, von Mirbach. And you know as well as I do about the shameful treachery of Social-Revolutionary Muraviev who, when responsible for the operations on the Volga front, abandoned the struggle against the Czechs and the Whites. Luckily a brave revolutionary got him with three revolver shots.'[1]

'Like the dog he was,' broke in Ermakov hoarsely.

'We have neither an organised army nor supplies nor munitions,' Golochtchekin went on. 'The Revolution has only a fifty-fifty chance of surviving this ordeal. . . . We have to foresee the worst and act accordingly. For everything leads back to the problem of our prisoners and the fate of Nicholas Romanov, assassin of the people. A week ago we cabled the Commander of the Red Army of the Volga to send us reliable men to form a guard for a special train,[2] but today we can't even dream of evacuating the Romanovs westwards. The railway to Moscow is no longer safe and the one going north ends up in territory controlled by the Whites.'

For the first time in the endless session Beloborodov got up. He clenched his fists before he said his few decisive words:

'Comrades, long ago the Revolutionary Military High Committee authorised us to decide for ourselves what to do if the situation became critical. . . . It is certainly critical now. To be more precise still, comrades Sverdlov and Zinoviev have sent a coded cable to me personally as chairman of the Ural Soviet,

1. By an irony of fate Golochtchekin was executed at dawn on October 15, 1939 by three revolver shots in the neck. The deed was performed by an execution squad in the cellar of an NKVD prison.

In Golochtchekin's biography recently published in the Soviet Union we read: 'This valiant Bolshevik of the earliest date, close collaborator with J. M. Sverdlov and V. I. Lenin, indefatigable in the workers' struggle, hero of the civil war, Regional Secretary for Kazakstan and one of the builders of the "Turksib" railway, fell victim to Stalin's personality cult.'

2. Telegram No. 4640 of July 8 (Photo No. 44).

making it clear that we have *carte blanche* as regards the Romanovs.[1]
Their only order is that they shall be kept informed.'

Yurovsky nodded his agreement and returned to the charge:

'For my part, comrades, as commander of the Ipatiev house, I
should inform you that within a few hours I shall no longer be
in a position to guarantee our hold over the Romanovs. The
conspiracies of the Socialist traitors, allies of the monarchists
and the Western powers, constitute an ever-increasing threat to
the place of detention, for all its guards and fencing.'

Whereupon Golochtchekin spoke again, and in a confidential
voice:

'Our glorious comrades at the Kremlin have one overriding
concern—that of preventing the German army from invading
central Russia. Now the Germans have warned comrade Joffé
that if Nicholas Romanov falls into the hands of the Whites—
that is to say of the Allies who would immediately appoint him
Commander-in-Chief of the rebellion—they would consider the
treaty of Brest-Litovsk null and void and would march on
Moscow and Petrograd. From now on the Romanovs will be of
more use to us dead than alive. Naturally we will not publish the
news of Nikolachka's[2] execution until it will be in our interests
to do so. In the meantime it must remain an absolute State
Secret.'

Golochtchekin swept his glance over his audience. Beloborodov, though officially his superior, was listening quietly. He went
on:

'I know that you will all keep your mouths shut. We have all
agreed to eliminate comrade Bogolepov who was not up to
his responsibilities. We must inform comrades Zinoviev and
Molotov of this matter and ask them to send us comrade
Kostina[3] as a replacement in the chancellery and cypher office.
You know as well as I do that Vladimir Ilytch has just given

1. The coded cable sent from the Kremlin was in all likelihood destroyed
immediately in accord with instructions. But its existence was proved both
by evidence collected by Sokolov and by the original of the answer signed
'Beloborodov' announcing that the execution had taken place and that the
whole family had perished. (Photo No. 45—the coded cable was decoded by
the French in 1923 at the request of Sokolov who was then a refugee in
Paris.)

2. Nikolachka: a pejorative name for Nicholas II.

3. Telegram No. 4852 (photo No. 55) provides confirmation on this
point.

comrade Molotov the job of supervising the *Vzik* commission for the Ural and Siberian regions. Zinoviev, still at the Smolny in Petrograd, is overwhelmed by the work involved in his main duties as the man responsible to the Third International.'[1]

Golochtchekin sat down heavily. His neighbour was mopping his face. Yurovsky, as Commissar for Justice in the local Soviet, drew up a few lines on a piece of paper. He underlined three words, then handed the paper to Piotr Voïkov. Voïkov read what was written and then signed with a weary hand. Beloborodov scribbled his initials in his turn, and handed the document to his neighbour, Ermakov, who made haste to do the same.

While Yurovsky was fiddling with his pince-nez, Golochtchekin grabbed the piece of paper between thumb and finger. The paper was of poor quality and his pen went right through it.

So, after a whole day's discussion, the verdict was reached. The fate of the Romanovs was sealed by those three words, '*Prisuzhdenni k smerti*' ('Condemned to death'). It was July 15, 1918, and according to the bronze clock on the mantelpiece it was just after eight in the evening.

Without haste, Commissar Golochtchekin—his eyes turned towards the window from which he could see the rainbow that had followed the storm—tore the historic act up into tiny pieces and scattered them over the check tablecloth.

1. Grigory Zinoviev, Lenin's right-hand man, was a distinguished custodian of Soviet doctrine and 'specialist' in German affairs at the *Vzik*. Fourteen years later he was liquidated by Stalin. Molotov was confirmed as director of Ural and Siberian affairs on August 18, 1918. The commission he headed included Sucharverkov, Ditman, Dmitrieva and Rabinovitch.

Chapter IV

STATE SECRET

*

IN PARIS the night of July 16 was one of the warmest and
loveliest of the Great War. The city was still celebrating the
French national festival. But the last notes of the kermesse
were punctured by the sound of cannon. Since the day before
furious fighting had been raging round Château-Thierry, fifty
miles from the capital, where the French were containing the
last great German offensive without giving an inch of ground,
while on the south bank of the Marne their American brothers-
in-arms were launching a victorious counter-attack.

At enemy Headquarters General Erich von Ludendorff was
sitting the night out chewing cigar after cigar. The Kaiser's
supreme commander had a presentiment that victory was slip-
ping through his hands. In vain had he massed his divisions for
the *kolossal* push. The German spearhead had been blunted by
repeated blows struck both east and west. The Treaty of Brest-
Litovsk (March 3) had come too late to resharpen it.

A back-glance at the Paris daily, *Le Matin*, gives us an overall
picture of what was happening on that 1456th day of the war.
In Siberia the Czechs, in alliance with the White Army, were
making an armed break-through in the direction of their native
Bohemia. Longing for their native Carpathians, they were
approaching the Ural region and threatening to cut the Bol-
shevik-held territories in two. In the United States President
Wilson had authorised the parents of soldiers killed in combat to
wear a special distinction—a black band sewn with a gold star.
On the French Riviera the conflict between Germany and
Monaco had come to a head and German subjects had been
expelled from the principality. In Paris there was good news for
civilians: the abolition of meatless days. But it was a bad day for
the defeatist politician, Malvy: at the High Court of Justice they
were dusting the benches in readiness for the first hearing of his
trial. Finally during the night a man was preparing to face the

final penalty—he was the journalist Duval, who had been involved in the treasonable *affaire* of the 'Bonnet Rouge' and the Malvy scandal. At dawn Monsieur Badin—for that was how he signed his articles—was shot at Vincennes. He asked for his eyes not to be bandaged.

But that was not all that had happened. On that same night an illustrious family—an Emperor, an Empress and their five children—had also faced a firing squad. *Le Matin* made no mention of this.

And yet on the morning of July 17 some of the inhabitants of Ekaterinburg knew that it had happened: a handful of *muzhiks* who had nothing to do with the Red police or the executioners. Henceforward they lowered their eyes when they saw men of the Cheka, for fear that its redoubtable chief, comrade Beloborodov, would guess their terrible secret.

One of these men was called Piotr Feodorovitch Tsetsegov. He had the modest job of night watchman on the Voznessenski Prospekt, Ekaterinburg's main artery.[1]

'In the middle of the night,' he was later to relate,' 'I heard the noise of gunfire coming from the basement of the finest building in the Prospekt, the former house of the merchant Ipatiev. A few minutes later a truck that was stationed in front of the house with its engine turning over started off in the direction of the country. I immediately guessed what had happened but I never mentioned a word to anybody.'

Another of these men was called Viktor Ivanovitch Bouÿvid and he lived opposite the Ipatiev house. The evening before he had drunk too much vodka and in the middle of the night felt ill. While he was relieving his stomach in a corner of the garden he was suddenly startled by the sound of shots coming from the basement of the house opposite. For an instant a piercing female cry rose above the noise. When he went back to bed Bouÿvid found his room-mate awake. The two men couldn't help talking:

'Did you hear it?'

'Yes, I heard.'

---

1. Ekaterinburg, originally named after Catherine the Great who founded it, was rechristened Sverdlovsk by the Soviets in memory of Yakob Sverdlov, Lenin's assistant, who played such an important part in the execution of the Romanov family.

'Did you guess?'

'Yes, I guessed.'

The third person who learnt of it was a woman, Capitolina Alexandrovna. She was the sister of an unemployed turner Anatole Yakimov, who had enrolled in the Red Guards. Early on the morning of July 17 Yakimov came to see her at her lodging in an Ekaterinburg suburb. His face was distraught and he was staring wide-eyed in a way she had never seen before. She knew that something terrible must have happened and pressed him with questions. Yakimov closed the windows and seemed about to speak, then changed his mind.

'Is it to do with the Romanovs?' Capitolina urged.

'They've all been shot,' Yakimov whispered,[1] 'the Tsar, the Tsarina, the Tsarevitch, the four Grand Duchesses, Olga, Tatiana, Maria and Anastasia, as well as the Tsarevitch's doctor and three servants. Only Leonid, the little kitchen boy, was spared.'

And in a still more hushed voice Yakimov continued:

'The basement of the Ipatiev house is covered with blood. The bodies have been taken away, but I don't know where. Although I'm a revolutionary, I went as pale as a sheet when I heard. The comrades laugh at me, and if it gets round that I've told you our lives won't be worth living. Commissar Goloch-tchekin has given orders that it is to be kept a State Secret.'

In the *izbas* of the little village of Koptiaki, situated in the heart of an immense forest some twelve or fourteen miles north-west of Ekaterinburg, there lived peasants who in their turn witnessed mysterious goings-on. Early that morning Anastasia Zykova had left the village to go and sell fish at the Ekaterinburg market, but on reaching the spot called 'The Four Brothers'— roughly three miles from the village—she had run into a very unusual procession: a few motor vehicles surrounded by an imposing detachment of Red Guards were jolting along the track. Two Red Guards seized her horse by the bridle and forced her cart to turn back. Without mincing their words, they told her to go away and stay away. On regaining Koptiaki

---

1. All the evidence here given was collected at the end of August 1918 by the police service of Admiral Kolchak's forces after the capture of the town by the Whites. Its veracity was confirmed by the detailed inquiry made by the White Army's examining magistrate, Nicholas Sokolov.

Anastasia Zykova warned her neighbours not to go out and work in the fields, whereupon a few incredulous *muzhiks* decided to set off and see for themselves what was afoot. At some distance from the village they were met by a Red sentry, a big bully of a man armed with rifle, sabre, revolver and two grenades at his belt. He ordered them straight back to Koptiaki.

The village was isolated from the town by cordons of Red Guards until the morning of July 19. On that day the Bolshevik forces began their withdrawal from the region. A small garrison remained in Ekaterinburg until the evening of July 21. On the morning of July 25 the White Army and a Czechoslovak detachment entered the town.

It was not until July 21 that *Le Matin* and the other Paris dailies devoted a few lines to events in Ekaterinburg. In small print on its third page *Le Matin* said:

RUMOUR THAT THE TSAR HAS BEEN SHOT

There has been yet another announcement of the death of Tsar Nicholas of Russia.[1] We herewith reprint the dispatch received from the Havas agency: LONDON, JULY 20: A radio telegram of the Russian Government thus reports the circumstances of the ex-Emperor's death, according to a direct telegraphic message from the Regional Council of the Ural. On the discovery of a counter-revolutionary plot whose object was to abduct the ex-Tsar, the Revolutionary Council of the Ural decided to have him shot. The decision was carried out on July 16.

The ex-Empress and the ex-Tsarevitch have been consigned elsewhere for safe-keeping.

The radio telegram picked up in London was strictly authentic and the news editor of *Le Matin* showed a lack of flair in giving it such a modest showing. But at least the readers of *Le Matin* knew of the affair before the people of Ekaterinburg. These heard the official Bolshevik announcement on the evening of July 21,

1. The execution of the Tsar by the Bolsheviks had been announced on a number of occasions since his abrupt transfer to Ekaterinburg on April 26, 1918.

at a final meeting of the workers held in the municipal theatre just a few hours before the Red Guards' withdrawal.[1]

Here is the text of the announcement:

Decision of the Presidium of the Workers', Peasants' and Red Guards' Soviet of the Ural Region: Given that the Czechoslovak irregulars are threatening Ekaterinburg, Red capital of the Ural region; given that the crowned butcher might escape the people's tribunal (a White plot aiming to abduct the whole Romanov family has just been discovered), the Presidium of the Regional Committee, in accordance with the will of the people, decided as follows: ex-Tsar Nicholas Romanov, guilty before the people of countless crimes, will be shot.

The decision of the Presidium of the Regional Soviet was carried out during the night of July 16/17. The Romanov family has been transferred from Ekaterinburg to another and safer place.

Apart from one or two strong epithets, the telegram as printed by the Western press is identical with the Presidium's communiqué. The Soviet authorities admitted the execution of the ex-Tsar but maintained that the lives of the other members of the family had been safeguarded.

There were diplomatic reasons for this lie. Particularly delicate negotiations were taking place in Moscow between Dr Ritzler, the German Ambassador, and the Bolshevik *Sovnarkom*, in the course of which the German-born ex-Tsarina would sooner or later play a part as small change.

For years to come this lie was to vitiate any objective study of the Imperial family's death. Until the end of September 1918 there was a curious period in the Soviet capital known as that of the 'reanimated corpses' (Kerensky's phrase).[2] The revolutionaries Karl Radek and Chicherin on the one hand, and Ritzler on the other, argued bitterly as to how German demands might be modified if the former Empress and her children were restored to the Kaiser.

1. Cf. P. M. Bikov, 'The Last Tsar's last days' (article), Moscow, 1921.
2. But it should be emphasised that the Germans had excellent correspondents all over Russia and were only taken in by this farce for a few weeks.

By the end of September the German military situation had become so bad that the *Sovnarkom* began to feel much freer. Chicherin, Commissar for Foreign Affairs, 'put an end to those merry speculations about the *living corpses* of the massacred women and children'. He told the German Ambassador that the Tsarina and her children, together with the detachment of Red Guards detailed to look after them, had been cut off from the bulk of the Bolshevik forces after the capture of Ekaterinburg by the Whites, and that the Soviet Government itself did not know what had become of them.

It was difficult for the Soviet authorities to go back on this first version of the facts. The first accurate account of the execution of the whole Romanov family was published in Moscow in 1921 in an article by P. M. Bikov, former chairman of the Ural Soviet, called 'The Last Tsar's Last Days', in a collection of essays entitled *The Workers' Revolution in the Ural Region*. But no sooner had this book appeared than it was seized and destroyed by the authorities. It was not until 1930 that this same author was able to publish his testimony in book form.[1]

When a member of a Western delegation at the Genoa Conference in 1922 questioned Chicherin, who was representing the Soviet Union, as to the fate of the ex-Tsarina and her children he answered coolly that as far as he knew the children were in America!

Ekaterinburg remained in the hands of the Whites from July 25, 1918, until September 25, 1919. Only a few hours after the city had been taken by the White Army some Koptiaki peasants told Kolchak's officers about how the Bolsheviks had lit mysterious fires in the forest near their village. Copies of the newspaper *The Ural Worker*, containing the Regional Soviet's communiqué on the execution of the ex-Tsar, were still littering the streets. As soon as they entered Ekaterinburg, White officers hurried to the Ipatiev house in quest of news of the Imperial family. Ipatiev the merchant, who had emerged from hiding in an isolated farm the day before and gone back to the house, showed them suspicious clues and bloodstains in the basement. It was obvious that something sinister had happened. Slowly people's

1. Published by the State Publishing House, Moscow, and by Payot, Paris, in the series *Mémoires, Etudes et Documents*.

tongues loosened. In mid-August the new chief of police of
Ekaterinburg interrogated first the night watchman Piotr
Tsetsegov, then the peasant Viktor Bouÿvid. On information
received he was able to arrest a Red Guard, Mikhail
Letemin, who had had no time to get away and who had
appropriated the spaniel, Joy, belonging to the Grand Duke
and heir.

On July 30, 1918, a judicial inquiry was officially set up by
White Army authorities. It was entrusted to the only examining
magistrate to be found in the region, one Nametkin, previously
employed by the higher court at Ekaterinburg. Judge Nametkin
was far from grateful for this task, as he was a coward and
'manifestly lacking in perspicacity and zeal', as Robert Wilton
put it—*The Times* correspondent and the only journalist on the
spot at the time. On August 8 the brief was taken from Nametkin
and entrusted to Judge Sergeiev, who initiated a six months'
inquiry with scarcely more brilliant results. Sergeiev, a former
president of the civil court, lacked the experience needed for
criminal inquiries, and his fear of falling into Bolshevik hands
made him cautious and lacking in initiative. He never dared
enter the forest near Koptiaki, the presumed burial place of the
Romanovs, 'for fear of running into prowlers'.

It was not until 1919 that the case was taken up to real purpose.
The examining magistrate, Nicholas Sokolov, was appointed on
February 7 by Admiral Kolchak and General Martianov (director
of the White Army chancellery), and he was a brilliant legal man
who devoted himself to the case body and soul. Several years
later when he was a refugee in France and had every reason to
rest on his laurels—so intensive had been the inquiry he initiated
at Ekaterinburg and in Siberia during the spring and summer of
1919—he was still collecting evidence from Russian witnesses in
exile.

In 1918 Nicholas Sokolov was a convinced monarchist aged
thirty-six, holding the rank of examining magistrate, first class,
at the Penza Court in Central Russia. After the October Revolution of 1917 he took refuge in a nearby village, Medviedevka,
where he had contacts among the peasants. When, in 1918, he
learnt that the Bolsheviks had lost control of some of the towns
along the Volga where the Social-Revolutionaries were in
revolt, he set out disguised as a *muzhik*, in rags and a rough

sheepskin hood, to reach the rebellious areas. He reached Sviajsk by short stretches, crossed the Volga in an interval between two battles, and joined other opponents of the Soviet regime at Ufa and continued in their company. Eventually he arrived at Tobolsk, then in Czech hands, presented himself to the White Army Command and was sent on to Omsk, seat of the Provisional Government. In December of that year Sokolov met Kolchak, who promised him an important post. (There is an astonishing photograph of Sokolov as a refugee, still in *muzhik* dress, taken immediately after his arrival in Tobolsk—plate 1).

His task was not made easier by his immediate superiors, the functionaries at the Department of Justice of Kolchak's Omsk headquarters, who were mostly Socialists and violently anti-monarchist. At times he feared the worst for his precious archives and even for his life. When a refugee at Tchita in the autumn of 1919, he was all but shot by the White Guards of Ataman Semenov, an Asiatic satrap who was determined that his mercenaries should believe that Tsar Nicholas was still alive. After fleeing to Harbin with his chests of archives and his relics of the Imperial family, Sokolov owed his safety to General Janin, head of the French mission and commander of Allied troops in Siberia. General Janin took those inestimable historical documents into his personal safe-keeping.

A final alarming episode for Sokolov occurred on March 16, 1920. As he was boarding General Janin's military train with the English journalist Robert Wilton and the Tsarevitch's former tutor, the Swiss Pierre Gilliard, he suddenly found himself surrounded by a group of suspicious-looking people. But as good luck would have it some French sentries came forward and the danger was averted.

The French Minister at Peking, M. Boppe, had put the documents under diplomatic seal and at Tientsin they were sent aboard a French troop transport, the *Armand Béhic*. They journeyed to Marseilles in the ship's strong-room. Arrived at Marseilles, General Janin refused to hand them over to a representative of the French Foreign Ministry but kept them in his family house in Grenoble with the intention of giving them personally to Grand Duke Nicholas.[1] But he sent a detailed and

1. The research article by M. Xavier de Hautecloque and General Janin's original letter were published in the *Petit Journal* of December 1930.

documented report on Sokolov's investigations to Clémenceau, who was thus the first Western leader to know the true history of the Ekaterinburg affair.

Strictly speaking, Sokolov's dossiers and relics should have been sent back to Russia to General Wrangel as new leader of the anti-Bolshevik struggle. But the White Army collapsed before this could be done. After some hesitation Grand Duke Nicholas, now leader of the monarchist emigration, decided that the 'Sokolov suitcases' should be entrusted to M. Michel de Guirs, doyen of Russian ambassadors in exile.

Years passed. Nicholas Sokolov died in Paris in 1924 after summing up his researches in a book.[1] During the German occupation of France (1940–4) most of the documents, which had been lodged in the strong-rooms of the *Sécurité Générale* insurance company, fell into the hands of the German police. As for the relics, they seem to have been restored to various members of the Romanov family.

So, as we have seen, the truth about the tragic death of Nicholas II and his family only emerged very slowly. The difficulty of proving the death of people whose bodies had been destroyed, and the deliberate misinformation propagated by the Soviet Government, gave free rein to improbable impostures. During the summer of 1919 a false Tsarevitch stirred up all the monarchists in the Omsk region, and when he was unmasked by M. Pierre Gilliard the functionaries were already providing him with hospitality. He was the first of an endless series of pretenders who were to turn up in Russia and abroad. Among them we think particularly of the pathetic, suffering face of Mme Tchaikovsky who has believed for forty years that she is the Grand Duchess Anastasia. The strange and tangled story that this old lady insists on reiterating before Hamburg judges and in television interviews has no claim on the serious historian's attention. But it is far from lacking in psychological interest. It is a measure of the seductive power that myths still retain in our century of progress and the exact sciences—retain over people's minds and still more over the sensational press.

The glossy magazines are really taking their revenge when they

1. *Enquête judiciaire sur l'assassinat de la famille impériale russe*, a work that appeared simultaneously in French (Paris, Payot) and Russian (Berlin), 1925.

devote so many pages to a mystery that is no longer a mystery. What happened was that in 1918 destiny snatched the drama from the journalists only to restore it many years later to the historians.

Chapter V

RASPUTIN'S PREDICTION

*

IT WAS around one o'clock in the morning that a hail of bullets cut down Emperor Nicholas Romanov and his family. A few minutes later, in a room adjoining the execution chamber and used by the Red Guards as an office, a bloodstained hand tore a leaf off the calendar to display the fateful date, July 17, 1918.

The number 17 had already been lethal for the last of the Tsars. One year five months before the tragic night at Ekaterinburg, the sinister confidant of the Imperial family, Rasputin, had himself been shot down (December 17). The two men who condemned him to death were no revolutionaries—they were a monarchist deputy and that dazzling aristocrat Prince Yussupov.

Oddly enough, Rasputin had foretold that the figure 7 would bring the Tsar bad luck. In one of the incredible notes he sent almost daily to Nicholas II, he had written (December 12, 1916):

Be careful, Papa, about the 7th day. Whenever the figure 7 comes up, there is trouble on the horizon. Dissolve the Duma[1] tomorrow, don't wait for December 17 which is a date of ill-omen.

Docile as usual to the miracle-man's instructions, and in the teeth of protests from the Prime Minister, Rodzianko, the Emperor and Autocrat of All the Russias dissolved the Duma. On December 18 Nicholas hurriedly left the military headquarters at Mohylev in Bielo-Russia to return to Petrograd. And on the evening of December 21 he noted with a tear-drenched pen, in the black morocco-bound book that he used as a diary, the reason for his journey:

1. The Russian Parliament, which was continually being prevented from sitting.

At nine o'clock my family and I were present at a sad spectacle: the coffin containing the body of the unforgettable Grigory, murdered by monsters at Yussupov's house during the night of December 16/17, was let down into the grave. Father Alexander Vassiliev recited the prayers for the dead.[1]

On the very day on which this equivocal figure was buried in a corner of the park of the Tsarskoye-Selo Palace, the Empress, dressed in black, sent for one of the best architects of the capital to whom she outlined plans for a splendid mausoleum to contain Rasputin's mortal remains. The architect apologised for the length of time the work would take: the mausoleum, carved in Paros stone, could only be completed by July 1918.

Like a hurricane, the February Revolution swept aside this costly project. Not even a spadeful of work was ever expended on it. And by the time the date foreseen for its inauguration had arrived, Red Guards were drilling in the Tsarskoye-Selo Park, and in far-away Siberia the Romanovs themselves had joined the graveless dead.

The fantastic story of Rasputin has already been told twenty times over and this is no place to repeat it—the story of how the drunken and debauched peasant from the depths of Siberia came to enjoy unbelievable success in the Imperial capital. But Rasputin played such an important part in the events immediately preceding the fall and execution of the Tsar, and his grotesque shadow lay for so long over the acts and thoughts of the Romanov family, that it would be no exaggeration to view him as a posthumous participant in the Ekaterinburg tragedy.

Before he usurped the prerogatives of a man of God and sought his fortune in St Petersburg, Grigory Efimovitch was an unruly and almost illiterate country lout in the province of Tobolsk, where he was born in 1864 in the little village of Pokrovskoye. His real name was Novikh—'Rasputin', a word stemming from *rasputny* (debauched), being a nickname given to other members of his family before him and which he wished to retain. Nature had endowed Novikh-Rasputin with unusual virility and un-questionable hypnotic gifts, and, like Stendhal's Julien Sorel, he chose the clerical state as a way of escaping from the wretched conditions of the peasantry. His dealings with the Khlisty, a

1. *Journal Intime de Nicholas II: Juillet 1914–Juillet 1918*, Payot, 1934, p.73.

sect particularly widespread in the Ural region—a sort of flagellant sect still influenced by ancient 'Shamanist' beliefs—decided him to choose the profession of *staretz* (a peasant monk or pilgrim), but a long period in a convent, in which he absorbed the rudiments of the Christian message, only caused a temporary change in his gross habits. The silver cross he wore over his country shirt was hardly enough to deceive the good people of Pokrovskoye. Even in Siberia it was not the cowl that made the monk. In view of this hopeless situation he left his wife and children one day in 1904 and boarded the Transiberian railway. He began preaching his doctrine—a highly personal blend of religious frenzy and eroticism—in Moscow and other provincial cities. Most of his disciples were women whom he called 'balm-carriers', urging them to practise that true repentance that follows immediately on sin. His reputation spread to sophisticated circles in the capital. A journalist on the *Novoie Vremia* made investigations regarding him and published the following picturesque statement by the peasant monk:

Even before I left Siberia I had many women disciples, among whom were ladies of high society. They came to me because they wanted to approach nearer to God. But the only road to God passes by way of humiliation. So I took them to the public baths, undressed them, and ordered them to wash me. In that way they showed themselves humble in the eyes of the Lord.

It was in 1906 that Rasputin, who was earning the nickname of 'holy devil' among the women in the capital, first met the Tsarina. He was presented to her by two female 'admirers' who were also close friends of the Empress: the Grand Duchesses Militza and Stana Nicolaievna, daughters of the King of Montenegro. With Anna Virubova, her lady-in-waiting, Empress Alexandra Feodorovna returned more and more frequently to the Montenegrin drawing-room to meet the holy man. Sometimes the Tsar accompanied his wife, and his timid nature, influenced by her German determination, inclined him to revere the dubious personage in his turn.

Ten years passed. In 1916, on the eve of the Revolution, the whole of Petrograd and the whole of Russia had one word only on its lips: Rasputin. With the exception of a small circle of courtiers and prebendaries at Tsarskoye-Selo, the name was mud. Rumour accused him—and rightly—of having relations with the 'Green centre' of Moravian flagellants and, through them, with Colonel Nicolai, the Kaiser's master-spy. He was blamed when a German U-boat sank the British cruiser *Hampshire* in the Orkneys as it was taking Lord Kitchener to Archangel to put some order into Russian affairs. He was well known for his vicious influence over crucial political decisions, and in the whirlwind of successive war cabinets no Minister could be nominated unless he had first paid court to Rasputin in his apartments in the Ghorinkaya and the Nevsky Prospekt.[1]

Rasputin was also rumoured to be the Empress's lover and even the father of the unfortunate Tsarevitch Alexis Nicolaievitch whose terrible onsets of haemophilic bleeding he treated by hypnotism. The Tsar was a complaisant husband, they whispered in St Petersburg. And when news films showed Rasputin wearing the St George Cross recently conferred on him by the Grand Council of the Order there were uproarious scenes.

Study of the endless evidence published since the Revolution enables us to clear the Tsarina's memory of this accusation. Grand Duke Alexis, born in 1904, was conceived before Rasputin's first visit to the capital. And after the birth of this, her last child, it seems hardly likely that Alexandra Feodorovna's relations with the horse-thief's son went beyond false paternal caresses and rather too familiar embraces.[2] The Empress was by nature a mystic and a neurotic and she was too attached to her 'holy man' for him to need more intimate links. A tall, angular German, tortured by sciatica, was no very attractive prey for the 'holy devil' who could have the company of the capital's prettiest girls, both of the aristocracy and the demi-monde. But what seems probable is that Rasputin, with his taste for young girls,

---

1. Documents published since the Revolution have confirmed that Rasputin had a hand in the Kitchener affair (cf. the present author's article in *Lectures pour Tous*, March 1963). Some authors have maintained that Rasputin had foreknowledge of the Sarajevo assassination plot (June 28, 1914) in which both the Serbian Government and the Tsarist Secret Service had a hand; but on this occasion Rasputin is alleged to have been against taking action.

2. Commissar Voïkov stated before reliable witnesses that in Alexandra Feodorovna's private papers he had come across evidence that Rasputin had taken advantage of her *after having hypnotised her*.

was attracted by the eldest daughters, especially the Grand Duchess Olga, whose twentieth birthday occurred in 1915. But their governesses[1] kept a close watch over the Grand Duchesses' apartments, and on the rare occasions when the monk attempted to get into the girls' bedrooms, on the pretext of 'blessing' them, he was confronted by ferocious female watchdogs.

But the most serious aspect in having this libertine established in the corridors of power in a country involved in the biggest war of its history lay not so much in his incredible influence over the Tsarina as in the Tsarina's own preponderance in State affairs. In 1915, with the first Russian reverses in Galicia, the Emperor and Autocrat had withdrawn the supreme command from his uncle, Grand Duke Nicholas Nicolaievitch, and added the post of *generalissimo* to his own many powers. Yet even when he was installed at Staff Headquarters in Mohylev and could both savour the military atmosphere he had enjoyed in his garrison days and carry out the divine mission he believed to be his, he could never escape his despotic wife. Alexandra Feodorovna's daily telegrams and letters influenced him on a thousand and one points.

The Tsarina never reproached him directly, and was careful to preserve the tone of a dutiful wife whose German education had restricted her to the three K's.[2] She did not more than 'wish', or, in matters nearest her heart, 'counsel'. The result was as could be expected. When very delicate matters were at stake she had a special train prepared and hurried to Mohylev where the Tsar would soon yield to the long English phrases she had prepared in advance. Anna Virubova, who served her mistress with dog-like loyalty, has left an account in her diary[3] of one of the Tsarina's journeys to Army Headquarters. It is dated November 3.

1. Besides their English nurses, 'Fräuleins', and tutors such as Gilliard and Gibbs, the Grand Duchesses had governesses. The lady-in-waiting Tutchev lived in the palace and discharged the functions of governess to the Tsar's children.

2. Despite her Heidelberg doctorate in philosophy, the Empress behaved like a German *petite bourgeoise* brought up for *Kinder, Kirche, Küche* (children, church, kitchen).

3. *Le Journal Secret d'Anna Virubova*, published in Russia in 1927 and in French translation in 1928 (Payot editor). This is an extraordinary document written from day to day by the Tsarina's famous 'shadow' and considered absolutely authentic by the majority of historians. 'Papa' and 'Mama' were the pet names by which the Tsar and Tsarina were known to their intimates; 'Kalinin' was the 'code name' for Minister Protopopov, official protégé of

Papa has decided to get rid of Kalinin. . . . As soon as Mama got wind of this she was alarmed . . . so she is going off to Headquarters. Once they are together there they will be able to comfort each other. . . . He will calm down and submit. He will come under Mama's influence again. And he will do everything she demands (or, rather, asks, for she never demands anything of Papa, she asks, but in such a way that Papa understands that a refusal would be taken as an offence. And he will never offend Mama!)

A few years earlier, in an entry dated July 9 (probably 1912 though no year is mentioned), Anna Virubova had already noted the following in her private jottings: 'When one sees Papa and Mama at close quarters, one realises that they were made "neither for greatness nor for glory" as the noble poet K.R. puts it.'[1]

Rasputin's unlimited power over the mind of the Tsarina, and the Tsarina's decisive influence over her Imperial husband constitute the two first clues to the division of authority at the Russian court during 1916–17, and even to the Revolution. To these we need only add one more to complete the mournful trilogy: the weak character of Nicholas II.

The 1917 Revolution, and the events that followed it, aroused such world-wide passions and produced such a vast literature that it seems difficult even today to make a choice between the fierce denunciations of the Soviets and the touching hagiographies of the monarchists in exile. So in order to get a true portrait of Tsar Nicholas we shall appeal to a reliable and

Rasputin and Alexandra Feodorovna. This is what Gérard Walter says about Anna Virubova's secret diary: 'When it was published by the Bolsheviks, the author, who had by then joined the emigration, denounced it as apocryphal. Of course she could hardly have done otherwise, as it was a private document and had at no time been intended for publication. Yet there are solid reasons for viewing it as authentic. On occasion, perhaps, the original text was sensationalised or amplified by the editors.' Walter's view is shared by others including the distinguished historian Constantin de Grunwald. Obviously the revelations this diary contains, which affect the interests of many people still alive, will be found displeasing by many. Whatever heated discussions it arouses either now or in the future, nobody with any acquaintance with Russian affairs will feel inclined to deny its indisputable value as a historical document.

1. Grand Duke Konstantín, a poet of merit. He signed his verses Konstantin Romanov.

impartial witness, Charles Rivet, for many years the St Petersburg correspondent of the French daily, *Le Temps*.

In his outstanding book on the last of the Romanovs,[1] written and published between the February and October Revolutions of 1917, Charles Rivet paints him as follows:

A fleeting figure looming behind the mysteries of an in-accessible palace, Tsar Nicholas II will some day confound the historians. The French press has portrayed him as an enlightened autocrat to whom war revealed the dangers of an irresponsible bureaucracy and who therefore set out to bring the living forces of the nation into politics. Is this view the product of illusion or credulity? Unfortunately the real Nicholas II bore no resemblance to this fictional character. He had the same name, but that is all.

In reality the Tsar did not understand his people at all, had no system and no policy, except perhaps—through self-infatuation as much as through the religion of autocracy that he had built up—a whole-hearted assertion of absolutism . . .

It was only when he was afraid that he had recourse to collaborators of any value. Then he became trusting and attentive, often putting forward the very proposal that he had rejected the day before. But as soon as his fear diminished he began setting traps for any Minister who spoke his mind; he set traps for him, and then came the day when he would 'resign' him. Though a despot, he was incapable of the sovereign gesture of the self-assured master who strikes and breaks. Nicholas II attacked his adversaries in the dark. He was false and shifty, cold and elusive. When Stolypin was assassinated under his eyes [in Kiev in 1911], the monarch made no move towards the man who had sought to consolidate his throne; he left the theatre where the murder had taken place without even approaching the wounded man who—though in the grip of the death-rattle—was still valiantly trying to bless with the sign of the cross the Caesar for whom he was dying. 'Stolypin eclipsed me' was the funeral oration the dead Prime Minister received from the Imperial lips the day after his burial.

Nicholas II failed to make himself loved even by his closest

1. *Le dernier des Romanov*, Librairie Académique Perrin, Paris.

attendants.[1] Outside his immediate family he displayed no
affection for anything or anyone. His egoism was as great as his
boredom. He had no known tastes. He did nothing with
passion, nor even with zest. What pleased him was flattery.
To keep his favour it was necessary to distract him and, above
all, not to speak to him of serious matters or point out difficulties or obstacles . . . Curtained off from his people by Court
intriguers, the Tsar was but a fleeting vision for his public. On
such occasions he seemed shy, worried, and his movements
were nervous and jerky. He only felt really at home with his
army. In a Guards' officers' mess, or at some regimental
banquet, Nicholas II could let himself go and become loqua-
cious, free and easy. Sometimes he even got drunk.

At the very moment that Charles Rivet was writing these
lines in a Petrograd that had not yet become Leningrad, the
Provisional Government's Extraordinary Commission, set up to
study the years before the Revolution, was carrying out a whole
series of interrogations of former Ministers, Councillors,
Generals, and high functionaries and dignitaries of the Imperial
court and Government. The typed account of these hearings make
a fascinating document.[2] It emerges from the evidence that in
the course of the years 1915 and 1916 the Tsar became more and
more submissive to the Empress's demands and progressively
abandoned all his powers into the hands of his neurotic wife.

Alexander Kerensky, leader of the Provisional Government
during the summer of 1917, was later to sum up the findings of
the inquiry carried out under his orders.[3] 'As the war progressed,
the Tsar's resistance to Rasputin's will diminished. In January
1916 he returned to his capital and within less than two weeks
had approved all the decisions taken by the Tsarina-Rasputin-
Virubova trio. Stürmer was nominated Prime Minister, the
bishops who did not suit the Metropolitan Pitirim, Rasputin's
candidate, were thrown out of the synod, and all secret military
plans were revealed to the Tsarina and by her to Rasputin.'

Rasputin was assassinated eleven months after the nomination

1. We shall come across one or two rare exceptions to this rule in the
course of this book. Dr Botkin and a few servants followed their monarch
into captivity, and even to death.
2. *Padenie Tsarskovo Regime*, Moscow, 1925–6, seven volumes.
3. In *La Vérité sur le massacre des Romanov*, Paris, Payot, 1936.

of Stürmer and three months before the Revolution. Witnesses, notably Anna Virubova, testify that he looked extremely nervous during the last months of his life. He had begun playing for the highest stakes and wanted the Tsar to abdicate in favour of the Tsarevitch Alexis. In that event Alexandra Feodorovna would become regent and he, Rasputin, the *muzhik* of Pokrovskoye, would control the levers of power. At times, according to Anna Virubova, his nervousness developed into an access of depression and he foresaw the worst. Twice already he had escaped violent death and he more than expected a fresh attempt on his life.

Yet he seems to have felt no forebodings when he went to Prince Yussupov's house on the night of December 16, 1916. Whereas Anna Virubova noted in her diary: 'I don't like this friendship. I am afraid for the *staretz*.'

When at two in the morning he had already swallowed two glasses of cyanide which had had no effect on him, and survived the revolver shots fired straight at his chest, he was finished off by another shot as he fled across the snow.

He had prophesied a few days earlier: 'If anything happens to me, it will be a bad look-out for Papa and Mama. My life is bound up with theirs.'

Chapter VI

A SLEEP-WALKING TSAR

*

THE fate of the Romanovs gathered momentum between December 17, 1916, and July 17, 1918. Sixteen months and a half separated Rasputin's death from that of his illustrious patrons.[1]

Unnerved by the death of the *staretz*, and prostrate with grief, the Imperial family shut itself away in the luxurious apartments at Tsarskoye-Selo. Heavy silk curtains were drawn across windows looking out on to a never-ending snow-storm. Alexandra Feodorovna and her children, huddling over blazing fires, recalled the Holy Memory of the deceased and invoked his Holy Protection. Anna Virubova, on the express demand of the Tsar, installed herself in the Imperial residence whose atmosphere, on her own evidence, she found 'suffocating'.

More broken than he cared to show, the Tsar provisionally gave up his residence with his soldiers at the Mohylev Headquarters and moved to Tsarskoye-Selo for the two months following Rasputin's assassination. During this brief period the cold, impenetrable mask that this shy, suspicious man had forced himself to wear, fell off at times, revealing the Autocrat of all the Russias in a strange light.

Throughout his whole reign the Tsar had felt fear and an instinctive repulsion for intellectuals. Ever since the morning of March 1, 1881, when as a boy he had witnessed the assassination by a nihilist of his grandfather, Alexander II, he had always been convinced that philosophers and writers generally had a pernicious influence over public opinion.

Heir to Hamlet's blood on his mother's side—she was Princess Dagmar of Denmark—he was educated by tutors[2] who

1. In February 1918 the Bolsheviks aligned the Russian calendar with that of the rest of the world by skipping thirteen days.
2. Mainly by the jurist Pobedonostsev, a champion of orthodox autocracy.

failed to form his character, let alone his intelligence, and in his hesitations at least he recalled Shakespeare's hero. Apart from hunting, cards and dominoes he lacked any systematic interests. Books bored him. The library at Tsarskoye-Selo was well stocked, but he read unwillingly, and if at all, then briefly. He 'couldn't stick it', threw the book down, and hurried off to rejoin his wife and children playing a parlour game—as he noted in his diary. He discovered the pleasures of reading only in the last months of his life when a prisoner of the Red Guards.

In her colourful secret diary Anna Virubova described the way in which Nicholas spoke of the intelligentsia, the 'intellectual classes' of St Petersburg, even well before the Revolution. 'He articulates the word in a very special way,' she wrote. 'When Papa says *intelligentsia* he makes the face my husband used to make when he said *syphilis*. You can hear the fear and a sort of disgust in his voice. . . .'[1]

Another 'complex'—to use the word that had recently been put into currency by Freud—had branded Nicholas for life. Born weak and weedy, as a very young man he felt that, though heir to the throne, he was the least 'successful' of Alexander III's sons. Every time he had to look right up at his father, who was prodigiously tall and who, they said, was thinking of 'passing him over' in favour of his brother, he felt humiliated. On reaching manhood Nicholas fled from worldly pleasures and was the chastest of Crown Princes. He had only one liaison before his marriage —with the famous ballerina Kshessinskaya. But the chroniclers of the time all agree that the dancer threw herself at the Tsarevitch's head on the command of Alexander III, who wanted her to make a man of him.

The dry and angular German, who at a very young age set her cap at the graceless Crown Prince, was to be the only woman who played a part in his life, as in his death.

To the description of Nicholas II as shifty and shut in on himself—a description that fits alike the autocrat of the first years of the war and the prisoner of 1917–18—a final touch, and a surprising one, should be added. For a few weeks—precisely those between Rasputin's assassination and the outbreak of the February Revolution—Nicholas began behaving in an extraordinary way.

1. *Journal Secret d'Anna Virubova*, op. cit., p. 34.

The evidence is beyond doubt. It was the time of 'the sleep-walking Tsar'.

The first witness is Count Kokovtsev, a convinced monarchist and former Prime Minister. In his *memoirs* published in 1933 he told of his last interview with the Tsar at Tsarskoye-Selo on January 17, 1917.

> I shall never forget that meeting . . . I was so dismayed at the Tsar's appearance that I was afraid to ask after his health. It was twelve months since I had last seen him and he was quite unrecognisable. His face was terribly thin and worn and covered with lines. His eyes, normally velvety and deep brown, seemed faded and wandered listlessly from one object to the next, instead of remaining, as in the past, on the person with whom he was talking. The whites of his eyes had yellowed, the black pupil had lost its lustre and become grey and lifeless. There was a lost expression on His Majesty's features, and his lips preserved a sad, forced smile . . . He heard me to the end with this new desolate smile and with his glance wandering in every direction. Then I asked him for immediate instructions about the task he had given me, which question—and it was a simple one for it never crossed my mind that the Tsar, with his marvellous memory, could have forgotten what he had said to his own Minister for the Interior two or three days before—threw him into a state of confusion to me inexplicable. The strange, forced, expressionless smile was still there as he looked at me as if begging for my help to call back something that had completely slipped his mind . . .

After he had grasped the hand of the Tsar who took leave of him with the same lost look, Kokovtsev, his eyes filled with tears, could not resist questioning Dr Botkin, the Imperial physician.

'Do you mean to say you don't see the state His Majesty is in? He's on the edge of a mental breakdown, if it hasn't happened already. . . .'

Kokovtsev was one of the first to notice the Tsar's dazed condition, but others soon followed. Eight days later the French Ambassador, Maurice Paléologue, who had an eye for detail, also saw Nicholas II for the last time, and he too noted the 'deep feeling of sadness and worry' that seemed to beset him.

Everything he said, and especially the long intervals of silence, his vague, unseeing eyes, his wandering thoughts, his strange overwrought appearance—all these confirmed the idea in circulation for some months, that the Tsar already felt he was being swept away by destiny, had already lost all faith in his mission or in anything he did, had abdicated in spirit, resigned himself to imminent catastrophe, and was awaiting martyrdom.[1]

This purely psychological explanation of the Tsar's abnormal condition during the last weeks of his reign can hardly satisfy historians. The black forebodings that must have darkened his mind at this time, and his state of physical and moral prostration, are not enough, taken alone, to explain that 'inexplicable confusion' of his speech and manner, his eyes that 'wandered listlessly' and so on. If they were, why should his appearance have returned to normal a few months later, when he had lost his throne and his freedom and was worried about his family? For after the abdication no visitors to the Imperial family reported any abnormality.

In the summer of 1917 Alexander Kerensky saw the captive Tsar a number of times and found him relaxed and 'without any inner conflict'. Determined to look more closely at the mystery of the 'dazed Tsar', Kerensky put forward another explanation, a really disturbing one: that in the December and January preceding the February Revolution, Nicholas II was *drugged*.

Kerensky deals with this explanation at length in his excellent book already mentioned. He reviews the evidence put forward by Kokovtsev and Paléologue as well as that of an officer who, a few days before the Revolution, was present when the Tsar was inspecting troops at the front. 'The Emperor simply wasn't there; he behaved like a mere automaton', the officer reported; and Kerensky concludes:

Shortly before his assassination, Rasputin had decided to get rid of the Emperor and make the Empress regent. In some vague way Nicholas was hostile to him, so he believed; what was more, the Tsar lied, he said. 'He's capable of making the

1. Maurice Paléologue: *La Russie des Tsars pendant la grande guerre*, Paris, 1923.

sign of the cross just to take me in.' To kill him was out of the question, but there was another solution: to paralyse his will—and there was a man to hand capable of doing it, the Tibetan magician Badmayev, a tool of Rasputin's.

Badmayev, the liveliest figure in the whole Rasputin clique, treated his patients with herbs, roots and balms. He had first-hand knowledge of the age-long secrets of the lama healers, and in St Petersburg a number of people had blind faith in him. One day, in a moment of indiscretion, the *staretz* told Yussupov about Badmayev's herbs and roots and how they could 'cause mental paralysis as well as stop or aggravate haemorrhages'—the latter being the evil from which the Tsarevitch suffered. As for the former, it would be hard to imagine a more terrible example of the effect of Badmayev's nostrums than the Tsar with his wan smile, his constantly shifting eyes and his failure to recall the purpose of his conversation with Kokovtsev.

By February 1917 Rasputin was dead, but at Tsarskoye-Selo things went on exactly as they had when he was alive . . . No business of importance was decided without the Tsarina having a hand in it. And now she had only one aim: to maintain the autocratic system of government for her son Alexis . . . Grand Dukes were exiled to their country estates or sent to distant provinces; the army was suspect; public bodies working for national defence were marked down for dissolution; the Duma, too, was to be dissolved. 'We are at war with all of them and we must be firm'.[1]

And Kerensky concludes, in italics:

Rasputin dead proved to be more powerful than Rasputin alive. In his name Tsarskoye-Selo broke its last links with the nation and the army . . . for ever.

'Rumours, rumours, rumours. Our heads are bursting with them. And the town is boiling and bubbling like a cauldron of tar.' So Anna Virubova noted in her diary for February 10, 1917.

1. Here Kerensky is quoting from Alexandra Feodorovna's letter to Nicholas II dated December 14, 1916.

The Romanov dynasty was sitting on a volcano, and a flaming torrent was soon to sweep away the descendants of Catherine the Great. But some members of the family realised the danger and tried (though very much in vain) to warn the Tsar. The most vigorous and intelligent of the Romanovs was the Tsar's first cousin, Grand Duke Nicholas Mikhailovitch. He was a man with Western ideas, a historian of merit and a 'corresponding' member of the French Institute. As 'the intellectual of the family', he had made repeated attempts to remove the scales from the eyes of his august cousin, but at each conversation the Tsar politely stifled yawns and hurried to provide a light every time Nicholas Mikhailovitch took out a fresh cigarette. Finally the Grand Duke became exasperated and lost his temper:

'And now, Nicholas Alexandrovitch, call the Guard and have me killed and buried in your garden!'

The Emperor merely smiled as he escorted his cousin to his study door. But a few days later he ordered him to stop coming to court and to consider himself under arrest at his estate in Gruchevaya. Whereupon the Grand Duke dispatched a long letter to the Tsar which is now a historical document. Here are its salient passages:

Are you properly informed about the situation within the Empire and particularly in Siberia, Turkestan and the Caucasus? Do you know the whole truth, or do they hide most of it from you? Where does the root of the evil lie? Let me explain in a few words:

So long as your method of choosing your ministers was only known to a small coterie, things could carry on for better or worse. But as soon as such matters were generally known and discussed in public, it became obvious that Russia could not go on being governed in that way. You often told me that you trusted no one and were constantly being betrayed.

If this is true, the remark should apply above all to your wife who, though she loves you, is constantly leading you into error—surrounded as she is by people in the grip of the spirit of evil. You believe in Alexandra Feodorovna. That is natural. But the words she utters are the outcome of clever intrigues, they are not the truth. If you are powerless to rid yourself of

such influences, at least be always on your guard against the
unceasing and systematic intriguers who use your wife as a
tool . . .

If you could prevent the persistent intervention of these evil
influences, Russia's regeneration would take a great leap forward, and you would regain the confidence you have lost with
the immense majority of your subjects. You would find yourself faced with a people who, with a new regime, would be
happy to work under your guidance . . .

I have hesitated for a long time before telling you the truth,
but have now decided to do so on the persuasion of your
mother and sisters. You are on the eve of new trials—even
new attempts against your person. Believe me, if I stress my
desire that you should cast off the chains that imprison you, it
is not for personal motives—as you know, I have none—but
only with the hope of saving you and your throne and our dear
country from the terrible and irreparable catastrophe that lies
ahead.

When Nicholas had read these almost prophetic words, all he
did was to give a wry smile. He did not even dare show the letter
to the Empress. The Romanov relatives made a final effort in
January 1917. The Grand Duchess Victoria, wife of Grand Duke
Cyril, was sent to Tsarskoye-Selo. She tried to reason with the
'German woman' or *nemka*, as everyone called her. She sketched
a picture of Russia with the nobles in the van—the very ones who
had taken part in all the liberating movements—all demanding an
up-to-date regime to replace this grim Byzantine farce. Alexandra
Feodorovna, whose eyes were red with weeping for the *staretz*,
broke in drily and started enumerating in her turn all the 'enemies'
of the Imperial family and all those she suspected of condoning
Rasputin's assassination.

'However high their positions,' she said in a threatening voice,
'they had better look out!'

And when Victoria persevered in her warnings the Tsarina
dismissed her with:

'I have been on the throne twenty-two years. I know Russia.
I know how the people love our family. Who would dare to side
against us?'

A few days earlier when the British Ambassador had come to

present his New Year wishes and a few observations, Nicholas had adopted much the same tone as his wife:

'You tell me, my dear Ambassador, that I ought to earn my people's trust. But isn't it rather my people who ought to earn my trust?'

Chapter VII

THE ABDICATION

*

I
T WAS the terrible winter of 1916–17 that hastened the death-blow hanging over the Russian monarchy.

Already in decline before 1914, the monarchy had become incurably sick as a result of the war (that incomparable 'speeder-up of history', as Lenin put it). Indeed the regime had become so worm-eaten that it needed a blow only slightly rougher than former blows to bring the entire fabric down, and the exceptionally severe weather of January and February served this purpose and precipitated the collapse.

At Tsarskoye-Selo, as in all the great Russian cities, it froze to minus thirty degrees. On February 22 two hundred trains on their way to the capital stopped in their tracks, frozen like blocks of ice. During the night the thermometer had gone down to minus forty degrees. Fifty-seven thousand supply trucks, taking food to the front, the capital and the great urban centres, were blocked. At Petrograd the bread shops were empty. In the working-class suburbs on the other side of the Liteini Bridge the people murmured, infuriated by the announcement made the previous week that bread cards were to be issued. The reserves of flour ordered by the municipality had been sold to provincial traffickers by unscrupulous administrators. On that day which was, for Socialists, the eve of the 'workers' festival',[1] the women of Petrograd smashed the bakers' windows before moving on to plunder other food shops.

In his mahogony-panelled study at Tsarskoye-Selo, Nicholas II was pacing nervously up and down. He had got up at dawn. From time to time he went to one of the windows, pulled back the heavy curtains, and glanced towards the avenue. Hooded men and women were hurrying across it so as to make way for a

1. The date had been fixed by the various European Socialist movements a few years earlier.

military convoy. Clouds of steam poured from the horses' nostrils.

A polar blast tore at official posters caught in the skeleton trees—proclamations signed by Stürmer, Prime Minister, and Protopopov, Minister for the Interior: the glue had frozen before they could be stuck to the walls. At a corner of the palace a motionless sentry in a long grey cloak suddenly came to life and waved a salute to some passing sailors and soldiers piled in a Peugeot truck. The soldiers and sailors seemed ill-tempered and answered the sentry with catcalls.

The Tsar's reflection trembled in the polished parquet floor as if he had been attacked by a shivering fit. By now Nicholas II was afraid of his own soldiers. He now saw himself as a weary traveller caught in all the fury of a storm and with no idea where to find his road. He turned back to his black marble table and with nerveless fingers sorted through the pile of telegrams from the front which were awaiting his attention.

The news from Headquarters was bad. The hopelessly under-equipped Russian soldier no longer believed in his saints and heroes, nor in the St George medals distributed to the disabled; he made every possible effort to stay in the rear. Fifty per cent of the effectives disappeared from their billets on the eve of the great counter-attacks. Probably the sentry at Tsarskoye-Selo knew the facts better than the Emperor. Probably when he saw his comrades he felt rather ashamed of his fine uniform and brand-new boots.

How much was the Tsar, as commander-in-chief, responsible for the disintegration of the Imperial army? Having pitted the great tide of his Russian troops against German and Austrian technical perfection, and having seen trenches brimming with the corpses of his *muzhiks*, he now found himself at the head of a gigantic rout. A few months earlier the soldiers had cheered him when he visited their billets. Even after the tragic Galician retreat, when the Russian artillery had run out of munitions and could make no answer to General von Mackensen's cannonades, the artillerymen had waved their caps when he passed by. In the spring of 1916 the infantrymen were still marching to death with their icons under their tunics and spears in their hands—waiting to pick up the rifle of a fallen comrade. But it was two and a half years since the fine popular enthusiasm of the summer of 1914.

The Russian armies had lost two and a half million men, almost as many as all the other allies put together.

The Emperor passed his ringed hand over his damp forehead. He had a headache and was tired of trying to solve so many insoluble problems. He felt in a drawer of his desk, found the phial he wanted, and, with trembling hand, counted a certain number of drops into a crystal glass. Badmayev's nostrum would calm his jangled nerves. Then he got up and went into the billiard-room where the maps of the fronts, dotted with little flags, were hanging from the walls. No one was allowed in this room except the Emperor, and he alone had the keys; yet there was a light on and the door was ajar. Alexandra Feodorovna rose when her husband came in.

'I was tidying up a little,' she said, 'as the servants aren't allowed to come in here.'

And as the Tsar seemed on the point of asking a question she changed the subject.

'Niki, I'm worried. Alexis and Olga are feverish. I shall send for Dr Botkin this evening.'

A passing military convoy shook the icy road outside and the Empress's last words were inaudible. 'Niki' struggled against the feeling of numbness that came over him every morning at the same time, and said in a firm voice:

'Alix, I shall be leaving immediately after lunch for Mohylev. I am needed at Headquarters.'

The news amazed Alexandra Feodorovna, as indeed it amazed the whole Imperial suite. The Tsar seemed to be getting a grip over himself and wanted to escape from the stifling atmosphere of Tsarskoye-Selo and his wife's burdensome solicitude.[1]

The Tsarina took a breath before answering in her dry voice:

'But, Niki, we promised Anna Virubova we would spend the evening with her. She is having the little Rumanian orchestra we are so fond of.'

'I've got to go, my dear Alix. It's cold, but at least the sun is shining. Tomorrow it may be snowing again.'

The Empress, after her moment of rebellion, gave way. She

1. According to some historians it was Grand Duke Michael who called on Nicholas to leave Tsarskoye in a hurry, so as to permit action against the Empress's household.

knew better than anyone that she must never have a head-on clash with her impulsive husband. The tall thin Tsarina felt it was more tactful to bend down and kiss him on the cheek.

'As you think, darling boysy.[1] But promise you won't forget what Protopopov told you last night after dinner. You must be firm, firmer than ever. That pretentious windbag of a lawyer, Kerensky, must be put in prison. We must strike out against our enemies and against all those who have condoned the horrible crime against our friend.'

'But, Alix, the question is . . . how?'

'Protopopov is your faithful servant. Give him dictatorial powers.'

'Could he calm the workers? Isn't it too late?'

'It's never too late, Niki, to repress the follies of the mob. You can trust Protopopov.'[2]

In the course of this conversation,[3] the last between the Tsar and Tsarina—for when they met again on March 9 they had fallen from power—the Tsarina had, as many times before, fervently pleaded the cause of the man she trusted, the Minister of the Interior.

What sort of man was this Protopopov who was to play such a significant part in the events of February 1917? Gérard Walter, one of the historians who best understood the *dramatis personae* of the time, has left us the following portrait:

Only one man stands out, but he stands out with brilliance, from the drab backcloth of the successive Ministers in the Imperial Cabinet: the Minister of the Interior, Protopopov.

It would take a Balzac to describe the lightning career of this starving student who gave lessons at fifty kopeks an hour and by the age of forty had become an all-powerful Minister. He has been described as unbalanced, even mad, and this he in fact became after the hammer-blow of February. But up till then all that could be seen in him was unbridled ambition,

1. One of the pet names Alexandra gave her husband. Whenever possible she liked to talk to him in English.
2. Cf. the extraordinary document (photo No. 12) which shows better than any words the atmosphere of the conversations between husband and wife in the Emperor's study.
3. Following unpublished evidence of a story told later by the Empress herself.

great ability, the most winning manners, and a great talent for pleasing. When he first entered the Duma he was an obscure deputy; in a very little while he had won the sympathy of the majority and was elected Vice President. When at the end of 1916 a delegation of Russian members of parliament was chosen to visit the Allies, not only was he one of them, but he was made leader of the delegation and was its spokesman in London and Paris. Which didn't prevent him—in Stockholm on the way back—from having a chat with a German diplomat whom he managed to charm just as much. He pleased Rasputin who saw him as just the man to govern the Russians, and he pleased the Empress who fell for his air of mystical inspiration.[1]

At two o'clock in the afternoon the Tsar boarded one of the few trains still running from the station at Tsarskoye-Selo. He had heard Mass in the palace chapel and kissed his children, as he did every time he went to Headquarters. The Master of all the Russias and last autocrat of Europe had not the faintest idea that when he returned home to his family sixteen days later it would be as a mere prisoner of a republic that was finding it very difficult to control the forces of revolution.

While the Tsar in his over-heated drawing-room coach was sleepily listening to General Lukemsky reading the latest reports from Staff Headquarters, the unrest in Petrograd was spreading from suburb to suburb. The lack of supplies at the height of a glacial spell had made even the timorous rebellious. In the endless queues stretching outside the few shops that had not yet been closed or pillaged, no one talked of anything but of hanging Stürmer and Protopopov. Politics, which a few days earlier had only caused a stir in drawing-rooms, had now swept down to the streets. A hundred thousand workers were either on strike or unemployed: the Putilev works, the biggest metallurgical combine in the capital, had shut down and the workers had joined the enraged housewives.

Next day, February 23, while at Mohylev Nicholas entertained the leaders of the British and French military missions to dinner, a great wave of rioters was streaming along the Nevsky Prospekt in Petrograd and shouting 'We want bread' on the steps of

1. Gérard Walter, *Histoire de la Révolution russe*, Paris, 1953.

Parliament. The next day, February 24, the Tsar noted in his diary that he had been decorated with the Belgian *Croix de Guerre* and then taken a stroll in his garden. Meanwhile in the capital the weavers, given orders to strike, had thrown two hundred thousand workers on to the streets in their turn. The riots were becoming a revolt.

On February 25 Nicholas rose late and—as he noted in his diary—prayed prostrate before the icons in the Mohylev monastery. That afternoon he took a stroll along the Orcha road before going to evening service. In Petrograd there was now a general strike; in the great avenues spreading out from the Admiralty red flags, held aloft, were waving like a sea. The first dead fell in front of the great shops of the Nevsky Prospekt. For the first time the troops used for keeping order showed signs of hesitation. When the 'pharaohs'—the police—were baited, the troops merely smiled.

On February 26, a Sunday, the now daily riots continued. There was a serious incident: the Pavlovtsy, one of the crack regiments of the Imperial Guard, openly refused to obey orders and cheered the rioters. They were confined to barracks and there was talk of shooting the ringleaders. When news of this reached the Tsar he showed no signs of anxiety, he played dominoes all evening in the conviction that the order he had sent to General Kabalov, military commander in the capital, to 'put an end to the troubles' was a perfectly adequate step.

The decisive day was February 27. The Pavlovtsy, fearing a court martial, rallied brother-regiments to their cause. The great avenues were now invaded by a double uprising—of workers and soldiers. The Volhynia regiment—the Tsar was its colonel—mutinied and won over the Ismailovsky, the Semenovsky and the Lithuanians: these were the very troops that had been used in the ferocious repression of 1905. Even the Preobrazhensky regiment, most loyal of them all, ended up by cheering the Duma deputies and their president, Rodzianko. The rioters occupied all the public buildings. The Stürmer Government resigned. The Revolution had begun so spontaneously that the extreme Left, the Social-Revolutionaries and the Bolsheviks, were not yet ready. The labour leader (*trudevik*), Kerensky, cleverly put himself at the head of the movement, thereby 'short-circuiting' the leaders of the clandestine organisations. Late that night armed

workers and mutinous soldiers brought the first political
prisoners to Kerensky's office at the Duma.

Meanwhile, at Mohylev, Nicholas II was beginning to show
signs of anxiety at last. That evening he noted in his diary:

'There have been disorders in Petrograd during the last few
days and to my great distress the troops have joined in. It is
frightful being so far away and only receiving fragmentary
news. I didn't spend long on the report. This afternoon I took a
stroll along the Orcha road. There was bright sunshine.'

Events followed thick and fast. Early on February 28, while
the Tsar was setting out in his special train for Tsarskoye, a
provisional Executive Committee, including all the popular
leaders, assembled in Room 13 in the Parliament. In a neighbouring room Duma deputies were somewhat apprehensively setting
up another committee whose simple aim was to 're-establish
order in Petrograd'. In the Taurid Palace, less than a mile from
Parliament, the leaders of the old Socialist clandestine movements were meeting in their turn to form a Soviet for the capital.
The whole of the next day, March 1, was spent in passionate
discussions, and on the morning of March 2 the Provisional
Government was established under Prince Lvov. This Government was a makeshift organisation intended to take interim
charge until a Constituent Assembly could be got together, and it
was only created after laborious negotiations between the various
Petrograd Committees. It depended on the representatives of
the traditional Parliament as well as on a Soviet representing the
Revolution triumphant, and during its three months of life it
suffered from this duality. The stubbornness of the Petrograd
Soviet and the inflexibility—and cowardice—of the Duma
monarchists rapidly led to a general compromise, for which the
person of Nicholas II, and then the monarchical system itself,
were to pay the price.

Nicholas's decision to leave Mohylev at five in the morning of
Tuesday, February 28, was the last and clumsiest of his whole
reign. Doubtless it was prompted by family considerations—his
wife was isolated at Tsarskoye-Selo and the children had all
fallen ill since his departure—rather than by political imperatives.
At Mohylev the Tsar was surrounded by relatively loyal troops
who had to keep a certain discipline owing to the proximity of
the enemy. Had he stayed on there, he could have made some

attempt to control the situation. By leaving his safest refuge he merely involved himself in a useless adventure. 'At the moment when the fate of the monarchy depended above all on speedy decisions, the Imperial train approached Petrograd with all the majestic slowness of a Russian express.' Towards ten o'clock in the morning Nicholas awoke. The journey proceeded without incident through the snow-bound plains of White Russia.

At three in the afternoon, and then again at nine in the evening, he dictated telegrams to the Empress telling her that 'he would be home the following morning'. These telegrams—like the innumerable cables sent by Alexandra Feodorovna to Mohylev—were never delivered. The latter were returned to the Imperial home with the insolent note in blue pencil: 'Addressee unknown.'

At Malaya-Vichera, about a hundred miles from the capital, the two trains bearing the Tsar and his suite had to turn back. Further along the line the revolutionaries were in occupation and they would certainly block the convoy. The trains struggled through Valdai and Dno and finally reached the town of Pskov, headquarters for the northern front under the command of General Russky, reputed to be an inflexible monarchist.

And it was in Pskov, historic city of White Russia and famous for its churches, that Imperial Russia died after a thousand years of life. On March 2, late in the evening and after forty-eight hours of fruitless search, two deputies of the Duma, Shulgin and Gutchkov,[1] finally found the Tsar. They had been charged by the Provisional Government to negotiate his abdication. Their task was painful, but extremely easy. All general officers of the Russian Army, consulted by telegram by Alexeiev, Imperial Chief of Staff, had shown themselves in favour of the abdication. And the more monarchist they were the more categorical they were. Disturbed for a long time about the Sovereign's incompetence, and desirous at all costs to save Russia from disintegration, they hoped that this wise decision would re-establish national cohesion. Shulgin and Gutchkov did not have to *persuade* Nicholas. During the afternoon Nicholas, 'whose features were twisted by a strange movement of the lips', had been repeatedly 'thumbing through the pile of telegrams from army commanders'.

1. The latter was the Empress's *bête noire*. She had frequently considered having him imprisoned.

'They are all against me,' he muttered, 'Grand Duke Nicholas, commander on the southern front, Brussilov on the south-western front, Evert on the western front, Sakharov in Rumania, Admiral Nepenin of the Baltic fleet . . . all of them. Very well, I shall abdicate in favour of my son Alexis.'

In the spacious drawing-room coach, with its green silk hangings, the Emperor, wearing a grey *tcherkesska* (cossack tunic), welcomed the deputies and shook their hands in a not uncordial manner. The three men sat down at a small square table and others joined them—the old Count Frederiks, tall, grey and sallow, and General Russky. Gutchkov spoke first, not without some emotion, and explained the purpose of the meeting. Nicholas II listened without raising an eyebrow. 'His face was impenetrable and perfectly calm', as Shulgin, from whom we take the description of this scene, was to put it. 'The only thing, in my opinion, that his expression suggested was: This long speech is superfluous.'

In a calm, clear voice, 'in which only the accent was a little odd, suggestive of a Guards Officer', Nicholas replied:

'I have made my decision to abdicate. Until three o'clock this afternoon I thought I could abdicate in favour of my son Alexis. But now I have modified my decision in favour of my brother Michael.'

After a moment's pause, and in a graver voice, he went on:

'I hope you will appreciate this decision of a father.'

Everyone, Shulgin tells us, got up. Gutchkov handed the Emperor a rough draft of the abdication act. Nicholas took it and left the room. After a moment he returned and handed the two deputies a telegram form on which the text had been typed and signed in pencil. It was exactly twelve minutes to midnight.

Before going to bed the Emperor entered a description of what had happened in his black morocco notebook. It shows no apparent emotion. The final words were:

'At one o'clock this morning I left Pskov, my soul oppressed by what I had just lived through. All around me there is nothing but treachery, cowardice and deceit.'

The return of the two deputies to Petrograd was not without incident. Gutchkov was arrested by workers of the railwaymen's Soviet who demanded that the act of abdication should be handed over to them. The revolutionaries did not take to the idea of the continuance of the monarchy. But they failed to get hold of the document.

At Petrograd railway station the paper was handed to a messenger sent by the monarchist deputies, Bublikov and Lebedev. The latter hid the historic document in Bublikov's office, not in a safe but in a dusty file of back numbers of the *Official Journal*.[1]

1. P. M. Bikov, op. cit., p. 41.

Chapter VIII

'DEPRIVED OF LIBERTY'

*

THE dramatic events of March 2 did not make undue inroads into Nicholas's nervous resistance, nor did they undermine his astonishing capacity for sleep. 'I had a long, deep sleep,' he noted on the 3rd in his diary. And again, on the 4th, 'I slept well.'

A general characteristic lethargy, or torpor due to barbiturates? That excellent St Petersburg poet and chronicler, Blok, who wrote a number of studies on the last days of the old regime, opted for the former. Whatever the influence of Badmayev's drugs, the objective historian is bound to point out that long before the Tibetan magician appeared on the scene the Tsar had been an 'abnormal man lacking in sensibility and conscience'— the man who so astonished the deputy Gutchkov. Foreign journalists, including Charles Rivet of *Le Temps* whom we have quoted already, reported that at the time of the bloody affrays of 1905 the Tsar declared to his cronies: 'What interesting times we live in!' and added in French: *'Moi, ça m'asticotte!'* ('It worries me!')

The ex-Tsar left Pskov on the night following the fateful signature and was back at Mohylev on the evening of the next day. Headquarters personnel met him on the little station platform in formal array. The staff officers, who were nearly all monarchists, felt it their duty to pay this last honour to a sovereign who had given the army the best of himself, or at any rate the least mediocre part of himself. Dinner with a few intimates in the dining-room of the Imperial manor was more relaxed than might have been expected. There was no departure from normal etiquette. General Ivanov, Nicholas's private military adviser, tried to place the conversation in the context of the war, and spoke about recent French successes in Champagne. Ivanov was famous not for his gifts as a warrior but for his Tolstoy-type beard and his peculiar patronymic (his father's

Christian name being Judas, the General, according to Russian custom, was called 'son of Judas').

But the end of the evening was overshadowed by a telegram from Rodzianko containing the latest news. The new Tsar, Grand Duke Michael, had renounced the throne in his turn, and all he asked for was the election of a Constituent Assembly in accord with the fourfold formula of 'universal, equal, direct and secret' suffrage. 'God alone knows what put the idea of signing such a disgraceful thing into my brother's head', wrote Nicholas in his diary before once more enjoying the sleep of the just.

So, without the smallest monarchist resistance, power passed from the descendant of Peter the Great into the hands of the Revolutionary Committees and the Provisional Government stemming from them. As Kerensky, unrivalled participator-witness-historian in and of the times, wrote:

> Russian autocracy collapsed without any pocket of resistance such as La Vendée, and the last Emperor had no Swiss Guards to defend him. At Tsarskoye-Selo the men of the Imperial escort strutted about decked in red ribbons before the Palace entrusted to their guard . . . Consultation with the army command showed that Rasputin and 'the German woman' had isolated the Tsar from his army as much as from the rest of the country . . . Neither in St Petersburg nor at the front was there a single regiment on which the Emperor could depend. In the whole army there was only one instance (at least so far as I knew) of 'a subject of His Majesty' sufficiently loyal and conscious of his duty to fight to the end. This was Count Keller, commander of one of the cavalry corps. He refused to bow to the 'mutiny' and the evil will of 'cowardly drunkards'. Vainly he appealed for organised resistance; no officer would follow him. Count Keller committed suicide . . .

Nicholas II, notes Kerensky, seemed so 'harmless' and so 'completely outside the nation's preoccupations' that the new Government left him and all his staff completely free, and even permitted him to live unguarded at Staff Headquarters, the heart and brain of the army. 'Of course,' Gutchkov had answered when Nicholas asked if he could go back to Mohylev.

So there was no guard nor even any 'observer' from the

Revolutionary Government when, on March 4, the Tsar stood on the station platform waiting for the special train to bring his mother from Kiev. The Dowager Empress's eyes were full of tears. The old Danish woman could not help reflecting that this sad reunion was due to the deplorable influence of her daughter-in-law, the hypochondriac, 'irascible' ex-Tsarina. For days on end Alexander III's widow wept hot tears while her son 'kept his eyes fixed on the ground and smoked in silence—as he always did in uncongenial circumstances'.

On the evening of March 7, after a game of bezique with his mother, Nicholas shut himself up in his private study. He had one last task to perform, to draw up a farewell ukase to the Russian armies. Next day, the 8th, he signed the typed copy. A duplicate of the message was found by Judge Sokolov among the ex-Tsar's private papers after the Ekaterinburg drama. Here is a translation of the little-known document:

This is the last time I shall address you, my beloved soldiers. Since signing the abdication in My Name and that of My Son, supreme power has passed into the hands of the Provisional Government formed on the initiative of the Duma of the Empire. May God help it to lead Russia in the path of glory and prosperity. May God help you, too, brave soldiers, to defend our country successfully against a tenacious enemy. For two and a half years you have been engaged in the unremitting hardships of military service. Much blood has been shed, and many efforts made in vain. But the hour is not far off when Russia and her glorious allies will reap the fruits of their endeavour. This war must be carried on to a victorious conclusion. Anyone who talks of peace, anyone who asks for a truce, is a traitor to the motherland. I know that you all think as I do. Do your duty, defend your motherland, obey the orders of your leaders and the Provisional Government. Remember that weakness or insubordination can only play into the enemy's hands. I am convinced of the great love you have for your motherland. God bless you and may St George lead you to victory.

This rather prolix and rhetorical—yet sincere—farewell was never communicated to the troops. It should have been included in the order of the day No. 371, March 8, 1917. But Gutchkov, the new War Minister, forbade its publication by telegram. Instead came a decree from the Provisional Government.

Meanwhile Nicholas had been savouring the bitterness of separation. Discreet interventions by army leaders had obliged him to dismiss his 'evil genius', General Voïkov, Head of the Imperial Chancellery. This protégé of Rasputin was particularly unpopular at Staff Headquarters. He was accused of being an intriguer and also a shameless trafficker. He had even made use of his privileged position to impose on staff messes a brand of mineral water from one of his estates to replace the German and Austrian mineral waters that had been unobtainable since 1914.

Late at night on March 7 (old style) the telephone rang in Nicholas's apartments. General Alexeiev, Chief of Staff, had good news. Negotiations with the Provisional Government for the ex-sovereigns to leave for abroad were going well. Soon they would receive a safe-conduct to the port of Murmansk on the Arctic Ocean, where they could board a British warship.

Reassured, Nicholas stretched out on a divan and fell into a deep sleep. At dawn, March 8, he was fresh and ready for a hard day. He had to leave Mohylev, say goodbye to his Generals and part from his mother. It was high time to be getting back to Tsarskoye-Selo, to his frantic wife and feverish children. At 1 p.m. lunch was served in the restaurant car of the Dowager Empress's train. While mother and son conferred together for the last time, and the engine of the ex-Emperor's train was warming up, a third special train drew into the station. The Mohylev railwaymen had never been so hard-worked. It brought Bublikov, representing the Duma, and three obscure deputies, Vershinin, Gribunin and Kalinin. A large crowd cheered the emissaries of the new Government. There was applause and speeches. Nicholas, who was sitting facing his mother in a leather armchair, could not help wincing. For the first time in his life the fallen autocrat was attending popular rejoicing as an onlooker.

At 4.45 in the afternoon Nicholas's train, which had been protected from the crowd all the morning by a detachment of the third Baltic regiment, began moving. A group of workers with red armbands occupied the first and last coaches. The four Duma deputies also took their places in the tenth and last coach.

Nicholas wiped his eyes with a handkerchief as Maria Feodorovna's train disappeared from sight. Mother and son were never to meet again.

The journey was slower even than usual. Precautions had to be taken to ensure that the stations of Orcha, Licslav and Bologoye were adequately guarded by security detachments. There was news of bands of fugitives and army deserters roaming pretty well everywhere—obeying anarchist orders, so it was said. At Vitebsk people gathered on the platform outside the ex-Tsar's coach. Nicholas appeared at the window. Some of them sneered. But a fat woman in a fur coat burst into tears.

'Don't go away, *Batiushka* [Little Father],' she cried. 'You are the glory and hope of our motherland; you can still lead our men to victory.'

The fallen Tsar smiled bitterly. Under his fur coat his left hand clutched the icon that his mother had hung around his neck a few hours earlier. He closed the window of his drawing-room coach and went back to his armchair. He had been brought a file of newspapers from Petrograd, already out of date. In the capital special editions had been rushed out in numbers unheard-of in the history of journalism. The *Vestnik* announced in headlines: 'All power in the hands of the Provisional Government.' Others told of 'the suicide of the monarchy' or 'the collapse of the Empire'. Editorials spoke of the 'new and mysterious Russia' that had now come into being. War correspondents described the enthusiasm of the troops and their oath of allegiance to the new Government. This was the only piece of news that really affected Nicholas. As the journey continued he was brought more recent papers. Events in St Petrograd now danced before his eyes like a ballet. 'Kronstadt sailors condemn their officers to death'; 'Protopopov gives himself up'; 'Political prisoners return from Siberia'; 'Vladimir Ulianov Lenin returning from Switzerland.'

Now and again the train stopped at country halts, little stations hastily put up since war broke out, where men wearing top coats jostled with fat peasant women carrying baskets. A swarming, tight-packed crowd, full of emaciated faces but with the eternal good temper of the Russian people. Nicholas looked at the grey mass of his former subjects spread out on the icy platforms. He felt no bitterness against the immense peasantry that had betrayed the monarchy. He merely failed to understand. How could they reject a leader imposed on them by God Himself? During the last few days he had felt very remote from the old Holy Russia— somewhere at the antipodes amongst strangers with bizarre names. Sometimes, as at Vitebsk, he was recognised. An occasional old man would make the sign of the cross, or a peasant woman would kneel; but more often there were urchins raising dirty bony fists, or railwaymen who knew who was in the train and held Nicholas's eye while they spat. Then, shivering, the ex-Tsar would pull his English woollen shawl over his shoulders. Until he reached Tsarskoye-Selo his comfortable railway carriage was a warm and safe refuge.

Nicholas was dozing in his armchair when General Lukemsky came and woke him as respectfully as ever. Despite the late hour the four Duma deputies wanted a word with him. Inwardly the Emperor cursed the new men for their lack of courtesy. In that case he would make them wait.

'Tell them I shall receive them in a quarter of an hour,' he said.

He spent a few moments in the washroom in the adjoining compartment. Then he strolled in the corridor. At the far end a Baltic rifleman in a grey cloak and red armband was on guard. Two soldiers were dragging a heavy machine-gun along the carpet of the corridor. Nicholas had not seen them before and was astonished at this increase in measures for his protection.

The sentry was chewing sunflower seeds, his eyes lost in the night. Nicholas wanted to make a gesture of friendship to a man who called to mind all the soldiers who had died for him.

'So, my fine fellow, do you belong to one of the glorious regiments that is to take part in the spring offensive?'

Instead of saluting, the soldier jeered:

'I'm not your fine fellow, but a comrade rifleman. And I'm not going to the front, but to Petrograd, to bring about the Revolution.'

Choking, Nicholas returned to his sitting-room, where the Duma delegates were awaiting him. Their faces looked waxen. Even before Bublikov opened his mouth, Nicholas knew that they were bringing bad news.

'Your Highness, we are here to show you the resolution passed

by the Government,' and the deputy handed over an official
paper dated March 7. It read as follows:

1. The deposed Emperor and his wife are to be considered as
   deprived of liberty, and the deposed Emperor is to be taken
   from Mohylev to Tsarskoye-Selo.
2. Adjutant-General Alexeiev will receive orders to place a
   detachment of soldiers to serve as a guard for the deposed
   Emperor, under the command of Bublikov, Vershinin,
   Gribunin and Kalinin, members of the Duma. These
   deputies are hereby ordered to Mohylev.
3. The members of the Duma chosen to accompany the
   deposed Emperor from Mohylev to Tsarskoye-Selo shall be
   asked to submit a written report on how their orders have
   been carried out.
4. This resolution shall be made public.

So Nicholas was the last person to hear what everybody else
knew already. His deep brown eyes took stock of the four men
who remained standing with their bowler hats on. A certain
uneasiness was perceptible beneath the rigidity of their bearing.
Gribunin was fumbling with his watch-chain; Kalinin was
flicking away traces of snow from his pale grey gaiters; Vershinin
was swaying backwards and forwards. With his thumb in his
braided waistcoat, Bublikov broke the silence:

'I think our mission, unpleasant as it has been, is now over.'

The Tsar acknowledged the deputies' salute with a short bow.
There was no handshaking. A few minutes later a young captain
knocked at the door.

'I have orders,' he said, 'to take charge of any firearms that
may be in your luggage. As well as any official documents. . . .'

Nicholas looked at the infantry officer. He had the St George
Cross pinned on his chest. Nicholas wanted to be affable and, as
usual, he was clumsy:

'The Carpathian campaign, Captain?'

'Yes, Highness. Two mentions in dispatches. The second
recalling the glorious retreat from Galicia. . . .'

At eleven-thirty the following morning the special train drew
into Tsarskoye station. Colonel Kobylinsky, Military Commander
of the small town, the station master, and two lesser officials were

waiting. Scarcely had the train stopped than a dozen officers leapt out on the wrong side and fled nimbly over the railway tracks. The court was no more, and with unrivalled turpitude the courtiers abandoned the man whom they had always called 'our adored Tsar' like a sinking ship.

Nicholas Alexandrovitch Romanov emerged in the uniform of a Cossack colonel. He spoke to no one, merely saluted and got into the waiting car. Ten minutes later he heard the gates of his beloved Alexandrovsky Palace close behind him. He was a prisoner.

Chapter IX

SHE WHOM
THE PEOPLE HATED

*

A COMMON microbe, the *virus morbillus*, also played its part
in the events of February and March 1917, and unexpectedly facilitated the formalities of the Tsar's abdication.
At the moment when revolution broke out in Petrograd the
four daughters and only son of the Imperial family fell seriously
ill one after the other. While the Nevsky Prospekt produced a
rash of red flags, measles was raging in the palace at Tsarskoye-
Selo. The Empress, now a nurse, was worried about the state of
the Grand Duchesses but tormented by the new affliction that
had befallen her haemophilic Alexis. To that unbalanced woman
the Tsarevitch was the object of more than all a mother's love;
he enshrined her ambitions and explained all her mad 'policy-
making' of the preceding years. It was terrible for her to have to
forsake Nicholas—'the Tsar under marital tutorship'—at the
very moment when the throne was toppling: she was well aware
that the endless messages she sent off to Mohylev could not make
up for her presence. She had a foreboding of her husband's
apostasy and tried to guarantee the future—Alexis's future—by
writing:

> Alone, defenceless, ensnared, what can you do? It is the
> most monstrous, the most unheard-of ignominy that history
> has ever known. If they force you to make concessions, you
> must not consider yourself bound by them. They will have
> been extracted from you by shameless means.

From the depths of her tabernacle, isolated and ill-informed,
the Tsarina had been following the progress of the uprisings in
the capital. For years she had done everything to keep her
husband's relations away from Tsarskoye-Selo . . . so the Grand

Dukes laughed, instead of coming to her help, and concentrated on how best to shift for themselves. As the *Temps* correspondent wrote: 'They can be presumed to be feeling some secret satisfaction as they see events proving them right in the German woman's eyes.'

The Empress heard of the defection of the military on February 28. The Guard was ordered to prepare for defence and surround the palace with machine-guns and armoured cars. But most of the soldiers went over to the revolutionaries once these appeared. A few loyalists had already trained their arms on the newcomers. With the precious person of the Tsarevitch in mind, the Tsarina besought them to do nothing.

The next day Alexandra summoned her uncle-in-law, Grand Duke Pavel Alexandrovitch, to the palace.

'Go to Staff Headquarters,' she begged. 'Bring me back loyal troops. Everything must be done to save the throne and Alexis.'

Pavel Alexandrovitch knew perfectly well how useless such a move would be and thoroughly enjoyed refusing. On March 3 he was again summoned to Tsarskoye-Selo, and immediately showed the Empress the last edition of the newspapers with the news of the abdication.

'The Tsarina knew nothing,' he said afterwards. 'When I stopped reading she shouted out: "I don't believe it, it's all lies, invented by the papers. I believe in God and the army. They have not abandoned us." I had to explain that not only God but even the army had joined the Revolution. I saw the Empress again and for the last time on March 5. She was incapable of speech. She sobbed and kept asking me what she should do.' Defeated and humiliated, she had to wait on the Duma's decision.

The first evening after the revolutionary troops had seized Tsarskoye-Selo, the Empress heard the sound of shots outside her windows. Volkov, the valet, went to find out what had happened and reported that it was only the sentries amusing themselves by firing on the deer in the park. With her 'dear Anna' (Anna Virubova), Alexandra then devoted herself to a crucial task: she burnt all her personal correspondence, all Rasputin's letters, and all her diary notebooks. More than ten boxes of precious documents, invaluable, no doubt, for throwing light on the Empress's relations with her 'clique', went up in smoke that night.

When the car bringing Nicholas stopped in front of the palace steps (according to the account of Lily Dène, the lady's maid), Alexandra ran down the stairs to meet her husband like a fifteen-year-old. The Tsar modestly refrained from mentioning this detail when writing his diary that evening.

> Lord! What a change! Sentries everywhere, in the road, round the palace, in the park. And in the entrance hall I couldn't count the midshipmen! I went upstairs and saw my beloved Alix and my dear children. Alix looked well and not at all cast down, but the children were all in bed in a dark room. We lunched and dined in Alix's quarters, in the play-room.

We have two more accounts of this reunion. Volkov, the Tsar's personal valet, relates: 'Husband and wife embraced and kissed one another, smiling. Then they went to see the children. It was only later, when they were alone together, that they gave their feelings free rein and wept for a long time in silence.'

Anna Virubova in her *Souvenirs de ma Vie*[1] recounts how the Tsarina came to visit her in her sickroom at four in the afternoon (she had measles too) and told her that 'the Emperor had cried in front of her like a child'.

Moreover the Tsarina had told her husband of a 'very terrible thing' that he had not yet heard. During his absence a band of revolutionaries had passed beneath the windows of the Alexandrovsky Palace dragging a coffin. 'It was Grigory's,' Alexandra said, wringing her hands. 'I was told they took it off to a field and made a huge bonfire and burnt it.'

This news seems to have upset the Tsarina more than her husband's abdication, perhaps because—and this is a fact of history confirmed by a number of witnesses—the strange 'man of God' had predicted that his remains would be burnt and his ashes scattered on the wind. Kerensky relates that one of those partaking in the macabre ceremony found a small icon on the body and gave it to him. On the reverse side were the signatures of Nicholas, Alexandra Feodorovna and the five children.

---

1. An infinitely less interesting book than her secret diary. It was a defence *pro domo* and pure hagiography of her Imperial protectress.

'The Emperor has regained his calm,' the ex-Empress told Virubova. 'He is taking the air in the park.'

From the window of her confidante's room she could watch her husband, who, axe in hand, was felling a tree that had suffered from the inclemencies of the winter. Cutting down trees and chopping wood were the fallen autocrat's favourite pastime in the weeks that followed. Frequenters of the house often photographed him, and Nicholas, as usual, posed obligingly.

Her husband's arrival helped to restore Alexandra's calm and make her forget Rasputin's sinister prediction. Nicholas had informed her of the promises made by the New Government to General Alexeiev, and of the firm hope entertained by the Generals at Staff Headquarters that an agreement would soon be reached for the Imperial family to leave Russia. The 'resolution' of March 7 had not actually used the word 'arrest'; and the expression 'deprived of liberty' surely indicated protective measures aimed at reassuring the people and preparing the way for a safe-conduct as far as Murmansk.

This reasoning, fully justified on March 7, very soon ceased to correspond with the facts. What had happened was that Prince Lvov, head of the Provisional Government, ex-monarchist, and having no more intention than Kerensky of being a 'new Marat', had committed a major gaffe. He had sent to General Alexeiev at Mohylev an uncoded telegram saying: 'The Provisional Government has decided to grant the former Emperor free transit for a stay in Tsarskoye-Selo, thereafter to travel to Murmansk.'[1] Everyone seemed to approve of the 'Save-the-Romanovs' operation. The British Ambassador, Buchanan, had cabled his Government and received a favourable reply. A British warship cruising in the Barents Sea was ready to pick up the fugitives. No one in the Cabinet had opposed this measure of humanity and political wisdom.

But the 'conspirators' (to use the rather over-colourful expression employed by Soviet historians) had left one very important element out of their calculations—the Executive Committee of the Petrograd Soviet. When this Committee learned of Prince Lvov's telegram, on the night of March 8, it immediately took action. As Gérard Walter points out:

1. Published in *Russian Annals*, Leningrad, 1927.

[The Soviets] were not harbouring any specially cruel designs regarding the former monarch but, as always—and here they were perfectly justified—they were afraid of popular reaction in Petrograd. It was easier to get agreement from the plenary Soviet Assembly (a good child, taken all in all, and easy to handle) than to face the angry and suspicious masses which were always ready to come pouring in from the suburbs and out of the barracks. . . .[1]

At the risk of upsetting the delicate relationship established with the Provisional Government, the Executive Committee went into action forthwith, and on its own initiative. Radio telegrams were sent to the Soviets of the big provincial cities instructing them 'to arrest Nicholas Romanov at all costs' should he pass through. Troop detachments obeying orders only from the Soldiers' and Workers' Soviet were posted in the railway stations of Tsarskoye-Selo and Petrograd.

During its meeting of March 9 which took place while the ex-Tsar was sobbing in his wife's arms, the Executive Committee considered the possibility of re-arresting Nicholas and his family and transferring them to the Trubetskoy bastion in the famous Peter and Paul Fortress. One of the Committee members, Social-Revolutionary Mstislavsky, was detailed to set off for Tsarskoye-Selo at the head of an imposing detachment of soldiers of the Semenovsky regiment as well as machine-gunners. Mstislavsky, whose real name was Maslovsky and who has left us a very interesting book of memoirs, was a 'progressive' colonel wounded on the Bielo-Russian front and subsequently a member of the least extreme of the Socialist parties. He was chairman of a secret commission of the Petrograd Soviet aimed at 'setting up a People's Tribunal to judge the perjured Tsar'. His vice-chairman was the enigmatic Yacovlev, about whom we shall have more to say later. The two men and their 'army' proceeded to Tsarskoye-Selo where their first act was to arrest the commander of the local garrison, Colonel Korovitchenko.

His spurs ringing out on the marble floors of the Alexandrovsky Palace, the 'democratic colonel' Maslovsky-Mstislavsky ordered his men to take up positions in the entrance hall and on the stairways. The scene was now set for the 'inspection' that he

1. *Histoire de la Révolution russe*, op. cit., p. 253.

had to make (his mission, though he was endowed with 'full powers', was in fact ill-defined and he could not seize the persons of the Romanovs unless the conditions of their detention seemed to him unsatisfactory). All that remained was for him to dictate his orders to General Count Benkendorf, 'Grand Chamberlain' of this gilded prison, and insist that Nicholas Romanov should be produced before him. Here is his account:

When the door opened with a sinister groan and we were at last in the entrance hall, we found ourselves surrounded by a respectful but curious throng of court retainers—their numbers seemed fantastic after the simplicity of the revolutionary days we had been living through. An enormous *haidouk*, the size of Alexander's monument at Trubetzkoy, wearing a bearskin as tall as a barrel; 'runners'; court Negroes in crimson velvet jackets embroidered with gold, turbans on their heads and long pointed slippers on their feet; footmen in three-cornered hats and red capes embroidered with the Imperial arms; valets in snow-white gaiters and polished shoes with felt soles— these preceded us up the stairs, running along the carpets. After mounting the stairs we went through innumerable drawing-rooms, banqueting-rooms, retiring rooms: outside the door of each room stood a motionless pair of lackeys wearing varied costumes answering to the purpose of the room to which they were posted, sometimes traditional black suits, sometimes white, black or red *kuntuches*. In front of one door there were two magnificently costumed valets in white stockings, polished shoes, and absurd crimson head-bands held in place by hooks of tinsel.

In a glass-roofed upper corridor used as a picture gallery, a little group of courtiers, with Benkendorf at their head, was awaiting us. They were wearing black frock coats buttoned up to the neck.

A few yards beyond this group the corridor was crossed by another one, and it was from there that the ex-Emperor was to appear. I put myself in the middle of the corridor with Benkendorf on my right and Prince Dolgoruky (Grand Marshal of the Court) and a civilian whose face I did not know, on my left. The officers who had accompanied me stood a little behind me.

Somewhere on one side a lock clicked. Benkendorf fell silent and smoothed his grey whiskers with a trembling hand. The officers quickly buttoned their gloves and stood to attention. Hurried steps could be heard, and a faint clinking of spurs. Romanov was wearing the khaki summer uniform of the Imperial hussars and his head was bare. With his habitual shoulder-movement, and rubbing his hands together as if he was washing, he stopped at the intersection of the corridors and turned towards us. His face was red and chubby; his swollen, inflamed eyelids heavily framed his lustreless, leaden, bloodshot eyes. He paused and seemed to hesitate a moment, rubbed his hands together, then walked towards our group.

He seemed on the point of addressing us. I looked at him, he looked at me. There was a dead silence. Then suddenly the Emperor's eye—yellow and fixed like that of a tired and hunted wolf—lit up. In the depths of his pupils there suddenly shone a mortal hatred; it was as if a flame had suddenly melted the leaden indifference of his gaze.

Nicholas stopped a moment, trod the ground, then abruptly turned and went away, jerking his shoulder. I thereupon drew out my right hand from below my belt where it was thrust, raised it to my fur cap to salute the courtiers, and, to the tune of ill-mannered throat-clearing from Benkendorf who also spat, I turned to go. 'You did wrong not to take off your cap,' an officer told me; 'the Emperor seemed to want to talk to you, but seeing the way you behaved . . .' And another chimed in with, 'You'd better be careful. If the Romanovs come back to power, you'll be found at the bottom of the sea.'

The Soviet 'raid' on the Tsarskoye-Selo palace was over. The Social Revolutionaries and Mensheviks, who formed the majority on the Executive Committee, purported to be 'satisfied' by Colonel Maslovsky-Mstislavsky's report. But the Georgian chairman, Tscheidze, felt he had to underline the results of the control operation in a lengthy discourse, in the course of which he said: 'That dangerous family is now under the supervision of the people of Petrograd. Henceforward the Government is under an obligation to take account of the people's wishes. The working masses shall not be betrayed.'

The truth was that the Petrograd Soviet was delighted to have the tiresome business over. For the time being they had lost interest in the Romanov affair, totally absorbed as they were in settling the inner disputes between the Social-Revolutionaries and the Mensheviks on the one side, and on the other the Bolshevik minorities who were waiting impatiently for Lenin's arrival so as to try to establish their control over the Assembly.

Only one thing mattered to the Executive Committee: appeasing the mobs in the streets. The snarl of popular anger was inflamed by revelations in the Press. For some days now all the main Petrograd newspapers had been devoting column after column to the 'Tsarskoye-Selo scandals'—unearthing details, true or fictitious, about the 'Tsarina's clique', Rasputin, and his titled lady friends. Sometimes they turned on the fallen Tsar and tried to show that his return to Mohylev after his abdication was intended as a 'plot against freedom'. But the populace was less easily roused on this point. All bitterness and hatred were concentrated against the *nemka*, the woman who had come from Germany twenty-three years before to install herself on the Imperial throne. We need have no hesitation in saying that loathing for the Tsarina was the real reason which prevented the Romanovs' departure abroad in March 1917.

Chapter X

UNDER THE
SIGN OF THE SWASTIKA

*

T HIS rheumatic woman in her forties whom Nicholas helped
into her wheelchair as evening fell; this mother execrated
by a people well known for its generosity of spirit; this
fallen Empress, executed like a criminal in a cellar at Ekaterinburg, had had the reputation of bringing ill-luck ever since her
youth.

At Darmstadt, where she was born to the Grand Duke of
Hesse, she was already viewed somewhat coldly by the common
people who nicknamed her *Pechvogel*, 'bird of ill-omen'. Eye-
witnesses have told how, when the Princess left the Grand Duchy
with her Tsarevitch fiancé, onlookers were heard to shout: '*Geh
und nimm dein Pech mit dir*' ('Go, and take your ill-luck with you').

In that same year, 1894, further murmurings took place in St
Petersburg drawing-rooms as Alice of Hesse arrived in Russia.
This time the theme was the terrible illness, haemophilia. It was
taken for granted in the Grand Duchy of Hesse-Darmstadt, and
known in all the courts of Europe, that the women of that
princely house handed on the incurable sickness to their eldest
sons. In the previous century a Hessian Princess, Marie, wife of
Tsar Alexander II, had given Russia a haemophilic Tsarevitch
who died without reigning at the age of twenty.[1] His brother
Alexander III—father of Nicholas II—had inherited the throne.
Alexandra Feodorovna's brother, the Duke of Hesse, had died
of the disease, and so had her uncle, Duke Leopold, while her
nephews, the sons of her third sister Irene, had had to contend
with haemophilia all their lives.

---

1. The fact is that the death certificate of Grand Duke Nicolai
Alexandrovitch, Alexander II's eldest son, contained the words 'meningitis
and tuberculosis of the bones', though Grand Duke Nicolai had suffered from
haemophilia as well as a weak heart. He died and was buried in Nice.

If we are to understand the—entirely passive—part played by the Tsarina in the imprisonment of the Romanovs and the break-down of the plans for evacuating the family abroad, we need to take a glance back in time.

In June 1917, before the events of Ekaterinburg were even on the horizon, the *Temps* correspondent wrote a tirade for the prosecution:

> It is a delicate matter to bring in a woman, above all the Empress Alexandra Feodorovna who was doubly hostile to us [the French], first as a German, then as a sovereign.
>
> Yet we cannot paint a lifelike portrait of the ex-Tsar without sketching in the woman who symbolised the atmosphere in which he lived.
>
> The minor Princess from Hesse was for long a shadowy figure moving in the wake of a monarch who, himself, showed no signs of any vocation to play a transcendent part in his country's history. In the early days the young Empress, married like others of her rank, exercised no power over the man to whom destiny alone had tied her. Nicholas was retiring and had been given a ravishing mistress by a father who wanted to make a man of him.[1] He kept up the liaison and at first his marriage to a foreigner who was his intellectual superior was no more than one of the unavoidable obligations of his position. As for her, the Tsarina seemed to nurse for her Imperial husband the feelings that a life in common can bring into being—no more. At court she had found a hand-some officer whom she built up into her 'romantic hero', lavishing a deep affection on him that fed the secret chronicles of the capital.
>
> Though they whispered at Petrograd that the paternity of Grand Duke Alexis was unwarrantably attributed to the Tsar, the child's birth certainly strengthened the marriage bond. With Alexandra Feodorovna, motherhood eclipsed all else—and anyway the former object of her thoughts disappeared round about this time in a somewhat mysterious way.
>
> His death, coupled with the religious stirrings that were

1. In private Nicholas called Kshessinskaya his 'canary'.

already coming to the surface, kept the Tsarina beside the cradle of the weak little Romanov offspring who created an intimacy, and a common concern for the future, between husband and wife. It was with the birth of Alexis that she began to take the place in the Tsar's mind and life that had previously been occupied by her mother-in-law, the Dowager Empress Maria Feodorovna.

Unfortunately she did not make use of this situation to turn Nicholas's indecisive mind away from a narrow conception of autocratic rule and towards more up-to-date ideas. Herself open to western currents of thought, she could have brought some fresh air into the Asiatic court which had taken over from its western counterparts only their vices and failings. As a woman with a head on her shoulders, she should have grasped the danger threatening herself and her family if they isolated themselves with outmoded conceptions in the midst of a world that wanted to live in modern times.

She failed to grasp this. The loss of someone dear to her, her anxieties for her beloved son, her vague fear of that mysterious Russia which remained closed to her but whence confused rumblings reached her ears—these things gradually brought the cold German of the past, and the neophyte of the Orthodox Church, to a state of mystical exaltation which bordered on the pathological. This warped state of mind deprived her of any faculty for impartial observation. The former Huguenot submitted to the grotesque or sadistic practices of Grigory Rasputin, the Cagliostro from Siberia, whom she imposed on her weak husband as her influence grew to be decisive. Alexandra Feodorovna was never liked, and very soon she was hated . . .[1]

The 'romantic hero' to whom Charles Rivet makes discreet allusion was a man who left his mark: General Prince Orlov. He was a brilliant officer in command of the Uhlan regiment of the Imperial Guard, and his fine presence coupled with a ready flow of conversation captivated the Empress. Orlov was in all things the very opposite of the Tsar. 'It would have been so sweet to be with him . . . But I was never his mistress. Our love was sad, like everything else. I liked talking to him and singing for him . . .'

1. Charles Rivet, op. cit., pp. 32–5.

—so the Tsarina told Virubova, who noted in addition: 'It's true, Mama becomes quite beautiful when she sings . . .'[1]

Alexander Afinoguivitch Orlov, called 'Solovushka' ('gentle nightingale') by the Empress, died in a convenient if bizarre way. His body was found in January 1908 . . . in Egypt. The General had no reason to be in that country, though, according to the official version of what happened, 'he had gone there to convalesce from a sudden illness'. In opposition circles it was whispered that the Prince had been assassinated at Odessa on the Tsar's orders and that only his remains had made the journey east. There is no means of checking this assertion. In those more fortunate days all that was needed to enter the Khedive's country was a visiting card—as Baedeker pointed out. There were no police to record the arrival or residence of foreign citizens. The Orlov affair remains a mystery.

Even with her 'nightingale' the young Tsarina had made little attempt to learn the language of her adopted country. As she had passed some years at the English court she spoke English as fluently as German, and it was in English that she wrote the four hundred letters she addressed to her husband between April 26, 1914, and March 4, 1917. This vast and illuminating correspondence was found in a black wooden coffer at Ekaterinburg. Her ignorance of Russian served Alexandra badly with her subjects. In the years 1906–7, after the tragic shootings in the square outside the Winter Palace, rumour went round the country that the *nemka* despised her new compatriots and the impression spread that the throne was not the right place for her.

Her relations with her Danish mother-in-law (though she, too, was a foreigner and highly anglicised) soon became very strained. The Dowager Empress, who was the child of her Scandinavian education and influenced by her Grand Chamberlain, the Caucasian liberal Prince Chervachidze, would have liked to open her son's eyes and urge him to give a Western-type Constitution to his country. But the 'German woman' pressed her husband in the

1. Anna Virubova, *Journal Secret*, op. cit., p. 38. The pet names 'Papa' and 'Mama' for the Tsar and Tsarina dated from 1903. In that year a *yurodivi* (holy innocent) called Mitya Kozelski was a guest at the Winter Palace in St. Petersburg. He 'prayed' for the birth of an heir and his prayer was answered. The memory of this simpleton who could pronounce no words correctly except 'Papa' and 'Mama' was cherished by the little circle of courtiers in the Tsarskoye-Selo 'retreat'—chosen after the events of 1905.

opposite direction, thereby causing 'two hostile camps' at court. On October 21, 1894, when she was received into the Orthodox Church, 'Mama' took an oath to save Russia. 'She also thought that a single drop of royal blood was more precious than the lives of millions of common people.' (Anna Virubova)

'I ought to mention in parenthesis', Virubova wrote in her diary around 1910, 'that I have never known anyone with so much faith in miracles and wonders generally than Papa and Mama—Mama even more than Papa. Mama isn't a great talker. When she talks of something ordinary it is very boring and un-interesting. But when she touches on something miraculous or extraordinary her attitude completely changes, she seems almost on fire. Papa, too, has noticed this. He says to her, "If you weren't the Tsarina, you would be a prophetess!" '

After the births of four successive daughters—Olga in 1895, Tatiana in 1897, Maria in 1899, and Anastasia in 1901—the Tsarina was undoubtedly embittered. The arrival in the world of little Alexis, who was welcomed as a gift from heaven and as a just reward for the intercession of Mitya Kozelski and others like him, changed Alexandra Feodorovna's outlook if not her character. She now began to see herself as charged with a sacred mission, that of guaranteeing the Tsarevitch's future. Whereas she had previously been indifferent to the interplay of politics, she now took a very personal interest. She sought the company both of politicians and of holy innocents, 'God's emanations' through whom she tried to fathom the Almighty's intentions. Once these flatterers and simpletons had been the centre of attention in the Tsarina's little salon, they started acting in collusion. The Rasputin-Badmayev clique was an amazing mixture of politics and magic. But a whole cohort of grotesque characters had preceded the *staretz* Grigory under the gilded ceilings of Tsarskoye-Selo: Aginuchka called 'the owl'; a Coun-tess-voyante who was on terms of complete intimacy with the Empress; Philippe the magician, a cunning and greedy fellow from Lyons; Prascovia, the 'pilgrim from Kiev'; and many others.

Alexandra's taste for this kind of company cannot be entirely laid at the door of Russian mysticism. According to the chronic-lers, her father's palace at Darmstadt was 'a place haunted by charlatans'. And it was a Moravian flagellant who had provided the adolescent Princess with the talisman which, throughout her life, she supposed would bring her luck: a swastika. Long before it was flaunted across the façades of the Third Reich, the crooked cross was traced on a wall in the Ipatiev house at Ekaterinburg by the fallen Empress.[1]

Someone else besides Rasputin played an important part in the long prelude to the tragedy of the Romanovs: Anna Virubova. She was the Tsarina's all-powerful and equivocal Egeria, and then subsequently—during the tragic period—'a faithful if blundering friend'. As we shall see, most of the Russian monarchist attempts to set the Imperial family free were 'supervised'— and lamentably—by this meddlesome, credulous and excitable young woman.

'Ania', aged thirty-three at the time of the first Revolution, was the daughter of A. S. Taneiev, State Secretary and chief of the Emperor's private cabinet, a descendant of Marshal Kutuzov, Napoleon's conqueror, and of General Tolstoy. In 1903, when still under twenty, she became official lady-in-waiting and, two years later, lady of the bedchamber. From that time onwards she renounced all personal life, drew nearer and nearer to the Empress, and finally became her 'beloved sovereign's' confidante. She had a short, non-consummated marriage with a naval officer, Virubov, but this scarcely impinged on her other functions. Her husband went to the palace to make a stormy scene and obtained the Tsar's permission for a divorce.

This is how Anna Virubova described herself in the pages of her *Journal Secret* (entry for February 9, 1917):

> Since the death of the *staretz* I am prepared for anything. I fear nothing for myself and expect nothing. But *'situation oblige'*! Fate has placed me close to power. I am called 'Mama's shadow'.

Pierre Gilliard, the Tsarevitch's Swiss tutor, who shared the general scepticism about her, wrote:

> She was narrow-minded, not very intelligent, kind-hearted, very talkative, sentimental and mystical . . .

1. A detail recorded by Judge Sokolov. The swastika was accompanied by a date: April 17, 1918, the day Nicholas and Alexandra arrived at Ekaterinburg.

The severest of all those who knew her at this period was Charles Rivet:

> This graceless wench looked more like the landlady of a genteel hotel than an Empress's confidante, yet anyone who wanted to obtain some post or favour outside the ordinary run of things had to apply to her . . . All-powerful over the Tsarina's heart, she was to share her power with that gross and dirty creature, Rasputin, of whom—who would have suspected it to see her stout figure?—she was the passionate lover . . . Virubova was one of the first to wish to be exorcised by this vigorous male who contrasted so strongly with the affected gallants of her world.

Here this excellent journalist is mistaken. During her first imprisonment in the Peter and Paul Fortress, Virubova was questioned by the Extraordinary Commission of Inquiry set up by the Provisional Government to investigate the last years of Tsarism. The 'wench' vehemently maintained that she had never been Rasputin's mistress. Her denials made the members of the Commission smile. However, she was accorded the benefit of a medical examination which produced a definite if surprising result: Mme Virubova had all the physiological characteristics of a virgin.

These proceedings, unseemly though they may have been, were of some historical importance. They allowed historians to revise views that were taken for granted before the February Revolution. Rasputin's influence—the 'lusting he-goat', as Paléologue called him—was found to be rather that of an extraordinary practitioner of hypnotism. That, too, of a 'political adviser'. And today there are historians studying what 'defence' the *staretz* could make were he put on trial. At least he was no warmonger—he was the sworn enemy of the military clique led by Grand Duke Nicholas Nicolaievitch. It may even happen—should the part played by the Tsarist Secret Service in the Sarajevo assassination be confirmed—that a more favourable portrait of Rasputin will emerge. In that case the Tsarina's portrait would also need retouching.

The 'man of God' was one of the posthumous participants in the Ekaterinburg tragedy, not as the Tsarina's lover but—more in conformity with history—as the Devil's Advocate. But in 1914 the 'Devil's Advocate' had predicted: 'If Russia goes to war, it will be the end of the monarchy, of the Romanovs and of Russian institutions. In other words, there will be "revolutionary chaos".'[1]

1. cf. the letter in photograph 5.

Chapter XI

ABANDONED BY THE ALLIES

*

FROM the point of view of the Russian monarchists in exile, one of the men 'responsible' for the Ekaterinburg tragedy, in that he could have prevented the Imperial family from being led to the macabre cellars in the Voznessensky Prospekt, was David Lloyd George. For after being 'betrayed and abandoned' by their subjects, the Romanovs, in the spring of 1917, were 'pitilessly abandoned by their Allies'.

The 'deprivation of freedom' which began on March 9, 1917, was to last four hundred and eighty-one days and end with the execution squad despatched by the Ural Soviet on July 17, 1918. First came restricted residence under guard, then strict imprisonment. At first the intention was protective rather than punitive. With the exception of the Soviet extremists, the left-wing Social-Revolutionaries and the anarchists, all the leaders of the new Government were in favour of a prompt departure of the Romanovs for the West.

The only suitable country as a refuge for the fallen sovereigns was Great Britain. Russia, after all, was still at war with Germany. Only an Allied nation could house the Romanovs and at the same time give the Provisional Government guarantees that Nicholas II would not fall into the hands of his 'cousin', Kaiser Wilhelm. There was no question of refuge in France: not only was the ex-Imperial family considered undesirable on republican soil, but in Paris Alexandra Feodorovna was detested and known as '*la bochesse*'. So the British Ambassador in Petrograd, Sir George Buchanan, contacted his Government in the early days of March 1917. The Coalition Cabinet in London was led by Lloyd George and his Liberal Party, which had a close association with Labour opinion.

But there seemed every ground for supposing that the British Royal Family would intercede in the Romanovs' favour. In the Petrograd banks King George V was known as the 'twin brother' of Nicholas II. Their bearded profiles on gold sovereigns and roubles were absolutely identical.

On March 6, 1917, Sir George Buchanan was informed by P. N. Miliukov, the new Foreign Minister, that the Provisional Government was disposed to allow the Romanovs to leave for England. And after an exchange of telegrams the Ambassador received the British Government's approval three days later.

The Anglo-Russian negotiations that followed are more obscure. The arguments and retractions on the point would deserve a historical study of their own. The bitter reflections of Alexander Kerensky, who played an intimate part in the whole business, must command our attention. His opinion of Mr Lloyd George's behaviour is particularly severe. This is what he writes:[1]

In the early days of the Revolution we were obliged to postpone the Romanovs' departure until we could organise all the practical details and choose the most favourable moment from the psychological point of view (vis-à-vis the Petrograd Soviet).

Meanwhile, when the British Government expressed its readiness to harbour the ex-Tsar, the news had been received very coldly in certain British circles, notably among the Liberals and members of the Labour Party—their reactions were examined fully in *Daily Telegraph* leading articles. Then, on April 10 (Russian March 28), the British press published a semi-official statement by the Foreign Office that could only be interpreted as a withdrawal. In connection with Miliukov's reply to Sir George Buchanan, it announced that 'the British Government is not insisting on its offer of hospitality previously made to the Imperial family'.

But what did this mean? 'Is not insisting on its offer previously made'? Anyone would think that the British Government had been insistently begging the Russian Provisional Government to agree . . . whereas in reality the exact opposite was the case.

For a long time people tried to create a legend according to which the British Government 'would never have withdrawn

1. Kerensky, op. cit., pp. 160–6. This book was published in 1936 when all the documents were at Kerensky's disposal. When his political days were over he became a remarkable historian.

its offer of hospitality'. Lloyd George affirms it in so many words in his *Memoirs*. In his view the Tsar and his family died because of the 'weakness' of the Provisional Government which did not dare, or was not able, to follow up the courteous proposal of the British cabinet. Lloyd George's legend was accepted in reactionary circles of the Russian emigration. Their hatred for the democratic revolution blinded them to such an extent that they did not see that Russian honour demands that light should be thrown on the tragic fate of the Imperial family. I had established the truth by 1921. But information from official English sources continued to claim that the Provisional Government was responsible for the Tsar's death. When Sir George Buchanan wanted to relate in his *Memoirs* the facts as they really were, he was told that he would be deprived of his pension for divulging a State Secret. Sir George's daughter, who witnessed her father's activities at close quarters, confirmed word for word all that I wrote on the subject at the time and have repeated here.

Lloyd George has now become franker in his *Memoirs*, but he still does not tell the whole truth. With regard to the negotiations in March, he tells only half the truth, and preserves total silence as to what happened in the summer. He admits that towards the end of March it 'became more and more difficult to carry out this proposal . . . Opinion in France, opinion in working-class circles throughout Europe, the attitude of the Russian revolutionaries'—all these served as pretexts to cover up the British Prime Minister's real feelings.

On March 28 (old style) an Embassy messenger brought a decoded message to Sir George's study. Miss M. Buchanan reports that her father's face changed when he read it.

'The cabinet no longer wants the Tsar to enter Great Britain,' he said.

'Why?'

'They are afraid. . . . Afraid of disorders at home. There might be strikes—at the docks, in munitions factories, in the mines. There might even be rioting if the Romanovs landed. I shall have to inform the Russian Government that the agreement is no longer confirmed.'[1]

1. M. Buchanan, *Petrograd, City of Trouble*, London, 1918.

Lloyd George had made a very pessimistic report to the King. George V showed no ardour to defend his Russian cousins. Possibly the house of Saxe-Coburg had decided to drop its compromising German connections.

Sir George tried to soften the blow to the Russian Government and save appearances. Kerensky writes: 'He expounded the idea that the parties of the extreme Left as well as German agents would profit by the departure of the Tsar to incite Russian public opinion against Great Britain; and hence that it would be preferable to transfer Nicholas and his family to the Crimea.'

The affair took on a dramatic turn a few weeks later, in early summer, and it was this final setback in the Anglo-Russian negotiations that Lloyd George decided to pass over in silence. By that date Prince Lvov's Government had more control over the situation than in March, and the masses were less interested in the Tsar and Tsarina. The Petrograd press had given up dwelling on past scandals and was concerned with present problems.

Furthermore Miliukov had been replaced by Terestchenko. The new Minister for Foreign Affairs proved patient and skilful. Through the mediation of the Danish Minister, Skavenius, he had obtained assurances that the cruiser on which the Romanovs were to embark at Murmansk would not be molested by U-boats. But unfortunately the whole arrangement broke down at the beginning of July. Here is Kerensky's account:

'The British Ambassador called on Terestchenko in a state of deep distress. He brought a letter from a high official of the Foreign Office *who was also in close contact with the court* [our italics]. With tears in his eyes, Sir George Buchanan told the Russian Foreign Minister that the British Government had decided once and for all that it was unable to offer asylum to the ex-Tsar. The letter even contained a sly dig at the Russian Provisional Government, by pointing out how impossible it was for the British Prime Minister to advise His Majesty to offer hospitality to people whose German sympathies were only too well known.'

What had meanwhile happened in London? Why had George V, grandson of Queen Victoria and Prince Albert of Saxe-Coburg, abandoned his cousin Alexandra who had lived at the British court and, long ago, been dandled on his knee? Here the author must stand in for Kerensky so as to deal with another affair into which he has made some research: the disappearance of Lord Kitchener. As we mentioned earlier, Field Marshal Lord Kitchener disappeared on June 5, 1916, when HMS *Hampshire* was sunk off the Orkneys. He was, as we said, on his way to St Petersburg to help the Russians to put some order into their military affairs. In Petrograd public rumour accused Rasputin of leaking information to the Germans which enabled them to torpedo at one and the same time both the warship and the plans for reorganising the Russo-German front.

The circumstances in which the *Hampshire* sank were never quite cleared up. Various biographies of Lord Kitchener have repeated the official Admiralty version that the cruiser had struck a drifting mine. But the Secret Service and Scotland Yard conducted a special inquiry into a shipwreck so providential for the enemy. Twenty years later the minutes of this investigation were still an official secret.

Today it seems extremely likely, if not certain, that the British authorities quickly came to the conclusion that the St Petersburg rumours were well founded. Someone close to the Tsarina knew of Kitchener's impending journey and the name of the ship in which he was to travel. Information cabled to the 'Green Centre' at Stockholm, re-transmitted to Colonel Nicolai in Berlin and thence to German naval headquarters, had made the German submarine fleet's sensational operation possible. A close watch had been kept on all the exits from Scapa Flow through enemy periscopes. The submarine responsible for the exploit, it appears, was the U.22.[1]

It goes without saying that there was no question of ventilating this sort of collusion on the part of an Allied sovereign in wartime. After the war anti-Bolshevik feelings in British policy and the need to keep an open door for a change of regime—even to the profit of the Russian monarchy—were sufficient reasons for the British cabinet to maintain a black-out on information.

It appears that on humane grounds King George V felt disposed to take in Alexandra Feodorovna and her children—though this does not mean that he would have shown them any excess of affection. But Lloyd George and the left-wing members

1. This detail was revealed by Herbert Fitch, formerly inspector in counter-espionage at Scotland Yard, in his memoirs published in 1933.

of his cabinet put sharp pressure on the King to suppress his good feelings.

The comparatively easy-going, democratic, 'Western-style' Russia on which the British Left had laid its bet for the future was swept away during the following autumn by Lenin and his group.[1] Held under arrest in their gilded prison at Tsarskoye-Selo, then in a comfortable residence at Tobolsk (Siberia), the Romanovs were to be handed over, bound hand and foot, to their most ferocious enemies.

1. The Second, or October, Revolution took place on November 7, 1917 (October 25, old style).

Chapter XII

KERENSKY'S SECRET AIMS

*

AFTER the exceptionally severe winter the spring of 1917 was warm and sunny. 'Delicious morning, without any wind'; 'a superb day, but fresher'; '24 degrees in the shade'; 'occasional rain': so Nicholas noted in his diary, as he had done at Staff Headquarters. For historians it will always be an out-standing document—meteorologically!

For the prisoners the new season was in happy contrast with the preceding months and their cascade of tragic events. Time now passed uneventfully, monotonously, very little news reaching them from the outside world. For during the months of April, May and June, Tsarskoye-Selo was like a fortified camp into which only an occasional emissary could penetrate. The former Emperor was now a glum and bearded woodcutter working away in a corner of the great park.

In her 'official' memoirs published in 1926, Anna Virubova wrote:

> Every day I watched the Emperor from my window as he swept away the snow. Along the narrow path that ran round the lawn, Nicholas II and Prince Vassili Dolgoruky (Grand Marshal of the court) shovelled towards one another, while soldiers and non-commissioned officers of the Guard drilled around them. Often the Emperor would look up at the window where we were gathered and smile or wave dis-creetly. The Empress spent her afternoons in my apartments. I was near her, resting, and felt happy. In the evenings both their Majesties visited me, the Emperor pushing the wheelchair in which the Empress sat, as by the end of the day she was too tired to walk. We talked of the past. From my apartments they went to visit other members of the court who had remained with them. These were the Count and Countess Benkendorf (the Countess arrived after the palace had been curtained off

by troops), Baroness Buxhoevden, Countess Hendrikova, and Mademoiselle Catherine Schneider, the Empress's reader.

Curled up in her bed of convalescence (still from measles) the stout favourite sometimes questioned Nicholas apprehensively on the future of Russia. When would the 'disorders' cease? When would the good Russian people turn its back on this 'crisis of immorality'?

'I doubt if order will be restored under less than two years', answered the ex-Tsar, stroking his beard. His prostration of the early days had now given place to an imperturbable calm.

Virubova felt such intense attachment to her protectors that she was deeply resentful of the way in which the old familiars had dispersed, or been dispersed. General Count Frederiks,[1] General Voïkov (the mineral-water seller), and General Groton—Nicholas's three favourites at Headquarters, had been arrested. Aide-de-camp Linevitch and Count Zamoisky—two of the Empress's special cronies—had been ordered away from Tsarskoye-Selo by the revolutionaries. Others—a large number it must be admitted—had simply fled. At Tsarskoye station, when Nicholas arrived there for the first time as ex-Tsar, General Narishkin (commanding the Tsar's mixed regiment) and Tsabel (commanding the Railway battalion) had given the signal for a general rout when they themselves leapt down on to the railway lines. Their example had been followed by N. P. Sablin, a Guards officer who had been one of the Imperial couple's closest friends, Colonel Mordvinev, an aide-de-camp, General Count Grabbe, Count Apraxin and even Duke Nicholas of Leuchtenberg. Courtiers who had participated in all Tsarskoye's pleasures and never been refused the smallest favour dismissed the past from their minds in a matter of seconds.

Some of the servants had followed suit. 'Generally speaking,' as Virubova put it, 'all the Empress's servants stayed on, but all the Emperor's disappeared with the exception of his faithful valet Tchemodurov who followed Nicholas into captivity at Tobolsk and then at Ekaterinburg.'

Derevenko, the mustachioed sailor who served as Alexis's nurse and slept in his room so as to prevent him ever even

1. In 1918–19 he was to play an important part in the Siberian White Army and in the inquiry concerning the Romanovs' execution.

bruising himself, treated the Romanovs with contempt from the moment the abdication was announced. Virubova records that when she last saw him, in April 1917, 'Derevenko was sprawling in an armchair giving orders to the Tsarevitch.' Emulating Louis XVII's shoemaker-'tutor', he was teaching the boy gross language. 'The child, his eyes wide with melancholy and astonishment, kept running from one object to another, doing whatever the sailor told him.'

But the cruellest separation of all for the Empress occurred on April 3 (March 21, old style). That morning had already seen the dismissal of Colonel Kotzebue, First Commander of the revolutionary garrison at Tsarskoye, who had adopted a particularly kindly manner towards the 'internees'. It was his own soldiers who turned him away and spat on him. But to return to the major separation. One of the revolutionary Petrograd dailies—which Alexandra avidly read every morning while letting out exclamations of rage—had just published a new article on Virubova denouncing her as a Brinvilliers, a poisoner, an accomplice of Rasputin and Badmayev. Anna had dark forebodings when, at two o'clock in the afternoon, Kerensky arrived unexpectedly at the palace. The ex-Tsarina had hastily scribbled her confidante a message: 'The Minister of Justice is here. God help us!'[1] A few minutes later there entered her sickroom 'a close-shaven little man with an insolent air and surrounded by soldiers'. The Minister of the Revolutionary Government seemed to relent when he saw her bedridden. He dispatched Count Benkendorf to ask Dr Botkin[2] if Anna Virubova could be moved. The doctor was only too delighted to rid the Romanovs of such a discredited and compromising person, and hastened to say yes. There was a dramatic farewell between Virubova and the ex-Empress. Alexandra Feodorovna was wheeled in by Nicholas's valet, Volkov, shaking with sobs. The two women clung to each other and exchanged rings. The ex-Tsar, who only tolerated 'Ania' out of deference to his wife, judged it superfluous to show himself.

1. One of his informers at the Alexandrovsky Palace had told Kerensky that the Imperial couple had been burning documents.
2. Dr Evgen Sergeievitch Botkin, the family doctor and a man of high moral standing, was one of the four associates shot with the Romanovs at Ekaterinburg. His son, Gleb Botkin, and his daughter, Tatiana Melnik-Botkin, who followed the Romanovs to Tobolsk, have recently been in the headlines over the Tchaikovsky affair (the Anastasia claimant).

Virubova was borne by soldiers to a car and driven to the Trubetskoy bastion in the Peter and Paul Fortress. During the journey a revolutionary officer, Colonel Peretz, said ironically:

'Grichka[1] and you deserve a monument for your help in bringing about the Revolution.'

Anna Virubova was imprisoned in Cell 70 near Manuilov, the black marketeer, and General Voïkov—two other Rasputin protégés. She was set free on July 24 of that same year. After an adventurous stay in Finland she returned to Petrograd and remained in hiding in the suburban slums. Together with her faithful valet Bertchik, and her friend Chura Gagarin, she used all her blundering goodwill to help her former protectors and plan risky escapes.

Apart from Virubova and Lily Dène, the lady's maid, no other member of the Romanov household was seriously incommoded. The courtiers and servants who left the military enclosure of the palace only did so of their own free will and after obtaining authorisation from the Tsarskoye military command. On April 1 (14) Nicholas noted with due melancholy in his morocco-bound diary that on the previous day forty-six lackeys, valets and servants of different kinds had taken leave of their masters. True, almost as many preferred to remain cut off from the outside world so as to enjoy the Imperial food allowance during this time of shortage. Dethroned though they were, the Romanovs were still prodigiously rich.

In mid-April, at the moment when Vladimir Ulianov Lenin returned from Switzerland via Germany in an 'extraterritorial'[2] train coach, the little court was still following its outmoded routine, with the minutest details regulated by etiquette. Lenin and Trotsky, as well as Kamenev and Stalin who had recently emerged from Siberian prison camps, had only one formula on their lips: to encourage the revolutionary ferment and 'maximalise' the transformation of the old Tsarist Empire. At Tsarskoye, fifteen versts from the stormy meetings of the Petrograd Soviet, Count Benkendorf, monocle in eye, went on playing his part of Grand Court Marshal with all the pomp and solemnity of the past. With due respect for protocol he would receive the emissaries of the Revolutionary Government at the door of the

1. Diminutive of Grigory, i.e. Rasputin.
2. The famous 'sealed' coach was not sealed at all.

Imperial apartments and inquire whether His Majesty was disposed to receive them. A strange spectacle—this monarchical microcosm at the heart of an immense country quivering with revolt—with the Provisional Government's powers disputed by the Soviets in the large cities, and they themselves torn by the quarrel between Mensheviks and Bolsheviks.[1]

After the end of March the Alexandrovsky Palace fell under the direct control of Alexander Kerensky, Minister of Justice. This apparently anodine decision nevertheless gave a faint premonition that one day the Imperial couple would have to face a reckoning with the people. Two regular army officers with quite different temperaments, except that both had rallied to the Revolution, were given the delicate task of watching over—as well as protecting—the Romanovs. The troops inside the palace were now under the command of the luckless Kotzebue's successor, Lieutenant-Colonel Korovitchenko. This man came from the legal side of the army and had once been a colleague of Kerensky at the bar. Like Kerensky he was a good republican and Kerensky trusted him. He always maintained a tone of dry politeness when addressing Nicholas. Nicholas loathed him.

Outside the palace the command was in the hands of Colonel Eugen Stepanovitch Kobylinsky. This man was a Guards officer who had distinguished himself on the Polish front, and a henchman of the new commander of the Petrograd military district, General Lavr Kornilov. Kornilov (who was involved in the abortive *Putsch* of late August 1917 and eventually commanded the White Army in the South) and Kobylinsky were two honest soldiers who had become temporary democrats paying lipservice to the Revolution. Kobylinsky, who succeeded Korovitchenko at the end of May, became the Imperial family's 'guardian angel', first at Tsarskoye-Selo and later at Tobolsk. 'Our good Commander' was how Nicholas referred to him in his diary (entry for June 26—July 9—1917), when noting that Kobylinsky had been given the unpleasant job of asking the Romanovs to stop shaking hands with the soldiers and officers on guard. Ex-imperial affability had provoked a series of incidents with young revolutionary officers who brusquely ignored

1. What made the situation in Russia even more fluid was that the February revolutionaries had not yet dared to proclaim the Republic. That was done only in September 1917.

the outstretched hand and looked away. The private diaries have preserved the names of these 'ill-bred' men: Lieutenant Yarinitch, Midshipman Shumovitch and Midshipman Domodiantz. Domodiantz, an Armenian militant syndicalist, was young Alexis's *bête noire*. The ex-Tsarevitch used a coarse word about him in his diary—one doubtlessly learnt from Derevenko.

As for Lieutenant Yarinitch, when Nicholas expressed paternal astonishment at his rudeness, he replied:

'Citizen Nicholas Alexandrovitch, when the Russian people offered you their hand in 1905, it was you who turned your back.'

Within the buildings of the Alexandrovsky Palace the Romanovs were left entirely free to come and go and to organise their little court as they liked. But walks in the park were restricted to the enclosed part of the gardens and they were kept under strict surveillance.[1] On Sundays and feast days a disorderly and inquisitive crowd would press up against the park railings and spit at the ex-Tsar if they caught sight of him, while the young Grand Duchesses were greeted with coarse jeers. As for Tsarina Alexandra, suffering both from sciatica and the terrible wound to her self-esteem, she happily never ventured beyond a little sunny terrace screened from 'spectators'. Had she appeared in public, the scenes would certainly have been much more riotous.

It was the sentries who were harshest with the Romanovs. 'Even in the park', Kerensky wrote,[2] 'the guards deliberately exaggerated their orders by following on the heels of the prisoners, taking them rudely to task, and showing their contempt for the fallen Sovereign in every possible way.' Their crude bad manners were all the more painful for Nicholas as they mostly came from the regiments he knew best—the first, second and fourth Light Infantry regiments of the Imperial Guard. On June 3 (June 16) it was Alexis who had an incident with the guards as they were following just behind him as usual. While Nicholas was cutting up pine logs on the far side of the tennis court, the Tsarevitch amused himself with a small-scale carbine on the island in the middle of the lake. This 'bloodthirsty' game enraged the sentries who confiscated the child's weapon and took it to the guard-room. Some days later the

1. See the photograph of the Tsarevitch and his dog Jimmy (No. 14).
2. Op. cit.

carbine, which Midshipman Domodiantz had taken to the revolutionary town hall of Tsarskoye-Selo as 'evidence for the prosecution', was restored to the Romanovs, but in pieces.

There was another incident on June 10 (23). This time the victim was Anastasia. Here is the entry in Nicholas's diary:

> Saturday, June 10. Last night and until three this morning the heat was stifling. In the morning I went a long walk. We lunched, as we did yesterday, in the children's dining-room. In the afternoon we worked in the same place.[1] There was a storm nearby but we only had a few drops of rain. Fortunately they freshened the temperature. At six-thirty we went to church. And towards eleven in the evening there was the sound of a shot in the garden. After a quarter of an hour the Commander of the Guard asked permission to come in. He explained that a sentry had fired because he thought somebody had been signalling with a red light from the children's window. When they saw how the electric light was placed, and the way Anastasia moved her head, a non-commissioned officer who had come in with the Commander of the Guard realised what the explanation was and they both went away with apologies.

Korovitchenko and Kobylinsky were constantly obliged to manœuvre—to use Kerensky's expression—between the garrison, which was under pressure, and the Imperial cabinet which had been reduced to a caricature—so both, but especially Korovitchenko, were the object of each group's resentment. They had to take care to avoid any repetition of what had happened to poor Kotzebue, and so they approached their own subordinates as little as possible and then with caution. As the weeks and months passed, their functions became more and more a matter of form.

As a last resort when they had complaints to make, the Romanovs could appeal to Kerensky. This they often did. Between March 21 and July 31 (old style) the Minister of Justice visited the prisoners regularly. After July 9 his visits became solemn

---

1. We learn from earlier entries that three dead trees had fallen near the Arsenal and been sawn up with the help of Prince Dolgoruky, the valets Volkov and Teriatnikov, the lackeys Martychkin and Korneev, and several other 'volunteers' recruited by the Tsar.

events as he had succeeded Prince Lvov as President of the Council.

This great champion of the people, whose strong personality left its mark on the only democratic and parliamentary government Russia has ever known in a thousand years of history, was naturally curious when he first visited the Imperial family. For some ten years, first at the Petrograd bar and then in the Imperial Duma, he had been a passionate defender of democrats and the new ideas. Nevertheless, as he himself relates,[1] his aim in his first interview with the ex-Tsar was to show himself as 'meticulously correct and nothing more'. When Count Benkendorf went off ceremoniously to inform 'His Majesty' of the visit, and Kerensky followed him along endless corridors, he had to struggle with himself to overcome his emotions—'too many harsh and terrible things had been associated with the name of Nicholas II'.

After keeping him waiting behind closed double doors the Count threw open both wings and intoned:

'His Majesty bids you welcome!'

Through the door Kerensky glimpsed 'a confused, perplexed group' sitting at a round table near one of the great bays of the Alexandrovsky Palace. 'From the midst of these timid creatures,' he relates, 'and not without some hesitation, there emerged a man of average height in military uniform who approached me with a faint, odd smile.' After a moment's embarrassment the ice was broken and the two men shook hands. The introduction to the Tsarina—'stiff and tense, proud, dominating, intractable'—was more difficult. In that brief moment Kerensky grasped the difference of temperament between Nicholas II and his wife, and, as he says in so many words, got an insight into 'the psychological undercurrents of the tragedy that had been going on for years within the walls of this palace'.

In the course of later interviews—'which were not very many' —the two men got to know each other better. Kerensky's visits had at least one advantage in the eyes of the Romanovs, they broke the monotony of life at the palace. 'The Tsar's whole family had a happy memory of these visits, between eight and ten of them', wrote the Soviet memorialist, P. M. Bikov. Sur-

1. Op. cit., p. 173. Kerensky, originally a member of the Russian Labour Party, joined the Social-Revolutionaries in 1917.

vivors who were close to the Romanovs at that time testify that
Kerensky treated them with kid gloves. 'As Bikov wanted to do
as much harm as possible to his political enemy in exile, he was
only too pleased to be able to quote a statement made by the
valet Volkov who escaped the tragedy at Ekaterinburg: "One
day the Tsarina said to me of Kerensky, I have no complaint to
make against him, he's a decent man and one with whom one
can talk." '[1]

'I'm convinced that Kerensky was a hypocrite and was merely
playing a part at Tsarskoye,' affirmed Sokolov to one of his
White Army colleagues after taking down Volkov's statement.
And though he was less categorical when writing up the account
of his inquiry, Sokolov nevertheless let it be understood that
Kerensky's courtesy to the Romanovs seemed to him insincere.
Numbers of other *émigré* historians have accepted his view and
laid many sins at Kerensky's door.

There are not enough documents available to settle this
question. On one side we have Soviet historians claiming that
Kerensky was the 'valet' of the Romanovs; on the other there are
those who maintain that he was a hypocrite who might sooner or
later have signed their death-warrants. In his own book, from
which we have quoted, Kerensky seems deliberately to omit
certain details. What were his real intentions concerning the
continued captivity of the Romanovs?

As he is alive, and very much so, the present writer decided
to ask him this question himself. It was a very vital old man, for
all his eighty-two years, who received me in his elegant apartment on New York's 93rd Street. Though now half blind, he is
still actively employed in putting together a new book of
memoirs. Incidentally he is a close observer of Soviet politics.

'Yes, of course I had precise intentions about Nicholas II and
Alexandra Feodorovna,' he answered.

'Did you want to set them free, or shoot them?'

'Neither. I thought that every possible light should be thrown
on the last years of Tsarism and the domination of the Rasputin
clique. But in the spring and summer of 1917, when we were
still engaged in a terrible war, it was impossible to divulge my
plan, which was to bring the Tsar, and above all the Tsarina,
before a revolutionary and democratic court whose task would

1. Reported by Sokolov.

be to clear up a whole epoch of Russian history. It was with this in mind that I instructed Colonel Korovitchenko to confiscate all political documents still in the Emperor's hands. Our Extraordinary Commission of Inquiry was to conduct a preliminary investigation. It was for this reason that, for a short period, I gave orders that Nicholas II should see his wife only at family mealtimes.'

Chapter XIII

DEPORTED TO SIBERIA

*

A S THE trees at Tsarskoye-Selo, meticulously cleared of
their dead wood by the woodcutter-gardener Nicholas
Romanov, began to sprout their buds and new green leaves,
a fresh forest of multicoloured banners sprang up along the
great avenues of Petrograd.

On April 18 (or May 1, Western style) the Workers' and
Soldiers' Soviet of the capital staged an enormous but orderly
procession, which, as it proceeded, cheered all resolutely pacifist
slogans. By next morning the Nevsky Prospekt and the big
shopping streets seemed restored to relative calm. But on April
19 and 20 the demonstrations suddenly began again and rapidly
took on the violent character of an uprising.

What had happened? Before we try to analyse the 'April
days' which were soon followed by the equally famous 'July
days' of 1917—and show how they affected the fate of the captives
in the Alexandrovsky Palace—we must always keep in mind that
the Russian-German war was still being waged. Of all the
difficulties facing Prince Lvov's Provisional Government the continuation of hostilities was the most oppressive. The new regime
which was 'neither fish nor fowl'—uncomfortably poised halfway between monarchy and republic—had received speedy
recognition in London, Paris and Rome (March 11–March 24–
1917). But in return the Allied governments had insisted that
Russia should resolutely pursue military operations against the
Central Powers.

But the war which, in the Western countries, had brought
about a temporary reconciliation between Socialists and Conservatives, had grown more and more intensely unpopular in
Russia. The national flame that had burned so brightly in 1914
had well and truly gone out. Given their overriding concern for
social reform, both workers in the large cities and *muzhiks* in the
country could hardly have cared less about the 'war aims' of the

Tsarist cabinets of 1914–16: annexation of Constantinople and the Straits as well as of Armenia and northern Persia; dismemberment of Turkey and the Austro-Hungarian Empire. The only person who still identified himself with these aims was the maladroit Minister for Foreign Affairs of the Provisional Government, P. N. Miliukov.

Miliukov was a university man with a mania for things English, and he was quite at sea when it came to assessing the aspirations of a newly awakened people. He made blunder after blunder. On the eve of the May 1 celebrations he declared to the Press that 'the possession of Constantinople was still a task for the nation'. Worse, he had no hesitation in faking an official note of the Provisional Government—which had rallied in part to the pacifist demands of the Soviets—and proclaiming on his own authority 'the determination of the whole Russian people to carry on the war to a victorious conclusion'. The text of this declaration was published in Petrograd on April 19 (May 2). It came like a bombshell.

For the first time since the revolutionary days in February, blood flowed. General Lvar Kornilov, Military Commander in Petrograd, did not scruple to provoke the masses. The Soviet of the capital skilfully kept control of its followers and forced the resignation of Gutchkov and Miliukov. The Government was re-formed on the coalition principle. Prince Lvov remained Prime Minister, while Kerensky, whose popularity was growing every day, took over the War Ministry. But the real victors behind the scenes were Lenin and Trotsky, and the only beneficiary of the rising was the Bolshevik Party, which was able to increase its membership.

The 'July days' followed almost exactly the same pattern. But this time the unpopularity of the Government did not follow from a mere declaration of intentions, as had happened with Miliukov, but from a tragic reality. The offensive on the Galician front was a failure. This military action was particularly unpopular with the Petrograd masses as it had been conducted under the command of General Kornilov. Despite the Bolshevik leaders' traditional prudence, the people of Petrograd poured out once more into the great avenues and besieged the Taurid palace (July 4, old style). Tchernov, the Socialist Minister of Agriculture, was nearly lynched. Prince Lvov decided on repressive measures against the Bolsheviks. The offices of the newspaper *Pravda*, which was edited by Stalin and Kamenev, were sacked and occupied by troops brought in from the provinces. By now things had got beyond Prince Lvov's control and he resigned. There was a Government crisis. A new coalition cabinet, dominated this time by the Socialists, was not set up until July 24 (August 6, Western style).

The Provisional Government, whose left-wing had now lost touch with the people of Petrograd, was dying on its feet— though Kerensky's energy (he was now Prime Minister), and the support of the Social-Revolutionaries and the Workers' and Peasants' Soviets, enabled it to get the better of Kornilov's right-wing *pronunciamento*. But the October rising, led by Lenin, was to sweep it away like straw in a Siberian wind.

As new Premier of the Provisional Government, Kerensky aimed at being a national referee, set above the political mêlée, and one of his first actions as such was to remove the Romanovs and get them away from the riots that had now become chronic in the streets of Petrograd, and might spread.

The position of the Romanovs at Tsarskoye had been made even more critical by the intrigues of the 'rearguard' of Russian monarchists. Though the activities of these amateur agitators were insignificant enough, the revolutionary garrison resented them as intolerable provocations. There were, for instance, anonymous letters to the ex-Tsarina promising her that she would soon be back on the throne; there were visits from sub-emissaries such as Bertchik, Anna Virubova's valet, who got into the palace on the pretext of bringing provisions to the kitchens. For the machine-gunners of the Guard, these small but routine conspiracies became matters of State.

'One day,' Kerensky relates, 'a car broke through the garden railings just near the palace. Needless to say the whole of Tsarskoye-Selo was in turmoil and there were cries of treason. It had been an attempt to rescue the Tsar! Though this was nonsense, a sentry had to be set over the gap in the railings.

'So it was really impossible to delay any longer. The Tsar's family had to be sent far away—to some island of tranquillity which, incidentally, was hard indeed to find in Russia at that time.'

Shortly before he resigned, Prince Lvov had put Kerensky in

charge of 'all the negotiations bearing on this urgent problem'. Kerensky made a careful study of the alternatives. He decided against installing the Romanovs on the estates of one of their relations such as Grand Duke Michael or Grand Duke Nicholas. The population in the central provinces that the special train would need to pass through was dense and particularly restless.

Nicholas II soon heard of the change in store for him. On July 11 (July 24) he had a visit from Kerensky which, as usual, cheered him up. Three days earlier, after Prince Lvov's resignation, he had written in his diary: 'Kerensky is to be Prime Minister. As things now are, it will be the right place for the the right man. The more power he has, the better.' Kerensky tactfully let the Tsar know of an impending move, and hinted that the Romanovs would be taken *south*.

The ex-Tsar loved the climate of the Crimea and his castle at Livadia (his mother's refuge), and began packing the Imperial luggage. He even showed signs of impatience: 'I am longing to know when we shall be leaving,' he wrote in his diary for July 28 (August 10). Kerensky's warning, 'Don't forget to provide yourself with plenty of warm clothing,' seems to have caused him no alarm. Alas for his hopes! On July 28 (August 10) he was informed by Count Benkendorf that there was no question of going to the Black Sea and its stretches of tamarisk, but that he was to be sent to a town in the east, three or four days' train journey from Tsarskoye. Disappointment was intense, and it was a clever move of Kerensky's to communicate the bad news through a third person. As long as the world war lasted—so doubtless reasoned the astute young politician—it would be pointless to alienate Nicholas. After all, the Emperor still had some vague credit with the Allies. There would be time enough to wash the Romanovs' dirty linen when war was over.

In order to make his final interview with the Tsar less of a strain, Kerensky took an unexpected and consoling visitor with him. He hoped that by contriving this happy surprise he would mitigate the captives' recriminations. The visitor in question was Nicholas's favourite brother, Grand Duke Michael.

So on the evening of July 31, only a few hours before the Romanovs' departure, a moving scene of reunion took place in the little study that Nicholas had arranged for himself at the top of the palace. Nicholas and 'Misha' embraced with tears in their eyes. It was their first meeting since the February Revolution. 'They stood facing each other,' Kerensky tells us, 'moving from one foot to the other, in a state of strange embarrassment, sometimes taking each other by the arm, or by a button on their clothing . . . Grand Duke Michael wanted to see the children, but I was unable to give permission.'

Once Michael had left, Kerensky profited by the Tsar's emotion to give him details about his new place of detention.

'Nicholas Alexandrovitch, my Government has decided to send you to Tobolsk. You and your family will be very comfortably installed in the former Governor's residence. And above all you will be protected from injury. . . .'

The ex-Tsar, who had never learnt how to 'take' several simultaneous emotions except by withdrawing into a strange state of apathy, said nothing—just as he had said nothing in his special train when signing the act of abdication. His face was only a little more glum than usual. He smoothed his moustaches with automatic hand and looked out of the window at the great park under the moonlight. He realised that once again he had been mistaken about a man's character. But this Kerensky, whom he had treated as a friend and almost as an accomplice, had never even considered betraying his trust as legal head of the Government brought in by the Revolution. The passionate young democrat of the Duma had shown himself, as in the past, just but severe. So ended what Bikov, the Soviet chronicler, called the 'Kerensky-Romanov idyll'.

Tobolsk could hardly have been less like a charming holiday resort. It was a little patriarchal city washed by the silver Tobol, a tributary of the river Ob that gives into the Arctic Ocean. Though not in the tundra, or the far east of Trans-Baikalia, it was nevertheless the land of the *taiga* (the huge sub-Arctic forest of pines and birches) and of interminable winters. Though Kerensky later tried to defend himself from the accusation, there is no reason to suppose that he minded 'paying back the Tsar in his own coin' by sending him to distant Siberia where the Tsar himself had previously consigned his political enemies.

But this consideration had been reinforced by other urgent needs. The isolation of Tobolsk, which was cut off from the rest of the nation by snows and the absence of any railway, would make 'punitive action' against the Romanovs on the part of

Petrograd or Kronstadt extremists almost impossible, as also any effort to rescue the prisoners on the part of monarchist factions. As usual, Kerensky had organised his defences both to the right and the left.

The prisoners' departure, after various delays, had been finally fixed for the night of August 1. After that last meeting with Grand Duke Michael, hardly anyone slept. During the afternoon Nicholas had cut down three large pine-trees on the edge of the clearing in the park, and was rather tired. Nevertheless at midnight he joined the rest of the family gathered in the circular ground-floor hall of the Alexandrovsky Palace. The Tsarevitch was very restless, lying first in one chair and then in another, until finally his new guardian, the sailor Nagorny, covered him with a plaid rug.

Kerensky was nervous too, and passed the 'disordered and troubled' night first in the garden near the palace and then in the Tsar's study. He had been busy since nightfall. First he had presided over a cabinet meeting, then inspected the Tsarskoye troops, then had a long conference with Colonel Kobylinsky. He was uneasy about possible reactions in the first and fourth battalions of the Guard and insisted on addressing them himself. Three hundred and thirty men had been selected to take part in the journey (the destination was not divulged to them). Newly equipped and with loaded rifles, most of them had recently come from the front. Their officers, six in number, all wore the St George Cross.

The special train arrived late. There were several false alarms, and the Romanovs returned to their armchairs. The railwaymen of the big Petrograd station tried to obstruct the journey, but Kerensky's trusted men, Makarov and Vershinin, themselves supervised the coupling of the coaches, avoided embarrassing questions and finally obtained obedience. At five-thirty in the morning the train drew into a siding on Tsarskoye station. A motorcade rapidly crossed the sleeping little town. Cossacks preceded and followed the captives' cars, in one of which Alexandra Feodorovna was sobbing noisily.

The formalities of boarding the train were quickly accomplished. As soon as the list of travellers had been checked the train got on the move in the warm light of the rising sun. With a gesture of his hand Kerensky gave some final instructions to

V. M. Vershinin who was the last to board the train, and in the last coach. Henceforward Vershinin, who had escorted Nicholas from Mohylev to Tsarskoye, was to be responsible for the Romanovs to the Provisional Government.

Besides the military escort and the two Government representatives, thirty-nine people voluntarily travelled with the ex-Imperial family in the special train. These included Prince Vassili Dolgoruky, who had recently replaced Count Benkendorf as Grand Marshal, Count Ilya Tatichtchev, who had joined the prisoners on the station platform, Dr Botkin, Pierre Gilliard, the Tsarevitch's Swiss tutor, Mademoiselle Catherine Schneider, the Imperial reader, and Countess Hendrikova, the ex-Tsarina's lady-in-waiting. A considerable number of servants were also travelling: three valets, Alexis's nurse, eight lackeys, three cooks, a kitchen boy, a cellarer, three kitchen helpers, a boots, three housekeepers, four chambermaids, two messenger boys, a secretary, a hairdresser, a needle-woman and so on. As a Petrograd newspaper put it: 'Never in all history has a detained man had such a large staff at his disposal as was granted to Nicholas.'

The Romanovs' journey was none too comfortable. They were installed in a sleeping-car and could take their meals in the dining-car next door (it bore the crest of the Chinese railways). But 'the weather is oppressive and there is a lot of dust (26° Réaumur in the sleeping-car),' noted Nicholas. According to Kerensky's instructions the train stopped every afternoon in open country so as to allow the prisoners and their suite to take a half-hour stroll. The ex-Tsar used this freedom to stretch his legs in a field just before Viatka, and then again near Kungar beside the river Sylva.

Early in the morning of Friday August 4 (17) the train passed very slowly through Ekaterinburg. From the window of his compartment the ex-Emperor stared vacantly at the industrial city where he was to be taken the following spring. The train then proceeded to negotiate the passes of the Ural mountains before reaching the small town of Tiumen after nightfall. Finally it came to a halt alongside a landing-stage where two river steamers were vibrating under full pressure.

The Romanovs and their suite went aboard the *Russ* which was scheduled to reach Tobolsk on the evening of Sunday August 6 (19). On Saturday at midday the *Russ* hove to in the grey waters of the Tura to allow for a picnic and a series of snapshots (reproductions 18, 19 and 20). Despite the cool weather the whole Imperial family, including Alexandra Feodorovna, passed Saturday evening on deck, for the *Russ* was passing by Pokrovskoye, Rasputin's native village.

The two boats were awaited by an enormous crowd on the quays of Tobolsk. The astonishing news that the ex-Imperial family was to take up residence in the 'Governor's house' had spread through the population like wildfire. Nicholas looked out of a porthole at the little town he had visited many years earlier, soon after ascending the throne. He could see the cathedral and the large house on the hillside where his family was now going to live. He was haunted by memories. There had been a disagreeable incident at Tobolsk during one of the big shoots organised in his honour (at that time he had enjoyed slaughtering fifty-odd ducks more than anything in the world). A clumsy gamekeeper had accidentally let off his rifle and only just missed the Tsar's legs. He was punished on the spot, and under the Tsar's eyes, by twenty strokes of the knout. This wounded and humiliated man might well be on the quayside now, waiting to take his revenge . . . perhaps on the delicate body of Alexis? Decidedly Nicholas was dogged by bad luck. How many lieutenants like Yarinitch, how many Russians with implacable memories, were still going to reproach him for governing his vast Empire as he had been brought up to do?

Vershinin and Kobylinsky found the ex-Governor's residence in such a lamentable state of disrepair that they decided to postpone the settling-in of their prisoners. The Romanovs spent a further week on board the *Russ*. Every afternoon they were taken on a cruise away from the curiosity of the crowd. On August 12 (25) they went as far as the tumultuous waters of the river Irtych. Nicholas and his family were allowed to disembark and make a little excursion. They climbed up the high bank and spent a long time seated on a bare hillock gazing over the nostalgic Siberian landscape.

Chapter XIV

HOPES OF ESCAPE

*

THE ex-Tsarina had once wanted to see Kerensky hanged from the highest oak at Tsarskoye, yet it was thanks to him that the Imperial family now found itself safe and sound, thousands of versts away from the demonstrations raging in the capital. Of course, the Romanovs were exiles—'de luxe deportees', as the left-wing Petrograd papers called them. But exile was better by far than the ever-increasing promiscuity of Tsarskoye. As good Colonel Kobylinsky kept telling the Tsar, 'After all, Siberia is preferable to *samossoudd* [lynch law].'

The population of Tobolsk—'traditionally a backward and reactionary city'—had received the family with intense curiosity but without enmity. There had only been a few bantering remarks as Nicholas, with his daughters, set out on foot for the Governor's residence: '*Zdorova Tsar! Dobro pozhalovat!*' ('Good day, Tsar! Welcome to Siberia!')

Nicholas lived in the spacious building that made the corner of Nobility Street and Gubernatorskaya Street, in the manner of a well-to-do middle-class man disposing of a large staff. As a gesture to the taste of the day, rather than to humiliate the newcomers, the sign 'Nobility Street' had been repainted 'Liberty Street'. Makarov and Vershinin requisitioned the house opposite, that of the merchant Kornilov, to accommodate the Romanovs' suite.

At first Nicholas was not altogether convinced by Colonel Kobylinsky's words of wisdom. He felt it was humiliating in the extreme to be sent to a distant province which had hitherto been considered only just good enough for intriguing politicians and wicked liberals. For several evenings his indignation burst out unchecked in the pages of his diary. 'Everything here has a battered and abandoned look. . . . A lot of the rooms in the Kornilov house have not yet been done up. . . .' He was particularly irritated by the contrast between the park at Tsarskoye and the small garden of the Governor's residence—'a pocket handkerchief', he called it, or 'a miserable vegetable patch'.

Nicholas devoted his first days at Tobolsk to his hobby. He photographed the Tsarevitch and Trupp the lackey putting up a swing and the Tsarevitch playing with a bow and arrow in the courtyard under the amused eye of two soldiers of the Guard.[1] He sorted out and classified some pre-war snapshots which he had brought back from a tour in the Far East. Indeed by the end of August he was in that state of oriental imperturbability which was his substitute for good humour. In spite of his complaints against the garden, he found work there that suited him—there were a pine and a birch to be cut into logs, and the flower-beds to be dug with the help of his secretary Kirpitchnikov.

Other minor discoveries warmed his heart. Through the great open bay windows of the Governor's house he caught sight of old friends from Tsarskoye who had come to Tobolsk under their own steam. Despite their peasant headscarves he recognised the faces of two of the Tsarina's chambermaids—Nadia Utkin and Anna Romanov (the name Romanov, which was given to the dynasty by Tsar Mikhail Feodorovitch, is very common in Russia).

Less discreet than the two maids was one of the ex-Empress's ladies-in-waiting, Marguerite Khitrovo, who promenaded along Liberty Street in Paris fashions and called on the suite in the Kornilov house. Her sensational comings and goings made the new local authorities uneasy and they obliged the elegant 'Rita' to rejoin her boat and go back to Tiumen. At Tobolsk both legal and real power were still in the hands of the Municipal Council whose main concern was keeping on good terms with Commissars Makarov and Vershinin. At the time of the Romanovs' arrival there was no Bolshevik cell at Tobolsk. The local Soviet, which was run by a few Social Democrats and Social-Revolutionaries, played an insignificant part. Kerensky's orders were carried out much more promptly in this part of Siberia than in Petrograd or Moscow.

Almost every week brought fresh arrivals at Tobolsk from the Alexandrovsky Palace. First Dr Vladimir Derevenko, another of the Tsarevitch's doctors whose son, Kolya, was one of Alexis's

---

1. This touching snapshot is part of the material reproduced here for the first time (photo 28).

playmates. Then a courtier with big grey moustaches and volumi-
nous luggage—Baron Nicholas Bode, 'our good Baron Bode' as
the ex-Tsar wrote on the first page of exercise book No. 51,
which was to last him up till two days before his execution. Bode
had formerly been attached to the court administration, and he
brought a whole cargo of household utensils, books and clothes
left behind at Tsarskoye. He also brought four cases of St
Raphaël wine, Nicholas's favourite drink—he used to have two
or three glasses of it every evening at Mohylev Headquarters.
But unfortunately this last luxury brought down the wrath of
the soldiers of the *druzhima* (the unit of reservists) stationed at
Tobolsk. They complained to Midshipman Nikolski—one of the
strictest of the officials sent by the Provisional Government and
very hostile to the Romanovs—and on September 23 Nicholas
related with some bitterness in his diary:

'This afternoon there was a big fuss. After endless talk between
the commissar and other functionaries it was decided that the
cases of wine should be confiscated and thrown into the Irtych.
They were duly loaded on a cart, and before tea we saw the
convoy from our windows as it set out: the commissar's assistant
(Nikolski) was perched on top of the load, brandishing an axe
. . . A military escort accompanied him . . .'

On October 6 (19) came Sidney Gibbs, the Tsarevitch's
English tutor. He brought letters and messages. Three days
later came Klavdia Bitner, ex-headmistress of the girls' lycée in
Tsarskoye-Selo, with a letter from Xenia Alexandrovna,
Nicholas's eldest sister. And the following week came the 'healer'
Kostritsky from the Dowager-Empress's household in the
Crimea. He stayed some time before returning south.

The ex-Empress derived enormous consolation from the re-
assembly of her familiar staff and the coming and going of the
faithful little band. Reclining in her cane armchair, with the
dogs Jimmy and Ortipo snuggling against her legs and her
greying chignon resting on a satin cushion stuffed with rose
petals from the Caucasus, she wrote interminable letters to Anna
Virubova. She also sent her cases of provisions—flour, macaroni
and sausages. For while Petrograd was approaching famine,
there were no shortages at Tobolsk.

The failure of the attempted *pronunciamento* by Kornilov and his
accomplice General Krynov (who led the notorious 'Savage

division') was very distressing to the ex-Tsarina. She had begun to lose all faith in the chances of a political reorientation in Petrograd. Her mind was dominated by one hope: to get her beloved Alexis to some safe place so that, when the day came, he could ascend the throne of his ancestors. This meant escape. She could count on friends in Petrograd, Moscow and the Crimea— people who had not forgotten their Empress. With their help, and protected by the aura of the deceased *staretz*, 'Ania' could surely find a way of getting them out of Russia.

Besides its proximity to the village where Rasputin was born, Tobolsk had another attribute in which the superstitious German woman thought she saw a good omen. For some months now the episcopal see of Tobolsk had been occupied by Bishop Hermogene, the member of the Holy Synod who had helped the *staretz* gain admittance at the Tsarskoye court, and 'blessed' his irresistible rise to power. Having subsequently fallen foul of Rasputin—who never showed any gratitude towards his early protectors—Hermogene had been obliged to resign the bishopric of Saratov and, on the Tsarina's orders, betake himself to a Lithuanian monastery. . . . But such storms in a teacup were now things of the past. Hermogene was an intimate friend of Father Theophane who for long had been Alexandra Feodorovna's chaplain. So he hurriedly sent his blessing to the Governor's residence and let it be known that he still viewed Nicholas as his sovereign and that all the Siberian clergy could be counted on to help the family.

As Bishop Hermogene could not visit the Romanovs without arousing the suspicions of Kerensky's representatives and stirring up trouble among the few extremists in the Tobolsk garrison, he chose naturally enough as his intermediary Father Alexis Belaiev, Nicholas's confessor. Father Alexis carried on a daily shuttle-service between the Romanovs and the Church of Our Lady's Intercession, where the Bishop lived. Soon the Bishop was receiving visits from a large number of monarchist envoys, including lieutenants Kirilov and Mefodiev, and the brothers Rayevsky who travelled as representatives of the All-Russian Confraternity of Orthodox parishes and were officially bearers of a letter from Bishop Nestor of Kamtchatka to Bishop Hermogene (a number of names, mostly aliases, were found among the Bishop's papers after his arrest by the Bolsheviks).

The Dowager-Empress Maria Feodorovna herself wrote to Hermogene. Her message, which was probably sent through the healer Kostritsky, amounted to a command: 'You bear the name of St Hermogene who struggled to liberate Russia. It is a good omen. Now it is your turn to save our motherland. All Russia knows you: plead, act, convince. May your name be glorified.'

Soon there developed a thorough-going conspiracy to free the prisoners, in which friends and enemies of the late *staretz*—from the neurotic German woman to her mother-in-law, the 'irascible Dane'—found themselves reconciled. In spite of the remoteness of their abode, the Romanovs were now in much closer liaison with the faithful. The ferocious Tsarskoye guards had established a veritable *cordon sanitaire* round the Alexandrovsky Palace, whereas here in Tobolsk discipline was hypocritical and paternal. Alexandra Feodorovna's letters were hidden in apples or pots of jam and took some two or three weeks to reach 'Ania' and Bertchik in their Petrograd slum. As the monarchist Markov testified to Judge Sokolov after the Ekaterinburg tragedy: 'As autumn came on things began moving; we sent a man to Tobolsk to establish a link with the Imperial family, study the ground and make preparations for seizing them in case of danger. Our choice was N., an officer of the Empress's Crimean regiment . . . He was half successful in his task, and a little later he was followed by another officer, Serge Markov.'[1]

Thus several networks were set up to organise the escape of the Romanovs. Evidence, apart from articles published abroad by the monarchist Bulygin and by the Soviet press, is hard to come by, but it seems that the best organised of the projects was a military one led by Colonel Puritchkevitch, Victor Pavlovitch Sokolov, former Hussar officer in the Sumskoy regiment, and Colonel Kappel. This project was financed by K. Y. Yarochevsky, the banker, who contributed nearly two hundred thousand gold roubles to the cause. The monarchists were to strike at Tobolsk, that 'nest of Siberian monopolists, open door to England' (P. M. Bikov). The rebels were to seize the Governor's residence, disarm the men of the local Soviet, and hold the town for some hours—long enough to destroy the telegraphic installations and let the fugitives get a good start. The plains of western Siberia are difficult to cross in summer owing to the innumerable

1. Nicholas Sokolov, *Enquête Judicaire*, pp. 121–7.

swamps; but from October onwards journeys could be made by sleigh. A convoy protected by a hundred resolute cavalrymen stood a reasonable chance of reaching northern Turkestan, a region of Moslem tribes hostile to the Revolution.

Why was this plan never even attempted? The terrible civil war of 1918–20 was to show that there was no lack of bold, indeed intrepid, men in the ranks of the counter-revolutionaries.

We cannot accept the explanation according to which the monarchists of the capital and the other large cities made a miscalculation, and preferred to temporise, owing to some mistaken hope that the Revolution would 'fizzle out' of its own accord. After the failure of Kornilov's *Putsch* even someone as gullible as Anna Virubova no longer cherished illusions of that kind.

No, the real answer to our question is that the Cheka was watching—that is, the men who were later to constitute the famous 'Extraordinary Commission against reaction, speculation and sabotage' set up by the Bolsheviks on December 7, 1917. Even before they seized power, the 'Maximalists' and their left-wing Socialist allies had a brilliantly organised 'Secret Service'. The revolutionaries were past-masters in this field owing to their decades of conflict with the *Okhrana*—the Tsarist political police. The notorious case of the spy Azev, who had been in charge of a secret revolutionary committee for some fifteen years, had shown them to their cost how useful 'double agents' could be.

By the autumn of 1917 the Bolshevik specialists in the 'struggle against the counter-revolutionaries'—specialists who included the terrifying Dzershinksy and young Stalin—were actively uneasy about the fate of the royal family. The spies dispatched by the Petrograd Soviet to Tobolsk—they were provided with false papers or disguised as soldiers on leave so as not to alarm Kerensky's officials—sent back disturbing reports. Bishop Hermogene and his clergy had their fingers in a network of plots. A secret 'monarchist bureau' had been set up in the little town of Tiumen. . . . As Tobolsk was beyond the reach of the Bolshevik commandos of central Russia, Dzershinsky opted for trickery. He resolved on setting up monarchist organisations, on repeating the Azev affair but this time to the profit of the revolutionaries. He had the right man for the operation at his disposal, a certain Lieutenant Soloviev.

Boris Soloviev, whose father had been treasurer of the Holy Synod, was none other than Rasputin's son-in-law. Born in 1891, he had lived an adventurous life in contradictory activities. When war broke out he was in Germany and on excellent terms with various Prussian officers. On returning to Russia he donned the uniform of a lieutenant in the second regiment of machine-gunners, but took care not to expose himself to the bullets of his German friends. Through his father he was admitted into the little circle of Rasputin's friends. Rasputin's secretary, Aron Simanovitch, was one of his cronies.

We have no means of proving that Soloviev belonged to the 'Green' organisation and the network of German espionage operating round the *staretz*. What is certain is that the young officer lost no time in abandoning his protectors in the Alexandrovsky Palace once the February Revolution broke out, and he found his way into the revolutionary caucus in the Duma even before Nicholas's abdication. As a reward for his zeal he was made aide-de-camp to General Potapov, later a famous Bolshevik military leader. There is even evidence that Soloviev maltreated officers and police who remained loyal to the monarchy.

Then, at the end of the summer of 1917, Lieutenant Soloviev suddenly resumed his friendships within the 'Rasputin circle'. Anna Virubova, just released from prison, opened her heart to him. She told him of her hopes, of how she and her friend, Chura Gagarin, had been making every possible contact that might help the Imperial family. She dwelt at length on Bishop Hermogene and Father Alexis Belaiev. It was in Anna Virubova's slum dwelling that Soloviev met once more his old acquaintance Matriona Rasputin, the *staretz*'s daughter. The girl fell madly in love with the dashing officer, and a few weeks later, in the Taurid Palace church, she became Matriona Solovieva.

On the pretext of paying a visit to his mother-in-law, Boris Soloviev took his wife to Pokrovskoye for their honeymoon—some ten versts from Tiumen and Tobolsk. With judicious flattery and bribery he soon gained ascendancy over one of the Romanovs' chief advisers, and was certainly their best 'peephole' on to the external world. As winter set in, Soloviev discreetly moved to Tiumen where he played the part of 'turn-table' for the monarchist networks.

Tatiana Melnik-Botkin, daughter of the Tsar's doctor, who

also lived through the months of exile at Tobolsk, has left an acute description of Soloviev's nefarious activities.

'The monarchist organisations in Petrograd and Moscow', she writes, 'had sent a considerable number of supporters to Tobolsk and Tiumen. Many of them spent months there under false names in appalling conditions of poverty and privation. But all fell into the same trap: the group led by Father Alexis and his beloved lieutenant Soloviev, who had wormed their way into the confidence of the over-simple monarchists . . . Soloviev was deliberately working for the destruction of the Imperial family, and it was with this in view that he established himself at Tiumen, a strategic point where all new arrivals passed through his hands. This enabled him to send very useful information to Petrograd and Moscow.'[1]

Soloviev's real character was only shown up much later. When Judge Sokolov came across him in 1919 at Omsk he did not dare have him arrested. It was not until 1926 that this double agent paid for his treachery with his life.[2]

---

1. Tatiana Melnik-Botkina, *Souvenirs de la famille impériale*.

2. Boris Soloviev went over to the Whites when the Bolsheviks seemed on the point of collapse, and subsequently emigrated to Germany and France. Russian *émigrés* accused him of having again worked for the Cheka and of having disclosed his sister-in-law Varvara Rasputin's hiding place—she was shot by the Reds in 1920. Soloviev became a car salesman for a Paris branch of Fords, and one evening some White Russians attacked him and left him for dead on the pavement. He died at the Hôpital Cochin on August 31, 1926 and was buried in Bagneux cemetery. In 1957 his remains were removed to a communal grave. His wife, who accepted no responsibility for his grave, lives in the Seine-et-Oise with two dogs called Youssou and Pof.

Chapter XV

THE MYSTERIOUS YACOVLEV

*

THE astonishing and tragic news about the situation in Petrograd reached Tobolsk towards the end of 1917 like echoes from another world. Despite the speed with which the crackling Hugues telegraph system transmitted it, the information seemed diluted by contact with the vast spaces of Siberia and muffled by the snowy eiderdown spread over the landscape.

The brevity and rarity of the instructions transmitted by Kerensky—head of a ghostly government execrated by the revolutionaries—to the dwarf-like Pankratov, who had succeeded Commissars Makarov and Vershinin, had only increased the uneasiness of the Tobolsk authorities. Both jailors and prisoners felt united in the same isolation. They were like passengers on an ice-breaker lost in the Arctic winter, and on both sides there was an inclination to fraternise.

By the last days of October telegrams and newspapers from the capital were no longer reaching Tobolsk. Travellers who had crossed the Urals on horseback or sleigh told the Romanov household how Kerensky had been overthrown by a masterly *coup* of the Bolsheviks. On the evening of October 25—it was the famous day on which the Baltic sailors, led by Lenin and Trotsky, had seized most of Petrograd—the ex-Emperor wrote in the handwriting of an average but painstaking schoolboy:

'Wednesday, October 25. Another fine day with slight frost. In the morning we showed Kostritsky over the house [this was the healer]. In the afternoon, sawed wood.'

And during the next few days the same ignorance was displayed by Nicholas about events in his former capital. But at some time or other he must have learnt the truth: of how Kerensky, 'the lesser evil', had escaped in a diplomatic car flying the American flag. On November 11 the ex-Tsar alluded for the first time to 'the gravity of the situation' before adding that the Grand Duchesses had spent their leisure jumping from swings into a heap of snow. October 1917 was none the less a turning-point in Russian history. This second Revolution to all intents and purposes sealed the ex-Tsar's fate. Two days of rioting, a few short bursts of fire, endless galloping over the frozen pavements, and thirty-six cannon shots (badly aimed, at that; only two grazed the façade of the Winter Palace) had given the power to a 'little man' with a shaggy beard who—in the words of Bruce Lockhart, the British Consul General—looked like a provincial grocer. But that steely-eyed little man had a solid hold over Petrograd and all Central Russia.

While at Tobolsk the thermometer was going down and down, and the infantrymen of the fourth regiment were waiting their turn to shake the ex-Tsar's hand and wish him a happy feast of St Nicholas, the whole world was watching Lenin—chairman of the Council of People's Commissars in Petrograd.

The first man to interview him was a French journalist, Ludovic Naudeau, special correspondent of Le Temps.

His trunk was enveloped in one of those woollen or camel-hair vests that have a neck of the same material—the sort the English call sweaters. I thought M. Lenin looked very pale and thin, and he had the red nose of someone suffering from a bad cold. I felt I was in the presence of someone impenetrable and difficult to describe, and I was uneasy.

Lenin, whom his followers called 'the Reformer', spoke at length with the journalist. In excellent French he explained how he was laying the foundations of a new Communist State, and how the whole world would sooner or later partake of the 'Socialist tart' [sic]. Not a word was said about the former Tsar and the fate reserved for him. The truth was that nobody in Petrograd seemed concerned about the Romanovs. Naudeau also met Trotsky, People's Commissar for Foreign Affairs, but learnt nothing about them there either (though the boldness of his questions earned him imprisonment in the sinister Butirky prison). It is only from Trotsky's journal published much later from exile that we learn, with approximate dates, the views of the impetuous Leo Davidovitch.

During my short visits to Moscow[1] I remarked casually to the Politburo that in view of the unfavourable conditions in the Ural region we would have to hurry up the Tsar's trial. I proposed a public court trial which would give a picture of the whole reign (policy regarding peasants, workers, the nation, culture, the two wars, and so on). An account of the trial would be telegraphed all over the country; and in local capitals the reports would be read and commented on every day. Lenin expressed the opinion that it would be a very good thing if this could be done. But time might run short . . . At that period he was in a rather depressed mood.[2]

What undoubtedly emerges from the above is that as soon as Lenin and the Bolshevik leaders seized power they agreed in principle to trying Nicholas (and very probably the hated Tsarina also), but that more pressing problems than the punishment of the Romanovs obliged them to postpone their plan.

Moreover Tobolsk did not come into the hands of the Bolsheviks in any practical way until four and a half months after the October Revolution. The victory of the Bolsheviks, or Maximallists, had been so sudden and unforeseen that the populations of towns far removed from the capital tended to see it as something transitory. Moscow and Petrograd apart, none of the big cities of the former Empire was solidly behind the new regime. Everyone in the provinces was waiting for the meeting of the Constituent Assembly in which the Social-Revolutionaries were expected to have an enormous majority—for, in the November elections, they had won twenty-one million votes as against the nine million that went to the Bolsheviks. On January 5, after Lenin had closed the door of the Taurid Palace and suppressed the Constituent Assembly, distant regions such as the Donetz basin and Siberia lived in a climate of passive resistance to the Bolshevik regime—with here and there cores of active resistance. For months the Tobolsk authorities, who had been appointed by the Kerensky Government, went on administering the town and the neighbouring country as though nothing had happened. The regime established in Siberia by the first Socialist Govern-

1. Lenin transferred the Government to Moscow on March 12, 1918. At that time Trotsky became People's Commissar for War.
2. *Journal d'Exil*, Gallimard, 1960.

ments had been so well consolidated that the *Sovnarkom* representatives sent to Tobolsk made a halt at Ekaterinburg so as to prepare false papers and disguises. As we saw in the previous chapter, the monarchist envoys, like those of the People's Commissariat, had been compelled to equal secrecy. At Tobolsk the word of Socialists with a Social-Revolutionary tinge was law. In December 1917 Commissar Pankratov received an ultimatum by telegram from the Omsk Soviet ordering him, under pain of arrest, to transfer the Romanovs to the common prison. He threw the telegram into the waste-paper basket and nothing happened.

Apart from periodical conflicts with the committees of the soldiers of the Guard (set up by Bolshevik agents dispatched from Ekaterinburg), Nicholas and his family had no moral sufferings to undergo between September 1917 and January 1918. The reign of terror set up in Petrograd and Moscow after the October Revolution had no repercussions in Tobolsk and there were no victims in the household. The Romanovs spent the days before Christmas and the New Year rehearsing a play called *Les Deux Timides*, with repartee between Nicholas and the Tsarevitch's Swiss tutor, and there was in general a festive air in the apartments on the first floor of the Governor's residence. Alexandra Feodorovna left her chaise-longue and herself decorated the Christmas tree that the family presented to the first platoon of the fourth regiment of the Guards. The royal couple spent the afternoon of December 24 toasting the NCOs and sentries as they came off duty.[1] The following morning the family went in procession to the Church of Our Lady's Intercession while the town re-echoed to the peal of bells. After the service a Te Deum was sung before a precious icon specially brought from the Abalak monastery. Then Father Alexis recited a final prayer for intercession for 'their Imperial Majesties the Emperor Nicholas II and the Empress Alexandra Feodorovna . . .' This fantasy on the part of the Romanovs' confessor involved him in mild trouble with Commissar Pankratov.

Vassili Semenovitch Pankratov had arrived at Tobolsk on August 19, 1917, to relieve Makarov and Vershinin. At first Nicholas and his family hated him as a crusty old Socialist

1. 'We have some good soldiers and I play draughts with them in the guardroom', wrote the Tsarevitch to Virubova on January 22 (February 4), 1918.

militant, but he was a good-natured man and ended up on good terms with his captives. He enjoyed telling the Grand Duchesses the story of his life and doubtless the girls secretly trembled with fear as they listened. For Vassili had been a victim of the Tsarist regime. At the age of eighteen he had killed a 'pharaoh' who was ill-treating a working woman, and had been condemned to fifteen years' confinement in the redoubtable Schlüsselburg Fortress on the Baltic.[1] Ten years later his sentence had been commuted to life deportation to Yakutsk, and here he spent twenty-seven years 'forsaken by God and man'. Yet his vivid stories were recounted with perfect good humour. We can leave these conversations between the old revolutionary—who had been set free only a few months earlier—and the royal girls, brought up in luxury and in the belief that their family was all-powerful, yet now captives in their turn, to the imagination. Pankratov prudently resigned his post on January 24, 1918, and a few months later fled the country.

In January the situation at Tobolsk underwent a rapid change and the relatively comfortable conditions of the Romanovs' internment deteriorated day by day. The early weeks of the New Year saw a succession of irksome incidents. First came the affair of the epaulettes (the Guards officers, the courtiers, and Nicholas himself had to remove all badges of rank from their uniforms); then the soldiers' meetings pressing for Pankratov's dismissal; and finally orders from Moscow to ration the Imperial family and allot it the same food-allowance as the soldiers (February 10, 1918). It was from then that the real imprisonment of the Romanovs must be dated.

During their internment at Tsarskoye and, so far, at Tobolsk, the Romanovs had been able to keep up the fiction of a court and lead the life of boyars confined to their estates. The Kerensky Government had left them to enjoy their enormous fortune deposited in various Russian and foreign banks (by the most conservative estimates this amounted to fourteen million gold roubles). The telegram signed by the People's Commissar for the Property of the Republic,[2] which was received in Tobolsk on

1. Schlüsselburg lies on the river Neva between lake Ladoga and the Gulf of Finland which is part of the Baltic.

2. This was a certain Marelin, a Social-Revolutionary of the Left and a friend of Vassili Yacovlev, the Commissar Extraordinary who was to 'accompany' the Romanovs to Ekaterinburg.

February 10 (February 23), cut the Romanovs down to six hundred roubles a month for each member of the family and excluded all servants and dependants. A rate of four thousand two hundred roubles a month to keep forty people at a time of shortage was little indeed!

Alexandra Feodorovna—for it was she who kept the keys of the Imperial money-chest—had to dismiss ten servants immediately, with rage in her heart. She also had to inform the courtiers at the Kornilov house opposite that in future they would have to make do on their own resources. Many of them crept away without waiting for this injunction. As with all tragedies, the end of the Romanovs involved a certain number of doubtful characters. Side by side with Dr Botkin, the foreign tutors, Countess Hendrikova and a few others—whose loyalty to the family now began to demand real heroism—the suite had also had its spongers.

The new arrangements had to be applied in a hurry. The Romanovs only had a few days' respite before March 1 (February 15, old style). On that day the Swiss tutor, Pierre Gilliard, wrote in his diary: 'March 1. The new regime comes into effect. As from today, butter and sugar are banished from our table as luxuries.' Pierre Gilliard saw the collapse of all his youthful dreams, but he had decided not to show ingratitude to his protectors or disloyalty to his fiancée who was one of the assistant teachers to the Grand Duchesses. He only escaped death the following summer by a hair's breadth.

For a short period real hardship reigned in the Romanov household. The cook, Kharitonov—who was to meet his death in the Ekaterinburg basement—made desperate efforts to obtain credit from the Tobolsk tradespeople, but the Romanovs already owed them large sums of money and they were intractable. Good Colonel Kobylinsky made a round of Siberian notables to beg for help.[1] In the end manna fell from heaven in the shape of baskets of provisions brought by the popes and monks of the neighbourhood. Until the end of their lives at Ekaterinburg the Romanovs were amply provided for by the Orthodox hierarchy.

By and large Nicholas was detached from these material

---

1. Alexandra Feodorovna had secretly put aside a substantial sum on which she drew for the benefit of her 'protégés' only, refusing to take out any sum as contribution to the daily life of the household.

difficulties, but he was angry too and for a nobler reason. The news of the long negotiations for an armistice at Brest-Litovsk touched him to the quick. For all his mediocrity of character and his autocratic views, Nicholas Alexandrovitch was a loyal soldier. That Russia should thus desert her allies appalled him and was 'a real nightmare'. We may well wonder whether it ever occurred to him that the initial artisan of this desertion had been himself; and that, had he put his kingdom in order at an early stage, Russia would never have collapsed so quickly. We may be allowed to doubt it. The last of the Romanovs was not given to meditating on philosophical or historical matters. As winter drew to a close and the future prospects of his family became blacker and blacker, he sought refuge in adventure stories, like a dunce trying to forget his failure at exams. In less than two weeks, sunk deep in a red velvet armchair, Nicholas devoured *The Three Musketeers*, *The Adventures of Sherlock Holmes*, and two other light English novels. From time to time he would throw his book down on the thick carpet and approach his study window through whose frost-covered panes a pale sun was shining. From there he could survey the excitement and endless arguments of the soldiers. The little Tobolsk garrison was boiling up.

As winter drew to an end the great railway stations dotted along the silver rails of the Trans-Siberian railway were the meeting-point of two great torrents of human beings. From the two capitals, Petrograd and Moscow, the citizens of the young Soviet State were fleeing to the fertile regions of the Volga and the frontiers of Siberia so as to escape hunger and, so they hoped, find food. Former statesmen and soldiers, bankrupt tradespeople, dispossessed landed gentry, dismissed officials, young people who sensed adventure beyond the Urals—in a word a whole cross-section of Russian society from the great cities of the west—were making their way east.

In the van of this throng came the solid masses of the Fifth Red Army, recently founded by Mikhail Tukhachevsky, together with arms, field-guns and munitions. In the marshalling yards huge bottlenecks facilitated the infiltration of emissaries and spies taking messages to Ataman Dutov and Admiral Kolchak. Villagers and army deserters flocked to the stations to barter bread and bacon against arms, salt or clothing. Robbers and bandits prowled along the lines. Those caught red-handed were lynched by the infuriated travellers. Red police patrols were rare and too thinly scattered to guarantee discipline. The road and rail blocks they set up were soon stampeded by the crowd.

Those immense stretches of horizonless steppes between the banks of the Volga and the Irtych became a land of chaos where everything was possible. The peasants wore their caps over one ear with a swagger and had their rifles at the sling. They could do what they liked. One day the *bedniaki*, the poor peasants, went too far and elected a regional Soviet. Next day Dutov's White Guards dispersed the Soviet with bayonet thrusts, but only to be dislodged in their turn by detachments of revolutionaries made up of sailors and workers.

A tall slim man in an officer's cloak and a cap decorated with the red star was lying full-length in a requisitioned compartment of a Trans-Siberian train. This train was making its way towards Ufa, but often stopped in the open country, at which times a whitish landscape, made blotchy by the thaw, could be seen through the filthy windows, and a fresh wind smelling of mud and damp blew in through the broken glass. Suddenly a flock of ravens rose into the air with wild croaks, roused by the engine.

The train hammered along the rails and shuddered at the bifurcations. On a nearby road carts drawn by shaggy little horses were making their way through the melting snow and mud.

Vassili Vassilievitch Yacovlev, Commissar Extraordinary from the Kremlin, was dozing with his head under a blanket. His delicate features were disfigured by several days' growth of beard. There were deep lines on either side of his rigid lips. Everything about him betrayed the weariness of interminable travel. After four days' train journey to Ufa, he then had to do two hundred versts on horseback to get to Tobolsk.

'The Siberian town of Tobolsk', writes Kerensky, 'which was forgotten at first, became an object of outstanding interest in Moscow, Ekaterinburg and Omsk four months after Lenin seized power. The first arrivals were representatives of the Regional Executive Committee of the Ural Soviet, furnished with false papers. Amongst them was the worker Avdeiev who was to become the first "commissariat officer" of the Ipatiev house. Soon afterwards, on March 11 [March 24], came the sober and silent

Commissar Dutzmann from Omsk. He installed himself in a flat facing the Governor's house and watched, without interfering.'[1] Two days later a detachment of a hundred Red Guards, all Bolsheviks, set out from Omsk under the command of a certain Demianov. Dutzmann and Demianov made immediate contact with ensign Alexander Matveiev of the second regiment of the Guard who, in recent months, had been forming a Bolshevik cell within the garrison. The three men decided to 'recast the revolutionary administration'. The democratic town council and *zemstvo* of Tobolsk were disbanded. The local Soviet, with its majority of non-Bolshevik Socialists and anti-Communists, was dissolved. New elections, rushed through in a few hours, gave the chairmanship of the Soviet to Avdeiev's henchman, leading stoker Khokriakov, who also hailed from Ekaterinburg. This former sailor, once attached to the cruiser *Alexander II*, was an odd figure who will appear in our story like a marionette who has to make three pirouettes and then disappear again.

A second detachment of Red Guards then arrived, having been armed at Ekaterinburg and put under the command of Zaslavsky, a pseudo-tradesman. Zaslavsky demanded that the Romanovs should be transferred to the local prison forthwith, but oddly enough Khokriakov, supported by the first detachment of Red Guards, opposed this demand. The two groups of revolutionaries came into violent conflict. Khokriakov was arrested and jailed. The Romanovs were on the point of joining him when a new dramatic event took place—the unexpected arrival of a third detachment of Red Guards. This was composed of the flower of the revolutionaries of Ufa, a town on the other side of the Urals, south of Ekaterinburg and nearer Moscow. It was better armed and disciplined than the previous Red Guards, its hundred and fifty men obeying their leader without asking questions. A Commissar Extraordinary straight from Moscow, with secret orders from the *Vzik* (the Soviet Central Executive Committee), this leader was empowered to shoot anyone who stood in his way.

Vassili Yacovlev was the man, tall, thin, clean-shaven, with an intellectual forehead and immaculate clothes. He refused to argue with Zaslavsky and his underlings but immediately came to an understanding—it seemed almost as if they were old

1. Kerensky, op. cit., p. 204.

friends—with the ex-sailor chairman of the local Soviet, Khok-riakov. If the least difficulty arose with other Bolshevik representatives, he threatened to telegraph direct to the *Vzik* in Moscow. He had a telegrapher with him who could work the Hugues system direct to the Kremlin.

Yacovlev's official mission was to transfer the Romanovs without delay from Tobolsk to Ekaterinburg, where they would be much nearer the new capital and much safer from any monarchist attempt at rescue. This at least is how Yacovlev put it to the Tobolsk Bolsheviks.

Nevertheless Zaslavsky and Avdeiev wondered . . . Yacovlev's arrival with his imposing escort had been an unpleasant surprise for them. After all the *Vzik* could have ordered the Bolshevik representatives already installed in Tobolsk to transport the Imperial family back across the Urals. There would have been no opposition to such an order. Why had Yacovlev's instructions been kept secret from such men as themselves who were hardened Bolsheviks? Why make a drama of such a simple operation?

Even today in the Ural region there must be Communist Party veterans who still ask these questions. They can hardly have been convinced by *The Last Days of the Romanovs* in which P. M. Bikov's account of Vassili Yacovlev and his mission is extremely confused. We wonder if Bikov himself believed his account!

Although more than forty-five years have elapsed since these events, we shall have to proceed with a veritable counter-inquiry if we are to find the truth.

Chapter XVI

JOURNEY TO THE
END OF THE STEPPE

*

THE elegant Commissar with the man-of-the-world manners, who had so unexpectedly thrust himself on the rustic revolutionaries of Siberia, made it plain from the start that he was going to waste no time.

Vassili Vassilievitch Yacovlev arrived in Tobolsk on the evening of Monday, April 22 (new style, as are all dates mentioned as from now), and left, long before dawn, four days later, having loaded the fur-wrapped Emperor, Empress and Grand Duchess Maria on to his sleighs. What had happened was as follows. Very early in the morning of Tuesday, April 23, he had made an official call on Colonel Kobylinsky, handed him an official order and spread out on the desk his own credentials signed by one of the highest personalities of the proletarian State, Yakob Sverdlov, chairman of the *Vzik*.[1] He demanded to be conducted to Nicholas without delay. This is how the ex-Tsar described the first interview:

'At ten-thirty this morning Kobylinsky arrived with Yacovlev, who was accompanied by his staff. I received them in the drawing-room with my daughters. We were expecting him at eleven o'clock and Alix was not yet ready.

'He came in, clean-shaven, smiling, and somewhat confused, and asked me if I was satisfied with the house and the Guard. Then, almost at a run, he burst into Alexis's room, and examined the other rooms, then came down again apologising for the trouble he had caused. He looked over the other floors with the same speed. At the end of half an hour he came back to present himself to Alix, then burst into Alexis's room again, then came down again.'

1. And counter-signed by Ovanessov (vice-chairman of the *Vzik*) and Steinberg (Commissioner for Justice of the *Sovnarkom*).

Subsequent events suggest that on his first visit Yacovlev wanted to talk with the Emperor alone and was put out by the presence of his staff. For two days later he came again unexpectedly, and this time only with Kobylinsky. Kobylinsky was to tell Judge Sokolov later that Vassili Vassilievitch warned Nicholas of his imminent departure to a new destination some four or five days' journey from Tobolsk—but above all he wanted to give him reassurances.

'You will come to no harm. I will answer for your safety with my head,' he went so far as to say,[1] 'and if you want to bring anyone from your entourage, I shall not oppose it. Unfortunately your son, owing to his haemorrhage, can only join you in about three weeks. . . .'

The *Vzik* envoy's voice was coaxing and convincing, which did not allay the Tsarina's fears, however. She got it into her head that the Tsar was to be separated from his family so that he could be made to sign some important political document.

'It'll be the abdication absurdity all over again,' she groaned, clinging to Kobylinsky's tunic. 'They'll try to persuade him to do something wrong by worrying him about his family. But the two of us together could hold our own. I must be beside him to help him. The boy is still ill . . .;[2] I entrust him to you.'

Yacovlev granted the ex-Empress's request without the slightest concern. The only thing he feared seemed to be that the Romanovs would use the Tsarevitch's illness as a pretext for insisting on spending more days in Tobolsk.

Tatiana Botkin, the doctor's daughter, has provided a moving description of the hurried departure at five in the morning on Saturday, April 27.

Towards two in the morning we could already hear the creaking of sledge-runners and the noise of horses' hooves. The drivers and horsemen formed part of Yacovlev's regiment. The day before the whole town had been combed for the best sleighs and drivers, and it was only with great difficulty that a little covered sleigh was found for the Empress . . . Soon the courtyard sprang into life, and we could see the silhouettes of soldiers and servants dragging packages.

1. Conversation reported by the valet Volkov.
2. See photograph No. 34.

Amongst them could be seen the tall figure of Tchemedurov, the Emperor's old valet. My father went out of the house several times, wearing Prince Dolgoruky's rabbit-skin coat for his sable had gone to wrap round the Empress and the Grand Duchess Maria whose furs were anything but warm. The convoy passed under my windows and turned left up the main street. In the first two sleighs there were four soldiers with rifles, and then the Sovereign and Yacovlev. His Majesty was sitting on the right, wearing a military cap and an old military cloak. The Sovereign turned as he talked to Yacovlev. I can still recall his kind face and brave smile.[1]

As far as Tiumen, where Yacovlev had a special train waiting, the journey was made in *tarantasses*, the sleighs with rush seats used throughout the whole of western Siberia. The last two were armed with machine-guns at the ready. Soon after leaving Tobolsk the convoy had to cross the river Irtych, thin and melting though the ice was. Shortly before the relay station at Jolevo, the main convoy was unexpectedly joined by a cavalry regiment under Zaslavsky's command: the 'toughs' of the Tobolsk Soviet had decided at the last moment to keep an eye on Yacovlev's doings. In addition to this a second detachment of Ural cavalry, commanded by the Red Guard Bussiastsky, followed the sleighs at some distance. The whole extraordinary turn-out halted at Pokrovskoye, Rasputin's native village, to change horses. From their window the *staretz*'s widow and daughters watched the passage of the *tarantasses* and their rival escorts. We do not know whether Soloviev was with them. At 9.15, 'by the light of the moon', as Nicholas emphasises in his diary, the travellers, spattered with mud and snow, reached Tiumen railway station.

It was at Tiumen that the conflict between Yacovlev and his 'guardian angels'—Zaslavsky's men and Bussiastsky's men— came out into the open. After telegraphing to Moscow, the Commissar Extraordinary told his men to arrest the 'representative of the Ural revolutionary forces', deputed to the train by Zaslavsky and who was none other than the famous Avdeiev whom the Romanovs were to find a few days later in the Ipatiev house. He then informed the Bolsheviks of his personal escort

1. Tatiana Melnik-Botkina, op. cit.

'that he had been ordered not to take the special train in a westerly direction, that is to say towards Ekaterinburg, but in an easterly direction to Omsk where he could join the railway to Samara and Moscow—which was to be the ultimate destination of the Romanovs'. This route, though somewhat longer than the one from Tiumen to Moscow via Ekaterinburg, Perm and Vologda, had the advantage of by-passing the Ural region and its local Soviet.

Unfortunately for Yacovlev—and for the Romanovs—Avdeiev managed to give his guards the slip and shouted the news through the door of his compartment to one of Zaslavsky's men. At the same moment the special train shunted off in the direction of Omsk. But the Ural Communists were now wise to Yacovlev's machinations, and without a moment's delay they telegraphed the Ekaterinburg and Omsk Soviets—the latter was led by the ferocious revolutionary Kossirev.

Yacovlev had lost the game. (*What* game? We shall try to answer this question later.) Warned by the railwaymen that categorical orders had been telegraphed to stop the special train at Kulomzino, shortly before Omsk, Yacovlev ordered a halt at the wayside station of Liublinsk. Accompanied by three trusted henchmen, he then boarded the engine and proceeded to Omsk by himself. There Kossirev was awaiting him, but only after lengthy persuasion did he give him permission to communicate on the direct line to Moscow. For an hour all that could be heard was clickings and cracklings as the Commissar's personal operator made contact, and a hubbub of distant voices now and again dominated by the words: 'Hang the traitor Yacovlev.' What an odd scene it must have been—the man who had been denounced as an outlaw through Siberia and the Ural region calmly communicating with the supreme chiefs of the Revolution! The local Bolshevik authorities, while mobilising the 'fury of the Revolution' against him, nevertheless felt obliged to treat him as a man with special powers. . . .

From the other end of the wire the answer took a long time coming. Doubtless Yakob Sverdlov, although the strong man of the *Sovnarkom*, wanted to cover himself and consult either Lenin or Trotsky. In the end the Kremlin ordered Yacovlev to abandon all resistance and yield to the demands of the local authorities. So the Commissar Extraordinary had no choice but to remount his engine and return with all speed to Liublinsk and the body of the train—in which the ex-Imperial couple was still peacefully sleeping oblivious of the strange conflict that had just taken place, whose outcome had sealed their last hope of rescue.

At 8.40 in the morning of Tuesday, April 30, the special train rolled into Ekaterinburg station under the sneering eyes of the local revolutionaries.

Yacovlev showed no emotion whatsoever as he courteously took leave of the Romanovs. Perhaps his eyes melted a little as he shook hands with the ravishing Grand Duchess Maria with whom he had had many asides. A black, mud-spattered limousine bore the Romanovs off towards their destiny.

But what happened to the 'traitor to the Revolution', Vassili Vassilievitch Yacovlev? 'His fate confirmed yet again that he had not acted at his own risk and peril, and that he had extremely close relations with Moscow', writes Kerensky; and even more convincing is the testimony of P. M. Bikov.

On the administrative side the astonishing zigzag journey across the Siberian steppe had only a brief epilogue. On the evening of April 30 the Executive Committee of the Ural Soviet held a packed meeting to discuss the Yacovlev affair. From the very outset he was referred to as the 'loyal subject of their Imperial Majesties', as 'sold to the monarchists' and suchlike phrases. Though he had been prudent enough to preserve records of some of his telegraphic conversations with Moscow, his defence, which he put forward with the utmost coolness, was pretty inconsistent. Beloborodov and Didkovsky stated that they were 'very dissatisfied' with his explanations. Yet they released him and in addition granted him the *satisfecit* he almost flippantly requested: a receipt signed by the local authorities certifying that he had accomplished his mission and conveyed the Romanovs to their destination.[1]

Back in Moscow the Commissar Extraordinary was received by Sverdlov and came to no harm whatever. A few weeks later it became known that the *Vzik* had given him another important mission in the Volga region, now troubled by the onset of the civil war.

What, then, was Yacovlev's real aim? 'Was his tragic failure',

1. Cf. the photograph-copy of this curious document, signed by members of the Executive of the Ural Communist Party (plate No. 35).

asks Kerensky, 'the outcome of a double game played by those who had appointed him, or was it the outcome of a struggle between certain groups or certain persons in the Kremlin?'

We should first consider the official Soviet version of what happened.

'The *Vzik*, in appointing Yacovlev as Commissar Extraordinary, doubtless made a mistake. . . . Subsequently he betrayed the Revolution. Nominated after his return to Moscow to an important post on the Samara front, he deserted to the Whites in October 1918, together with various other officers.' (P. M. Bikov)

But, as Nicholas Sokolov, the punctilious examining magistrate, asks: 'Was Yacovlev his real name? However that may be, he was an intellectual who was always keen on talking French or English . . . Until the Revolution he lived abroad; he seems to have committed a political crime in Finland which carried a death sentence . . . His actions were directed by some non-Bolshevik force, as were those of the sailor Khokriakov.' We should point out that Sokolov, whose investigations were so meticulous that he is often quoted by Soviet historians, tried in vain to meet Yacovlev after he had gone over to the Whites. This hitherto unknown detail was recounted by Sokolov's friend, Robert Wilton, correspondent of *The Times* and *Le Matin*. Sokolov seems to us a trifle evasive when writing of Yacovlev, and we cannot help wondering whether he knew more about the Commissar's real personality than he admits. This is at least probable. A loyal monarchist, and a poor and tubercular exile, the former judge—when writing his book in Paris in 1924 —doubtless had reasons of his own for not divulging important political secrets. . . .

In *The Truth about the Massacre of the Romanovs* Kerensky devotes some twenty pages to the Yacovlev affair, and concludes with the depressing reflection: 'The reasons why the Kremlin sent Yacovlev to Tobolsk will remain a mystery until all the archives of the Soviet Government become accessible to historians—granting that all documents have been preserved in the archives. . . .'

It is some thirty years since Kerensky wrote those lines. The present writer has obviously had no chance of consulting the Kremlin files. Yet he has been lucky enough to unearth various unpublished documents which allow the evidence—among which there is some that has hitherto passed unnoticed—to be better co-ordinated. Among unpublished documents there are, first and foremost, the—alas, fragmentary—memoirs of Piotr Laravitch Voïkov, Ural Soviet Commissar for Supplies, who, it may be remembered, became Soviet Ambassador in Warsaw and was assassinated in 1927 by the monarchist Koverda. One of Voïkov's assistants hid his notebooks and brought them with him a few years later when he came to the West. As for what has passed unnoticed, we should recall to readers' minds the highly colourful personality of Colonel Maslovsky-Mstislavsky whose name came up when we described the inspection of the detainees at Tsarskoye-Selo. Maslovsky's vivid memoirs, entitled *Five Days*, refer at length to a young assistant he had at the time, whose name was none other than Vassili Vassilievitch Yacovlev.

Who was Vassili Yacovlev? Was it really his intention—as certain monarchist exiles, as well as Bolsheviks, claim—to help the Tsar and Tsarina to 'escape'? Today both questions can in all likelihood be answered; but to answer them we must ask a third, more delicate, question: was Yacovlev the secret agent of some Western power concerned to get hold of the Tsar? And, if so, which power, Germany or Great Britain?

We are going to try to plumb this fascinating enigma.

Chapter XVII

'GREEN CENTRE' OR
INTELLIGENCE SERVICE?

*

THE examining magistrate Nicholas Sokolov, who was every
bit as intrigued as were the rough Bolsheviks of the Ural
region by the behaviour of the *Vzik* envoy to the Romanovs, soon came to the conclusion that Vassili Vassilievitch was a
pseudonym.

This was current if not invariable practice in revolutionary
circles. Ulianov and Bronstein called themselves Lenin and
Trotsky. But when it comes to such an enigmatic character as
Yacovlev the custom confuses the evidence. In 1919 there was a
rumour in Moscow[1] that 'the traitor Yacovlev'—there was no
longer any doubt about it now, as he had recently deserted to the
Whites—was in reality an aristocrat from Kiev called Moskvin
who had eliminated the real Yacovlev and taken his place. A
fairy story, no doubt, invented by Dzershinsky, head of the
Cheka, so as to conceal from his Bolshevik comrades that the
People's Commissars had been duped by a revolutionary of
sound stock who had passed into foreign employ.

Yacovlev was born around 1890 probably at Ufa (between the
Volga and the Urals) and there he spent at least part of his childhood. His father was a Lithuanian technician called Zarrin who
changed his place of work a number of times. After some schooling, Vassili was apprenticed to his father and became skilled in
electricity and mechanics. His next step was to enter the navy
through the hawse-hole where, as a mechanic, he rapidly rose in
rank. He was a brilliant young man and got into the good books of
his superiors who had no idea that at night by candlelight he was
devouring Socialist pamphlets. Next he was admitted to the
officers' school of mechanics. With the grade of ensign he served
with various naval units in the Baltic and the Black Sea and

1. A detail related by Voïkov.

probably on the cruiser *Alexander II* where there was a quarter-master called Khokriakov. . . .

Maslovsky-Mstislavsky tells us that Vassili Zarrin played an active part in the insurrection at the Sveaborg Fortress in Finland, an outstanding episode in the 1905 uprising. It was then that he adopted the name Yacovlev and deserted the navy. He was condemned to death *in absentia* during the bloody repression that followed the revolt, but managed to escape—in this he was luckier than his comrade, Lieutenant Schmidt, the artisan of the Black Sea mutiny, who was shot on the island of Berezan in 1906. Eventually Zarrin-Yacovlev reached Canada where he found no difficulty in getting a profitable job as a technician in Saskatchewan. No one knows the details of these years of exile. He must have become somewhat anglicised, for when he returned to Russia in 1917 he was quite unlike his former comrades. But the most extraordinary thing about his return to the fold was its speed. Yacovlev—so he was known in revolutionary circles—arrived in Petrograd in March, 1917, after a short stay in Stockholm where his wallet crammed with bank-notes and his Canadian passport had produced a very favourable impression. How had he managed to foresee events so quickly? Where did he get the money for such a comfortable journey? Homesickness for the land of his birth and the chance to get rich quick in the New World can hardly be the whole explanation.

At any rate, a former revolutionary had re-entered his country and in the nick of time. There he found comrades who had kept his name green and who gave him a picked place on their new committees. At that time everyone was living so frantically in the present that no one bothered to ask questions about his stay in Canada, his elegant clothes, or—most important of all—about his stay in Stockholm, meeting-ground of world espionage.

Like Yacovlev, Colonel Maslovsky belonged to the left-wing of the Social-Revolutionary party. On recommendation he found a job for the ebullient young technician: he set him to work as his assistant in the library of the Petrograd Headquarters of which he was custodian. He found Yacovlev helpful in classifying foreign books, and Yacovlev also displayed a thorough grounding in naval and submarine warfare.

Maslovsky-Mstislavsky goes on to relate the events of March and April 1917 and how, at meetings of the Petrograd Soviet, the left-wing of the Social-Revolutionary party pressed for the Tsar's arrest and internment in the Peter and Paul Fortress. It will be remembered how Kerensky, though not without difficulty, managed to sidestep this draconian measure. Maslovsky was chosen as chairman of the Secret Commission for the imprisonment and trial of the Imperial couple. It was as such that he went to inspect Tsarskoye-Selo. Yacovlev was his assistant in this political work too.

'Vassili Yacovlev, my assistant on the Commission,' writes Maslovsky, 'went to Kerensky and put it to him that if he failed to arrest the Tsar the people would take the matter into their own hands. In that case a *samossoudd* [lynching] would be inevitable. Kerensky turned pale. . . .'[1]

The bitter tone of this reproach came as an unpleasant surprise to Kerensky. Vassili, as we have every ground for supposing, played the part of a fiery and intriguing revolutionary to perfection.

It was then—doubtless on Yacovlev's suggestion, though Maslovsky says nothing about this—that the two men decided to act on their own. They planned to storm the Tsarskoye Palace with the help of ten sailors from the Kronstadt naval base. With two armoured cars and the support of a handful of extremists in the Guard, they would force Colonel Kotzebue's hand and demand that the Emperor and Empress should be handed over. Their transfer to the Peter and Paul Fortress would be followed by a brief trial before a people's tribunal. The mode of execution had also been decided: they would be hanged in the very yard where the first Russian liberals, the famous 'Decembrists', had met their death in 1826.

The plan broke down owing to the strong opposition of General Kornilov (future rebel and 'Putschist') who got wind of it. He dispatched a *sotnia* (squadron) of Cossacks to Tsarskoye and gave the alarm to his protégé, Colonel Kobylinsky. Skilfully worked on by Yacovlev, Maslovsky put off any further attempt till later. He favoured the appointment of extremist officers to the palace Guard, and 'protected' the midshipman Domodiantz of whom we have already spoken (as inflicting sundry vexations

1. During his short period as Minister and then as head of the Provisional Government, Kerensky met so many people that it seems hardly surprising that he should later have forgotten Yacovlev's name.

on Nicholas). When General Kornilov was retired on the instance of the extremists and replaced by General Polovtsev, Maslovsky and Yacovlev thought their chance had come at last. But at that precise moment Maslovsky was arrested for his part in various revolts against Kerensky. And Kerensky exiled the Romanovs to the safety of Tobolsk.

The first period of Yacovlev's revolutionary(?) activities ended with Maslovsky's imprisonment. We must now note that as early as the spring and the beginning of the summer of 1918, Yacovlev was taking a very close interest in the circumstances of the Romanovs' captivity. Was he already planning to facilitate their escape? We must leave it to the reader to form his own opinion.

Let us pass for a moment to another hitherto unknown detail. *Who was the mysterious Smirnov?*

It will be remembered that when the Romanovs left for Tobolsk a large number of their household, domestic and otherwise, was permitted to go with them, either in the train from Tsarskoye station or else following on later. Judge Sokolov was able to draw up an exact list of the 'court' at Tobolsk with the help of documentary evidence and detailed questioning. It amounted to forty-six persons. The forty-fifth was Anna Utkin, 'the Tsarina's maid'. The forty-sixth and last, given no Christian name nor description of office, was simply: Smirnov.

Now a few days before the Romanovs were deported to Tobolsk, Anna Utkin had been married to an *efreitor* (soldier of the first class) called Vassili Smirnov. This man's job was that of office caretaker in the library of the Petrograd Headquarters. So far as we can gather, Yacovlev had close links with all the library's employees, and particularly with Smirnov. With the prestige of his uniform, and arguments in the form of hard cash, Smirnov would have no difficulty in getting himself accepted by the maid —whom anyway he knew already.[1]

Now why did Yacovlev—who, pending Maslovsky's release, was operating on his own—thus appoint a personal observer at Tobolsk? Obviously so as to have a spy on the spot[2]—and one

1. Information provided by Piotr Voïkov, probably obtained years earlier from the Cheka.
2. He also learned a great deal from his friend Karelin, a high official responsible for the liquidation of the Imperial properties.

who was not a Kerensky supporter—who could keep him informed of the precise points that were of capital interest to him.

Plainly Smirnov was acting in good faith as regards the Social-Revolutionaries in Petrograd and thought he was a 'hard-boiled' revolutionary keeping watch over the 'weaklings'. The fact is that his mission to Tobolsk was not particularly useful and he returned to Petrograd in December 1917.

As for Yacovlev, we have little information as to his activities during the autumn of 1917. It is known that he was one of the officials of the left-wing faction of the Social-Revolutionaries co-opted by Lenin after the October Revolution. He was one of the twenty-nine Social-Revolutionaries who, with seventy-one Bolsheviks, formed the first Central Executive Committee of a hundred appointed by the Second Soviet Congress on October 27. Yet we come across him—or at least we come across someone called Yacovlev who is as like him as a twin brother—as a member of the Soviet delegation at the negotiations of Brest-Litovsk. For interminable weeks after December 9 the German Empire and the new proletarian Russia sat face to face in a miserable town half-buried in snow. After constant break-downs in the discussions, disagreements between the Bolshevik leaders, and arrogant demands from the German spokesmen, Kühlmann and General Hoffmann, the Peace Treaty was finally signed on March 3, 1918.

In his history of the Russian Revolution Leo Trotsky describes an incident that occurred during the negotiations:

'Brest-Litovsk was crossed by a strategic road barricaded by barbed wire. Sometimes we made an outing along this road in German cars and accompanied by German non-commissioned officers. On the other side of the barbed wire was a notice in German and Russian saying, "Any Russian found here will be shot." A member of our delegation, Yacovlev, had an altercation with a German of our escort on the subject, for this Yacovlev got out of the car and entered the forbidden zone. General Hoffmann lodged a written complaint with me about the incident, claiming that Yacovlev had insulted the German non-commissioned officer.'

The signing of the Peace Treaty was a turning-point in the foreign policy of the Bolshevik State. The subject of the ex-

Imperial family came up again. As Kerensky puts it, 'After Brest-Litovsk a sort of struggle began in Moscow around the ex-Tsar—in Moscow or somewhere still further away.' Kerensky says that he was inclined to the belief that Lenin was playing a double game in the Kremlin and using Sverdlov as his stooge. (In this case, Lenin must have decided to eliminate the Romanovs without a trial—an impression which seems to be confirmed by Trotsky's account of the discussion in the Kremlin from which we have already quoted). Another of Kerensky's convictions was that there was an unquestionable co-relation between two days: April 22 (Yacovlev's hurried arrival in Tobolsk) and April 24 (the arrival in Moscow of Count Mirbach, the new German Ambassador, determined to dictate his own terms to the Kremlin).

However justified Kerensky's reflections about Lenin's double game, Maslovsky-Mstislavsky's evidence forces us to conclude that Yacovlev had his own private interest in the Romanovs. But there is nothing contradictory in these two situations, for Yacovlev could have cleverly intrigued to be Lenin's man in the affair, which would in no way have prevented him from pulling out when the moment came.

Was Yacovlev an agent of Colonel Nicolai, head of the German Secret Service? Was he recruited by the famous 'Green Centre' in Stockholm, and by Kleist, the man who had placed so many of his spies round the Tsarina Alexandra Feodorovna? This hypothesis seems extremely unlikely. First of all because Wilhelm II would have had no interest in saving the Tsar. He was a cold-hearted man who refused to respond to the humanitarian appeals made by King Christian X of Denmark[1] on the Romanovs' behalf (letter of March 17, 1918, published by Kerensky). Besides, had the Kaiser really wanted to save Nicholas and, above all the Princesses with their German blood, all he needed to do was to demand that they should be handed over (during the Brest-Litovsk negotiations, or even later). All evidence goes to show that at that time Lenin had to concede whatever Germany wanted. And finally, there is no trace in the secret archives of the Wilhelmstrasse (as published in 1935 by the *Berliner Magnatshefte*) of any interest shown in the Romanovs by the German Ambassador in Moscow. Had the Germans been anxious about

---

1. Dowager-Empress María Feodorovna was King Christian's aunt, and also, we must not forget, sister to the English Queen Mother.

the safety of the Imperial prisoners, they would have said so sooner or later, if only during the second German-Russian war.[1]

What seems infinitely more likely is that Yacovlev was a British agent. The Commissar Extraordinary on his special mission was, after all, a Canadian citizen also and a subject— perhaps a loyal one—of George V.

Let us turn for a moment to that rather obscure but one-time successful author, William Le Queux. A British writer and journalist, he played an important part in the Intelligence Service from which he was dismissed at the end of the First World War for breach of discretion. He was a specialist in Russian affairs and after the war published several books. The first, *The Tragic Tsarina*, was a thorough-going indictment of Alexandra Feodorovna and the Rasputin clique, and it aroused public protest in Russian *émigré* circles still reeling from the shock of the slaughter at Ekaterinburg. The second, less well-known and entitled *The Dead only Talk at the Last Judgement*, disclosed various episodes in Secret Service activity directly experienced by Le Queux when—under the names of Strandford and Robertson— he was an 'honourable correspondent' in His Majesty's Service.

Strandford-Le Queux relates that the Secret Service had managed to place an agent among those watching over the Russian Imperial family. He does not give his name, but says that this man was a member of the left-wing faction of the Social-Revolutionary party who had been repatriated from Canada on the eve of the 1918 Revolution. . . . He was later nominated to the Soviet Central Executive Committee. . . . He played a part in the Brest-Litovsk negotiations. . . . He was involved in the assassination of Count Mirbach the German Ambassador by the Social-Revolutionaries (July 1918). A few months later all trace of him was lost during battles along the Volga.

This agent offers some astonishing points in common with Yacovlev—that is the least that one can say. There is nothing improbable about the British keeping a second master-spy in the ranks of the Russian revolutionaries. We say a *second*, for the first

1. Before obtaining the documentation used in this book, the present author studied *in extenso* the hypothesis that Yacovlev was a German agent (*Tribune de Genève*, 1958) or an envoy of the Social-Revolutionaries Muraviev and Savinkov whose foreign policy was very different from Lenin's.

was Sydney Reilly, an Oxford graduate who established himself in Russia in 1909, spied on Lenin's circle under the name of Relinsky until 1924, was unmasked, condemned to death, escaped to Riga disguised as a pope, but met his death on a new mission in December 1925.[1]

Our hypothesis suggests that after the British Government had *officially* refused to save the Imperial family at the end of June 1917 it made an underground attempt to 'recoup' the loss. This type of policy, involving two stages, is thoroughly in the British tradition. We should not forget that the London cabinet had had a lively interest in Russian affairs ever since the eighteenth century. Tsar Paul I was assassinated in 1801 by conspirators directed by Count Pahlen but inspired by the British Ambassador.[2]

Information obtained from our—unintentional—Soviet source, that is to say from Voïkov's memoirs, completes the picture of Yacovlev as a British agent without in any way distorting it. According to rumours current in Cheka circles in 1919, Yacovlev was in fact a British subject. He was said to have fled to Rumania where he was taken in charge by a man called Gibson, the Secret Service representative in Bucarest.

And the Cheka—still following Voïkov's account—eventually laid hands on a suitcase belonging to Yacovlev which had been hidden in an attic of the Granada Hotel in Moscow. Among his papers they found a manuscript, the rough draft of a novel telling of an idyll between a young revolutionary and a princess. The princess, who was described in detail, bore an astonishing resemblance to the Grand Duchess Maria Nikolaevna. As Yacovlev had manifestly tried to torpedo the negotiations for a separate peace at Brest-Litovsk, his whole identity and character was made a State Secret; and this explains why books about the Secret Service published in London (always very discreet) have never given him the mention he deserves.

---

1. We should also mention the names of Lockhart, Captain Cromy and Edward Crawford—all brilliant Secret Service agents in Russia.

2. See certain historical works such as *L'assassinat de Paul Ier* by Constantin de Grunwald (Hachette), p. 180, which is borne out by Albert Sorel's French classic *L'Europe et la Révolution Française*, vol. VI, p. 121.

Chapter XVIII

THE LAST RESPITE

*

FORTUNATELY for Nicholas, it never crossed his mind that the transfer to Ekaterinburg and the new humiliations boded ill for himself and his family.[1]

A few weeks before he was shot he was almost sprightly. On May 1, after his first night in his last prison, he hastened to record in his diary that he had 'slept marvellously'. The night before he had written: 'The house is handsome and well-kept. Four large rooms have been put at our disposal—a corner bedroom, a bathroom, a dining-room with windows looking on to a little garden and from which we can see the lower part of the town, and finally a huge drawing-room.' When no one was looking he took the air and enjoyed the brilliant sunshine by hoisting himself up to a fanlight window. Finally, on the day after his arrival, which was Good Friday, he noted that he and his family had lunched very late 'because of an influx of provisions in honour of the festival'—the good nuns of Ekaterinburg having taken over from the priests of Tobolsk.

Another omen that Nicholas missed—for he had never shone at history—was that the merchant Ipatiev, who had been moved out of his house so as to provide accommodation for the Romanovs, had the same name as, and might be a direct descendant of, the Ipatiev who owned the Kostrowa monastery where Michael Romanov had sought refuge before he was elected Tsar of Moscow and thereby founded the Romanov dynasty (1614).

Stiffer and prouder than ever, Alexandra Feodorovna seemed as incapable as her husband of grasping the sad realities. Whereas the months of internment and, above all, the absence of responsibilities, had relaxed the Tsar, the Empress had become bitterness personified. She was continually nagging at her

1. The testimony of one of his Bolshevik attendants in July 1918 is conclusive; he, the Tsar, amenable, kindly, gentle; she, the Tsarina, arrogant and stand-offish.

daughters and whispering reprimands. But only once did she knit her brows and heave a sigh. On arrival at Ekaterinburg she began practising a sort of hunger strike and would rise from the table without having touched the dishes prepared with such care by Kharitonov. Between meals the young kitchen boy, Leonid Siednev, had to bring her specially prepared macaroni and a sort of white gruel. We owe this glimpse of Alexandra Feodorovna to Eugen Platonovitch N., a monarchist who joined the Ekaterinburg Red Guard with the aim of helping the Romanovs. But for all his sympathy he felt obliged to add: 'She has nothing of a Russian Empress about her. She is rather like a German general's wife—such as one finds among governesses full of their own importance.'[1]

Alexander Kerensky was very much struck by the phrase 'the Bridegroom is at hand' which occurred at the end of a long tirade of fiery mysticism in a letter to Anna Virubova.[2] The time had come, he says, when the Romanovs had no choice but to prepare for death. But here we have to join issue with the distinguished historian, and strongly. The intelligent reader has only to look at the context of this letter to see that the phrase in question reflects no tragic forebodings. It is merely the peroration of a pre-Easter 'sermon' which the exalted Alix had begun in her previous letter: 'It is Lent. We must purify ourselves so that we can sing throughout Holy Russia that Christ is risen.' This letter ends: 'The King of Glory is at hand. . . . He is bearing your cross, he can sustain us all. . . . He will save the motherland. . . . The Bolsheviks are in our town, but do not worry: the Lord is everywhere and he will work a miracle. That is our common way of salvation: he who can endure shall be saved.'

Moreover, in writing to her 'sweet little darling', Alexandra Feodorovna outlined her plans for the future, especially for the

1. Recorded by Valentin Speransky, *La Maison à destination spéciale* (Ferenczi et Fils, 1929). This former Petrograd university professor made a secret visit to Russia to investigate the death of the Imperial family.

2. 'The Bridegroom is at hand. Let us prepare to receive him. Let us cast off our raiment soiled by the dust of here-below, and let us purify our souls and bodies. Let vanity be far from us. All is vanity in this world. Let us open the gates of our souls to receive the Bridegroom. Let us invoke the help of the Saints . . .' (This letter was written in Russian. Alexandra usually preferred to write in English but her correspondence was now often censored and she had to use the language of the country. The letter, dated March 20 (April 2), 1918, was published in Anna Virubova's *Souvenirs*.)

summer holidays of 1918. Now that we know of the events of
July 17, this makes painful reading. But history is made up of
brutal juxtapositions.

In the very last letter that Anna Virubova received—Alix
wrote often from Ekaterinburg but none of her letters reached
their destination—there is the passage: 'Moscow has sent a new
commissar, a certain Yacovlev . . . In summer the heat reaches 40°
in Tobolsk. Dust, damp, and no greenery. We are putting out
feelers with a view to spending the summer in some monastery.'
And she concluded, later that same day: 'We have now seen the
new commissar. He doesn't look too bad.' Coming from Alix, no
compliment could be greater!

The last news to reach Anna Virubova in her Petrograd slum
was sent by Grand Duchess Maria. It is a young girl's letter, full
of restraint and melancholy:

'Good morning, darling. It is a long time since I wrote to
you. It made me very happy to hear from you. It is sad never
to see each other, but we shall meet again when God wills. What
a joyful day that will be! We are living in the house where you
lived, we are all right especially since the arrival of our belongings.
We go out a walk twice a day. There are some kind people here.
. . . Mr Gibbs gave us your photographs, it was so good to see
them. We wear the brooches that we received, we have smelt
your scent, and it so brings your face to mind! I hope the Lord
will grant you all that is best and I give you a big kiss. Don't
worry, Jesus is with you. I love you very much.'

This undated letter was written late in May or early in June
(according to Nicholas's diary the Princess's belongings reached
Ekaterinburg on May 25). It provides us with another hitherto
unpublished detail: that Anna Virubova had once stayed in the
Ipatiev house. This must have been on one of her journeys to
Pokrovskoye when Rasputin was on 'retreat' in his native village.
Thus the macabre and forced pilgrimage of the captive Romanovs,
who had twice passed through Pokrovskoye and who had
placed all their hopes of escape in the *staretz*'s treacherous son-
in-law, even ended up in a place redolent of Rasputin and his
clique. Without indulging in cheap literature we may none the
less remark how steeped in memories of the dead monk the
Imperial tragedy was. Sometimes destiny has a good memory.

Who were the intermediaries who transmitted this letter to

Virubova and who brought the brooches to the Grand Duchesses? Who were the 'kind people' to whom the prettiest of the Tsarina's daughters refers? Almost certainly the monks and nuns of Ekaterinburg—the same as those who also brought to the bodyguard of the Ipatiev house the *kulitch*, the *paskha* and the red eggs without which Easter could not be properly celebrated in Russia.

It should also be mentioned in passing that semi-official envoys of the Allied Governments sometimes went to Ekaterinburg so as to confirm on the spot that the ex-Imperial family was still alive and in good health. These missions could hardly have been called secret so must have taken place with Chicherin's consent, as he was responsible for Soviet foreign policy. For instance a man called Boar(?) stayed at 27 Voznessensky Prospekt in Ekaterinburg, a stone's throw from the Ipatiev house, and sent an uncoded telegram to the French consulate in Moscow on July 7 to the effect that 'the rumours about the Romanovs are false' (see facsimile of this telegram, illustration No. 43).

Daily life in the Ipatiev house rapidly deteriorated to prison level. At Tsarskoye they had been 'confined to their residence' in luxury; at Tobolsk they had been interned in comfort. Now they experienced a political prisoners' regime (though it must be admitted that their living conditions were infinitely better than those formerly accorded to the Tsar's political enemies). As Bikov himself admits: 'The relative ease and freedom that the Romanovs had enjoyed at Tobolsk no longer existed.'

With the help of the evidence culled by Judge Sokolov from the old valet Tchemodurov, we can form a pretty good idea of the meals served to Nicholas and his family in the dining-room of the Ipatiev house:

'The food was very ordinary; it was brought in ready cooked from a nearby restaurant'—though Kharitonov added delicacies provided by the nuns. 'Their Majesties ate with the servants'— Tchemodurov seemed very shocked by this. 'A soup tureen was placed on the table. There were not enough knives, forks or spoons. The meal was usually made up of meat stock followed by a joint or, more often, cutlets [the Russian word for rissoles]. Morning tea was served with black bread left over from the day before. As we had no napkins or table linen, and nobody gave us any, we ate without a cloth!'

The faithful servant, his bearing and manner of speech resembling those of an impeccable English butler, was fuming with rage as he continued:

'Sometimes the commissars ate at the same table as Their Majesties'—so we suspect that the daily bill of fare was not so very bad for a time of shortage and black market. 'One day when Avdeiev was at one of these meals he kept his hat on and smoked a cigarette. As we were eating cutlets [rissoles], he seized his plate, pushed his arm between Their Majesties and served himself. In putting the cutlet on his plate he crooked his arm and knocked the Emperor's face with his elbow.'

Life was not rosy in the Ipatiev house which the local Soviet had just encircled with a huge fence. If we bear in mind Nicholas's incredible education and how he had been brought up to be 'Emperor and Autocrat of all the Russias, Tsar of Moscow, King of Poland, of Siberia, of Georgia, Grand Duke of Smolensk, Lithuania, Finland and Kurland, Lord of Turkestan . . .' etc.,[1] the proximity of the Red Guards and even the promiscuity with his own servants must have been appalling humiliation. And yet, at the risk of repetition, we should again point out how favourably these conditions compared with those of the liberals imprisoned at Schlüsselburg or, later, those of Stalin's enemies. Until the last minute, when the girls and the boy were brutally and savagely sacrificed in holocaust to Reasons of State and made to atone for the errors of their parents, the Romanovs were not treated badly.

The most touching picture we have of the Ipatiev house is the description of the young Tsarevitch Alexis by Eugen Platonovitch N., the monarchist masquerading as a Red Guard.

Poor Alexis stayed in bed all day. His father helped to carry his bed from one room to another. When I saw this poor sick child I had to sigh. His waxen face was transparent and his eyes were sad like an animal pursued by wolves. Yet he smiled at me and joked when I gave him a deep bow. His sisters were full of vitality and exhaled a gusto for life, whereas he looked as though he no longer belonged to this world. Anastasia was a charming little devil, such a bag of mischief that no one could

1. A shortened version of Nicholas II's official titles as published in the last *St. Petersburg Almanach* (1916).

ever be bored in her company. Lively and always on the move, she was continually pulling funny faces at her favourite dog as they do in the circus.

Alexis, Anastasia, Olga and Tatiana had joined their parents and Maria on May 23. Their Swiss and British tutors, Pierre Gilliard and Sydney Gibbs, had accompanied them from Tobolsk by sleigh and train on a journey that was a real ordeal for young Alexis. The Swiss tutor was forcibly parted from his pupils on Ekaterinburg station and so saw them for the last time:

Nagorny, the sailor attached to Alexis Nicolaievitch, passed by my carriage bearing the little invalid in his arms. After him came the Grand Duchesses loaded with suitcases and other objects. I wanted to get out but was brutally thrust back into the carriage by a sentry. So I returned to the window. Tatiana Nicolaievna came last carrying her little dog[1] and laboriously dragging a heavy brown suit-case. It was raining and I saw her sinking into the mud at every step. . . .'

The man responsible for transferring the Romanov children to Ekaterinburg was our old friend Khokriakov. This former member of the crew of the cruiser *Alexander II*, and in all likelihood an old acquaintance of Yacovlev, was going, like him, to disappear into the horizon. Odd chairman of the Tobolsk Soviet, he appeared at just the right moment, then disappeared for ever, abandoning his office. Nicholas Sokolov was convinced that this man had been sent to Tobolsk on some special mission concerning the Romanovs. His contacts with some mysterious Letts such as Rodionov (an alias) have been established, but there is no way of following up this clue. We may suppose that he belonged to the Yacovlev and Maslovsky circle and, like Maslovsky, was in the dark about the double-personality of Zarrin-Yacovlev. Tricked by Yacovlev and compromised by the assassination of Count Mirbach, the left-wing of the Social-Revolutionaries broke off from the Bolsheviks in July 1918 and joined the other enemies of the new proletarian State.

The soldiers who formed the last kernel of those loyal to the

1. The King Charles, Jimmy, a present from Anna Virubova. Jimmy was killed at the same time as his masters.

ex-Tsar, and his most devoted subjects, were the Tekintzi—a word used at Tsarskoye-Selo for the Moslem cavalry of the Emperor's personal guard. After playing an important part in Kornilov's abortive *Putsch* (August 1917), the Tekintzi were imprisoned by Kerensky at Bychov, but they rose up again, liberated some monarchist officers, and managed to reach the Don and the Kuban.

A witness that the present author himself discovered— Lieutenant Sokolov (no relation to the judge of the same name) who at present keeps a restaurant at Cannes—confirmed that the Tekintzi, who were scattered all over the Ural region and even in the suburbs of Ekaterinburg, constructed a plan to free the Romanovs which failed owing to the delay in the Czech offensive. Lieutenant Sokolov himself took part in this politico-military plot.

There was yet another last-minute plan to release the Romanovs in June 1918. Its main lines were revealed by General Diterichs, the Emperor's former aide-de-camp, in his book on the assassination of the Romanovs published in Vladivostok during the civil war. From May 1918 onwards a large number of the Russian monarchists and relatives of the Romanovs were concentrated in the Urals around Ekaterinburg, Alapaievsk and Perm, notably Grand Dukes Michael Alexandrovitch, Sergei Mikhailovitch, Igor Konstantinovitch, Konstantin Konstantinovitch, Ivan Konstantinovitch, Prince Paley (Grand Duke Paul's son) and Elisabeth Feodorovna, the widow of Grand Duke Sergei Alexandrovitch who had been assassinated in 1905. These noblemen, helped by some rich tradesmen of the Ural region, boasted that they had set up a group 'ready for anything' to save the Tsar. Their bombast and rhetoric, which was later complacently echoed in the monarchist review *Imperial Eagle* published outside Russia, did the Romanovs enormous harm. Remarkably well-informed, the local Cheka had agents in the salon of every one of these aristocrats. Their police reports, carefully collected by Yurovsky and sometimes not a little exaggerated, were used as the pretext for the sentence pronounced by the 'judges' in the Hotel Amerika.

When the question of transferring the Romanovs to the Ural region had first come up, the idea had been to send them to Alapaievsk, a small town on the Irbit–Nizhni–Tiagil railway, and a suitable place had been found in the Napolnoi school there. But later on, when the front came too near, it was decided to leave the most important members of the family at Ekaterinburg.

Subsequently the Ural Soviet picked on Alapaievsk as detention place for the Grand Dukes. But they were only taken there on May 20, 1918. Meanwhile the Tsar's closest relatives—Grand Duchess Elisabeth Feodorovna, ex-Grand Duke Sergei Mikhailovitch, Helen (ex-Serbian Princess Royal), the sons of the late Grand Duke Konstantin Konstantinovitch (Ivan, Igor and Konstantin), and Vladimir Paley (son of the ex-Grand Duke Paul Alexandrovitch)—passed a few weeks near Ekaterinburg where they were left in relative liberty. Even at Alapaievsk, where they were established in a new stone building called 'The School on the Fields', which was located on some factory land, they still had some benefits of freedom. They could go to church without an escort of guards and go for walks in the country round the 'School'. There, as everywhere else, a compact group of friends gathered round them whose kindness brought them plentiful gifts—in goods, flowers and condolences. Moreover, the monarchist couriers kept them in constant contact with Ekaterinburg and Perm as well as with groups from the Ural middle classes set up to save the Tsar and his family.

Another striking example of the sort of freedom accorded to other members of the Romanov dynasty was that of Grand Duke Michael Alexandrovitch, the Tsar's brother, who was also put to death in the Ural region. Michael Alexandrovitch, together with his family, lived at Gatchina—he had been there since March 1917 and it was only a year later, in February 1918, and as a result of monarchist insurrection on his behalf, that he was arrested on the orders of the Petrograd Soviet and sent to Perm with his secretary, Johnson. The document dispatched to the Perm Soviet referred to Michael Romanov being deported to Perm under the responsibility and guard of the Soviet.

At the same time the Soviet was recommended not to make Michael Alexandrovitch's life too difficult. Yet the Perm Soviet felt unable to grant him his freedom but kept him under arrest in the furnished rooms of the 'Nobility Club'. Michael Romanov protested and insisted on being accorded his freedom—quoting the decision made by Petrograd about him.

The Perm Soviet was well aware of the danger that life in freedom at Perm constituted for Michael Romanov as there were endless possibilities of assassination by the 'Greens' or the anarchist terrorists, and offered to transfer him to the prison hospital which had already been suitably repaired. But Romanov complained to the Council of People's Commissars and to the Extraordinary All-Russia Commission (the Cheka). By way of answer the Perm Soviet received a proposal signed by Bontch-Bruyevitch, head of chancery of the Council of People's Commissars, to release Michael Romanov and grant him unrestricted freedom at Perm. This document was signed by Uritzski, chairman of the Petrograd Cheka. Whereupon the representatives of the Executive Committee gave Romanov his freedom but told him that they were unable to guarantee his safety and that the Soviet could in no way henceforward be held responsible for whatever might occur.

Once freed Romanov set up house—together with his secretary, Johnson, Tchelitchev, his valet, and Borunov, his chauffeur—in Siberia Street, one of the principal Perm thoroughfares near the river Kama, in the best furnished apartment known as the 'Korolev'. At first he was guarded by the local militia, but subsequently the Executive Committee informed the Central Government that in view of the new situation it declined all responsibility for Romanov's safety. Whereupon, on suggestion from Petrograd, the watch was entrusted to the Perm Extraordinary Commission—at whose offices Grand Duke Michael had to appear on given days for a report.

Though he enjoyed freedom Michael Romanov kept up close links with his friends and relatives, so that there was permanent contact between Perm, Ekaterinburg, Alapaievsk, Petrograd and Moscow. We need hardly say that this contact was constantly fostered by the monarchists who were ready for anything. Another important factor in the constant link between the 'Ural detainees' and the outside world was Countess Brassova, Michael's wife, who went to Perm in May (through Ekaterinburg) and returned to Moscow where she had an interview with V. I. Lenin whose permission she had requested for her husband's emigration abroad. Naturally, the request was withheld. Later Brassova was arrested but she managed to escape from Russia.

Meanwhile the Perm workers had begun agitating for Michael's death and formed a group with this end in view. This group, which was composed of five men, was independent of the Soviet and Party organisations and carried on in high secrecy with all the risks that course involved. During the night of June 12–13 the group arrived at the hotel with forged papers as if from the Gubcheka (the Extraordinary Commission of the Region).

Michael Romanov was already asleep. They woke him up and showed him the documents ordering his immediate departure from Perm. Romanov was suspicious and refused to accompany them. Whereupon the newcomers announced that they would take him away by force, at which the secretary Johnson declared that he, too, would follow his master.

The two prisoners were put into cars ready for them and taken outside the town. After they had passed the Nobel petrol works they made for the woods and there Michael Romanov and Johnson were executed.

So as to mislead searchers, one of the group telephoned to the militia and the Gubcheka and said that some persons unknown had arrived at the Korolev Hotel during the night and carried away Michael Romanov in the direction of the Siberia highway.

The kidnapping came completely unexpectedly to all the Perm organisations. A pursuit was immediately set afoot, but in the wrong direction and the search was fruitless. At the same time telephone calls were put through to Petrograd and in all other directions announcing Michael Romanov's escape. To what extent was the 'kidnapping' of Grand Duke Michael truly unexpected to the Perm organisations, and had the workers' group no real link with any Soviet or Communist organisation? At least one member of the group, Lukianov, was also a member of the Perm Cheka, according to Nicholas Sokolov in his book already cited.

According to Diterichs, Colonel Ivan Siderov, a well-known monarchist, arrived in Ekaterinburg from Odessa in June 1918. He had a number of meetings with Dr Derevenko, the only person apart from Dr Botkin who still had the right to visit the Ipatiev house (so as to tend Alexis). With Dr Derevenko's help Sidorov smuggled food to the Imperial family (perhaps he was one of the 'kind people' Grand Duchess Maria mentions in her letter) and reached an understanding with them. According to P. M. Bikov the hot-headed monarchists in Ekaterinburg were becoming more and more reckless at this time on account of outside events. The civil war was in full swing, the Czechs were cutting their way through the Ural district and the front was rapidly approaching Ekaterinburg.

It was at this moment that the Cheka skilfully cast its net and hauled in a pretty good catch: various monarchist agents and, if we are to believe P. M. Bikov, an important Serbian group commanded by Major Michich, NCO Bogetchich, and one Smirnov, formerly steward to the Serbian Princess married to Grand Duke Ivan Konstantinovitch. Simultaneously with this round-up of enemies of the regime, the Cheka removed the Grand Dukes present in Ekaterinburg and dispatched them to Alapaievsk where they were soon to be assassinated.

How far were the Romanovs aware of these plans on their behalf? It is very difficult to make a judgement on this point. But General Diterichs is in no doubt, and in his book quotes a letter sent secretly by the Tsar to his friends outside. In this letter the Tsar gives exact information about how to get into their apartment, the time-table of the sentries' rounds, and so on; but the authenticity of the document is not proved.

The Ekaterinburg Soviet became aware of the security loop-holes and on July 4 it appointed a new 'commander' over the Ipatiev house, Y. M. Yurovsky. In the days that followed, this dumpy, red-faced man made history and sealed the fate of the Russia of the past.

Chapter XIX

THE EXECUTION

*

A s I was approaching the end of my historical inquiry my eyes fell on a series of American press cuttings. There is yet another Anastasia claimant. A certain Mrs Smith maintains that she had a miraculous escape from the bloody basement in Ekaterinburg. In New York there is also a Pole, a Mr Goloniewsky, who claims to be the Tsarevitch Alexis.

Alas, in the past forty years false Anastasias and pseudo-Alexises have been cropping up almost everywhere, from the Manchurian snows to the sunny coast of California, only to disappear again as soon as they are unmasked.

But mythomania has its tenacious heroines. Ever since 1920 Frau Tchaikovsky-Anderson has been bringing tears to shop-girls' eyes as the sensational Press—and perhaps businessmen too, on the scent of the Romanovs' secret accounts said to be lying fallow in Swedish and British banks—periodically tries to build up her grotesque story.

The only way of putting an end to these legends would be to produce some irrefutable document, for instance the Kremlin official minutes, which would be even more categorical than the crucial book by P. M. Bikov, former chairman of the Ural Soviet at Ekaterinburg. But many years will surely have to elapse before historians get access to the Kremlin archives.

So we had better give an account of the execution as it has been described by Bikov, both in his article and his book.

As soon as Golochtchekin returned from Moscow—this was about July 12—he reported to the Ural Regional Soviet the Kremlin's view on the execution of the Romanovs.

As the front was already far too near and the slightest delay might involve new complications, the Regional Soviet decided that a trial, as envisaged by Moscow, was now out of the question. It decided to consult the Army Command as to the

real situation at the front. The military authorities produced
the report as requested. This proved that the outlook was very
black indeed. The Czechs had already by-passed Ekaterinburg
to the south and were attacking on two fronts. Red Army
forces were insufficient and the fall of Ekaterinburg could be
expected within three days. In view of this the Regional
Soviet decided to shoot the Romanovs without any public
trial.

A preliminary conference of the Regional Soviet decided on
ways and means of carrying out the execution and the destruction of the bodies.

Decision concerning the latter was made in view of the
imminent fall of Ekaterinburg, so that the Whites should not
be given the opportunity of exploiting popular ignorance by
producing 'relics' of the ex-Tsar.

In the event, after their occupation of Ekaterinburg, the
Whites took quite a time before discovering the 'holy bodies'
of the Imperial family.

On the evening of July 16 those appointed to carry out the
death sentence assembled in the commander's room in 'the
house of special assignment'. It had been agreed that the upper
floor, where the family lived, was unsuitable as the place of
execution. It was therefore decided to take the family down into
one of the rooms in the basement. Until the moment of
execution the Romanovs knew nothing of the Soviet's decree.
Towards midnight they were asked to dress and go down to
the basement, and in order not to arouse suspicion they were
told that this measure was being taken in view of a possible
attack by White Guards.

When they were all assembled in the room fixed on for the
execution, the decree of the Ural Regional Soviet was made
known to them. The house commander, who was at the same
time the Ural Soviet representative, read out the death sentence
and added that all hope was vain and that they must all die.
The unexpected news left the victims dumbfounded, though
the ex-Tsar had just time to ask, 'So we aren't being taken
anywhere?'

After which all the eleven: Nicholas Romanov, his wife,
their son, their four daughters, and four members of their
household, were executed on the spot. They were finished off

with revolver shots. There were only four people present at the execution, those who fired on the victims.

After the execution the bodies of the Romanovs were wrapped in blankets, carried into the courtyard, and placed on a truck. By an itinerary decided on, the truck left Ekaterinburg through the Verkh-Issetsk suburb and made in the direction of Koptiaki. Halfway there, at some eight versts from the town, there is a plot of land known as the 'Four Brothers'—the name comes from four tall pine trees that used to stand there. To the left of the road, in the same area, are some disused pits, abandoned a long time ago, where iron ore used to be mined. This area gets its name from the little pond in the middle of the mines, called Ganina Yama. It was there that the bodies of the Romanovs were taken, by a little woodland path leading off the Koptiaki road. They were placed provisionally in one of the pits, and their destruction was carried out next day. On the bodies of the ex-Tsarina and her daughters large quantities of jewels, of gold and diamonds, were discovered, concealed in their clothes and especially in the bodices of the girls' dresses, diamonds in the buttons and so on . . . All the clothes were carefully scrutinised and all objects of value gathered up.

On July 18 the 'obsequies' were definitely over. They were so carefully carried out that in spite of professionally excavating in the area, the Whites took two years to find the Romanovs' place of burial.

After the execution of the sentence the Regional Soviet sent Golochtchekin and Yurovsky to Moscow with the more valuable objects taken off the Romanovs, their correspondence, diaries, and all the documents justifying the Soviet's decision to shoot the ex-Tsar and his family.

At the session of the Praesidium of the All-Russian Central Executive Committee (*Vzik*) on July 19, the president, J. M. Sverdlov, read out a telegram announcing the former Emperor's execution. After examining all the circumstances which had compelled the Ural Regional Soviet to take this decision, the *Vzik* Praesidium ratified and approved it. That same evening news of the execution was communicated to the Council of People's Commissars.

While the meeting was discussing a proposal of the Commissariat for Public Health, and at the very moment when Comrade Semachko was making his report, Sverdlov entered and sat down in his usual place behind Ilytch [Lenin]. When Semachko had finished his report Sverdlov turned to Ilytch and said a few words to him.

'Comrade Sverdlov asks leave to speak. He has some information.'

'I have to tell you,' Sverdlov began in his smooth voice, 'of some information that has come through to us: Nicholas has been executed at Ekaterinburg on the decision of the Regional Soviet. Nicholas wanted to escape; the Czechoslovaks are drawing near the town. The Praesidium of the *Vzik* has approved the measure.'

There was general silence.

'Now let us return to the proposal,' said Ilytch.

They returned to the proposal. . . .

On July 19 the Council of the People's Commissars promulgated the decree on the confiscation of the property of Nicholas Romanov and the members of the Imperial family. All their possessions were declared the property of the Soviet Republic.

The official communiqué on the Romanovs' execution was published in Ekaterinburg on July 22 [we have already quoted it on p. 99, so omit it here]. This same communiqué had been made the day before at a workers' meeting in the Town Theatre where it was acclaimed with enthusiasm. The meeting adopted the following resolution: 'Bloody Nicholas's punishment is the answer and the warning to bourgeois and monarchist counter-revolutionaries who are trying to drown the workers' and peasants' revolution in blood. All the enemies of the working people have united under the flag of the restoration of bourgeois and aristocratic autocracy. All the working people have united under the flag of the Socialist and Soviet Republic. The struggle will be to the death, and all who are not with the people in its fight for existence are in the camp of the people's enemies . . .'

Bikov's evidence, confirmed by the Ural regional press of the time, is historically authentic.

As for all the evidence collected by the examinining magistrates of the White Army, we have to admit that, accurate though it is, it does nevertheless leave a remote possibility that one of the Grand Duchesses could have escaped the slaughter and fled to the West.

In the present writer's view, however, this remote possibility is ruled out by another interesting account of the execution, still in manuscript. It is a document that deserves to be made known, for it fits in so well with what we know already that there can be no doubt of its authenticity.

As we have seen, the USSR Ambassador in Warsaw from 1924 to 1927 was Piotr Lazarevitch Voïkov, former Commissar for Supplies in the Ural Soviet. When this diplomat was assassinated by the Russian monarchist, Boris Koverda, on June 7, 1927, it was precisely because he had been one of the participants in the execution in the Ipatiev house. Among the documents which escaped the destruction of Warsaw by the Nazis, a portion of the archives of the Warsaw Assizes containing copies of documents referring to the 'Koverda/Voïkov' affair was found in the house of a certain Gutek, secretary of the substitute interrogating magistrate.[1]

The Gutek file[2] is based on confidences made by Voïkov to his friend Rosengoltz and to other friends in the Polish Communist Party. It coincides with Bikov's declarations as well as with other evidence, for instance that of a former secretary at the

1. This inquiry took place in June 1927 at Warsaw and Vilno. It was carried out under the instructions of the Procurator of the Republic of Poland, Sviontkovsky. The chairman of the court which judged the Koverda/Voïkov affair was I. Guminsky. The Judges were Kozakovsky and Skavinsky. The Advocate General at the Court of Appeal was K. Rudnícky. Boris Safronovitch Koverda, aged nineteen, a pupil of the Russian school at Vilno, who at 9.55 a.m. in Warsaw central station had fired six revolver shots at the Soviet Ambassador to Poland and mortally wounded him, was defended by senior advocates Andreev, Nedzelsky, Paskalsky and Etlinger. The trial opened on June 15, 1927 at Warsaw Assizes, with a vivid account of the facts. Boris Koverda described the motives which led him to kill P. Voïkov. The world press and political observers were present, as the assassination nearly led to plunging Europe into a new Russian-Polish conflict. There were big headlines calling young Koverda 'the assassin of the assassin'. In the eyes of the Poles it was the trial of the century. The Kremlin saw it as a further proof that the White emigration abroad was not ready to disarm. Large numbers of White organisations were arming terrorists such as Boris Koverda, so as to combat the young Soviet State.

2. Gutek himself was a victim of the SS 'Operation Reinhardt' whose aim was to rid Polish justice of all former members of the Polish Socialist Party.

USSR Embassy in Warsaw who came west in the thirties and had collected and typed out some of Piotr Voïkov's private conversations.

It appears from these revelations that in view of the imminent occupation of Ekaterinburg by the anti-Communist Czech troops as well as Admiral Kolchak's, the Ural Soviet had decided to have the Imperial family executed without waiting for Lenin's opinion. A special commission was set up, composed of Yakob Yurovsky, Golochtchekin, Beloborodov, Voïkov and Ermakov. Voïkov was chosen to make the speech for the prosecution. He had asked for this—so that he would never be forgotten in the history of his country. No one, however, asked for the job of defending the Tsar. The strange 'special commission' met at the Hotel Amerika.

Here is Voïkov's story as reconstituted from the Gutek file:[1]

The Cheka had made the Hotel Amerika its headquarters. Provisionally we had been allotted rooms 3 and 10 for our meetings. In fact only two meetings were devoted to my speech for the prosecution. Judgement was pronounced after a discussion *in camera*. It was unanimous.

We reached our verdict on July 15, 1918. We then submitted it for ratification to the Central Committee of the Bolshevik Party and the Soviet of the Ural Region. It was ratified immediately. That same evening Golochtchekin, the Kremlin's special envoy, telegraphed to Moscow. Moscow approved our decision and stressed that the whole family must disappear at the same time as the Tsar. In Moscow, as with us in the Ural Region, they were afraid of a plot to release the Tsarevitch, the Tsarina and the Grand Duchesses after Nicholas's death and then to make the Tsarina regent.

We now know that numbers of plots had already been hatched. Moreover the Germans, though they raised no protest against the execution of Nicholas II which they viewed as a purely Russian affair in which they did not want to be involved, were on the point of demanding the transfer of the Tsarina and her children to Germany. In order to prevent Wilhelm II from trying to use the Imperial family against us,

1. We came upon it, or upon part of it, in 1946 while reporting in Warsaw.

the Government resolved to have the whole family put to death.

On Wednesday July 13 Sverdlov wired Beloborodov and insisted again on this point. But he added that we must be discreet and conceal the execution for as long as possible. Beloborodov replied that to achieve secrecy we would have to do away with all the attendants in the Ipatiev house.

'You know as well as I do what you have to do,' Sverdlov answered on the Hugues telegraph.

The position was clear. Together with the Ural Soviet we had examined ways and means of concealing the execution of the Imperial family. My proposal was that we should invent some excuse to get them out of the house, then shoot them in the great forest north-west of Ekaterinburg, then weight the bodies with metal bars and drop them into the Isseth lake. But Yurovsky protested. He shouted rather than talked. He would not answer for the consequences, he cried, for part of the Guard might revolt, rape the Grand Duchesses, search their bodies for jewels, who knew what else, and anyway ditch the whole enterprise.

At this Beloborodov suggested that it should be left to Yurovsky and myself to work something out for the execution and the complete destruction of the bodies. 'Think of some way,' he concluded, 'whereby not a trace of the bodies shall ever be found.'

When the Grand Duchesses arrived from Tobolsk with Alexis to rejoin 'citizen' Romanov, there was a rumour that they were carrying an enormous quantity of jewels. Yet they were not searched. Yurovsky was obsessed on this point: there were no women in the Guard and he would not trust men near the Tsar's daughters. He kept saying there was no counting on discipline and that it would end in rape.

But Yurovsky had added: 'One day we'll get all the jewels that they have sewn into their nightgowns and corsets.' It was a fact that the Tsarina made her daughters wear very special underclothes. She had even had a sort of chastity belt added to their corsets. She was afraid of sudden onslaughts anywhere —in the garden and even in the house. The Grand Duchesses were always accompanied by attendants when they went to the lavatory. The door stayed ajar . . . Anything could happen.

One of the guards, the Lett Kalnin, often told his comrades that they should avenge themselves on the Grand Duchesses for the centuries of suffering the people had had to endure. 'I don't care a f—— about their attractions,' said the Lett, 'for myself I much prefer the Ekaterinburg girls. But we've been through so much in my country at the hands of German barons putting our peasant girls in the family way—now it's our turn to have our revenge on the German woman. The treatment of our peasant girls must be wiped out on her daughters.'

We had decided to hold the execution in the basement of the Ipatiev house. Then the bodies would be taken by truck to the Koptiaki forest and burnt. I ordered my secretary, Zimin, to ask for sulphuric acid and petrol at the central drug store to make it easier and quicker to destroy the bodies. On July 14 Yurovsky and I visited the Koptiaki forest some twenty kilometres from Ekaterinburg. There we earmarked two clearings where the bodies could be piled up on some sort of pyre, and an abandoned mineshaft into which the ashes and other remains could be thrown. This didn't really present a difficulty: the country round Ekaterinburg is full of forests and mines, and the roads are deserted. The essential thing was to execute Nicholas, his family and his companions as rapidly as possible.

Yet it was not all that easy. The guards at the Ipatiev house were not dependable. They might talk. Yurovsky began planning to liquidate some of them as well, but Beloborodov drew the line at this. They were workers from the Zlokasov factories. Their liquidation would provoke an uproar in the town . . .

During the day of July 16 Yurovsky looked thoroughly nervous. In the afternoon he asked me to go and see if everything was all right in the Ipatiev house.

In the evening, Ermakov announced that all was ready. A detachment of Letts and Magyars of the Cheka, and ten members of the Regional Committee of the Bolshevik Party, were to take part in the execution. Mausers, Nagan revolvers and two machine-guns were handed out. Around midnight Yurovsky went up and woke the Tsar, his family, and four members of his household—one of them being Dr Botkin.

He told them that an attack against the Ipatiev house was being planned and that they were going to be taken elsewhere. The prisoners were calm, having no suspicion of their danger. Towards one-thirty in the morning Nicholas II, his family and his attendants emerged from their rooms. Led by Yurovsky they went down into the courtyard and then into the basement. Yurovsky ordered three chairs to be brought, for Nicholas II, the Tsarina and the Tsarevitch. Dr Botkin stood behind the Tsarevitch.

As soon as they were lined up, Yurovsky gave the signal. We opened the door. I was to give the order to open fire and execute the last Russian Tsar. But Yurovsky was ahead of me. Taking a piece of paper from his pocket he read rapidly: 'Nicholas Alexandrovitch. By decision of the Ural Regional Soviet you have been condemned to death.'

The ex-Tsar made the sign of the cross and turned towards his family. Yurovsky turned to me. 'Ready?' I checked my Mauser.

At that moment the Tsar turned to Yurovsky and began to say something in a trembling, convulsive voice. I heard Yurovsky saying, 'Enough of this talk. The Revolution is dying, you will die with it.' Then, to us: 'Go ahead.'

As he spoke he discharged his own revolver into the Tsar. It was my turn to command. 'Sustained fire!'

We fired for several minutes. The basement was full of acrid smoke and the sickening smell of blood. The Grand Duchesses were still groaning. They had to be finished off with pistol shots. The Tsarevitch received his *coup de grâce* from Yurovsky. It was I who gave the *coup de grâce* to Nicholas II.

At that moment Ermakov exclaimed, 'The Tsarina's maid and the youngest daughter, Anastasia, are still breathing.' Two Letts from the Cheka ran forward to finish off Anna Demidova and the youngest daughter, Anastasia. One of the Letts drove his bayonet through Anastasia's face.

By about two all was over . . .

It was nearly four o'clock in the morning; the dawn of July 17, 1918, was breaking. The sun was just about to rise. Yurovsky wanted to take the bodies to the wood before daylight. He had two big trucks sent along. The driver, Lukhianov, was in charge of the removal. Yurovsky and I chose twelve of the most reliable guards and left with the trucks. It was already daylight when we reached our destination. We piled the bodies of the Tsar, the Tsarina, the Tsarevitch and the Grand Duchesses in the bigger of the clearings; those of the four members of the household we threw on the little patch of grass beside the disused mine—the pit of the 'Four Brothers'.

It was then that Yurovsky gave orders to undress the bodies and look for the jewels sewn into the top clothes and under-wear. We cut the material. We tore the dresses in our haste. We found a large quantity of jewels. We had not expected to find so many.

I remember that all the Grand Duchesses were wearing topaz necklaces, Ural topazes, presents from Rasputin![1] When we had finished Yurovsky hurriedly drew up an inventory, handed it to me to sign, and put the jewels in a big bag to take to Ekaterinburg and later to Moscow.

Now came the business of destroying the bodies. Axes were produced and we chopped the bodies into pieces so that they would burn better in the fire. Ermakov directed this part of the operation as Yurovsky and I were still busy with the inventory. But before the bodies were thrown on the pyre and sulphuric acid poured on them, Yurovsky wanted to satsify himself that everything had been done properly.

He approached the macabre heap of human remains—heads, trunks, legs, arms—and rummaged for a full quarter of an hour. Then he said, 'I think there is something wrong.' I was on edge. 'Come on, let's finish,' I said. He gave the order and the bodies were thrown on the fire. The next day I asked Yurovsky what he had meant by what he said. He replied that he had failed to locate the head with the bayonet thrust, the head of the youngest Grand Duchess.

When we undressed the bodies of the Romanov family to look for jewels, the bodies had lain naked on the grass. Perhaps the soldiers thought there were jewels concealed in the private parts of the bodies.

This incident was mentioned to the Ural Regional Soviet. It was whispered that one of the Lett soldiers had been seen talking to Anastasia on a number of occasions when on guard duty at the Ipatiev house, and that once he had put his arm

1. We leave the responsibility for this assertion with Voïkov.

round her in the garden. The Romanov girl, who was then sixteen, cannot have reported this to her mother, for Yurovsky had no complaints from the Romanov family. It was just a passing flirtation on the part of a young girl already destined for death . . .

And here ends Voïkov's story as found among the papers of the Gutek file. It puts an end to the possibility of survival of any of the Grand Duchesses, all of whose corpses were counted in that macabre forest, even if Yurovsky was right about the disappearance of a head.

Chapter XX

A DIPLOMATIC COMEDY

*

BY a curious coincidence the Soviet diplomat who collected and typed out Piotr Voïkov's confidences—and to whom we referred in the last chapter—was to come across traces of the pseudo-Anastasia again, at the time when he was Soviet chargé d'affaires in Tokyo.

His diary is still in manuscript, but I have been able to consult it, as Kerensky, Burtsev and Melgunov did before me. This is what it says:

On a warm Japanese afternoon—June 27, 1927—a handful of diplomats dressed in white were slowly climbing up the hill leading to the Tiger Gate and going towards Tansumatchi street in Tokyo's Aoyama quarter. They were on their way to watch a tennis match between the Dutch Legation and the Belgian Embassy.

I and my friend Baron Giovanni di Giura, First Secretary at the Italian Embassy, had stopped so that I could light a cigarette. The baron wanted to get a close-up view of the historic Tora-no-Mon crossroads where in 1924 the Prince Regent, the future Mikado Hirohito, had been wounded by a student called Namba-Kiro, a half-cracked follower of the Black Dragon.

I gave Giura a short account of the attempted assassination. He listened attentively. Suddenly his eyes became dreamy and he gazed into the distance. I told him to hurry up—it was getting late and the tennis would begin without us.

The baron threw out his arms. 'Listen, do you really want to see the match?' he asked. 'The Dutch couple are pretty poor, and the Comte de Bassompierre's[1] secretary and his partner are even worse. I suggest you come along to the Embassy and we'll split a bottle of Asti Spumante.' I agreed

1. The Belgian Ambassador in Tokyo.

and we retraced our steps without saying goodbye to our colleagues.

The Italian Embassy was not far from the crossroads, but I asked the baron to drop in first at the Soviet Embassy in Ura-Kassoumi-Gasseki Avenue.

I was crossing the Embassy courtyard when the cries of the newsvendors reached my ears. I caught the words 'Raïssi sovietouré' and the name 'Voikobou'.[1] Several other words meaning 'assassination' were followed by 'Voikobou'.

I turned back and bought a paper. I couldn't read the Japanese hieroglyphs but I already knew the 'Hiragana' alphabet which serves as a clue.[2]

The Soviet Ambassador in Warsaw, Piotr Lazarevitch Voïkov, had been assassinated by a White terrorist. The *Maïnitchi* newspaper gave the assassin's name as Borissou Kobersa. The name meant nothing to me though, from my days at the Warsaw Embassy, I had a thorough knowledge of the activities of the White terrorists, whose centre was Vilno.[3]

I dashed up to my office as I thought there would be a telegram from Moscow, from Chicherin or Karakhan,[4] but there was nothing. So I decided not to be 'more royalist than the king' but to continue peacefully with my day's occupations. But some of my colleagues at the Embassy had arrived in a

1. 'Raïssi' means 'Ambassador'. The word 'Voikobou' referred to Voïkov.

2. 'Hiragana' is a Japanese syllabic alphabet.

3. In the course of a long conversation between the present author and Boris Safronovitch Koverda in New York in 1966, Koverda admitted that he had not been single handed. An anti-Bolshevik organisation had helped to arm him for the events of the summer of 1927. He added that it was still too early to reveal the names of his secret accomplices but that one day he would perhaps do so. In any case he would not have killed Voïkov had Voïkov not played a part in the massacre of the Romanovs. Ten years of solitary confinement in a Polish prison have left their mark on the enigmatic personality of Koverda. He has greying hair, an affable smile and his features look drawn. But though in the West the name of the 'man who did justice' has been forgotten, the same cannot be said of the Soviet Union. In 1943 Red partisans broke into the farm of Safron Koverda, his father, and when they learnt that they were really face to face with the father of Voïkov's assassin, they shot Safron Koverda.

4. At that time Chicherin was Commissar for Foreign Affairs, and Mikhailovitch Karakhan was Vice-Commissar and Director of the Far-Eastern Department from which the Soviet Embassy in Tokyo depended.

panic. They thought Voïkov's assassination might lead to war. I calmed them down. I knew that Stalin had decided to avoid war of any kind, even with countries such as Poland and Rumania that could be easily overrun. The dictator was already preparing his five-year plan for industrialisation and had no intention of taking military risks.

I had told my wife that I was going to dine with Giovanni di Giura and was just leaving the office when the telephone rang. It was Dr Solf, the German Ambassador, with whom I was on excellent terms. He was almost as worried as our people in the Soviet Embassy. He already visualised Budienny's Red cavalry on the Minsk–Smolensk–Warsaw road. When I had calmed him down and assured him that to my knowledge the rumours of a general mobilisation in the USSR were pure fantasy, I set out for the Italian Embassy. There the baron was waiting for me. As he didn't understand a word of Japanese he hadn't taken in what the newsvendors were shouting. The only English-language paper in Tokyo, the *Japan Times*, had not yet come out.[1]

I didn't feel in a hurry to tell my Italian friend about the drama in Warsaw central station. So I sat down and we began a game of chess with the baron's excellent Asti Spumante beside us.

Giovanni di Giura wasn't a very good chess player and in a few minutes he had lost both knights and a castle. I was just moving my queen up for the checkmate when the Italian Ambassador, Count Torre di Lavagna, burst in. He was in a state of great agitation.

'Do you mean to say you haven't heard the news?'

I began explaining that although Voïkov's assassination was a terrible thing and though there had been other serious incidents,[2] there was no threat to peace. I said that I had already received a special communiqué in case the Japanese

1. In fact the political situation became so tense with the assassination of P. Voïkov that Marshal Pilsudski himself called at the Soviet Embassy to express the condolences of the Polish Government. In Polish industrial centres meetings and strikes followed the news of the assassination. Despite the vigilance of the political police workers protests were organised throughout Poland.

2. These incidents were attacks on the Soviet Embassy in Pekin and on a USSR Trade Delegation in London.

Government asked about the situation on the Soviet-Polish frontier.

When he heard all this Count Torre di Lavagna was very relieved. He was a calm and peaceful man. He was looking forward to retirement and a well-merited rest on his property in Sorrento. A war would more than upset the peaceful evening of his career.

Torre di Lavagna, putting on a suitably conventional expression, thereupon expressed his Government's condollences for what had happened. Then he went on, 'Forgive me, Monsieur le Chargé d'Affaires, I know that Voïkov was a friend of yours and your former chief in Warsaw, but even so I think that his death is . . .' he felt around for the right way of putting it '. . . his death is in some ways history's revenge for the crime . . .'

I interrupted. 'I know of no crime committed by Voïkov. If executioners execute people who have been condemned to death it is a sad duty, it isn't a crime. You have a law degree, Count, unless I am mistaken . . .'

Torre di Lavagna made a gesture and shook his head. I had already got up to leave when a plump rotund outline appeared in the Embassy garden. The Ambassador and his First Secretary exchanged glances. Di Giura announced: 'His Excellency Monsignor Giardini, the Holy Father's Delegate to Japan, will be here in a minute, he wants to meet you . . .'

I had to hide a smile when I saw the deference with which Mussolini's representatives referred to the Vatican envoy. I knew about the arduous negotiations that had been going on in Rome between Pius XI and Mussolini, but the Concordat and Treaty of the Lateran were still two years ahead: relations between the Vatican and Palazzo Chigi were not all that cordial.

The Holy Father's Delegate entered the room and, without stopping to let the two Italian diplomats kiss his ring, came straight up to me:

'Monsieur le Chargé d'Affaires, I have just telephoned the Soviet Embassy and they told me you were here. I wanted urgently to see you: it is my duty to express the Holy See's condolences for the terrible crime against your Ambassador at Warsaw, his Excellency Voïkov . . .' Then, without a pause,

Monsignor Giardini went on, 'Monsieur le Chargé d'Affaires, I have a second mission of another kind. Could you receive me privately in a few days' time?'

'I would be delighted, your Excellency,' I said.

When I left the Italian Embassy I felt very intrigued by the behaviour of the Apostolic Delegate. True, at an earlier date I had had some negotiations with Monsignor Giardini about a Concordat between the USSR and the Vatican, for the negotiations in Berlin had reached a stalemate.[1] The Tokyo negotiations had been hardly more successful. There was fresh hesitation about the question of Polish priests. The Kremlin, following the policy of Nicholas I, did not want to allow them into the Soviet Ukraine. As the Pope's representative had now expressed his condolences—and that on the territory of the Italian Embassy—I felt there was something brewing and looked forward with some impatience to Giardini's visit on the date arranged.

My impatience only increased when I was informed by telephone that he would not be coming to the Embassy before June 15. I had telegraphed to my chief, Leo Mikhailovitch Karakhan, about the proposed visit of the Apostolic Delegate. What was my astonishment when I received a confidential letter by diplomatic bag saying approximately as follows:

'Your telegram about the Apostolic Delegate's visit was no surprise. Since you replaced Nicholas Nikholaievitch [Krestinsky], in negotiations with the Vatican you are a sort of unofficial representative for us at the Holy See. But I must warn you to be very cautious in your conversations with Giardini. A political intrigue is being developed by certain services of the Vatican and the Archbishop Primate of Poland[2] of which "the neighbours"[3] have got wind through their informants at Mohylev, seat of the Catholic bishop. Do not be surprised, dear comrade, by what I am going to tell you. Though it

1. Eugenio Pacelli, later Pope Pius XII, who was then Apostolic Nuncio in Berlin, had been conducting secret negotiations for over two years with Krestinsky, the Soviet Ambassador, for the conclusion of a Concordat. When Krestinsky was put on trial during the Great Purge he was accused, among other crimes, of being a Vatican agent.

2. The Cardinal Archbishop of Cracow, Hlond.

3. The word used by the Commissariat for Foreign Affairs for the GPU or secret police.

sounds like something out of a novel, the neighbours' information is beyond question.

'It concerns the usurpation of the identity of one of the daughters of Nicholas II who was shot in 1918 with all the Romanov family. According to the neighbours, one of the guards at the Ipatiev house, who was on friendly terms with the Tsarina and her daughters, deserted after the evacuation of the Ural region and went to live in Rumania. When he escaped he took his mistress with him, a mentally unbalanced Polish girl. They went to live in Bessarabia and Rumania. As his money had completely given out, the soldier, who was of Polish origin himself, approached the Polish Secret Service in Rumania—it was represented by a White Russian called Brukhatov-Rostovsky. The latter sent an agent, Essaul Yacovlev,[1] to interview the soldier. Yacovlev's report on this interview resulted in a conference at Warsaw aimed at obtaining recognition for the mentally defective girl as one of the Grand Duchesses who had allegedly escaped execution. The choice fell on Grand Duchess Anastasia, partly because of her age and partly because certain physical characteristics were similar.

'But after the setback suffered by Pilsudski's expedition and the signing of the peace at Riga, the "Anastasia intrigue" lost all interest. The Polish Second Bureau dropped the Polish soldier and his mistress and the soldier was subsequently killed in a drunken brawl. On February 17, 1920, his mistress was rescued from the Landwehr Kanal in Berlin and taken to a lunatic asylum at Dalldorf.

'With the assassination of Comrade Voïkov there are fresh rumours of a crusade against the USSR. We know for certain through Mohylev that the Vatican, which is very sensitive to all changes in the international set-up, has a revived interest in the false Anastasia . . .'

Karakhan's letter revealed an intrigue of whose existence I hadn't the faintest idea. I was impatient for the next move.

When he called on June 15, Monsignor Giardini said a few affable words and then plunged *in medias res*.

'I would like to make a very discreet request, Monsieur le

1. This Yacovlev has no connection with our friend Yacovlev. He had the rank of Essaul, that is, captain of Cossacks, and commanded a cavalry brigade in Pilsudski's army.

Chargé d'Affaires. Is it possible to see a copy of the written report on the business at the Ipatiev house in Ekaterinburg? The Secretary of State would like to know for certain whether the whole family really perished . . .'

'Yes, Monsignor, the whole family perished.'

'Yet the Soviet Government has never published an official communiqué on the disappearance of the whole Imperial family. The only ones mentioned are the Tsar, the Tsarina and the Tsarevitch.'

'That may well be. But I can give you my personal assurance that the whole family perished.'

Monsignor Giardini could hardly conceal his disappointment. He went on: 'If possible I would like to see a copy of the written account of the disappearance of the family—a copy of the original with signatures so that I can assure the Secretary of State that I have seen it.'

'I will ask Moscow if it is possible, Monsignor. And now I have to say something to you. My Government is ready to resume negotiations on the Concordat.'

Giardini's face changed abruptly. 'We have broken off negotiations, Monsieur Chargé d'Affaires. There is no hope of resuming them.'

After he left I sent a long telegram in cypher to my chief, Leo Mikhailovitch Karakhan. I hadn't to wait long for his answer. He approved of my tactics and ended his telegram with the words: 'The Vatican knows perfectly well that we have no formal statement signed by members of the Government on the execution at Sverdlovsk,[1] nor any death certificate signed by a doctor. They want you to say this so that they can have freedom of action about the false Anastasia. In these matters doubt is always on the side of usurpers.'

I was astonished at his answer. If no written account or minutes existed in 1918, they could have been fabricated as of 1926. I telegraphed in this sense to Karakhan. His answer was short. My orders were to imply clearly that we had a written document, and to add that 'the Soviet State cannot follow the example of the laws in decadent bourgeois countries'.

Poor Karakhan had no idea then that years later he would be inventing 'spontaneous confessions' as a Japanese spy in

1. The new name for Ekaterinburg.

order to save the lives of his family. But to return. I had to keep my contact with Giardini. I telephoned to say I would like to see him and added that I was now in a position to satisfy his curiosity. Monsignor Giardini's voice was fresh and jovial. He would be delighted if I could come to lunch. Lunch was fixed for June 30.

On the day arranged I went to the Apostolic Legation. We were served by a Japanese boy who pointedly wore a cross round his neck. The food was insipid, an unsuccessful blend of Japanese and Neapolitan cooking. Giardini hardly ate anything. Over the dessert I expected to be questioned about the documents, but the Apostolic Delegate avoided the subject. As soon as lunch was over we moved into the next room and without waiting for the Apostolic Delegate to make any further move, I took a sheet of paper from my pocket and said:

'Here it is. They have sent me the document you are interested in, but I have been strictly forbidden to show it to anyone whatever. But to show my esteem for your Excellency I have prepared and signed a note in which I certify that I have read the written account and minutes. The whole Romanov family, including the Grand Duchess Anastasia, perished in the Ipatiev house.'

A quarter of an hour later I took my leave of Monsignor Giardini. He came with me to the door. His face bore no trace of any Christian feelings towards me.

EPILOGUE

*

W E HAVE reached the end of the file on the Ekaterinburg tragedy. There can henceforward be no 'reasonable doubt' about how the Imperial family—and the whole of it—met its end in July 1918.

Nicholas II, last of the Romanovs, had as obscure a death as the humblest of his subjects who were swept away by the million during the fratricidal civil war of 1918-21. He was one of the richest men in the world. A few years before he disappeared it had been possible to estimate his personal fortune at two and a half milliard roubles. He owned immense landed estates and industrial property, for instance: miles of vineyards in the Crimea, entire districts in the Altai region, vast quantities of real-estate in towns, gold mines, silver mines and mines of precious stones in Siberia, steel works in the Ural region and a considerable percentage of the railways throughout the Empire. These properties, called *Kabinetskie zemli* (lands of the Imperial cabinet), were managed by an army of officials, middlemen and bankers. One of the Tsar's financial advisers was the banker Dmitri Rubinstein, Rasputin's protégé. The Emperor was richer than the Fords and Rockefellers put together. Indeed, he possessed more money than the Russian State itself—at the outbreak of war the Russian budget amounted to some two milliard gold roubles.

Memories of this enormous fortune lingered on, long after the end of the civil war. Even today they give rise to tendentious interpretations. All these false Tsarevitches and Grand Duchesses who have made their bow on the international stage may well have supposed that one day they would lay claim to the ruins of the Romanov fortune.

As the burst of gunfire in the Ipatiev house wiped out the greatest of the boyars and all his direct heirs, that fortune was left in escheat.

And what was the fate of the Russian revolutionaries most closely involved in the Ekaterinburg tragedy? Let us take the most famous of them first—Yacob Sverdlov and Vlacheslav Molotov. Sverdlov only survived the Romanovs for a few months—he was carried away by tuberculosis on March 16, 1919. As for Molotov, if he was one of the distant 'antennae' of the Ural Soviet (as telegram number 4852 may lead us to suppose) he could today make an interesting contribution to the labours of modern historians. Over seventy, and still going strong, he passes his days peacefully in the 'Estrada' block of flats on a Moscow hill whence he can see the Kremlin even if he no longer has access to it.

As the reader may recall, telegram No. 4852 contained the name of Zinoviev, i.e. Grigory Zinoviev, President of the Executive Committee of the Third International (1918) and an outstanding figure in Lenin's team. The accusation of being a 'Zinovievist' led the following to the firing-squad (everyone his turn!): comrades Beloborodov (1938), Ermakov and Golochtchekin (1939). Voïkov, as we have seen, was assassinated in Warsaw in 1927.

Last comes Yakob Yurovsky, the revolutionary who will remain in history as the High Executioner of the Ipatiev house. By keeping an eye on the Moscow press, we learnt that he died in his bed in 1962 'after a long and painful illness'. The obituary notice of this 'old Bolshevik, hero of the Ural revolution', made no mention of his part in the execution of the Imperial family. But the Press reported that he was rewarded by an official funeral at the Novo-Dievitchi cemetery, which is something like Moscow's Kensal Green.

At the moment of going to press another piece of historical research that we have undertaken has led us to revise our view about the responsibilities for the Sarajevo assassination. There is now plentiful proof of the complicated game played by the Russian Secret Service in the Balkans.

Were new light ever to be thrown on the Sarajevo assassination, and were it shown that Tsarist agents were in the thick of it, then it would not be difficult to throw new light on the assassination of Rasputin: the *staretz* might emerge as an inconvenient witness at a moment when the war was going badly.

The 'third man' on the night of the Rasputin assassination is still alive. He is Dr Stanislav Lazover. If some day he consented to talk, historians would be able to make a big step forward towards discovering the truth. Then we might also learn who armed the hand of Jaurès' assassin and why the German Socialists supported Wilhelm II when war was declared in 1914.

Were Germany no longer held responsible for the First World War, history would indeed have to be re-written.

INDEX

References to illustrations are numbered in italics

*

PRAISE FOR THE MORALIST

"O'Toole is a lucid and elegant writer. . . . She gives each of her many characters their due, rendering them vivid and also memorable . . . . On Wilson's tortured entrance into World War I, she is truly superb, assiduously tracing his journey from stubborn neutrality to zealous wartime president. As a study of Wilson's relationship with Europe, and the intrigues of his foreign policy administration, the book is exemplary."

—*The New York Times*

"Ms. O'Toole does full justice to Wilson's complexities, but it is with the coming of the war that her narrative takes on something close to Shakespearean dimensions . . . scrupulously balanced . . . elegantly crafted."

—*The Wall Street Journal*

"*The Moralist* comes at a ripe moment, now that the harsh revisionism of recent years has cast a dark light on Wilson's legacy. . . . Grim and often gripping, *The Moralist* goes a long way in explaining the America we're awakening to."

—*USA Today*

"A skillfully crafted account of the president's life and legacy. . . . a compelling page-turner . . . O'Toole's revelations break fresh ground. . . . A balanced, welcome new addition to the Wilson shelf."

—Kirkus Reviews (starred review)

"*The Moralist* is a brilliant and vital biography of Woodrow Wilson. With surgical precision she analyzes Wilson's intellectual greatness, military cunning, and evangelical fervor aimed at promoting global democracy after World War I. Every chapter crackles with first-rate scholarship."

—Douglas Brinkley, author of *Rightful Heritage:*
Franklin D. Roosevelt and the Land of America

"What a wonderful book. With a sure hand and clarity of thought, Patricia O'Toole has given us a Woodrow Wilson in all his complexity. In one way or another, from our role in the world to our views of each other at home, much of our America can be traced to the epic events of the Wilson presidency, and O'Toole tells that story with grace and insight."

—Jon Meacham, author of *American Lion* and *Thomas Jefferson: The Art of Power*

"By turns eloquent, aloof, incisive, racist, romantic, and, above all, moralistic, Woodrow Wilson dominated political life a century ago. Patricia O'Toole brings him alive, with a cogent mix of propulsive narrative and penetrating insight. This is a fresh and invigorating take on a monumental if flawed president."

—Jonathan Alter, author of *The Defining Moment: FDR's Hundred Days*

"Enlightening . . . a commentary-infused biography that illuminates an ugly and reckless side of Wilson. Her book stands as a welcome corrective. . . . By devoting a biographical study to Wilson's exaggerated sense of moral rectitude, O'Toole has done students of American history a great service. She has exposed, in meticulous detail, the vanity and vacuity of Wilson the moralist."

—National Review

"In graceful prose and deep scholarship, Patricia O'Toole casts new light on the presidency of Woodrow Wilson. . . . The most important value of O'Toole's new book is its sharp-edged treatment of Wilson—severely critical of his character and policies when appropriate, praising his idealism and persistence when appropriate."

—Minneapolis Star-Tribune

"A great strength of Patricia O'Toole's new biography is the argument announced by her title. She sets out to investigate Wilson by focusing on his strong moral streak, an attribute that proved to be his greatest asset and his greatest failing. . . . a master class in political analysis."

—America Magazine

"A comprehensive biography of Woodrow Wilson and a fresh perspective on his moral vision and legacy. The book provides an intimate portrait of Wilson's life and identifies his 'deep sense of moral responsibility' as the guiding factor behind his actions and decision-making . . . O'Toole writes with compassion and impartiality . . . this gracefully written account will likely renew debates on Wilson's role in a century of U.S. foreign policy and the role of the United States in international affairs."

—Publishers Weekly

"This splendid biography tells a story of triumph and tragedy—the triumph of democratic reform at home in Wilson's first term and of victory in the war to make the world safe for democracy in his second, but tragedy in his failure to secure a just peace and American participation in the League of Nations. Of special value are O'Toole's incisive analyses of the crucial and sometimes fraught relationships among Wilson, his wife Edith, his personal physician Cary Grayson, 'Colonel' Edward House, Secretary of State Robert Lansing, and private secretary Joe Tumulty."

—James McPherson, author of The War That Forged a Nation

"Can one man use his moral force to change the world? The question seems outlandish but Woodrow Wilson very nearly did. A vivacious writer who digs deep, Patricia O'Toole has given us a grand, flawed, fascinating Wilson."

—Evan Thomas, author of Ike's Bluff and Being Nixon

"Patricia O'Toole's new biography captures the essence of Wilson's approach to politics and the world."

—New York Journal of Books

"Excellent. . . . O'Toole offers a fair-minded portrait of a vain moralist and political visionary whose certitude could exceed his judgment."

—The American Conservative

ALSO BY PATRICIA O'TOOLE

In the Words of Theodore Roosevelt:
Quotations from the Man in the Arena (editor)

When Trumpets Call:
Theodore Roosevelt After the White House

Money and Morals in America:
A History

The Five of Hearts:
An Intimate Portrait of Henry Adams and His Friends, 1880–1918

Corporate Messiah:
The Hiring and Firing of Million-Dollar Managers

PATRICIA O'TOOLE

THE
MORALIST

- - - • • • • • • • • • • • - - -

Woodrow Wilson

and

The World He Made

SIMON & SCHUSTER PAPERBACKS
New York   London   Toronto   Sydney   New Delhi

Simon & Schuster Paperbacks
A Division of Simon & Schuster, Inc.
1230 Avenue of the Americas
New York, NY 10020

First Simon & Schuster trade paperback edition April 2019

SIMON & SCHUSTER PAPERBACKS and colophon are registered trademarks
of Simon & Schuster, Inc.

For information about special discounts for bulk purchases,
please contact Simon & Schuster Special Sales at 1-866-506-1949
or business@simonandschuster.com.

The Simon & Schuster Speakers Bureau can bring authors to your live event. For
more information or to book an event, contact the Simon & Schuster Speakers
Bureau at 1-866-248-3049 or visit our website at www.simonspeakers.com.

Interior design by Lewelin Polanco
Maps by David Lindroth

Manufactured in the United States of America

3 5 7 9 10 8 6 4 2

Library of Congress has cataloged the hardcover edition as follows:

Names: O'Toole, Patricia, author.
Title: The moralist : Woodrow Wilson and the world he made / by Patricia O'Toole.
Other titles: Woodrow Wilson and the world he made
Description: New York : Simon & Schuster, [2018] | Includes bibliographical
references and index.
Identifiers: LCCN 2018006628| ISBN 9780743298094 (hardcover : alk. paper) |
ISBN 9780743298100 (trade pbk. : alk. paper) | ISBN 9781501130021 (ebook)
Subjects: LCSH: Wilson, Woodrow, 1856-1924. | Presidents--United
States--Biography. | United States--Politics and government--1913-1921. |
United States--Foreign relations--Moral and ethical aspects.
Classification: LCC E767 .O95 2018 | DDC 973.91/3092 [B] --dc23 LC record
available at https://lccn.loc.gov/2018006628

ISBN 978-0-7432-9809-4
ISBN 978-0-7432-9810-0 (pbk)
ISBN 978-1-5011-3002-1 (ebook)

For the Squad:

Hilary O'Toole, Randy Hartwell, Chris Milenkevich,
Tara Smith, Val Monroe, Bridget Potter, and Sarah Perry

If it be a sin to covet honour, I am the most offending soul alive.

William Shakespeare, *Henry V*

Contents

List of Maps

Author's Note

A Moralist in the White House

The idea of writing a biography of Woodrow Wilson grew out of my long-standing interest in World War I and a conversation with Alice Mayhew, my editor at Simon & Schuster. I originally imagined that I would focus on Wilson as commander in chief, but Alice encouraged me to follow the trail wherever it led. It forked while I was looking at the index of *Presidential Greatness* by the historian Thomas A. Bailey. To my surprise, Wilson took up more space than any other major president. I soon understood why: he was the most controversial of the lot because his triumphs as well as his defeats were so large and lasting.

Struck by the intensity of the praise and condemnation that Wilson has aroused since his first days in the White House, I wanted to know the cause. Was it the dissonance between his old-fashioned social ideas and his modern notions of what government should do? Was it the era, with its constant clash between the status quo and the progressive push for reform? Several possibilities came to mind, but for me, the one that stood out was a personal quality—his great sense of moral responsibility. While admirers have treated it as a virtue and a political asset, critics have often seen it as arrogance. Both camps agree that morality was a conspicuous feature of his character and a hallmark of his presidency. And both say that it left an unusually big mark on the country and the world.

The depth of Wilson's moral concern is almost always traced to the fact that he was the son and grandson of Presbyterian ministers. The precepts of the Judeo-Christian tradition did permeate his boyhood, and he remained a devout Christian all his life. But he was not a zealot. Nor did he claim to know God's will. His religion was a largely private matter, a source of comfort in the face of adversity and unfathomable events.

Ultimately I came to see the moral ideals of President Wilson as more secular than religious, the effect of his long formal education in history, government, and law. As Professor Wilson (of Bryn Mawr, Wesleyan, and Princeton), he lectured and wrote extensively on government. Democracy was a frequent theme, and his faith in democracy ran as deep as his faith in God. Because democracy rests on the consent of the governed, he thought it the most moral form of government, and like many Americans before and since, he believed that the success of the American democratic experiment made the United States a morally superior nation. Wilson also believed in the power of "moral force," by which he meant the power of ideas and actions aligned with commonly accepted moral principles. In his judgment, the greatest power of the United States was not its wealth but the moral force of its democracy.

In Wilson's first term, his moral sensitivity served him and the country well. He persuaded Congress to enact a substantial program of economic reform by arguing that his course was morally right and that doing the right thing would pay off politically and materially. In short order he won the creation of the Federal Reserve Board, the income tax, the Federal Trade Commission, and an antitrust law designed to prevent monopoly.

No previous president and only two of his successors (Franklin D. Roosevelt and Lyndon B. Johnson) compiled legislative records as impressive as Wilson's. But moral force was not the only force in play. The reforms were long overdue, his party controlled both houses of Congress, and two persuasive members of his cabinet lobbied unceasingly for his demands. Yet I think it fair to say that the moral force of Wilson's case mattered. Set forth in a series of speeches, it won broad public support for his legislative agenda and made it difficult for Congress to oppose him without sounding morally deficient.

I found these moral victories significant for another reason: they were purchased in an immoral bargain. Southerners in Congress saw that Wilson's reforms would bring a wholesale expansion of federal power, and federal power was anathema to men who used states' rights to justify laws that made second-class citizens of African Americans. The Southern bloc agreed to support Wilson's economic reforms in exchange for segregation of the civil service.

The bargain was made by the same two cabinet secretaries who worked Capitol Hill. Wilson acquiesced and, I discovered, he paid a personal price. Denounced by African Americans and others who voted for him on the strength of his promise of equal justice, he was so upset that he took to his bed for days. He knew the segregation was morally indefensible, but ending it would have cost him the votes of every Southerner in Congress. The injustice lasted for decades, as Southern Democrats in Congress forced one president after another into bargains that preserved racially discriminatory state laws. It also exposed a hazard of claiming the moral high ground: when an outspokenly high-minded leader fails to meet his own standards, he is seen as a hypocrite.

Wilson's preoccupation with morality also figured prominently in his conduct of foreign relations. Early in World War I, he justified U.S. neutrality not on grounds of national interest but as a noble response to a senseless war. And he presented himself as uniquely qualified to broker a peace because the United States was the only major power unstained by the slaughter. Both sides found his condescension insufferable.

In 1917, when U.S. neutrality was no longer tenable, Wilson grounded his call for a declaration of war in another noble idea: "The world must be made safe for democracy." Although the thought stirred souls on both sides of the Atlantic, it was profoundly distressing to Americans who objected to fighting Europe's quarrels and those who opposed war on principle. New espionage and sedition laws sent protestors to jail in record numbers. The stifling of dissent raised another question for my investigation: what happens when two moral visions collide? Wilson sometimes resisted the hard line taken by his attorney general and postmaster general in dealing with antiwar protest, but he let virtually all of their decisions stand. As a result, he has gone into history as the president whose administration outdid all others in prosecuting dissent.

When the war ended, in November 1918, President Wilson had just lost his majorities in both houses of Congress, and as he struggled with the new opposition, his righteousness hardened into a self-righteousness that compromised his political judgment. By ignoring advice to appoint an influential Republican to the American Commission to Negotiate Peace, he alienated virtually every Republican in the Senate. At the Paris Peace Conference, his demands for a moderate settlement irked the Allies, who were intent on making Germany pay for the war and preventing it from rebuilding its army and navy. Britain's prime minister, David Lloyd George, complained about Wilson's "sermonettes" and his sense of himself as the only morally upright statesman in the group of four who set the peace terms.

Wilson's greatest triumph in Paris was the creation of the League of Nations, the first global organization committed to the preservation of peace. He also persuaded the Allies to moderate some of their demands, but the terms of the treaty signed at Versailles were generally punitive, and the authors came in for no end of blame when Germany launched World War II. Wilson had tried, but moral suasion was not enough; it rarely is when stakes are high.

Home from Paris, Wilson found himself in the fight of his life over the ratification of the treaty. Three months in, he suffered a stroke that permanently paralyzed his left side and forced him to the sidelines. Republicans were willing to ratify a treaty with reservations, but Wilson refused all pleas for compromise. While some historians have blamed his intransigence on his illness, I side with those who have pointed out that his obstinacy was nothing new. An exasperated Henry Cabot Lodge, leader of the Republican drive for reservations, rose in the Senate to remind the country that "We too have our ideals, even if we differ from those who have tried to establish a monopoly of idealism." The Senate defeated the treaty three times. The lesson was lost on Wilson, who had persuaded himself that his was the only position with moral force. He came to believe that he had erred, but only in proposing the League before his fellow Americans were ready for it.

Woodrow Wilson felt most alive when he was waging a moral war. What follows is a story of battles won and lost by moral force, of exhilaration and dread on the high road, of great tenacity undercut by willfulness and spite. An author does not know what a reader will take away from a book, but I hope that this one—the story of a president who succeeded *and* failed by hewing to his moral convictions—will start a serious conversation about the possibilities and the complexities of moral leadership in a fractured world. Faced with a crisis, Wilson often asked himself, "What ought we to do?" I cannot think of a better place for the conversation to begin.

1

Son of the South

Thomas Woodrow Wilson entered the world in Staunton, Virginia, on December 28, 1856. His father, Joseph Ruggles Wilson, was a Presbyterian minister, and his mother, Jessie Woodrow Wilson, was the daughter of one Presbyterian divine and a descendant of several more. Tommy, as the baby was called, was their third child and first son. Before his second birthday, the family left Staunton for Augusta, Georgia, a move that put Joseph in a more prominent pulpit and brought him an honorary Doctor of Divinity degree.

In the autumn of 1860, Tommy was standing near the front gate of the Augusta parsonage when a passerby said that Abraham Lincoln had been elected and there would be war. Not yet four, the boy did not understand, but the force of the stranger's voice sent him running into the house for an explanation. The war soon dominated the family's life. After the national governing body of the Presbyterian Church declared its opposition to slavery, Joseph Wilson hosted the founding assembly of the Presbyterian Church in the Confederate States of America. He spent a summer as a chaplain to the Confederate Army, his churchyard occasionally served as a stockade for Union prisoners, and when necessary, a corner of the church was fitted out as a military hospital. Jessie assisted in caring for the wounded.

In 1870, when Tommy was thirteen, the family moved to Columbia, South Carolina, where Joseph joined the faculty of a Presbyterian seminary. Torched in the last weeks of the war, Columbia was still a blackened wreck. Although the adult Woodrow Wilson rarely reminisced about the destruction on view in Columbia, the ruins and the maimed soldiers he saw daily left him with a permanent horror of war.

Tommy grew up in the care of parents who were loving but not at ease in the larger world. Jessie was often abed with maladies that defied diagnosis, and Joseph, despite his eminence in Presbyterian circles, was hounded by a sense that he did not measure up. Shy except in the pulpit, he overcompensated by holding forth in schoolmaster fashion or by telling jokes, the same jokes, again and again. He was the sort of man who is more respected than enjoyed.

President Wilson's moral certitude has often been ascribed to his religious upbringing, but Joseph Wilson's Presbyterianism was not as exacting as the Scottish original. Joseph did not imagine that he knew the will of Heaven, nor did he tyrannize his congregations with visions of Hell. He savored at least two pleasures of the flesh, pipe smoking and Scotch drinking. In the furor loosed by Charles Darwin's *On the Origin of Species* (1859), Joseph stood with the religious progressives who maintained that science was compatible with religion because all truths were part of a higher Truth.

Until the birth of the Wilsons' fourth and last child, Joseph Jr., in 1867, Tommy was schooled by his parents, both of whom were intelligent, cultivated, and well educated. Joseph Sr. graduated at the head of his class at Jefferson College, in Canonsburg, Pennsylvania, and went on to study at two schools of theology. Jessie was a graduate of a respected school in Ohio, the Steubenville Female Seminary. The Wilsons prized moral education above other forms of instruction but also passed on their love of language and English literature. Joseph had a melodious, well-trained voice, and on Sunday afternoons, with the family gathered round, he entertained by reading a few chapters of Charles Dickens or Sir Walter Scott. Jessie had been born in England, but the Wilsons' literary Anglophilia probably owed no more to that fact than to the educated American's view of the Old World as the repository of high culture. The garden of American letters was still small, and to Southerners of the nineteenth century, it must have seemed choked with Yankees.

Tommy was odd man out in this bookish household. He did not learn the alphabet until he was nine, could not read until he was eleven or twelve, and at thirteen still struggled with reading and writing. Flagging every error in Tommy's compositions, Joseph demanded revision after revision. It has been suggested that Tommy's reading difficulties were the unconscious rebellion of a powerless boy against a powerful father, but it appears that Tommy's reading problem was more physiological than oedipal. Edwin A. Weinstein, a neuropsychiatrist and close student of Wilson's medical history, concluded that Wilson suffered from developmental dyslexia, a childhood disorder not understood at the time. Joseph suspected his son of laziness, a reasonable guess in light of the boy's facility with spoken English. Tommy was precocious in conversation, had an exceptional ear for dialect, and was quick to master grammar and syntax. The adult Woodrow Wilson fondly recalled the hours he and Joseph had devoted to dissecting sermons and speeches to see how they worked and where they might be improved. No schooling would contribute more to Woodrow Wilson's political triumphs than these oratorical studies.

If Woodrow Wilson ever wrote an unkind word about his father, it did not survive. The son voiced his admiration often and at length, and always referred to Joseph as the finest of all his teachers. Jessie rarely figured in Woodrow's recollections, and the handful of stories that came down through the family suggest that she was humorless and touchy. Yet she must have been more than the sum of her faults. As a young man, Wilson freely confessed to having been a mama's boy, and he and three other members of his extended family named daughters for her.

Tommy's adolescence was a mix of escapist fantasy and small forays in the direction of independence. While physically present in his parents' home, he led a covert parallel life in his imagination, first as Vice Admiral Thomas W. Wilson, who sailed the world, exterminated pirates, and recorded his exploits in dispatches to the Royal Navy. As Lieutenant Thomas W. Wilson of Her Majesty's Royal Lance Guards, he upbraided subordinates for wearing civilian dress and warned that further infractions would bring a drop in rank. All his life, Woodrow Wilson felt himself in a tussle to control the side of his temperament he thought of as volcanic, and in his adolescent wish to command others, it is easy to see a wish to master his own unruly self.

At sixteen, Tommy hung a portrait of Prime Minister William Gladstone over his desk and announced that he too would be a statesman. The last of his invented selves, Commodore Wilson of the Royal United Kingdom Yacht Club, appeared shortly thereafter, and the commodore's maritime preoccupations were soon crowded out by a consuming interest in writing the yacht club's constitution. No longer content to rule his imaginary realms, Tommy yearned to organize them as well. The yearning, which became a lifelong passion, would culminate in his constitution for the world, the covenant of the League of Nations.

In spite of Tommy's scholastic difficulties, his parents assumed that he would go to college, and his wish to be a politician rather than follow his father into the ministry drew a predictable reaction: Joseph sent him to Davidson College in North Carolina, a small Presbyterian establishment whose graduates typically went on to divinity school. Sixteen and now calling himself Tom, Wilson entered Davidson in 1873. He turned in a creditable academic performance and was an enthusiastic participant in a debating society. But in his second semester, when he suffered from an endless cold, his notebooks filled up with self-denigration, inspirational verse, and spiritual advice transcribed from Protestant periodicals.

Tom's need for such solace coincided with the greatest crisis in his father's life. In the spring of 1874, after years of success as a minister, church leader, and professor of theology, Joseph Wilson found himself out of work. He had clashed with his students over chapel attendance, the dispute went to the governing body of the church for adjudication, and when church authorities ruled in the students' favor, Joseph resigned. The resignation was a matter of principle, he wrote Tom; the seminary had given him a responsibility but no power to carry it out. With a large household to support, Joseph hastily accepted a call from the Presbyterians of Wilmington, North Carolina. They offered a generous salary, but the church lacked the prestige of his posts in Columbia and Augusta, and Wilmington was regarded as a cultural backwater. Joseph was devastated.

Tom joined his family in Wilmington for the summer, expecting to return to Davidson in the fall, but it was soon decided that he would spend a year at home, studying Greek with a tutor to fit himself out for Princeton. Princeton appealed to Joseph because it was the finest Presbyterian college in the United States, and it appealed to Tom because it had produced an extraordinary number of statesmen. In the Republic's first two decades alone, forty-three Princeton men had been elected to Congress (twenty-three to the House, twenty to the Senate), thirteen had become governors, and three had been appointed to the Supreme Court of the United States. The roll of honor also included a vice president (Aaron Burr) and a president (James Madison).

Tom worked at his Greek, and with the aid of mail-order instruction manuals spent hours mastering shorthand, a valuable skill for a boy who

wrote slowly. He rarely socialized with his contemporaries during the fifteen months between Davidson and Princeton, and when he ventured out
of the manse on his own, it was often to take a solitary walk around Wilmington's harbor. To the Wilson family's butler, the tall, quiet boy of eighteen
seemed like "an old young man." When not studying Greek or practicing
shorthand, Tom spent long stretches of time with his father, and it is possible that Joseph's crisis and his need for the companionship of his loving,
much loved son were the chief reasons for the long interruption in Tom's
college education. Profoundly upset by his failure at the seminary, afraid that
he would never again know success, Joseph suffered greatly yet refused to
abandon his faith in God's love. He grimly lashed himself to the mast and
submitted to the will of Providence. Tom did not write about this time in
their lives, but the experience of watching his father hold fast despite his anguish left an indelible impression. President Wilson would sometimes yield
to expediency, but he never shrank from his deepest moral convictions, a
trait that made him a formidable opponent and an unpredictable ally.

Tom set off for Princeton in September 1875, and apart from a brief detour
into law, he would stay in academe until he entered politics, in 1910. After
graduating from Princeton, he would study at the University of Virginia
and Johns Hopkins, teach at Bryn Mawr and Wesleyan, and then return to
Princeton for twelve years as a professor and eight as president. Each of these
institutions suited him for a time, but Princeton was the only one he loved,
and with good reason. His intellect, his passions, his political gifts—Princeton unfurled them all.

Soon after arriving, Tom met another statesman-in-waiting, Charles
A. Talcott, who would serve a term in the U.S. House of Representatives
when Wilson was president. As undergraduates, Wilson and Talcott vowed
to groom themselves for politics by mastering all the arts of persuasion, especially oratory. Tom competed in campus debates, dissected great speeches,
and took classic orations into the woods, where he could practice his delivery
without being observed. He also labored over his compositions, honing his
powers of argument and striving for the bright clarity he saw in the histories
of Thomas Macaulay. Tom's wish for a place in the governing class ran so
deep that he sometimes fantasized himself already there. At a stalemate in a
political tiff with one of his friends, he joshed that they would resume their
debate in the Senate, and on a card that served as a bookmark, he signed
himself "Thomas Woodrow Wilson, Senator from Virginia."

Aware of Tom's overreaching, Joseph occasionally reminded him of the
need for patience and a sense of proportion. "Dearest boy, can you hope to

jump into eminency all at once?" he inquired after Tom sent a petulant account of being passed over for an oratorical contest. "My darling, make *more* of your class studies. Dismiss *ambition*—and replace it with hard industry, which shall have little or no regard to *present* triumphs, but which will be all the time laying foundations for future work and wage."

Unenthusiastic about most of his classes, Tom would finish thirty-eighth in a class of 105. But in history and philosophy, which abounded in lessons for would-be statesmen, he applied himself to excellent effect. Proudly he wrote his father, "I have made a discovery; I have found that I have a mind." He also had a powerful will, although he could not force it to concentrate on mathematics or French or Greek. Instead he devoured works of English history and transcripts of debates in Parliament, which often appeared in the British press. An essay on oratory in one English periodical struck him with such force that he would always remember where he was when he read it—at the head of a staircase in the library. From his father Tom had learned that great oratory was closely reasoned and deeply felt as well as pleasing to the ear. The essay affirmed Joseph's observations and went on to declare that great oratory was the fount of great statesmanship. Few notions could have ignited more hope in an aspiring politician who loved oratory and excelled at it.

As a Southerner, Tom often felt out of place at Princeton. He was stunned to find that his fellow students made no effort to conceal their contempt for the South, and when he failed in his attempts to broaden their minds, he wrote his mother that he sometimes longed to drive his arguments home with a punch. "Tommy dear, don't talk about knocking anybody down—no matter what they do or say," Jessie replied. "Yankee ignorance" must be borne in silence, she said, and in her experience, the less one said about politics, the better.

Tom kept his fists at his side but constantly thought, talked, and wrote about politics. In 1876, as the United States celebrated the centenary of the Declaration of Independence, he sourly predicted that the Republic would be destroyed by universal suffrage. Granted in 1870 by the Fifteenth Amendment, universal suffrage was hardly universal. It excluded women. But in giving the vote to all men, it threatened white supremacy in the South, where blacks outnumbered whites in many states. Many white Southerners, Tom Wilson included, argued that universal suffrage was a mistake not because blacks were black but because 80 percent of them were illiterate. That was true—a legacy of state laws that had made it a crime to teach slaves to read. But it was also true that 20 percent of whites were illiterate, and their fitness for the franchise was rarely challenged. Tom's antipathy to universal suffrage was so strong that when he was asked to defend it in a campus debate, he declined.

Making friends came no more easily to Tom Wilson than to his parents, but a half-dozen classmates brought him into their circle, and once he was sure of their affection, he revealed that behind his decorous facade there was a great big ham. He loved theater and by osmosis had become a gifted mimic. His new friends were regularly entertained with impersonations, jokes told in several dialects, and a large store of limericks. His performances, like his father's, masked his shyness, but he could summon more charm than his father. Tom's friends reveled in his antics, admired his discipline, and encouraged his political ambitions. Several of them would energetically deploy their influence and wealth to speed his rise to prominence. The friends Wilson made at Princeton were the only friends he kept for life.

In his last year at Princeton, Wilson felt sufficiently sure of his literary and intellectual powers to submit a political essay to the *International Review,* a prestigious journal of opinion. Entitled "Cabinet Government in the United States," the essay pointed out a deficiency in the American political system and proposed a remedy. Pressing national issues were being ignored, the author said, because senators and congressmen no longer engaged in serious public debate. Instead they did business in committee, usually behind closed doors, an arrangement that allowed them to indulge in a perpetual orgy of self-dealing. To solve the problem, Wilson said, Americans had only to emulate the British, who did not pass laws until they had thrashed them out in debate on the floor of the House of Commons. He argued that public debate would end the undemocratic secrecy that had crept over the Congress and would thwart the rise of the mediocre man, because only the ablest could prevail when "arguments are the weapons and the people the judges."

Wilson also urged the United States to adopt the British practice of linking the legislative and executive branches through the cabinet. Cabinet members and the prime minister all held seats in Parliament, an arrangement that gave a prime minister a decided edge over a president in advancing his legislative proposals. And when a prime minister lost his majority in Parliament, out he went—unlike a president, who stayed on till the end of his four-year term. Wilson pronounced the British model superior because it minimized the potential for the impasses that develop when elections wrest control of the Congress from the president's party.

The young author's prescription was inspired by a diagnosis made a decade earlier in *The English Constitution,* by the British political economist Walter Bagehot. Bagehot pitied the United States, where the separation of powers had weakened both the executive and the legislature. Weakness produced deadlock, and when there was little opportunity for meaningful accomplishment, first-rate men had scant interest in running for office, Bagehot thought. In spite of the fact that "Cabinet Government in the United States" leaned heavily on Bagehot, the essay was still a triumph for Thomas W. Wilson, as he now signed himself. By sheer willpower, the boy who could hardly read had turned himself into a writer with a confident, clear, persuasive voice.

Wilson was elated when he received a letter of acceptance from one of the editors of the *International Review,* Henry Cabot Lodge. Forty years later President Wilson would pit himself against Senator Lodge in an epic struggle over American foreign policy, but in the spring of 1879, Lodge was a man of letters and a freshman representative in the lower house of the Massachusetts legislature. The review paid its contributors next to nothing, airily explaining that the financial rewards were inversely proportional to the honor of appearing in the same pages as Henry James, Oliver Wendell Holmes, and John Greenleaf Whittier. Wilson spent his mite on a bookcase, which he kept close at hand all his life.

The would-be senator from Virginia collected his Princeton diploma in June 1879 and started down a path taken by many a political hopeful: he studied law. But he found his law books tedious, skipped class, and disliked his new school, the University of Virginia. "There's no *college* life here, as *we* know college life, at all," he complained to Charlie Talcott. "It's simply a place where men happen to have congregated for study—and for nothing else." Troubled by his inability to give himself to the study of law, he wondered if he had chosen the wrong road to politics, and his doubts filled him with anxiety about his ambitions. When Tom returned to Charlottesville after his summer vacation, Joseph urged him to concentrate on his studies and put aside his literary and oratorical endeavors for the year.

Concentration proved impossible. Tom had fallen in love. The object of his affections was his cousin Hattie Woodrow, who was attending a female seminary in Staunton, the town where Tom was born. Many an hour that the law student might have devoted to his books was spent on the forty miles of road between Staunton and Charlottesville. Tom had not yet declared himself to Hattie, but after his first year of law school, he began calling himself Woodrow Wilson. He later explained the choice by saying that he wanted to honor both sides of his family and that "Woodrow Wilson" struck him as more distinguished than "Thomas W. Wilson." Whether he recognized it or not, the new name also represented a fusion with Hattie.

Ill health—chronic indigestion and chronic colds—forced Wilson to withdraw from law school after the fall semester of his second year. He began reading law on his own, and with no classes to attend, he was free to go to Ohio in 1881 for an extended stay with Hattie and her family. She had not encouraged his attentions, but he had interpreted her reserve as a social stratagem, a way of showing him that she was a proper young lady. When he proposed, she immediately declined on the grounds that they were first cousins.

Deeply pained by the rejection, Wilson told no one outside the family for almost a year. Robert Bridges was the first of his Princeton friends to learn of it, in March 1882, and as he put his experience on paper, Wilson seemed surprised to discover that he was still upset. "[E]ven at this distance of time I am unable to speak of it without such a rush of feeling as makes clear expression next to impossible," he wrote.

Two months later, Woodrow Wilson left home for good. He was twenty-five. He had decided to settle in Atlanta, where Henry W. Grady, editor of *The Atlanta Constitution,* was trying to persuade the rest of the United States that a New South, democratic rather than feudal, was on the rise. "The South found her jewel in the toad's head of defeat," Grady declared. "The shackles that had held her in narrow limitations fell forever when the shackles of the negro slave were broken. Under the old regime the negroes were slaves to the South; the South was a slave to the system." The New South was "less splendid on the surface, but stronger at the core—a hundred farms for every plantation, fifty homes for every palace—and a diversified industry that meets the complex need of this complex age." Woodrow Wilson had expressed similar views and imagined that playing a part in the emergence of the New South would give him a toehold in politics.

With another fledgling lawyer, Edward I. Renick, Wilson opened a law firm in the center of Atlanta in June 1882. Renick, an acquaintance from Charlottesville, would succeed as a lawyer, but Wilson immediately found himself at odds with every aspect of practicing law. He shrank from the idea of courting potential clients. He was appalled by the greed and pettiness on display in the courtroom. And on a visit to the State Senate, he made the unhappy discovery that the senators of Georgia had none of the finesse of the oratorical statesmen he idolized. The final shock was the realization that he would need a small fortune to enter politics. He was still living on an allowance from his father.

Given the feverishness of his political ambition, Wilson showed surprisingly little gumption in the face of rather ordinary obstacles, and his passivity brought concerned letters from home. "It is hardly like you, my brave boy, to show a white feather before the battle is well joined," Joseph wrote. In

Joseph's judgment, the situation called for *Totus in illo*—all in. He promised his support if the law proved intolerable but did not think it right for Woodrow to quit before getting his feet "fully upon the ladder."

After only a few months in Atlanta, Woodrow was putting his *Totus* into an endeavor unlikely to win a single client. A congressional commission was coming to town to hold hearings on the tariff, the federal government's principal source of revenue in the era before the modern income tax (which President Wilson would bring into being). Imposed on most imports, the tariff protected American manufacturers from competition, producing handsome profits for them while raising prices for everyone else. The South, which had few factories and considerably less wealth than the rest of the country, was especially hard hit. Agriculture was the mainstay of the South and West, and farmers, unlike the manufacturers of the Northeast, had to sell in a free market and buy whatever they needed at prices inflated by the tariff.

Like most Southerners, Wilson advocated free trade. He was thrilled by the prospect of sharing his views with members of Congress and undoubtedly hoped to dazzle them with his oratory and expertise. Although he doubted that he would end American protectionism, he was pleased by the idea that his words might be immortalized in the federal record. (Not all of the testimony would be published. As the official stenographer explained, some of it was not even recorded, "but where the insanity does not crop out too plainly we will allow it to go in.") Wilson's speech won compliments from the local congressman, passed the stenographer's sanity test, and made the front page of Henry Grady's *Constitution,* which reported that Mr. "Goodrow" Wilson had been long-winded but intelligent.

The experience was a great disappointment to young Mr. Wilson. He had imagined himself testifying before a large audience, but the hearings took place in a smallish hotel dining room. No one was looking for the next Daniel Webster, and the young Mr. Wilson lacked the nerve to introduce himself to the congressmen present. Later in his career, Wilson would speak fondly of his Southern upbringing and would claim (usually in the company of other Southerners) that he was a proud son of the South. But he was also a confirmed nationalist by the time he left Princeton. He did not feel a piece with the New South.

Discouraged and unable to focus on the law, he continued to spend most of his time reading history and writing political essays, several of which were published by Robert Bridges, then an editor at the *New York Evening Post.* "I am unfit for practice," he wrote Bridges in April 1883. "I have had just enough experience to prove that." Law had been a stepping-stone to politics, and if he could not enter politics, perhaps he would take up writing, his other great love. Bridges sympathized but warned Wilson that a man of letters led a financially precarious life.

All doors seemed closed until the spring of 1883, when his uncle James Woodrow, president of South Carolina College, suggested an academic career. The idea immediately appealed to Wilson. He would have an income, a ready-made audience, and time to write. With his fantasies once again galloping far ahead of his prospects, he dared to hope that by writing history and political commentary, he would become a respected voice in national affairs. The term "public intellectual" had not yet been coined, but that was the role Wilson now envisioned for himself. With Uncle James's encouragement, Woodrow applied to the doctoral program in history at Baltimore's Johns Hopkins University, a new institution devoted to graduate study.

The fretful year in Atlanta came to a surprisingly happy end. He won admission to Johns Hopkins, and during a stay in Rome, Georgia, where he had gone on a legal errand for his mother, he went to church one Sunday morning and found himself attracted to a young woman in a veil. After a few inquiries, he was at her family's door on the pretext of paying his respects to her father, the Reverend Samuel Axson, who had once been an assistant to Joseph Wilson. In the course of the chitchat, Woodrow inquired after the health of the daughter he had seen in church. The Reverend Axson called her into the parlor and made the introduction.

Ellen Louise Axson was twenty-three, and her charms included a petite figure, glowing complexion, expressive brown eyes, and a profusion of coppery curls. A stranger needed only a few minutes in her company to see that she was warm, intelligent, and well read. Woodrow dallied in Rome for ten days, made two more trips from Atlanta to Rome in the next six weeks, and left Georgia feeling that he had found "a new and altogether delightful sort of companion."

Ellen was intrigued by Woodrow, although as eligible bachelors went, he was hardly a prize. Tall and spindly, he considered himself homely, and unless he smiled, he was. His eyes were a chilly blue-gray, his nose and ears unduly large, his face all angles and planes. At twenty-six, he had yet to earn a living, and graduate school would again postpone the day of his self-sufficiency. He did not know if his professorial plan would succeed, and there was reason to wonder whether he would find the next chapter of his life any more satisfying than the last.

Ellen, trapped in a grim situation with no foreseeable end, was also a questionable prospect. Her mother had died two years before, dropping her widower into an incapacitating grief. As the oldest child, Ellen was expected to care for him and her three siblings. When she could, which was not often, she escaped into painting and drawing, her greatest loves. She was genuinely talented, especially at portraiture, and her artistic accomplishments delighted her new suitor.

Both Woodrow and Ellen had plans to retreat to the cool hills of North Carolina in August, she with a friend in Morganton, and he with his mother in Arden, fifty miles away. They had no opportunity to see each other there, and on September 14, Woodrow left Arden for Johns Hopkins with no assurances from Ellen except a promise to write to him. Waiting for a train in Asheville, he strolled the streets and happened to catch sight of a coiled braid through a hotel window. He recognized it as Ellen's, raced toward it, and found her in one of the hotel's public rooms. Her vacation in Morganton had been cut short, she explained; her father had fallen ill, and she was in Asheville to catch a train home.

Helpless against his joy and hope, Woodrow declared his love, proposed, and vowed to help care for her family. Ellen hesitated, unsure of her love for Woodrow and afraid that he would regret his haste. Pressing hard, he said her doubts would cloud his studies. She gave in, and he pronounced himself the country's happiest man. Telling a friend about his engagement, he described Ellen's attainments and her beauty but said that he had fallen in love with her simply because she was "irresistibly lovable." Why she loved him was a mystery, he went on, but he had decided to accept her love "without seeking to understand it—as something sent to strengthen and ennoble me."

2

When a Man Comes to Himself

Preoccupied by his love for Ellen, Woodrow was as restless and impatient at Johns Hopkins as he had been in Charlottesville and Atlanta. During his first month in Baltimore he wrote her long, pining love letters that omitted all mention of his studies and revealed next to nothing of his new life. If anyone on the streets of Rome, Georgia, had asked Ellen for news of her fiancé, she would have had little to report except that he was taking long walks and living in a cheerful, well-furnished room with a large window overlooking a handsome square.

The reason for his large omission became clear in a letter he wrote her on October 18, 1883. He had been feeling downcast, he said, because Johns Hopkins did not offer any course of study in comparative politics—"my chief amusement and delight during leisure hours for the past five or six years." His professors expected students to root around in the archives, up to their elbows in "dusty records of old settlements and colonial cities . . . which seemed very tiresome in comparison with the grand excursions amongst imperial policies which I had planned for myself." Wilson also balked at the number of books he was expected to read. But when he sat down to write Ellen, he had just come from baring his soul to his advisor and gaining an extraordinary concession: exemption from most of the history department's coursework. He had asked for it in order to write a book.

"How very fortunate that they haven't a cast-iron system in vogue there, and that you are enabled to follow your bent," Ellen replied. She was pleased that he would be studying "vital questions, *live* issues, the deeper relations of past and present, and the workings of great laws and principles." Her appreciation emboldened Woodrow to tell her that he had set aside his ambition for public office but still wanted to play a role in American politics, as a man of ideas, contributing "what no American has ever contributed, studies in the philosophy of our institutions, not the abstract and the occult, but the practical and suggestive."

As for the oratorical skills he had worked so hard to acquire for his life in politics, Woodrow now saw that they would prove useful in the lecture hall. A great orator was more than a lecturer, he explained to Ellen. He was a master of persuasion, of "putting things so as to appeal irresistibly to an audience. And how can a teacher stimulate young men to study, how can he fill them with great ideas and worthy purposes, how can he draw them out of themselves and make them to become forces in the world without oratory?"

Woodrow guessed that his nineteen egotistical pages would draw a wry smile from Ellen, but she replied that she had read them with "profound interest and pleasure." She also assured him of her sympathy and promised to keep all his thoughts in her heart. "When I think of your various gifts and the high, pure and noble purposes to which they are dedicated, I feel a quiet little glow and thrill of admiration tingling out to my very fingertips."

Proof that he had finally found his calling can be seen in his performance: in little more than a year he wrote an excellent book and sold it to a prestigious publisher, Houghton Mifflin. More political science than history, *Congressional Government* (1885) proceeded from a refreshingly simple question: how had the Founding Fathers' checks and balances worked out in practice? Wilson concluded that they no longer existed except as ideals. For all practical purposes the national government reigned supreme over the states, and Congress dominated the president and the courts. Presidents had exercised great power in the early days of the Republic, but only because of a peculiarity of the times: the new nation faced challenge after challenge from abroad, and the Constitution had entrusted foreign affairs to the president.

But once the country turned inward to settle the West, a president had few duties beyond executing the directives of Congress. It seemed to Wilson that as long as the United States concentrated on domestic affairs, the presidency would be a minor office, and no first-rate man would exert himself to win it. History bore him out: Lincoln had been preceded by eight mediocre presidents and followed by five more.

Congress had grown powerful by the classic strategy of divide and conquer, scattering its authority across dozens of standing committees. Wilson disapproved of the committees' habit of crafting legislation in secret, and he complained that each committee was its own little legislature. The sheer number of committees left scant time for debate, so when Congress assembled in its entirety, it generally contented itself with saying yea or nay to the bills that emerged from committee.

Wilson conceded that the checks and balances had prevented the rise of despots, but he also noted that the Founding Fathers had not foreseen that the division of power could be carried so far that citizens would find it impossible to hold anyone in government accountable. Point a finger, and the sin would be admitted, but the blame would immediately be hung on someone else. "How is the schoolmaster, the nation, to know which boy needs the whipping?" Wilson inquired.

Once again, Wilson declared that Congress—and American democracy— would be much improved by debate, because only the best men could succeed in a true contest of ideas. And once again Wilson presented the British Parliament as the paragon of self-government. "Each session of the Lords and Commons becomes a grand inquest into the affairs of the empire," he wrote. "The two estates . . . sit with open doors, and spare themselves no fatigue in securing for every interest represented a full, fair, and impartial hearing."

Plainly the author of *Congressional Government* still yearned to test himself in politics. But how would he stir the nation from a back room in the Capitol? And what good was oratory in a committee meeting? Committee members did not make speeches. They haggled and wheedled, and victory went to the shrewdest negotiator. Woodrow Wilson detested negotiation and always would.

In spite of the demanding schedule Wilson set for completing his book, he regularly wrote long letters to Ellen. He also made time for oratory, which gave him more pleasure than anything else at Johns Hopkins. Public speaking "sets my mind—all my faculties—aglow," he wrote her after addressing the campus literary society. In front of an audience he got a thrill that kept him awake long into the night. For some time he had known that having an audience gave him a sense of power that he did not feel when dealing with individuals, and he thought he knew why. As he put it to Ellen, "One feels no sacrifice of pride necessary in courting the favor of an assembly of men such as he would have to make in seeking to please one man."

The publication of *Congressional Government* brought great joy to Ellen and to Joseph and Jessie Wilson but left the author feeling anxious and conflicted. "The question is, What next?" he asked Ellen. Like a general who had just gained a foothold in enemy territory, he felt he must push on: "to linger would be fatal. There is now a responsibility resting upon me where before there was none." The writing of the book had awakened his old political ambitions, and much as he wanted to believe that Congress had no place for a reforming politician of the sort he wanted to be, he knew that he would run for office if he had the money.

Contemplating his future as an intellectual, Woodrow said that he would feel complete if his writing inspired the country, but it saddened him to think that his political talent would be the handmaiden of his literary work. In his dreams it was the other way around. And in spite of his wish to bask in the warm reception of *Congressional Government,* Wilson could not stop thinking about the handful of negative comments. Any word that seemed to threaten his success "hurts me like a slap in the face," he wrote to Ellen.

Wilson lasted two years at Hopkins. The doctorate required three years of study plus examinations and a dissertation, but he chafed at the thought of more cramming. A new institution of higher learning for women, Bryn Mawr College, was urging him to join its faculty, he was inclined to accept, and his father endorsed the idea. Ellen, however, was skeptical. Could a young professor make his reputation at a women's college? she asked Woodrow. And wouldn't he find it unpleasant to serve under a woman dean? "It seems so unnatural, so jarring to one's sense of the fitness of things—so absurd too."

Woodrow admitted that he did not relish the prospect of teaching young women, but Bryn Mawr had promised him ample time for writing, and writing was the way he intended to distinguish himself. He reminded Ellen that teaching was merely a way "to get a start in the literary work which cannot at first bring one a living."

Now assured of employment, Woodrow was eager to marry, and Ellen was at last free to do so, although the liberating event had been a sad one. Her father, unable to overcome his grief for his wife, had taken his life in May

1884. After a summer in mourning, various Axson relatives agreed to care for Ellen's three siblings while she went to New York to study at the Art Students League. Encouraged by her teachers, she gave serious thought to setting herself up as an artist, and when a group of classmates invited her to join them for a summer of painting in the country, she was eager to accept. Woodrow, who was longing to marry, protested, and Ellen yielded. She returned to her grandfather's home in Savannah in the spring of 1885 and on June 24 became Mrs. Woodrow Wilson.

The couple honeymooned for the summer in a cottage near Asheville, where Woodrow had proposed, and in the fall they went north to Bryn Mawr. Woodrow worried that his salary of $1,500 a year would not support a family, and the worry was more pressing for him than for most new husbands. He and Ellen were already caring for her eleven-year-old brother, Edward, and they were about to be joined by a child of their own.

Wilson had been at Bryn Mawr for only a semester when he began to worry that he had made a mistake in not finishing his doctorate. Sensing that he would be at a disadvantage in competing for a professorship in the future, he asked Johns Hopkins if *Congressional Government* could serve as his dissertation and if he could receive the degree through some special arrangement. The university met him halfway, allowing the book to stand for a dissertation but not waiving the examinations. He forced himself to cram and in June 1886 became Woodrow Wilson, PhD.

Bored and frustrated at Bryn Mawr, Woodrow sometimes entertained thoughts of a career in government, reasoning that if he could not enter politics, perhaps he could watch it from a front-row seat. He went to Washington to see his old law partner from Atlanta, Edward Renick, who had taken a position in the Treasury Department. With Renick's help, he met officials in several agencies, but no one offered to take him on. "Thirty-one years old and nothing done!" he lamented.

Wilson's attitudes toward women were decades behind those of Bryn Mawr's founding dean, Carey Thomas, and he had no interest in preparing women for roles in the larger world, but his greatest grievance against the college was the same as his complaint against Johns Hopkins and Virginia: it was not Princeton. Although a faculty position at his alma mater was not yet within reach, Wilson left Bryn Mawr in 1888 for a full professorship at Wesleyan University in Middletown, Connecticut. The post returned him to a largely masculine world, increased his pay from $1,500 to $2,500, and allowed him to teach his two favorite subjects, history and political economy.

As 1889 began, he and Ellen had two small girls and a third on the way,

Ellen's brother Edward* still lived with them, and they were soon to be joined by her brother Stockton. Financially unable to continue his studies after his junior year at the University of Georgia, Stockton was about to take a job in the cotton business when Wilson took him in and arranged for him to complete his studies at Wesleyan. Unable to support them all on his salary, Woodrow wrote and lectured constantly to make ends meet.

In 1890, after more than a year of discreet lobbying by his friend Robert Bridges, Princeton hired Wilson to teach jurisprudence and political economy. He was deeply grateful to be returned to the scene of the four happiest years of his life, and the appointment came with a full professorship, a salary of $3,000, a month's leave to teach a short course at Johns Hopkins, and time for his writing.

Woodrow Wilson began his professorial career at Princeton as a contented man. He and Ellen had three small children—"the baby, the little baby and the littlest baby of all," he called them. Margaret was four, Jessie three, and Eleanor (Nell) not quite a year old. Woodrow thoroughly enjoyed fatherhood and discovered that playing with the children revived forgotten delights of his own early years. Woodrow and Ellen usually dined with their girls, and the family spent most evenings playing backgammon or card games or sharing stories. Woodrow often read aloud, as his father had done. He told funny stories, recited limericks, and enjoyed showing off his mastery of dialects. In his silliest moods he donned a top hat for a few minutes of buck and wing.

Wilson's salary was twice what he had earned at Bryn Mawr but not enough to dispel his worries about providing for three children and the parade of impecunious relatives. Ellen made all of the girls' clothing and most of her own. Nevertheless, Woodrow's moonlighting and Ellen's economizing enabled the Wilsons to leave the summer heat of New Jersey's interior for the Adirondacks or some other cool spot, and in 1896, the year Woodrow turned forty, they built a comfortable, pretty house on Library Place in Princeton. Its half-timbering and diamond-paned windows nodded toward the Wilsons' love of English literature, and the floor plan, drawn by Ellen, placed Woodrow's study far from the bustle of the rest of the house.

---

* Edward Axson was the first of a half-dozen relatives who would live with Woodrow and Ellen Wilson for months, sometimes years. The others were Woodrow's widowed sister, Annie Howe, and her daughter; Ellen's cousin Mary Hoyt; Ellen's brother Stockton; and Woodrow's aging father.

From the outset he was a popular professor, and his growing reputation as a public speaker and a commentator on political affairs brought him more and more invitations to lecture and write. He had arrived in Princeton with a commission to write a book called *Division and Reunion,* one of three volumes in a series called *Epochs of American History. Harper's Weekly* paid generously for a life of George Washington in installments, and popular magazines as well as scholarly journals regularly commissioned articles and reviews. As his reputation grew, Wilson was invited to speak in parts of the country he had never seen—Chicago in 1893, Colorado a year later.

The letters that Woodrow and Ellen exchanged when he was away lecturing or she and the girls were visiting her relatives in Georgia, visiting her side of the family, show the undimmed ardor of their love. During a lonely stay in Baltimore, he asked her, "When you get me back you'll smother me, will you, my sweet little lover? And what will I be doing all the while—simply submitting to being smothered? Do you think you can stand the innumerable kisses and the passionate embraces you will *receive*? Are you prepared for the storm of love making with which you will be assailed?" One Valentine's Day he wrote, "Never blame me, darling, for being too passionate in my love making—in my kisses and embraces. The hot fire that is in my heart *must* find *some* passionate expression. Read it for what it truly is: my poetry—the ecstasy of my heart breaking all bounds to find its satisfaction. Would I not be odiously commonplace were it not for this side of me: would you not yawn if I did not sometimes make you blush?" She was not only the perfect confidante and counselor for an intellectual, he told her, she was also *"Love's Playmate,* led on to all the sweet abandonments and utter intimacies of love—as if you had been made for nothing else."

Ellen rarely responded in kind, but during one of the interminable Februarys when Woodrow lectured at Johns Hopkins, he asked if she wanted all of him, and she promptly replied, "Yes, sir, I do want 'all of you.'" She missed their kisses and embraces as much as he did.

Happy at home, the Wilsons had little interest in the social life of Princeton. Ellen said she felt too "country-bred" for Northern drawing rooms, and Woodrow had not overcome his fear of taking the initiative in making friends. "All his life he dreaded the first plunge of personal contact," wrote his first major biographer, Ray Stannard Baker, who knew him well. Wilson was only slightly less wary when other men made the overture. To one of his women friends, he confided that many people offered their friendship, but he seldom responded. He suspected that he hesitated partly because of shyness and partly because "when I give at all I want to give my whole heart, and I feel that so few want it all, or would return measure for measure."

Years later, several acquaintances interviewed separately for a book about Wilson at Princeton observed that he seemed more at ease with women than men. One said that with women, he seemed "almost a swashbuckling gallant." Another claimed that he was "at his very best at tea with an intelligent lady talking about literature." Ellen's sister would remember him as "such fun in the home. The house was always full, mostly with women. He used to say that he was 'submerged in petticoats.'"

Wilson's closest friend on the faculty, John Grier Hibben, tried to sell him on the importance of sprucing up, getting out, and cultivating the plutocrats who were building country estates near Princeton. The counsel went unheeded. But after a few years at Princeton, he had a sense that his life was changing. His success on the lecture circuit, where he preached muscular citizenship and expatiated on democracy, had carried him well beyond the cloistered life of the scholar. It still excited him to give speeches, though his full calendar was wearing him out and making him wonder what drove him. Only half in jest he told Ellen that her husband was "hungry—*too hungry*—for reputation and influence."

Early in 1896, as he struggled to meet his magazine deadlines and get through his lecture season at Johns Hopkins, he was a physical wreck—gaunt and wan, besieged by stomach trouble and distracted by a chronic facial tic. When friends urged him to rest, he waved them off because he could not see how else to support all who counted on him. He was finally persuaded to go abroad by his Princeton classmate Charles Mitchell, a physician. Impressed by Mitchell's forcefulness (and temporarily relieved of financial pressure by a check from a friend of the university), Wilson decided to spend the summer in Britain, home of the poets and politicians he revered.

On May 27, 1896, three days before sailing, Wilson suddenly lost the use of his right hand. Several fingertips went numb, and his upper arm hurt. Diagnosed as "neuritis," the attack was attributed to an overuse of the nerves and muscles involved in the act of writing. Decades later, Edwin Weinstein, the neuropsychiatrist who theorized that Wilson was dyslexic, concluded that the episode was actually a small stroke brought on by high blood pressure and stress. The symptoms indicated a blockage of the left middle coronary artery.

Only thirty-nine at the time, Wilson took the attack in stride. He sailed as planned on May 30, and by the time his ship docked in Glasgow, he had taught himself to write with his left hand—slowly but with an engraver's precision. Although his arm would not fully recover for a year, his exhaustion faded within weeks. "Really this out-of-door life is a delicious tonic," he wrote home from York. After cycling 120 miles in four days, he was exhilarated. The serenity of the countryside, the hedgerows, the quaint old villages and great estates—all of it "makes the wheel run easily and with zest, as if to hurry from beauty to beauty," he reported. From Rydal he sent Ellen a tiny flower plucked near the home of William Wordsworth, their favorite poet. Wilson found Cambridge "beyond measure attractive," and of Oxford he wrote, "dear me, a mere glance at Oxford is enough to take one's heart by storm." If he could teach at Oxford, he told Ellen, "America would see me again only to sell the house and fetch you and the children."

Well rested, he returned to Princeton in early September and resumed his grind. He read the proofs of his life of Washington, taught his classes, and carved out time to concentrate on the composition of "Princeton in the Nation's Service." The most notable address of his academic career, it was delivered in October 1896, at Princeton's celebration of its sesquicentennial, to a huge audience of alumni, college presidents, and distinguished guests. Inspired by Oxford, he called for a revival of Princeton's tradition of preparing young men to play a leading role in national affairs. The country's age of easy expansion had ended with the closing of the American frontier, Wilson said, and the ideal American college for the new age would inculcate a spirit of service and a vibrant sense of "the duty of man towards man."

Praised for its thoughts on the role of a university in a democracy, "Princeton in the Nation's Service" was widely republished, in full and in snippets, and it became a classic in the literature of higher education. It was also a textbook example of the power of the unconscious to reveal what the conscious mind does not perceive. With his right arm still out of commission, Wilson had typed the first eleven pages of the speech with his left hand before giving up and dictating the rest. His doctors had not diagnosed his debility as a stroke, and he downplayed it as writer's cramp, but the speech brimmed with images of constriction. He spoke of "forces long pent up," of "unrelaxing" purposefulness, of a sense of duty as "a fretful thing in confinement," of a responsible man's unwillingness to be "clapped up within a narrow round." The speech was also laced with pessimism and fear. Newness was a "risk," commerce was "strife," excessive growth carried "the threat of death."

Wilson tried to conserve his energy in the hope of making a full recovery, but before long he was overbooked and near despair. Though his salary, now $4,300, was Princeton's highest, he and Ellen still struggled to help their needy relatives, and in 1895 the household had gained yet another member, Woodrow's father. Seventy-three years old, widowed, and slowly dying of coronary artery disease, Joseph Wilson would live with Woodrow and

Ellen and their daughters until his death, in 1903. Wilson asked Princeton to match the lucrative offers he occasionally received from other colleges, but Princeton declined. When one of his friends on the board of trustees asked the university's president, Francis L. Patton, about Wilson's pay, Patton explained that Wilson was already reaping more rewards than any other member of the faculty. Beyond drawing the top salary, he had been granted a light schedule and a month's leave for his lectures at Johns Hopkins.

Not wanting to leave Princeton, Wilson took on more assignments from magazines and more invitations to lecture. In 1898, Cleveland Dodge, Cyrus Hall McCormick, Jr., and other prosperous friends from Wilson's undergraduate days came to his rescue with an arrangement designed to please Princeton as well as their old friend Tommy. Wilson agreed to stay on for five years, and the friends pledged to supplement his salary with an annual gift of $2,500. Even that did not relieve Wilson's anxieties. By 1899 he was as run-down as he had been in 1896. His right arm was painfully sore, he never felt rested, and he had lost a worrisome amount of weight. His friend Jack Hibben raised money for another summer in Britain and told Wilson that he could do the university a great service by finding a suitable Englishman to teach colonial administration at Princeton.

It was an inspired assignment. The United States had just annexed Hawaii, and in the treaty that ended the Spanish-American War of 1898, the United States had acquired Cuba, Puerto Rico, Guam, and the Philippines. The notion of expanding beyond North America disturbed many citizens, including Senator George Frisbie Hoar of Massachusetts, who predicted that ratification of the treaty would make the United States "a vulgar, commonplace empire controlling subject races and vassal states, in which one class must forever rule and other classes must forever obey." The junior senator from Massachusetts, Henry Cabot Lodge, filed an equally fervid brief for the other side: if America rejected the treaty, it would still be at war. "At the same time we repudiate the president and his action before the whole world and the repudiation . . . brands us as a people incapable of great affairs or taking rank where we belong, as one of the greatest of the great world powers."

Wilson agreed with Lodge. Whatever the scruples of the naysayers, Wilson wrote, "the thing is done; cannot be undone; and our future must spring out of it." Asia was going to be transformed, and a new age had begun. In his mind, the great question was, "Which nations shall possess the world?" He saw Britain, Germany, and Russia as the chief competitors in the new race for world domination, and although he did not believe that the United States would build an empire, vulgar or otherwise, he thought that Americans would be obliged to play some role by virtue of their presence in the

Philippines. *"What ought we to do?"* he wondered. In his mind, the question was one of morals, not of geopolitical strategy.

The West would try to modernize the East, and Wilson thought that the United States and Great Britain ought to try to ease Asia's transition from old to new by instilling Western principles of law and order and Western habits of self-help and self-restraint. He recognized the challenges. Americans believed that they understood self-government, but their democracy had developed in isolation, an experience that had given them "a false self-confidence, a false self-sufficiency because we have heeded no successes or failures but our own," he wrote.

It also seemed to Wilson that the United States would need strong presidents again. "When foreign affairs play a prominent part in the politics and policy of a nation," he wrote, "the Executive must of necessity be its guide: must utter every initial judgment, take every first step of action, supply the information upon which it is to act, suggest and in large measure control its conduct. . . . Interesting things may come of the singular change."

Wilson eventually developed a fascination with the presidency, but in the summer of 1899 he was preoccupied with restoring his health. With Ellen's brother Stockton, he sailed for Glasgow in June and stayed abroad for two months. He did not find an instructor in colonial administration and resented even the small amount of time he spent on the errand Princeton had asked him to do. "How I *hate* business," he wrote Ellen after a day of searching in vain for men who had been recommended by an Oxford don. "I have done what I could." He made his first visit to the House of Commons, an institution he had long venerated, but if the experience moved him, he did not say so in his letters. His glowering hinted at the magnitude of his fatigue.

He was refreshed by a few weeks of cycling in Ireland and by his return to the Lake District, Cambridge, and Oxford. Struck anew by the physical beauty of Oxford's gardens and trees and great lawns, he wrote Ellen that the seclusion of the quadrangles and cloisters filled him with "a very keen sense of what we lack in our democratic colleges, where no one has privacy or claims to have his own thoughts."

Back in Princeton, Wilson made one more attempt to come to terms with his unfulfilled and seemingly unfulfillable political ambitions, this time in an essay entitled "When a Man Comes to Himself." The phrase, from the New Testament's parable of the prodigal son, refers to the happiness a Christian is said to know once he makes Christ's teachings the center of his life. Wilson reworked the tale in largely secular terms, writing of the joy that comes to a person who recognizes that he is not the center of the universe.

Only when a man abandoned such illusions could he see the limits of his powers and understand that he was simply "the part he plays among his fellows," Wilson wrote. "He is not isolated; he cannot be. His life is made up of the relations he bears to others." To thrive as a human being, a man had to turn away from himself and become "part of the motive force of communities or of nations. It makes no difference how small a part, how insignificant, how unnoticed. When his powers begin to play outward, and he loves the task at hand, not because it gains him a livelihood, but because it makes him a life, he has come to himself." For Wilson, the outward turn explained why men loved power: "it affords them so pleasurable an expansion of faculty, so large a run for their minds, an exercise of spirit so various and refreshing; they have the freedom of so wide a tract of the world of affairs." Real satisfaction came not from the excitement of action or self-aggrandizement, he said, but from "consciousness of right, of powers greatly and nobly spent."

Woodrow Wilson's first taste of power came to him out of the blue. The president of Princeton, Francis L. Patton, was a genial fellow who had steered the university with a light hand but not in any particular direction. On June 9, 1902, after months of negotiation, the university's trustees thanked Patton for his service, sent him off with a large check, and asked Wilson to succeed him.

The trustees had made an excellent choice. Wilson had long been a close student of leadership. He was one of the most eminent and best-liked members of the faculty. His writings and public lectures had won admiration far beyond Princeton. And his ideas about education were sufficiently modern to please progressives but not radical enough to alarm the conservative alumni who bankrolled Princeton. The fact that Wilson would be the university's first Southern-born president was taken by many as another sign that the old differences between North and South no longer mattered. Wilson was also the first Princeton president without a degree in theology, but as the son, grandson, son-in-law, and nephew of clergymen, he seemed unlikely to put the young men of Princeton on the road to perdition.

Wilson was Princeton's thirteenth president, and thirteen was Wilson's lucky number. There were thirteen letters in his name. His invitation to teach at Princeton had come on February 13, 1890 (a Friday, and therefore doubly auspicious, in his view). And he would be inaugurated during his thirteenth year on the faculty. Accepting the office "has done a very helpful thing for me," he wrote Ellen. "It has settled the future for me and given me a sense of *position* and of definite, tangible tasks which takes the *flutter* and restlessness from my spirits." At last he would have an opportunity to govern something, and as he worked on his inaugural address, he said he felt "like a new prime minister getting ready to address his constituents."

As a college president, Wilson could do more than envy Oxford's long history of producing statesmen. Oxford had inspired his sesquicentennial address, "Princeton in the Nation's Service," and his inaugural speech, "Princeton for the Nation's Service," imagined an even larger place for the university in American life. A proper university had a graduate school to train specialists as well as an undergraduate college to give its students "a breadth of vision" and "a surplus of mind" to invest in the affairs of the country. A great university needed laboratories, natural history museums, and observatories, but it also needed the humanities in order to pass on the wisdom of the past, he said. Above all, it had a duty to impart a philosophy of conduct. "We are not put into this world to sit still and know; we are put into it to act."

Joseph Wilson, too ill to attend the inaugural ceremonies on October 25, 1902, died a few months later, at the age of eighty. With Ellen's help, Woodrow had nursed him to the last, spending hours at his side, singing hymns and reciting Wordsworth's "Character of the Happy Warrior," a poem father and son cherished. The happy warrior was their ideal, a self-mastered man "Whose high endeavours are an inward light/That makes the path before him always bright," a man who conquered his pain and fear, whose suffering made him alive to tenderness, who owed his victories to his virtues, who if called upon to face some awful moment is "happy as a lover." "[I]t has quite taken the heart out of me to lose my lifelong friend and companion," Woodrow wrote a friend. "I have told you what he was to me. And now he is gone and a great loneliness is in my heart."

In spite of his grief, Princeton's new president made an impressive start. He won praise for shifting the control of curriculum from trustees to faculty, for striking a new balance between elective and required courses, and for raising academic standards. Special dispensations for pedigreed young men who flunked the entrance examination were abolished, and students who did not pass at least half their courses were dismissed. He also persuaded alumni to raise unprecedented sums for new fields of study and a long-overdue construction program.

The most innovative of Wilson's changes, and the one that pleased him most, was the hiring of fifty energetic young preceptors. Like the tutors of Oxford and Cambridge, the preceptors would serve as "companions and coaches and guides of the men's reading," he explained. As a student, he had loathed cramming, and as an educator, he felt that examinations based on lectures and textbooks rewarded cramming rather than mastery of a subject. He hoped that additional reading and discussions with preceptors would take students beyond "schoolboyish" classroom learning.

Within four years, most of these changes were in place, and Wilson enjoyed the esteem of his Princeton constituencies and of college presidents throughout the country. And then, on May 28, 1906—ten years and a day after his stroke—Wilson awoke to discover that he was blind in his left eye and had no feeling in his right arm. The blindness indicated that the disease, a degenerative and irreversible affliction, had spread to yet another artery. A specialist in Philadelphia prescribed retirement, but the doctor he consulted for a second opinion predicted that three months' rest would restore his health. "Of course 50-year-old arteries do not go back to an earlier condition," the doctor said, "but I expect that you will be as well as you need be for any work you can reasonably wish to undertake next fall. The warning simply indicates that an excess of work is dangerous."

When the trustees urged Wilson to rest until fully recovered, he and Ellen took the girls to Britain and rented a cottage near the home where Wordsworth had lived. Woodrow was soon tramping fourteen miles a day without feeling overtaxed. He went to Edinburgh to see specialists in hypertension and learned that although his blood pressure was on the high side, there was no compelling reason to give up his work.

The news pleased Woodrow but troubled Ellen. She understood that he was suffering from a hardening of the arteries, and as she wrote to one of her cousins, the disease was "an awful thing—a dying by inches." She attributed it to his high-stress life and made him promise to take a short vacation every winter and a long one each summer. Woodrow also agreed to hire a full-time secretary—his first. He also stopped meeting with people unless they had appointments.

The streamlining enabled Wilson to devote his energies to his next big project: building quadrangles akin to those at Oxford and Cambridge in the interest of strengthening the sense of community among Princeton's students. Outside the classroom, the students congregated mainly in eating clubs, which had sprung up out of necessity in the days before dormitories had dining rooms. Over time the clubs had become bastions of snobbery, open only to upperclassmen who passed muster with current members. Wilson did not propose to abolish the eating clubs, but he might as well have. His plans called for the quads to house all students, graduate as well as undergraduate, and each quad would have its own dining hall. Unveiling the plan in June 1907, he told the trustees that he was "not seeking to form better clubs, but academic communities. We are making a university, not devising a method of social pleasure. The social life of the quads will be all-inclusive, and it will serve as the medium of things intellectual."

The trustees were amenable until they began hearing from alumni with warm memories of their eating clubs. Once unleashed, the opposition was unrelenting. As the fight dragged on, the *New York Evening Post* joked that Wilson was about to ruin "the most agreeable and aristocratic country club in America by transforming it into an institution of learning." Sure that Wilson would lose a fight over the issue, the trustees suggested that he settle for democratizing the clubs. Wilson, furious with the trustees for deserting him and certain that the quads would do more for Princeton than reformed clubs would, refused. Defeat, he decided, was more honorable than settling for an inferior idea.

In the fall, Wilson tried again, going to the faculty in hopes of overwhelming the opposition from trustees and alumni. One professor made a motion in favor of Wilson's plans, another seconded it. But when Professor Henry van Dyke of the English department made a motion against it, the faculty member who rose to second it was Wilson's best friend, Jack Hibben. Wilson went pale. "Do I understand that Professor Hibben seconds Professor van Dyke's motion?" he asked. Hibben replied in the affirmative. As far as Wilson was concerned, their friendship was over.

Despite Hibben and Van Dyke, Wilson won the faculty vote by a wide margin. But the trustees, responding to steady pressure from alumni, rejected Wilson's proposal but left the door open for another vote. Wilson thought he could prevail and began meeting with alumni clubs in hopes of winning them over with well-reasoned oratory, as William Gladstone and Daniel Webster had done with their opponents. It took only a few speeches on the road for Wilson to see that reason was no match for the alumni's sentimental attachment to the clubs. Wilson still believed that he was right about the quads, but his conviction gave him little solace. He could conceive of no better plan than the quads, he told a friend, "and in these circumstances it has been a struggle with me all the year to keep in any sort of spirits."

Wilson took one more do-or-die stand, in 1909, over the location of a long-delayed building for Princeton's graduate school. In his inaugural address, he had promised to place it as close as possible to the center of campus. But the dean of graduate studies, Andrew Fleming West, thought the school should be built on a site a mile away, near the university's golf links. Wilson believed that the distance would work against the spirit of community he was trying to foster, but West maintained that a graduate school built in the center of an already crowded campus would have no room for expansion.

Wilson was optimistic. The trustees and the faculty agreed with him, and before going into the fray, he had taken the precaution of stripping West of most of his power. West had a well-deserved reputation as an autocrat, making it difficult for Princeton to attract graduate students. Wilson had taken the problem to the trustees and persuaded them to transfer much of West's authority to a faculty committee.

West had also given offense with his architectural aspirations for the graduate school. An aesthete and bon vivant, he had ordered up a cathedral of learning to out-Oxford Oxford, with sumptuous quarters for the students and an oak-paneled dining hall with grand Gothic windows. Wilson played a cool hand, allowing the faculty committee to deliberate on its own. Only after it voiced its opposition to West's proposal did Wilson ask the trustees to see the architect and request something less palatial.

But West played an even cooler hand. His boyhood friend William Cooper Procter, president of Procter & Gamble, was contemplating a $500,000 donation to Princeton, and West encouraged him to offer it with strings attached. Procter cooperated, pledging the sum for a graduate school, but not on the spot Wilson had selected. Wilson tried to convert Procter, and when that failed, alumni began urging the university not to turn away $500,000. The trustees gave in, accepting Procter's offer just before Christmas.

Wilson felt betrayed. By taking the $500,000, the trustees were telling the world that money trumped the university's president. Deeply despondent, Wilson wrote to one of the trustees, "I seem to have come to the end." But the battle had not. It raged for several more months, with offensives and counteroffensives, an abortive plot against West, more unsuccessful attempts to orate the alumni into submission, and a surprise ending. In May 1910, one Isaac Wyman, class of 1848, died at his home in Salem, Massachusetts, and left Princeton an estate said to be worth millions. West had cultivated Wyman for years and was one of the executors of his estate. Wilson, at home when West telegraphed news of the bequest, could hardly stop laughing. "We have beaten the living, but we cannot fight the dead," he told Ellen. "The game is up."

3

Ascent

The defeats left Wilson in an unenviable position. If he resigned, his opponents would feel triumphant, but if he stayed, he would be nothing more than the caretaker of the most agreeable, most aristocratic country club in America. Wilson had fought hard for his convictions (too hard, in the opinion of Princeton's old guard), and he had lost. Twice. But beyond Princeton, he had been praised for standing up to wealth and privilege at a moment when wealth and privilege were about to get a comeuppance.

For decades, the country had been piling up immense riches, which were increasingly concentrated in the hands of the few. Although Democrats, populists, and socialists had been decrying the inequity since the 1890s, Republicans had managed to hang on to the presidency and, more often than not, both houses of Congress. The Republican reign might have gone on indefinitely if President William Howard Taft had not handed himself over to the party's conservatives, who were working for a return to the days of laissez-faire and the figurehead presidents scorned by Woodrow Wilson in *Congressional Government*. Taft's abandonment of moderate and progressive Republicans set off a war between them and the party's reactionaries. The progressives were hoping to ditch Taft and nominate one of their own to run for president in 1912, and the feud gave Democrats a good chance to capture the White House for the first time since 1892.

The Democratic politicos of the Northeast had been eyeing Woodrow Wilson for some time. He was upstanding, bright, well spoken. He was also progressive, but unlike the party's leader, William Jennings Bryan, he set off no alarms. The kinds of reform that interested Wilson typically involved a recasting of an old ideal rather than a swan dive into the unknown. "We now expect to see Woodrow Wilson elected Governor of the State of New Jersey in 1910 and nominated for President in 1912," *Harper's Weekly* had declared in the spring of 1909. The editor, George Harvey, had been calling attention to Wilson for three years. Both parties were still run by bosses, and the Democratic bosses of New Jersey considered Wilson's inexperience an asset. He had no followers, so no one but the bosses could get him elected. And that, they thought, would make him their man.

Aware of the politicos' interest, Wilson accepted a handful of invitations to speak at Democratic dinners but studiously avoided showing any eagerness to run. When Harvey, a confidant of Big Jim Smith, New Jersey's chief boss, privately asked Wilson what he would do if he were offered the nomination with no strings attached, Wilson said only that he would seriously consider the idea. Looking to 1912, Smith asked Democratic power brokers in other states if they would support Wilson and found a fair amount of enthusiasm for the idea.

But in June 1910, when New Jersey Democrats began clamoring for a different candidate, Smith told Harvey that unless Wilson immediately agreed to run, he would lose the chance. Harvey relayed the message, and Wilson gave his consent. Smith and Harvey promised him the governorship and told him that he had a good chance at the party's next presidential nomination. The Wilsons were vacationing in Old Lyme, Connecticut, a place Ellen found congenial for painting, when Woodrow was summoned back to New Jersey to confer with the bosses. The family was overjoyed, but as Nell remembered it, her father, Woodrow, was serenity incarnate. "I never saw him excited about his own destiny," she wrote. "He had a calm way of accepting everything, a philosophic sort of fatalism."

September 15, the day that Wilson went down to Trenton to accept the nomination, was a day of firsts—his first political convention and his first meeting with most of the men who had put him on the ticket. Those who worried that a professor might not be able to connect with the crowds at union halls and county fairs worried even more after he fumbled his first speech. But he never again lost his bearings onstage. He spoke simply, did not run on or overheat, and his refusal to resort to ridicule was a refreshing departure from the campaign oratory of the day. His audiences liked him, and he was pleased to see how quickly laborers grasped his arguments. Unafraid to present himself as a moralist, he insisted that corruption be rooted out and that government put the public interest ahead of special interests.

New Jersey gave Wilson a huge victory. He was the first Democrat in fourteen years to win the governorship, and only one gubernatorial candidate in the state's history had won a larger share of the vote. His coat-tails carried New Jersey's Democrats to a majority in the State Assembly, and five of the state's seven seats in the U.S. House of Representatives went to Democrats. Nationwide, the Democrats recaptured the House and gained ten seats in the Senate. They also picked up four governorships, for a total of twenty-five. That left twenty-one Republican governors, sixteen of whom identified themselves as progressives. The Socialist Party also made a strong showing, electing its first congressman, Victor Berger of Wisconsin, along with a thousand state legislators, mayors, and city councilmen.

President Taft described the election as "not only a landslide but a tidal wave and holocaust all rolled into a general cataclysm." To Wilson it seemed that the voters had not endorsed any particular program of the Democrats but had turned away from the Republicans in despair. "The Democrats have not so much won a victory as they have obtained an opportunity," he told a reporter. Those were the words of a man looking to 1912.

Wilson's victory left him more pensive than elated. At a celebratory dinner hosted by Princeton seniors, he reflected that when a man had to decide upon a course of action, he might believe that he had several choices, but only one of them would be right. He also wanted the students to know that their lives would be governed by forces beyond their control. In entering politics, Wilson said, he felt as if he had boarded a boat for points unknown, with someone else at the helm.

And now how did he feel? they asked.

Trusting and happy to be on the voyage, he said.

New Jersey had no governor's mansion, so after eight years in the spaciousness of the president's home on the Princeton campus, the Wilsons shoehorned themselves into a small sitting room and three bedrooms at the Princeton Inn. "The first evening we sat and looked at one another in despair," Nell remembered. "No fireplace, no garden, and meals in a hotel dining room surrounded by other people." The governor commuted by train to Trenton, ten miles away, and the girls, now in their early twenties, fell into a similar routine. Margaret studied music in New York. Jessie and Nell spent most of their time in Philadelphia, Jessie as a settlement house worker and Nell as an art student. To keep up their spirits, the girls pretended that the family no longer needed a house.

Wilson began asserting his independence from the bosses even before his inauguration. One of New Jersey's seats in the U.S. Senate was open, and in those days, senators were elected by state legislatures. Big Jim Smith, the boss whose $50,000 campaign contribution was Wilson's largest by far, wanted the seat and believed that Wilson had promised to help him get it. Wilson had no such recollection and throughout the campaign had presented himself as a candidate without political debts. Insisting that he had been elected by New Jersey's progressives, not by Smith's money or his machine, Wilson gave his support to the progressives' choice, James Martine. If he did otherwise, Wilson said, he would hardly be a credible progressive presidential candidate in 1912. Smith never forgave him, but the political tide was running with Wilson, not Smith.

The idea that Woodrow Wilson or anyone else could win the Democratic presidential nomination after only two years in politics was, on its face, preposterous. But the Democratic sweep of 1910 had been equally preposterous. The *New York Evening Mail* had interpreted the vote much as Wilson did: "the country is not Democratic—it is discontented." With a progressive presidential nominee and a platform addressing the discontent, they had an excellent chance to consolidate their control of Congress and take the White House in 1912.

Governor Wilson was of three minds about the presidential nomination. Looking at the world, he saw revolutions in Mexico and China, wars in the Balkans, an arms race in Europe, and mounting discontent in Russia. He feared that the next president of the United States would have a war on his hands, and he was not sure he could be a good war president. He also understood the long odds against a newcomer. But long odds were not the same as impossible odds, and despite his doubts, he could not resist positioning himself for the prize. Soon after his inauguration he persuaded the New Jersey legislature to do as progressives elsewhere were doing: establish primaries, pass a workmen's compensation law and a corrupt practices act, allow the state public utilities commission to set rates, and authorize the use of grassroots ballot measures in municipal elections.

Once the legislative work was under way, Wilson left Trenton for a series of speeches in the South, where he was relatively unknown. At Ellen's insistence, he interrupted the trip to meet William Jennings Bryan, who was giving a lecture at Princeton's theological seminary. Wilson had little respect for Bryan's mind, but Ellen persuaded him that it would be rude (and unwise) for a Democratic governor to ignore a visit by the party's leader. At Ellen's insistence, Wilson invited Bryan to dinner. Bryan accepted, and both men went away pleasantly surprised. Wilson wrote a friend that Bryan had "extraordinary force of personality, and it seems the force of sincerity and conviction. He has himself well in hand at every turn of the thought and talk, too; and his voice is wholly delightful." Bryan, expecting Wilson to be as dour as his photographs, was charmed by his playfulness.

A few weeks after Governor Wilson took office, he was visited by an admiring former pupil named William F. McCombs, a thirty-five-year-old lawyer who practiced in New York. McCombs had come to see him about a bill pending in the New Jersey legislature, but when Wilson mentioned that he was inundated with requests for speeches, McCombs, believing that Wilson would make a formidable presidential candidate, advised him to introduce himself to the western half of the country. McCombs volunteered to arrange the tour, found civic groups and universities willing to extend invitations, and underwrote much of the trip.

In May, after only four months as governor, Wilson set off on a nine-thousand-mile speaking tour that took him to the West Coast and back. Wilson avoided speaking under the auspices of any political group, but reporters everywhere along his route asked if he would run for president. When he claimed to have no such thought, cynics rolled their eyes. After the *New York Sun* suggested that Wilson was overdoing his "bashful maiden" act, he evaded the question of his candidacy by observing that the convention was more than a year away. But in an interview with a reporter in Oregon, he left no doubt about his availability: "The presidency of the United States is not an office for which a man can start out and declare he is fitted. On the other hand no man can refuse such a nomination for the office if it be offered him."

As an undeclared candidate, Wilson could not very well say how he would run the country, but in Kansas City, he identified the country's foremost problem: "the control of our politics, therefore our life, by great bodies of accumulated and organized wealth." Wilson's agility as an orator served him well whenever he wanted to respond to newspapers critical of his ideas. After the *Los Angeles Times* branded him a radical, he did his best to give radicalism a good name. In a speech to college students, he asked, "Do you know what a radical is? He is a man who goes to the root of things, and when you go to the root of things you get to the body of the people. . . . If you don't subscribe to radicalism, you don't subscribe to Americanism."

On occasion Wilson praised former president Theodore Roosevelt, whose mounting unhappiness with conservative Republicans was turning him into an outspoken progressive, but Wilson wanted his audiences to understand that not all progressives were alike. He himself was a Democrat, he said, because the Democratic Party believed in government by the people as well as for the people, while the Republican Party "grants that government should be for the people, but doubts the wisdom of letting the people do the governing." Orthodox Republicans still opposed the direct election of senators and saw such measures as the initiative and referendum as usurpations of powers that ought to remain in the hands of a legislature. "You must let the people into the game or they will break in," Wilson told an audience in San Francisco.

Guessing that his audience wondered how a professor could succeed in politics, Wilson regularly explained that as a lifelong student of American government, he was well versed in its ways and that after years of urging Princeton men toward public service, he had felt obliged to heed his own counsel when asked to run for governor.

The great surprise of the tour was personal. "What pleases me to the core is that the men I meet, both singly and in the mass, seem to *like* me and accept me as genuine," he wrote a friend. He was startled by how much the people of the West had read about him. But he doubted their prophecy that he would be the next president. That, he said, was "almost amusing." To his family, he confessed that he took a "wicked pleasure" in imagining how annoyed his Princeton foes would be if he won a presidential nomination. But he was not counting on it, because he knew that public adulation did not always translate into political success. "Crowds and enthusiasm do not mean very much," he told Nell. "Mr. Bryan had more of that than anyone else in American politics but he never attained the presidency."

Informed by Ellen that New Jersey disapproved of his gallivanting, Woodrow soon discovered that she was right. The state treasurer had docked his May paycheck of $880 by $800. June would cost him another $89. New Jersey's constitution required the state to give the money to the official, who acted as chief executive in the governor's absence. Wilson did not protest, and the story ended happily, with the acting chief executive returning the money to the governor.

In July the family left its warren at the Princeton Inn to stretch out at the Governor's Cottage in Sea Girt. A large, airy house flooded with sunlight, the cottage had been moved to the Jersey shore from Chicago, where it had been used to show off the state at the 1893 world's fair. As architectural pastiches went, the house was not bad—two stories of white clapboard and shutters with a long front porch accented by graceful columns and a sensible waist-high railing. After Ellen installed crates and crates of the family's objets d'art, it felt almost like home.

Sea Girt was a much needed reprieve from Princeton, where the townspeople still remembered the bitterness of the fights over the eating clubs and the graduate school. Wilson wrote a friend that he was always conscious of "how full the place is of spiteful hostility to me." He walked around town with a lump in his throat. At Sea Girt, the awkwardness disappeared. To relax, Woodrow golfed whenever he could. He found it impossible to worry and golf at the same time, he said, because every shot required his full attention. The partial blindness in his right eye, a consequence of the stroke he had suffered in 1906, was a considerable impediment. "My right eye is like a horse's," he explained. "I can see straight out with it, but not sideways. As a result, I cannot take a full swing because my nose gets in the way and cuts off my view of the ball."

The cottage had its drawbacks. The railroad tracks were so close that every passing train drowned out the family's conversation. A surprising number of strangers presumed that the governor's residence, like his office in the capital, was open to the public. One small boy who dropped in would tell his family that the governor had given him some cake but that the governor's husband had not been at home.

It was the lack of privacy that Ellen and Woodrow minded most. She escaped to her sitting room, while he took refuge on the golf course and in memories of his youth. As he wrote one of his friends, Mary Peck, "Sometimes . . . my whole life seems to me rooted in dreams—and I do not want the roots of it to dry up. I lived a dream life (almost too exclusively, perhaps) when I was a lad and even now my thought goes back for refreshment to those days."

Mary Allen Hulbert Peck, recipient of two hundred warm letters from Wilson, would attract increasing public notice as he made his political ascent. They had met on his first winter vacation in Bermuda, in 1907. Woodrow had just turned fifty. Mary was forty-four and recently separated from Thomas Peck, a textile manufacturer in Pittsfield, Massachusetts. Stylish and gregarious, she was not a beauty, but she was a close reader of men and had a genius for making them feel enchanting. A long list of male personages, from Mark Twain to the governor of Bermuda, dined at her table.

Mary has been portrayed as Ellen's opposite, the grasshopper who played and laughed while the drab ant toiled. It was whispered that Mary had had an affair with Woodrow, and Ellen had suspected as much after his second trip to Bermuda, in 1908. Woodrow vigorously proclaimed his innocence. While there is no compelling evidence to the contrary, a gap in his and Ellen's correspondence for that year has led some biographers to wonder if the most telling letters were burned.

Seemingly driven to prove the platonic nature of the friendship, Woodrow introduced Mary to the family and attempted to fold her into their circle. He often invited her to visit, a gesture that Ellen sometimes seconded in a note of her own. Ellen treated Mary graciously, but the girls regarded their new friend as a mixed blessing. Nell would remember how becoming Mary looked, "daintily puffing at one cigarette after another," and how irritating she could be with her inexhaustible fund of ideas for beautifying the Wilson girls.

In the fall, the family returned to Princeton, but not to the inn. Nell had found a house for rent on Cleveland Lane. Anticipating her parents' objection to the expense, she had persuaded them to invite two old friends, the Smith sisters of New Orleans, to share it with them. With its bay windows and half-timbering, the new place was reminiscent of the family's house on Library Place, and Wilsons and Smiths were soon happily settled in.

The governor's return to Trenton was less agreeable. New Jersey would hold state and local elections in November, and Big Jim Smith was in a crucifying mood. Wilson campaigned up and down the state, warning that any vote for a Democrat backed by the Smith machine was a vote for bossism. In one of the last speeches of the campaign, he declared that any vote for a Republican was pointless: "You can't do anything with a party made up of men who do not agree with each other, and that is the way with the Republican Party now." When the Republicans carried both the State Senate and the Assembly, some wondered if Wilson's presidential bubble had just burst. Wilson showed no fear. While he regretted his party's loss, he said, he looked forward to helping the Republicans keep their campaign promises: "If they want, the session should be productive of legislation of considerable importance."

The new legislature, which convened in January 1912, was indeed productive, quickly passing 130 bills. Just as quickly, the governor vetoed thirty-eight of them. In April the Republicans lashed back, accusing him of using the veto because he was not home long enough to study the legislation. "Absolutely false," Wilson said. He had been away for only two days during the legislative session.

A look at the governor's calendar suggests that however conscientious he was, he was also highly distracted. The news that Mary Peck was suing Thomas Peck for divorce had recently appeared on the front pages of *The New York Times* and the *New-York Tribune*. The Pecks were hardly page-one material, so the placement seemed to hint at something. If the newspapers began openly speculating about Mrs. Peck's relationship with Governor Wilson, his denials would carry no weight; even an unfounded rumor of an extramarital dalliance would end his political career.

In Bermuda when the stories appeared, Mary was upset to be the object of such publicity. Woodrow sent a reassuring letter, reminding her that she had done nothing to be ashamed of. He did not mention politics, but she grasped the delicacy of his situation, and she wondered if the Wilsons wanted her to drop out of their lives. "It would cost me dear," she wrote Woodrow, "but rather than have the least shadow of unpleasant feeling, I would never write to or see you again, save as chance brought us together."

In January 1912, the friendship of Governor Wilson and Mrs. Peck was no more than a potential problem. His actual problems included an angry legislature and two brushfires of the sort that break out in every election year. Once extinguished, they seem trivial, but while they burn, there is no telling how far they will spread, when they will be contained, or what the damage will be. The first was the disclosure of a five-year-old letter in which Wilson had wished that William Jennings Bryan could be muscled aside: "Would that we could do something, at once dignified and effective, to knock Mr. Bryan once for all into a cocked hat!" Bryan had won the Democratic presidential nomination three times but never won the election. Wilson had made the remark in a note to a Princeton alumnus who had just given a speech excoriating Bryan's call for nationalizing the railroads. When the letter appeared in the newspapers, on January 7, Wilson calmly explained that his views of Bryan had changed in the years since the letter was written.

The letter had come to light on the same day that Bryan told the Washington press corps that he would not run in 1912. The press wondered whether Bryan would back Woodrow Wilson or Speaker of the House Champ Clark, who was well liked by Democrats across the country. Bryan declined to choose, prompting the newspapermen to laugh at the idea that he would sit out 1912. With the Democrats poised to take the White House after a generation in exile, Bryan's silence seemed like a ruse to keep his longtime followers from falling in behind Wilson or Clark.

Bryan admitted to only one desire: party unity. The Democrats had a splendid chance in 1912, but the party's prospects always seemed rosy at the start of an election year, he said. "Everything depends on the manner in which we conduct ourselves." He and the rest of the country's leading Democrats, including Governor Wilson, were in Washington to choose a city for their national convention, tend to a host of procedural details, and hold their annual Jackson Day Dinner. Baltimore won the convention by turning up in Washington with a certified check for $100,000 and an invitation to use a local armory.

The veteran politicians on hand understood that the "cocked hat" letter had been leaked to spoil their gathering, and they feared that any sign of a chill between Bryan and Wilson would be taken as proof that Democrats were incapable of working together. The two men greeted each other warmly and talked, hand in hand, for ten minutes. Bryan's face showed "unmistakable pleasure," *The Washington Post* reported. "The great throng was plainly puzzled."

Wilson gave an adroit performance. After a warm-up of a minute or two, he paid Bryan a high compliment. During their sixteen years in the political wilderness, the Democrats had argued and wandered in all directions, but they had not forsaken the progressive ideals of William Jennings Bryan, Wilson said. "I, for my part, never want to forget this: That while we have differed with Mr. Bryan upon occasion . . . he has gone serenely on pointing out to a more and more convinced people what was the matter."

And what was the matter was that big business controlled the political as well as the economic life of the country, Wilson said. The great financiers and industrialists controlled government by lobbying and by funding the political campaigns of men who would do as they were told, and the economy was controlled by trusts that stifled competition and limited access to credit. They were, said Wilson, a "combination of combinations," a league of monopolies joined through interlocking boards of directors, and they used their power to keep others out of the game. Acknowledging the difficulty of dismantling the combination of combinations, Wilson suggested that the Democrats approach the task as a prudent surgeon approached a life-saving operation. The surgeon had to be conservative as well as radical, had to cut deep but also carefully.

Wilson drew ovation after ovation, but so did his chief rival, Champ Clark, who called on Democrats to "stand together, pull together, and work together" and urged progressive Republicans to join them. The political banquets of the day were part lovefest and part endurance test, and it was two in the morning when Bryan rose to eviscerate the "Plunderbund," as he called the combination of combinations. He still had the crowd with him when the clock struck three, and the cheers rolled on and on as he wound his way to the end with a few rousing lines from Byron:

> *The dead here have been awaken'd—shall I sleep?*
> *The World's at war with tyrants—shall I crouch?*
> *The harvest's ripe—and shall I pause to reap?*
> *I slumber not; the thorn is in my Couch;*
> *Each day a trumpet soundeth in mine ear,*
> *Its echo in my heart—*

4

Against All Odds

The winner of the 1912 Democratic presidential nomination would need the votes of two-thirds of the delegates to the national convention. In most states, the party's voting would begin in caucuses and state party conventions, but for the first time, thirteen states would hold Democratic presidential primaries, an innovation long advocated by the most progressive wings of both major parties. The hope was that if the people chose candidates in primaries, the bosses would lose their hold on presidential politics.

As the electioneering began, Wilson's campaign was operating mainly on the generosity of his Princeton friends—his old classmates and young William F. McCombs. After he choreographed Wilson's tour of the West, McCombs had opened a small office in New York to mail Wilson's speeches to newspapers from coast to coast. McCombs also collected the names and addresses of 147,000 progressives around the country—a base of people who could help Wilson in the primaries and, if all went well, in the general campaign. The progressives of the era were a loose collection of reform-minded optimists, Republicans as well as Democrats, who had been working through hundreds of organizations to cure a host of societal ills, from the concentration of wealth and the exploitation of labor to racial injustice and living conditions in the slums. Recalling the energy and optimism of the era, the progressive journalist William Allen White wrote that 1912 was a moment when forward-thinking Americans coalesced around the idea of using the president and the Congress to end the reign of the plutocrats and pass laws that would make the federal government "an agency of human welfare. Lord, how we did like that phrase." White and his fellow progressives believed that if they could send enough like-minded representatives to Washington, they would get the laws needed to heal the body politic.

The spadework done by McCombs and the success of the Western tour led Wilson to think that he could win the primaries. He knew he could make an excellent case for his ideas, and he hoped that if he made it directly to the people, they would carry him to victory. Oratory would always be Wilson's weapon of choice. Wilson also reasoned that if he kept his distance from the bosses and party hacks, he would not be beholden to them.

Pleasant as it might have been for Wilson to imagine that oratory had won him the governorship, it is unlikely that he or any other novice could have succeeded without the progressive tidal wave of 1910 and the power of the Smith machine. A year later, with Smith working against him, Governor Wilson had not been able to conjure a Democratic victory out of pure oratory. Nor had oratory carried the day in his political battles at Princeton. Twice he had gone on the road to ask Princeton clubs for their support in his battles with the trustees, and twice he had been beaten back. Although the losses bothered Wilson, they did not rattle his confidence in the power of oratory.

In his pursuit of delegates, Wilson traveled to eighteen states to speak to the people. They cheered lustily wherever he appeared, but his competitors regularly bested him in the primaries. They had the support of local politicians, most of whom were strangers to Wilson, and they shrewdly avoided the primaries they knew they would lose. In Georgia and Florida, Wilson hoped that his Southern roots would give him an edge over Champ Clark of distant Missouri. But Clark was not even on the ballot; he had ceded the Deep South to Oscar Underwood, a congressman from Alabama. Underwood stayed out of the contests in and around Missouri, and Governor Judson Harmon of Ohio monopolized his region but steered clear of Clark's and Underwood's territories. Standing alone against favorite sons, Wilson took drubbing after drubbing.

Wilson suspected that Wall Street had ganged up on him, but when told that he needed more friends in the Democratic Party, he hastened to Washington to meet with a dozen senators and thirty-odd congressmen. Hoping to win the Illinois primary, he spoke four times in Chicago and whistle-stopped up and down the state, making twenty-odd speeches from the train, on courthouse steps, and in halls packed with cheering audiences. He was stunned when Clark, who had not even set foot in Illinois, beat him three to one. The state's Democratic establishment knew Clark, and they were old hands at getting out the vote.

Focused on replacing the bosses' choice with the people's choice, the progressives who were making primaries a fixture of presidential politics did not see that they were replacing one set of hurdles with another. Primaries prolonged the physical ordeal of campaigning, and the exorbitant cost of a national primary campaign increased the chances that the successful candidate would owe his soul to one wing or the other of the moneyed class. As *The Atlantic Monthly* explained in a long-winded sentence: "Willingness on the part of adequate men to serve the public in office is rare enough at best, and willingness on the part of adequate men to undergo a protracted and necessarily expensive campaign of personalities with Tom, Dick, and Harry for the right to undergo another protracted and expensive campaign for the right to serve the public in office is more than can be expected normally except from those at once very rich and very patriotic." Wilson did not complain about the physical strain but was dismayed by the small number of votes cast in the primaries. "Possibly the people will wake up later to the significance of the whole thing," he wrote an old friend, "but for the present there seems to be extraordinary lethargy and indifference."

As Clark's victories piled up, Wilson wore a confident mask in public but privately began to say that he wanted to drop out. "He intimated it more than once," McCombs wrote in his account of the campaign. "He thought it was too much to call on his friends to do." McCombs persuaded him that his friends would rather lose than quit in the middle of a fight. Wilson's stock rose briefly with triumphs in Pennsylvania and Oregon, then plunged with Clark's wins in Massachusetts and Washington. After two more losses, in early May, it was rumored that Wilson had suffered a physical collapse. In fact, he was in bed with a bad cold. But the rumor had many grains of truth. Under pressure, Wilson often suffered from digestive upsets severe enough to land him in bed, and "a bad cold" was often the explanation given to the public.

Though Wilson quickly recovered, his presidential prospects dwindled day by day. Clark won the primaries in Maryland and California. Harmon, as expected, took Ohio. Toward the end of May, with nothing to lose, Wilson made a frontal assault on big business, confronting five hundred oligarchs at the annual dinner of the Economic Club of New York. Wilson the prosecutor charged them with crushing the hopes of the have-nots, manipulating financial markets, corrupting government, and making a mockery of American ideals. Wilson the historian chronicled the origins and the course of the trouble, Wilson the statesman explained why a modern government could not stand apart from business affairs, and Wilson the preacher held out the possibility of redemption. The speech had the urgency of a last lecture, and it laid out the two great questions that the presidential candidates of 1912 would have to answer: how should the excesses of large-scale capitalism be reined in, and who should hold the reins?

The problems were nearly a century old, Wilson said. They had begun with a tariff that promised to raise revenue for the government and foster its growth by protecting American industry from foreign competition. The government became dependent on tariff revenue, and manufacturers increased the dependency by demanding ever-higher walls of protection. The legislator disinclined to play along was likely to meet a fierce, well-funded opponent in the next election. Had wages kept pace with rising prices, few Americans would have minded the high tariff, but the disparity between rich and poor steadily widened, and while shareholders grew rich, the tariff cost the typical American family dearly—more than 10 percent of its income, on average.

The public was increasingly uneasy about the concentration of power in the business world, Wilson said. Bankers sat on the boards of railroads, railroad men sat on the boards of commodities companies, and so on. "I do not suspect that any man has deliberately planned these things," he said, but these interlocking directorates had created "so extraordinary a concentration in the control of business in this country that the people are afraid that there will be a concentration in the control of government." And control was the issue. "Do not get impatient, therefore, gentlemen, with those who go about preaching, 'We must return to the rule of the people.' All they mean . . . is that we must consent to let a majority into the game."

The socialism dreaded by the American ruling class was, in Wilson's view, a logical reaction to the present state of affairs. "If you want to oust socialism you have got to propose something better. It is a case, if you will allow me to fall into the language of the vulgar, of 'put up or shut up.' . . . Many of you do know what is going on. You know what part is wrong and what is right, if you have not lost your moral perspective, and you know how the wrong can be stopped."

Government could not allow business to police itself, Wilson said. It was the business of the businessman to further his own interests, but it was the business of government to make policy in the interest of all citizens. Wilson conceded that government might not do a perfect job of regulating business, and he warned that government officials would err unless they were properly instructed by the business world. But, he said, "they must go forward whether instructed or not." Besides insisting that Washington serve as watchdog, Wilson proposed that the laws be rewritten in a way that would open the gates of opportunity to all so that

> in some distant day, men shall look back to our time and say that the chief glory of America was not that she was successfully set up in a simple age when mankind came to begin a new life in a new land, but that, after the age had ceased to be simple, when the forces of society had come into hot contact, when there was bred more heat than light, there were men of serene enough intelligence, of steady enough self-command, of indomitable enough power of will and purpose to stand up once again and say: "Fellow citizens, we have come into a great heritage of liberty, our heritage is not wealth, our distinction is not that we are rich in power, our boast is, rather, that we can transmute gold into the lifeblood of a free people."

The gentlemen of the Economic Club gave Wilson a huge ovation. He had dressed them down, but so what? He was about to be returned to the obscurity whence he came.

Wilson carried the last two primaries, in New Jersey and South Dakota, but not because momentum had suddenly shifted in his direction. He had run unopposed in New Jersey, and he had won South Dakota by a scant 419 votes. In mid-June, when the Wilsons moved out to the Governor's Cottage for the summer, Woodrow was sure that his run for the presidency was over. "Just between you and me," he wrote Mary Peck, "I have not the least idea of being nominated, because . . . the outcome is in the hands of the professional, case-hardened politicians who serve only their own interests and who know that I will not serve them except as I might serve the party in general. I am well and in the best of spirits. I have no deep stakes involved in this game."

Writing to his friend Cleve Dodge, who had already put up thousands of dollars for Wilson's campaign, Wilson admitted his disappointment: "sometimes when I see vast sums of money poured out against me, with fatal success, and it begins to look as if I must merely sit on the sidelines and talk as a mere critic of the game I understand so intimately, throw all my training away and *do* nothing, well, I do not repine, but I grow a little sad." His whole life was in the game, and he was pained by the turn it had taken.

The newspapermen following Wilson were more optimistic. They had begun calling the Governor's Cottage "the Little White House," and by June 15, when the Wilsons arrived, the first of a half-dozen press tents had been pitched on the lawn. The Democratic convention, in Baltimore, would not open for ten days, but the reporters wanted to watch the governor and coax him into sharing his thoughts on every little twist in the presidential race. In Chicago, where the Republicans had convened to bestow their nomination on President Taft, Theodore Roosevelt had just quit the GOP and stormed off to form a new party. Did Governor Wilson have any comment? The governor did not. That night, Roosevelt told an audience of thousands that the new National Progressive Party was a necessity because Republicans were turning the country into a plutocracy. "We stand at Armageddon, and we battle for the Lord," Roosevelt thundered. Would Governor Wilson care to comment? No, except in private, where he said, "Good old Teddy—what a help he is!" and entertained his family by chanting the Armageddon line in Roosevelt's high-pitched staccato. Roosevelt could not win but was sure to bleed millions of votes from the Republicans.

Although pleased by the Republican split, Wilson was still torn about his own part in coming events. Winning the nomination would be gratifying, but in a letter to Mary he confessed his devout wish to escape. He did not dread the burden of high office, he wrote her; what depressed him was the thought of all the trivia and distractions he would have to endure—hateful work that counted for nothing. Then, as if embarrassed by his petulance, he gave her a happier reading of his emotional state: "underneath, deep down, my soul is quiet." If Roosevelt was the Lord's warrior, Wilson was His faithful servant, held steady by the conviction that his fate would be ordained in heaven, not Baltimore.

Wilson's managers, William F. McCombs and William Gibbs McAdoo, the entrepreneur who built the first rail tunnels under the Hudson River, were men of littler faith. While Wilson waited and trusted, they left nothing to chance. McCombs went to Baltimore early to hone their tactics for the convention floor, and McAdoo sped to Chicago to take the pulse of William Jennings Bryan. In town to cover the Republican convention for a newspaper syndicate, Bryan would go on to Baltimore in three capacities: journalist, Nebraska delegate, and party patriarch. It was also possible that he would angle for one more presidential nomination.

The days in Chicago had been a reckoning of sorts for Bryan. It was here, at the Democratic National Convention of 1896, that he had delivered his great jeremiad, warning the predators of Wall Street that they were doomed because America would not consent to be crucified upon a cross of gold. Now fifty-two, Bryan ought to have been at the pinnacle of his political career, and 1912 ought to have been his year. His call for a government that would take on the Plunderbund, a cause that had sounded like political extremism when he began, was finally at dead center. But his three failed presidential campaigns had put him out of the running.

McAdoo found Bryan in his hotel suite, shirt-sleeved and sitting at an open window in hopes of catching a breeze from Lake Michigan. It was only eight-thirty in the morning, but Bryan was already surrounded by suppliants. When McAdoo introduced himself, Bryan escorted him out to the corridor for a private talk. He explained that as a member of the Nebraska delegation, he was pledged to Champ Clark, at least on the first ballot. But after that he would feel free to vote his conscience and, he said, "if, during the course of the convention, anything should develop to convince me that Clark cannot or ought not to be nominated, I shall support Governor Wilson."

McAdoo caught a train for Baltimore and spent much of the trip reading newspaper predictions of the death of the Wilson movement. The prophets' case rested on the fact that Clark was coming to the convention with 450 delegates, Wilson with only 324. McAdoo bored in on another set of numbers: Republicans chose their nominee by a simple majority, but Democrats required a majority of two-thirds, or 726 of the 1,088 delegates. The gap between 324 and 450 was smaller than the gap between 450 and 726, and McAdoo thought that with the right kind of missionary work among the delegates, he and McCombs could stop Clark.

The Democratic convention, which opened on Tuesday, June 25, turned out to be as contentious, sweaty, and peculiar as its Republican counterpart, and while the Democrats did not end in a fatal schism, it seemed as if their convention would never end at all. After the seventeenth ballot, Wilson joshed with the reporters at Sea Girt about being nominated just after the 175th ballot. The convention dragged on for more than a week in sessions that seldom adjourned before midnight and once lasted till breakfast. Delegates trapped day after day in the hotbox of the armory began disappearing for naps on the grass. Many ran out of money. After seven days and forty-two ballots failed to produce a nominee, the Los Angeles Times carried a testy headline: "Democrats in a Stupor."

Party leaders tried to keep moving toward a decisive vote but were stalled again and again by Bryan. The champion of party harmony six months earlier, Bryan was now in a pugnacious mood. To one reporter covering both conventions, Bryan seemed older, paler, and sterner than he had been a few days before in Chicago. Whether he was secretly scheming for the nomination is still subject to debate, but his campaign against the party's reactionaries was waged in the open, probably with the aim of dominating the news from Baltimore. No one was better than Bryan at rousing the moral indignation of Americans west of the Alleghenies, a constituency known to Eastern reporters as "mother and the cornfields." Bryan knew that once roused, these plain folk, thousands upon thousands of them, would flood their delegates with high-minded telegrams.

Parliamentary squabbling delayed the start of the balloting until almost midnight on Thursday, the third day of the convention. Alabama, first in the alphabet, nominated its favorite son, Oscar Underwood. Next came Arkansas, which yielded to neighboring Missouri, home of Champ Clark, whose name touched off cheers and parades lasting sixty-five minutes. Sometime after two in the morning, New Jersey nominated Wilson and set off a demonstration that his followers kept going for ten minutes longer than Clark's. Ohio nominated Harmon, and it was well after sunup when the results of the first ballot were announced: 440-1/2 for Clark, 324 for Wilson, 148 for Harmon, and 117-1/2 for Underwood. The rest went to a scattering of favorite sons.

McAdoo found McCombs sobbing on his bed, sure that all his work had been for nothing. McAdoo tried to persuade McCombs that Wilson could still win, but McCombs was inconsolable. McAdoo's optimism was rooted in a poll that McCombs himself had taken before the convention. He had asked the delegations that were pledged to other candidates how they thought they would vote if their man fell out of the running. Most favored Wilson. With that in mind, McAdoo and the best-organized Wilson supporters, the Pennsylvania and Texas delegations, had devised a strategy for wooing these Wilson-second men. Texans and Pennsylvanians paired up and each pair worked a delegation amenable to Wilson. Men were also assigned to walk the aisles after each ballot to talk with the Wilson point man in each delegation and try to get a sense of how the delegation might vote on the next ballot.

In Friday's balloting, Clark and Wilson each picked up a handful of votes until late at night, on the tenth ballot, when Boss Charles Murphy of New York shifted his delegation's 90 votes from Harmon to Clark. Clark's tally shot from 452 to 556, giving him the first simple majority of the convention. Wilson was stuck at 350. The Clark forces cheered their lungs out and paraded around the armory, wrapped a flag around the speaker's eighteen-year-old daughter, and cheered even louder as she was marched around on the shoulders of her father's friends. The candidate who reached the halfway mark first had gone on to win the nomination at the last sixteen Democratic conventions.

Convinced that Wilson could not win, McCombs telephoned him early the next morning to say it was time to release his delegates. "So, McCombs, you feel it is hopeless?" Wilson asked. McCombs did. Ellen, who was listening to Woodrow's end of the conversation, was in tears, but Woodrow was the epitome of the self-mastered man. "After all, it is God's will, and I feel that a great load has been lifted from my shoulders," he told her. He promised her a vacation in Wordsworth's corner of England as soon as his term as governor expired. Then he composed a message authorizing McCombs to release his delegates. When he joined the family at breakfast, he was amused to see that the morning's mail had brought a catalogue from a coffin maker.

The phone rang again. McAdoo was on the line. He had just learned of McCombs's call to Sea Girt, and he was livid. Yes, Clark had the New York vote, McAdoo said. And yes, Clark had more than half the delegates. But Wilson was holding his own. To McAdoo the conclusion was obvious: Clark had peaked. Wilson decided to go a few more rounds.

Clark's strength diminished inch by inch on the eleventh, twelfth, and thirteenth ballots, and on the fourteenth, when the roll call of the states reached Nebraska, Bryan rose to announce that he could not vote for Clark. Nebraskans had chosen Clark in the primary, Bryan said, but they had done so with the understanding that Clark stood with progressive Democrats. But as long as Boss Murphy of Tammany Hall stood with Clark, Bryan said, "I shall withhold my vote from Mr. Clark." He cast his vote for Nebraska's second choice, Woodrow Wilson, and declared that if Tammany later shifted its ninety votes to Wilson, Wilson, too, would lose the support of William Jennings Bryan.

Bryan's move set off two hours of cheers, boos, and fistfights. Fearing for his safety, the Texas delegates moved in as bodyguards. But as often happened in the public life of William Jennings Bryan, the theatrics had slight effect. The fourteenth ballot shifted the balance by only one tenth of one percent. Enraged by the suggestion that he was beholden to any group, Clark demanded that Bryan either retract or prove his allegation. Bryan refused. When Bryan's switch to Wilson was not followed by mass defections from Clark, many in the armory suspected that Bryan was merely prolonging the deadlock in hopes of forcing the convention to turn to him.

Word that Wilson had finally overtaken Clark clattered into the telegraph machine at Sea Girt on Monday afternoon. Twenty reporters shouting the news bounded into the house, where they found the paterfamilias reciting a limerick to his wife and daughters. He received their bulletin with

maddening composure. "That's the stuff," he said, and resumed his recitation. The reporters threw a gentlemanly tantrum. For a week, they told
the governor, they had played the game his way, writing pretty little stories
about the sweeping lawns at the Little White House, the play of the moon on
the surf, the cheerful thwack-thwack of balls on the tennis court, the governor's departures for the golf links. There was no scenery left to paint and no
more to say about the equanimity of the Wilson family. Would the governor
please show some excitement?

Wilson thought for a moment, smiled, and offered a suggestion: "You
might put it in the paper that Gov. Wilson received the news that Champ
Clark had dropped to second place in a riot of silence."

Wilson was right not to celebrate. After another marathon day—fifteen
ballots—he led 494 to 430 but was miles from the 726 needed for the nomination. For the first time, though, the momentum had been with Wilson
all day, a change that visibly perturbed Bryan. The convention adjourned at
1:00 a.m., and by two accounts, Bryan spent most of the recess between the
Monday and Tuesday sessions waging an eleventh-hour campaign on his
own behalf. One account is in McCombs's memoir, the other in a biography of Wilson by the journalist William Allen White. McCombs's book is
marred by errors and a few outright fabrications, but his portrait of Bryan as
a man at the end of his tether is corroborated by White's version.

McCombs claimed that he was asked to call on Bryan at his hotel, where
he found him in a grim mood and a brown undershirt, baggy trousers, and
slippers. Bryan stated his business, with his index finger pressed into Mc-
Combs's chest. "McCombs," he said, "*you* know that Wilson cannot be
nominated. *I* know that Clark cannot be nominated. You must turn your
forces to a progressive Democrat like me." McCombs was deferential but
expressed his loyalty to Wilson and left. "Mr. Bryan was in a rage," he wrote.

White's informant was George Harvey of *Harper's Weekly,* who said that
Bryan asked to see him on Tuesday morning. The two spoke privately, in
Bryan's bathroom, "each with a foot on the tub, and Bryan proposed to Col-
onel Harvey that he pass the word to the friends of Clark to propose the
adjournment of the convention for thirty days," White wrote. It seems that
Bryan considered Clark a corpse, figured that the adjournment would turn
Wilson into a corpse, and believed that the Democrats would then turn to
William Jennings Bryan.

Harvey did not pass the word, and on Tuesday, July 2, at 3:30 p.m., New
York boarded the Wilson bandwagon, on the forty-sixth and last ballot. Wilson carried the convention with 890 of the 1,088 votes.

Forty-five minutes before the final vote was in, Wilson had received a telephone call with a connection so poor that he could not identify the speaker or hear all that was said. But he gathered that his nomination was imminent, and he went upstairs to tell Ellen that they would not be going to Wordsworth country anytime soon. When they came down arm in arm, Ellen was beaming, and a reporter detected "a suspicious moisture in the governor's eyes," along with "strain under perfect control." Wilson felt honored and intensely aware of his new duties, he said. "I hope with all my heart that the party will never have reason to regret it."

A few hours earlier, he had gone over to the telegraphers' tent to explain his uncommunicativeness during the week. Watching the votes accumulate in his column, he said, he had grown more and more aware of the responsibilities that lay ahead of him. Poor Woodrow Wilson. Defeat pained him, and victory brought no thrill. It was as if he feared that the gods would punish him for the sin of pride. The Democratic Party had just crowned him with its highest honor, and he was weighed down by the same dreary sense of responsibility that had overtaken him thirty years before, when his first book was published.

Ellen and the girls were more ebullient. They smiled and smiled. They embraced one another jointly and severally, and Jessie, who had recorded the results of every ballot, was clapping with delight. Nell divulged that the family had been excited all week. "Papa was excited, too," she told a reporter, "and it was only his marvelous willpower that kept him from shouting it."

Back in Baltimore, the Democrats stayed in the armory to approve the party's platform and nominate a vice president. Wilson hoped to run with Underwood, but Underwood had no intention of giving up his power in the House of Representatives, where he chaired the Ways and Means Committee. A smooth-talking Texan was deputized to telephone Wilson and say that the convention leaned toward Thomas Riley Marshall, governor of Indiana. Wilson, who had met Marshall, protested that he was a "small-caliber" man. The Texan countered that Marshall was a skilled campaigner and would help Wilson win Indiana, which typically voted Republican. Marshall was nominated at 1:56 a.m., and the delegates were at last free to go home.

The New York Times, long suspicious of Bryan's motives, expressed astonishment that a novice like Wilson had prevailed over Bryan. The editors considered Wilson "one of the ablest men in the country" but cautioned that he could not win unless he carried more than the Democrats' long-solid South. "[I]f the people of Michigan and Iowa and Indiana and Pennsylvania will vote in November as their delegates have been shouting here . . . there need be no fear of the result. But will they?"

5

A New Freedom

While Theodore Roosevelt stood at Armageddon and battled for the Lord, while Eugene V. Debs and his Socialist Party called for the abolition of capitalism, while William Howard Taft marched under the limp banner of IT IS BETTER TO BE SAFE THAN SORRY, Woodrow Wilson promised to level the economic playing field. In his acceptance speech, he noted that the United States had grown immensely rich. But to what end? he asked. "Prosperity? Yes, if by prosperity you mean vast wealth no matter how distributed." The financial struggle of the average American of 1912 was the great issue of the election, and the great question before the voters was, What should government do about it?

There had been no presidential contest more critical since the one in 1860, which had propelled four-year-old Tommy Wilson into the manse to ask what the stranger in the street had meant when he said Lincoln had been elected and there would be war. The house was again divided, this time between the rich and everyone else, and if the gaping disparity was unlikely to sunder the Union, it nevertheless corroded the country's belief in itself as the most democratic nation on earth. America was supposed to be a place where "the strong could not put the weak to the wall," Wilson said, and unless she lived up to her ideals, she would lose the right to hold her head high.

President Taft defended his record and assured the country that the economic machinery needed no more than a tweak. His minimalism appealed only to the most conservative Republicans, and two months before Election Day he wrote his wife, "I think I might as well give up so far as being a candidate is concerned. There are so many people in the country who don't like me."

It was true. "The country will have none of him," Woodrow Wilson wrote his friend Mary early in the summer. "But just what will happen, as between Roosevelt and me, with party lines utterly confused and broken, is all guess work." Wilson worried that he would seem colorless next to the pyrotechnic Roosevelt, who was still loved by Americans of all descriptions. "He is a real, vivid person, whom they have seen and shouted themselves hoarse over and voted for, millions strong," Wilson wrote. "I am a vague, conjectural personality, more made up of opinions and academic prepossessions than of human traits and red corpuscles."

When Roosevelt bellowed that he felt as strong as a bull moose and pledged to give his all to his new National Progressive Party, Wilson said without embarrassment, "I haven't a Bull Moose's strength." Roosevelt would travel north, south, east, and all the way west to the Pacific, speaking in thirty-eight states. Wilson hopscotched around the Northeast and the Midwest, ventured no farther west than Colorado, and did not put so much as a toe in the South, which was sure to vote Democratic. Free to follow his own wishes, Wilson would have done even less. He loathed the idea of repeating himself to audience after audience, feared that his health would give out, and doubted that his exertions would net any more votes than he could get by making a few substantive speeches and letting the newspapers do the rest. But McCombs and McAdoo insisted that he tour. Most Americans had never laid eyes on a doctor of philosophy, and only a few had lived long enough to remember the last presidential nominee born in the South (California's John C. Fremont, a native of Savannah, who had run in 1856).

Wilson made more than seventy major speeches during the campaign. Wherever he went, thousands came out to have a look at him—more than 175,000 in a single week. They saw a rather plain fellow—fifty-five years old, not quite six feet tall, a bit too thin. His chestnut-brown hair was graying, and the odd combination of his pensive expression and his golfer's tan gave him the look of a bookworm who had been made to play outdoors. Many who met him in close quarters were struck by his inquiring blue-gray eyes, hard in some lights but kind when he smiled. When tense, he sometimes left an unfortunate impression. The journalist William Allen White, a genial man, recalled that when he was introduced to Wilson, "the hand he gave me to shake felt like a ten-cent pickled mackerel in brown paper."

Wilson was at his best on a stage. He had studied elocution as diligently as any actor and without seeming to raise his voice could make himself heard by a crowd of fifteen thousand even in a hall with poor acoustics. A genius at the harmonics of political speech, he could easily work idealism and self-interest into the same chord, and he had the rare ability to stir emotion even as he appealed to reason. As the literary critic Edmund Wilson pointed out in the 1920s, Woodrow Wilson's speeches were often lackluster on the page but "magnificently successful" when delivered; his voice was "quiet, well-mannered and beautifully distinct, with an edge that made his words seem incisive. He had just enough of a Southern accent and a grace and ease learned in the South to make one forget his square face and rather rigidly looming figure; and . . . a persuasiveness that was almost hypnotic. He gave the impression of a deep conviction and burning zeal, under imperturbable control."

To Woodrow Wilson, oratory was "the greatest power granted unto man" and the sine qua non of great leadership. The oratorical statesman never spoke over people's heads or proposed drastic change or presented unfamiliar ideas. He spoke common sense uncommonly well. He was also a keen observer, "a sort of sensitive dial registering all forces that move upon society." Once registered, the forces could be rightly interpreted by any leader worthy of the name, explained in his speeches to the people, and used to persuade their elected representatives to make government responsive to the collective will. As he had written years earlier, "There are men to be moved. How shall [the statesman] move them? He supplies the power; others supply the materials upon which that power operates. It is the *power* which dictates, dominates: the materials yield. Men are as clay in the hands of the consummate leader." Oratory was the wheel on which the clay was worked.

For more than a decade, senators and congressmen beholden to big business had done their shameless best to obscure the connections between the tariff, the trusts, and the banks. The tariff had been sold as the protector of American jobs, monopoly's economies of scale were said to reduce the cost of living, and the bankers who lent only to the privileged few presented themselves as bulwarks against folly and catastrophe.

Wilson blew away the smoke. Tariff, trusts, banks—he treated them all as causes of the hardship felt by everyone but the rich. The tariff enabled American manufacturers to sell their own goods at inflated prices, monopolies stifled potential rivals, and banks denied credit to new businesses in order to protect their investments in monopolies, Wilson said. "We naturally ask ourselves, how did these gentlemen get control of these things? Who handed our economic laws over to them?" Not the people, he said. "The high cost of living is arranged by private understanding."

Roosevelt, whose analysis was similar, prescribed two new commissions of experts, one to regulate the trusts and one to see that labor got its fair share of the high profits thrown off by the tariff. Courteously but firmly, Wilson disagreed. The experts who worked for the monopolists would easily manipulate the experts on the commission, and the idea of regulating monopoly was absurd, Wilson said. Monopoly was illegal. It needed destruction, not regulation. He would raze the trusts with laws giving all businesses equal access to markets and credit.

Roosevelt claimed that his new National Progressive Party occupied the sensible middle ground between Republicans who would do nothing and Democrats who, by doing too much, would throttle the goose laying the golden eggs. Wilson accused the monopolists and protectionists of being sissies, the Republicans of coddling the sissies, and the Progressives of being Republicans in all but name. In his judgment, the tariff had turned powerful American manufacturers into weaklings "afraid to venture out into the great world on their own merits and on their own strength." Look at them, he said: "paralyzed by timidity" and "tied to the apron strings of the government at Washington."

Wilson gravitated toward large ideas, and his large idea in 1912 was brought to him by Louis D. Brandeis, the son of Jewish Czech immigrants. Born in 1856, he was a Kentuckian who never lost his Southern accent. After graduating from Harvard Law School at twenty, with high honors, he joined a law firm in Boston, where his suits against railroads and other corporations led him to study the mismatch between commonsense morality and the privileges enshrined in corporate law. His success in the courtroom and his formidable skill as a polemicist infuriated New England's business establishment, which retaliated by turning a cold shoulder. At the Dedham Polo Club, Brandeis was left to "flock by himself," one Brahmin reported to another; "he ceased to frequent the Club—and his absence was not regretted."

By the time Brandeis was in his mid-thirties, he was earning more than $50,000 a year and had accumulated a fortune of $2 million. With his family amply provided for, he scaled back his legal practice to devote more time to issues of economic justice, and at the time he and Wilson met, Brandeis was studying the cabal between the banks and the trusts. The big banks were lending to the trusts, investing in the trusts, and sitting on the boards of the trusts, a state of affairs that gave the banks every incentive to collude with the trusts in crushing their competitors. The banks often did their part simply by depriving new enterprises of capital. Brandeis persuaded Wilson that it made sense to regulate competition instead of monopoly. If the government passed laws creating truly free markets, it could stand back as long as competition remained open to all. Wilson was soon painting the picture in black and white: Roosevelt's way meant "industrial absolutism," his own would bring "industrial liberty."

After a few exchanges with Brandeis in late August, Wilson committed himself to an ambitious program that would banish monopoly, expand access to credit, and speedily reduce tariff rates. His was a campaign for freedom, he said: freedom from the "thralldom of monopoly," from the favoritism embedded in the tariff, from the strangulating grip of special interests, from all the powers that "have set us in a straitjacket to do as they pleased." By October, he was calling his program the New Freedom, which he described as the old freedom "revived and clothed in the unconquerable strength of modern America." He aimed for a restoration of "absolutely free opportunity," he said, with laws that would make it possible for individuals to prosper on their merits.

Roosevelt, architect of the New Nationalism, denounced the New Freedom as "a queer kind of Toryism," by which he meant that it would crimp the powers of the federal government and return the country to the days when states' rights and property rights took precedence over human rights. Roosevelt argued that an industrialized country needed a powerful central government to ensure that the strong did not exploit the weak or otherwise abuse the public interest. Wilson's talk of regulating competition struck Roosevelt as airy, and he warned that it would "leave unchecked the colossal embodied privileges of the day."

Wilson countered with a warning: Roosevelt's New Nationalism, with its powerful federal government, would curtail individual freedom. "The minute you are taken care of by the government, you are wards, not independent men," Wilson said.

Both Wilson and Roosevelt ignored Debs. An Indiana native who spent much of his life as a railway worker and union official, Debs had gone to jail in 1895 for defying federal authorities seeking to end a strike at the Pullman Palace Car Company in Illinois. While in jail, Debs read Karl Marx and concluded that capitalism was beyond redemption. He decided that private enterprise should become public enterprise, and he dreamed of accomplishing the transformation peacefully, at the polls. In front of an audience, Eugene Debs radiated so much goodness and character that even skeptics of socialism fell under his spell. One such citizen who was puzzled by his strong attraction to Debs told a reporter, "That old man with the burning eyes actually believes that there can be such a thing as the brotherhood of man. And that's not the funniest part of it. As long as he's around I believe it myself." The speeches of Eugene Debs were well reasoned, well informed, and moving, but something went awry between the lyceum and the ballot box. In 1908, on his third try for the presidency, he had polled no more votes than he had in 1904—about 400,000.

Issues unrelated to the economy barely registered, and when they did arise, the public seemed inclined to side with the newcomer. Roosevelt spoke out strongly in favor of women's suffrage. Wilson did not, yet he would carry five of the six states where women already had the vote. African Americans traditionally supported the party of Lincoln, but with little to show for their decades of loyalty, they opened themselves to other possibilities in 1912. It was time, said the *Afro-American* of Baltimore. "Too many black people have been on one side of the boat." And there was a practical reason to look elsewhere, the editors said: "The poverty of the colored man makes it imperative for him to support the party which takes the least from his pocket, and therefore the Democratic Party should receive his support."

Most black leaders endorsed Wilson in spite of the fact that he was a Democrat born in the South, where the Democratic Party was a powerful force for white supremacy. Wilson assured Bishop Alexander Walters, president of the National Colored Democratic League, that he earnestly wished to see justice done to his colored fellow citizens—"not mere grudging justice, but justice executed with liberality and cordial good feeling." Should he become president, Wilson said, "they may count upon me for absolute fair dealing and for everything by which I could assist in advancing the interests of their race in the United States."

Although the candidates refrained from personal attacks, the personal sometimes threatened to become political, and the campaigns of both Wilson and Roosevelt narrowly escaped derailment. In July, when a court in Massachusetts granted Woodrow Wilson's friend Mary Peck a divorce, the steadfastly Republican *New-York Tribune* put the news on the front page and identified her as "a friend of Governor and Mrs. Woodrow Wilson." It was true, but the item's prominence and the mention of the social connection seemed calculated to cause mischief and raise a titillating question: had Mrs. Peck's friendship with the governor figured in the divorce? One of Roosevelt's confidants shared rumors of a romance, apparently in the hope of using the gossip against Wilson. T.R. instantly cut him off. He did not doubt Wilson's decency, he said, and besides, the mere thought of this prim Presbyterian in the role of swain was absurd. The picture set Roosevelt to laughing so hard that he could barely speak.

At the end of September, Wilson learned that Republicans were whispering about his relationship with Mary, and the account he sent her might be the most panicked and jumbled letter he ever wrote. In one passage he seemed to choke on his thoughts: "It at once came into my mind that this might be an attempt to set gossip afloat, if nothing more, which would, no matter how completely discredited later, abundantly suffice, just at this juncture, to ruin me utterly, and all connected with me. . . ." He caught his breath but still could not think straight. Noting that she was on Nantucket and that he had just spoken in Fall River, he asked, "Is it not from Fall River that the boats ply to Nantucket? I thought that you might have heard of the meeting, and looked eagerly around among the women of the audience in the hope that I might see you there. How jolly, how delightful that would have been! No such luck!" He seemed oblivious to his great luck in *not* seeing her. A meeting at that point might well have sunk his candidacy. When his mind righted itself, he assured her that he was pegging away at the campaign: "There *are* great issues, the greatest imaginable, issues of life and death, as it seems to me, so far as the sound political life of the country is concerned; and therefore I keep heart and strength. The people believe in me and trust me."

William Allen White never warmed to Wilson, but years later, as he was writing a biography of Wilson, someone showed him some of the letters Mrs. Peck had received from the man who signed himself "Your devoted friend." Finding nothing unseemly, White speculated that Wilson's fascination with Mrs. Peck owed much to the fact that she was "something quite outside the Calvin cycle"—a free spirit.

Roosevelt's candidacy was threatened on October 14 by a delusional loner who shot him at close range while he was campaigning in Milwaukee. Roosevelt came literally within an inch of his life: a bullet that might have pierced his lung came to rest in a rib. Taft and Wilson put their campaigns on hold, partly out of a sense of decorum and partly because they feared a backlash if they carried on as Roosevelt lay wounded. William Jennings Bryan, as wily as ever, declared that to suspend the campaign was to let the would-be assassin decide the election. Roosevelt, as wily as Bryan, announced that he agreed with Bryan. The campaign resumed before the month was out.

Taft's campaign was a misery, and the last week was surely the most miserable of all. On October 30, he lost his running mate, Vice President James Sherman, who had been ill for months. Two days later, at the suggestion of his campaign managers, Taft gave a long interview to the *New York World*. He was supposed to tell the full story of his break with Roosevelt, and the *World* was supposed to syndicate the story to newspapers across the country. The idea was to slam Roosevelt hard on the eve of the election. But there was not an ounce of meanness in Taft's 335 pounds, and he could manage no more than a few faintly critical remarks about his old friend. Even that made him blue. At his request, the interview was spiked.

On Election Day, November 5, the Democratic candidate for president of the United States allowed himself to sleep until nine o'clock. After breakfast he walked over to Princeton's firehouse, which had been outfitted as a polling place, and took his spot at the end of the line. At 10:15 a.m., Woodrow Wilson cast ballot 112 for himself and the rest of the Democratic ticket.

In the afternoon, Wilson's bodyguard and two aides accompanied him on a long walk. He was in excellent shape. His fear of buckling under the stress of the campaign had gone unrealized, and he had put on seven needed pounds. Although he appeared unconcerned about the election, his itinerary suggested that he was thinking of little else. For a time he led his companions along a road taken by George Washington's army during the American Revolution. The walking party also made stops to see the Princeton diploma of James Madison and the death mask of Grover Cleveland. One presidential destination might be a coincidence, but three?

By evening, a telegrapher had set up a ticker in Ellen's studio, and nine reporters were working quietly at the large table in the library. Margaret, Jessie, and Nell were home, and Ellen's brother Stockton Axson, two of Woodrow's cousins, and a few close friends had been invited to dinner. When the party moved from the dinner table to the hearth in the living room, Wilson stayed on his feet, warming his back at the fire. He was convivial, amusing, at ease—the self-mastered man.

At ten o'clock, the governor's chief aide, Joe Tumulty, hollered, "He's elected, Mrs. Wilson!" Ellen reached for Woodrow's hand, and Nell watched the gaiety drain from his face as he took in the news. While the reporters elbowed their way to Wilson's side, Nell fled to the calm of the upstairs and opened a window. The university's bell was ringing, and scores of townspeople were hurrying toward the house. Among them was a contingent of Princeton men marching by torchlight. Wilson went out to the porch, climbed onto a chair, and stood in silence while the crowd settled. His face, red in the torchlight, looked "utterly, utterly unfamiliar," Nell thought. "I had a sense of awe, almost of terror—he was no longer the man with whom we had lived in warm sweet intimacy—he was no longer my father. These people, strangers who had chosen him to be their leader, now claimed him. He belonged to them."

The president-elect seemed almost as lost. He voiced no joy, and to prime his oratorical pump, he had to borrow from one of his old heroes. "I have no feeling of triumph tonight, but a feeling of solemn responsibility," he said. "I know the great task ahead of me and the men associated with myself." William Gladstone had used almost exactly the same words on becoming prime minister. To the students in the crowd, Wilson said, "I look almost with pleading to you, the young men of America, to stand behind me." He urged them to work quietly for the political change they sought, to accept that success would be long in coming, and to persevere. When he finished, scores of people waited for a turn to shake his hand, and he thanked each of them "for caring so much."

Taft and Roosevelt wired their congratulations, Roosevelt's being memorable for calling attention to the fact that Wilson's victory was a plurality. At 42 percent it was a "great plurality," Roosevelt said, but he was undoubtedly relieved that Wilson had fallen far short of his own commanding majority (56 percent) in 1904. Neither Roosevelt nor Taft saluted the sweep of Wilson's victory: forty of the forty-eight states, 435 of 531 electoral votes, and majorities in both houses of Congress. Roosevelt came in second, with 27 percent, an impressive finish for a candidate whose party was a mere three months old. No incumbent president had ever fared worse than Taft, who won only 23 percent of the vote. In four states, Taft suffered the indignity of finishing behind Debs, who drew 6 percent nationwide. The Socialists had never done better in a presidential election and would never do so well again.

Ever since 1912, historians have said that Roosevelt's candidacy cost Taft the election by splitting the Republican vote. The Republicans were indeed divided, but the deciding factor was Taft's unpopularity: 77 percent of the electorate rejected him. Taft would have made a stronger showing if Roosevelt had not run, but in that case, a sizable share of Roosevelt supporters surely would have chosen Wilson's progressivism over the reactionary Republicanism of 1912. In a Taft-Wilson race, Wilson could have achieved a majority with only a third of the votes that went to Roosevelt. The people did not want Roosevelt *or* Taft. They wanted a change and believed that Wilson would deliver on his promise of a New Freedom, an emancipation from rule by the rich for the rich. No one, not even Wilson, could say precisely how this emancipation would come about, but by their votes the people showed their confidence in Wilson's ability to put government back into their hands. And they believed that when he succeeded, they would, too.

Woodrow Wilson had waged a consistently intelligent, consistently inspiring campaign. Most American newspapers concurred in his diagnosis of the country's ills, considered his prescription sensible, and saw him as well schooled if not well practiced in the art of governing. The emphasis on the president-elect's learning was not misplaced. He had more years of higher education (eight) than any of his White House predecessors, and as a scholar of American and English political institutions, he had thought deeply about what democratic government was, what it ought to do, and how the doing ought to be done.

But as Wilson thought ahead to the presidency, he told a friend that it would be "an irony of fate" if world affairs dominated his presidency, because his scholarship had focused on domestic politics. This offhand remark would be accorded unduly great significance because of the world war and the controversies that followed, controversies that ultimately overwhelmed his presidency. The truth was that he entered the White House with a rich understanding of the role a president might play in foreign relations, an education gleaned largely from close observation of President Theodore Roosevelt, who had steadily enlarged the part played by the United States on the world stage.

The great deficiency in the education of Woodrow Wilson was not in foreign relations but human relations. While he was more socially adept than his self-absorbed father had been, he showed no interest in mastering the arts of friendship, collaboration, and disagreement. Unsuccessful in his romance with Hattie Woodrow, he had pronounced her "heartless." Unsuccessful as a young lawyer, he blamed the law. In neither instance is there evidence that he sought to understand his own part in the failures.

As a member of Princeton's faculty, Woodrow Wilson enjoyed more success than his father had ever known. His classes were oversubscribed, publishers clamored for his work, and he was a favorite on the lecture circuit. As president of Princeton, Wilson had gone on to even greater success and was showered with acclaim. But success is a poor teacher. It discourages analysis and self-examination, and it tempts the successful to overestimate their abilities.

Eight years as president of Princeton and two years as governor had not taught Woodrow Wilson how to deal constructively with opposition or how to make friends. During his presidential campaign, he promised to "take counsel" before making decisions, and at times he would do so, but he would also cling to his preference for acting on his own. And despite the fact that his speeches to alumni had not led to victory in either of his big battles at Princeton, he still believed he would be able to govern the country and win the cooperation of Congress through oratory. When he resigned from Princeton, he acknowledged his hurts and had upsetting dreams about his foes, but there is no evidence that these disturbances led to self-reflection or efforts to change. Instead he had been defiantly proud, writing Ellen, "We have no compromises to look back on, the record of our consciences is clear in this whole trying business. We can be happy, therefore, no matter what may come of it all." What came of it, quite by chance, was the political career he had always wanted. Happenstance allowed him to start near the top of the political ladder, giving him a governorship on his first try and the presidency on his second. What was Woodrow Wilson supposed to learn from that?

6

A President Begins

S worn in at 1:34 p.m. on March 4, 1913, the twenty-eighth president
of the United States delivered an inaugural address that was half civics
lesson, half sermon. Power had passed from the Republicans to the
Democrats, but a party's power mattered little unless the nation used it for
a large purpose, Wilson said. The nation had accumulated great wealth, it
had acquired great "moral force," and its government had become a model
for all peoples who sought to "set liberty upon foundations that will endure." But Americans had been wasting their natural resources, ignoring
the human toll of their industrial might, and contenting themselves with a
government that was too often used to advance private interests at the expense of the public good. "Our great thought has been, 'Let every man look
out for himself, let every generation look out for itself.'" With the change of
government came a vision of American life as a whole: "We see the bad with
the good, the debased and decadent with the sound and vital. . . . Our duty is

to cleanse, to reconsider, to restore, to correct the evil without impairing the good." He pledged that lost ideals would be recovered and injustices would be redressed, but all changes would be accompanied by a "fundamental safe-guarding of property and of individual right."

That night, for the first time in living memory, there was no inaugural ball. A fixture of Washington life since the days of Dolley Madison, the ball had been called off only once—in 1853, by President Franklin Pierce and his wife, who were in mourning. Inaugural balls were largely underwritten by friends of the president, but the use of any federal monies for such a func-tion did not sit well with Woodrow Wilson, and the new first lady thought it vulgar to put the highest office in the land at the center of an occasion so conspicuously commercial.

Wilson had other reasons not to preen. His election had left him 9 per-centage points shy of a popular majority. He was also the first Southerner to live in the White House since Andrew Johnson, who had endeared himself to no one. And the reforms Wilson had promised would pit him against the most powerful men in the country. Small wonder, then, that Wilson had ended his inaugural address with the thought that the day was one of dedica-tion, not of triumph. And small wonder that while the guests at the Wilsons' private inaugural dinner were, in the words of the chief usher of the White House, "bubbling over with joy and all trying to talk at once," the president himself seemed preoccupied and fatigued.

Come morning, though, Wilson seemed rested and robust, and at nine o'clock, after stoking himself on coffee, porridge, and raw eggs in orange juice, he set forth to show the country what sort of president he intended to be. It was customary for new presidents to see the hordes hoping to be appointed to office, but Wilson had decided to skip that task. As he explained to his first visitor, a president needed time for thought and for leisure, so he would concentrate on essentials and delegate everything else. Wilson's break with custom made front pages across the country. In Columbia, South Car-olina, where he had spent much of his boyhood, the headline read, "Seekers After Pie Get Cold Shoulder."

At ten he met briefly with his cabinet, a collective of men he barely knew. The exception was William Jennings Bryan, who had been rewarded with the post of secretary of state. The men at the meeting were pleasantly surprised. The secretary of the interior, Franklin K. Lane, wrote a friend that Wilson was not the "cold nose" he was rumored to be. "He is the most sym-pathetic, cordial, and considerate presiding officer that can be imagined. And he sees so clearly. He has no fog in his brain." The secretary of agriculture, David F. Houston, marveled in his diary that the new president had "no mark of the recruit about him." Wilson conducted the meeting as if he had been president all his life, Houston thought.

At noon the president went back up to the family quarters of the White House for lunch with Woodrow relatives, and shortly after two o'clock he plunged into a reception in the East Room, where he shook 1,123 hands, a performance suggesting that while he would not be running a pie shop, he would not be in seclusion, either.

This day required the new president to make a nod to the rest of the world, and in a move that was both sensible and comfortable, he received the British ambassador, James Bryce. The two had met in 1883, when Wilson was a Johns Hopkins student and Bryce a visiting lecturer. A generation older than Wilson, Bryce was the sort of man the young Wilson had longed to become: don, politician, man of letters. Bryce had written a favorable review of Wilson's first book and borrowed some of its ideas for his own writings.

Toward the end of the afternoon, the president took a ride out to the Washington Monument and back in one of the White House limousines. Wilson had never owned an automobile, but he became a motoring enthusiast as soon as he entered politics. Riding in a car relaxed him—so much so that he frequently drifted off into a nap. Back in his office by five-thirty, Wilson met with his campaign chairman, William F. McCombs, who had hoped to be named secretary of the treasury. When the position went to William G. McAdoo, McCombs asked for a face-saving written statement, Wilson promised him one, and McCombs had come to collect. Wilson was ready. McCombs had been offered a major embassy, the statement said, and Wilson hoped that he would accept.

Once that prickly business was done, the rest of the Democratic National Committee was brought in, and promptly at seven o'clock the president went upstairs to host a dinner for the Wilson side of the family. At eight-thirty he excused himself, went to his study for a look at the day's paperwork, and received a governor for a short visit. He turned in at ten, his usual hour.

Taft had warned Wilson that the White House was the loneliest house in the world, and Wilson felt isolated from the start. It seemed to him that everyone in the capital was on the make night and day, lusting after more power, more influence, more success. Washington changes people, he told Nell. "They either grow or they swell—usually the latter." At times he feared that the man he thought of as Woodrow Wilson had vanished. He felt betwixt, lost somewhere between the self he recognized and the role he played.

Although scores of people came to see him and he shook thousands of hands, these encounters were too fleeting to alleviate his sense of disconnection. During the Wilsons' first three months in Washington, they hosted forty-one receptions and a total of 24,000 guests. As he wrote his friend Mary Allen Hulbert, the former Mrs. Peck, he and Ellen lived "at the beck and call of others (how many, many others!) and almost never have a chance to order our days as we wish, or to follow our own thoughts and devices. The life we lead is one of infinite distraction, confusions,—fragmentary, broken in upon and athwart in every conceivable way." To be alone without fear of interruption, they often resorted to outings in one of the presidential automobiles.

But if he felt disoriented, he looked like a man at the height of his powers. "When I saw him come out of his study and stride down the hall toward us, I noticed that his walk had acquired more than its usual buoyancy," Nell would recall. "His eyes were strikingly clear and bright, and there was a sort of chiseled keenness in his face. He was finer looking in those days than ever before in his life." He was also better dressed. The White House valet, unhappy with the informality of the president's wardrobe, had persuaded Ellen to find a tailor who would make a fresh start. Informed that the process would require numerous fittings, Wilson consented on the condition that the tailor make enough clothes to last through his presidency. By July, in his new white linen suit or his new navy blazer, white trousers, and straw boater, he could have passed as a summering oligarch.

The White House handed over to the Wilsons had been renovated by the Roosevelts and dressed up by the Tafts. By giving the house more softness, Ellen made it feel like a home. In the family quarters, dark walls were brightened with pale grass cloth, pastel paint, and airy wallpaper. Icy-white woodwork was redone in warm ivory. Carpeting was ripped up, floors were refinished, and area rugs were rolled out. Armchairs were reupholstered in gay chintzes, and here and there Ellen used fabrics and quilts made by women in Appalachia. The president's bedroom was redecorated in white and Delft blue.

For the main floor, Ellen ordered white slipcovers, white curtains, and pleated white dimity to cover the dark silk panels on the walls. The animal heads that Roosevelt had put up in the State Dining Room were exiled to the Smithsonian. Only the Oval Office, built by Taft, proved irredeemable. Too new to justify the expense of redecorating, it would remain in the gloom of its olive green velvet draperies, dark paneling, and furniture upholstered in caribou hide stained a dark red.

With her painter's eye and love of flowers, Ellen drew up an ambitious plan for beautifying the White House grounds, but the small congressional appropriation available for such purposes limited her to a garden on either side of the south Portico. Her rose garden lasted until the 1960s, when John F. Kennedy revised it with television cameras in mind. His version included a lawn large enough for a crowd of a thousand.

Before coming to Washington, Ellen had rarely involved herself in public causes. But after learning that thousands of Washington's poor were living without water or electricity in the city's alleys, she lent her time and prestige to a civic group lobbying Congress for a bill to clean up the alleys and move the inhabitants to better housing. She soon had the satisfaction of seeing bills introduced in both the House and the Senate.

The Three Wilson Girls, as the newspapers called them, were expected to contribute to the larger good, and two of them pitched in energetically. Margaret, who was twenty-seven, hosted musicales at the White House and joined a successful campaign to keep Washington's schools open after hours as social centers for adolescents. Jessie had dreaded moving to the White House, where she pictured herself sentenced to four years of small talk at her parents' teas and receptions. At twenty-six, she had been a social worker for five years and wanted only to carry on. With her parents' blessing, she involved herself in the work of the YWCA. Nell, the only Wilson whose soul fattened on parties, resisted when her mother remarked that a woman of twenty-three ought to do more than amuse herself. Ellen persevered until Nell offered herself to a day nursery, where, she confessed, "I was a complete failure."

Woodrows and Wilsons and Axsons came to visit, and one of the president's first cousins, Helen Bones, moved in to assist the first lady's social secretary, Isabella (Belle) Hagner. Belle, who had perfected her role in the Roosevelt and Taft administrations, managed Ellen's schedule and instructed the girls in the ways of Washington society. Belle believed that presidential offspring ought to socialize with an eye on their father's political fortunes, and she advocated a policy of divide and conquer: if they went out en bloc, they would thrill one hostess, but if they split up, they could delight three.

The president was happiest when surrounded by women, and when Belle hinted to his wife and daughter that his circle ought to include a man or two, they shrugged. Belle was one of the first in Washington to notice Wilson's avoidance of powerful men. He collaborated with them when necessary and did not shrink from confrontation, but he did not seek them out for the sake of expanding his power. Nor did he make the spontaneous social overtures that enable a gregarious politician to build goodwill just by being himself.

President Wilson had three male confidants, all of whom were subordinates. Joseph Patrick Tumulty had been at his side since 1910. Tumulty's father, an Irish immigrant who had fought in the Civil War, was a Democratic leader in a Jersey City ward so rough it was called the Bloody Angle, after a stretch of ground where Union and Confederate soldiers had fought hand to hand. The Tumulty family's grocery store became a gathering place for local Democrats, and Joe grew up in their midst. He went on to the local Jesuit college, read law at a local firm, established his own practice, and in 1906, at the age of twenty-seven, won a seat in the State Assembly.

In the White House, Tumulty functioned as Wilson's chief of staff, political advisor, and manager of press relations. He also served as the warm face of a president whose reserve and self-discipline intimidated some people and annoyed others. Everyone liked Joe Tumulty. The White House ran smoothly under his direction, he was unfailingly cordial, and if he could lend a hand, he did. Why not? His boss would need favors, too. Tumulty treated reporters well and, sharing Wilson's belief in the importance of molding public opinion, he took the national pulse daily by scanning newspaper articles clipped by his staff.

Set up in a room adjacent to the Oval Office, Tumulty was the only staff member with unrestricted access to the president. If Wilson had a visitor he did not want to see, Tumulty cut the meeting short by barging in with an allegedly urgent piece of business. Wilson often did his paperwork upstairs in his study and asked his staff and the cabinet to communicate by memo. Even when he was in the Oval Office, he liked Tumulty to submit his questions and suggestions in writing. Typically the memos were sent back with a penciled "No" or "Okeh." Perhaps because he believed that his father had taught him all that could be known about the English language, Wilson insisted that the expression came from an American Indian language and that "Okeh" was the orthodox spelling.

Wilson also permitted himself a friendship with Captain Cary T. Grayson of the U.S. Navy, a physician who had occasionally attended the Roosevelts and Tafts. Taft introduced Grayson to Wilson, and Wilson immediately had him assigned to the White House. Like Tumulty, Grayson was a generation younger than Wilson. He had grown up in Virginia, in a family of doctors, and held degrees in pharmacology as well as medicine. Half an inch shy of five-feet-eight, Grayson had jet-black hair and strong features offset by a welcoming smile. Called to Wilson's bedside on the sixth day of his presidency, Grayson found a patient with a hammering headache and an intestinal upset that he described as "turmoil in Central America." The doctor urged the president to stay in bed for the rest of the day. For the long term he prescribed a change of diet, regular exercise, and more rest. He also emptied Wilson's medicine chest. Soon after Grayson's house call, Wilson told the cabinet that he would absent himself from many of the president's customary social appearances. "While I am not ill, my health is not exceptionally good, and I have signed a protocol of peace with my doctor," he explained. "I must be good."

Wilson had total confidence in his new physician's medical knowledge. He was also attracted to Grayson's Southern courtliness and his skill as a raconteur. Wilson preferred golf to other forms of exercise, and he and Grayson were soon playing several times a week. They went out for their first round on May 31 and over the next six months played ninety times. A cannier politician would have taken along a senator or congressman from time to time, but Wilson balked at enlarging the twosome. His mealtimes were only marginally less exclusive. Grayson was a frequent guest, but the president ate virtually all of his breakfasts, lunches, and dinners alone or with his family. He delegated the social side of his political work to Tumulty, who lunched daily at a nearby hotel with a rotating cast of journalists, politicians, and other men of influence.

No friend would have more sway with Wilson than Edward Mandell House, a slight, dapper man who fulfilled his life's ambition when he became Wilson's confidential advisor. Two years younger than Wilson, House was the son of one of the richest men in Texas. A childhood bout of malaria left House with a permanently weakened constitution and an inability to tolerate summer heat. His career as a self-appointed éminence grise allowed him to make the most of his fascination with politics, his financial independence, and his physical limitations. House had entered his chosen profession in the early 1890s, helping four Democrats win the governorship of Texas. One expressed his thanks by making House an honorary colonel, but House disliked the title and everything else that made him an object of curiosity. He wished to be an insider known only to other insiders.

After a decade in Texas politics, House felt prepared to assist a national figure but had no interest in making himself available to William Jennings Bryan, the only Democrat with a large following as the twentieth century began. Patient as well as rich, House waited him out. For nine years he read history and politics, traveled, and widened his circle of political acquaintances. He wintered in Austin, summered abroad or in New England to escape the Texas heat, and passed much of the rest of the year in New York.

House watched Wilson's ascent and at the end of 1911 wrote him to say that he was already urging Texas Democrats to support his nomination in 1912. House also invited Wilson to New York for a long talk, and both men went away with the intoxicating sensation that they understood each other perfectly. Describing the governor to a confidant, House said, "He is not the biggest man I have ever met, but he is one of the pleasantest and I would rather play with him than any prospective candidate I have seen. From what I had heard, I was afraid that he had to have his hats made to order; but I saw not the slightest evidence of it." Ill for much of 1912, House had played only a minor role in Wilson's campaign but afterward did most of the scouting for cabinet members. When Wilson offered him a cabinet post, House said he preferred to be a minister without portfolio. Endowed with an abundance of self-esteem, House thought of himself as Wilson's peer.

Few incoming presidents had studied government as closely as Woodrow Wilson, who had thought, lectured, and written about it for three decades. In his youth he had seen the president as little more than the vassal of Congress. He could veto an act of Congress, but with enough votes, Congress could override the veto. A president was in charge of foreign relations, but in the 1880s, when Wilson's serious political studies began, the world beyond the Atlantic and the Pacific barely registered in the American mind.

Wilson found the presidency more appealing after 1898, when the Spanish-American War returned foreign relations to center stage. He had watched closely as President Roosevelt made one unprecedented foray after another, and if Wilson did not applaud all he saw, his conception of executive power was undoubtedly enlarged by Roosevelt's insistence that a president could do anything the Constitution did not expressly prohibit.

In 1907, soon after the Democrats of the Northeast began their "Wilson for President" talk, Wilson advanced a view of the chief executive that would have startled his younger self: "His office is anything he has the sagacity and force to make it," he said. "The president is at liberty, both in law and conscience, to be as big a man as he can. His capacity will set the limit; and if Congress be overborne by him, it will be . . . because the president has the nation behind him, and Congress has not." The president was the only official elected by all the people, and once he had their admiration and confidence, "no other single force can withstand him, no combination of forces will easily overpower him," Wilson wrote. And even though the Constitution assigned the legislative domain to Congress, it had authorized the president to recommend that Congress pass measures that he deemed necessary. In short, the president's place was "the vital place of action in the system."

Looking on as the Roosevelt and Taft administrations battled the trusts, Wilson concluded that the increasing concentration of power and wealth in the United States called for a new interpretation of the separation of powers ordained by the Constitution. As he explained in a 1911 interview with *Harper's Weekly,* a modern government needed "a single lever to control the whole complicated machine, so that you can start it by a single motion or stop it by a single motion. . . . We have made a great, complicated machine, and each part separately answers to our hands. But there is no one lever to control the whole machine, therefore it is not controlled at all." Wilson believed that the problem could be solved by putting one person in charge and holding him accountable.

Wilson took all of these concepts to the White House, where he trained his formidable will on becoming as big a president as his sagacity and force could make him. He intended to be the representative of all the people, the vital center of action, the man at the lever of the great machine. He began with a drive to win enactment of his New Freedom and within eighteen months would transform the tax system, expand access to credit, and establish the Federal Reserve Board.

On the advice of his allies in Congress, Wilson pursued his big reforms one at a time. He started with the tariff, an issue that irritated Americans almost as much as it bored them. It caused widespread discontent because it raised the cost of living, but it was also the Treasury's main source of revenue. Congress had agreed on a new source—an income tax—in 1909, but establishing the right of Congress to impose such a tax required a constitutional amendment, which was not ratified until the eve of Wilson's inauguration. Armed with their new authority to impose taxes on any kind of income and their big majority in the House, Democrats were confident that they could at last lower the tariff and devise a tax schedule that would enjoy broad public support.

Within days of his inauguration, Wilson exercised his constitutional power to call a special session of Congress, and a few weeks later he sent word to the Capitol that he would like to address the House and Senate on April 8, the first day of the special session. He was not the first president to deliver a speech to Congress, but he was the first since Thomas Jefferson had abolished the custom on the grounds that such speeches smacked of orders from the throne. (Wilson suspected that the change had been prompted by the fact that Jefferson, for all his eloquence on paper, was a poor public speaker.) Wilson's request was granted, but not without some senatorial grumbling about the return of monarchy.

Washingtonians curious about Wilson's departure from tradition began packing the House galleries around noon. His family attended, as did most members of the cabinet, who came individually because of the president's wish to avoid any hint of a royal procession. Shortly before one o'clock, Wilson entered the House chamber from a door behind the rostrum, shook hands with Vice President Marshall and Speaker Clark, and took his place at the clerk's desk. He struck onlookers as commanding and wholly at ease.

Wilson began by saying that he was glad to have the opportunity to address the Congress and glad to confirm that the president was not a department of the government but "a human being trying to cooperate with other human beings in a common service." He added that he might come back on other occasions but for the moment wished to speak only of the tariff bill. The world's economy had changed, and the tariff made American goods uncompetitive abroad. "Only new principles of action will save us from a final hard crystallization of monopoly and a complete loss of the influences that quicken enterprise and keep independent energy alive," he said. Undoubtedly there would be mistakes as tariff rates were adjusted, but the motives for the reform—eliminating special privilege and promoting prosperity for all—were in his view unassailable.

Barely six minutes after he'd begun, Wilson thanked Congress, bowed again, and exited to somewhat warmer applause. "Whereupon," *The Boston Globe* reported, "diverse and sundry gentlemen of both houses turned to each other and said in effect, if not altogether in words, 'What the h—l?'"

Wilson returned to the Capitol the next day in a motorcade that was a marvel of simplicity: a limousine trailed by two Secret Service agents in a taxi and two policemen on motorcycles. He had invited the Democrats from the Senate's Committee on Finance to meet with him in the President's Room, a chamber rarely used except on inauguration day, when the outgoing president signed the bills passed in the final hours of his administration. Assured that the House would act quickly on tariff reform, Wilson wanted to urge the committee's Democrats to speed the measure through the Senate. His listeners replied that the Senate would do as the Senate thought best.

Two days later a hundred White House correspondents trooped into the East Room for their third press conference with President Wilson. His predecessors had often granted interviews, and sometimes they spoke with several journalists at once, but Wilson was the first to meet regularly with the press corps. The press conferences (sixty-four during his first year in office) gave all reporters access to the president and gave the president an opportunity to command public opinion.

The new president's early dealings with reporters revealed a surprising amount of wishful thinking on his part. At the first press conference, he had asked reporters to be his partners in serving the country, a notion seriously at odds with the independence required for a free press. He also urged them to focus on bringing the opinions of the country to Washington rather than on reporting Washington's news to their readers back home. "You have got to write from the country in and not from Washington out," he said. In this he was extrapolating from his own desire to stay in touch with political sentiment across the country, but Washington correspondents could not write from the country in. They existed for the purpose of sending Washington's news out.

The president's iconoclastic week ended on Saturday night, when he dined out for the first time since taking office. His host was the Gridiron Club, and he used his time at the lectern to explain his visits to the Capitol. The Constitution's checks on the powers of each branch of government had been carried to an extreme, he said. The president and the Congress no longer understood each other, so they were no longer able to work together, and unless that changed, neither he nor they could serve the country well.

The speech to Congress, the meeting in the President's Room, the press conferences, the Gridiron speech—all emanated from Wilson's conviction that the leader who commanded public opinion would command the government. He had dominated the headlines, but editorial reactions were reserved, politicians hesitated to comment, and the press conferences would prove as frustrating to the press as they were to the president. Reporters soon discovered that although Wilson was more available than his predecessors, he was no more forthcoming.

7

Lines of Accommodation

U nlike a British prime minister, an American president does not have a cabinet whose members also sit in the legislature, but Wilson clearly had cabinet government in mind when he assigned Treasury Secretary William G. McAdoo to lobby the Senate and Postmaster General Albert S. Burleson to manage his relations with the House. The Democrats controlled both houses of Congress, but they were a contentious lot. They often split along sectional lines, and one faction could be as conservative as the most reactionary Republicans. Unless Wilson could hold all of them together, the New Freedom would not materialize. McAdoo had demonstrated his political agility in managing Wilson's floor fight at the Democratic National Convention, and Burleson was a seven-term veteran of the House. Working long into the night to win votes for the president's legislation, the two would soothe the anxious, encourage the timid, and cajole the stubborn. In private Wilson called them his "wet nurses."

It fell to Burleson to give the president his first hard lesson in party unity. After sixteen years out of power, the Democrats had an opportunity to replace thousands of Republican appointees. Wilson was eager to fill the ranks with high-caliber progressives, and he informed Burleson that if a first-rate Democrat could not be found, he would appoint a progressive Republican. For two hours Burleson tried to persuade Wilson that it did not matter who served as postmaster of some hamlet in the sticks—except to the locals and their congressman. Wilson would not budge. Burleson tried again: "I know these congressmen and senators. They are mostly good men. If they are turned down, they will hate you and will not vote for anything you want. It is human nature."

Wilson understood human nature but fervently believed that those who enjoyed great power had a duty to rise above self-interest and act for the common good. Throughout his career he had held his temper, and he had stayed true to his ideals even when they cost him the presidency of his beloved Princeton. But after resisting Burleson for a week, Wilson gave in and abandoned the field. Burleson would oversee the appointment of 56,000 postmasters and thousands of other minor officials, and Wilson would confine his appointive efforts to judges, ambassadors, and others on the high rungs.

On May 8, only a month after Wilson's speech to Congress, the House voted to cut the tariff and finally exercise its new power to create an income tax. Hundreds of members of the National Association of Manufacturers raced to Washington for the seemingly innocuous purpose of holding a convention. In truth, they were massing their forces to lobby the Senate, where the Democrats had an edge of only six seats and where every tariff fight since the Civil War had ended in a victory for the manufacturing establishment.

Wilson staged a one-man counterattack, accusing the lobbyists of buying votes and of spending heavily on publicity to create the illusion of a popular backlash to tariff reform. This was a serious matter, Wilson said, because the people had no lobby to rebut the clever men distorting the facts. Mother and the cornfields sided with the president, but the Senate embarked on a testy debate, with Democrats reciting the benefits of free trade and Republicans warning that a sudden influx of cheap foreign goods would drive American companies out of business, depress stock prices, and create massive unemployment. Wilson and the wet nurses interceded where they could but resigned themselves to a long wait.

As the tariff fight dragged on, Wilson prepared for the establishment of a central bank. During the campaign, Wilson had focused on the big banks' monopoly on credit, but neither he nor his opponents had said much about the need for federal control of the nation's money supply. By the time Wilson came to power, politicians and financiers were largely agreed on the need for a central bank but differed on the question of who would control it. Bankers wanted a private collaborative run by bankers, while progressives and would-be borrowers argued for federal control.

Wilson decided that he wanted the government in the saddle and asked Congress to authorize the creation of the Federal Reserve Board and the issuance of currency backed by the full faith and credit of the U.S. government. Once again he went to Capitol Hill, this time to request that Congress stay in session in order to pass the legislation as soon as possible. Once again he was the picture of self-possession. And once again he was brief. It was, he said, "perfectly clear that it is our duty to supply the new banking and currency system the country needs. . . . The only question is, When shall we supply it—now, or later, after the demands shall have become reproaches that we were so dull and so slow?"

On June 20, the White House announced that on the advice of Dr. Grayson, Mrs. Wilson would give up her philanthropic activities. She was not seriously ill but would remain quietly in the White House until she went to Cornish. Cornish was Cornish, New Hampshire, where the Wilsons had rented a large house with the idea of summering in a place cooler than Washington. Wilson planned a working vacation. But after he lectured Congress on its duty to stay on the job until a banking bill was passed, a friend pointed out the obvious: Congress, baking in Washington, would resent his absence. On June 28, the Three Wilson Girls and their exhausted mother departed for Cornish and left the president to his tug-of-war with Congress.

Although the House had given Wilson a swift victory on tax reform, the Senate had yet to act, and neither chamber had begun work on the Federal Reserve bill. Bryan tried to shepherd the errant into the fold with the argument that a Democratic president, a Democratic House, and a Democratic Senate had to act in accord with the principles of the Democratic Party.

At the end of July, Senate Republicans announced that they would ask for an adjournment after finishing with tax reform. Wilson replied that if Congress adjourned, he would immediately invoke his power to call an extra session and would direct the country's attention to the dereliction of duty on Capitol Hill. Burleson helped to wear down the president's adversaries by sidelining their patronage requests.

Wilson did not flinch, but he felt the strain. As he wrote Ellen, the pressure was "great, very great: eternal watchfulness, incessant shifts of personal sensitiveness and jealousy, incalculable currents to be watched for and offset and controlled." Why, he wondered in a letter to his friend Mary, should U.S. senators have to be dragooned into doing their duty? Why should they find it so hard to see the straight path? "To whom are they listening?" he wondered. "Certainly not to the voice of the people."

Going well beyond the call of duty, Grayson and Tumulty moved into the White House for the summer to keep the president company. Grayson was still unmarried, and Tumulty's wife and children had gone to the Jersey Shore. Tumulty kept the work side of Wilson's life in excellent order, and Grayson saw to his relaxation, golfing with him, arranging daily sessions of deep breathing and calisthenics, and taking him out for long automobile rides in the country and evenings at the theater. Sometimes they weekended on the presidential yacht *Mayflower*. Woodrow reported to Ellen that Grayson and Tumulty were "lovely fellows, both of them, and good company all the while."

The neuritis that plagued Wilson at Princeton reappeared, and he and Grayson finished many of their summer nights with a half-hour massage done with the aid of a contraption that pumped electric current into glass tubes and balls. A medical textbook of the time instructed the physician to adjust the current to produce "the thickest disruptive charge from the largest ball electrode [and then] apply single thick, thumping sparks slowly, with intermissions, but persistently, over the course of the affected nerve trunk and on each point of tenderness until the greatest possible relief is obtained."

Woodrow mentioned his symptoms in letters to Mary, but not to his wife. Ellen missed him keenly, and after a month in New Hampshire asked to come to Washington for a few days. "Indeed, dear, I must go!" she wrote. "I love you unspeakably." He longed for her, too, but asked her not to come. She needed rest, and her presence might break his concentration, he said. "If I succeed in this session, the rest is easy. We must act together and without a touch of weakness. . . . Be a Spartan wife . . . and it will make it easy for me to be a Spartan statesman."

Wilson's breakthrough in the Senate came on September 9, with the passage of the Underwood-Simmons Tariff Act. The new law cut the average tariff rate by 25 percent and imposed a graduated income tax. Those who earned less than $3,000 (the vast majority of working Americans) would be exempt. The tax rate started at 1 percent and stopped at 7, a rate to be paid only by those whose annual earnings topped $500,000.

Printed on gilt-edged parchment and bound in blue leather, the Tariff Act reached the White House early on the afternoon of October 3. On the advice of his attorney general, the president postponed the signing until customhouses across all of the country's time zones had closed for the night, so it was nine o'clock when cabinet members, the vice president, and the congressional Democrats who had led the fight crowded into the Oval Office. The proceedings were more solemn than celebratory. No backslapping, no newspaper photographers. A hush settled in when the president sat for the signing. He wrote "Woodrow" with one gold pen, "Wilson" with another, and handed the pens to Underwood and Simmons.

The president expressed his thanks in a short talk that left no doubt about his gratitude to Congress, and he paid an oblique compliment to himself, quoting Shakespeare's *Henry V*: "If it be a sin to covet honour, I am the most offending soul alive." "I have had the accomplishment of something like this at heart ever since I was a boy," he said. It was true: the English statesmen who had inspired him in his youth were ardent free traders. But the Democrats' work would not be finished until they broke the money monopoly, he reminded his guests. "So I feel tonight like a man who is lodging happily in the inn which lies halfway along the journey and [knowing] that in time, with a fresh impulse, we shall go the rest of the journey."

The outlook for the rest of the journey was mixed. The optimists, including Ellen, pointed out that the Federal Reserve bill had sailed through the House by a wide margin. "The Senate surely cannot stand out against that," she wrote from New Hampshire. She was right, but three more disputatious months would pass before the Senate approved it.

Wilson suspected that lobbyists were responsible for the foot-dragging in the banking committee, and he worried that with enough time, they would find a way to derail the bill. He called a few friendly senators to the White House on the morning of October 7 and told them he wanted the committee's Democrats to stand together and cast a vote that would send the bill to the Senate floor. The visitors advised letting the hearings run their course. The president might well pick up a few more votes as the undecided made up their minds, they said, and his opponents would ultimately have to admit that their views had been heard.

The morning's disappointment was followed by a lunch with Tumulty and Oswald Garrison Villard. A grandson of the abolitionist William Lloyd Garrison, chairman of the National Association for the Advancement of Colored People (NAACP), and publisher of the *New York Evening Post* and *The Nation*, Villard had helped Wilson win the support of black voters in 1912. But the two men had been at loggerheads for months over the administration's treatment of African Americans in the civil service.

Black voters who cast their ballots for Wilson assumed that the New Freedom, with its rhetoric of emancipation and equal opportunity, included all

Americans, and they were shocked when Burleson and McAdoo began segregating their departments. The Wilson administration was only five weeks old when Burleson informed the cabinet of his segregation plan, which he said was a response to complaints from white workers. De facto discrimination had long existed in the civil service—the white face at virtually every supervisor's desk attested to that—but blacks and whites in the clerical ranks had coexisted peacefully for years. The overt segregation introduced by the Wilson administration has been ascribed to the fact that the president and half of his cabinet, including Burleson and McAdoo, were native Southerners who took white superiority for granted and regarded segregation as the secret of racial harmony: minimize the interaction, and you minimize the hostility.

While such attitudes undoubtedly played a part, there was another potent force at work. Virtually all of the new segregation occurred in the Treasury and the Post Office, which happened to be run by McAdoo and Burleson, the same two who were twisting congressional arms on behalf of the president's legislation. Most of the Democrats opposing Wilson's economic reforms were Southerners who feared that Wilson's drive for more federal control of the economy would eventually lead to federal abolition of state laws that segregated virtually every aspect of life. Emboldened by the South's new dominance of the executive branch, Southerners in Congress wanted the civil service segregated in exchange for their votes on Wilson's economic measures. McAdoo and Burleson accepted the terms with no apparent qualms and cooperated in thwarting federal appointments of African Americans throughout the South.

An NAACP investigation in the summer of 1913 confirmed that the new segregation in Washington was concentrated in the Post Office and the Treasury. Black civil servants were shunted to the edges of the big rooms where the clerks worked, barred from lunchrooms, and directed to separate lavatories. Those who protested the indignities often used the same figure of speech: they felt like lepers.

Southern Democrats in Congress praised the changes and pressed for more. A freshman congressman from Oklahoma demanded segregation of all federal offices, as did Senator James K. Vardaman of Mississippi. Vardaman, proud to be known as the Great White Chief, introduced bills to repeal two constitutional amendments—the Fourteenth, which granted all citizens equal protection under the law, and the Fifteenth, which gave the right to vote to all male citizens. Pointing out that the army and navy had been segregated years before by Republicans, they called on Democrats to finish the job by segregating the whole civil service.

When NAACP leaders decided to make a public protest, Villard wrote Wilson to say that before going ahead, they wanted to be certain that they had the facts and understood the president's position. Distressed by the prospect of a public fight over the issue, Wilson replied that the segregation was not a movement against Negroes. "I sincerely believe it to be in their interest. . . . [W]e are rendering them more safe in their possession of office and less likely to be discriminated against." Villard had no sympathy for Wilson's distress and no patience with his argument.

The NAACP's protest took the form of an open letter to Wilson. "Never before has the Federal Government discriminated against its civilian employees on the ground of color," Villard and his NAACP colleagues wrote. "Every such act heretofore has been that of an individual state." Where would it end? the letter asked. "Shall ten millions of our citizens say that their civic liberties and rights are not safe in your hands? To ask the question is to answer it. They desire a 'New Freedom,' too, Mr. President."

As soon as the protest was made public, Villard sent Wilson a friendly private note suggesting that the White House try to regain the confidence of black citizens by appointing a nonpartisan commission to study the well-being of African Americans. The two men had discussed the idea before the election, and Wilson had acknowledged its value but had asked Villard to give him time to get to know the Congress. Now he told Villard that Southern senators were bound to see a study of social conditions in black America as an indictment.

Infuriated by Wilson's timidity, Villard asked why the delicate feelings of the South's senators should be allowed to postpone any search for truth. And what of the new despair among African Americans? "Are they not to be recognized by you in any way? Are you not going to appoint any one of them to office? Are you going to continue the policy of segregation?" Villard asked to bring some of his NAACP colleagues to the White House for a talk that might lessen the tensions on both sides. Wilson had replied with an invitation to Villard only.

In the hour he spent with Wilson, Villard was unsparing. Early in the conversation, the president threw himself on Villard's mercy. "I am in a cruel position," he said. "I am at heart working for these people, but I cannot come out and say so for publication because that would naturally betray my plan and method to the senators." Showing no sympathy, Villard blamed Wilson personally for the outrage felt by black citizens. Wilson struck back with a novel defense: the new segregation was social, not racial, and it was just plain unfortunate that the social cleavage coincided with the color line.

Villard, refusing to follow him into the shallows, asked for his answer to the open letter from the NAACP. Wilson, clearly upset, said he wanted to act but did not know what to do. Figuring out what to do was the fundamental task of the statesman, Villard observed. The word "statesman" hit another nerve, for there was no title Wilson coveted more. "I say it with shame and humiliation, shame and humiliation, but I have thought about this thing for twenty years and I see no way out," he said. He predicted that the situation would not change until Southern politicians needed black votes.

Villard landed one last blow. Wilson had stopped nominating African Americans as soon as he realized that the Senate would refuse to confirm them. Grover Cleveland and Theodore Roosevelt had been braver than that, Villard said. They had nominated the men they wanted and forced the Senate to do the rejecting. Wilson admitted that he could follow their example but did not promise that he would. At that point Villard realized that Wilson had no intention of undoing the segregation imposed by Burleson and McAdoo.

Shortly after Villard left, Wilson went out for a round of golf with Grayson, but the next day a roiling stomach forced him to stop work early and confined him to the family quarters. He was ill for a week. During his first ten months as president, Wilson was sick in bed at least six times, felled by headaches, "turmoil in Central America," neuritis, and exhaustion—maladies caused more by stress than overwork. He rarely spent more than six hours a day in his office, and the time that he and Grayson devoted to golf and other diversions was recreation at its most literal, a recreation of physical and mental energy. But despite Wilson's abbreviated workdays and regular exercise, his body often gave out after emotionally taxing events.

Although Grayson was quick to see the pattern, it is not clear what (if anything) he knew of the strokes Wilson had suffered during his years at Princeton. Edwin A. Weinstein, the neuropsychiatrist who made an exhaustive study of Wilson's medical history, concluded that Wilson had a minor but ominous stroke about a month after taking office. As the first attack on Wilson's left side, it indicated that arteries on both sides of the brain were diseased, a change that greatly increased the risk of further strokes. Grayson described it as neuritis, and Wilson used the same term in letters to friends.

In December Wilson suffered a two-week siege of influenza complete with fevered nightmares about his defeats at Princeton. He had barely recovered when the Senate passed the Federal Reserve Act and sent it to the White House for his signature. With the passage of the tariff and banking acts, Congress had at long last ended the contest between class and class, Wilson said. "The men who have fought for this measure have fought nobody. They have simply fought for those accommodations which are going to secure us in prosperity and in peace. Nobody can be the friend of any class in America in the sense of being the enemy of any other class. You can only be the friend of one class by showing it the lines by which it can accommodate itself to the other class. The lines of help are always the lines of accommodation."

But one class had not been accommodated. It is unlikely that any of Wilson's economic reforms would have passed without Burleson's and McAdoo's willingness to segregate their vast bureaucracies in exchange for Southern votes.

8

Our Detached and Distant Situation

The Federal Reserve Act was signed at six o'clock in the evening on December 23, and by ten, Wilson and his family (minus Jessie, who had just married) were aboard a train bound for Pass Christian, Mississippi. Congress adjourned, and the president was at last free to take the long vacation he had denied himself during the summer. He intended to loaf for three weeks.

The Wilsons would have a sedately merry Christmas and mark Woodrow's fifty-seventh birthday on December 28, but there would be no exulting over the birth of the New Freedom. A few weeks before Christmas he had written Mary that his life as president was a path with "few flowers but some grim satisfactions." The gray cloud that hung over Wilson's triumphs has been variously attributed to his exacting father, his chronically unhappy mother, and the rigors of Calvinism, but his emptiness at the end of 1913 is more readily accounted for: he was worn out. Despite Dr. Grayson's constant attention and their thrice-weekly golf outings, Wilson was far from robust, and while waging the long, strenuous fight with Congress, he had also had to cope with a series of foreign problems that caused him enormous anxiety.

The most dangerous erupted two weeks before his inauguration, with a military coup in Mexico. After a long siege of the capital, General Victoriano Huerta had captured the National Palace, forced the president and vice president to resign, then sent them under armed guard to the penitentiary. En route they were shot dead, allegedly in an attempt to escape. Virtually everyone in Mexico suspected Huerta of ordering the murders. The first great revolution of the twentieth century, the Mexican upheaval had begun in 1910 and would last until 1920. If the violence had taken place an ocean away, it would have stirred little interest in the United States. But a revolution next door was a security threat, and Mexico in 1913 was home to forty thousand U.S. citizens, nearly all of whom were associated with American companies extracting Mexican oil and minerals or operating large agricultural enterprises. By the time Wilson took office, scores of American civilians had died at the hands of the rebels, and the American residents of Mexico were seeking $500 million in damages from the Mexican government.

Wilson made the revolution in Mexico and rumors of revolution elsewhere in the region the subject of his first statement on foreign policy. The United States wished to cultivate the friendship of her sister republics in Latin America but only if the ties were supported by the rule of law, he said. Americans could not sympathize with those who overthrew constitutional governments and installed themselves as dictators. While most Americans applauded Wilson's position, a few skeptics wondered what he intended to do if the autocrats did not fall in line with his ideals. To show the skeptics the kind of thing he had in mind, he refused to recognize Huerta's government.

John Bassett Moore, a scholar of international law and counselor of the State Department, explained to Wilson that the U.S. government, itself the product of a revolution, had always acted on the principle of de facto recognition—acknowledging that a new government existed whether the United States approved of it or not. "We regard governments as existing or not existing," Moore wrote to Wilson. "We do not require them to be chosen by popular vote." Deplorable as the assassinations had been, Huerta seemed to be in control, and the need for the United States to deal with Mexico had not disappeared, Moore added. Wilson stuck to his decision but asked the State Department to assure the world that Huerta had not been singled out. Henceforth the United States would deny recognition to any government that forced its way into power. The U.S. ambassador to Mexico, Henry Lane Wilson, a Taft appointee (and no relation to Woodrow), tried to persuade Washington that failure to extend recognition would merely prolong the violence. He admitted that Huerta fell short by every measure of statesmanship but maintained that no other rebel faction was powerful enough to pacify the country.

For the most part, Wilson's predecessors had heeded the advice in Washington's Farewell Address (1796), which urged the United States to approach the rest of the world without stars in its eyes. Self-interest was the only sure guide, Washington wrote. "Nations as well as individuals act for their own benefit, and not for the benefit of others, unless both interests happen to be assimilated." He urged the United States to build its trade with other nations but keep political connections to a minimum. Why forgo the advantages bestowed by geography? he asked. "Our detached and distant situation invites and enables us to pursue a different course." But in a rarely quoted passage of the address, Washington showed that he was not without the idealism that burned so bright in Woodrow Wilson: "Observe good faith and justice towards all nations; cultivate peace and harmony with all. Religion and morality enjoin this conduct, and can it be that good policy does not equally enjoin it? It will be worthy of a free, enlightened and, at no distant period, a great nation to give mankind the magnanimous and too novel example of a people always guided by an exalted justice and benevolence."

In 1823, Americans fortified their natural geographic advantage with the Monroe Doctrine, which declared the Western Hemisphere off limits to further colonization. By the end of the nineteenth century, the United States was in a truly enviable position: no powerful rivals north or south and thousands of miles of ocean east and west. By another stroke of good fortune, Britannia ruled the waves, and Britannia's strong friendship with America spared the U.S. government the expense of a large navy.

The great departure from Washington's ideas came at the close of the nineteenth century, when the United States acquired its first outposts in the Pacific, Hawaii and Samoa, and emerged from the Spanish-American War with three new possessions (Guam, the Philippines, and Puerto Rico) and one protectorate (Cuba). In a book called *The Influence of Sea Power upon History* (1895), Captain Alfred Thayer Mahan of the U.S. Navy had made a cogent case for the idea that the British Empire owed its might to its naval supremacy. He also argued that if a great nation did not wish to have an empire, it could extend its global power and influence simply by building naval bases in strategically significant locations. Mahan's book convinced Theodore Roosevelt and his advisors that the United States could not be a world power without a great navy. The American acquisitions in the Pacific were made with U.S. power in mind, as were the decisions to build a canal through the Isthmus of Panama and to gain control of the Caribbean.

Such was the portfolio handed to Woodrow Wilson, and he hoped that it would not require much attention. He was fairly well grounded in European political history and in recent international developments affecting the United States, but he was a novice at diplomacy. He would have done well to choose an experienced international lawyer as secretary of state, but instead he gave the post to William Jennings Bryan, a personable man with keen political instincts but scant knowledge of foreign affairs and no patience with complex ideas. Bryan had been appointed for political reasons: as a member of the administration, he could not easily challenge Wilson for the next Democratic presidential nomination, and as a former party leader who still enjoyed the affection of Democrats in Congress, he was helpful in securing votes for Wilson's legislation.

The U.S. Department of State in 1913 had one pinstriped leg in the twentieth century, the other in the nineteenth. Roosevelt and Taft had professionalized the Foreign Service with entrance exams and a merit system for promotions, but the department's so-called specialists were responsible for preposterously vast swaths of the world. On the Near East desk, for example, the specialists managed relations with the present Middle East plus Greece, Italy, and the German, Russian, and Austro-Hungarian Empires. The two largest of the four bureaus dealt with Latin America and the Far East, a mirror of the main U.S. strategic concerns of the early twentieth century: a desire to dominate the Western Hemisphere and a fear of Japanese expansion in the Pacific. The department's minuscule staff and low salaries summed up a common feeling among Americans: when it came to foreign affairs, they didn't want any.

Wilson hoped to end the practice of awarding embassies to rich men who had contributed generously to the victor's presidential campaign. "I must have the best men in the nation!" he told a friend. But when he offered Great Britain to Charles W. Eliot, former president of Harvard, Eliot excused himself on the grounds that he was nearly seventy and busy with other endeavors. The polite refusal turned out to be for the official files; privately he told Wilson that he could not see himself as an errand boy for Bryan.

Walter Hines Page, a progressive editor and successful publisher who had known Wilson for many years, wanted to accept when asked to represent the United States in Britain, but initially demurred because he could not afford the grand house and lavish entertaining expected of an ambassador. Page's appointment was made possible by an annual subsidy of $25,000 from Wilson's friend Cleveland Dodge. Paris was the post Wilson had in mind for William F. McCombs, and while McCombs liked the idea, he could not afford it. Wilson left Taft's appointee in place in Paris and forced himself onto the usual path of appointing rich supporters to serve in the other capitals of Europe.

Soon after joining the cabinet, Bryan met with the Senate Committee on Foreign Relations to propose a series of bilateral treaties that could be invoked if the two parties found themselves in a quarrel they could not resolve through diplomacy. Under the terms of these "cooling-off treaties," as Bryan called them, the adversaries would refrain from going to war for a least a year, presumably long enough for an impartial commission to determine the facts of the case and recommend a solution. Although neither country would be bound by the recommendation, Bryan and other peace activists believed that the commission's findings and the passage of time would, nine times out of ten, enable the contending parties to reach a peaceable settlement. The scheme was generally well received, and within six weeks, twenty nations announced plans to negotiate cooling-off treaties with the United States.

Wilson came to the presidency well informed about China. American Presbyterians funded a major missionary effort there, and Wilson, as a Presbyterian and president of the leading Presbyterian university in the United States, had numerous connections with missionaries. They recruited at Princeton's divinity school, and he often heard from former students who joined the clergy and served in China. Wilson was also an admirer of the Open Door policy, which the United States had initiated at the turn of the century to prevent the Great Powers from carving up China and parceling it out among themselves, as they had done with Africa. When the Qing dynasty fell to Chinese revolutionaries, Sun Yat-sen, the provisional president of the new republic, wrote Woodrow Wilson, and Wilson sent a warm reply, saying that he had long sympathized with the Chinese people and their desire for a democratic government. Wilson was the first head of state to welcome the Republic of China to the family of nations.

The Wilson administration was only a few days old when a pair of bankers from the House of Morgan turned up at the State Department to ask Secretary Bryan whether the Wilson administration wanted American banks to remain involved in an international loan consortium that was about to lend $125 million to the new Chinese government. It was an odd question. The loan had been several years in the making, and it had taken Taft's secretary of state months to persuade the other powers to include American lenders.

It does not appear that Bryan asked his visitors if they had worries about the transaction, but he had one: what if China defaulted? In that case, the Morgan men said, the American banks might ask the U.S. government to use its army and navy to protect their interests. As a pacifist and a vocal critic of Wall Street, Bryan was appalled. Where the Taft administration took it on faith that private American capital lent to foreign governments would enhance U.S. influence, Bryan feared that a China beholden to the largest banks of the world's most powerful nations would have no independence worth having. When he reported the conversation to the cabinet, his fellow secretaries unanimously agreed that the administration should not support the loan. Wilson followed up with an announcement that the administration would not ask American banks to remain in the consortium.

If Wilson and Bryan had consulted the State Department's file on the loan, they would have realized that they were being used to extricate the House of Morgan from a deal it no longer found attractive. The Chinese loan was an enormous gamble, the new republic's fragile hold on the country was causing delay after delay, and the other powers in the consortium were at swords' points over control of various aspects of the loan. But rather than ask a favor of Bryan, who had risen to fame on his denunciations of Wall Street, they posed their question in a fashion calculated to stir his antipathy to imperialism.

Wilson's first full-blown foreign crisis happened on American soil. In the spring of 1913, as the state of California prepared to pass a law barring Japanese residents from acquiring more farmland, the government of Japan filed a vigorous protest through its ambassador in Washington. California was acting on a prejudice that had taken hold in the Gold Rush, which brought the first big influx of Chinese immigrants. Working for pennies, they were the bane of white laborers, whose complaints led to the federal Chinese Exclusion Act of 1882. Japanese immigrants, most of whom arrived later, found themselves lumped with the Chinese, and in 1906, San Francisco's board of education decreed that Asian and white children could no longer attend school together. Japan's protests and its negotiations with the United States in 1907–1908 culminated in the so-called Gentlemen's Agreement: Japan stopped issuing passports to citizens wanting to work in the United States, and San Francisco stopped segregating Asian schoolchildren.

Reinforced by a federal law denying Asian immigrants the opportunity to become citizens, the racial prejudice persisted, and when Japanese farmers began outproducing their white neighbors in central California, white farmers clamored for protection. Despite the fact that the Japanese cultivated less than one-half of one percent of California's arable land, pleas for common sense went unheard. Explaining the situation to Woodrow Wilson during the 1912 campaign, one of the state's leading Democrats, James D.

Phelan, likened the Japanese presence to an invasion. The success of Japanese farmers was lowering the standard of living for members of the white race, Phelan said, "and ultimately the same race question which arose in the South will arise." Candidate Wilson replied that he favored the exclusion policy and hoped that a new "race problem" could be avoided. "[S]urely we have had our lesson," he said.

The news of California's intention to ban Japanese ownership of farmland triggered huge anti-American demonstrations in Tokyo. Thousands cheered as speakers demanded that Japan defend its honor by declaring war on the United States. When Japanese officials called for restraint and an amicable resolution, the protesters accused them of servility.

Phelan sent Wilson a telegram: THE TIDE MUST BE CHECKED, OTHERWISE CALIFORNIA WILL BECOME A JAPANESE PLANTATION. But President Wilson was not as free as Candidate Wilson had been. He had spoken with the Japanese ambassador, Baron Sutemi Chinda, who was profoundly upset. The government of Japan viewed the proposed ban as a violation of its commercial treaty with the United States, and while Japanese officials had no desire for war, Chinda said, they feared that they might not be able to contain the militarists.

Hoping to calm Tokyo, Wilson sent Bryan to Sacramento, but there was little that the administration could do, because the commercial treaty had not mentioned farmland. In early May, a few days after Bryan reached Sacramento, both houses of the California legislature voted overwhelmingly in favor of the Alien Land Act, which limited the right to buy agricultural land to aliens eligible for citizenship and deprived those Japanese who already owned farms of the right to leave them to their families. All that remained was the right to lease farmland for up to three years. "We have accomplished the big thing," the governor boasted to the press. "We have prevented the Japanese from driving the root of their civilization deep into California soil."

Ambassador Chinda reported Japan's "painful disappointment" to Bryan and questioned the equity of a law that did not treat all aliens alike. Bryan, like Wilson a stout defender of states' rights, replied that the federal government could not interfere in the matter. When Chinda protested again, Bryan suggested that Japan take its case to the federal courts. To the Japanese the idea of having to sue for rights enjoyed by other aliens seemed yet another humiliation. In Tokyo the walls of the U.S. embassy were defaced, and signs reading GIVE ME LIBERTY OR GIVE ME DEATH summoned Japanese patriots to public protests. One newspaper urged Japan to demand the Philippines as compensation for the mistreatment of Japanese aliens in the United States. Another called for an end to the ruling "White Man's Clique," by force if necessary.

In Washington the Joint Board of the Army and Navy, forerunner of the Joint Chiefs of Staff, began considering the possibility of war with Japan. At a meeting on May 13, the army's chief of staff informed the board that he had quietly begun moving men and matériel to Hawaii and the Philippines. One of the board's admirals wanted the navy to make similar preparations, but Wilson and Secretary of the Navy Josephus Daniels resisted, Wilson because he believed that any show of force would further inflame the Japanese, and Daniels because he doubted that the U.S. Navy could win even a small skirmish in the Pacific. With the fleet concentrated in the Atlantic and the Panama Canal still a year away from completion, Japan could seize the Philippines and Hawaii long before a single American battleship could round Cape Horn.

At a cabinet meeting on May 16, Secretary of War Lindley M. Garrison spoke up in favor of shifting a handful of U.S. naval vessels from Chinese waters to Manila. That was the recommendation of the Joint Board, he said, and he respected its judgment. Bryan lost his temper, grew red in the face, and thundered that while the president had been trying to keep the United States out of a war, the generals and admirals had been making plans to get in. In Bryan's opinion, the army and navy should not have taken such steps until called upon to do so by the commander in chief. Half the cabinet agreed with Garrison, seeing no reason why the United States could not move its own vessels to its own ports without provoking a war. Daniels sided with Bryan, partly because of his own pacifism but also because the U.S. ships in China, poky old tubs with antiquated guns, were no match for the modern Japanese navy. When Garrison insisted that the Philippines had to be protected, Daniels lost *his* temper. In his view, the situation proved that the U.S. acquisition of the Philippines in the peace treaty signed after the Spanish-American War had been stupid as well as immoral. The sooner the United States repaired the wrong done in the treaty and granted independence to the Philippines, the sooner the United States would return to true democracy, he said.

Wilson let the debate run on and then, rather than risk a vote that might not go his way, adjourned the meeting. Garrison and Daniels were invited to return to the White House after lunch for more discussion. When they arrived, the president took them out into the sunny warmth of a spring afternoon and let them spar till they had nothing left to say. Only then did Wilson say that he wanted the problem with Japan settled by diplomacy, not war. The crisis subsided on its own, but the refusal of the White Man's Clique to accept the Japanese as equals would continue to rankle.

9

Moral Force

Chance favored the new president in his dealings with China and Japan, but his luck ran out in Mexico. To Wilson, General Victoriano Huerta was the Latin American political problem incarnate—a brutal, corrupt dictator sure to provoke more brutality and corruption—and when the U.S. refusal to recognize Huerta's government had no effect on the Mexican Revolution, Wilson decided that Huerta must go. Wilson had no doubt about the moral correctness of his position, no doubt about his moral duty to insist on the return of constitutional government to Mexico, no doubt that moral exhortation would force Huerta to step down. He took it for granted that democracy was the best form of government and would ultimately prevail.

By getting rid of Huerta, Wilson aimed to reform the whole continent. As he explained to a British envoy, "I propose to teach the South American Republics to elect good men." Huerta's demise would show Latin America that revolution did not pay and, lesson learned, the Latin Americans would change their governments with ballots rather than bullets.

Neither teacher nor pupils succeeded. The scale of the U.S. military intervention in Europe during World War I—two million men—has obscured Wilson's armed interventions closer to home, in Cuba, Haiti, the Dominican Republic, Mexico (twice), Panama (twice), and Honduras (five times). No other president had sent troops abroad as often as Woodrow Wilson. But as a new president, Wilson seemed oblivious to the risks he was running in Mexico. He assumed that Huerta's departure would be followed by a restoration of constitutional government, but it was much more likely that the blood would run indefinitely. Rebel chieftain would topple rebel chieftain, then prove unable to win the allegiance of the whole country. More American residents of Mexico would be killed, more American property would be destroyed, and the United States might well be dragged into a war.

Huerta deserved the world's opprobrium. He had risen to the rank of general by his brutal treatment of uncooperative indigenous peoples and his liberal use of assassination. "He is a man-eater," one of Huerta's officers confessed to a foreign journalist, "but he is what we need." If European diplomats in Mexico were more tactful, they too believed that Mexicans could be governed only by a mailed fist. Those who remembered the old dictator, Porfirio Díaz, saw little difference between him and Huerta, and few believed that Huerta's chief rivals—Emiliano Zapata in the south or Venustiano Carranza and Pancho Villa in the north—would prove any less savage.

Huerta drank constantly, but those who knew him claimed that no matter how much alcohol he consumed, he never lost his cunning. He openly referred to his cabinet as pigs and complained that he had to rely on pigs because respectable citizens refused to associate with him. The German minister in Mexico City said he had never seen a government as corrupt as Huerta's and sensed that he and his associates were stealing as fast as they could because they sensed that their opportunity would be short-lived.

Morally speaking, Wilson's opposition to Huerta was unassailable, but by flatly insisting on Huerta's resignation he had left no room for negotiation. Nor had he given Huerta any incentive to cooperate. Spurned by the United States, Huerta courted the governments of Europe, which recognized his regime and lent him millions in exchange for mineral rights and other economic concessions.

"What to do with Mexico is the great problem," Josephus Daniels sighed in his diary after a tempestuous cabinet meeting in April 1913. Wilson and Bryan were dead set against diplomatic recognition, while Secretary of War

Lindley Garrison argued that it might be necessary in order to avoid a military intervention. Having no intention of marching into Mexico, Wilson dismissed Garrison's concerns. But the revolution had already claimed the lives of more than a hundred American residents of Mexico. How many would prove too many? Garrison wondered. And in the event of an accidental but deadly skirmish between Huerta's army and the American soldiers patrolling the border, what would the United States do? What *should* it do? Garrison worried for the same reason Daniels had worried about a naval clash with the Japanese: the army was as unready as the navy to fight a war.

Leaving Garrison to fret over remote contingencies, Wilson turned to a more immediate headache, the U.S. ambassador to Mexico, Henry Lane Wilson. President Wilson had distrusted Ambassador Wilson from the start because of allegations that he had not done enough to prevent the assassinations of the president and vice president ousted by Huerta. The White House was also troubled by discrepancies between the embassy's optimistic reports of Huerta's progress in pacifying the country and dispatches from U.S. consuls in northern Mexico, who wrote of defections from Huerta's army and growing popular support for the rebel forces who called themselves the Constitutionalists.

Unable to name a new ambassador to a government he did not recognize, the president left Henry Lane Wilson in place and recruited a series of personal emissaries, none of them versed in diplomacy. A personal agent would report directly to the White House, and this president had great faith in amateurs. Speaking to the U.S. Navy during the world war, he would say that America was "the prize amateur nation of the world. Now when it comes to doing new things and doing them well, I will back the amateur against the professional every time, because the professional does it out of the book and the amateur does it with his eyes open upon a new world and with a new set of circumstances. He knows so little about it that he is fool enough to try the right thing."

The first of the emissaries was William Bayard Hale, a former Episcopalian priest who had ingratiated himself with Wilson by stitching excerpts of his campaign speeches into a bestselling book called *The New Freedom*. Barely a month into his presidency, Wilson asked Hale to go to Mexico and pose as a journalist. Hale's first report to the White House implicated the ambassador in the assassinations, and his second suggested that Huerta's government was on the verge of collapse. Deducing that Hale was a spy for the White House, Ambassador Wilson treated him courteously but warned the president that Hale's ignorance of the revolution was profound. The president disregarded the warnings and in July, after the State Department learned that Huerta had just dined at the embassy, Henry Lane Wilson was sacked.

Responsibility for the embassy passed to the chargé d'affaires, Nelson O'Shaughnessy. Hale had vouched for O'Shaughnessy's trustworthiness, but President Wilson, wanting his own man in the embassy, chose John Lind, a former Minnesota governor who had persuaded the state's delegates to vote for Wilson at the Democratic National Convention. Lind was also the perfect amateur: ignorant of Spanish and of Latin America. On August 4, the State Department announced Ambassador Wilson's resignation and Lind's appointment as the president's personal representative and advisor to the embassy.

Lind's appointment riled the Senate, because unofficial envoys escaped confirmation hearings and were accountable only to the president. Members of the Committee on Foreign Relations asked for a briefing and were soon huddled with Wilson and Bryan. After a two-hour talk, the senators filed out to the North Portico and told reporters that the president had been cordial and talkative. He opposed intervention. He opposed recognition. He opposed ending the U.S. ban on weapons sales to Mexico, an option favored by those who believed that the United States should allow all factions to arm to the teeth and fight until one of them achieved a decisive victory. In other words, the president had said only what he planned not to do. Wilson made a surprise appearance on the portico but was not in an elaborating frame of mind. Asked what Lind would propose to the Mexican government, the president said, "There ain't no proposals."

That was loosely true. Lind had gone off to Mexico with a letter that surely ranks as one of the strangest ever composed by an American president. After an extravagant profession of Mexican-American friendship, Wilson made a series of demands, insisted that they were made for Mexico's own good, and offered U.S. assistance in meeting them. He wanted an immediate cease-fire throughout Mexico, a pledge of a clean presidential election at an early date, a promise that Huerta would not run, and assurance that the Mexican people would abide by the results. The letter closed with an insulting challenge: "Can Mexico give the civilized world a satisfactory reason for rejecting our good offices? If Mexico can suggest any better way in which to show our friendship, serve the people of Mexico, and meet our international obligations, we are more than willing to consider the suggestion."

Nonplussed, Senator Lodge said nothing in public but wrote a friend that he found Wilson's letter "almost unbelievable . . . not merely amateurish but crude and ignorant." For a man who had devoted his life to the study of history and politics, Wilson was "extraordinarily green," Lodge thought.

On Thursday, August 14, Lind presented the letter to the Mexican secretary of foreign affairs, Federico Gamboa, and a few days later Wilson learned that Gamboa had checkmated him in one move. Mexico could not consider Wilson's demands, Gamboa said, because it rejected his premises. With a disingenuous bow in the direction of Wilson's openness to suggestions, Gamboa proposed that the two countries begin by exchanging ambassadors. "Hard day on P. over Mexican situation," Dr. Grayson noted in his diary. "Rec'd reply from Huerta—bad—Poor game of golf." That was no trivial matter in Grayson's mind. Golf was the only form of exercise Wilson enjoyed and his only relief from stress, which medical research had already linked to coronary artery disease.

At an impasse with Gamboa, Lind left Mexico City for Veracruz on August 26, taking Hale with him. Anti-Americanism was on the rise, and the Americans living in Mexico blamed it on the meddling of Wilson's amateurs. Lind had made an especially unfavorable impression. He arrived in Mexico with a strong prejudice against Catholics and took an instant dislike to Mexicans. Hale returned to the United States, but Lind stayed on in Veracruz, imagining that it would be a good listening post and that Gamboa would eventually summon him back to the capital. But Gamboa had no desire to negotiate with an unofficial emissary of a nation that did not recognize his government. And in the eyes of one seasoned diplomat in Mexico City, Lind's notion that he could be useful in Veracruz was as absurd as posting a Frenchman in San Francisco to keep an eye on U.S. relations with Japan.

In hopes of putting a good face on his humiliation in Mexico, Wilson headed for the Capitol on August 27 to explain to a joint session of Congress that after months of waiting for conditions to improve, he had felt obliged to offer his assistance in arranging a peace and establishing a government accepted by all Mexicans. He had sent Lind to make the offer, but two things had gone awry: Mexico suspected the United States of ulterior motives, and Huerta did not believe that Wilson's proposals represented the will of the American people. Until such misunderstandings were cleared up, Wilson said, "[w]e cannot thrust our good offices upon them. The situation must be given a little more time to work itself out." Huerta would find himself increasingly isolated, Wilson predicted. "The steady pressure of moral force will before many days break the barriers of pride and prejudice down, and we shall triumph as Mexico's friends sooner than we could triumph as her enemies."

No one asked for a definition of "moral force." The newspapers optimistically characterized Wilson's improvisations as a policy and dubbed it "watchful waiting." Congress honored the old principle that politics stops at the water's edge, and the two Senate Republicans most knowledgeable about foreign affairs, Lodge and Root, publicly expressed admiration for the address. But Lodge had no faith that Huerta's departure would cure Mexico's ills, and in a letter to a friend admitted that his motives for praising Wilson were hardly selfless: he wanted to deny Wilson the opportunity to claim that he had been hampered in any way by Republicans.

Occasionally Wilson sought advice from John Bassett Moore, counselor of the State Department, and Moore sometimes volunteered his opinions in hopes of preventing an accidental war with Mexico. Moore did his best to school the president and secretary of state: A government's first duty is to protect its citizens at home and abroad. Other peoples are not subject to U.S. control. Interference in the domestic affairs of another nation, even for a noble purpose, provokes resentment and tends to thwart desired ends. Wilson was a willing pupil, but Bryan so disliked the tutelage that he stopped talking to Moore.

In early October, with Mexico's election only two weeks off, General Venustiano Carranza and his Constitutionalist army captured Huerta's major stronghold in the northern provinces. In a panic, Huerta dissolved the Congress and jailed more than a hundred of its members. Sure that Huerta intended to steal the election, Wilson instructed the State Department to inform Huerta that the United States would not recognize the results.

Come election day, Huerta's name did not appear on the ballot, but his political lieutenants had papered the country with notices urging voters to write him in. To no one's surprise, he received a commanding majority. Virtually all of Mexico had stayed home, however, fearing violence at the polls, and the number of votes cast fell short of the constitutional minimum. Huerta had abided by the law that prevented a provisional president from standing for election, he had won as a write-in candidate, and he cheerfully accepted the nullification of the election. Why not? He was still the provisional president of Mexico.

And Woodrow Wilson was still determined to prevail by moral force.

The day after the Mexican election, Wilson left for Mobile, Alabama, to address a convention of Southern businessmen. He used the occasion to paint two pictures of Latin America. One showed the United States and Latin America arm in arm, drawn together by the economic opportunities they would have once the Panama Canal opened. The other depicted a Darwinian jungle in which commerce spawned dangerous national rivalries and rich nations preyed upon poor ones. "You hear of 'concessions' to foreign capitalists in Latin America," he said. "You do not hear of concessions to foreign capitalists in the United States. They are not granted concessions. They are invited to make investments."

Wilson envisioned a day when the commerce that would begin passing through the canal in 1914 would eliminate the poor nations' dependence on foreign capital, and all nations would set human rights above economic interests. It was the New Freedom expanded to global proportions. "I want to take this occasion to say that the United States will never again seek one additional foot of territory by conquest," he went on. "She will devote herself to showing that she knows how to make honorable and fruitful use of the territory she has, and she must regard it as one of the duties of friendship to see that from no quarter are material interests made superior to human liberty and national opportunity."

Americans praised Wilson for raising the moral bar in international relations, but Europeans felt unjustly castigated. Their governments were not seeking another foot of the Western Hemisphere by conquest, either, and they had been no more exploitative than Americans doing business in Latin America. The French ambassador to the United States, Jean Jules Jusserand, said nothing for publication but privately told Moore that France regarded Wilson's criticism as unfortunate. The British wondered if the United States meant to extend the Monroe Doctrine to finance, banning new European investments as it had long before banned new colonies. The Germans accused Wilson of "imperialistic delirium"—imperialistic because they were certain that he would turn Mexico into an American protectorate and delirious because they had no faith that a nation armed only with moral force could play a meaningful part in world affairs.

Wilson had seemed a tower of confidence in Mobile, but his nights were sleepless and filled with prayers for a peaceful end to the standoff. He drafted a demand that Huerta hand over his authority to the Mexican Congress and wanted to ask the U.S. Congress for a joint resolution to that effect. After the chairman of the Senate's Committee on Foreign Relations persuaded him that it would go nowhere, Wilson asked Nelson O'Shaughnessy to quietly deliver an ultimatum: if Huerta did not resign immediately, there would be, in Wilson's words, "terrible consequences." Of what sort he did not say. O'Shaughnessy moved on tiptoe, hoping that he and Gamboa could arrange a face-saving exit for Huerta and thereby prevent a war.

Lind heard about O'Shaughnessy's talks with Gamboa and headed for Mexico City. When an American journalist assigned to watch his movements asked if there was some new plan afoot, Lind confirmed the hunch, and the newspapers were soon filled with speculation that Huerta was about to resign. Furious, Gamboa called off the negotiations with O'Shaughnessy, explaining that if there was even the slightest suggestion that Huerta was bowing to the wishes of the United States, he would refuse to step down. Lind, unrepentant, stayed in Mexico City for several days, demanding Huerta's resignation and threatening that if he did not step down, the United States would sever relations with Mexico.

Lind had no such instructions from Washington, but instead of dismissing him, Wilson summoned Moore to find out what it meant to sever relations. Moore explained that such a break was often a prelude to war. Wilson also asked what Huerta would think if the United States ended its arms embargo. Huerta was likely to regard the change as hostile, Moore said, because it would help his rivals. And if the United States let arms flow only to Carranza and the Constitutionalists? Wilson asked. Definitely hostile, Moore said. Wilson wondered if a president had the authority to ask the navy, which had several ships in Mexican waters, to open fire on Veracruz. Only when the situation called for self-defense, Moore replied. Wilson decided to hold his fire, keep the arms embargo in place, and hope for a diplomatic solution.

On December 2, in his first State of the Union speech, Wilson devoted half of his twenty-eight minutes at the rostrum to foreign affairs. He reminded Americans that the United States was at peace with all the world and remarked that the world itself seemed to be entering "an age of settled peace and good will." The Senate would soon renew several arbitration treaties, and more than thirty nations had agreed in principle to negotiate cooling-off treaties with the United States. All in all, the pending agreements covered four-fifths of the earth's population. The only cloud on the horizon, Wilson said, was Mexico, and there could be no hope for peace in the Americas until Huerta resigned and the world understood that the United States would not deal with usurpers. The president assured Congress that the United States would have no need to alter its policy of watchful waiting, because Huerta's prestige and his regime were in tatters. And when the end came, Wilson said, he hoped that constitutional government would be restored.

As 1914 began, there was no sign that Wilson was rethinking his approach to Mexico or questioning the merits of a foreign policy consisting almost entirely of moral pronouncements. He still assumed that moral force would triumph over brute force. He still assumed the United States had the right to decide which Latin American governments were legitimate and which were not. He still believed in amateurs. He still assumed that because the Constitution entrusted the conduct of foreign relations to the president, the president should do the job alone. Wanting only to spread democracy, he would have been astounded to hear a diplomatic historian of a later era pronounce him guilty of "the imperialism of idealism." Despite his surrender to the realities of self-interest in domestic affairs, he still believed that U.S. foreign relations—and the world itself—could be run on higher principles. And he still hoped to show the way by putting an end to dictatorship and revolution in Latin America.

Which left only one question: how?

10

A Psychological Moment

As the sun rose and set on March 4, 1914, the first anniversary of his inauguration, Wilson took no special note of his year in the White House. He was not given to reflecting on his past, and while he often recognized his mistakes, he was more inclined to move on than pause for a round of self-examination. Like the greatest presidents, he spoke of the future with eloquence and optimism, and he exercised his power in the hope of moving the United States closer to its ideals. The present was not without joy for Woodrow Wilson—he adored his wife and daughters, and they adored him—but for President Wilson, the present was one long vexation. Though he fought hard for his legislation, he did not relish his battles or try to befriend his adversaries, as Theodore Roosevelt had. To Wilson, every victory seemed hard won. He forced himself to stay in the ring, often fell ill when a fight ended, then steeled himself for the next bout.

"Sometimes I get desperately tired, and sometimes deeply discouraged," he wrote his friend Mary. "But discouragement is weakness and most days—most normal days,—I manage to keep the thing at arm's length and despise it." He was also weighed down by an illness in the family. Ellen had taken a fall and been in bed for two weeks. "Coming as it did at the end of an exhausting social season of all sorts of functions and exacting duties, when she was fairly worn out and in sore need of rest, the shock and the effect on her nerves went all the deeper." The pain had subsided, and it appeared that a long rest would put her to rights. Still, he found the experience unnerving: "work has gone harder than usual with me . . . and sometimes I have gone to bed at night as tired a man as there was, I venture, in all the Republic."

He still did not feel at home in the White House. In an impromptu visit to the new quarters of the National Press Club, he said he did not recognize the Woodrow Wilson he saw in the papers. The newspaper version was a remote and chilly man with "a thinking machine inside . . . which he does not allow to be moved by any winds of affection or emotion of any kind." In truth, Wilson said, he expended enormous energy in restraining his emotions: "You may not believe it, but I sometimes feel like a fire from a far from extinct volcano." He felt passionately connected to the struggles of his fellow Americans, and when he thought of his responsibility for them, he said he trembled—"not only with a sense of my own inadequacy and weakness, but as if I were shaken by the very things that are shaking them, and if I seem circumspect, it is because I am so diligently trying not to make any colossal blunders." The best safeguard he had found was to listen more than he talked. "That, I dare say, is what gives the impression of circumspectness, and of the 'velvet slipper.' I am listening."

The reporters were touched. President Wilson had climbed down from his plinth and shown them a man of warm blood. With a bit of coaxing, he allowed them to publish his remarks, and the country got a close-up of a Woodrow Wilson it had never seen.

Wilson's feelings, particularly the feeling that his fellow Americans were not being justly dealt with in the economic sphere, had inspired the New Freedom, but it was Wilson the thinking machine, the political calculator, who had surrendered to the segregationists whose votes he needed to turn his ideas into law. The surrender had given Wilson an excellent year in Congress, and the passage of the new banking and tax laws opened the way for the rest of the New Freedom: a straightforward antitrust act, the creation of the Federal Trade Commission, and the eight-hour workday at companies engaged in interstate commerce. In the twentieth century, only Franklin Roosevelt's New Deal would do more to change the economic arrangements of the United States.

But in foreign affairs, there had been no triumphs. "Watchful waiting" was soon mocked as "deadly drifting," and Japan, still angry about the administration's inaction on California's Alien Land Act, had begun injecting itself into Mexican affairs, selling weapons to Huerta at bargain prices. Wilson doubted that the Japanese would make a lunge at the West Coast of the United States, but he worried that they might be waiting for a moment when Americans were so ensnared in Mexico that they would be powerless to prevent a Japanese raid on one of the U.S. possessions in the Pacific.

In the hope of improving his performance abroad, Wilson rescinded the ban on arms sales to Mexico, arguing that the Mexicans should be left free to settle their own affairs. When the flow of arms failed to produce major gains for Carranza and the Constitutionalists, Lind pressed Wilson for more—a military foray into Mexico City to pry Huerta from his throne, perhaps, or robust support for the Constitutionalists' plan to capture the oil port of Tampico, two hundred miles up the coast from Veracruz. A rebel victory at Tampico would deprive Huerta of a third of his revenue. Again and again Lind argued that the Constitutionalists would fail unless the president backed his morals with muscle. The president hesitated, but his inexplicable respect for Lind's judgment contributed not a little to the administration's first international disaster.

The trouble began on April 9, 1914, when the USS *Dolphin,* a cruiser attached to a small squadron near Tampico, sent the ship's paymaster and seven sailors into port for supplies. Foreign warships were a common sight along the Gulf coast of Mexico during the revolution. Germany and Great Britain occasionally sent cruisers, and the U.S. Navy kept several ships on hand for reasons that might be summed up as glowering at General Huerta.

The men from the *Dolphin* docked their whaleboat, did their errands, and were loading their cargo when they were arrested by a Mexican colonel. Within ninety minutes, the army's local commander, General Morelos Zaragoza, had released the Americans and apologized wholeheartedly for his colonel's ignorance of a point of international protocol: except in war, sailors aboard a vessel flying their nation's flag were immune to arrest.

Outraged by the arrests, the *Dolphin*'s commander, Rear Admiral Henry T. Mayo, sent an armed officer ashore with an imperious note demanding a formal apology and assurance that the arresting officer would be severely punished. Mayo also demanded that Zaragoza hoist the American flag and give it a twenty-one gun salute. He promised to return the salute from his ship.

Huerta quickly added his apology to Zaragoza's, put the hapless colo-nel under arrest, demanded an investigation, and promised a fitting pun-ishment if punishment was in order. But he balked at raising the Stars and Stripes on Mexican soil, saying that it would humiliate all Mexico. Huerta made his case to chargé O'Shaughnessy on Easter Sunday, April 12, and O'Shaughnessy shuttled to and from the Ministry of Foreign Affairs, trying to persuade Mexico to make the salute. No humiliation was intended, he ex-plained. The custom was an old one, a gesture of goodwill to ease two nations past an incident that might otherwise fester. On the same day, O'Shaugh-nessy informed the State Department of two more slights to Americans: the government-owned telegraph company had delayed delivery of a cable for the embassy, and a sailor from the USS *Minnesota* was arrested when he went into Veracruz to pick up the ship's mail.

In Washington, Bryan, Daniels, and Garrison spent much of their Easter Sunday and the first hours of Monday piecing together the reports from Mexico. From time to time they telephoned the president, who had taken his family to the hills of West Virginia in the hope that fresh air and a change of scene would speed the first lady's recovery. It had been six weeks since her fall, and she was unaccountably weak. The president returned alone to the White House at seven-thirty Monday morning, and on Tuesday issued a statement as stiff as Mayo's. The three incidents were of a piece, Wilson said—a pattern of "ill will and contempt." He called on the government of Mexico to correct the wrongs in a manner that would satisfy the United States and show the rest of the world "an entire change of attitude."

On Tuesday, Huerta said he would not authorize a salute because he did not believe the United States would return it. Gamboa suggested to O'Shaughnessy that Mexico and the United States could salute simultane-ously. But the custom called for the offending country to fire first. Bryan told O'Shaughnessy to assure the Mexicans that Admiral Mayo had prom-ised a return. With all the bellicosity that his pacific soul could muster, Bryan added that the United States was "disappointed" by Huerta's refusal. Huerta was indifferent to American disappointment.

On Wednesday, O'Shaughnessy warned Huerta that the time for salutes was running out. Daniels had just ordered all available warships from the Atlantic Fleet to head for Mexico. Huerta expressed puzzlement. He and Zaragoza had fully apologized for the mistake at Tampico, and the other incidents had been quickly sorted out. He could not understand why the apologies did not suffice.

Nor, frankly, could Secretary Daniels, who wished that Admiral Mayo had consulted him before barking orders at the sovereign state of Mexico. As commander in chief, Wilson could have ordered Mayo to back off, but a year's worth of frustration with Mexico had pushed the president to the brink. After magnifying three trivial mistakes into a grand show of contempt, Wilson persuaded himself that a show of force would speed Huerta's downfall. He expected no casualties, because the Mexican general in charge of the local garrison had told Lind that in the event of a U.S. attack, he would retreat rather than suffer the heavy losses sure to result from a contest between his light artillery and the big guns of the U.S. Navy's battleships.

By Saturday, the temper of the United States had worsened from "disappointed" to "greatly disappointed," and Bryan instructed O'Shaughnessy to deliver an ultimatum: if by six o'clock on Sunday evening Huerta did not announce his intention to comply with Admiral Mayo's demand, President Wilson would ask Congress for authority to take "such action as may be necessary." O'Shaughnessy spoke with Gamboa, who floated yet another proposal. Would O'Shaughnessy guarantee in writing that the salute would be returned? O'Shaughnessy said he would—if Huerta and the State Department approved.

The State Department did not approve. Furious, Gamboa accused O'Shaughnessy of duplicity and noted the absurdity of the U.S. demand for a salute from a government it did not recognize.

On Monday, April 20, the president updated the cabinet on events in Mexico and startled them by asking for their prayers. Next he briefed the press. He had no enthusiasm for war, would not ask for a declaration of war, and did not expect one, he said. In his view, the country did not face a war but "a special situation," and if dealt with firmly and promptly, it would not become a war.

At two o'clock the president met with the chairs and ranking minority members of the House and Senate foreign affairs committees. Lodge routinely composed accounts of his significant meetings, and after this gathering he wrote that Wilson had read a resolution authorizing him to use armed force to secure Huerta's recognition of American rights. Lodge, pointing out that the resolution was essentially a declaration of war against an individual, said he thought that the United States should act on a higher principle, namely the duty of a government to protect the lives and property of its citizens. Wilson replied that the broader language would lead to war. Lodge thought, but did not say, that it would be war no matter what Wilson called it.

Wilson trumped Lodge with the news that the *Ypiranga,* a German freighter laden with arms and ammunition, was about to leave Havana for Veracruz, where three long trains waited to carry the cargo to Huerta's arsenals. Wilson was determined to intercept the ship. Lodge asked how that could be lawfully accomplished if the United States was not officially at war. Wilson said that the U.S. Navy would seize the Veracruz customhouse and impound the cargo as soon as it touched the wharf.

At three o'clock, when the president went to the Capitol to ask Congress to support his resolution, the House galleries were packed. Ellen Wilson, making her first public appearance in weeks, invited several women who were standing to join her in the seats reserved for the White House. The president strode in briskly, showing no sign of strain. In reviewing the Mexican affronts, he said that if they were ignored, they might multiply and grow more serious until they caused a war. The Constitution empowered the president to act on his own in redressing such grievances, he said, but he wished to act with the support of Congress. "I therefore come to ask your approval that I should use the armed forces of the United States in such ways and to such an extent as may be necessary to obtain from General Huerta and his adherents the fullest recognition of the rights and dignity of the United States."

Within hours, the House granted the president's request with a vote of 337 to 37, but in the Senate, Lodge persuaded the entire Committee on Foreign Relations to reject any resolution targeting an individual. Wilson raced up to the Capitol to press the Senate's Democratic leaders for speedy acceptance of his version, while McAdoo, Burleson, and Tumulty lobbied the rest of the caucus by telephone. Back at the White House again, the president and his secretaries of state, war, and navy met long into the night with senior officers of the army and navy to complete plans for the intervention.

At two-thirty on Tuesday morning, April 21, the White House telephone operator roused Tumulty at home and connected him with Bryan, who reported that the *Ypiranga* had left Havana for Veracruz. Daniels and Wilson were patched into the conversation, and as Tumulty sat in his pajamas and listened to their solemn consideration of the orders they were about to give, it occurred to him that all three were pacifists at heart. Wilson and Daniels had painful childhood memories of the Civil War, and while Bryan had served in the army during the Spanish-American War, he had worked assiduously for peace ever since. When Wilson asked Daniels and Bryan what they thought should be done, both said the arms should not be allowed to reach Huerta. Taking the leap, Wilson said, "There is no alternative but to land." Daniels wired the commander of the navy's ships in Mexican waters: SEIZE CUSTOMHOUSE. DO NOT PERMIT WAR SUPPLIES TO BE DELIVERED TO HUERTA GOVERNMENT OR ANY OTHER PARTY.

American sailors and marines began piling into small boats and heading for shore at about eleven o'clock in the morning, and at one-thirty the USS *Utah* stopped the *Ypiranga* outside the Veracruz harbor's breakwater. The German cruiser *Dresden* was on the scene, and its quick-thinking captain told the Americans that the *Ypiranga* had no orders to unload in Veracruz. He volunteered to take custody of the ship and promised to make it available to transport Americans wanting to return to the United States, offers that were gratefully accepted.

In minutes, the Germans had eliminated the reason for the U.S. Navy's landing at Veracruz, but a thousand American sailors and marines had gone ashore just before noon, and by four o'clock had taken possession of the customhouse, the telegraph and post offices, the railroad station, and the hotel nearest the harbor. Contrary to Lind's predictions, the fighting was fierce. The sight of U.S. troops in Mexico had enraged the army as well as the cadets at the naval academy, which was next to the customhouse. The Mexicans started the shooting.

In Mexico City, O'Shaughnessy saw Huerta within hours of the landing. Huerta took the chargé's hand, called him amigo, and asked how he was holding up. Then the atmosphere turned arctic. "You have seized our port," Huerta snapped. "You have the right to take it, if you can, and we have the right to try to prevent you. *Su Excelencia el Señor Presidente* Wilson has declared war, unnecessarily, on a people that ask only to be left alone, to follow out their own evolution in their own way, though it may not seem to you a good way." Huerta now claimed that he had been willing to give the salute until he concluded that if he had done so, *el Señor Presidente* would have drummed up some other pretext for the invasion.

Five battleships from the Atlantic fleet reached Veracruz during the night, and with the three thousand reinforcements who went ashore early Wednesday, April 22, the Americans brought the fighting to an end before noon. Nineteen American sailors and marines were dead, 71 wounded. Mexico's dead numbered 126, its wounded 195. No war had been declared, and the word "invasion" had not been used by the White House, but there had been a battle.

One of the reporters at the White House press conference on April 23, the day after the fighting ended, described the president as "preternaturally pale, almost parchment. . . . The death of American sailors and marines owing to an order of his seemed to affect him like an ailment. He was positively shaken." Another reporter said he supposed that Huerta would announce that a state of war existed. "Well, will he?" the president asked. "I don't know whether he will or not."

None of the correspondents asked if the interdiction of the *Ypiranga* or the U.S. control of Veracruz would end Huerta's regime, nor did they ask what the United States planned to do about the salute. Their main concern was a searing message from General Carranza. Although his desire for Huerta's downfall was at least as fervent as Wilson's, Carranza did not hesitate to call the U.S. landing an invasion and a violation of Mexican sovereignty. He demanded that the United States evacuate.

The final question was another unsuccessful attempt to get Wilson to call the invasion an act of war. The European press generally insisted that it *had* been an act of war, and the editors of the *New York Evening Post* wrote that to call the seizure of the port anything else was to say that "a blow in the face is a love token."

Years later, recalling a White House meeting a day or two after the casualty reports were in, Lodge wrote, "We found Mr. Wilson in a state of great agitation. . . . He had never meant to have a war. Owing to his misinformation he was taken completely by surprise by the fighting at Veracruz and he was thoroughly alarmed. His one idea seemed to be that there must be no further warlike operations and he was then looking for an escape." Luckily for Wilson, escape came soon. Acting on a suggestion from Ambassador Jusserand, the ABC Powers of South America—Argentina, Brazil, and Chile—offered to mediate the dispute between Mexico and the United States. Wilson accepted on April 24, Huerta a few days later.

Within hours of Huerta's decision, Wilson sat down with Samuel G. Blythe, a staff writer for *The Saturday Evening Post,* to talk about Mexico. They met after dinner in Wilson's study, and Blythe was struck by the contrast between the pallid Wilson he had seen at the press conference, and the Wilson who sat before him in evening clothes—tan, clear-eyed, aglow with self-assurance. Wilson made a fist and leaned forward, tensing his body. "I could see the cords stand out on the back of his neck," Blythe wrote. "His eyes were narrowed, his lips slightly parted." And then "Bang! He hit the desk with that clenched fist. The paper knife rattled against the tray and a few open letters stirred a bit from the jar of the blow."

"I challenge you to cite me an instance in all the history of the world where liberty was handed down from above," Wilson said. "Liberty always is attained by the forces working below, underneath, by the great movement of the people. That, leavened by the sense of wrong and oppression and injustice, by the ferment of human rights to be attained, brings freedom." Wilson relaxed and mused on an irony he had noticed in Mexican affairs: every demand for order in Mexico was a demand for the kind of order desired by those who had caused the disorder—the aristocrats, hidalgos, and overlords who plundered the country's natural resources and exploited the people. Their idea of order was repression, he said. "My ideal is an orderly and righteous government in Mexico, but my passion is for the submerged eighty-five percent of the people of that Republic, who are now struggling toward liberty." Coping with the chaos in Mexico had been complicated, Wilson went on. The United States had been forced to wait for an opening, and the incident at Tampico had supplied it. "Really," he said, "it was a psychological moment, if that phrase is not too trite to be used."

Wilson hoped that the ABC mediation would succeed, but whether it did or not, he said, he deemed it the duty of the United States to help the Mexican people until peace and constitutional government were restored. And for those who believed that Mexicans were innately unsuited to self-government, Wilson had a message: when properly directed, all peoples were capable of self-government. He would not go so far as to say that Mexico's submerged 85 percent, almost all of them illiterate, were at that moment ready for democracy, but in his judgment, the idea that they would never be ready was "wickedly false."

The ABC Powers selected the neutral ground of Niagara Falls, Ontario, for their conference, which opened on May 20 and lasted six weeks. Bryan and Wilson had one agenda, Huerta another. Carranza, whose armies had advanced to the point where they controlled two-thirds of Mexico, had agreed to take part in the conference, but he refused to send delegates when he learned that the mediators expected a cease-fire and the United States expected a say in Mexico's future. Closing in on Mexico City, Carranza was determined to have his military victory, and he had no intention of allowing foreigners to interfere in Mexico's internal affairs.

From first to last, Wilson's intervention at Veracruz was a fiasco. Although Huerta soon agreed to resign, he did so because of Carranza's military strength, not because of Wilson or the U.S. Navy. The future of Mexico would be decided by six more years of revolution, not by the ABC Powers or the United States. The *Ypiranga,* after sailing north to Mobile to drop off American refugees, headed south again, steaming past Admiral Mayo's flotilla near Tampico, past the American flag flying over Veracruz, and down to the city of Puerto Mexico, where it unloaded its munitions. The United States had assumed that the *Ypiranga* would return to Germany after leaving Mobile, but when Washington complained to Berlin, Berlin feigned surprise. Admiral Mayo never got his salute.

11

Departures

On May 7, after an engagement of six months, Eleanor Randolph Wilson, the youngest of Woodrow and Ellen's three daughters, married William Gibbs McAdoo in the Blue Room of the White House. Out of solicitude for Ellen's health, Nell and Mac arranged a small wedding, inviting only their relatives, a handful of Nell's childhood friends, the cabinet, and the president's closest associates—Tumulty, Grayson, and House. Grayson served as best man and lent his navy dress sword for the cutting of the cake. Nell's bridal party included only Jessie and Margaret.

The mother of the bride cried openly. The father managed to control every physical manifestation of his sadness except in one eyelid, which quivered with the strain of keeping the tears back of the duct. He let them fall in his letters to Mary. "Ah! how desperately my heart aches that she is gone," he wrote a few days after the wedding. Nell was his ideal chum, a wonder, too good for any husband, and although he would not say it, his favorite.

She was, he said, "simply part of me, the only delightful part; and I feel the loneliness more than I dare admit even to myself." Though he disapproved of his selfishness, he could not suppress it: "I have lost her, for good and all. She will love me as much as ever, but she will not be at my side every day in my life, and I am desolate."

Wilson had no evident wish to stand in the way of Nell and Mac's marriage, but he would never be entirely at ease with it. He had been supplanted by a fifty-year-old widower, a man whose age made him a surrogate father as well as a husband. At twenty-four, Nell was younger than some of Mac's children. Wilson was also heavily indebted to McAdoo—for the presidential nomination in 1912, his service as secretary of the treasury, the passage of the New Freedom, the organization of the Federal Reserve Board, and the creation of a system to collect the new income tax. Wilson was grateful and clearly wanted to feel all that a father-in-law is supposed to feel, but his affections were laced with uneasiness. McAdoo was an astute politician with presidential ambitions. It was not long before Wilson began blaming his indigestion, an old problem, on his new son-in-law's habit of talking politics at the dinner table.

After the invasion of Veracruz, peace activists, clergymen, labor unions, and social reformers wrote Wilson to protest and to demand an immediate evacuation. Wilson refused. He had decided that the troops would stay until Huerta was gone and a new provisional government agreed to conduct a fair national election. The USS *Montana* carried the American war dead to New York for a funeral procession and a service at the Brooklyn Navy Yard on May 11. Daniels asked Wilson to take part, and against the advice of the Secret Service, he accepted. Haunted by the deaths in Veracruz, he felt that he had a duty to pay his respects in person. Ellen begged him to heed the Secret Service, which worried about his safety in the crowd. He refused. Wilson and Daniels rode through a crowd estimated at one million, in an open carriage behind the caissons bearing the coffins.

At the Navy Yard the president and the secretary of the navy shared the platform with the families of the fallen. The coffins, wrapped in flags, had been lined up shoulder to shoulder in one long row. After a hymn and an invocation, Daniels turned to Wilson and read the names of the dead. "All were in their prime of vigorous young manhood," Daniels said, and "[t]hey gave not only all they were, but all they hoped to be."

The commander in chief found himself in an uncharacteristic struggle for words. He sounded familiar chords of gratitude and patriotism, and offered an explanation for resorting to armed force: "We have gone down to Mexico to serve mankind, if we can find out the way." At last he used the word he had so assiduously avoided—war—but only in the abstract, to draw a distinction between a war of aggression and "a war of service."

No amount of abstraction could soften the hard fact of the coffins, but Wilson pressed on: "War, gentlemen, is only a sort of dramatic representation, a sort of dramatic symbol, of a thousand forms of duty." After quoting Kipling at his toplofty worst and spouting clichés about the ultimate verdict of conscience, Wilson found his way back to the eulogy. "These boys have shown us the way, and it is easier to walk on it because they have gone before and shown us how," he said.

But what *was* the way, and where did it lead? If the sailors' deaths were real, how could their war be merely a symbol? How had the killing in Veracruz served Mexico or mankind? And why should a president anchor his foreign policy in the idea of serving another nation, much less mankind? What if the other nation did not wish to be served? Or saw the alleged service as interference? Was it not enough for a president to tend to the interests of his own nation? Those who had come to the ceremony for comfort or clarification left empty-handed.

General Huerta soon resigned and took flight with eight of his generals. No one in the Wilson administration, including the president, could offer a convincing explanation of how the seizure of Veracruz had hastened Huerta's abdication, but Wilson's admirers gave him credit anyway. The truth was that Huerta had been brought down by the strength of Carranza's army, and Huerta and his generals fled to escape assassination.

There was no celebrating in the White House or the State Department. Carranza's ally Pancho Villa had just turned against him, raising considerable doubt about the durability of a Carranza government, and Wilson, having backed Carranza, would be blamed if he failed.

From Brooklyn Wilson went to Colonel House's apartment in Manhattan for lunch. Grayson was there, and he and House devoted the afternoon to relaxing the president with a drive out to Long Island for a walk around a golf course. In the evening House listened for nearly an hour as Wilson read poetry aloud. About to leave for Europe, House had a long list of political and diplomatic matters to discuss with the president but waited patiently for him to wind down.

House had had his first taste of diplomacy in the summer of 1913, when Wilson sent him to London to tell Sir Edward Grey, the foreign secretary, that he thought Britain had the better case in a dispute with the United States over the tolls to be paid at the Panama Canal. Britain claimed that in 1901, when it relinquished its interests in the Canal Zone to the United States, it had done so with the understanding that the ships of all nations would use the canal on equal terms. Congress later construed "ships of all nations" to mean "ships of all nations except the United States," arguing that American ships deserved an exemption because Americans had built and paid for the canal. Wilson had sent House to the Foreign Office with two messages: the president would ask Congress to repeal the exemption as soon as he could, and he would appreciate it if the British press maintained a discreet silence on the subject.

When the Foreign Office proved amenable, House was like a man awakened to the wonders of Champagne: he wanted more and longed to know all its varieties. So he was instantly galvanized when Walter Hines Page, the American ambassador to the Court of St. James's, urged him to find a way for Wilson to stop the ruinously expensive, increasingly dangerous European arms race. Page hoped that if Wilson put his army and navy at the service of humanity, the Europeans would follow suit. For starters, Page said, they could collaborate in "cleaning up the tropics," doing everything for the good of tropical peoples, with no thought of conquest. If Europe's large armies and navies had a job, said Page, "they'd quit sitting on their haunches, growling at one another." He asked House to draw up a plan.

House began to think about how the United States might ease the tensions that drove the Great Powers to build more dreadnoughts, fill more arsenals, invent more methods of killing. The arms race had been going on for more than a decade. The Hague Conference of 1899 banned the use of poison gas, aerial attacks, and dumdum bullets but had not banned their development, so the developers carried on.

While Page imagined turning militarism into humanitarianism, House imagined transforming the competition into a grand project for spreading prosperity. The Great Adventure, as he called it, would bring together the world's richest nations—the United States, Great Britain, Germany, and France—to invest side by side in the poorer quarters of the globe. The rich nations would finance development on reasonable terms, everyone would prosper, and everyone would have a stake in maintaining amicable relations and stable governments.

When Colonel House tried out his idea on German and British envoys to the United States, they encouraged him to pursue it. He leaned heavily on the advice of Sir William Tyrrell, Grey's private secretary, who spent the fall of 1913 at the British embassy in Washington. Tyrrell urged him to go to Berlin first, and, reaching for the moon, suggested that House encourage the kaiser to call off the arms race and invite Germany to join the United States and Britain in the economic development scheme. Tyrrell promised the colonel that Britain would cooperate with the United States. There is no sign that House wondered how a private secretary to a foreign minister could pledge his country to anything, or what "cooperate" might mean in this instance. House was equally incurious about Wilson's detachment from the Great Adventure. Wilson tepidly endorsed it, then seemed to tuck it into the same mental file where he kept Bryan's cooling-off treaties, a file that might have been labeled "Probably Harmless and Possibly Useful."

When Colonel House reached Berlin in late May, he was shocked by the militarism in the air. As a guest at the U.S. embassy, he undoubtedly heard Ambassador James W. Gerard's oft-stated view that the summer of 1914 would be an ideal moment for Germany to start a war. The Kiel Canal, widened and deepened to speed the new German dreadnoughts from the Baltic to the North Sea, had just reopened. No one but Germany had dirigibles or stores of poison gas. No other nation had more submarines or better airplanes. And with their big guns, they were confident that they could pulverize the great fortresses of France. Gerard also believed that the kaiser would have to move soon. Militarism had permeated the country, but there was also mounting popular resistance to it, and the kaiser and his circle feared that they would lose their hold on Germany unless they quickly marched the country into a short and successful war.

After a few days in Berlin, House wrote Wilson that the atmosphere was "jingoism run stark mad. Unless someone acting for you can bring about an understanding, there is someday to be an awful cataclysm." He had an hour's private conversation with Admiral Alfred von Tirpitz, champion of German naval expansion, about the hazards of the dreadnought competition with Britain. Disclaiming any desire for conquest, Tirpitz insisted that the best way for Germany to maintain peace was to put fear in the hearts of her enemies. House let Tirpitz know that if any complications arose between the United States and Germany, Germany would have to deal with Woodrow Wilson, whom he described as "a man of iron courage and inflexible will."

Gerard took House to meet the kaiser at his country palace in Potsdam on June 1. After lunch, House was taken to the terrace for a tête-à-tête with the kaiser, who spoke of soldiers and Mexico and his obsession with preserving the Anglo-Saxon race. For twenty years the kaiser had been warning Europe that if it did not stand up to the "yellow peril," it would be overrun by the hordes of Asia. With House he spoke of Japanese "fanaticism" and the "semi-barbarous" character of Slavs and Latins. As the only countries able to advance Christian civilization, the United States, Germany, and England ought to unite against the rest of the world, the kaiser said. House replied that the United States did not form alliances but was more than willing to do its part for world peace.

House left Potsdam with a mixed message from the kaiser. The positives were a promise to consider any peace plan that did not compromise German security and a declaration that he did not want a war because it would interfere with trade. The great negative was his paranoia. "Every nation in Europe has its bayonets pointed at Germany," he told House. "But we are ready."

Colonel House thrived on dualities: mixed messages, ostensible agendas and real agendas, dealings on the table and under the table. He was often duplicitous, and had he been asked to defend himself, he undoubtedly would have cited the purity of his ambitions: success for a president he admired, peace, freedom, and global prosperity. His diary, which summarizes hundreds of conversations with powerful men, reveals a man who listened and suggested but almost never inquired. His account of the afternoon at Potsdam was all "I told the kaiser and the kaiser told me." House told the kaiser that Wilson, as an outsider to the quarrels of Europe, might play a useful role in defusing its tensions. I agree, said the kaiser. House told the kaiser about the Great Adventure, and the kaiser said that if the undertaking had the support of Germany, England, and the United States, it would succeed. House told the kaiser that he would write him about his talks with the British. That would be good, said the kaiser. Despite the kaiser's talk of bayonets and Tirpitz's impatience with the idea of halting the dreadnought competition, House told Wilson that the visit to Berlin had been a triumph. It would have been more accurate to say that the kaiser had been cordial but noncommittal.

In Paris, House saw only the U.S. ambassador, and if they discussed the Great Adventure, there is no sign of it. House left France with the mistaken idea that while the French people still dreamed of revenge and the recovery of Alsace-Lorraine, territory lost forty years earlier in the Franco-Prussian War, French political leaders had moved on. According to House, they were content with the boundaries of France and resigned to Germany's preeminence on the Continent. "France, I am sure, will welcome our efforts for peace," he wrote Wilson.

In London, House found the British less preoccupied with Germany than with their subjects in Ireland, who were on the brink of revolution. Despite the Irish crisis, they were remarkably attentive to House, and they readily agreed when he suggested that naval talks with Germany might ease tensions between the two countries. House's notion that Wilson, as an outsider, might serve as mediator would be rejected again and again. The Great Powers did not regard the United States as an equal, and they disliked Wilson's self-righteousness in foreign affairs. But the warm welcome that House found in the country palace of the kaiser and the garden parties of English aristocrats gave him an outsized sense of his own importance and led him to think that all things were possible.

Nor did House grasp that he was a bearer of old news and superficial impressions. He spoke of the military fever in Berlin as if the Foreign Office had received no word of it, and he seemed to think he was enlightening Grey when he reported that Germany would soon have aircraft capable of crossing the sea and bombing London. "The idea, then, is that England will be in the same position as the Continental Powers?" Grey asked. House replied with a self-satisfied "Quite so." A man less self-deceived than Colonel House would have understood Grey's question as a social gesture made simply to keep the wheel of conversation turning. Nor did House seem to realize that the Europeans' willingness to listen was only that. They lost nothing by making themselves agreeable to the confidential advisor of the American president. The United States was not yet the most powerful nation on earth, but it was the wealthiest, and no genius was required to understand the value of its goodwill.

House made one more attempt to interest Grey in high-level talks with Germany. He presented his brief at a luncheon hosted by Grey, and reported in his diary that the guests, all men in the top echelon of the British government, agreed that special representatives should be sent to Germany "to talk over the situation and give assurances of good intentions." Privately, House proposed to Grey that the two of them run up to Kiel, where the German regatta was under way. They would go on the pretext of seeing the races but behind the scenes would lay the groundwork for the Anglo-German talks House had in mind. House did not record Grey's response but left in a buoyant mood. "It is difficult for me to realize that the dream I had last year is beginning to come true," he told his diary. "I have seen the kaiser, and now the British government seem eager to carry on the discussion."

There would be no trip to Kiel. On June 28, 1914, the archduke of Austria-Hungary and his wife were assassinated in Sarajevo by Serbian nationalists, and the kaiser, who received the news while racing his yacht at

Kiel, sped back to Berlin. House's diary does not mention Sarajevo or the kaiser's alarm, and it would be weeks before the White House press corps asked Wilson about the assassinations.

Grey was not expecting a war, but he suddenly hesitated to write the kaiser—for fear of offending the French, he said. Tyrrell was sent to ask House if *he* would write Berlin about his talks with the British. House was more than willing. "I feel we have gone a long way in the right direction and that much good has already been accomplished," he reported in his diary on July 3. "I trust more will follow."

House sailed for Boston on July 21 and landed on July 29, the day after Austria declared war on Serbia. "The kaiser does not want war," he told reporters who met him at the pier. But as soon as Austria announced that it was at war with Serbia, the dominoes began to fall: the Russians mobilized in defense of the Serbs, Germany declared war on Russia, and France pledged to support Russia. The Germans promptly declared war on the French, then sought the Belgians' permission to pass through Flanders en route to France. Belgium refused, and the Germans invaded. On August 4, the British decided to come to the defense of the Belgians with a declaration of war against Germany.

Colonel and Mrs. House settled into their summer rental in Prides Crossing, Massachusetts, and for several days the colonel ignored his diary. But before the week was out, he offered a flattering version of his role in recent events: "I clearly foreshadowed the present catastrophe. I knew then that the high tension under which Germany was working could lead to but one result unless something was done to stop it. I recall with what surprise Sir Edward Grey and other members of the British government listened to my story of the German situation as I saw it. They believed that matters were in better shape than they had been for a long while, and it was hard for them to think I was diagnosing the situation correctly. I take it that I will have some reputation as a prophet with Sir Edward and his confreres."

In a letter to Page he spoke as if the two of them had almost prevented the war: "just think how near we came to making such a catastrophe impossible! If England had moved a little faster and had let me go back to Germany, the thing, perhaps, could have been done." Page understood House's disappointment but rejected his hypothesis: "No, no, no—no power on earth could have prevented it. The German militarism, which is the crime of the last fifty years, has been working for this for twenty-five years. It is the logical result of their spirit and enterprise and doctrine. . . . Don't let your conscience be worried. You did all that any mortal man could do. But nobody could have done anything effective. We've got to see to it that this system doesn't grow up again. That's all."

From Washington came a sympathetic note urging House not to despair. The war was far removed from their hopes, Wilson wrote, "but we must face the situation in the confidence that Providence has deeper plans than we could possibly have laid ourselves."

EUROPE IN 1914,
ON THE EVE OF WORLD WAR I

MILES 200

KM 200

ATLANTIC OCEAN

UNITED KINGDOM

London

North Sea

NORWAY

SWEDEN

DENMARK

NETHER-LANDS

Amsterdam

Rotterdam

Antwerp

BELGIUM

Brussels

Lux.

ALSACE-LORRAINE

Paris

FRANCE

Marseille

SPAIN

PORTUGAL

Mediterranean Sea

St. Petersburg

Riga

Baltic Sea

Vilna

Minsk

RUSSIA

Moscow

Kiev

Warsaw

L'vov

Berlin

GERMANY

Munich

SWITZ.

AUSTRIA-HUNGARY

Vienna

ITALY

Rome

Adriatic Sea

BOSNIA-HERZEGOVINA

Belgrade

Sarajevo

SERBIA

MONTE-NEGRO

ALBANIA

TRANSYLVANIA

RUMANIA

Bucharest

BULGARIA

Sofia

Odessa

Black Sea

GREECE

Istanbul

OTTOMAN TURKEY

Izmir (Smyrna)

N E S W

12

·············

The General Wreck

Tuesday, August 4, 1914, gave Washington something it rarely got: a perfect summer day. Light breeze, temperature of seventy-nine degrees. Few savored it. Most of officialdom had taken wing, as it did every summer, and although Congress was still in session, its members were not spending much time outdoors. They went to the Capitol early and stayed late in hopes of finishing the work that stood between them and a bit of vacation before their campaigns for reelection.

The president was also immured, absorbed in matters that rendered the loveliness of the day grotesque. In a single week, Europe had self-destructed, and millions of soldiers were now on the march. Wilson had followed the collapse hour by hour, and while there was little he could do, he had not been idle. On August 3, he issued a proclamation of U.S. neutrality, forbidding Americans from joining or recruiting for the belligerents' armies, arming ships for any nation at war, or planning a military expedition in support of a combatant.

The president also asked reporters to abstain from passing along reports or rumors that might incite an American version of the lawlessness sweeping the capitals of Europe. In Paris, an overzealous patriot had assassinated the Socialist leader Jean Jaurès for his pacifist leanings. In Berlin, embassy windows were smashed, and English tourists were evicted from their hotels. There and in Paris and London, foreigners were being spat upon and roughed up. Crowds roamed the streets at all hours, waving flags, singing national airs, and looking for foreign-owned establishments to vandalize. The Continent's finance ministers staved off a panic by closing stock exchanges, raising interest rates, and curtailing withdrawals, but Europeans fearing the worst were emptying the stores.

Thousands of American tourists in Europe were cut off from their money, and as the captains of dozens of transatlantic liners ducked into port to await instructions from their home offices, departure dates and reservations disappeared. Americans poured into their embassies, which worked nonstop to relieve the destitute and to issue passports. When Holland declared its neutrality, Ambassador Gerard bought hundreds of steerage tickets on Dutch liners and sold them to Americans. Ambassador Page wrote Wilson that "Crazy men and weeping women were imploring and cursing and demanding. . . . Men shook English banknotes in my face and demanded U.S. money and swore our Government and its agents ought all to be shot."

On August 4, Wilson wrote the heads of the warring states to say that he would welcome an opportunity to act for peace. In tendering the good offices of the United States, he was taking a cue from The Hague Convention for the Pacific Settlement of International Disputes, which recommended that in case of an armed conflict, a disinterested third party should offer to mediate.

Wilson customarily wrote on a typewriter, but on this day he was composing in pencil, at his wife's bedside, and straining to concentrate. Ellen's failure to recover from her fall in March had led Grayson to diagnose a nervous breakdown caused by the demands of her life as first lady. She had rallied in May for her fifty-fourth birthday and Nell and Mac's wedding, but by June good days were rare. Then the diagnosis was revised to Bright's disease, an incurable disorder of the kidneys. Grayson summoned the specialists and reassured Wilson, hoping to protect him from anguish for as long as possible. Toward the end of July, Grayson moved into the White House to care for Ellen around the clock.

The most important visitor on August 4 was Edward P. Davis of Philadelphia, the Wilsons' family physician for many years and one of Wilson's inner circle during their student days at Princeton. "We sat all day waiting," Nell wrote. The day would remain in her memory as "a terrible nightmare—Europe in flames, and all hope fading from our own hearts." Grayson came and went from the sickroom, his face inscrutable, and late in the afternoon, after Davis arrived, it was decided that he should tell the girls that their mother's death was imminent. Their father wept, which he had never done in their presence.

Wilson had known for weeks that Ellen's illness was fatal, but knowing was not the same as believing: "we are still hoping and the doctors are doing noble work," he wrote House on August 6. On the same day, the Senate passed the legislation Ellen had sought to clean up Washington's alleyways, and when Woodrow gave her the news, she seemed to understand. Ellen died at five o'clock, with Woodrow and Margaret and Jessie and Nell at her side. He wept again, uncontrollably. Turning away, he walked to a window and burst out, "Oh, my God, what am I to do?" When he could speak again, he was resolute: "I must not give way."

Ellen's funeral took place in the East Room on August 10 at two in the afternoon. The ceremonies were simple, the guest list abbreviated. The Wilson family entered moments before the service began and did not linger when it ended. By four-thirty they were on a private train bound for Rome, Georgia, Ellen's hometown. She would be buried next to her parents. The president's official retinue numbered exactly two: Tumulty and Grayson.

The coffin traveled with the president, at one end of his private car, where he continued the vigil he had kept since her death. The Secret Service had orders to admit no one but family except at his invitation. Rome had draped itself in black, and row upon row of townspeople lined the streets between the railroad station and the Presbyterian church where Ellen's father had served as pastor. Wilson maintained his composure throughout the service but broke down at the grave.

Traveling back to Washington he stood alone for hours on the train's rear platform. Grayson, who went out at one point to keep him company, was sent away. "I want to think," Wilson said. Once home, though, he clung to Grayson. They golfed together, dined together, and read together in Wilson's study. "I never understood before what a broken heart meant, and did for a man," Wilson wrote his friend Mary. "It just means that he lives by the compulsion of necessity and duty only, and has no other motive force. . . . Every night finds me exhausted—dead in heart and body." He blamed Ellen's early death on his demanding political career, and he sought escape from guilt and grief in his work.

Twenty-one of Bryan's cooling-off treaties were pending in the Senate when the world war began, and as soon as Wilson returned from Georgia he urged

William J. Stone, chairman of the Senate's Committee on Foreign Relations, to secure ratification quickly and without any watering down. The incessant hopscotching of Bryan's mind exasperated all who dealt with him, but he had moved the treaties forward with the single-mindedness of Woodrow Wilson. Great Britain, France, Russia, and Austria had accepted the treaties in principle, and Bryan regularly nudged their ambassadors to press their governments for final approval. He also made repeated approaches to the chief resisters, Germany and Japan. Germany had spurned him on the basis of a military calculation: after years of preparation and an investment of billions of marks, it had the most powerful army in Europe. A cooling-off treaty would require Germany to put war on hold if it found itself at an impasse with the United States. The German army had prepared itself to strike quickly and was not about to forfeit its advantage. Tokyo rejected Bryan's approaches because the United States disapproved of Japanese ambitions in China and because Japan still resented California's Alien Land Law. Nevertheless, Bryan had stuck to his last, and on August 13 the Senate ratified eighteen of the treaties. The rest were returned to the State Department for fine-tuning.

Bryan had spent the afternoon conferring with senators at the Capitol, and as he walked to his automobile after the vote, the *Christian Science Monitor*'s correspondent caught up with him. The reporter was puzzled. Germany had ridiculed Britain for entering the war in defense of "a scrap of paper" (a reference to an old treaty protecting the neutrality of Belgium). The reporter wondered why the United States was busily signing peace treaties at a moment that seemed to prove their pointlessness. The cooling-off treaties were "absolutely new," Bryan said. He was sure that if the belligerents had had time to think, they would not have gone to war.

Unless one of them decided that the treaty was a scrap of paper.

Though Americans would grow rich on the war, its first economic effects were devastating. The value of exports shipped from New York sank by 30 percent in three weeks. Imports also plummeted, and the decline in revenues from customs duties threatened to leave the Treasury well short of its projections for the fiscal year. Wharves and warehouses were soon piled high with exports of every description.

Overnight, European cargo ships had disappeared from the Atlantic. Many French and English vessels were pressed into war service, and scores of German ships docked in American ports to avoid destruction or capture by the British, who still ruled the Atlantic. American ships were in short supply, because the growth in trade had far outstripped the growth of the

U.S. merchant marine: only 10 percent of American exports traveled in American bottoms. Shipping rates soared as marine insurers canceled policies and U.S. shipping companies either suspended operations or demanded compensation for the added risk.

McAdoo proposed a heretical solution: government intervention. The country was in crisis, business had gone into hiding, and no one but government could save the day, he told Wilson. He thought that the administration should establish a federal agency to provide the necessary insurance and a corporation to buy and build ships. Wilson liked the ideas but foresaw a huge fight with Republicans, who would accuse him of putting the country on the road to socialism. But after considering the proposition for a day or two, he decided to pursue it. Although Congress quickly approved the insurance agency, the debate on the shipping corporation dragged on for months and thrust the administration into quarrels with Big Business, Big Finance, and the governments of France and Great Britain.

Days after the war began, the House of Morgan telephoned the State Department to ask if a $100 million loan to the French government would be at odds with the new state of neutrality. The laws of war allowed neutrals to do business with all belligerents, but Bryan strongly believed that the United States should not allow its banks to lend to the warring countries. "Money is the worst of all contrabands because it commands everything else," he wrote Wilson. Bryan argued that barring such loans would shorten the war and set a fine example for the rest of the world. Wilson agreed, and on August 15 the United States banned loans to all belligerents.

Given their antipathy to war, Wilson and Bryan might have banned the sale of munitions as well, but they did not, and when called upon to explain, they turned to the new counselor of the State Department, Robert Lansing. An experienced international lawyer, Lansing pointed out that banks typically turned large loans into bonds for sale on Wall Street. Because the bonds would probably be purchased by investors who sympathized with the government borrowing the money, thousands of Americans would become fierce partisans of one side or the other, Lansing argued. But a sale of munitions was different, he said. The manufacturer would sell to one belligerent as readily as he would to another. No chauvinism would be aroused. The moral conundrum of being an amoral accomplice to all parties in the slaughter was never addressed.

Grayson and House pleaded with Wilson to take a vacation, and House proposed a cruise along the Massachusetts coast in the presidential yacht. "You owe it to the country to do this, and I trust you may find it possible to do so this week," the colonel wrote the president soon after Ellen's death. "Our automobile can follow the *Mayflower* from place to place, so that you may have diversion both by land and sea." Wilson declined, saying that he had to keep a close watch on Europe. And, he added, "my great safety lies in having my attention absolutely fixed elsewhere than upon myself. I believe this is good 'doctor' sense as well as good reasoning about the public welfare."

He was more candid with Mary Hulbert: "In God's gracious arrangement of things I have little time or chance to think about myself. The day's work and responsibilities exhaust all the vitality I have and there is none left to spend on pity for myself. I am lamed and wounded more sorely than any words I have could describe. I never dreamed such loneliness and desolation of heart possible. I suffer all the time a sort of dumb agony of longing." He was grateful for the magnitude of his labors, he said, because they forced him to stay in harness. "Nothing less great, I imagine, could. The world itself seems gone mad, and there is a sort of grim pleasure and stern compulsion to keep sane and self-possessed amidst the general wreck and distemper."

Wilson expected the United States to face the general wreck with the same stoicism he imposed on himself. On August 18, a week after Ellen's burial, he issued a statement exhorting Americans to serve the national interest by acting and speaking in "the spirit of impartiality and fairness and friendliness to all concerned." Some 35 million Americans—one in three— were immigrants or, like Wilson himself, children of immigrants. With ties to one or another of the countries at war, they were bound to differ in their sympathies, Wilson acknowledged, and he asked them to rein in their passions. "We must be impartial in thought as well as in action," he said.

The belligerents answered Wilson's call for a neutrality of spirit by starting a propaganda war in the United States, hoping to persuade Americans to do the very thing their president had asked them not to do: take sides. Within days of his appeal, Britain, France, Germany, and Japan had set up "information bureaus" in Washington and other American cities.

The president granted himself a few days' leave at the end of August and went up to the house he and Ellen had rented in Cornish. Jessie and her husband, Frank Sayre, a lawyer who devoted his career to public service and higher education, were already there. Wilson took Margaret and Grayson with him and extended an invitation to House, who was also in mourning— for the Great Adventure, which had been blasted to pieces by the Great War. He was distraught, too, about Ellen's death, and deeply unhappy that his hypersensitivity to heat had kept him from going to Washington to comfort his friend.

House did not mention (as others did) that Wilson looked older, but he was clearly moved by Wilson's grief. As Wilson spoke of his loss, he cried and told House that he felt like a machine that had given out. As far as he could tell, he was still doing good work, yet he looked to the rest of his term in office—two and a half years—with dread. "He did not see how he could go through with it," House told his diary.

Wilson put House in the suite he had shared with Ellen, a pair of bedrooms joined by a bath. The president rose early to take care of his ablutions before the colonel got up, which House saw as a perfect illustration of Wilson's thoroughgoing courtesy. At night they played billiards, read, and talked about the war. Wilson was sickened by the week's news from Belgium, where the Germans were systematically destroying villages and executing scores of civilians, punishing whole towns for casualties inflicted by a handful of snipers. The worst of these depredations, the sacking of the medieval city of Louvain, had begun on the night of August 25 in a moment of confusion over who had fired on whom. Five days later, German soldiers were still moving through the streets, smashing windows and tossing incendiary devices into every house. More than a thousand homes were destroyed, along with the cathedral and most of the University of Louvain.

Wilson predicted that such barbarism would erase centuries of civilization. House, too, was in despair, unable to imagine any good ending for the war. If the Allies won, he thought that Russia, not England and France, would dominate the Continent. And if the Central Powers won, German militarism would force the rest of the world to become an armed camp.*

Between the first and last days of August 1914, nine European nations had mobilized eighteen million men, fought eighteen battles, and inflicted hundreds of thousands of casualties. The French dead and wounded in a handful of short engagements collectively known as the Battle of the Frontiers numbered 140,000.

By the time Wilson returned to Washington, on September 1, he was under attack from every quarter. There were demands for an official protest of the German rampage through Belgium, and while Wilson deplored the wantonness of the destruction, he maintained that neutrality required the

---

* Ultimately the six Allies (Britain, France, Russia, Italy, Japan, and Portugal) would have twenty-two Associates (Belgium, Bolivia, Brazil, China, Cuba, Czechoslovakia, Ecuador, Greece, Guatemala, Haiti, the Hejaz [an Arabian kingdom], Honduras, Liberia, Nicaragua, Panama, Peru, Poland, Romania, Serb-Croat-Slovene State, Siam, the United States, and Uruguay).

United States to refrain from commenting on the acts of any belligerent. Germany accused American newspapers of favoring Britain. Britain feared that American exports to the neutral nation of Holland would be floated up the Rhine to Germany. And France cried foul when it learned that the U.S. government might purchase the German ships lying idle in American ports. Ambassador Jusserand wondered how the United States could justify paying huge sums to German shipping interests when it refused to let the French government borrow money in the United States. "What is our duty, what are our obligations, what are our rights under the circumstances?" asked *The Baltimore Sun*. "... We have got to consider other nations, and we have got to consider ourselves. And Uncle Sam will have to put on his best thinking cap to reach the right conclusion."

13

· · · · · · · · · · · · ·

At Sea

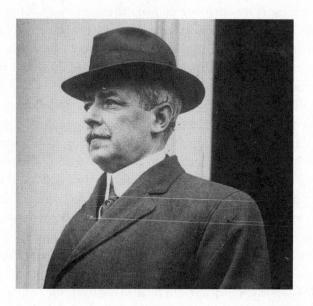

H ome from New Hampshire, Wilson handed himself over to the
exigencies of the war. When McAdoo told him that the disruption
of trade would leave the U.S. Treasury $100 million short for the
year, Wilson hastened to the Capitol and asked for an emergency tax bill. He
needed only twelve minutes to lay out his case, the gist of which was that
although the United States had not caused the problem, it was obliged to
solve it. He left the particulars to Congress but requested that the new levies,
whatever they were, produce revenue immediately, steadily, and for as long
as necessary. Within weeks the House and Senate agreed to tax a long list of
financial instruments and nonessential consumer goods.

None of the nations at war had accepted Wilson's offer to assist in re-
storing peace, and at the end of August, Bryan forwarded the refusals to the
White House with a note saying that they called to mind "that passage in the
Scriptures which says 'that they all with one accord began to make excuses.'

Each one declares he is opposed to war and anxious to avoid it and then lays the blame upon someone else." As undownable as Mr. Micawber, Bryan still believed that an opportunity for peacemaking would turn up and that when it did, Wilson would be able to capitalize on the antipathy to war expressed in all the letters.

But the war was scarcely a month old when Ambassador Page informed the State Department that the Allies would not welcome a peace overture anytime soon. Page had raised the subject at the Foreign Office only to be told by Sir Edward Grey that Britain had exhausted every honorable means to avoid war and now saw the kaiser as it had seen Napoleon: as "a world pest and an enemy of civilization." The French were of a similar mind, and France, Great Britain, and Russia had agreed that they would make peace together or not at all.

Away when the war began, most of the European diplomats serving in Washington were back at their posts by the beginning of September. On landing in the United States, the German ambassador, Count Johann Heinrich von Bernstorff, had something to declare: Russia had started the war by meddling in a quarrel between Austria and Serbia, and when Russia mobilized its army, Germany had been forced to do the same, in self-defense. Bernstorff expressed confidence that Americans would understand as soon as they had the facts.

The British and French ambassadors, Sir Cecil Spring Rice and Jean Jules Jusserand, returned from Europe together on a crowded ocean liner. While their wives were quartered in relative comfort, the ambassadors were assigned to stifling cabins next to one of the ship's funnels. They did much of their sleeping on deck. Spring Rice was distressed to find Jusserand and his wife "shattered and nervous." Like Bernstorff, Spring Rice and Jusserand believed that their enemies had started the war. All three ambassadors carried instructions to hold the United States to its pledge of strict neutrality.

Spring Rice met with Wilson on September 3 and came away relieved. Wilson had told him that all he loved most in the world was at risk. Wilson also said that if the Germans won the war, the United States would be forced to enlarge its defenses to a point that would be fatal to American democracy. Both utterances confirmed the impression the ambassador had carried away from a meeting a few days before, when he mentioned Wordsworth's "Sonnets Dedicated to Liberty," written during the Napoleonic Wars. Wilson had replied that he knew the poems by heart and thought of them constantly. Seizing the moment, Spring Rice said, "You and Grey are fed on the same food and I think you understand." Wilson teared up.

"I am sure we can, at the right moment, depend on an understanding heart here," Spring Rice wrote Grey after the meeting. But he warned that Wilson should not be taken for granted. Americans saw no reason to involve themselves in a European war, and two huge blocs of American voters, German Americans and Irish Americans, had no sympathy for England. The president had to be "rather conspicuously neutral, and that he is trying to be," Spring Rice explained. "Our line is to say that we are confident he will favor neither one party nor the other, and that we only ask a fair field."

An able and experienced diplomat, Spring Rice had delighted Washington society in the 1880s, when he served as a junior secretary in the British legation. His pedigree included Eton and Oxford, a clerkship in the Foreign Office, and, after his first posting to Washington, assignments in Tehran, Cairo, Berlin, St. Petersburg, and Stockholm. Spring Rice should have been a highly successful ambassador to the United States, but his arrival in Washington in 1913 coincided with the onset of hyperthyroidism, which can elevate blood pressure and body temperature, affect digestion and muscle strength, and provoke operatic mood swings. Now categorized as an autoimmune disease, hyperthyroidism in Spring Rice's day was seen as a nervous disorder, and nervous disorders were commonly regarded as character defects. Spring Rice's friends knew him as a sharp analyst of geopolitics, a perceptive reader of his fellow humans, and a great wit—judgments borne out by his correspondence. But in his new condition, which triggered fears and angry outbursts that he could neither foresee nor control, he sometimes offended officials at the State Department. Not knowing the old Spring Rice, many in Wilson's Washington regarded him as unfit for diplomacy. He was also suspect because of his long friendships with two vocal critics of Wilson, Roosevelt and Lodge.

Jusserand, who was also fond of Roosevelt, fared better. Born in Lyon, he had come to the United States as ambassador in 1903, after serving France in Tunisia, Britain, and Denmark and spending several years at the French Foreign Ministry. In his spare time, Jusserand had pegged away at a doctorate in literature and over his life would write books on Shakespeare, Chaucer, diplomacy, sports, French literature, and other subjects. Although he had an American-born wife, she had been raised in France, and he came to Washington knowing next to nothing about the United States. To begin filling the void, he and his wife spent much of their first year in the United States traveling the country. He also read voluminously and, like Wilson, taught himself American history by writing it. One of his books, *With Americans of Past and Present Days,* would be awarded a Pulitzer Prize in history. Robert Lansing ranked Jusserand first among the ambassadors in Washington.

Depressed by the German army's destruction of the cathedral at Reims ("his favorite spot on earth," according to Spring Rice), Jusserand nevertheless waged a brilliant one-man battle for France in the first months of the war. In public he protested the Wilson administration's plan to purchase the German ships, which were said to be worth at least $25 million. To anyone who would listen, Jusserand argued that it would be decidedly un-neutral for the United States to send millions of dollars to Germany while refusing to allow American banks to make loans to the Allies. In private he retained an American banker to find a way around the loan ban, and before long the banker persuaded the State Department that armies in need of supplies would purchase them elsewhere if they could not arrange financing in the United States. The banker suggested that the administration leave the loan ban in place but allow American banks to extend lines of credit.

So began the U.S. investment in an Allied victory. Although free to grant similar credits to the Central Powers, few American banks did. From the fall of 1914 until the spring of 1917, when the United States entered the war, American banks arranged $2.3 billion in financing for the Allies, nearly a hundred times more than the amount they furnished to Germany.

Neutrality, which seemed to ensure the safety of the United States, was actually a minefield. The laws of naval warfare barred neutrals from mounting military expeditions or recruiting troops for a foreign army but allowed them to ship whatever they chose, munitions included, wherever they pleased. The rub was that the same body of law allowed belligerents to interdict any neutral ship on the high seas and confiscate cargo deemed militarily useful to the enemy. Belligerents naturally cast a wary eye on neutral ships, and neutrals naturally resented the searches and seizures.

It stood to reason that a nation at war would ignore all rights that threatened its survival, but it also stood to reason that if a neutral did not vigorously defend its rights, belligerents would grow ever more aggressive in interfering with neutral trade. Stakes were high, tempers flared, and the neutral was in constant danger of being swept into the war. Sir Edward Grey would remember the management of this phase of the world war as "anxious work," with each British interdiction of an American merchant ship setting off a chain reaction: U.S. protest, British rebuttal, U.S. irritation, British regrets and resolve. As Grey explained in his memoir, he went at his task with his eye fixed on one objective: "secure the maximum of blockade that could be enforced without a rupture with the United States."

The defense of America's neutral rights fell to Robert Lansing. A graduate of Amherst College, he had read law in his father's firm and moved into international law through his father-in-law, John W. Foster, who served as secretary of state to President Benjamin Harrison. Over the next two decades Lansing represented the United States in four arbitration cases, represented several governments in his private practice, and co-founded the American Society for International Law.

Lansing had joined the State Department as counselor in 1914, at Wilson's invitation. A year shy of fifty, he was five-foot-nine and had gray eyes, close-cropped gray hair, and a gray mustache. At the State Department he wore a gray cutaway and striped trousers, and away from the office he favored a gray hat and gray tweeds. He was an elder of the Presbyterian Church, a coin collector, and an amateur horticulturist. His manner was so mild that even the lowliest employees of the State Department felt free to make fun of him. On one slow ride up the department's steam-driven elevator, Lansing remarked, in his gray voice, "Not much power this morning." When he got off, the elevator operator winked at the other passenger, nodded in Lansing's direction, and said, "Not much power this morning."

In truth Lansing possessed considerable force of will, all of it subterranean except for his exquisite penmanship, which revealed a wealth of self-discipline. His preoccupation with the fine points of international law made him seem dull and narrow to Wilson, but the successful defense of neutral rights often rested on small moves and intricate calculations. Wilson had little experience with the legal side of international relations, and Bryan's authority in the field was of the "I feel strongly" variety. Although Lansing shared Wilson's belief that democracies were less warlike than other forms of government, he did not share the president's idealism in foreign affairs. Lansing believed that ideals had no place in foreign policy unless they served the national interest.

Lansing worked under constant fire from the belligerents' ambassadors and from American exporters frustrated by the difficulties of delivering their goods to Europe. Copper, for example, was quickly shifted from the category of conditional contraband (materials that might be militarily useful) to absolute contraband (materials of obvious military value). Britain had realized that while copper did have industrial uses, it would be used primarily in munitions during the war. Britain could not ban U.S. exports to Holland, Denmark, Sweden, or any other neutral, but it served notice that a copper-laden ship was liable to seizure.

Hoping to avoid such interference, American exporters of copper began heading for the Mediterranean rather than the North Atlantic. But as soon as the British learned that most of the copper going ashore at the neutral ports of Genoa and Naples was forwarded to Germany, they began stopping merchant ships entering the Mediterranean at the Strait of Gibraltar. Americans skeptical of British intelligence were shown the numbers and the evidence. At one point, Grey learned that although the Swedish government had prohibited copper exports to Germany, it had not stopped the export of artworks. An enterprising Swede began manufacturing copper statues of German generals and shipping them to Germany, where, it seems safe to say, they were melted down for munitions.

The State Department instructed Page to tell Grey that the United States could not consent to the confiscations without proof that the copper was headed for Germany. Grey put the burden of proof on the Americans: unless they could show that the copper would *not* end up in German bullets aimed at British troops, Britain would confiscate it and compensate the owners of the cargo.

Lansing and Bryan were soon knee-deep in the tears of the copper lobby. The governor of Montana predicted that thousands of miners would be thrown out of work, the Chamber of Commerce reminded Bryan that the United States supplied nearly half the world's copper, and the American Mining Congress noted that the industry had a workforce of 100,000, who of course supported uncountable wives and children not to mention the grocers and barbers of towns across the West.

Spring Rice understood the American pique and begged Grey to find a means of depriving Germany without ruining the mining states, which had powerful supporters in Congress. Spring Rice also worked to persuade the United States that Britain was fighting for its life under conditions far more serious than Americans realized. In the very first days of the war, he told Lansing, shiploads of food unloaded in Holland had gone straight to the German army in Belgium. Copper, petroleum, and rubber entering Germany were also being used in service of the German conquest of Europe.

In the war's first year London ceded only one contraband quarrel to Washington. The commodity in question was cotton, which the world's armies treated with nitric acid and packed into munitions to increase their explosive power. Raw cotton was not only the leading export of the United States, it was also the crop most dependent on exports: two-thirds of it was sold abroad. In the spring of 1914, anticipating another good year, cotton planters had borrowed heavily to expand production, and when September 1914's cotton exports proved to be less than one-tenth the size of September 1913's, cotton prices collapsed.

For a time it looked as if the federal government would rescue the South, but Wilson decided to let the market correct itself. His refusal to intervene infuriated the Southern congressmen and senators who had voted for his economic reforms. Although the crisis would pass before the year was out, it lasted long enough to give Grey time for a diplomatic coup: ignoring the wishes of the French, he refused to add cotton to the contraband list. Grey feared that the United States would demand a ban on munitions exports or assign naval convoys to merchant vessels carrying cotton. To avoid war with the United States, Britain would have had to let the convoys pass, and once merchant ships enjoyed the protection of a convoy, they could carry any cargo with impunity.

The war forced Wilson to defer his legislative plans, but there was no way to postpone the midterm congressional elections of 1914. Still grieving, he had no energy for campaigning and contributed only a long letter detailing the administration's accomplishments. In a mere eighteen months, he and the Democrats in Congress put the federal government in charge of the nation's money supply, broadened access to credit, shifted a large share of the tax burden from imports to incomes, put labor and capital on a more equal footing, and required businesses large and small to play by the same rules. The White House encouraged Democratic candidates to use the letter to remind voters of the party's record and urge them to keep the Democrats in power.

On Election Day the country gave the administration mixed reviews. The Democrats retained their congressional majorities and even gained five seats in the Senate, but they lost sixty-one seats in the House. Republicans painted the losses as a repudiation of Woodrow Wilson and the New Freedom, which, they said, had upset trade and increased unemployment. Extrapolating from the voting patterns of the previous four decades, the editorial class predicted that Wilson would not be reelected in 1916.

Wilson took some comfort from the fact that the losses were confined largely to the Northeast, where the plutocrats still reigned, but when Colonel House went to Washington the day after the election, he found his friend weary and heartsick. What was the point of working so hard for so little reward? the president wanted to know. House reminded him that the voters had been electing members of Congress, not a president, an observation that drew a snappish reply. People were not stupid, Wilson said. They knew that a vote against a Democratic ticket was a vote against his leadership. He said he was no longer fit to be president. He could not think straight anymore, and his heart was not in the work. House tried to brace him up with visions of the great work to be done in foreign affairs but, he told his diary, "it was useless."

The problem of segregation in the civil service flared up again, on November 12, when Wilson met with a delegation from the National Equal Rights

League. Their spokesman, William Monroe Trotter, was a Harvard-educated real estate investor and co-founder of the *Boston Guardian,* one of the more militant voices of the era's civil rights movement. In 1912 the National Equal Rights League and several other black organizations had endorsed Woodrow Wilson on the basis of his progressive record and his promise that black citizens could count on his fairness. While disturbed by reports of segregation in the Post Office and the Treasury in the spring and summer of 1913, Trotter had taken heart from a conference with the president, whose parting words to him were, "I assure you that it will be worked out."

The situation did not improve, and Trotter returned to the White House in November 1914 with a delegation from the league. He began his side of the conversation by reminding Wilson of his campaign promise and asking him to undo the segregation. In 1912, black voters had hoped that Wilson would prove to be another Lincoln, but now, Trotter said, the black leaders who had advocated his election were "hounded as false leaders and traitors to their race."

Wilson was incensed. "If the colored people made a mistake in voting for me, they ought to correct it and vote against me," he said. In his view, friction between blacks and whites was "a human problem, not a political problem," and the president of the United States could not simply decree an end to it. Wilson advised Trotter and his colleagues to "see that the race makes good and nobody can say that there is any kind of work that they can't do as well as anybody else."

Ignoring the point, Trotter asked the president for his thoughts on Negro workers having to use separate lunch rooms and lavatories far removed from their offices. Were such practices not humiliating? Wilson testily replied that the new arrangements were not intended to humiliate. Trotter insisted that all segregation was humiliating. Wilson lost his temper and accused Trotter of being the only American who had ever come into the Oval Office and spoken to him in such a passionate tone. Perhaps Wilson had forgotten, but Oswald Garrison Villard had been ablaze with passion when he came to the White House for a talk about segregation. And on that occasion Wilson had linked the problem and its solution directly to politics, predicting that the South's elected officials would not change their attitudes until they needed black votes.

Trotter apologized and tried once more to explain. Black citizens wanted nothing more than a return to the old working conditions in the civil service, he said. "We would be false, Mr. President, false to ourselves and false to you, if we went out and led you to believe that we could convince the colored people that there was anything but degradation."

"I don't think it's degradation," Wilson replied. "That is your interpretation of it." Although he promised to look into the matter again, the promise was delivered with one more warning not to politicize race by threatening to vote Republican: "to put it plainly, that is a form of blackmail."

After his bruising quarrel with Villard, Wilson had gone to bed and stayed there for days. This time he asked Grayson to arrange a getaway to Manhattan. They boarded an overnight train, and at six o'clock the next morning, House met them at Penn Station. After breakfast in the president's car, they motored out to the Piping Rock Club on Long Island for a morning on the links. Back in Manhattan, at House's apartment, the president and the colonel settled down to work.

That evening, the two strolled from House's apartment on East Fifty-third Street to Broadway, pausing now and then to listen to a soapbox orator. As soon as the president was recognized by people in the crowd, he and House would move on, but eventually they had a crowd of their own. When escape seemed in order, they ducked into a hotel, caught an elevator, and made for an exit on another street.

The president seemed to enjoy himself while they were out, but as soon as they got home, House wrote, Wilson "began to tell me how lonely and sad his life was since Mrs. Wilson's death, and he could not help wishing when we were out tonight that someone would kill him. He has told me this before. His eyes were moist when he spoke of not wanting to live longer, and of not being fit to do the work he had in hand. He said he had himself so well disciplined that he knew perfectly well that unless someone killed him, he would go on to the end doing the best he could."

14

Moonshine

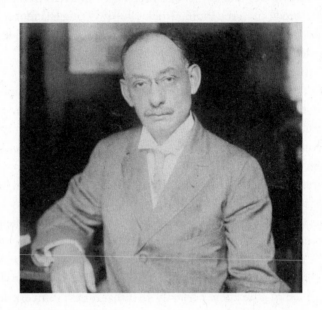

The Federal Reserve's regional banks opened for business on November 16, and a few days later Wilson ordered the army to withdraw from Veracruz, but neither of these welcome developments lifted his spirits. "All the elasticity has gone out of me," he confided to a friend. "I have not yet learned how to throw off the incubus of my grief and live as I used to live. . . . Even books have grown meaningless to me. I read detective stories to forget, as a man would get drunk!"

Colonel House, worried about his friend's state of mind, made six trips to Washington in as many weeks. Wilson was happiest in pursuit of high ideals, and now that the New Freedom was almost a fully accomplished fact, the colonel believed that the president would find more satisfaction on the world stage than in domestic politics. House was right, but his drive to fix Wilson's attention on foreign affairs was also a drive to put himself at the center of U.S. diplomacy and push everyone else—Bryan, Lansing, and the ambassadors—to the margins.

In September, just after seeing Wilson in New Hampshire, House had bared his ambition in his diary: "I am laying plans to make myself persona grata to all the nations involved in the European war, so that my services may be utilized to advantage and without objection in the event a proper opportunity arrives. I have been assiduously working to this end ever since the war broke loose. I do not believe in leaving things to chance. . . . I am trying to think out in advance the problems that the war will entail and the obligations which will fall upon this country, which I hope the president will properly meet."

House spent Saturday evening, September 5, with Konstantin Dumba, the Austrian ambassador, whose summer embassy was a few miles away from House's cottage in Prides Crossing. Writing Wilson the next day, House said that Dumba "talked very indiscreetly, and if one will sit still, he will tell all he knows. I sat very still." Bernstorff had just told the American newspapers that the German people were committed to winning the war and would fight to the end, but Dumba told House that the German government feared mass starvation. "England, it seems, lets no ship pass into neutral ports without first ascertaining whether or not it contains foodstuffs and when it does, she exercises her right to purchase it," House reported to Wilson. "What Dumba particularly wants is for the American ships to defy England and feed Germany."

Dumba's concern for his German ally hid his panic for Austria. A laggard in the arms race that preceded the war, the Austro-Hungarian Empire suffered one reverse after another on the battlefield, and the Habsburgs soon realized that unless Germany triumphed, their own empire was doomed. If House grasped this point, he did not mention it in his diary or his report to Wilson. House assumed that he was one step ahead of the diplomats he met—canny, self-effacing, and able to elicit state secrets simply by lending a sympathetic ear. It seems not to have occurred to him that the whispering diplomats might be lying. Years after his visit to Prides Crossing, Dumba wrote about it in his memoir. By then much of House's diary and the letter to Wilson had been made public, and Dumba wished to set the record straight. He thanked House for passing on all his "indiscretions" to the president. That, Dumba said, had been his objective.

A worldly man with a gift for languages, Dumba came from a family of Viennese merchants who were prosperous and socially prominent despite their lack of blue blood and their indifference to Catholicism, the religion of the Habsburg court. As a lad of seventeen, Konstantin visited Paris, learned of its new École Libre des Sciences Politiques, and promptly enrolled. After a six-month course in diplomacy, he traveled to London, where he soon realized that an aspiring diplomat would do well to study the British Empire, which was vastly more powerful than the swath of Central Europe ruled by the Habsburgs. In 1880, at the age of eighteen, Dumba began his diplomatic career as an aide in Austria's embassy in London. Tall, slender, and alert, he rose steadily for twenty-five years. And then, while serving as minister to Serbia, he fell in love with the Russian ambassador's wife. When the affair was exposed, Dumba was recalled but not dismissed, and his Catholic superiors looked the other way when his paramour secured a divorce and accepted Dumba's proposal of marriage.

Dumba arrived in Washington in the spring of 1913, just as Wilson took office. A lover of opera and the beau monde, Dumba had charmed his way into the inner social circles of a half-dozen European capitals, but in the United States he showed less interest in ingratiating himself with official Washington than with moneyed Americans. He vacationed on their yachts and estivated in their midst on Boston's North Shore. Unlike the ambassadors of the other major belligerents, he had not hurried back to Washington when the war broke out.

Perhaps it was mere coincidence, but on the same evening that Dumba motored over to see House, Bernstorff dined in Scarborough-on-Hudson, New York, at the estate of a prominent investment banker, a German-Jewish immigrant named James Speyer. Also at the table was Oscar S. Straus, whose family had moved to the United States from Germany when he was a small boy. The Strauses prospered and involved themselves in public life, and Oscar became the first Jew to hold a cabinet post. In 1906, Theodore Roosevelt chose him to head the new Department of Commerce and Labor. Straus went on to serve as Taft's ambassador to Turkey.

When the dinner conversation turned to the war, Straus asked Bernstorff how the kaiser might respond to an offer of mediation from the White House. He was asking, he said, because it had occurred to him that France could not win the war and that peace was the only way to prevent the destruction of Paris. Bernstorff replied that while he could not speak officially, he believed that the kaiser would agree to mediation if his enemies were similarly inclined.

Excited by the thought that the war could be ended if the moment were seized, Straus raced back to Manhattan, caught an overnight train to

Washington, and reached Bryan's doorstep early on Sunday morning. Bryan called Wilson with the news, and on Monday, with Wilson's approval, Bryan summoned Bernstorff and persuaded him to communicate the gist of the dinner conversation to his superiors in Berlin. Next Bryan instructed Ambassador Gerard to see the German foreign minister and ask him to pass the word to the kaiser. If the kaiser consented, Wilson would approach the other belligerents and would be pleased to bring them together to discuss a settlement of their differences.

Spring Rice and Jusserand were called to the State Department that afternoon for separate briefings and a plea from Bryan. At the very least, Bryan told them, their governments should be willing to state their war aims and peace terms. Even if this peace initiative failed, Bryan thought, such statements would show who was responsible for continuing the war.

As the confidential cables flew between Washington and the capitals of Europe, House dismissed the scheme in his diary. "Bernstorff is less clever than I thought," he wrote. He believed that Bernstorff had blundered by discussing a subject as sensitive as mediation at a dinner party and was compounding the mistake by talking about the possibilities for peace with still more people. The colonel did not suspect that Bernstorff might be feigning an interest in peace to put Germany's enemies in a bind: if the kaiser expressed an interest in peace and the Allies rebuffed him, the kaiser could blame them for needlessly prolonging the carnage. Bernstorff admitted as much in a memo to Berlin: "I wanted to leave the odium of rejection to our enemies."

The full truth was even more complicated. Bernstorff was deeply conflicted about the war. Despite his frequent public predictions of German victory, he privately worried that Germany could not win. But as soon as Straus raised the question of mediation at Speyer's dinner table, Bernstorff recognized that he had just been handed an opportunity to one-up the Allies in the propaganda war being waged in the United States.

Born in London in 1862, when his father was ambassador to the Court of St. James's, Bernstorff learned English before he learned German. As a young man he served in a German artillery regiment, an experience that left him with a strong distaste for the kaiser's militarism ("colossal stupidity," he would call it after the war, when he was free to speak his mind).

At twenty-five Bernstorff had married an American heiress and begun working for the German ambassador in Constantinople. Amiable and deferential, he struck some on the Wilhelmstrasse as too soft for Realpolitik, but he proved himself in Cairo, St. Petersburg, and elsewhere before being posted to Washington, in 1909. Bernstorff's geniality, his

American wife, and the pleasure he took in the theatrics of ambassadorial life made him a favorite of the American press. He looked the part of a German count—blond, blue-eyed, tall, and erect. And despite his dislike of the kaiser's militarism, he adopted one of his most arresting features, a mustache waxed and twiddled into two upswept points. Bernstorff was a serious student of American business and politics, but he was a sport, too. He took up poker, loved baseball, and wheeled around the capital in a convertible.

By the middle of September 1914, both the Allies and the Central Powers had rejected all thought of mediation, and for the same reason: each side believed the other would interpret a willingness to discuss peace as a sign of military weakness. Straus's peace initiative had coincided with the first major reversal of Germany's fortunes on the battlefield. Until September 6, the army of Kaiser Wilhelm II had rolled through Belgian and French defenses, and then, just fifty miles from Paris, the French and British held fast in six days of hard fighting at the Marne. It was the Battle of the Marne that persuaded Bernstorff the Germans could not win. Both sides dug in. The war of movement was over, and the long, ghastly war of the trenches had begun.

Unwilling to accept the belligerents' refusal to consider mediation by the United States, House continued to have separate conversations with Spring Rice and Bernstorff in hopes of creating an opening for Wilson. Wilson saw no harm in House's effort but no hope for it, either. At the end of September, House went to Washington with a new idea. If the impasse dragged on, he told Wilson, it might be possible for the United States to suggest a peace conference in Washington or offer to send an American peace commission abroad. Nothing came of the idea, House wrote, because "neither of us could quite figure out how this was to be brought about. It was tentatively agreed that I should keep the matter in my hands and advise him what was being done." The agreement was more than tentative. From that moment on, Woodrow Wilson's diplomat in chief was not William Jennings Bryan but Edward Mandell House.

Bryan had left town to rest up for six weeks of whistle-stopping on behalf of Democrats running in the midterm congressional elections. His long absence from Washington made it easy for House to insert himself into the disputes with England over neutral rights, allegedly to keep Anglo-American relations on an even keel but really to muscle aside Ambassadors Spring Rice and Page as well as the State Department. For a man who presented himself as the soul of straightforwardness, House was unduly fond of cabals and indirection. He regularly played one diplomat off against another, excluded them when it suited his purposes, and disparaged them in his conversations with Wilson. By avoiding Lansing, House spared himself the annoyance of being told that his grand schemes were amateurish or out of order, and by working out his ideas with the president rather than with the professionals in the State Department, he avoided resistance and troublesome questions. The intensity of his aversion to officialdom suggests both a fear of authority and a wish to dominate the president. The maneuvering would have gone largely unnoticed by posterity, but House could not resist the temptation to record it all in his diary.

Without question, Bryan was ill suited to the position of secretary of state. The precedents and minutiae of international law struck him as so many barnacles on the Bible. All men were brothers, were they not? And that being so, war was a monstrous sin, was it not? Back in Washington after the congressional elections, Bryan presented Spring Rice with a sword beaten into a plowshare six inches long—a paperweight, he explained. "It is adorned with quotations from Isaiah and himself," Spring Rice wrote home to London. Bryan had spoken to him—yet again—of peace. Spring Rice (feeling "rather cross," he wrote) reminded Bryan that the United States had signed the Hague Convention of 1899 but had yet to protest Germany's gross violations of it in Belgium and France. As Spring Rice saw it, the Americans, by failing to protest, had forfeited their right to adjudicate the war in the court of world opinion.

The argument made no sense to Bryan. War was evil, and evil must be stopped. On December 1, he urged Wilson to make a peace overture on the basis of national self-interest. The war had imposed a huge financial burden on the United States, he said. American trade had been thrown into disarray. Neutrality was disturbing U.S. relations with the belligerents, causing political quarrels in the United States, and sapping energies that the government ought to put into dealing with a deepening recession. After four months of appalling losses on both sides, it was plain that no good could come of continuing the war, Bryan said. The time had come for the United States to ask the belligerents to agree to a meeting that would enable them to lay down their arms.

Wilson set the letter aside to read to House, who came to Washington two days later. House was unreceptive. The idea of basing a proposal for peace talks on American considerations would irritate the Allies, he thought, and he was no longer willing to risk that. The United States was still a neutral, but he now shared the conclusion that Lansing and Page had reached in the earliest days of the war: American interests would be best served by a decisive Allied victory.

By this point, House was so sure of his indispensability in foreign affairs that he told Wilson he wished Bryan would find some excuse to resign. Wilson agreed but confessed that he had not yet told Bryan of his decision to entrust the question of peace to House. There was a chance that Bryan would gracefully relinquish the role of peacemaker, Wilson said, but only a chance, so he hesitated, afraid of giving offense.

"I advised not telling him for the moment," House said. The moment would come soon. House would choose it, and he would do the telling.

In Wilson's company, House made no secret of his hope for an Allied victory, but Wilson was keeping his own hope—for a military deadlock—largely to himself. He finally shared it in December, in an off-the-record interview with Herbert Brougham, editor of *Current History,* a monthly published by *The New York Times.* As Wilson saw it, no good could come of one side crushing the other, because the victor would impose a vengeful peace sure to seed another world war. But a deadlock after the most gargantuan clash of arms in history would be the final proof of the futility of war. Only then, when both sides were totally exhausted, would they be willing to make an equitable, enduring peace.

Two days into the new year, Ambassador Bernstorff and Colonel House had another in a long series of talks about the possibility of an American peace overture. As usual, Bernstorff played to House's vanity, encouraging his fantasy that Germany and England would bury their differences because they had more in common with each other than with the rest of Europe. As usual, the conversation went into House's diary straight, with no apparent curiosity about Bernstorff's motives. As a go-between in Democratic Party politics, House could be as shrewd as Bernstorff, but in diplomacy the colonel was almost as unwary as Bryan. He took the diplomats' smiles and compliments as affirmations of his brilliance and saw his tiffs with Spring Rice and Lansing as proof of their shortcomings, not his. Unfortunately for their historical reputations, House's diary has too often been taken as the last word.

After three months of shuttling between Spring Rice and Bernstorff, House got both ambassadors to agree that their governments *might* consider exploratory conversations about peace on the basis of three conditions: Germany would evacuate Belgium, Germany would compensate the Belgians for the damage it had done, and the Allies and Central Powers would work together on a plan for a permanent peace. The conditions had been set by Britain, and Bernstorff gave his word that Germany was willing to consider them.

With Wilson's consent, House contacted Whitehall and the Wilhelmstrasse to suggest that the time had come for him to return to Europe. "The president thinks that some result might be more easily brought about through me in an unofficial way, because there would be no embarrassment to anyone and no formal commitments," he explained to Arthur Zimmermann, the German undersecretary of foreign affairs. "If you could give me any assurances in this direction, I would leave immediately for England, where I have reason to believe I would get a sympathetic hearing." Believing that his talks with Bernstorff, Spring Rice, and Dumba had given him a fuller picture of the war than any of the belligerents had, House laid the peace problem to "a general misunderstanding of motives and purposes" and predicted that the confusions could be cleared up if the principals would speak frankly with one another.

On January 12, House went to Washington to discuss the trip with Wilson. The colonel reached the White House early in the evening, dressed for dinner, and headed for the president's study in hopes of a tête-à-tête before they sat down with the family. By House's watch, the conversation lasted exactly twelve minutes, during which it was decided that he should leave for Europe before the month was out. They returned to the study after dinner, and although House was surprised when there was no further talk of the peace mission, the president's silence on the subject led the colonel to an egotistical deduction: "He evidently has confidence in my doing the work I came to Washington for, without his help."

The next day House outlined his plans to Spring Rice, who was visibly annoyed by House's intention to bypass the ambassadors in Washington and deal directly with foreign ministers. House claimed in his diary that he brought Spring Rice around by remarking that it would be "a wonderful thing . . . to have the United States throw its moral strength in behalf of a permanent settlement." Spring Rice's brightening mood might have owed more to the ups and downs of his thyroid than to the notion of the United States as the moral arbiter of the war, an idea the Allies found irritating in the extreme. Spring Rice mustered enough goodwill to point out that House's exclusion of the French and Russian ambassadors would give offense. House agreed to meet them later in the day, with Spring Rice, and asked Spring Rice to put them in a receptive frame of mind.

Spring Rice turned up without having done the missionary work and, House complained, "was not particularly nice in helping me out. It was rather awkward at first. Both Jusserand and Bakhmeteff [George Bakhmeteff, the

Russian ambassador] were violent in their denunciations of the Germans and evinced a total lack of belief in their sincerity." House forged ahead, declaring that if the Germans were merely pretending to want peace, his mission would expose their lie. Jusserand and Bakhmeteff conceded the point and, House told his diary, "it was not a great while before we were all making merry, and they were offering me every facility to meet the heads of their government." Spring Rice did not record any merriment. His account says that Jusserand and Bakhmeteff decided that there could be no harm in letting the colonel find out for himself what they already knew: all of the belligerents firmly believed that they had more to gain by fighting than negotiating.

The colonel finished his wearying day by giving Bryan the news that Wilson had not been brave enough to deliver. House fetched Bryan from the State Department, allegedly to give him a lift home and brief him on his talks with the Allied ambassadors. All went well until House revealed that he was about to leave for Europe. Bryan was crestfallen. *He* had expected to be the president's peace emissary, he said. House replied that Wilson did not yet want to send a member of the administration to talk peace with other governments. Bryan protested, House persisted and, House wrote, "By this time we arrived at his home in Calumet Place, and he insisted upon my getting out and pursuing the conversation further." After more jousting, Bryan made a gentlemanly retreat.

Self-doubt rarely makes an appearance in the three thousand pages of House's diary, but as soon as Wilson agreed to let him go abroad in search of peace, House confessed to feeling great anxiety: "The undertaking is so great, and the difficulties so many, that to do it alone and practically without consultation or help from anyone, is as much of a task as even I, with all my willingness to assume responsibility, desire."

The colonel stayed the night at the White House and spent the next day getting a passport and doing political errands for Wilson. In the evening, Wilson seemed reluctant to part, so House stayed for dinner and lingered until the last train. "The president's eyes were moist when he said his last words of farewell," House reported in his diary. "He said, 'Your unselfish and intelligent friendship has meant much to me,' and he expressed his gratitude again and again, calling me his most trusted friend. He declared I was the only one in all the world to whom he could open his entire mind." Wilson accompanied House to Union Station and stayed at his side until House had to board.

For all their closeness, the two men made different assumptions about House's mission. While House went off with the grand ambition of leading enemies to common ground, Wilson thought of him merely as a "channel of confidential communication" for the vague purpose of finding out whether the two sides would consider even a preliminary exchange of their peace terms.

Colonel and Mrs. House boarded the *Lusitania* in New York on January 30, 1915. They had an eventful voyage—twenty-four hours of the stormiest seas House had ever experienced and, just off the Irish coast, a sudden change of flags. Warned of German submarines in the area, the *Lusitania*'s captain hauled down the Union Jack and hoisted the Stars and Stripes. Every German naval officer knew the silhouette of the *Lusitania,* but the captain hoped the American flag would signal that the ship was carrying American passengers and American exports. The *Lusitania* docked safely in Liverpool.

While the *Lusitania* was at sea, Germany informed Britain that from February 18 onward, it would consider the waters around the British Isles a war zone. All enemy merchant vessels sighted therein would be liable to destruction without warning. Neutral vessels would also be in danger because of the deceptive use of neutral flags. The announcement shocked the sensibilities of believers in "civilized" naval warfare, the laws of which had long required an attacker to attempt to save the lives of a merchant ship's crew and passengers before blowing it up. Submarine warfare had rendered the old laws obsolete. To show itself in advance of an attack would deprive a submarine of one of its main tactical advantages, stealth.

The Germans had established the war zone as a reprisal for Britain's violation of another law of naval warfare, the law governing blockades. The old rules required a blockading navy to station its ships near the enemy's coast and maintain a flotilla large enough to prevent access to the enemy's ports. The old rules also allowed a blockading navy to search merchant ships and seize contraband within the blockade zone but not on the high seas. The British had torn up the rules in November 1914 by declaring the whole of the North Sea a blockade zone. Alfred von Tirpitz, secretary of the German navy, turned his wrath on the United States for not protesting England's closing of the North Sea to neutral ships. "England wants to starve us," he told a journalist. "We can play the same game."

The idea of using submarines to starve England into submission had come to the Germans from a surprising source: Sir Arthur Conan Doyle. Already well known for his Sherlock Holmes stories, Conan Doyle was as British as it is possible to be. Knighted in 1902, he was the son of an Irishman, had grown up in Scotland, and would spend most of his life in England. In "Danger! Being the Log of Captain John Sirius," a short story

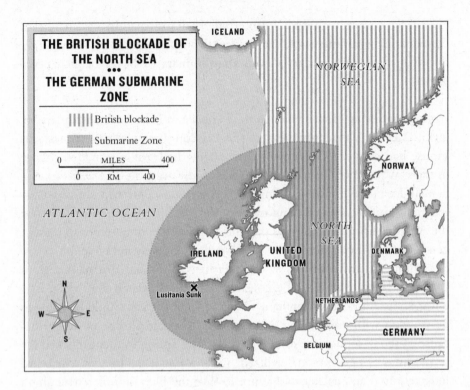

THE BRITISH BLOCKADE OF
THE NORTH SEA
•••
THE GERMAN SUBMARINE
ZONE

||||| British blockade

▨ Submarine Zone

0   MILES   400

0   KM   400

ICELAND

NORWEGIAN
SEA

NORWAY

ATLANTIC OCEAN

NORTH
SEA

IRELAND   UNITED
KINGDOM

DENMARK

N
W   E
S

✕
Lusitania Sunk

NETHERLANDS

GERMANY

BELGIUM

published in July 1914, Holmes imagined a war in which the Royal Navy
defeated the German Grand Fleet but Germany ultimately defeated England
with unremitting submarine attacks on merchant ships headed for English
ports. A German naval officer who read the story shared it with his superiors, and before long the notion that England could be broken with a handful
of submarines was an article of faith among German naval strategists. Britain
was more relieved than alarmed by the new war zone. It, too, was a violation
of the blockade rules, so Britain was no longer the only belligerent acting
with flagrant disregard for the laws of naval warfare. And Germany's violation invited even more opprobrium than Britain's because the submarine
posed a deadly threat to noncombatants.

The only major power unnerved by the kaiser's war zone proclamation
was the United States. Wilson and his cabinet immediately realized that if
German submarines began sinking American ships or ships carrying American passengers, the United States might have to declare war. Washington
advised Berlin that the German government would be held to a "strict accountability" for American deaths caused by German submarines.

Repelled by the idea of using starvation as a weapon, the United States
asked Britain to permit food to be shipped to Germany's civilian population

if Germany would promise not to divert any of it to its army. To ensure that the food went only to civilians, the United States offered to supervise the distribution through a humanitarian organization. The State Department sent the proposal to the American embassies in London and Berlin. As directed, Ambassador Page presented the American brief to Grey, but he could not press the case with enthusiasm. The proposal demanded more of England than Germany, Page thought, and his reports from relief organizations in Belgium suggested that there was no end to the German army's ingenuity in expropriating food meant for the Belgian people.

House pressed harder on Wilson's behalf, to no avail. On March 1 Britain and France informed the United States that Germany's submarine war on merchant ships forced the Allies to block commodities of any kind from reaching or leaving Germany. Henceforth, all ships with cargoes presumed to be going to or from Germany would be liable to search and possible seizure. The United States was assured that the interdictions would be carried out with no risk to the ships or the lives of the civilians on board.

Wilson wrote his friend Mary that the tension was like a fever, and "no one who did not sit daily here with me, each anxious twenty-four hours through, could possibly realize the constant strain." Once again he complained of feeling disconnected from his real self. He was also anxious about House's presence in London. Sensing (correctly) that the British would not want House to leave for Berlin until they felt that they were winning on the battlefield, the president feared that the German government would then see the colonel as England's envoy rather than as an advisor to the president of the United States. Wilson urged House to put the point squarely to Grey and move on.

But House was not ready to leave, and he was an easy conquest for Grey, who could invest even the wobbliest argument with the grandeur that Shakespeare gave Henry V at Agincourt. In a reply that Wilson could not have found reassuring, House explained that Grey "does not so much desire [a military] advantage before I go to Berlin but that there should neither be such a great disadvantage as now." The colonel counseled patience.

House stayed in England for three more weeks. Though he had not opened any door to the antechambers of peace, he told Wilson that he had put everything in London "in admirable shape." Evidently concerned that Page might file a less cheerful report, House claimed that he had met with many more officials and seen Grey much more often than Page knew. He had kept Page in the dark, he said, in order to spare his feelings and preserve their "very warm and cordial relations."

Page informed the president that the British had been taken aback by the American request to ship food to German civilians. The English did not doubt America's good faith, Page said, but they now regarded Americans as simpletons playing into Germany's hands. As for House, Page said he was going to Berlin empty-handed. The British were determined to defeat the Germans by starving them. Sir Edward Grey had put it to Page this way: "If we are defeated, it will be worse with us than it can be with Germany if she is defeated. The German people in any event will remain . . . on land that can practically feed them. We—if Germany should win—would have our overseas dominions cut off and we should be an island people without the means of self-support. . . . That is why we all prefer to die before disaster if need be, rather than after. That is why we must starve the Germans, lest we and our civilization starve afterwards."

House went to Berlin by way of Paris, where he had an icy meeting at the Quai d'Orsay with the foreign minister, Théophile Delcassé. The British had warned the colonel that Delcassé would not take kindly to any discussion of peace, and House had opened with a statement that Wilson did not wish to intervene on behalf of peace before he was welcome. Delcassé answered with platitudes and an announcement that he had no intention of speaking his mind until House had been to Berlin and back. House was so peeved that he enlisted an intermediary to tell the Quai d'Orsay that it ought to stay on the right side of the president of the United States, which meant staying on the right side of Colonel House. But to Wilson, House sent an astonishing report: "France has tentatively accepted you as mediator, and that, I think, is much." House's diary, the record of everything he considered a triumph, made no mention of any such acceptance.

When House calmed down, he set about cultivating one of Delcassé's associates and realized that he could use the same approach in Germany, cultivating the undersecretary of foreign affairs rather than the chancellor. "If I can establish such relations, the situation can scarcely get away from us," he wrote Wilson. The idea had promise. House was likable and more extroverted than his chief, and the bonds he forged with European leaders might well smooth the way for Wilson—*if* the warring nations ever reached a point where they desired his assistance. For the moment, though, Woodrow Wilson and the United States were irrelevant to Europe. Every belligerent believed that it had to win the war and would win if it kept fighting.

Despite Delcassé, despite the impasse on the battlefields, and despite a discouraging letter from Zimmermann, House went to Berlin in an exuberant mood. He had a fresh idea for ending the war, an idea that had briefly surfaced in discussions with Grey and, coincidentally, in a recent letter from

Zimmermann: freedom of the seas in war as well as peace. As envisioned by House, freedom of the seas would guarantee that no matter who was fighting whom, the seaborne commerce of the world would continue without interruption; belligerents would not even attack each another's merchant ships. House's notion was not original. The term "freedom of the seas" had been coined three centuries earlier by the Dutch legal scholar Hugo Grotius, and one of the most distinguished American lawyers of the prewar era, Joseph H. Choate, had proposed that all nations grant immunity to seaborne private property (except for munitions) in wartime. Theodore Roosevelt's secretary of state in 1907, Elihu Root, had sent an American delegation to The Hague with a similar proposal.

House reached Berlin at nine o'clock on the snowy morning of March 19 and before noon was chatting with the amiable undersecretary of foreign affairs, Arthur Zimmermann. Tall, blond, and outgoing, Zimmermann was a favorite of the junior members of the U.S. embassy's staff. He spoke English well and regularly helped them solve problems that his colleagues refused to address. House, who had met and corresponded with Zimmermann, found him personable if not entirely trustworthy. Among other things, Zimmermann delighted in taking radically different positions with individuals who were likely to compare notes, an excellent tactic for instilling fear and uncertainty.

House laid out his proposal for freedom of the seas and suggested that Germany and the United States join with the other naval powers of the world to persuade England to accept it. Once England agreed, House said, the German people would understand that there was no need for Germany to hang on to Belgium, even for its ports. And how much better it would be for Germany, House said, if it did not hold an alien people against its will. The proposition "gratified Zimmermann very much," the credulous House reported in his diary. The German chancellor, Theobald von Bethmann Hollweg, showed even more enthusiasm, telling House that as far as he was concerned, freedom of the seas could be the starting point for discussions of peace.

When a bit of reflection led Zimmermann to wonder aloud why Britain would accept any agreement likely to diminish her naval supremacy, House was reassuring. The logic and simple justice of freedom of the seas would make it impossible for England to refuse, he said. He would not only propose the idea to the British, he would also let them know that Germany and the United States would "thresh it out with them to a finish."

House waited until he left Berlin to tell Wilson how trying his visit had been. "I met there no one of either high or low degree who did not immediately corner me and begin to discuss our shipment to the Allies of munitions, and sometimes their manner was almost offensive," he wrote. But he felt that he had given them a better understanding of U.S. neutrality, and he hoped that he had persuaded the German government that it was in Germany's best interests to cooperate with the United States. "If we can keep this view before them, they will probably want you as mediator," he said. It seemed to him that the freedom of the seas proposal had been more warmly received than anything else he had said or done in Europe. If nothing disturbed the groundwork, he told the president, "your influence will dominate to a larger degree than it ever seemed possible."

On March 28, House headed to Switzerland and the south of France for a series of one-on-one meetings with the U.S. ambassadors to Austria, Italy, and Spain. He briefed them on his work and asked that they lobby discreetly for the idea that Woodrow Wilson do the mediating when the moment for mediation arrived. To his diary he confided that he was trying to eliminate Wilson's chief rivals for the job, the pope and the king of Spain.

House's conversations with the foreign offices in London, Paris, and Berlin in the early months of 1915 convinced him that all the belligerents had fallen into the same trap. Each had pointed a finger at an aggressor, called forth a vast army in the name of defending its honor, and promised a glorious victory. And all had insisted to House that there was no going back, because the people would not stand for it. "It is a dangerous thing to inflame a people and give them an exaggerated idea of success, and this is what has happened and is happening in almost every country that is at war," he wrote Wilson. As far as House could see, freedom of the seas offered the only hope for peace.

On his way back to London, House stopped in Paris to see Delcassé again and came away with the impression that their relations had improved. House had decided to stay on in Europe, waiting for a moment when the president would be able to make a mediation offer that both sides would accept. "[S]omething is sure to crack somewhere before a great while," he told his friend in the White House.

The colonel rented a flat in Mayfair and immediately launched his campaign for freedom of the seas. "I had but little difficulty in convincing [Grey] it was to Great Britain's advantage as much as to the rest of the world," he reported in his diary. But the distance between Sir Edward's words and his thoughts was not easily gauged, especially by a man as wishful as Colonel House. Buying time, Grey urged House to discuss the proposal with other British officials. Grey also put forward the fey idea that if

Britain agreed to freedom of the seas, it would want freedom of the land as well, so that trade moving by rail could go on without interruption in wartime.

House deserved more from Grey. Britain had nothing to gain from freedom of the seas in wartime. But House clung to the idea, and Wilson clung to House, entrusting his diplomacy to a man who could not read the diplomatic mind. When House's diary is read side by side with other accounts of the events he records, it becomes clear that he listened sympathetically but literally, not catching the things left unsaid, not questioning the veracity of what he heard, not wondering about ulterior motives. On the day that House and Grey had their long talk on freedom of the seas and freedom of the land, Page poured his exasperation into *his* diary: "The ingenious loophole discovered by House is—mere moonshine, viz., the freedom of the seas in war. That is a one-sided proposition unless they couple with it the freedom of the land in war also, which is nonsense. Nothing can be done, then, until some unfavorable military event brings a new mind to the Germans." As far as peace was concerned, Page said, House's travels had taken him from nowhere to nowhere.

15

Strict Accountability

After drawing their war zone around the British Isles, the Germans concentrated their U-boats on British cargo ships, but four Americans were killed in other attacks—one on a British passenger ship, three others on an American oil tanker. Wilson saw at once that the submarine had driven the American ship of state into the narrows. The U.S. government could either warn its citizens away from the ships of nations at war, or it could enforce the right of neutrals to travel on any ship. Putting human safety first, Bryan championed the warning. He was overruled by Wilson and Lansing, both of whom maintained that any concession would merely invite more attacks. Negotiations between the German embassy and the State Department over the small incidents were civil, but Washington and London began to wonder what would happen if a German submarine sank the *Lusitania*.

Largest, sleekest, most sumptuous ship of the Cunard Line, the *Lusitania* was a favorite of upper-class Americans, a source of pride to Englishmen, and a galling reminder to Germans that several of their own splendid liners were stranded in the United States. In February, when Germany warned the world of the risks of crossing its new war zone around Britain, Wilson asked Ambassador Gerard to inform the German government that the United States would hold Germany to a "strict accountability" for violations of the rights that Americans enjoyed as neutrals. To Lansing, "strict accountability" meant that the German government would have to compensate Americans for lives and property destroyed by the German navy, apologize, and give assurances that such acts would not be repeated. Wilson tried to make Bryan understand that the phrase carried a threat. "We have been doing a great deal of protesting," Wilson said, "and 'vigorous' protests are apt to be regarded as logically leading to action." Which raised two more questions: What would provoke the United States to act? And once provoked, what would it do?

Wilson was in no haste to decide. In a speech on April 20, he argued that American neutrality was not motivated by indifference or self-interest but by "sympathy for mankind." Neutrality appealed to him, he said, "because there is something so much greater to do than fight; there is a distinction waiting for this nation that no nation has ever got. That is the distinction of absolute self-control and self-mastery."

The words of the self-mastered man in the White House filled Ambassador Bernstorff with alarm. It seemed to him that the United States was counting too heavily on neutral rights. True, the rights were enshrined in international law, but the belligerents in this war were breaking the law whenever it threatened their success. The violations that had begun with the invasion of Belgium would eventually include the systematic starvation of civilians, the use of poison gas, and a host of other practices declared inhumane in the Hague conventions drawn up before the war.

Bernstorff had no worries about the safety of the big Cunarders, which could easily outrun the U-boats. His fears centered on workaday freighters and old steamers not built for speed. But when he tried to persuade the State Department to issue a warning to American travelers, he ran up against Lansing's insistence that citizens of neutral countries were free to sail on any ship they chose. Taking matters into his own hands, Bernstorff bought advertising space in several newspapers to remind Americans of the hazard in the war zone around Britain. His notice, signed by the Imperial German Embassy and dated April 22, first appeared in print on Saturday, May 1, which, quite by coincidence, was the day the *Lusitania* left New York for Liverpool.

The *Lusitania*'s captain, William T. Turner, appreciated the risks. He was the one who had raised the American flag and raced east across the Irish

Channel in February, when House was aboard. Turner had made several crossings since, and when his new passengers mentioned the German warning in the papers, Turner easily restored their serenity. The Royal Navy was on patrol and would alert him by wireless if any U-boats were spotted near the *Lusitania*'s course, and submarines poked along at nine knots an hour underwater, eighteen on the surface. The *Lusitania*, which cruised at twenty-one knots, could do at least twenty-three.

The *Times* of London derided Bernstorff's warning as an attempt to scare Americans away from British liners and guessed that it had been inspired by failure of the Germans' submarine campaign: so far, 99.7 percent of the 16,190 merchant ships going to and from the British Isles had eluded the U-boats.

Five days into its voyage, the *Lusitania*'s wireless received word that submarines had been spotted near Fastnet Rock off the southern tip of the Irish coast. Captain Turner steered wide of Fastnet and ordered the lifeboats stocked and swung out. The next afternoon, at 2:10, two lookouts spotted a streak of white racing toward the ship's starboard side. Their shouts of warning were instantaneous but too late.

Watching from the deck of *Unterseeboot-20,* which had fired the torpedo, Lieutenant Commander Walther Schwieger saw two explosions, walls of flame, and immense clouds of black smoke. In no time the ship listed heavily to starboard, the bow went under, and Schwieger guessed that the whole of it would be gone within minutes. He imagined the chaos on deck as he watched several lifeboats land bow first and capsize. Schwieger took his submarine down, and at 2:30 p.m., when the *Lusitania* slipped beneath the waves, *Unterseeboot-20* was churning away from the scene.

The American embassy in London learned of the disaster at four o'clock. The first report said that no lives had been lost, so Page's household staff carried on with preparations for the day's big event, a dinner in honor of Colonel House. By the time the ambassador left his desk, he knew that the death toll exceeded a thousand.

In Washington, where it was lunchtime when Page's workday ended, a reporter intercepted Bryan at a hotel to share a bare-bones bulletin: the *Lusitania* had been lost to a torpedo. A White House secretary gave the same news to Wilson, who canceled a round of golf to wait for more news. When none came, the president took a long automobile ride to try to calm his nerves. He learned the dimensions of the tragedy at eight o'clock, just after he returned. Shaken, he went to his study for a few minutes, then stole out of the White House for a long walk alone in the rain.

Bryan, coming home from a dinner party, wondered aloud to his wife if the *Lusitania* had been carrying munitions. The idea that England might be using noncombatants as a shield sickened him, and he instantly recognized that the presence of ammunition would give Germany a justification for sinking a passenger ship. He soon learned that the manifest filed with the collector of the Port of New York showed 4,200 cases of bullets and 1,250 cases of shrapnel in the ship's hold.

The day after the disaster, Page cabled Washington to say that Britain's senior officials were refraining from public comment but privately saying that the United States must declare war or lose the respect of the civilized world. If the United States joined the Allies, the Allies would soon triumph, and the United States would play a leading part in reorganizing the world, Page said. But if Washington turned the other cheek, "the United States will have no voice or influence in settling the war or in what follows for a long time to come." House filed a nearly identical brief and urged Wilson to act soon.

Wilson ignored them and nearly everyone else. Cabinet members who wanted to see him were turned away. The White House made no comment on the *Lusitania* for more than twenty-four hours, and the first word, which came from Tumulty, said only that the president keenly felt the gravity of the situation and was considering "very earnestly, but very calmly, the right course of action to pursue."

When Tumulty tried to talk to Wilson about the news from Queenstown, Ireland, where the dead were being buried in mass graves, Wilson could not bear it. If he were to stop and think about them, he said, "I should see red in everything, and I am afraid that when I am called upon to act . . . I could not be just to anyone." The catastrophe hung over him like a nightmare, he said. He could not sleep, nor could he fathom how a nation calling itself civilized could perpetrate such a horror. Wilson understood that the country wanted immediate action, but as he told Tumulty, he had to weigh all the facts, because whatever he did he could not undo.

Ambassador Spring Rice studied American reactions and canvassed his Washington sources for clues to Wilson's thinking. There were 128 Americans among the 1,198 victims. The Eastern press was demanding retribution while the Wilson administration seemed to be waiting for tempers to cool. Spring Rice presumed that the weakness of the U.S. Army ruled out a declaration of war, but he feared that another *Lusitania* might force the issue whether the United States was ready or not. And that would be hard on the Allies, he wrote Grey. "As our main interest is to preserve United States as base of supplies I hope language of our press will be very guarded."

Bernstorff maintained a facade of composure while frantically working to stave off the expected U.S. declaration of war. On Monday, May 10, he visited Bryan and expressed his regret at the loss of so many American lives. Bryan, whose cooling-off treaties were never far from his mind, lamented that Germany had refused to sign one. It would have given the two nations a year to settle the *Lusitania* question, Bryan said. Reporting the conversation to Berlin, Bernstorff urged his government to make a move toward some kind of negotiation.

The coincidence of the *Lusitania*'s departure and the German embassy's warning was too much for Ambassador Gerard, who assumed that Bernstorff had known of the plan for the attack and had "frankly, boldly, defiantly, and impudently" advertised it to the world. The available evidence suggests otherwise. For one thing, it is not clear that there *was* a plan to sink the *Lusitania.* The German admiralty's written orders to submarine commanders made no mention of passenger ships, an omission that might well have been deliberate, as it would allow Germany to claim that it had no plans to target ocean liners while leaving U-boat commanders free to attack. Bernstorff regarded the attack as a monumental blunder; American anger over the incident instantly destroyed all hope that Germany might win the propaganda war in the United States. Finally, two of the victims had been sons of Bernstorff's friends, and he had sent each of them off with a letter of introduction. Had he written the letters with foreknowledge of the *Lusitania*'s fate, he told an acquaintance, he would deserve to be hanged from the nearest lamppost.

From Berlin, Gerard forwarded a Foreign Office statement expressing sympathy for the American lives lost but placing the blame squarely on the British—for the blockade that had driven Germany to unleash the submarine and for their heedlessness in carrying passengers and munitions on the same ship. Privately, German officials reacted with emotions ranging from revulsion and disbelief to pride and cold resignation. As one wrote, "the scene of war is no golf links, the ships of the belligerent powers no pleasure palaces. The sinking of the *Lusitania* was for us a military necessity."

Wilson emerged briefly on Sunday, May 9, for a round of golf meant to assure the country that war was not imminent. On Monday he kept a long-scheduled date to address several thousand newly naturalized citizens in Philadelphia. Jimmie Starling, a Secret Service agent seated behind the president, could see that he was uncharacteristically nervous—squirming, rocking on his heels, unable to keep his hands still. It seemed to Starling that Wilson relaxed once he realized that the crowd was with him, but what happened next suggests that the president was still rattled. "There is such a thing as a man being too proud to fight," Wilson said. "There is such a thing as a nation being so right that it does not need to convince others by force that it is right." Wilson understood the gaffe as soon as he made it. "Too Proud to Fight" would be a page-one headline across the country.

Wilson often paraphrased himself, and "too proud to fight" was a slight variation on "there is something so much greater to do than fight," words he had used in a speech a few weeks earlier. There had been no criticism then. But with the sinking of the *Lusitania,* American indifference to the slaughter in Europe gave way to fear, and if most Americans did not want to go to war, neither did they want their president to take the blow with only a whimper.

The uproar over "too proud to fight" was cut off on May 13 by the dispatch of an official note to Germany. Drafted by Wilson and revised in consultation with Bryan and Lansing, the note cast the *Lusitania*'s destruction as the culmination of a series of German attacks on Americans at sea, events that he said the United States had observed "with growing concern, distress and amazement." After a nod to Germany's generally enlightened policies in the area of international rights, Wilson said he hoped that the German government would honor freedom of the seas. He acknowledged that Germany had resorted to extraordinary measures because of the British blockade but, he said, the submarine war zone violated neutral rights and the United States would continue holding Germany to "a strict accountability for any infringement."

Turning to his demands, Wilson said that the United States expected more than reparations and regrets. It also wanted Germany to disavow its attacks on neutral citizens and to take measures to prevent recurrences. The note closed with an unmistakable if somewhat circuitous threat: Germany should not expect the U.S. government "to omit any word or any act necessary" to protect the rights of the United States and its citizens.

From London, House and Page cabled their congratulations, and Page added that he had heard nothing but praise and gratitude for the note. In Berlin, Gerard presented the note to the foreign minister, Gottlieb von Jagow, who laughed at the mention of freedom of the seas. Gerard returned to his embassy certain that Germany's contempt would force the United States into the war.

As secretary of state, William Jennings Bryan had been obliged to sign the note, but he did so with an uneasy conscience. Just before cabling Berlin, he had requested one more paragraph, an expression of the long friendship between the United States and Germany. Wilson and Lansing rejected the suggestion. The day after the note went off, Bryan asked Lansing to compose a notice warning passengers away from ships carrying munitions. Lansing observed that Americans would wonder why the government had not sounded the alarm earlier. Bryan took his plea to Wilson. Yes, people would ask the discomfiting question, Bryan said, but wasn't that better than exposing American travelers to more attacks? Wilson stood firm.

It was not in the secretary of state's nature to sabotage the president, but at a moment when Bryan seemed to want the impossible—a note that was milder but not weaker—he was an easy mark for the Austrian ambassador, Konstantin Dumba. On May 17, Dumba called on Bryan, ostensibly to offer his assistance in dealing with Berlin but really to fish for some sort of statement that could be made to serve the purposes of the Central Powers. When Bryan said that the United States did not desire war, Dumba spread the rumor that Wilson had written a strong note to Germany only to silence his bellicose American critics, particularly Theodore Roosevelt. Roosevelt had raced into print to accuse Germany of mass murder and to tell Americans that "we earn as a nation measureless scorn and contempt if we follow the lead of those who exalt peace above righteousness, if we heed the voices of those feeble folk who bleat to high heaven that there is peace when there is no peace. For many months our government has preserved between right and wrong a neutrality which would have excited the emulous admiration of Pontius Pilate—the archtypical neutral of all time."

Dumba informed Vienna that Wilson's stern note to Germany was not to be taken seriously. Vienna forwarded the message to Berlin, and it reached the Wilhelmstrasse just as Ambassador Gerard turned up at the German Foreign Office to tell Arthur Zimmermann that if Berlin failed to meet Washington's demands, it would have to take the consequences. Zimmermann shared Dumba's message and the astounded Gerard immediately reported the exchange to the State Department.

Bryan, who had been made to look like a disloyal fool, was incensed. Dumba, asked to explain himself, professed his innocence and mused that Zimmermann must have been pulling Gerard's leg. Dumba extricated himself by agreeing to cable the German government about Zimmermann's "misinterpretation," a euphemism that allowed him to save Bryan's face as well as his own.

Wilson did not wish he had taken a softer line, but as he waited for Germany's reply, he gave House permission to revive a proposal the United States had made months before: an end to the British blockade on civilian foodstuffs for Germany in exchange for an end to the German submarine war on

Britain. Grey seemed generally amenable, although he said that the British were unlikely to consider the proposal anytime soon; it would have to be taken up by the cabinet, which was in the midst of reorganizing.

House's decision to press for the bargain sparked a quarrel with Page, who was sick of House's interference in affairs that ought to be managed by the embassy. Page said that he and Grey were managing perfectly well by themselves. When House sputtered that Wilson wanted these matters handled unofficially, Page replied that nine-tenths of his work was carried out in that manner. Clearly upset, House tried to acquit himself in a letter to Wilson. "I am very careful not to openly transgress upon any of [Page's] prerogatives, and Sir Edward understands this and aids me in every way possible," he wrote. House had done himself in by confiding in so many British officials that word of his covert talks inevitably got back to Page.

Refusing to admit to any unhappiness about the disagreement, he told Wilson that he had come around to Page's view. There was no doubt that neutrality had been the proper policy for the United States to take, House wrote Wilson, but the United States was now "bound up more or less in [the Allies'] success, and I do not think we should do anything that can possibly be avoided to alienate the good feeling that they now have for us. If we lose their goodwill we will not be able to figure at all in peace negotiations." With that, House showed that he was not the devoted neutral the president expected him to be. It was a surprising confession, but it elicited an even more surprising reaction from Wilson—silence.

Berlin rejected Wilson's proposal. "Germany in no need of food," Gerard cabled after a meeting in the Wilhelmstrasse. House could scarcely believe it, and his skepticism was well founded. The German government denied reports of starvation when there was a need to boast of Germany's self-sufficiency but insisted that civilians were starving when called upon to justify the submarine war. The truth was that food prices were soaring and bread rationing would soon go into effect. Soon after the war, the German National Health Office reported that the British blockade had starved 763,000 civilians to death.

On May 29, still waiting for the German answer to his note, Wilson and Bernstorff met secretly at the White House, and Bernstorff informed Berlin that Wilson was again entertaining the idea of mediation. The president wanted to build a coalition of neutrals which would demand that the belligerents begin peace talks, Bernstorff explained. If the belligerents refused, the neutrals would stop supplying them with food and munitions.

Did Wilson truly believe that the Allies or the Central Powers would bow to a coalition of neutrals? Or that the neutrals would agree to sacrifice their trade, which had grown ever more lucrative despite the disruptions caused by the war? Bernstorff declined to speculate about the neutrals but was certain the belligerents were in no mood for mediation. He advised Berlin to do nothing and "let the odium of rejection fall on England."

The German reply to Wilson's note reached Washington on May 31. Granting none of the U.S. demands, it summarized the minor incidents before the *Lusitania* and noted the status of each case, Germany's previous expressions of regret, and a willingness to make financial amends. Germany pointed out that it had already extended its sympathy for American lives lost in the attack on the *Lusitania* and wished now to call attention to certain overlooked aspects of the case. The *Lusitania* had been transporting ammunition and was armed and staffed with expert gunners. It was also carrying Canadian troops headed for the Western Front. And submarine commanders could not be expected to abide by the old rule requiring that a ship be visited and searched before it was destroyed, because the British Admiralty had ordered merchant ships to take one of two actions when faced with a U-boat on the surface: ram or flee.

In fact, the *Lusitania* was not armed, it had no gunners, and there were no Canadian soldiers aboard. There was indeed an order to ram or flee, but as Lansing observed, a submarine would be long gone before a liner could maneuver into position for a good swat. There was no denying the thousands of cases of bullets and shrapnel, however, and it was difficult to refute Germany's argument that it was acting in self-defense whenever it destroyed enemy munitions. Germany blamed the disaster on the Cunard Line, for carrying ammunition and passengers on the same ship. The German government asked the United States to examine the facts, reply, and give Germany the opportunity to make a final statement.

Wilson typed out his reply before he went to bed and took it with him to the next cabinet meeting. Bryan, who came in a bit late, was still smarting from the embarrassment inflicted by Ambassador Dumba, still heavy of heart about the sternness of Wilson's first note, and afraid that Wilson would adopt an even more rigid stance. He took his customary seat next to Wilson, leaned back, and closed his eyes. No one in the room considered Germany's reply satisfactory, but when it became apparent that the cabinet favored a stiff answer, Bryan hotly demanded a simultaneous protest to England for its unending confiscations of American cargo. Several members objected on the grounds that nuisances to trade were trivial beside the tragedy of the *Lusitania*. Bryan remarked that the cabinet seemed to favor the Allies.

Wilson upbraided him for doubting his colleagues' commitment to neutrality. Bryan did not retreat and told Wilson after the meeting that he thought he should resign. Wilson asked him to stay on and help avert a war, then followed up with a note asking Bryan how he would answer the Germans.

Bryan replied in writing, arguing once more that the U.S. government ought to warn Americans not to travel on the ships of nations at war. He begged Wilson to propose arbitration and to press Congress for a ban on transporting ammunition on passenger ships. He also asked Wilson to protest the practice in a note to Britain—before communicating with Germany. Otherwise the communiqué to Berlin might lead to war, he said. "This may be our last chance to speak for peace."

Wilson let Bryan know that his arguments had not carried, and Bryan went home to tell his wife that he had decided to resign. She began to cry and could not stop. Bryan fled the room, then fled the house and walked over to the home of Secretary McAdoo. As the son-in-law of the president, McAdoo enjoyed an intimacy with Wilson that no other cabinet member would ever achieve, and Bryan hoped that McAdoo could help him figure out how to resign without embarrassing the administration. Bryan poured out his woes. He had not slept well for two months. He worried constantly about war. He was hurt by Wilson's rejection of his ideas, upset by his clashes with the cabinet. And as a pacifist, he said, he could not in good conscience sign the note that Wilson proposed to send.

When McAdoo brought Wilson up to date, Wilson was unsurprised, but not entirely calm, and his first apprehensions were about his own prestige. Apart from Bryan, the cabinet was united, but what if Bryan's departure were read as a sign that the administration, and perhaps the country, disapproved of the president's management of the crisis?

Wilson consulted Tumulty and Secretary Houston of the Department of Agriculture, both of whom urged him to accept Bryan's resignation. Tumulty pointed out that Bryan was not useful in the State Department, and Houston thought that the public would support the president, not the secretary of state.

Bryan resigned in a letter to Wilson that began and ended graciously but took a disconcerting twist in the middle. It fell to the president to speak for the nation, Bryan said, but it would be his duty as a private citizen to promote the cause nearest his heart, the prevention of war. In other words, as Wilson persevered in his effort to keep the United States out of the war by winning concessions from Germany, Bryan would be out proselytizing for peace with or without concessions.

Wilson replied that his feelings about the resignation went much deeper than regret. "I sincerely deplore it," he said. "Our objects are the same and we ought to pursue them together. I yield to your desire only because I must and wish to bid you Godspeed in the parting."

Despite his frequent exasperation with Bryan, Wilson was genuinely fond of him and saddened by their rift. But the break disturbed him less for personal reasons than for the effect it might have on the impasse with Germany. Bryan electrified the crowds who came to hear him, and if his peace crusade attracted a large following, Germany might conclude that it could ignore Wilson's demands because the American people would not support him if he asked Congress for a declaration of war. In the days leading up to Bryan's departure, Wilson was beset by punishing headaches, and on the morning of June 9, when the news of the resignation appeared in the papers, he told a friend that it was "always painful to feel that any thinking man of disinterested motive, who has been your comrade and confidant, has turned away from you and set his hand against you; and it is hard to be fair and not think that the motive is something sinister. But I shall wait to think about *him* and put things to be *done* in the foreground. I have been deserted before. The wound does not heal, with me, but neither does it cripple."

Bryan was also wounded. To Josephus Daniels he remarked that instead of resigning he should have just told Wilson to give his desk to Colonel House. The sarcasm was out of character, as was his fleeting fantasy of taking revenge by writing a book, a notion he impulsively shared with Ambassador Jusserand. The two had run into each other just after Bryan's last meeting with Wilson. The book would recount his experiences as secretary of state and argue for peace at any price, Bryan explained. Jusserand observed that such an argument made the victims of a war as culpable as the perpetrators. Bryan offered no rebuttal. To Paris, Jusserand wrote that if Bryan's peace campaign succeeded, it would be a coup for the Germans, who "as we know all too well, are belligerents in Europe and pacifists in the United States." Jusserand could scarcely believe that Bryan had resigned in the middle of a foreign crisis. No other secretary of state had ever done so, Jusserand said. But, he added, no other American secretary of state had ever possessed Bryan's peculiar mix of "convictions and ignorance, mysticism and practicality, humanitarianism and puerility."

Ambassador Spring Rice sent Mrs. Bryan a charming note saying that he would miss the secretary's visits to the embassy and offering a cheerful apology for his ungovernable temper. "When I think how aggravating I have been," he wrote, "I am simply appalled by Mr. Bryan's good humor." At the same time, Spring Rice warned the Foreign Office that Bryan's return to the lecture circuit could hurt the Allies. As Spring Rice saw it, Bryan, now free to speak his mind, would "give a visible head to the 'long-haired men and short-haired women' who are agitating in this country for peace, prohibition, woman suffrage and the prohibition of the export of arms."

The president and the Allied ambassadors fretted for naught. Bryan soon disappeared from the front pages, a fate he himself had foreseen. As he told friends on the day he resigned, "I go out into the dark. The president has the prestige and power on his side."

16

· · · · · · · · · · ·

Haven

The question of who would succeed Bryan was answered before the month was out. Wilson named Robert Lansing secretary ad interim and sent McAdoo to New York to offer the full commission to House, who had just returned from Europe. House declined, preferring to conduct his diplomacy offstage. What about Lansing? he asked. McAdoo answered that Wilson did not think him "big enough." House, observing that Wilson was his own secretary of state, said the position did not require a big man and pointed out that the modest Lansing would have no trouble subordinating himself to Wilson. (Or to House. In his diary the colonel noted that because his involvement in foreign affairs was already known to Lansing, "he will be barred from complaining at the president's method of using me in the way he does.")

Keeping this selfish thought to himself, House lobbied Wilson on the basis of a single brief encounter with Lansing: "I have a feeling that if Lansing is at all acceptable to you that he could be used to better advantage than a stronger man. . . . I think the most important thing is to get a man with not too many ideas of his own and one that will be entirely guided by you without unnecessary argument, and this, it seems to me, you would find in Lansing." Wilson appointed Lansing on June 23.

Wilson's choice of a secretary of state whom he regarded as not "big enough" was one more example of his antipathy to powerful men. Faced with a significant problem, Wilson considered a range of solutions, often sought advice, and applied both his intellect and conscience to the situation. He acted only when he had persuaded himself that his chosen course squared with the facts and measured up to the highest American ideals. Unfortunately, once Wilson met the rigorous standards he set for himself, he was enraged by anyone who might thwart his carefully wrought plans.

Wilson saw influential members of both parties when necessary, but did nothing to cultivate their lasting goodwill, much less win their friendship. None of them was ever asked to join the president for a round of golf. Unlike Theodore Roosevelt, who often extended impromptu invitations for lunch, Wilson almost never invited a visitor to his office to join him for a meal in the family quarters. Dinner was also a family affair; the White House usher's diary records only a handful of exceptions during the eight years of Wilson's presidency.

Grayson, Tumulty, and House often came for dinner, but they were intimates and had nothing to gain by pitting themselves against him. Grayson and Tumulty were not only loyal insiders, they were also a generation younger than Wilson, who never lost the professor's delight in the company of bright young men. The president liked to think that he valued Colonel House because the colonel understood him and was unafraid to argue with him, and House liked to think of himself in the same terms, but House was hardly the tough-minded counselor he imagined himself to be. Reluctant to argue with Wilson, he generally contented himself with noting their differences in his diary. House's great gift to Wilson was not counsel but sympathy.

When Wilson could not avoid men who might gainsay him, he tended to minimize their contributions and keep them at arm's length, a pattern already evident in his dealings with Lansing. Throughout Lansing's tenure as counselor of the State Department, Wilson both relied on and resented his legal expertise. Although the president understood that lawyers were supposed to scrutinize details, raise questions, and provide for the unexpected, such work was of minor importance, in his opinion. "I have never had any patience with 'ifs' and conjectural cases," he told a friend soon after Lansing's appointment. "My mind insists always upon waiting until something actually does happen and then discussing what is to be done about that."

Coming from Woodrow Wilson, the criticism was downright perverse. He did respect facts, but only until they collided with his convictions. For months House and Page had been trying to persuade him that the belligerents, having fought the war, would insist on making the peace. The belligerents had plainly declared themselves on this point, but Wilson stubbornly maintained that they would have to turn to him because the United States, the only Great Power with no vested interest in the settlement, would be the world's only credible arbiter.

Lansing was hardly the pettifogging dullard that Wilson and House made him out to be, and his grasp of the facts was often superior to theirs, in part because of his attention to detail. Spring Rice admired Lansing's skill and cool head, and Jusserand regarded him as "very competent . . . thoroughly honorable . . . and robust in heart and spirit." Bernstorff treated him courteously but would always prefer dealing with the credulous Colonel House. In making his recommendation for secretary of state, House was right about only one thing: Lansing had no desire to upstage the president.

Apart from the headaches brought on by the rift with Bryan, Wilson felt surprisingly fit throughout the long diplomatic crisis that began with the attack on the *Lusitania*. In the past, the stresses of the presidency had often unsettled his stomach or triggered bouts of neuritis. In the spring and summer of 1915, he wrote only of fleeting twinges and numbness in his right arm, both of which he ascribed to overextending himself on the golf course. The depression that he often described to his friend Mary after Ellen's death disappeared from his letters. While Grayson doubtless deserves some credit for the president's hardihood, the emotional recovery owed even more to a wholly unexpected turn in his life: on March 7 he met a highly attractive younger woman, and eight weeks later he proposed. Woodrow Wilson, paragon and preacher of self-restraint, had not gone so wild since the day in 1883 when he proposed to Ellen Axson on a hotel porch in Asheville.

Edith Bolling Galt bore no resemblance to Ellen. Ellen had barely topped five feet. Edith, at five feet, nine inches, stood nearly as tall Woodrow. Ellen's hair was coppery, Edith's jet-black. Ellen had deep brown eyes. Edith's hovered on the line between violet and indigo. Ellen had gone through life sedately well dressed. Edith was exuberantly chic. To Ike Hoover, the White House usher, "Her every characteristic was pleasing beyond measure."

When Mrs. Galt met President Wilson, she was forty-two and he was fifty-eight. She, too, had been born in Virginia, and she, too, was widowed.

Beyond that, they had little in common. The seventh of eleven children, she grew up in straitened circumstances and spent only two years of her girlhood in school. The rest of her education she owed to an autocratic grandmother who lived with the family. In a household overflowing with children and boarders, Edith was forced to share her grandmother's bed and wait on her long into the night. But the old lady was well read, in French and Latin as well as English, and Edith absorbed her love of books.

At nineteen Edith traveled to Washington to visit her sister Gertrude and Gertrude's husband, Alexander Galt, whose family owned a well-known local establishment called Galt & Brs. Jewelers, Silversmiths and Stationers. Alexander's cousin Norman fell in love with Edith, who did not fall in love with him. He persisted, and after holding out for four years, she gave in. Norman eventually borrowed from his family to become the sole proprietor of Galt & Brs. In one prosperous year he bought Edith an electric automobile and in another took her on a grand tour of Europe. But Norman's fortunes proved erratic and he died young, in 1908, leaving his thirty-five-year-old widow in debt. She put a trusted employee in charge of the store, and while it would always have a fine reputation, it remained a financial worry for Edith.

Edith Galt's road to the White House was paved with coincidence. She happened to become the guardian of a young heiress, who happened to be romantically involved with Dr. Grayson, who happened to introduce her to the president's cousin Helen Bones. Helen, who had moved into the White House to assist Ellen, stayed on to keep Woodrow company after Ellen's death. Helen and Edith quickly became friends and fell into a routine of afternoon walks in Rock Creek Park followed by tea at Edith's. The president encouraged Helen to return the hospitality, and on March 7, in boots still muddy from their walk, the two women reached the living quarters of the White House at the same moment as Wilson and Grayson, also in muddy boots, came in from a round of golf.

Boots brushed, the four had tea, and the president was instantly smitten. Ellen had been dead for seven months, and if in his loneliness Woodrow ever wished for a new soul mate, he did not search for one or put the thought on paper. It was too soon. But Edith was a possibility unsought, brought to him by the same unfathomable forces that had taken Ellen away.

On March 23 Edith returned to the White House for dinner with the president, Grayson, cousin Helen, and one of Ellen's male cousins. The president took the ladies to the fireside in the oval sitting room for a post-prandial coffee and by Edith's account was a charming host. They talked, he told stories, and he treated them to a mellifluous reading of three English poems. She appreciated a good reading. Her father had excelled at the art, and she had rarely heard his equal.

Two weeks later Helen invited her for a drive in the country in one of the White House limousines. To Edith's surprise, the president was in the car, up front with the chauffeur, an arrangement he liked because it allowed him to nap unseen as his companions chatted away in back. At the end of the drive Woodrow and Helen begged Edith to stay for dinner. "So I went," Edith wrote, "and after a quiet little dinner we three sat around the fire and discussed books, and he read aloud several delightful things." Once again Edith was enchanted by Woodrow's voice, his love of language, and his skill in bringing out the beauty of the writing. She was also taken by the evening's main conversation, about the hardships their families had known in the South after the Civil War. "Thereafter," Edith wrote, "I never thought of him as the President of the United States, but as a real friend. That evening started a companionship which ripened quickly."

Edith dined at the White House again on April 30 and returned four nights after that for a dinner with the president and his daughter Margaret, cousin Helen, and some Wilson relatives who were spending the night. After coffee on the South Portico, the visitors were whisked off for a moonlit tour of the White House grounds while Woodrow and Edith stayed behind. He explained that he had asked Margaret and Helen to give him an opportunity to tell her that he loved her.

Edith blurted out her first thoughts. "Oh, you can't love me, for you don't really know me," she said; "and it is less than a year since your wife died." Unruffled, Wilson told her that he had lived a lifetime of loneliness and heartache since Ellen's death. "I was afraid, knowing you, I would shock you; but I would be less than a gentleman if I continued to make opportunities to see you without telling you what I have told my daughters and Helen: that I want you to be my wife." He raced on, listing the complications of a presidential courtship. He lived in a fishbowl. Gossip was inevitable. But she was a friend of Helen's, so she had a good reason for visiting the residential quarters of the White House, and they would have more privacy there than if he tried to visit her at home. Would she consent to such an arrangement?

Edith was miles behind, reeling. Years later, recounting her shock and embarrassment, she remembered that once her composure returned, they talked for more than an hour. "I told him if it had to be yes or no at once it would have to be no," she wrote. "Finally we agreed that as neither of us was a child, in spite of the public gaze we were entitled to continue the friendship until I should decide one way or the other." Once home, she was too keyed up to go to bed. Well after midnight she composed a note to her "dear kindred spirit" at 1600 Pennsylvania Avenue and enclosed an anonymous poem about a woman who felt unworthy of a great love that had come her way. Edith could not repay Woodrow's great gift in kind, she wrote, but she sent him as much as she could sincerely offer: "I pledge you all that is best in me—to help, to sustain, to comfort—and into the space that separates us I send my spirit to seek yours."

The suitor pressed on in ardent letters, sometimes two a day. On May 8, the day after the attack on the *Lusitania,* he confessed that he had loved her instantly and now believed that no one could help him as much as she could. "I know that you may be my haven," he wrote, "and the sanctuary in which my heart may realize all the purest passions that are in it, just as one knows (*how* does he know, do you think?) moving music when he hears it." The next day, while working on the first note to Germany, he wrote to say that he wished that she were with him. "I *need* you," he said.

On May 13, as the first *Lusitania* note was on its way to Berlin, Woodrow Wilson and his guests, including Edith Galt, boarded the presidential yacht *Mayflower* for a cruise to New York. Wilson was making the trip to review the U.S. Navy's Atlantic Fleet, which had gathered in the Hudson River before heading out for maneuvers at sea. The war games, a speech by the president, and the spectacle of the naval might of the United States had been staged to silence a small but persistent cadre of critics who were telling the public that the navy was ill prepared for the possibility of war. Wilson spoke on May 17, and Jusserand, who always dissected the president's speeches for the Quai d'Orsay, noted that there was no mention of the *Lusitania* or the war. Nor was there any reference to the attacks on Secretary Daniels, an avowed pacifist who had become the critics' punching bag. Wilson expressed confidence in Daniels and spoke of the navy as an upholder of American selflessness.

The fleet set sail on the morning of May 18, steaming smartly down the Hudson on the way to the open sea. Hundreds of thousands of New Yorkers cheered from the Manhattan side, and from the New Jersey side came the unexpected and strangely disconcerting salutes of eleven German ocean liners waiting out the war in slips at Hoboken. All had been decorated for the occasion, and all dipped their flags as the U.S. Navy sped by.

The president reviewed the fleet from the bridge of the *Mayflower,* which was anchored near the Statue of Liberty. He lifted his hat and smiled as the ships passed, and he called for binoculars and asked numerous questions when the navy's twelve submarines came into view. The *Mayflower* headed for Washington soon after the procession ended and could have docked at the Washington Navy Yard the next afternoon. At the president's request it stopped ninety miles short and spent the night at anchor in the Potomac. The official explanation was that the president wanted another night on the water before going back to work.

In truth, he wanted another night with Edith. The cruise had given them nearly a week together, a new luxury, and they were both saddened by its end. "Instead of golden sunlight and silver waters there has been rain and wet streets," Edith wrote him after a seemingly interminable day alone. "And my heart has been away—seeking you." In the month after their trip to New York, Woodrow and Edith saw each other at least fifteen times, at the White House and on long automobile rides—sometimes two a day.

Waiting for some assurance that Edith would marry him while waiting for Germany's reply to the first *Lusitania* note proved more than Woodrow could stand. After a night filled with agonizing fears, he was in no shape to compose a proper love letter, he wrote her on May 28. "My only message is this, For God's sake try to find out whether you really love me or not. You owe it to yourself and you owe it to the great love I have given you, without stint or measure. Do not be afraid of what I am thinking, but remember that I need strength and certainty for the daily task and that I cannot walk upon quicksand. I love you with all my heart."

Although Edith took only a day to reply, the wait was long enough to make Woodrow physically ill. He did not describe his symptoms to her or tell Grayson what had set them off. Edith's eagerly awaited note was not encouraging. She wished she could brighten his day, she wrote, "but my love seems inadequate. I have given it to you, and found such happiness in the giving, and instead of bringing joy to you, your note yesterday tells me that it is only a 'quicksand.'"

Woodrow Wilson learned little from his tribulations, but the prospect of losing Edith Galt knocked him off the high horse he often rode in quarrel. After hours of suffering, he realized that he shared the blame for the recent strain between them. "*I* have been blind as well as you," he wrote her. "I have *said* that love was supreme and have feared that it was not! . . . Henceforth we are not going to *discuss* our love, but live upon it and grow in it and let it lead us to strength and joy and peace by paths of its own."

They saw each other briefly on the evening of May 29, and on May 30 Woodrow reported that his heart was "*very* full." Edith answered in the same vein. "You made me so happy last night, and I came home with the assurance that we both understood—far better than ever before—and that *with* this understanding, and absolute faith in each other, we have nothing to fear."

A few weeks later Edith and Woodrow began a long vacation at the summer White House in Cornish. Edith and Helen set forth from Washington in a chauffeured automobile on June 20, and Woodrow followed by train a few days later. Jessie and Frank Sayre and their six-month-old son were there, Margaret came and went, and Grayson was on hand for golf. Tumulty stayed behind to fend off the legions wanting to talk to the president, and his efforts enabled Wilson to stay away for three weeks. He then spent a few days in Washington and scurried back to New Hampshire for another week with Edith.

Edith's curiosity about Woodrow's work prompted an invitation to join him in dealing with the letters, dispatches, and reports forwarded each day from Washington. Flattered, she accepted, and from then on she was a close collaborator. Although she found her new role immensely satisfying, she doubted the value of her assistance. Woodrow assured her that she had as good a mind as any man he knew and soon told her that he could not be happy without her full partnership in his work. It gave him wisdom as well as joy, he said, along with "a love that transforms the world and makes me better qualified to serve it."

The vacation produced two other developments of note. The first was an engagement. On June 28, just after Woodrow's arrival, Edith agreed to marry him but wanted to postpone the announcement of their engagement until after the election of 1916. As she explained in her memoir, "I was convinced that the Republicans would win, and had a sort of stubborn pride to show the world that it was the man and not the president I loved and honored." Although Edith's timetable disappointed Woodrow, it squared perfectly with the wishes of the president's political advisors, who feared that voters would turn against Wilson if he remarried too soon.

The second development was bound up with the first. Edith's presence on the *Mayflower*'s cruise to New York had elicited no press comment, but while she and Woodrow were in Cornish, their names appeared together in three small *Washington Post* items, all involving automobile excursions. The first listed Mrs. Norman Galt along with the other passengers in the president's car. In the second and third items, "Mrs. Galt" appeared in the subheads.

Unhappily for the gossips, Mrs. Galt left on August 2 to visit friends and take a trip with her mother and sister. Edith recalled the leave-taking as dreadful—in part because Woodrow was unhappy with the prospect of a long engagement, in part because they would be apart for a month. Everyone in the house gathered to see her off and, she wrote, "as we sped down the driveway, I looked back to see his figure alone, in his white flannels, outlined against the darkness of the door."

17

Dodging Trouble

Tender letters flew back and forth during the month Edith and Woodrow were apart, and elaborate precautions were taken to keep the seriousness of their relationship out of the newspapers. Her letters were sent in envelopes addressed to Margaret. His were often mailed from a post office in a town at some distance from Cornish. She was his "own Darling," he was her "best Beloved" and her "precious One." She sent love and chatted about her recreations in Geneva, New York. He savored every morsel: "How jolly, my Sweetheart, that you are taking golf lessons (and how I envy the teacher—you will be adorable as a pupil!). . . . If you'll give yourself as free a swing in hitting the ball as you give yourself in walking, you'll beat me all to pieces."

The day after Edith's departure, Woodrow started a letter to her at seven in the morning, added to it at lunchtime and again at bedtime, and did not reach the end of what he had to say until the next morning. "You have changed the world for me, my darling Edith, changed *this mad* world into a place of peace and confident hope for me," he wrote. "Every moment I *can* spend writing to you I must spend," he wrote a few days later. "I long for you so passionately, that I am as restless as any caged tiger if I cannot at least be pouring out my heart to you when I am free to come to my desk at all." Demure and unsure of herself, Edith held off for weeks before addressing him as "Dear Tiger."

Woodrow missed their working hours on the porch so much that he transplanted himself to another part of the house to take care of the day's business. He kept her up to date on his work—their work, as he thought of it—by sending thick packets of dispatches, correspondence, and newspaper clippings. She responded with comments and questions, and when it occurred to her that she was a confidante of the president of the United States, she could scarcely believe it. "I felt so queer this afternoon," she wrote him. There she was, in a quiet room in a tiny town beside a lake, an ordinary person "who has lived a sheltered inconspicuous existence, now having all the threads in the tangled fabric of the world's history laid in her hands for a few minutes."

The threads had never been more tangled. The tallies made on August 4, 1915, the first anniversary of the war, defied comprehension: 2.4 million dead, 5 million wounded, 1.8 million captured or missing in action. In a single year the belligerents had spent more on the war—$18.6 billion— than the Great Powers had put up for all the wars of the previous century. The kaiser took the occasion to issue a statement defending his actions: "Before God and history my conscience is clear. I did not will the war." In an exchange of telegrams, the president of France and the king of England vowed to fight until their enemies could no longer disturb the peace of the world. The Russians, who had lost 100,000 square miles of territory, affirmed their commitment to an Allied victory. Pope Benedict XV appealed for peace. He had issued a similar call when the fighting began and hoped that this echo would "induce kindly and more serene intentions." Enraged, the cardinals of France ordered their bishops to fix a day of prayer for victory.

To the English author H. G. Wells, it seemed that civilization would not survive unless humankind created a world government. Until all states were bound together as one, nations would be perpetually at war, he wrote. "Violence has no reserves but further violence. . . . Wars always end more savagely than they begin." Woodrow Wilson had had similar thoughts. In the first weeks of the war, he had told his brother-in-law Stockton Axson that world peace would require four things: an end to national expansion by conquest, governmental control of arms manufacturing, a recognition that all nations were equal, and a worldwide association of nations in which all were committed to the protection of each. After the attack on the *Lusitania,* Wilson's thoughts about peace were often crowded out by his fears of war.

For respite he turned to Edith. On an August evening soon after his return to the White House, he wrote her of working at his desk while listening to a band concert on the South Lawn.

> At the end, when they played the Star Spangled Banner, I stood up all alone here by my table, at attention, and had unutterable thoughts about my custody of the traditions and the present honor of that banner. I could hardly hold the tears back! And then the loneliness! The loneliness of the responsibility because the loneliness of the power, which no one *can* share. But in the midst of it I knew that there was one who *did* share—*everything*—a lovely lady who has given herself to me, who is my own, who is part of me, who makes anxieties light and responsibilities stimulating, not daunting, by her love and comprehension and exquisite sympathy.

Wilson's second *Lusitania* note to Berlin had brought an unsatisfactory reply, and in a third, dispatched July 31, he took an even stronger stand. Insisting once again that international law gave neutrals the right to travel the seas unmolested, he pledged to defend the principle "without compromise and at any cost." The kaiser covered his copy of the note with exclamations: "Immeasurably impertinent!" "Commands!" "It ends with a direct threat!"

On August 19 a German submarine sank the English liner *Arabic* off the coast of Ireland. The dead numbered forty-four, including two Americans. The *Arabic* was well known for transporting munitions and passengers on its voyages to Liverpool, but on this trip it was bound for New York, carrying only passengers and mail. Most of the 432 persons aboard survived because of calm seas and the forehandedness of the captain, who had left Liverpool with all lifesaving equipment at the ready.

In a plaintive letter asking House for advice, Wilson said he could see only one thing clearly: war would be a calamity. Most Americans strongly opposed the war, and the United States would cease to be the disinterested third party who could broker a just peace. "In view of what has been said, and in view of what has been done, it is clearly up to this government to act," House replied. "The question is, when and how?"

When *Arabic* survivors reported that the ship had been sunk without warning, American newspapers demanded Bernstorff's recall. The ambassador managed to hang on by persuading Lansing to wait until all the facts were in. Bernstorff also confided a state secret to Lansing: despite its icy replies to Wilson's notes, Germany had ordered its submarine commanders not to attack passenger ships without warning unless they tried to escape or resist. Passengers were to be allowed to board lifeboats before a ship was torpedoed. On September 1, with Bernstorff at his side, Lansing disclosed the policy to the press. With that, the crisis seemed to be over, although Wilson thought the newspapers went too far in hailing the moment as a diplomatic triumph. The submarine commander had yet to be heard from, there was no guarantee that the German order would remain in effect, and in the weeks between the loss of the *Arabic* and the happy moment that Bernstorff and Lansing shared with reporters, two other wildfires had broken out.

The first was set by Konstantin Dumba, the Austrian ambassador. In hopes of winning the propaganda war in the United States, the belligerents often funded the European travels of American reporters and photographers, and Dumba had agreed to underwrite the journey of a photojournalist named James F. J. Archibald. In August, just before Archibald's departure, Dumba asked him to deliver a letter to the Foreign Office in Vienna. Unfortunately for Dumba, the British interdicted Archibald's liner and found the letter, which was a request for funds to support labor agitation at American munitions factories. Lansing informed Vienna that its ambassador was no longer welcome in the United States.

Dumba's covert operation turned out to be only one strand in a large web of Austro-German sabotage and espionage in the United States. In the spring of 1915, Bernstorff's naval attaché, Captain Franz von Rintelen, recruited Wilson's old nemesis, General Victoriano Huerta, to help him start another Mexican-American war. Huerta, who had been living in Spain since his abdication, arrived in the United States in April, and it was widely rumored that he would soon go to Mexico to lead a rebellion against his successor, Venustiano Carranza. Huerta denied it, but Rintelen had already given him $800,000, Germany had pledged millions to the rebels, and there was a promise to deliver weapons to the Mexican coast by U-boat.

When newspapermen asked Huerta about the rumored insurrection, he first claimed that he was in the United States as a tourist. Then he rented a mansion in Queens, and Señora Huerta soon arrived with the extended family. The general became a New York landlord with a $300,000 investment in an apartment house in Harlem and a New York businessman with a civil engineering firm in a rented office on lower Broadway. On June 24, after telling friends that he had decided to take a pleasure trip to San Francisco, he boarded a westbound train.

Three days later, in a dusty border town, Huerta and one of his former generals were apprehended by Justice Department officials and a U.S. cavalry contingent. The Mexicans were charged with violating American neutrality laws banning the recruitment and arming of foreign military expeditions on U.S. soil. When Huerta appealed to the German embassy in Washington for protection for his family, Bernstorff cannily shared the message with the State Department. In disbelief, Lansing forwarded Huerta's message to Wilson, who forwarded it to Edith Galt. "Did you ever hear anything more amazing?" he asked her. "I've no doubt Bernstorff would have been deelighted, but didn't dare!" Huerta died in a Texas jail a few months later.

Rintelen lasted only a few months before falling into a British trap, but in addition to conspiring with Huerta, he organized a ring of saboteurs who planted time bombs on munitions ships and founded a union of longshoremen who went on strike to delay arms shipments to the Allies. The German embassy's military attachés were equally productive. They organized smuggling operations in American coastal towns to supply German cruisers lying offshore. They made plans to blow up tunnels and railways. And before they were deported, at the end of 1915, they plotted an invasion of Canada, to be launched from the American side of the Great Lakes. The attack was supposed to frighten the Canadian government out of sending more troops to the aid of British forces in France. As the one who approved and funded German sabotage in the United States, Bernstorff was responsible for much more havoc than Dumba, but he excelled at covering his tracks. With no hard evidence against Bernstorff, Lansing was reduced to watchful waiting.

The second wildfire proved impossible to contain. In the summer of 1915 Britain and France shifted cotton from conditional to absolute contraband after *Le Matin* of Paris claimed that two-thirds of German and Austrian gunpowder contained American cotton. The *Liverpool Gazette* printed statistics showing that Holland and Scandinavia were importing sixteen times more cotton than they had before the war, a strong indication that most of the shipments were going on to Germany. By ignoring the problem, the *Gazette* said, British authorities were contributing to the slaughter of their own armies.

Weeks before the change took effect, Ambassador Page reported that Britain had begun making arrangements to buy massive quantities of American cotton, a plan intended to prevent a crash in the cotton market. When

Bernstorff's spies learned that Britain would buy more than two million bales at ten cents a pound, he offered to take three million at the market price.

The State Department was open to Bernstorff's proposal, but when Wilson read it, he went into an exclamatory lather worthy of the kaiser. "What crude blunderers they are!" he wrote Lansing. "The idea of offering us a palpable bribe—or rather offering it to the Southern planters. How little they understand us!" But Bernstorff had simply asked that Germany and England be treated alike in the cotton market. Wilson's fury showed how far he had drifted from the ideal of impartiality he set at the beginning of the war.

Secretary McAdoo lost no time in making the case for putting even more support into the Allied cause. Wartime prosperity had just begun to take hold in the United States and would be even greater if American banks could furnish more credit to the governments making purchases in the United States, McAdoo told Wilson. England needed hundreds of millions of dollars to carry on its fight, and France and Russia were as needy as England. American banking houses had been granting modest lines of credit to foreign governments but had shied away from large bond offerings because of the former secretary of state's declaration that such loans were at odds with the spirit of neutrality. As a result, McAdoo said, "we cannot help ourselves or help our best customers."

To William Jennings Bryan, money was the worst of all forms of contraband because it enabled the warring parties to continue fighting even after they had bankrupted themselves. But McAdoo (seconded by Lansing) argued that the loan ban made no sense. On the one hand, the United States approved of selling American-made munitions and other goods to the Allies, but on the other, it refused to help the buyers finance their purchases. McAdoo assured Wilson that Wall Street could handle the transactions and that the securities would find a ready market.

Wilson acquiesced, but when Lansing asked him for a public statement supporting the $500 million bond issue McAdoo had in mind, Wilson refused. He wanted it understood that the government would take no action for or against such a transaction, he told Lansing, and he wanted that view conveyed orally, not in writing. There was to be no hint from the administration of any deviation from the strict neutrality that Wilson had proclaimed at the start of the war. When Senator George E. Chamberlain asked the president for details about the loans, Wilson directed McAdoo to reply, and McAdoo made it sound as if the lending was part of a settled policy: "The government has no power to prevent national banks from extending credits or making loans permitted by the national banking laws, and of course it has no power to interfere with loans made by private individuals or corporations not under its jurisdiction."

By the time England and France came to terms with the House of Morgan, the $500 million securities offering was being called a loan, and many went so far as to call it a war loan. Bryan protested that it amounted to placing a bet on the outcome of the war. Senator Robert M. La Follette read it as proof that the United States had "ceased to be neutral in fact as well as in name." Others who opposed such lending predicted that it would prolong the carnage and sweep the United States into the fighting. The critics got no comfort from the administration. A senator who sent a pointed query to the Federal Reserve was curtly informed that its board of governors would consider his views but had no jurisdiction over private loans to foreign governments.

Despite Wall Street's enthusiasm, American investors hesitated to put their money into a foreign war. They could earn similar returns on bonds issued by American corporations, and the foreign loans were backed by nothing but a promise to repay. Americans bought only $320 million of the $500 million offered, leaving the House of Morgan to pick up the rest. McAdoo showed no concern. An American economic collapse had been averted, and in September 1915, that seemed to justify the loan. But it was clear that the borrowers would be back for more and that each loan increased the American stake in an Allied victory.

Colonel House would soon complain in his diary of the president's tendency to "dodge trouble" rather than face it squarely, and it seemed to House that the tendency was growing more pronounced. He was right. Wilson's decision to stand by in silence as American banks lent $500 million to the Allies effectively brought U.S. neutrality to an end.

Only a few days after Lansing and Bernstorff smilingly informed reporters that German submarine commanders had been ordered not to attack unarmed passenger ships without warning, an explosion tore a hole in the starboard side of the *Hesperian,* an English liner bound for Montreal. But nearly all of the 1,100 persons aboard had been rescued, and when it was learned there were no Americans among the dead, Germany saw no reason to negotiate the case with the United States.

The submarine problem became a kind of chronic illness, flaring up and subsiding only to flare up again as Bernstorff made promises and Germany broke them. The United States kept up a pretense of neutrality by contesting the legality of British interference with neutral shipping but generally ignored Britain's most flagrant violation of international law, the blockade.

Blockades were supposed to be limited to the enemy's coastal waters, but Britain had cut off the whole North Sea. By the time the United States protested the blockade in the autumn of 1915, it knew of the spreading food shortages among civilians in Germany, but the White House and the State Department ignored the moral questions raised by a policy aimed at starving an enemy into submission. Following a pattern set at the beginning of the war, the United States continued to upbraid the British only for their disruptions of trade.

Lansing assumed that the war would drag on and the United States would eventually have to join with the Allies to bring it to an end. Wilson still hoped to stay on the sidelines. In a speech on October 11, he said, "We are not trying to keep out of trouble; we are trying to preserve the foundations upon which peace can be rebuilt." But he knew that the United States could not predict much less control the course of the war. As he told House, "My chief puzzle is to determine where patience ceases to be a virtue."

Lansing's negotiations with Bernstorff enabled Wilson to avoid a rupture with Germany, and McAdoo's success in selling the idea that American prosperity depended on huge loans to the Allies deflected most criticism from the White House to Wall Street. But there was one trouble Wilson could not dodge. By September 1, when Edith Galt returned to Washington, the fact of her romance with the president was an open secret, and the gossips were whispering about the couple's billing and cooing. They were also censorious about the president's hastiness in the wake of his wife's death. House regarded the romance as "extremely delicate" from the standpoint of the 1916 presidential election, but he wished the gossips could know the private Woodrow Wilson as well as he did. "I have never seen a man more dependent upon a woman's companionship," he wrote in his diary. "He was perfectly happy and contented with his wife. They had an ideal married life, as all her relatives will readily testify and have, indeed, to me. But his loneliness since her death has oppressed him, and if he does not marry and marry quickly, I believe he will go into a decline."

The situation grew even more delicate when the gossips resurrected the tales about Wilson and Mrs. Peck of Bermuda, now Mary Allen Hulbert of Los Angeles. Her finances deteriorated after her divorce from Mr. Peck, and chief among her liabilities was her only son, Allen Hulbert. Twenty-seven years old, he struggled with alcoholism and had not yet established himself in a career. In the spring of 1915 he moved to Los Angeles with ambitions of raising fruit, and Mary's letters to Woodrow about the venture suggest that she saw it as a last chance for herself as well as for Allen. In closing out her financial affairs in the East so that she could move west to assist him, she tried to raise cash by selling some small mortgages that she held as investments, but she had not found a buyer. When she mentioned the difficulty to her friend in the White House, he gallantly offered to purchase them, and she accepted. He sent her the money—$7,500—along with his best wishes.

The transaction was an exchange of assets, not a gift, but McAdoo was so afraid of what the gossips might read into it that he concocted a lie about it. Over lunch on September 18, he told Wilson that he had received an anonymous tip claiming that Mary Hulbert was sharing Wilson's letters to her and "doing him much harm." If the president's engagement were not announced soon, McAdoo said, the gossip would destroy Wilson's chances for reelection. Wilson could not imagine Mary stooping so low, but he panicked at the possibility that Edith would be swept up in the mess. His first impulse was to write Edith and tell her the whole story. Too distraught to frame his thoughts, he asked Grayson to see Edith that evening and "tell her everything and say my only alternative is to release her from any promise."

Dr. Grayson delivered the message but relayed a slightly different version of the story McAdoo had told Wilson. In Grayson's telling, reporters had warned House and McAdoo that if the rumors of an engagement proved to be true, Mary planned to take revenge by sharing her Wilson letters with the press. Edith, who apparently had not heard about Woodrow Wilson and Mrs. Peck, was deeply upset. She stayed up all night, despairing until she realized that she cared less about Woodrow's political fortunes than about their love for one another. At sunup she wrote a letter promising to stand by him "not for duty, not for pity, not for honor—but for love—trusting, protecting, comprehending love."

Woodrow, made physically ill by the conversation with McAdoo, was instantly cured. "Thank God there is such a woman and such love in the world," he replied. That night he slept like a child, and in the morning he wrote her, "A new chapter has opened in our wonderful love story." But the next chapter was dictated by politics, not love. Wilson capitulated to McAdoo and House, and the White House announced the engagement on October 6.

Years later, after Wilson left office, a journalist asked Mary Hulbert why Woodrow Wilson had not married her after his wife died. "Because Tumulty and McAdoo wouldn't let him," she said. There is every reason to think that Tumulty and McAdoo would have seen such a match as political suicide, but if Wilson ever explored the possibility of a courtship in a letter to Mary, it did not survive. After his death she offered a strikingly different explanation for the marriage that did not materialize: he and she were fundamentally incompatible, she wrote in *Liberty* magazine. He was the sort of man who needed a "doormat wife," and his habit of correcting grammatical lapses and other small faults "was warranted to drive certain temperaments to the verge of consideration of brutal murder."

The White House insiders who feared that the country would turn against the president for falling in love too soon were wrong. Three days after the engagement was announced, the president and his fiancée made their first public appearance together as a couple, at a World Series game in Philadelphia. To Agent Starling of the Secret Service, it seemed that "people showed increased affection for the president, and when they saw that Mrs. Galt was pretty, they loved her."

With no further need to conceal the relationship, Woodrow often spent his evenings at Edith's home, on Twentieth Street. "Almost every night we took him to see her, then waited outside the house until he reappeared," Starling wrote in his memoir. "That was never before midnight, and on Sundays the vigil was frequently from 1 p.m.—after church—to 1 a.m. We didn't mind. We were all romantic, and we were glad the boss had made good." The president often chose to walk the mile back to the White House, and Starling walked with him. When they paused at a corner to allow the traffic to pass, Wilson sometimes broke into a whistle and a tap-dance. The tune, always the same, was the vaudeville hit "Oh, You Beautiful Doll."

Woodrow and Edith were married at her home on the evening of December 18. The house was small, giving the bride and groom an excellent excuse for keeping the guest list to fifty. The honeymoon destination was kept under wraps, and the Secret Service created the illusion that the newlyweds would be leaving town by train, from Union Station. The *Superb*, a luxurious Pullman car, was coupled to a train. Golf bags and luggage were seen going aboard. Come evening, the lights were switched on at the presidential entrance, and two lines of policemen formed a protective corridor between the driveway and the door. But just as the president and the new first lady were stepping into an automobile on Twentieth Street, the train crew received orders to leave without them.

The automobile carrying the newlyweds was a black White House limousine with the shades drawn and sheets of carbon paper taped over the presidential seals on the doors. It sped to Alexandria, Virginia, hid behind the station, and when the Superb pulled in, President and Mrs. Wilson were hustled aboard. At seven the next morning, when the train came to a halt on a siding at Covington, Virginia, Starling entered the president's car and, he claimed, he heard the president singing a familiar tune: "Oh, you beautiful doll . . ."

The *Superb* and three cars transporting the Secret Service detail, the president's stenographer, and a party of White House servants were hitched to two ancient locomotives and hauled through a mountain gorge to the Homestead Hotel in Hot Springs. The Wilsons were given a large suite on the third floor, and their entire wing was closed to everyone who was not part of their entourage. To the *Baltimore Sun*'s correspondent, the hotel looked like "a mammoth hospital plant and the President's quarter might easily be taken for the isolation ward."

Isolation was exactly what Woodrow and Edith wanted. Reporters were ordered to keep their distance, and the Secret Service informed photographers that film would be confiscated and cameras broken if they were seen taking pictures of the president or the first lady. The press was reduced to reporting on Mrs. Wilson's wardrobe as the couple came and went from the hotel and relaying scraps of information deemed innocuous enough for public consumption: The Wilsons took a six-mile hike. The president removed his sweater and used it to shelter the first lady when they were caught in the rain on the golf course. The Homestead surprised the Wilsons with a Christmas tree. The first lady ordered an elaborately decorated cake for the president's birthday—his fifty-ninth—on December 28.

With his intimates, the president was more forthcoming. "We are having a heavenly time here," he wrote old friends. "Edith reveals new charms and still deeper loveliness to me every day and I shall go back to Washington feeling complete and strong for whatever may betide."

18

The World Is on Fire

The Wilsons hoped to stay at the Homestead until January 5, but on the night of January 3, after telegrams and telephone calls from Lansing and Tumulty, they hurried home. The submarine war had taken a dangerous new turn. A British liner, the *Persia,* had been torpedoed without warning in the Mediterranean, and there were two Americans among the 350 dead. Only a few months before, the crisis over the sinking of the *Arabic* had ended with Ambassador Bernstorff and Secretary Lansing announcing that Germany had ordered its submarine commanders not to attack unresisting passenger ships. Oswald Garrison Villard's *New York Evening Post* had celebrated the moment by running its first front-page photograph, a picture of Wilson, identified as "The man who, without rattling a sword, won for civilization." The attack on the *Persia* suggested that the Germans had no intention of keeping their promise.

Surprisingly, the telegram Lansing sent to the Homestead expressed less alarm about the possibility of war than the possibility that Wilson's absence would embolden Republicans to start their 1916 presidential campaign with an assault on his inaction in the face of repeated attacks on Americans. Even among Democrats, Wilson's patience was beginning to look less like a policy than an excuse for doing nothing, and many Americans had come to believe that more patience would invite more lawlessness. No one on Capitol Hill was calling for war, but senators and congressmen were making demands: Arm American ships. Stop Americans from sailing on the ships of the nations at war. Sever relations with Germany. Build up the armed forces of the United States.

The Wilsons reached the White House at eight o'clock in the morning. By ten o'clock, Tumulty was painting a bleak picture of the political temper in Congress and on the editorial pages. The situation called for action, he said. Wilson stiffened. "Tumulty," he said, "you may as well understand my position right now. If my reelection as president depends upon my getting into war, I don't want to be president. . . . I will not be rushed into war, no matter if every damned congressman and senator stands up on his hind legs and proclaims me a coward." When the facts came in, there was nothing to be done. The *Persia* had been armed with a cannon powerful enough to destroy a submarine, and it proved impossible to determine who was at fault.

Edith had only a few days to settle into her new quarters before the winter social season began. Her house would soon go up for sale, and the furnishings she kept—books, piano, sewing machine, and the contents of her bedroom—were transferred to Pennsylvania Avenue. The sewing machine drew howls from Margaret Wilson and Helen Bones. How absurd that the new first lady imagined she would have time to sew! Mrs. Wilson would have none of the leisure enjoyed by Mrs. Galt. After breakfast at eight, the president's stenographer arrived, and the first lady went off to discuss the needs of the day with the household staff, then joined her secretary to answer the mail, set her schedule, and arrange social functions. Around ten o'clock, after Woodrow finished his dictation, Edith often walked him to the Oval Office—through the garden when the weather obliged, through the colonnade when it did not. From the outset, she tried to match her schedule to his.

At her White House debut, on January 7, Edith joined Woodrow in welcoming more than three thousand guests at a reception for the Latin Americans who had come to Washington for a Pan-American Union conference. A dinner for the cabinet and the annual state dinner for the diplomatic corps soon followed. Edith seemed to enjoy the role of hostess in chief. She looked happy, the newspapers praised the stylishness of her wardrobe, and the country seemed pleased to have a first lady again.

Two weeks after his prickly conversation with Wilson, Tumulty tried again to rouse him to action. This time he put his critique on paper and proposed a major shift in policy. The vital issue was not diplomacy but national security, and the vital question was whether the United States could defend itself, Tumulty said. At the end of 1914, Wilson had stood before a joint session of Congress and mocked the handful of "nervous and excited" Republicans calling for a stronger navy and a bigger army. But after the sinking of the *Lusitania,* he had asked Secretary Garrison and Secretary Daniels for studies of the state of the nation's army and navy. The reports were not reassuring. The army's glaring weakness was its size. With 108,000 officers and men, it was on a par with the army of Montenegro. The navy was bigger but not in good shape. In the war games held in the Atlantic after Wilson reviewed the fleet in New York, the admiral in charge had been unable to prevent the landing of "enemy" marines on the shores of Chesapeake Bay. Summing up the sorry facts in a letter to the Senate Committee on Naval Affairs, Daniels noted shortages of ships and trained personnel, mechanical defects, and submarines so prone to breakdowns that the navy could not complete the necessary training

With recommendations from Garrison and Daniels, Wilson had gone to Capitol Hill on December 7 to ask for a larger defense budget, an acceleration of shipbuilding plans already approved by Congress, a larger standing army, and a 400,000-man force of reserves. He had also asked that the expansion be financed with higher taxes rather than government borrowing, on the theory that "this generation should pay the bills of this generation."

Most Americans cast a wary eye on Wilson's proposals. Many doubted that the world war would lead to an attack on the United States. Few identified themselves as pacifists, but many agreed with the pacifists' arguments against a larger defense establishment: Civilized nations ought to arbitrate their differences. Large armed forces gave generals and admirals too much political power. Big fleets and arsenals were an extravagance, and their very existence tended to provoke war.

Wilson also faced resistance from congressional Democrats. The Southern wing of the party recoiled at the thought of tens of thousands of African Americans in the army, while Midwestern Democrats were leery of offending their large German American constituencies in an election year. William Jennings Bryan publicly accused Wilson of "joyriding with the jingoes." At the other extreme, Theodore Roosevelt denounced the administration's requests as half-measures. He wanted a standing army of two million, universal military training, and military instruction in high schools.

Tumulty advised Wilson to make the case that despite the absence of immediate threats to American security, the future was full of question marks. Most Americans found Bryan and Roosevelt too radical, he told Wilson. "They are waiting for you." Tumulty urged him to tour the country and explain the need for a defense buildup, and he begged Wilson to go at once.

Wilson took the advice, setting off on January 27. From New York City he traveled as far west as Kansas City, speaking to huge, enthusiastic audiences in more than a dozen cities along the way. On his first outing he admitted that he had changed his mind about the nation's defense needs, because the war had thrust them into a new world, one they could neither control nor ignore. To protect all they held dear, they would have to come together on fundamental issues, and nothing was more fundamental than national security. How could Americans differ about the safety of America? he asked. And how dare they politicize the issue? In a show of nonpartisanship, he refused to meet with Democratic National Committee members along his route. Those afraid that the United States would become a military state had nothing to fear from him, he promised an audience in Pittsburgh. His plans called for a modest standing army augmented by a reserve force of men who were citizens first and soldiers second. And at the top, he reminded them, the Constitution had set a civilian commander in chief.

Wearing the mantle of statesman from first speech to last, Wilson said he regretted that 1916 was a campaign year. The dangers were such that Americans had to think like Americans, not like partisans. "The world is on fire, and there is tinder everywhere, he said. "The sparks are liable to drop anywhere, and somewhere there may be material which we cannot prevent from bursting into flame."

From the rear platform of his train, the president assured the inhabitants of Racine that he was not acting at the behest of the arms-makers. In Milwaukee, he warned that war might prove impossible to avoid. By the time he reached Iowa City, he was no longer asking audiences to back his defense program, he was voicing his confidence in their support. In Des Moines he added a new thought, a dream of a day when the world's governments would work together, through an association of nations, to guarantee the world's peace.

At Kansas City he confessed his impatience with the argument that enlarging the army would put the United States on the path to militarism. The present army was so small that it could not even prevent Mexican rebels from crossing the border to raid American towns for supplies, he said. The army had to be expanded, and it had to be trained. The crowd cheered, applauded, and waved small flags as he made the case that a strong army and navy were America's best hope for remaining at peace.

Wilson fared well everywhere but Topeka. Half of the five thousand members of the audience were farmers who had come to town for a convention, and the *New-York Tribune*'s reporter described them as "almost unmoved" except by the sight of the first lady. The highest praise the *Tribune* man heard after Wilson's speech came from a grizzled farmer in a flannel shirt: "he said a heap worth thinking over."

More than 100,000 people heard President Wilson speak. Hundreds of thousands more waited for hours in the cold to catch a glimpse of him and the new first lady. Editorial comment was overwhelmingly positive. Even the *Tribune* declared that he had "gained in every way—support for his policy, personal popularity, political standing and leadership, and, most important of all, in his ability to reach and move the people." For the many Republicans who assumed that Wilson's deeply divided party would cost him the White House in 1916, the *Tribune* added a warning: "President Wilson is not dead."

Congress would do as the president asked and shore up the nation's defenses, but not without a fight. The first casualties were Secretary Garrison and his 400,000-man army of reserves. For some it was too big, for others it was a poor substitute for a larger standing army, and for the National Guard, which was run by the states, it was an unwelcome competitor. With champions in every state, the Guard wielded enormous influence in Congress, and Wilson, needing Congress more than he needed Secretary Garrison, chose not to carry Garrison's torch. Garrison resigned on February 10.

That night the president and first lady dined with the cabinet at the home of Josephus Daniels. Wilson told stories and recited limericks, activities he found less taxing than conversation. To all appearances, he was in high spirits. But in a private conversation with one of the other guests, the journalist Ida Tarbell, he confessed to constant anxiety. "I never go to bed without realizing that I may be called up by news that will mean that we are at war," he told her.

Wilson's tour was brilliant political theater. Tumulty had asked him to give the country a show of leadership, and he had played his part perfectly. Onstage he warned of the dangers posed by modern warfare and offered a rational way out, making his case in a style that was thoroughly modern—cool, brisk—a welcome change from the overstuffed, overacted political speeches of the era. Wilson had always loved the theater, and as long as he had the stage to himself, he was superb. But when circumstances called for dialogue, he sometimes floundered. Questions from the twelve reporters covering the preparedness tour were fielded by Tumulty, not Wilson. Wilson never mastered the back-and-forth of a press conference. He met many a straightforward question with a sardonic question of his own, leaving no doubt that he found the reporter wanting. When a yes or no might suffice, he often let it stand unadorned; to expound was to risk being misinterpreted, he thought.

Colonel House shared Wilson's love of theater, although he preferred to stage his dramas for an audience of one. By training his attention on one person, he often succeeded in creating a feeling of intimacy well before any real intimacy existed. Wilson had been drawn in immediately. But not everyone was. House's eagerness to ingratiate himself put Edith Wilson on guard, and it repelled the Secret Service agent Jimmie Starling. Recalling his first encounters with the colonel, Starling wrote, "Deliver me from a man who smiles, rubs his hands together, and calls me 'Brother.'"

Given his talent for befriending powerful men and his success in serving them, House assumed that he would be invaluable to Wilson in foreign affairs. House enjoyed going toe-to-toe with powerful men. Having no official duties, he was free to travel. And in imagining that he would succeed at diplomacy, he resembled most of his fellow Americans. Filled with confidence, they liked to believe that there was no such thing as an irreconcilable difference. Whatever the problem, as long as reasonable men on one side were willing to confer with reasonable men on the other, they would arrive at a reasonable solution.

As Wilson was making plans for his preparedness tour, House was in Europe, hoping once again to find an opening for Wilson to intervene. The colonel's previous mission, a search for common ground, had come to a dead end, with each side insisting that it would defeat the other and dictate the peace. Although European attitudes had not changed, the attacks on the *Lusitania* and two other British passenger ships with Americans aboard had led the president to wonder whether it would be possible for the United States to stay out of the war.

For months Sir Edward Grey had been carrying on a warm correspondence with House, ostensibly to tell him that several neutral governments wished to form a group that would hold itself at the ready to mediate an end to the war. Grey told House that he believed that mediation would have to come about through the United States. But, he added, the Allies were determined to fight until they were certain that they could make a peace that would preclude a second world war.

Grey's next move had been a calculated appeal to Wilson's idealism. Come the end of the war, Grey said, there could be no lasting peace unless the belligerents pared their armies and navies to the minimum needed for self-defense and committed themselves to collective action against disturbers of the world's peace. "How much are the United States prepared to do in this direction?" he asked. "Would the president propose that there should be a League of Nations binding themselves to side against any power which broke a treaty . . . ? I cannot say which governments would be prepared to accept such a proposal, but I am sure that the government of the United States is the only government that could make it with effect."

It was said of Colonel House that he could walk on dead leaves and make no more noise than a tiger. But Sir Edward was even lighter on his feet—and much swifter. Believing that the letters gave him the makings of a "master-stroke of diplomacy," House failed to see that the master-stroke was Sir Edward's. Grey had not said that the Allies were open to mediation; he had said that if they *were* to consider it, they would want the United States in the lead. And even as he encouraged Wilson to propose a league of nations, he wondered about its acceptance.

"It has occurred to me," House wrote Grey (as if Grey had not put the idea into his head), "that the time may soon come when this government should intervene between the belligerents and demand that a peace parley begin upon the broad basis of the elimination of militarism and navalism. . . . What I want you to know is that whenever you consider the time is propitious for this intervention I will propose it to the president." "Intervention" now replaced "mediation" in House's vocabulary, and he craftily spoke of it without specifying whether he meant diplomatic intervention or the military kind. Worse, he volunteered to stack the deck against Germany: "I would not let Berlin know of course of any understanding with the Allies," he told Grey. "This might induce Berlin to accept the proposal, but, if they did not do so, it would nevertheless be the purpose to intervene. If the Central Powers were still obdurate, it would be necessary for us to join the Allies and force the issue."

When House revealed the scheme to Wilson, in October 1915, Wilson had seemed startled but did not protest. He lapsed into silence, which House chose to read as acquiescence. To a degree it was. Wilson inserted a "probably" before the "necessary" but otherwise offered no objections. The letter went off to Grey, and two months later House discovered that he and Wilson were no longer of one mind on the subject of military intervention.

While House considered it inevitable, Wilson thought that if the Allies could not win on their own, the United States would be of no use because of the long time it would take to muster and train a fighting army.

Now it was House who was startled. A victorious Germany would set its sights on the United States, he said, and when it did, the United States would need the Allies. Although Wilson understood, House told his diary, "I cannot quite get him up to the point where he is willing to take action. By action, I mean not to declare war, but to let the Allies know we are definitely on their side and that it is not our intention to permit Germany to win if the strength of this country can prevent [it]. The last time we talked he was quite ready to take this stand, but he has visibly weakened."

On December 22, a week before sailing, the colonel took the precaution of writing the president to ask "what to say in London and what to say in Berlin and how far I shall go." Wilson, still on his honeymoon, sent a muddled reply, saying first that instructions were superfluous because House understood him so well and then setting definite limits. House was not to discuss reparations or territorial questions. The United States was concerned only with the guarantees that might be made to secure world peace and, Wilson wrote, the only rational guarantees were disarmament and a league of nations.

House moved from capital to capital in a fog, apparently unaware that the Europeans assumed he was trying to end their war for the purpose of securing Wilson's reelection. Nor did House realize that the British, despite their cordiality and compliments, thought of him as "the Empty House." As one close student of American neutrality remarked, "His mind was not quite in the first class and his sudden transfiguration into a person of world importance left him just a little too pleased with himself." And to the dismay of Walter Hines Page, the U.S. ambassador in London, neither House nor Wilson guessed that Europeans might resent the idea of Wilson crossing the Atlantic to play peacemaker "and give a blessing to these erring children. There was a condescension in this attitude that was offensive."

House had been in London for only a week when Grey persuaded him that diplomatic intervention would not suffice and explained that the British could not recommend a peace conference to the French because France would panic at any hint that Britain was ready to give up the fight. But even if His Majesty's Government had been open to the idea of peace talks, some members of the cabinet would have balked at the thought of Wilson in the role of broker. As Page reminded House, the British had lost confidence in the president because of his weak response to the submarine attacks.

Near the end of his stay in London, House disingenuously informed Wilson that he thought diplomatic intervention would be possible and that military intervention would be a mistake. But, he added, "we should be ready to throw our weight at the right time in the right direction for the good of humanity. We are growing stronger as [the Allies] grow weaker, consequently our power is increasing in double ratio." The colonel was running amok.

In Berlin, House found that Germany, too, was dead set against peace talks. With victorious armies and a rapidly growing fleet of faster, more powerful U-boats, the Germans had nothing to gain by negotiating an end to the war, the chancellor told him. Nor could they imagine Wilson, whom they regarded as an Anglophile, in the role of peacemaker. The chancellor met House's unacceptable offer with an unacceptable offer of his own: a promise to evacuate Belgium and France—if the Allies would compensate Germany for the lost territory.

Arthur Zimmermann, the personable undersecretary of foreign affairs, was full of false compliments for the new American peace effort. House, taking the praise at face value and clearly relishing his own guile, replied that the world needed more statesmen of Zimmermann's caliber. Zimmermann said that he looked forward to a time after the war when the English, the Germans, and the Americans—"the white races," in his words—would be in accord.

In Paris, House talked war, not peace. With Jules Cambon, secretary general of the French Foreign Ministry, the colonel took up a point he had made to Sir Edward Grey: the Allies had to help the United States help them. If France could persuade the British to ease up on the blockade, House said, the United States would enter the war on the side of the Allies before the year was out. Cambon was so astounded by the mention of U.S. military intervention that he asked House to repeat the statement. House obliged. Cambon, wanting to be certain that he had it right, read his notes aloud. House confirmed them.

In order to take up arms against Germany, House said, the United States needed an "incident" of some sort, one more transgression that the president could use as a pretext for war. Cambon, undoubtedly thinking of the *Lusitania,* the *Arabic,* the *Persia,* and a long list of other "incidents," tartly observed that the Germans seemed quite good at pacifying the United States. House parried with a claim that times had changed. The kaiser had just ruled against all-out submarine warfare, but House was convinced that the German navy would soon persuade the kaiser to change his mind. And when the restraints were thrown off, House said, the United States would have a powerful justification for entering the war.

During his final talk with the French, House went even further in his offer of American support. As he put it in his diary, "I again told them that the lower the fortunes of the Allies ebbed, the closer the United States would stand by them." House told them that he had made the same pledge to the British.

France, like Britain, had assured its citizens that it would win the war, so Cambon wondered what plausible rationale the government could give the French people for a negotiated peace. Perhaps the Germans would be willing to return Alsace-Lorraine? Cambon and his colleagues asked. Here was a territorial question, the kind of question Wilson had instructed House to avoid, and here was House blithely assuring the French that the lost provinces could be regained by giving Germany a swath of Asia Minor. Taken aback once again, Cambon asked, "Then you would wipe out Turkey?" House said he had it in mind. The subject had come up in his talks with the British.

On his way back to London, House detoured to the Belgian coastal town of De Panne for a visit with King Albert. Fresh from dismantling Turkey, the colonel overflowed with ideas for imperial land swaps, and he asked Albert if he would consider selling the Belgian Congo to the Germans. The king answered that the Belgian people might object, but he did not. He asked only that the sale be consummated over his protest.

In Boulogne, waiting for the British troopship that would take him to England, House could hardly contain his excitement. He wrote separate letters to Wilson about his encounters with the Belgian king and the French Foreign Ministry, and in neither did he pause to reflect that he had gone to Europe in search of a path to peace but was now paving the American road to war. He reiterated his hope that the *Lusitania* would not be the pretext. The case was now nine months old—too old, in his view, to justify a plunge into war. American intervention would have to be based on "the highest human motives," he wrote. "We are the only nation left on earth with sufficient power to lead them out, and with us once in, the war would have to go on to a finish with all its appalling consequences. . . . A great opportunity is yours, my friend, the greatest perhaps that has ever come to any man."

In 1914 and 1915, Grey had often indulged House's preference for an audience of one, but in 1916 Grey invited other cabinet members into many of their conversations. "I wish I had but a single man to deal with here as at home," House grumbled in his diary after two weeks in London. He also complained about the pointed questions of Arthur J. Balfour, first lord of the admiralty. Nor did the colonel trust David Lloyd George, who was soon to become prime minister but was then doing double duty as minister of munitions and secretary of state for war. Lloyd George tended to listen sympathetically and agree wholeheartedly but often went home and changed his mind.

The enlargement of the cast put House in an awkward position with Ambassador Page. House generally conducted his British dealings behind Page's back, and while he could trust Grey not to give him away, he worried that one of the others might mention the nature of his business in London. Within an hour of his arrival at the Ritz, House took Page into his confidence. Shocked to learn of the course that House had set, Page told him that it would be morally wrong for the United States to get into the war by springing a trick on the Germans. Page also reminded him that the Allies expected to win the war, which meant that any British cabinet member who spoke out in favor of a peace conference would be pilloried. Page finished by telling House that Wilson no longer enjoyed the confidence of the British.

The next day House turned up at the embassy with a bland alternative: Wilson would invite both sides to confer and work things out themselves. "As if they would now confer!" Page shouted in his diary. When House airily announced that the two of them were to meet with the prime minister and key cabinet members in a few days, Page refused to attend. House seemed unsurprised, which Page took as a sign that House was having doubts about his grand plan. In fact, House was relieved to have Page out of the way.

The ambassador silently vowed to resign if the colonel made another trip to London, and in an obvious bid to put an end to House's scheme for intervention, he sent Wilson his own plan for ending the war: sever relations with Germany and impose an embargo on all goods from the Central Powers. German credit would collapse, and Germany would have to quit the war. "I do not believe we should have to fire a gun or risk a man," Page wrote. He warned that delay "or any other plan will bring us only a thankless, opulent and dangerous isolation." Page showed the cable to House and bluntly asked if he agreed. When House said he did not, Page demanded to know why. House lamely replied that it would take too long to explain.

The colonel's meeting with the foreign secretary culminated in a secret agreement known as the House-Grey Memorandum, in which Grey wrote, "Colonel House told me that President Wilson was ready, on hearing from France and England that the moment was opportune to propose that a Conference should be summoned to put an end to the war. Should the Allies accept this proposal and should Germany refuse it, the United States would enter the war against Germany. Colonel House expressed the opinion that if such a Conference met, it would secure peace on terms not unfavorable to the Allies; and, if it failed to secure peace, the United States would leave the Conference as a belligerent on the side of the Allies, if Germany was unreasonable." The colonel's final thought addressed Wilson's wish to avoid a useless American sacrifice on the battlefield. If the Allies delayed in accepting the U.S. offer and the war turned so sharply against them that U.S. intervention was unlikely to bring victory, "the United States would probably disinterest themselves in Europe, and look to their own protection in their own way."

House reported to the White House on March 6. His diary contains only a sketchy account of his conversation with Wilson. He claimed that he outlined his mission in detail, but there is no telling how frank he was about the British opposition to diplomatic intervention or the intensity of his own wish for military intervention. The briefing took place on a long automobile ride with the president and first lady, after which House was deposited at the State Department, where he summarized his travels for Secretary Lansing. There is no record of that conversation, either. Back at the White House, the colonel had another long meeting with the president, the details of which were not put on paper. What *is* known is that as House was leaving for dinner elsewhere, Wilson put an arm around his shoulder and said, "It would be impossible to imagine a more difficult task than the one placed in your hands, but you have accomplished it in a way beyond my expectations." House spoke of the pride he would feel on seeing Wilson at the head of a negotiating table at The Hague. "My dear friend," Wilson answered, "you should be proud of yourself and not of me since you have done it all."

House spent the night at the White House, and the next day, after a long discussion of the House-Grey Memorandum, the president took to his typewriter and tapped out a short note for House to send to Grey. Wilson made only one change to the memo. Where Grey had said that if Germany proved so unreasonable that the Americans quit the peace conference, they would enter the war on the Allied side, Wilson made it read "would probably enter." Some historians have taken Wilson's "probably" to mean that he was unwilling to commit to war, while others have argued that it merely acknowledged the fact that the Constitution assigns the war power to Congress, not the president.

Surely the most objectionable feature of the House-Grey Memorandum was not Wilson's "probably" but his willingness to go along with House's scheme for a dishonest peace. In assuring the Allies that he would devise a peace "not unfavorable" to them, he had consented to deceive not only the German government but the American people. As far as they knew, the United States had yet to take sides in the war.

Before leaving Washington, House briefed the British and French ambassadors on his mission and his conversations at the White House. He told Spring Rice and Jusserand that the United States would enter the war, and the only "probably" he mentioned was a reference to the timing. As Jusserand reported to the Quai d'Orsay, House had said that the United States would go to war *à un moment qui n'est peut-être pas fort éloigné* (at a moment perhaps not too far off).

Exhilarated by Wilson's praise and the thought of the United States fighting alongside the Allies, House began to imagine that he was the only one who fully understood the world's affairs. "The life I am leading transcends in interest and excitement any romance," he told his diary. "I cannot begin to outline here what happens from day to day, how information from every quarter pours into this little unobtrusive study. I believe I am the only one who gets a view of the entire picture. Some get one corner and some another, but I seem to have it all."

19

Stumbling in the Dark

O n Saturday, March 4, 1916, the Wilsons headed for the Navy Yard to board the *Mayflower* for a cruise of Chesapeake Bay. Edith considered these outings "red-letter days," and Woodrow savored the respite they gave him from the constant interruptions of life in the White House. On the *Mayflower,* he could think in peace for hours on end. Their luggage was always taken down in advance, the suitcases were unpacked, and the president's seagoing office, complete with his typewriter, was ready when he boarded. Even in cold weather they liked to begin their voyage on deck, watching the city of Washington shrink into nothingness. Nearing Mount Vernon, they stood as the crew paid the navy's traditional tribute to the first president with a dipping of the colors, taps, and a tolling of the ship's bell. Afterward Edith and Woodrow usually went to the chart room in hopes of finding a new port to visit.

Among the items in need of the president's attention on that weekend was the appointment of a successor to Secretary Garrison of the War Department. Wilson decided on Newton D. Baker, whom he had known since 1892, when Baker enrolled in the political economy class that Wilson taught at Johns Hopkins to augment his Princeton salary. Baker had gone on to a career in law and city government, and in 1911, at the age of thirty-nine, was elected mayor of Cleveland. At the Democrats' national convention in Baltimore, he had upended the Ohio delegation's plan to support a favorite son by giving an eloquent speech in favor of Wilson. Wilson took note and offered him the post of secretary of the interior. Baker declined, feeling obligated to finish his second term as mayor. He left office at the beginning of 1916 and returned to the practice of law.

On Sunday, from somewhere on Chesapeake Bay, the *Mayflower* radioed the Navy Department and directed it to send Baker a telegram from the president: "Would you accept Secretaryship of War. Earnestly hope that you can see your way to do so. It would greatly strengthen my hand." Baker decided to go to the White House and explain in person why he was the wrong man for the job. He was a pacifist. He had no interest in war. And the army had no interest in him: he had tried to enlist during the Spanish-American War but was turned down because of poor eyesight.

Wilson saw Baker at ten o'clock on Thursday morning, March 9. Only one sentence of their conversation has survived, but in all likelihood Baker rattled off his defects and Wilson pooh-poohed them. The hand he was trying to strengthen was not the War Department but Ohio, which had twenty-four electoral votes. "Are you ready to be sworn in?" he asked.

Baker surrendered, promising himself that he would leave at the end of Wilson's first term, which was only a year away. Secretary Daniels marched the prisoner next door to the War Department, where a clerk was waiting with five versions of the oath of office. Asked to choose one, Baker, who topped five feet by only four inches, joked that he would take the shortest, "since Nature has rather adapted me to short things."

After the ceremony, the new secretary was welcomed by the army officers based in Washington, and at some point in the morning's proceedings, a reporter delivered a bulletin from New Mexico: Pancho Villa and a band of hundreds had stormed the border town of Columbus at four o'clock in the morning, looting stores, setting fires, and killing seventeen Americans. Baker stayed at the office for the rest of the day and was soon buried in dispatches from Fort Bliss in San Antonio, headquarters of the army's Southern Department. Acutely aware of his ignorance, he sought out the army's chief of staff, Major General Hugh L. Scott, who had been a soldier since Baker's infancy. "[Y]ou know all about this," Baker said. "I know nothing. You must treat me as a father would his son."

The Mexican Revolution had faded from American newspapers after Wilson granted de facto recognition to the government of Venustiano Carranza, first chief of the Constitutionalist Party, in October 1915. The first chief was no George Washington, but his civics were on a higher moral plane than General Huerta's, and Wilson and Lansing hoped that Carranza's gratitude for American recognition would reduce Mexico's temptation to align itself with Germany, which was trying to provoke a Mexican-American war in order to disrupt American exports to the Allies.

After consulting the cabinet, Wilson authorized a punitive expedition, a tightly circumscribed military incursion to deal with a security threat that another government either could not or would not eliminate. The mission: capture Pancho Villa and put his rebel faction out of business. On March 15 nearly five thousand U.S. soldiers headed into Mexico under the command of Brigadier General John J. Pershing. Within two weeks the expedition had marched deep into Mexico and killed thirty Villistas in an old-fashioned cavalry charge. But Villa himself was still at large.

While Americans cheered, Carranza was deeply unhappy. A few days after Pershing and his men set out, the Mexican government had professed its surprise—a euphemism for irritation—that American troops were on Mexican soil. If the Americans did not capture Villa soon, they would be asked to withdraw, Carranza said. The expedition got little help from the Mexican army, and on April 12, the two armies actually came to blows, near the city of Parral. When the shooting ended, three Americans were dead or dying, one had disappeared, and several were wounded. Pershing called a temporary halt to his operations and retreated far to the north. Villa was still on the loose.

Some of Wilson's cabinet members questioned the wisdom of continuing the pursuit. The Villistas had been chased so deep into the interior that they no longer menaced the border, and Baker and Lansing feared more American casualties. Wilson argued that Pershing's exit would merely encourage the Villistas to regroup for a new spate of assaults. He also feared that Germany would see the withdrawal as a sign of American weakness, and he was facing yet another German challenge that demanded a projection of strength and resolve. Germany had ordered U-boat commanders in British waters to treat all Allied cargo vessels as warships, making them subject to attack without warning.

On March 24, a torpedo sliced open the bow of the *Sussex,* an unarmed

THE PUNITIVE EXPEDITION
March 1916 to February 1917

- - - ▶ Expedition route

British ferry crossing the English Channel. There were fifty fatalities, and four Americans among the wounded. Germany offered a succession of excuses: The *Sussex* must have hit a mine. The *Sussex* had been attacked by a British submarine firing a German torpedo. The U-boat commander had mistaken the steamer for a minelayer.

After reading a sheaf of incriminating dispatches, Lansing wrote the president that Washington had to act, and its action had to show that the United States would not tolerate the new submarine policy. Lansing wanted to set conditions, demand that Germany meet them by a certain date, and warn that Ambassador Bernstorff would be sent home if the U.S. demands were not met. "My impressions are not quite the same," Wilson replied. He wanted more evidence and time to formulate a response.

Colonel House, who was recuperating from minor surgery of some sort, did not feel up to going to Washington but went all the same. Like Lansing, he saw a need for action and was afraid that Wilson would procrastinate and then write an anemic note. His fears were well founded. Following their first talk about the *Sussex,* House sensed that Wilson would do little or nothing. "He does not seem to realize that one of the main points of criticism against him is that he talks boldly but acts weakly," House told his diary.

Wilson understood that he had to grasp the nettle but hoped to do it without a break in diplomatic relations, and even Lansing, the most hawkish member of the cabinet, understood the hesitation. Mexico was a powder keg, a rupture would almost certainly start a war for which the United States was unprepared, and Wilson still dreamed of bringing peace to Europe. He asked House to ask Grey if the Allies were ready to accept U.S. mediation. Grey not only rejected the idea, he dropped a large hint: unless the United States stood up to Germany in the matter of the *Sussex,* the Allies would have no faith in Wilson's mediation.

Refusing to be hurried, Wilson kept to himself as much as possible. On April 2, a Sunday, Grayson and one of Lansing's aides called on House in New York and begged him to come to Washington and persuade Wilson to act. Grayson expressed particular concern about Wilson's inaccessibility and his impatience with opposition.

As a presidential candidate in 1912, Wilson had stressed his intention to make decisions after "taking counsel," but by the spring of 1916, he had a decided preference for thinking things through alone. He had never seen the value of sharing meals with politicians, and he now saw cabinet meetings and press conferences as a waste of time. He wanted to use his time to arrive at the right thought, and once he had it, he was willing to put his all into fighting for it. In some notes for a forthcoming speech, he wrote, "Weave the world together in ideal, thought, and principle and you have woven it together in action. "Thought the real amalgam."

When House returned to Washington, on April 6, Wilson was still not ready to act. Lansing came to the White House to meet with them and deliver his latest draft of the diplomatic note he thought the United States should make to Germany. Wilson said he would read it later. House and Lansing had to persevere to get him to focus on Germany. House went home that night and returned on April 11 only to find that Wilson had been laid low for days by an upset stomach. He still looked wan but had driven himself to overhaul Lansing's draft and was ready to read it to the colonel and the first lady. Edith thought it weak, and House pointed out two defects: it did not call for an immediate response, and it left room for discussion.

Wilson knew that more talk would not avail, but he was afraid that a U.S. refusal to talk would mean war. He felt helpless, he said. House argued that forcing Germany to make the stark choice between peace and war would do more to preserve the peace. After two hours of talk, Wilson had to leave for a cabinet meeting, the very thought of which made him cross. He knew he had to share his plans but did not want to, he said, because he did not value the opinions of his cabinet members or trust them to keep the information to themselves.

After another anxious week, Wilson issued what he described as "practically an ultimatum": unless the German government immediately ordered an end to submarine attacks without warning, the United States would have to sever relations. Wilson discussed it with the cabinet and swore them to secrecy. The word was out within hours, and Bernstorff rushed to the State Department to plead for something short of an ultimatum—a commission to investigate the *Sussex* attack, perhaps. Lansing was immovable. The message went to Ambassador Gerard in Berlin at six o'clock that evening.

At ten the next morning, Wilson briefed the ranking members on the Senate and House committees on foreign affairs, and shortly before one o'clock, he went up to the Capitol to explain his decision. Edith was there, and for the first time since her engagement to Woodrow, the newspapermen had no comment on her clothes. Like the rest of the crowd, they were transfixed by a tension that seemed to emanate from the president himself. His first words were barely audible, he spoke slowly, and during the fifteen minutes it took to deliver the speech, his body scarcely stirred. There was no sound in the House chamber except his voice, which was so solemn that one congressman felt as if he were listening to an indictment.

"The Government of the United States has been very patient," Wilson said. It had accepted Germany's past assurances and had hoped that the German government would "square its policy with the principles of humanity as embodied in the law of nations. It has been willing to wait until the significance of the facts became absolutely unmistakable and susceptible of but one interpretation. That point has now unhappily been reached." He had given Germany a choice, he said. It could either order its submarine commanders to stop attacking passenger and cargo ships without warning, or it could forfeit its relations with the United States.

Most Germans read Wilson's ultimatum as a bluff, but the kaiser, who understood that Wilson was in earnest, was incensed by the accusation of inhumanity. In residence at the German army's base in Charleville-Mézières, France, Wilhelm was immediately set upon by his quarreling advisors. On April 27, Ambassador Gerard was summoned from Berlin, and he and his chargé d'affaires, Joseph C. Grew, were kept waiting for four days as the quarrel burned on.

In the evenings the Americans dined with the chancellor, Bethmann Hollweg, in a villa whose owners had left behind a mechanical hoochy-coochy dancer two feet tall and a toy clown with a ladder-climbing pig. Bethmann had them wound up every night after dinner. The ambassador offered entertainment in the form of Grew, an accomplished pianist. Grew had forgotten most of the music he once knew but managed to summon up an arrangement of "Liebestod." Bethmann brought up the ultimatum numerous times, leading Gerard to surmise that he was searching for more facts and for ideas that would help him win the argument for restraining the U-boats. Bethmann also tried to convince Gerard that Germany would make no concessions unless the United States forced Britain to loosen the blockade. Gerard declared that the United States would do no such thing.

Bethmann took Gerard and Grew to the kaiser's château on May 1. Wilhelm, dressed in a cavalry uniform complete with leather leggings, was walking in the garden, and he greeted Gerard by asking if he had come in peace or war. Gerard answered that he had come with the hope of adjusting their differences. The kaiser criticized the tone of Wilson's note on the *Sussex* and said that he had wanted to conduct the war in a chivalrous fashion but the blockade had forced him to more brutal tactics. In his view, the English effort to starve the Germans justified any kind of submarine war, and he was willing to destroy England, including the royal family, before he would permit his wife and children to die of starvation. His lecture to Gerard ended with a declaration that the submarine was here to stay and the laws of naval warfare must be changed to accommodate it. When the kaiser asked Gerard to promise that the United States would exact a concession on the blockade, Gerard resisted once again.

The State Department had given Gerard the protocol to follow in the event of a break, and the Wilhelmstrasse had instructed Bernstorff to prepare to sabotage Germany's most valuable asset in the United States, the liners and freighters tied up in ports along the East Coast. If Germany and the United States severed relations, the crews were to render the ships useless by destroying their engines.

The standoff ended on May 4, when Germany promised that its submarines would not strike passenger ships and said that it expected the United States to press the British to end their blockade of the high seas. If the United States was unsuccessful, Germany said, it would feel justified in taking other measures. Washington promptly rejected the demand for a quid pro quo. Wilson's boldness was widely praised, but *The New Republic* spoke plainly about where things stood: "The two countries are stumbling in the dark along a blind and treacherous footpath. The real difficulties are being evaded or postponed."

Colonel House proposed a cooling-off period, and Bernstorff agreed, for ulterior reasons: Berlin was working on a plan to lure Wilson into making another offer of mediation. By the Germans' reckoning, there was nothing to lose. Despite recent military setbacks, their overall gains were considerable, and they might be able to negotiate a settlement that left them with more territory than they had before the war. If the peace talks failed? Well, the angel of peace in the White House would hardly be able to lead his country into war, would he? And without the military intervention of the United States, the Allies were doomed. Bernstorff thought the calculations were sound and believed that there was no need for Germany to rush. As long as the United States was tied down in Mexico, he wrote the Foreign Office, Germany was fairly safe from an American attack.

Pershing was indeed tied down, stuck two hundred miles south of the border. The United States and Mexico had been communicating—testily— since the bloodshed at Parral, and Carranza instructed his minister of war to discuss the withdrawal of the American troops with the U.S. Army's chief of staff and the commander of the army's Southern Department. On May 2, the Americans agreed to a gradual exit, with the pace contingent on Mexico's success in putting down Villa's rebellion. Wilson gave his consent, but before Carranza could give his, two hundred Villistas killed six Americans in Texas. Fearing the worst, the War Department agreed to speed at least 150,000 troops to the border.

Wilson turned his attention back to Europe. "It seems to me that we should get down to hard pan," he wrote House on May 16. He wanted to challenge Britain—not on the blockade but on its recent interceptions of mail carried by neutral ships and its blacklisting of American firms that traded with Britain's enemies. Wilson had decided that the United States should either make a move for peace or insist upon the established rights of neutrals in wartime. But his idea of getting down to hard pan was as ethereal as anything he ever attempted. He made a speech calling for peace and for an association of nations charged with maintaining freedom of the seas and the peace of the world.

A crowd of two thousand turned up at the New Willard Hotel on May 27 to hear what the president had in mind. He had asked to speak last, to give himself time to read the crowd. Senator Lodge, who appeared just before Wilson, spoke of the world's need to move beyond voluntary arbitration. Arbitration was a fine thing, Lodge said, but it had reached its limit, and the next logical step was the one proposed by the League to Enforce Peace, an organization headed by William Howard Taft. As Taft, Lodge, Roosevelt, and many other influential Republicans conceived of it, the League to Enforce Peace would be equal parts world court and world army. The court would hear international disputes and render decisions, and the army would stand ready to enforce them. "Probably it will be impossible to stop all wars," Lodge said, "but it certainly will be possible to stop some wars and to diminish their number."

Wilson began by saying that he had come as the spokesman of the American people, to try to express their thoughts on the war and the peace. Echoing a theme from his preparedness tour, he said, "We are participants, whether we would or not, in the life of the world. The interests of all nations are our own also." It seemed to him that his fellow citizens shared three beliefs about the world: that every people had a right to choose its own government, that small states were entitled to the same respect as the Great Powers, and that the world had "a right to be free from every disturbance of its peace that has its origin in aggression and disregard of the rights of peoples and nations."

Venturing as close as he dared to the subject of ending the war, Wilson said that if the United States ever had the privilege of initiating a move toward peace, Americans would ask nothing for themselves. The United States wanted only a peace that could be maintained by a universal association of nations, he said. He had not come to spell out how the organization would do its work. He merely wanted to profess a creed and voice his faith that the world was closing in on "a great consummation, when some common force will be brought into existence which shall safeguard right as the first and most fundamental interest of all peoples and all governments, when coercion shall be summoned not to the service of political ambition or selfish hostility, but to the service of a common order, a common justice, and a common peace."

In twelve minutes, Woodrow Wilson had challenged the greatness of the Great Powers by asserting the equality of all nations, had affirmed the right of every people to choose its form of government, and had pointed out that in the modern world, there could be no security for any nation except in a community of nations, which would use its collective force for the defense of the community. Most radical of all was his abandonment of isolationism, the first principle of U.S. foreign policy. When his critics complained that American participation in an international peacekeeping league would create the entangling alliances George Washington had inveighed against, Wilson answered that the naysayers had missed his point. He was proposing a "disentangling alliance," he said, one that would free the world from the old balance-of-power alliances that overnight had plunged fifteen nations into war. By the time Wilson publicly proposed his league of nations, the war had touched five continents. *The New Republic* hoped Wilson would succeed and predicted that his speech would be remembered as a turning point in the world's history.

20

The Mystic Influence of the Stars and Stripes

Wilson sailed on to one of the most exhilarating seasons of his presidency. On June 1, after five months of wrangling, the Senate confirmed his nominee for the Supreme Court, Louis D. Brandeis. In 1913 Wilson had wanted him in the cabinet as attorney general or secretary of commerce but yielded to warnings that Brandeis's advanced progressivism would intensify the business world's hostility to the New Freedom. Known as "the people's lawyer," Brandeis had exposed the accounting hijinks and monopolistic practices of railroads, utilities, and banks, and he had represented labor in several lawsuits against employers. Wilson had stayed in touch, consulting him on the creation of the Federal Reserve Board, the drafting of the Clayton Antitrust Act, and the powers of the new

Federal Trade Commission. Few appointments pleased Wilson as much as this one. He admired Brandeis's intellect and commitment to economic justice, and he had few associates who understood his political philosophy as deeply as Brandeis did. Brandeis also shared Wilson's faith that capitalism could be made safe for democracy.

Over the summer, Congress authorized Wilson's buildup of the army and navy, passed the tax increases necessary to pay for the expansion, and established the U.S. Shipping Board to modernize and enlarge the nation's merchant marine. It also passed a half-dozen laws giving millions of Americans more economic security than they had ever had. The Workmen's Compensation Act aided federal employees injured on the job and would eventually be extended to the rest of the workforce. Goods made by child labor were banned from interstate commerce. The Federal Farm Loan Act and the U.S. Warehouse Act gave farmers their first access to long-term loans at low interest rates and allowed them to use their harvested crops as collateral. Wilson's congressional triumphs in the summer of 1916 would be his last, but no president before him had won so much substantive legislation in a single term, and among his successors, only Franklin Roosevelt surpassed him.

During the first days of June, it looked as if the presidential race of 1916 might resemble the campaign of 1912, with Theodore Roosevelt again at the head of the National Progressive Party's ticket. But Roosevelt refused the Progressives' nomination, and the Republicans chose Charles Evans Hughes, an associate justice of the Supreme Court.

The Progressives were disappointed, but not as disappointed as the Democrats. Roosevelt firmly believed that the United States ought to be fighting alongside the Allies, and given the antiwar mood of the country, Democrats were confident that a Roosevelt run would end with a Wilson victory. But Hughes, sequestered on the bench for six years, had taken no stand on the war or any other political issue. Nor had he made any enemies during the Republican feud of 1912. By four o'clock on June 10, Hughes's one-sentence letter of resignation from the Supreme Court had been delivered to the White House, and a few hours later he issued a statement taking aim at Wilson's "weak and vacillating" Mexican policy and his habit of appointing party hacks to diplomatic posts, which, Hughes said, "presented to the world a humiliating spectacle of ineptitude." Roosevelt capped the day by announcing that Hughes would have his full support.

Like Woodrow Wilson, Charles Evans Hughes was a minister's son who had received his early education at home. A much better pupil than

Wilson, Hughes was a mathematical prodigy and a precocious reader with a near-photographic memory. He entered college at fourteen, graduated at eighteen, and after two years of teaching the classics in a high school, had saved enough money to enter Columbia Law School. He passed the New York State bar exam with the unheard-of score of 99.5 percent.

Said to be delightful in private, Hughes cut an austere figure in public. Tall and erect, starched and creased, he parted his hair precisely in the middle and hid most of his face behind a full beard and a large mustache. To one of his Washington neighbors, he seemed like a mannequin. In 1905, after nearly twenty years of practicing and teaching law, Hughes was appointed by the state of New York to investigate two scandal-ridden businesses, utilities and insurance. The revelations of accounting fraud, price gouging, and other misdeeds culminated in major legislative reforms that brought him instant fame and, a year later, the governorship of New York. Like Governor Wilson, Governor Hughes had been moderately progressive. The two were so much alike that soon after Hughes's nomination, the pundits began calling him "the whiskered Wilson," and wondering if the public would see any difference between the two.

Wilson had no rivals for the Democratic nomination, so the party's leaders planned a convention that would celebrate his presidency and extol the glories of Americanism, a theme that had played well on his preparedness tour. On Memorial Day, Wilson had augmented the traditional presidential address at Arlington National Cemetery with a proclamation asking that every June 14 be marked as Flag Day, with patriotic exercises throughout the country "to give significant expression to our thoughtful love of America."

Walter Lippmann of *The New Republic,* puzzling over the attraction of a concept as vapid as "Americanism," ascribed it to his fellow citizens' uneasiness about their country's place in the world. Unsure whether neutrality was right yet fearful of going to war, Americans were taking refuge in platitudes. "There is a fervent desire on everyone's part to proclaim his adhesion to ideas which almost no one can dispute," Lippmann wrote.

The morning of Flag Day found Wilson at the head of Washington's patriotic exercises, a "preparedness parade" that marched past the cheering tens of thousands who lined Pennsylvania Avenue from the Capitol to the White House. As *The Washington Post* explained, "Flag Day was Wilson Day." It was not about preparedness or patriotism. It was about the president's bid for reelection. Watching her husband from the reviewing stand near the White House, Edith Wilson thought he seemed especially youthful and vigorous, and the photographs of the day bear her out. He is wearing white flannel trousers and a navy blue blazer, he is carrying a big flag, and he looks like he is having a ball.

After lunch at the White House, the Wilsons went to the Washington Monument, where the president gave a speech that began as a hymn to the flag and Americanism but evolved into an attack on an unnamed ethnic group. He was talking about German Americans, accusing them of "political blackmail" for saying that they would withhold their votes from a presidential candidate who ignored their interests. Although careful to point out that he was talking about a tiny minority of the unnamed group, he insisted that it was "a very active and subtle minority" but "must absolutely be crushed" because it was undermining the government's influence in international affairs. Wilson challenged the American people to "teach these gentlemen once and for all that loyalty to this flag is the first test of tolerance in the United States."

With this scurrilous speech, Wilson turned the chief symbol of American ideals into a symbol of unquestioning loyalty. By his novel construction, the good American was no longer the citizen who revered freedom but the one who refused to tolerate those who disagreed with their government. And sometime during the day, Wilson carried the speech a step further, with a last-minute addition to the Democratic platform: a plank summoning all who counted themselves truly American "to join in making clear to all the world the unity and consequent power of America. This is an issue of patriotism. To taint it with partisanship would be to defile it." Groups that promoted the interests of any foreign power or tried to turn Americans against each other were condemned as subversive. Together, the speech and the plank proposed to abolish the Constitution's guarantees of free expression and free assembly. Equally startling was the fact that no one in the mainstream press protested the demagoguery.

The finale of this overstuffed day, the opening of the Democratic National Convention, took place half a continent away, in St. Louis. The city's major convention hall, the Coliseum, was a riot of red, white, and blue when the delegates took their places, and for a time they followed their instructions to cheer every mention of the flag or America or Woodrow Wilson. The impresarios had planned a patriotic show to be played out in front of movie cameras (a first in the history of American political conventions), and their idea was to unite the country behind the president who had delivered the prosperity he promised in 1912 and had fortified the country against the dangers of a world at war.

The keynote speaker, Martin H. Glynn, a former governor of New York, began by reminding the delegates that they had entered the hall as

Democrats but would deliberate and act as Americans. "We stand for the Americanism which under the magic spell of citizenship and the mystic influence of the Stars and Stripes converts men of every country into men of one country, and that country our country; men of every flag into men of one flag, and that flag our flag." The crowd did not catch fire until Glynn brought up the subject of peace and presented it as something more heroic and more American than war. Glynn had intended to make the point in passing, but whenever he tried to move on to patriotism or prosperity, the crowd hauled him back to his stories of presidents who had chosen peace over war.

Neutrality was as American as the flag, Glynn said, and the voters of 1916 would be asked to decide whether their tradition of holding themselves apart from European wars was to be kept or abandoned. "This is the paramount issue," he said. "No lesser issue must cloud it, no unrelated problems must confuse us." George Washington had started the tradition during the Napoleonic Wars, Alexander Hamilton and John Jay and Thomas Jefferson had upheld it, and all had been scorned. Woodrow Wilson now stood where Washington had stood "when he prayed that this country would never unsheathe the sword except in self-defense." Neutrality did not mean that the United States would never go to war to protect its rights, Glynn went on, "but it does mean that America will exhaust every peaceful means of protecting those rights before it takes the step from which there is no appeal."

The audience applauded every point, and it went wild when he spoke of President Ulysses S. Grant, who as General Grant had been the greatest military hero of the Civil War. "When Grant was president, during the war between Spain and the Spanish West Indies, a Spanish commandant in cold blood shot the captain of the 'Virginius,' thirty-six of the crew and sixteen of the passengers. But we didn't go to war. Grant settled our troubles by negotiation, just as the president of the United States is trying to do today."

Next came the story of President Benjamin Harrison, who had done the same after a scuffle in which Chilean revolutionaries had killed U.S. sailors.

During the Civil War, the British had preyed on merchant ships from the Union states, destroying cargoes and seizing American-owned vessels. "But we didn't go to war," Glynn said. Lincoln had settled the troubles by negotiation, "just as the president of the United States is trying to do today." After another wave of applause, and when Glynn tried again to move on, the audience protested.

Glynn gave them the story of Franklin Pierce, who deported three British consuls for violating U.S. neutrality during the Crimean War, another tale that ended with the delirium-inducing refrain: "But we didn't go to war."

The impresarios watched in distress as their innocuous pageant for Old Glory turned into a celebration of a peace that might not hold. No one was more distressed than Wilson, who would soon tell Josephus Daniels, "I can't keep the country out of war. They talk of me as though I were a god. Any little German lieutenant can put us into the war at any time by some calculated outrage."

Now out of stories of presidents who had chosen diplomacy over war, Glynn asked whether the Republicans realized that when they arraigned Wilson for his neutrality they were arraigning their own heroes. Neutrality "may not satisfy the fire-eater or the swashbuckler," he said. "But it does satisfy those who worship at the altar of the God of Peace, and the mothers, fathers, and wives of the land."

From the crowd came a long wave of applause and cries of "Say it again!" and "Repeat it!" Glynn obliged and launched another attack on Republicans: going to war over every assault on Americans would mean war without end, he said. "It would give us a war abroad each time the fighting cock of the European weathervane shifted with the breeze. . . . It would mean the reversal of our traditional policy of government."

Knowing that Wilson had just broken with the American tradition of isolation in his speech advocating an association of nations, Glynn attempted to reconcile the contradiction by lamenting the Republicans' insistence that Wilson's efforts to avoid war had sullied the national honor. Were the Hotspurs saying that they were more honorable than Washington and Lincoln? Glynn asked. Eventually he worked his way around to preparedness and prosperity and Americanism and the greatness of Woodrow Wilson, whose name, he said, "will shine in golden splendor upon the page that is blackened with the tale of Europe's war."

The *New York Times* reporter on the scene realized the mass hysteria over a recitation of diplomatic precedents was a first in American politics, and he thought he understood it. The Democrats, who wanted no part in the war, had been jeered by Americans whose sentiments lay with the Allies. But Glynn was telling them that they were right, that one could be both a patriot and a pacifist, "and they could not contain themselves."

Next up at the podium was Senator Ollie James of Kentucky, who began with a masterly survey of Wilson's economic reforms. The delegates applauded throughout, but their applause was loudest when he spoke of peace: "Without orphaning a single American child, without widowing a single American mother, without firing a single gun, without the shedding of a single drop of blood," Wilson had made the kaiser yield to American rights and American demands. There was a huge burst of applause, and thousands of flag-waving, cheering Democrats stomped around the Coliseum for more than twenty minutes. By the time order was restored, it had been vouchsafed unto Senator James that there would come a day when the blood-spattered monarchs of the earth would march into the Court of God and there among them would be Woodrow Wilson, holding a painting of Christ on a battle-field, "with the dead and dying all about him, with the roar of cannon, the screaming of shrapnel, the wail of the dying, and above his head written these words, 'And He said unto them, love one another.'" The audience interrupted five times to applaud at length.

Spent, the Democrats gave themselves a recess and came back together at nine o'clock that evening, still feverish with peace. Someone started a cry for the party's most committed pacifist, William Jennings Bryan, who was covering the national conventions for his weekly newspaper, *The Commoner*. Surrendering to the mood of the crowd, the ringmasters gave him a turn on the stage. Bryan said he and Wilson had differed, but he joined the American people in "thanking God that we have a president who does not want this convention plunged into this war."

The convention moved on to the formalities of nominating Woodrow Wilson and Thomas R. Marshall for a second term. Unopposed, they were swept onto the ticket in a voice vote. All that remained was a reading of the twenty-six planks in the party's platform, most of which had been drafted by Wilson. The sordid plank on Americanism was inserted near the top. The platform contained the usual boasts and promises, including a pledge to recommend to the states that women be given the right to vote. That was better than nothing but nowhere close to satisfying the progressives in the suffrage movement, who wanted a constitutional amendment that would enfranchise American women in every state. Wilson's draft of the platform made several mentions of foreign affairs but was silent on the thorny sub-ject of Mexico. The members of the platform committee did not allow the omission to stand, but the plank they hammered into place gave the im-pression that the administration's course had been masterful. And to a sec-tion praising Wilson's leadership, they added a sentence commending "the splendid diplomatic victories of our great president, who has preserved the vital interests of our Government and its citizens, and kept us out of war." In spite of Wilson's fear that the peace between Germany and the United States might end at any moment, he would hold his tongue as his advertising men plucked the words "he kept us out of war" from the platform and turned them into the mainstay of his campaign.

"President Wilson has had his day in St. Louis," *The New Republic* told its readers. While the conservative Democrats of the South had objected to his drive to strengthen the power of the national government and the liberal Democrats of the North and West had criticized him for the arms buildup, the Punitive Expedition, and his ultimatum to Germany, both camps agreed that his leadership had given the party a unity essential for its survival. "The Democrats cannot get along without it," *The New Republic* observed. "They have no substitute for Mr. Wilson."

21

By a Whisker

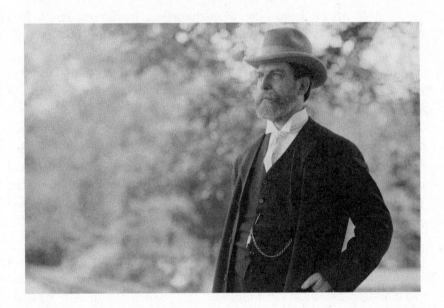

M r. Wilson was at his most agile in the summer of 1916, and thanks to his economic reforms and the Allies' insatiable demand for American crops and manufactures, more citizens were enjoying more prosperity than they had ever known. Even so, it was far from certain that he would be reelected. The chief obstacle was not the brilliant, politically independent Charles Evans Hughes but a quirk of American voters: although they often elected Democratic senators and representatives, they showed a preference for Republican presidents. In twelve of the fifteen elections since the party's founding, the people had sent a Republican to the White House. Wilson had won the four-way race of 1912, but to beat the odds in 1916, he would have to wring the most out of every opportunity for votes, steer wide of every foreseeable pitfall, and concoct a silver lining for every cloud that might come over the horizon.

Colonel House, more astute about American politics than European diplomacy, proved a valuable advisor. Reasoning that Hughes would dominate the Northeast and Wilson would again sweep the South, House persuaded the Democrats to bear down on the Midwest and the West. Some political observers assumed that Roosevelt's four million progressive followers would heed his instruction to fall in behind Hughes, but House sensed that the Roosevelt orphans might resist out of anger over his endorsement of the party led by the very forces he had abominated in 1912. House also had a feeling that voters would put more stock in Wilson's solidly progressive record than in any promises Hughes might make. Hughes was said to be a progressive, but the Old Guard dominated the party, and surely it would try to dominate Hughes.

In one of his appeals for the Bull Moose vote, Wilson pointed out that the Democrats had come close to carrying out the Progressives' platform. It was true: of the thirty-three items on T.R.'s 1912 agenda, the Democrats had enacted twenty-two in whole or in part. On another occasion, he reminded a crowd of young Democrats that the Progressives had sprung up out of Republican discontent with the Republican Party. Although the new party had not lasted, he said, "[t]he interesting thing for all politicians to remember is that the progressive voters of this country, all put together, outnumber either party."

Wilson faced three foreign crises during the campaign, the first of which erupted only a day after the Democrats finished their work in St. Louis. Mexico informed General Pershing, who was still marking time in the middle of nowhere, that it would not allow any more U.S. soldiers to enter the country or permit Pershing's troops to march in any direction but north, toward home. Failure to comply would bring an attack from the Mexican army. Wilson immediately mobilized nearly the whole of the National Guard, ordered it to the border, and dispatched sixteen warships to the east and west coasts of Mexico. President Carranza asked all available men to enlist, and to hinder an influx of U.S. troops the Mexicans destroyed the railroad tracks on their side of the bridge between Juárez and El Paso, Texas. Mexico countered the U.S. deployment of warships with an order forbidding American sailors to go ashore except to visit a U.S. consulate.

On June 21, an American cavalry patrol defied the new Mexican orders and marched east toward the town of Carrizal to investigate a rumor that the Mexican army was massing troops within easy reach of Pershing's forces. Mexican machine guns opened fire, and when the fighting ended, twelve Americans were dead, twelve were missing, and twenty-four had been taken prisoner. Wilson was devastated. "The break seems to have come in Mexico;

and all my patience seems to have gone for nothing," he wrote House. "I am infinitely sad about it."

Senators Stone and Lodge, the chairman and ranking member of the Committee on Foreign Relations, and Representative Henry Flood of the House Committee on Foreign Affairs were summoned to the White House that evening for a briefing. Lodge was disturbed to find that Wilson did not know where the Punitive Expedition was or how many troops Pershing had. Nor did the president seem to have an objective apart from staying in the good graces of the American electorate. In his notes of the meeting, Lodge wrote that Wilson was "in a nervous condition" and "torn between fear of losing votes and fear of war."

The first good news came the next morning, when Mexico agreed to free the prisoners. In an address to the New York Press Club, Wilson hailed the outcome as a triumph of American forbearance. The great lesson of history, he said, was that the most powerful force in world affairs was moral force, the force inherent in what the Declaration of Independence defined as "a decent respect to the opinions of mankind." Asserting that the leaders who started the world war had ignored the opinion of mankind, he predicted that nothing permanent would be achieved by the fighting. No good would come of that until the slaughter ended and the belligerents reached a settlement that took the world's opinion into account. Anticipating his Republican critics, who would say that he had once again let Mexico humiliate the United States, Wilson professed himself unafraid: "I am willing, no matter what my personal fortunes may be, to play for the verdict of mankind. Personally, it will be a matter of indifference to me what the verdict on the seventh of November is, provided I feel any degree of confidence that, when a later jury sits, I shall get their judgment in my favor. Not in my favor personally—what difference does that make?—but in my favor as an honest and conscientious spokesman of a great nation."

The Mexicans soon proposed a joint commission to mediate the differences between the two countries, and Washington accepted. So it was Venustiano Carranza, not Woodrow Wilson, who kept the United States out of war in 1916, but as long as the mediation continued, it was Wilson who got the credit, at least in the United States. Until the mediators completed their work, Wilson could leave General Pershing in Mexico, on guard against threats to the border. And as long as Pershing did not complete his mission, Wilson's critics could not declare the Punitive Expedition a failure. Pershing was ordered to sit tight, and Secretary Lansing, temporizing as skillfully as any European diplomat, allowed two months to be frittered away in making arrangements for the commission's first meeting.

Wilson and Lansing had barely doused the Mexican fires when the British presented the United States with a blacklist of eighty-five American companies and individuals suspected of aiding the Germans. Henceforth, His Majesty's Government decreed, British-owned enterprises were not to do business with the suspects. After two years of British interference with U.S. trade—contraband lists, interdictions of ships and confiscations of cargo, censorship of the mails—Wilson considered the blacklist the last straw. He thought about banning loans and curbing exports to the Allies but changed his mind because of the damage such reprisals would inflict on the U.S. economy. Instead he persuaded Congress to give him the power to ban Allied imports and bar ships that refused cargoes from the blacklisted firms. With the British, as with the Mexicans, Wilson defused the crisis without actually ending it.

The presidential nominees of 1916 delivered their acceptance speeches a few weeks after their parties' national conventions. The Republicans went first, gathering in New York's Carnegie Hall on the night of July 31. The hall was packed, and the party faithful seemed particularly pleased to see their black sheep, Theodore Roosevelt, in one of the boxes. Once the felicities were out of the way, Hughes offered a long critique of Wilson's foreign policy. Trying to exploit the administration's problems in Mexico, Hughes focused on Wilson's obsession with overthrowing Huerta but said nothing about the failures of the Punitive Expedition. Hughes also repeated his accusation that Wilson had filled the Foreign Service with good Democrats rather than good diplomats, and while the charge had merit, it was, like Huerta, old news. The speech was a dud.

Hughes suffered more serious wounds a few weeks later, on a visit to California, where Republican conservatives and Republican progressives hated each other even more than they despised Woodrow Wilson. The Southern Pacific Railroad's stranglehold on state politics had led the reformist faction to form the California Progressive Party, and by 1911 it had a following large enough to elect a governor, Hiram W. Johnson. Now Johnson was running as a Republican for the U.S. Senate, the conservatives were determined to annihilate him, and Hughes found himself in the crossfire. He asked both camps to cooperate during his California tour, but when the Old Guard refused, he did not push back.

Hughes's stand left him at the mercy of reactionaries who seized every chance to insult Johnson as they marched Hughes about the state. At one point, when Hughes attended a reception at a hotel in Long Beach, his escorts neglected to tell him that Johnson happened to be spending the night there. The governor waited in his room for word from Hughes, and when none came, he assumed the slight was deliberate. Appalled when he learned of his hosts' maneuver, Hughes tried to make amends, but the prickly Johnson refused his overtures.

To deal with the Mexican crisis, the furor over the blacklist, and the long list of crowd-pleasing bills that he and Congress wanted to pass before the election, Wilson began rising at five in the morning, and Agent Starling of the Secret Service would remember the sound of the president's typewriter well after most of Washington had gone to bed. Apart from a long bout of indigestion and one headache severe enough to send him to bed, Wilson was in good health. He kept up his exercise, golfing with Edith nearly every day. The summer was infernally hot, and when they could, they boarded the *Mayflower* for a weekend of fresh breezes on the Potomac.

In August, as Hughes traveled the West, Wilson was trying to stave off a nationwide rail strike. The unions wanted to shorten their workday from ten hours to eight with no reduction in wages, management refused, and the unions set a strike deadline of September 4. Wilson made four trips to the Capitol in four days to explain the emergency and press for action. "Cities will be cut off from their food supplies, the whole commerce of the nation will be paralyzed, men of every sort and occupation will be thrown out of employment," he told a joint session of Congress. Maintaining that experience and scientific study had shown that the eight-hour day improved productivity and the well-being of the workforce, he asked Congress to meet labor's demand and proposed a commission to assess the financial impact so that the railroads could raise their rates if the facts warranted. With the Adamson Act, Congress delivered what the president and the unions wanted, and just in time to avert the strike.

In a neat bit of political choreography, Wilson gave his acceptance speech on September 2, the day after the passage of the Adamson Act and the day before he signed it. The timing guaranteed that he would not be competing for headlines with his Republican critics, who viewed the new law as an assault on free enterprise. The Democrats held their festivities in Long Branch, New Jersey, at Shadow Lawn, a house that the Wilsons had rented on the advice of Colonel House, who did not think it proper for a president to use the Executive Mansion as a stage for his reelection campaign.

The president recited the Democrats' achievements and expressed confidence that the American people would want to keep the party in office. The Republicans had lost power by serving the few rather than the many, he said, and they would not deserve to rule again until they brought themselves up to date.

In Mexico, he said, he had tried to act with the sympathy he thought the American people would like him to show. Mindful of the public's opposition to U.S. involvement in the world war, he made no reference to such a possibility. Instead, he focused on the war's end. "It is not a future to be afraid of," he said. "It is, rather, a future to stimulate and excite us to the display of the best powers that are in us." The world would need a just peace, and the United States would have to do its utmost to ensure that the peace would last.

The newspapers gave Wilson a day of glory before turning their attention to the storm over the Adamson Act, which broke as soon as Wilson affixed his signature. Campaign donations from Wall Street and big business ceased, and Hughes lit into Wilson for bowing to labor, strong-arming Congress, and undermining the very principle of arbitration. Wilson parried by taking full responsibility. Labor had not asked him to go to Congress, he said. He had done so on his own, after the unions and the railroads refused to negotiate. He noted, too, that more than half of the Republicans in the House had supported the bill and that the Senate had allowed it to go to a vote without a fight. For good measure, he reminded the critics that it was the business of government to make sure that neither capital nor labor nor any other interest triumphed over the general welfare.

A few days later, Woodrow and Edith Wilson went to Atlantic City, where he addressed a convention of the National American Woman Suffrage Association. Edith, who was resolutely old-fashioned, opposed women's suffrage in private and did not discuss it in public. Woodrow had not only authored the suffrage article in the Democratic platform, he had voted for a suffrage initiative in New Jersey in 1915. (It did not pass.) As presidential candidates, he and Hughes had started at the same point: both parties supported women's suffrage, and both recommended that the question be settled by the states. But in early August, Hughes had decided to step out ahead of his party and campaign for a suffrage amendment to the Constitution, which would resolve the issue for the whole country. Margaret Wilson lobbied her father to take the same position, and now that he was neck and neck with Hughes, Margaret's case had practical as well as moral force: there were ninety-one electoral votes at stake in the twelve states where women already had the right to vote. But Wilson held back, saying that if he changed his stance in an election year, he would be accused of pandering.

His claim was disingenuous. On matters large and small, Wilson had often changed his mind. A leader who did not adjust in the face of new information or new circumstances was, in his phrase, "a dead letter." His refusal to budge on women's suffrage was undoubtedly meant to assure the South that he had no intention of mounting a federal challenge to states' rights on racial matters. Southerners feared that if he gave in to the women who wanted a suffrage amendment, it would not be long before blacks and the whites who sympathized with their struggles for equal rights would pressure him to take action against the welter of Southern state laws that segregated the races and made it all but impossible for Southern blacks to vote.

In hopes of persuading the suffragists that he sympathized with their ends if not their means, Wilson gave them a lecture. He began with the Founding Fathers and their preoccupation with legalities, then moved on to the nineteenth century and the great question of slavery, which, he said, had been more a human question than a legal one. "And is it not significant that it was then, and then for the first time, that women became prominent in politics in America?" he asked. Industrialization had raised new human questions, and women had again stepped to the fore.

Wilson assured the women at the convention that they would one day prevail:

> when the forces of nature are steadily working and the tide is rising to meet the moon, you need not be afraid that it will not come to its flood. We feel the tide; we rejoice in the strength of it; and we shall not quarrel in the long run as to the method of it. . . . The whole art and practice of government consists not in moving individuals, but in moving masses. It is all very well to run ahead and beckon, but, after all, you have got to wait for the body to follow. I have not come to ask you to be patient, because you have been, but I have come to congratulate you that there was a force behind you that will, beyond any peradventure, be triumphant, and for which you can afford a little while to wait.

The president had given the suffragists only half a loaf, but it was enough to stop them from endorsing Hughes.

September and October were trying months for Wilson. Maine held its state elections two months before the national election, and when voters went to the polls, the results were solidly Republican. The optimists around the president pointed out that the Republican majorities had thinned since 1912, but the old political adage, "As goes Maine, so goes the nation," was never far from mind. Wilson also suffered the loss of one of his sisters, who died suddenly of peritonitis. And there was a new round of rumors about Woodrow Wilson and Mary Allen Hulbert, who had come into his life as Mrs. Peck. The tale bearers were saying that Ellen Wilson had died of a broken heart, that Mrs. Hulbert had once initiated a breach-of-promise suit against Wilson, that her silence had been purchased for $75,000 in an arrangement brokered by Louis D. Brandeis.

After Wilson's death, Mrs. Hulbert revealed in a magazine article that a man calling himself Mr. Smith and claiming to represent the Republican Party had come to see her in 1916 and offered $300,000 for her letters from Wilson. When she asked why, he said that he and his associates believed it their patriotic duty to expose Wilson's true character and see that he was impeached. Mrs. Hulbert replied that the letters would not help their cause, because they showed Wilson to be a thoroughly honorable man.

Wilson's tribulations also included a surprisingly personal attack by his erstwhile friend Oswald Garrison Villard, in *The North American Review*. The gist was that Wilson lived in a world of his own, cut off from the rest of the government, the press, and the country. He did not so much lead the party as dictate to it, Villard wrote, and for a man who frequently said that a president ought to determine the will of the people and act on it, Wilson was mysteriously reluctant to meet with his fellow citizens and hear their thoughts. Because of Wilson's aloofness, Villard said, many congressmen and senators believed that they did not even exist in the president's mind until he wanted their votes.

It is not clear who in Wilson's entourage decided that the issue of his aloofness had to be met, but George Creel, the former journalist who wrote the president's 1916 campaign biography, audaciously declared it a virtue. "It is a matter of frequent comment that he has no friends," Creel wrote. "What is this but recognition of the bitter truth that friendship is the great American conspiracy in restraint of public duty? . . . Affection is a guide that has led many honest, sincere men into byways of broken faith and virtual dishonor." According to Creel, Wilson cloistered himself out of self-discipline; his emotions ran so deep that he had to guard himself against his "warmths and his impulses."

Creel was not entirely wrong. Quick to anger in the face of opposition, Wilson tended to avoid people and situations likely to set him off. When adversaries had to be seen, he treated them courteously but with no pretense of affection. It would be mechanistic to ascribe his debilitating headaches, bouts of indigestion, and attacks of neuritis wholly to his suppression of emotion, but it is striking that in 1915 and 1916, when his romance with Edith was in full bloom and complaints about his inaccessibility were common, Woodrow's physical ailments all but disappeared. Whatever the political drawbacks of his isolation, it appears to have been good for his health.

Wilson gave a half-dozen major campaign speeches at Shadow Lawn and made a few forays into other states, venturing as far west as Nebraska. The Democrats put William Jennings Bryan to work in the Midwest and the West, the regions where he had fared best in his own presidential campaigns. On the road for six weeks in September and October, Bryan drew large, appreciative crowds throughout his travels. In speech after speech he insisted that a vote for Hughes would restore the plutocracy, and he thanked the Lord for a president who had kept the country out of war. Wilson would carry fourteen of the nineteen states where Bryan campaigned.

The president's touring was confined to states where he and Hughes were in a dead heat. The idea that Americans were destined to play a large part in the world figured in nearly all of his campaign addresses. After a month of alluding to the prospect, he shared the whole of his ambitious dream and explained what had to be done to realize it. To an audience in Omaha he declared that the first requirement was undiluted Americanism, because a divided country could not make its full influence felt in the world. Americans would also have to make the world understand that they had not chosen neutrality because of their indifference but because those who had started the war had yet to explain why or state their aims. The United States was deeply concerned about the carnage, he said, but "when we exert the force of this nation, we want to know what we are exerting it for."

As if the delegates to the Democratic National Convention had not shouted themselves hoarse over the U.S. tradition of standing aside from the politics of the Old World, Wilson said that he did not read George Washington's warning against entangling alliances as an instruction to avoid the world's problems. The United States was part of the world, and nothing that concerned the whole world could be alien to Americans. "What disturbs the life of the whole world is the concern of the whole world," he said. "And it is our duty to lend the full force of this nation—moral and physical—to a league of nations which shall see to it that nobody disturbs the peace of the world without submitting his case first to the opinion of mankind. When you are asked, 'Aren't you willing to fight?' reply [that] you are waiting for something worth fighting for." Nebraska, a stronghold of isolationism and pacifism, cheered Wilson to the rafters.

A few weeks later, in Cincinnati, Wilson went even further: "I believe that the business of neutrality is over. Not because I want it to be over, but I mean this—that war now has such a scale that the position of neutrals sooner or later becomes intolerable." In an age when a single act of international aggression could set whole continents ablaze, the world needed a society of nations to hold the aggressors in check. If the aggressor defied the opinion of mankind, he said, it would find mankind leagued against it. "That is the kind of war I am willing to engage in."

The combination of Wilson's international aspirations and his progressive record appealed to many of the forward-thinking citizens who had rallied around Roosevelt in 1912, and it won the admiration of many Socialists as well. Knowing that the election would be close and fearing that Hughes would take the country back to the days of the robber barons, prominent Socialists urged their comrades to abandon their party's candidate and vote for Wilson.

Hughes rejected Wilson's internationalist dreams with a declaration that a Hughes administration would be "an American administration with exclusively American policies, devoted to American interests." He offered no specifics, nor did he seize the moment to point out the dangers of Wilson's overreach. The lapses were emblematic of Hughes's troubles throughout the campaign. Sometimes he talked over the heads of his listeners, and sometimes he was exasperatingly vague. After proudly committing himself to a women's suffrage amendment, he was silent when women asked what he would do to bring it into being. Cautious to a fault, Hughes hesitated to offend the Old Guard, hesitated to support progressive ideas, hesitated to say anything of substance that could be turned against him.

Theodore Roosevelt spent a month campaigning for Hughes in thirteen states, and some who watched thought that he was once again helping Woodrow Wilson to victory. Though T.R. did his work energetically, in private he called Hughes "the bearded iceberg" and wondered how he could have played his hand so badly in California. Roosevelt and Hughes agreed that Wilson's idealistic course in Mexico imperiled American interests and American security, and they shared the view that Wilson's tardiness in building up the army and navy had put the United States at a disadvantage in its wartime dealings with Britain and Germany. But while Hughes assiduously avoided any suggestion that he would lead the country into war, Roosevelt fulminated against Germany and asserted that "President Wilson by his tame submission to insult and injury from all whom he feared has invited the murder of our men, women and children by Mexican bandits on land and by German submarines at sea." Hughes grew increasingly irritated by Roosevelt's bellicosity but did nothing to rein it in.

The last foreign crisis Wilson faced before the election began on October 7, when an odd-looking ship flying a flag with a black Maltese cross appeared off the coast of Newport, Rhode Island. It was *Unterseeboot-53,* commanded by one Hans Rose, who brought it into the harbor and dropped anchor near the U.S. Navy's torpedo station. Over the next two days, the *U-53* torpedoed nine merchant ships in the general vicinity of the Nantucket Lightship, a floating lighthouse forty miles southeast of Nantucket Island. Nearly all ships leaving New York for the North Atlantic relied on the light to keep them off the Nantucket Shoals. The exploits of the *U-53* gave Americans an unforgettable demonstration of German sea power, and thanks to calm seas, Rose's willingness to give passengers and crews time to evacuate, and distress signals that quickly brought a dozen U.S. destroyers to the rescue, not a single life was lost.

The episode unnerved Wilson. Rose had conducted his raid outside the territorial waters of the United States, and by evacuating the ships before blowing them up, he had complied with the terms of the *Sussex* pledge. Still, the idea that German submarines operating so close to the United States might shut off the flow of munitions to the Allies sent the British into a state of alarm. Wilson met twice at Shadow Lawn with Ambassador Bernstorff, who reported to Berlin that Wilson had seemed "very anxious." The president's hopes for reelection rested on two considerations, Bernstorff explained to his superiors. Wilson had kept the country out of war, and he had persuaded Germany to halt unrestricted submarine warfare. Although the *U-53* had not, in a technical sense, violated the pledge, Wilson believed that more submarine attacks along the East Coast might drive the American public into a rage that he would not be able to contain.

When Ambassador Jusserand went to the White House to discuss the *U-53,* he pointed out that although Rose had kept to the letter of the *Sussex* pledge, he deserved no credit for preserving the lives of the passengers on the ships he sank. That, he said, had been due to the prompt aid from the American destroyers. Several of the torpedoed ships were British, but England was no more successful than France in getting Wilson to file a formal protest to Germany. The British found it galling that the U.S. Navy had come to the rescue of the passengers and crew, and they were incensed to learn that a U.S. destroyer had obeyed Rose's order to move aside so that he would have a clear shot at one of the ships, which happened to be British. Ambassador Page asked the State Department more than once when the United States would make an official statement on the incident. The department replied with a question: did the British feel that the U.S. Navy should *not* have assisted in the rescues?

Roosevelt, blaming the *U-53*'s raid on Wilson's weakness, told an audience in Louisville, "Instead of speaking softly and carrying a big stick, President Wilson spoke bombastically and carried a dish rag." Hughes felt that commenting on the *U-53* incident might complicate the administration's handling of the matter, so he settled for deploring the attack on the *Lusitania* and declaring that he would protect Americans on land and sea. How he did not say, but the Democrats seized on the remark and warned that Hughes meant to take a stronger stand than Wilson had. Wilson himself had suggested as much in one of his speeches at Shadow Lawn. The Republicans had been excoriating his foreign policy, he said, "and if it is wrong and they are men of conscience, they must change it. And if they are going to change it, in which direction are they going to change it? There is only one choice as against peace, and that is war."

Infuriated by such extrapolations, Hughes insisted that Wilson had not kept the country out of war. "We have had intermittent peace without honor, and intermittent war without honor," he said in Philadelphia. When Vice President Marshall, on a campaign swing through Nebraska, said in several speeches that a vote for Hughes was a vote for war, Hughes exploded. "I am a man of peace. I have been spending my life in maintaining the institutions of peace." As for "He kept us out of war," Hughes asked, "What was Carrizal—a peace festival?"

In the last days of October, Republican leaders panicked when they realized that they might well lose Ohio, which the party had won in every election since 1860. In 1916, the state's progressives and labor unions had convinced many voters that Hughes was a hawk and a tool of the plutocracy. While the Republicans worked frantically to save Ohio, the Democrats were loudly predicting a huge victory, but they, too, were alarmed. Wilson's attorney general announced a series of probes into allegations that the Republican Party had been scheming to win the election by transplanting thousands of Southern blacks to the hotly contested states of Ohio, Indiana, and Illinois. The Republicans were dumbfounded by the accusation, which was groundless. The great black migration from South to North had been under way for several years.

Black voters felt abandoned by both parties in 1916. They had no reason to reelect a president who had promised justice and then stood by as his treasury secretary and postmaster general segregated civil servants in the government's two largest bureaucracies. Wilson had refused to take any action against lynching. And blacks had noticed a wide streak of racism in Wilson's foreign policy. In his confrontations with Germany and Britain, he was content to use strong language, but when crossed by nations inhabited primarily by people of color, he often resorted to military force. In addition to sending troops to Mexico twice, he had authorized military interventions in Haiti and the Dominican Republic.

Hughes had met with a delegation of black leaders early in his campaign and gave at least one address to a black audience, but he never spoke out against the segregation of the civil service, and the issue of racial justice disappeared from his speeches. Put out with the Democrats and convinced that the Republican Party was the enemy of the working class, W. E. B. Du Bois of the National Association for the Advancement of Colored People advised black voters to support the Socialists or stay home on Election Day.

The campaign ended on a series of sour notes. At Madison Square Garden on November 2, Wilson castigated the Republicans for trying to return the country to the plutocrats. In a ghoulish speech at Cooper Union, where Lincoln had delivered the address that ensured his presidential nomination, Roosevelt lamented the gulf between Lincoln and Wilson, who, he said, had dragged American honor in the dust. "Mr. Wilson now dwells at Shadow Lawn," Roosevelt said.

> There should be shadows enough at Shadow Lawn—the shadows of men, women and children who have risen from the ooze of the ocean bottom and from graves in foreign lands. The shadows of the helpless whom Mr. Wilson did not protect lest he might have to face danger; the shadows of babies gasping pitifully as they sank under the waves. The shadows of women outraged and slain by bandits. The shadows of . . . troopers who lay in the Mexican desert, the black blood crusted round their mouths and their dim eyes looking upward, because President Wilson had sent them to do a task and then shamefully abandoned them to the mercy of the foes who knew no mercy. Those are the shadows proper for Shadow Lawn; the shadows of deeds that were never done; the shadows of lofty words that were followed by no action; the shadows of the tortured dead.

The Democrats made one last appeal to the undecided, with a newspaper advertisement aimed at their fear:

YOU ARE WORKING;
—NOT FIGHTING!
ALIVE AND HAPPY;
—NOT CANNON FODDER!
WILSON AND PEACE WITH HONOR?
HUGHES WITH ROOSEVELT AND WAR?

In his turn at Madison Square Garden, Hughes made a dutiful run through his campaign themes—wholehearted Americanism, a foreign policy centered on American interests, and a protective tariff to keep American wages high after the war, when cheap European goods would pour into the United States. He said nothing about women's suffrage, nothing about racial equality, nothing about entering the war or staying out of it.

Wilson had the last word, at Shadow Lawn. He scoffed at Republican predictions of a postwar economic collapse, calling them a blatant attempt to scare labor into voting Republican. He scoffed at those who called themselves statesmen but tried to make political capital out of unfolding foreign crises. And he scoffed at the notion that American foreign policy should concern itself wholly with American interests. "The world will never be again what it has been," Wilson said. "The United States will never be again what it has been." Splendid isolation was a thing of the past, "for now we are in the great drift of humanity which is to determine the politics of every country in the world."

The reporters at Shadow Lawn thought that Wilson looked like a man confident of victory, but two days before the election, he drew up a plan to be carried out as quickly as possible in case of defeat. He spelled it out in a letter to Lansing: "Again and again the question has arisen in my mind, What would it be my duty to do were Mr. Hughes to be elected? Four months would elapse before he could take charge of the affairs of the government, and during those four months I would be without such moral backing from the nation as would be necessary to steady and control our relations with other governments. . . . Such a situation would be fraught with the gravest dangers." The plan called for Lansing to resign as secretary of state and Hughes to be sworn in as his replacement. At that point, Marshall and Wilson would resign. Under the rules then governing the line of succession, the secretary of state would become president. After typing the final draft of the letter, Wilson put it into an envelope marked "most confidential" and sealed it with wax. He put it in the hands of Lansing's deputy, Frank Polk, and instructed him to deliver it personally to Lansing on Election Day.

November 7 was a beautiful day across the country, and voters turned out in record numbers. Wilson voted in his usual polling place, a firehouse in Princeton. He and the first lady set off from Shadow Lawn at seven-thirty in the morning, and by about nine o'clock he had finished marking his ballot and was headed back to Shadow Lawn. The Wilsons rode alone in one of the White House limousines and were trailed by a Secret Service car and a car full of reporters. As one of New Jersey's leading newspapers noted, "It required 16 men, three automobiles, four hours and 54 gallons of gasoline to deliver President Wilson's vote for himself."

Hughes, who was at the Astor Hotel in New York, rose early and walked the few blocks to his midtown polling place, a laundry on Eighth Avenue. He arrived at seven-thirty and was handed ballot number 13—Wilson's lucky number. He walked back to the Astor, where he allowed himself to sleep away the day.

The early returns gave Hughes a commanding lead: the whole of the Northeast from Maine to Pennsylvania. And with the exception of Ohio, he had carried the most populous states of the Midwest. Apart from Ohio, Wilson's early victories were all in the South. At nine-thirty in the evening, the *New York World* declared Hughes the winner, but he was not convinced that he had won.

Nor was Joe Tumulty, who was at work in the Asbury Park, New Jersey, offices used by the White House staff during the president's stay at Shadow Lawn. When a band of reporters burst in with the *World*'s bulletin and asked when the president would concede, Tumulty predicted that Wilson would win the West and the election. Soon after the reporters left, the president telephoned to predict the opposite. Tumulty offered encouragement based on a scattering of returns from the West. Wilson was skeptical but not ready to concede.

The suspense dragged on through Wednesday and Thursday. The president and his party left Shadow Lawn on Thursday night, boarding the *Mayflower* for the first leg of a journey to Williamstown, Massachusetts, to witness the christening of the president's third grandchild, Eleanor Axson Sayre. The election was still undecided. Three small states—New Hampshire, New Mexico, and North Dakota—had slipped into Wilson's column. Collectively they added 12 electoral votes, a gain that was canceled out by a bulletin confirming that the toss-up in Minnesota had gone to Hughes.

Wilson was leading in the popular vote, but he and Hughes were tied 254 to 254 for the electoral vote. Only California was still unaccounted for.

At five the next morning, Jimmie Starling of the Secret Service went to the *Mayflower*'s galley for a cup of coffee and learned from Arthur Brooks, the president's valet, that Wilson had won.

"Does he know?" Starling asked.

Brooks said no. The wireless message had come at midnight, and Brooks had a standing order not to wake the president.

"It was a funny election," Starling mused. "The Republicans celebrated and the Democrats won."

It *was* a funny election, across the board. The *World* hailed it as a defeat for "the cash-register patriotism of New York" and "a smashing victory for American democracy," but Wilson could not muster a scintilla of joy for his first public comments. He was glad, he said, that the campaign was over, so that "we can settle down in soberness and unity of spirit to work for the welfare of the country."

The popular vote, 9,126,868 to 8,548,728, gave Wilson an edge of 3.1 percent over Hughes, and Wilson received nearly three million more votes in 1916 than in 1912. But once again he had fallen short of a majority. His share came to 49.2 percent.

Democrats had placed their hopes on the dissension in the Republican ranks, but Hughes won nearly one million more votes than Taft and Roosevelt combined in 1912, evidence that the party's conservatives and progressives were willing and able to work together. Wilson's New Freedom had done more to enrich the average worker than Roosevelt's Square Deal or McKinley's Full Dinner Pail, and Democrats won a larger share of the labor vote in 1916 than in the three previous presidential elections, yet Hughes carried all the major industrial states except Ohio.

Hughes had taken the more progressive stand on women's suffrage yet carried only two of the twelve states where women voted. In Montana, which Wilson won in a landslide, voters also elected the first woman member of the House of Representatives, Jeannette Rankin, a Republican.

Wilson's California victory came down to 3,773 of the 999,603 votes cast—a whisker. It is always ascribed to Hughes's mistakes during his tour of California, and every analysis notes that his fellow Republican Hiram Johnson won his Senate race by a huge margin. Some historians blame Hughes for aligning himself with the wrong faction. Some blame Johnson's petulance. Some note that "He kept us out of war" strongly appealed to women voters in California. But there is rarely a mention of the benefit that Wilson derived from the steep decline in the state's Socialist vote, which fell from 78,641 in 1912 to 42,898 in 1916. If all of California's Socialists had voted their own ticket in 1916, Hughes would have carried the state and the election.

As a candidate, Wilson had not promised to keep the country out of war, but his cabinet members and others who campaigned for him had implied that a vote for Wilson meant peace and a vote for Hughes did not.

Hughes took his defeat graciously, but Roosevelt and Lodge were profoundly disturbed. Lodge regarded Wilson's reelection as a calamity and blamed it on small-town and rural Republicans who had failed to understand the hypocrisy of "He kept us out of war." To an English friend Lodge wrote that he feared he would never overcome "the depression caused to me by the nature of this deciding vote." Roosevelt lashed out in a letter to his Kansas friend William Allen White, accusing Americans west of the Alleghenies of voting for Wilson because they were "yellow."

The internationalism that Wilson preached with such fervor during the campaign probably did not capture many votes outside the small, overlapping circles of peace activists, intellectuals, and Socialists. But ordinary citizens who heard these sermons seemed pleased by his claim that the full force of American power would be exerted after the war, when it would be used for the noble purpose of safeguarding the world's peace. In due course Senator Lodge would have much to say about what the United States ought and ought not to promise the world, but in the heat of the campaign, the only one who articulated what was really at stake in the contest between Hughes and Wilson was a twenty-seven-year-old journalist, Walter Lippmann. In an afternoon they spent together at Shadow Lawn, Wilson had said that neutrality was becoming impossible. He underscored the point by showing him a recent dispatch from the American embassy in Berlin, a prediction that the U-boats would be turned loose after the U.S. election. Lippmann immediately understood and put it into words, but only for his colleagues at *The New Republic:* "What we're electing is a war president."

22

Verge of War

Edith and Woodrow Wilson returned to the White House on November 11, relieved to be home. But Woodrow was exhausted and full of dread. Two days after coming back to Washington he wrote a note instructing Tumulty to tell everyone who wanted to see him that he could not make appointments except when a question was too urgent to postpone. He underscored "everyone."

Wilson was suffering as only a person of conscience suffers when being driven toward a course of action at odds with his deepest convictions. He had strained every part of himself to keep the country at peace, yet every day increased the likelihood of war. Just before the election, U-boats had sunk two armed British merchant ships without warning (flagrant violations of the *Sussex* pledge) and there were fourteen Americans among the dead. Wilson was livid but did not believe that his fellow citizens would be willing to wage war over the two hundred American lives lost to submarines since 1914.

The liberals in the German Reichstag, a group that included the chancellor and the foreign secretary, shared Wilson's desire to avoid war, as did Ambassador Bernstorff. But the admirals argued that victory would elude Germany unless its U-boat commanders were allowed to strike without warning. The admirals believed that they had nothing to fear from the United States. Wilson was devoted to peace, and even if the Americans decided to declare war, the admiralty reasoned, their army and navy were too weak to matter.

The kaiser still sided with the liberals, but Joseph C. Grew, the American chargé d'affaires in Berlin, had just warned the State Department that the kaiser might well lose the submarine debate. The British blockade had reduced Germany's imports to a trickle, and despite rationing, food shortages were widespread. The admirals insisted that the only way to prevent starvation in Germany was to starve England first, by sinking every merchant ship bound for Britain. Preparations for the onslaught were already under way. German shipyards were building almost nothing but submarines, the new models could travel farther and faster than their predecessors, and the navy was training a huge corps of submariners. For Grew, the unanswered question about unrestricted submarine warfare was not "Will they?" but "When will they?"

Wilson, fearing the worst, wanted to put the belligerents on the path to peace before the United States was drawn into the war, and he had sequestered himself to figure out how to proceed. Within a week of the election, he was presenting his best idea to Colonel House: he would ask the belligerents, for the good of humankind, to state what they wanted from the fighting. He hoped that once the war aims were on paper, they would serve as a starting point for talks that would end the carnage, which had reached apocalyptic proportions.

House was unreceptive. Despite the impasse on the Western Front, the Allies ardently believed that they were making progress and, House said, they would suspect that Wilson was merely trying to stave off American involvement in the war. House and Wilson went round and round, with the colonel arguing that the United States should await further developments and the president countering that it would be good to make one more try for peace before a break.

The next morning House breakfasted alone. The president, he told his diary, "was unusually late, which bespoke a bad night. I was sorry, but it could not be helped." When they resumed their debate, neither ceded an inch. Wilson finally decided that they should set the matter aside until he had put his thoughts in writing. But he went back to bed, feeling so wretched that Dr. Grayson was called. The president slept all afternoon, and the colonel busied himself in a round of visits with other officials, including Lansing and Polk. When he disclosed the president's plan, he was pleased to find that they heartily disapproved.

Edith and Woodrow had dinner by themselves, leaving House on his own. The Wilsons proceeded in leisurely fashion, reading together and talking for a long while before the president roused himself for one more conversation with House. House mentioned that he had seen Lansing and Polk, but rather than come clean, he reported that they saw no imminent danger from Germany. He fancied that Wilson cheered up at his suggestion to leave well enough alone.

Wilson spent most of his time in the family quarters of the White House, pondering his German problem and writing his 1916 State of the Union address, which was notable only for its silence on foreign affairs, the subject now haunting him night and day. He did not feel well, and on November 23 canceled all his appointments and summoned Grayson, who persuaded him to call off a planned trip to the Army-Navy Game at West Point. Sending his regrets to House, Wilson described his malady as "a really overwhelming cold."

Excused from his trip, Wilson used the time to compose his note to the belligerents. He began with a memo to himself, posing a series of questions: What does a lasting peace require? War used to be seen as heroic and glorious, but where was there a glory large enough for the 700,000 casualties at Verdun? If the war ended with the defeat of German militarism or the end of Britain's hegemony at sea, would that yield lasting peace? He thought not: "The crowned victor in a mighty conflict too easily forgets the suffering and the agony endured in achieving the end. The memory of the death struggle which all but overpowered it is dimmed by the growing sun of glory and is finally eclipsed altogether."

Never before had two great foes been so equally matched. Never had there been so much death and destruction. In this war of attrition, the victor would suffer nearly as much as the vanquished. Wilson dared to hope that the shared suffering and the shared realization of the futility of modern war presented the best opportunity for a lasting peace. And given the magnitude of the suffering, Wilson thought that the statesmen involved ought to end the war "with the objects of each group of belligerents unaccomplished and all the magnificent sacrifices on both sides gone for naught. Only then would war be eliminated as a means of attaining national ambition. The world would be free to build its new peace structure on the solidest foundation it has ever possessed."

It is hard to fault Wilson's aspirations, but his conversations with House and the dispatches from his ambassadors in Europe ought to have convinced him that his appeal would fail. Both sides believed as fervently as ever that they must—and would—win. Lost in dreams of peace, Wilson had allowed himself to be transported from the world as it was to the world as he thought it should be. He had an uncanny gift for voicing the things Americans wished to believe about their country, and as president he had used it to great effect. Congress had rewarded him by translating his soaring rhetoric into the laws he wanted, and the people had rewarded him by returning him to office. But he was not president of the world, and when he stepped onto the world stage at the end of 1916, he failed to appreciate that aspirations he regarded as fundamental and universal would be deemed unaffordable by the nations at war.

Knowing that Wilson's request was pointless, Lansing suggested to the president on Friday, December 8, that the time had come for the United States to break with Germany. Although Berlin characterized the recent submarine attacks as mistakes, Lansing had his doubts. There had been five since late October, and he maintained that more American patience would simply lead to more attacks. Wilson replied on Saturday, ignoring the suggestion and requesting a detailed critique of the latest draft of his appeal.

On Sunday, Lansing resorted to cajolery. "I have little comment to make on this communication as a whole because it is so admirably presented," he began. But he worried that the replies might leave the United States in an increasingly precarious position. For months he had been trying to convince Wilson that Germany's imperialistic ambitions were a menace to the whole world and that there was only one right course for the United States: join the Allies and rid the world of German autocracy. "The amazing thing to me is that the president does not see this," Lansing wrote in one of his memos to himself.

On Tuesday, Germany threw a large wrench into Wilson's works. Chancellor Bethmann Hollweg had just returned from the kaiser's field headquarters, where he had found His Imperial Majesty in a jubilant mood. Despite the failure of the Germans' assault on Verdun, Bucharest had fallen to their army a few days before, and the rest of Romania would follow. The kaiser had authorized the chancellor to tell the Reichstag that the Central Powers, having demonstrated their invincibility, were willing to negotiate for a lasting peace. If rejected, he said, the Central Powers would drive on to victory "while solemnly disclaiming any responsibility before mankind and history."

One by one, the Allies rejected the offer. Wilson had hoped to make the next peace move, and now he feared that his overture would make the Allies think that he was merely echoing Berlin. Lansing prayed that the president would tear up the note, but Wilson pressed on. "Having made up his mind as to what he should do, nothing could swerve him from his purpose," Lansing would write after Wilson's death. "This characteristic of Mr. Wilson was a defect which he evinced on other occasions. It was an unfortunate stubbornness of purpose which defied facts."

The note went off to American ambassadors in the belligerent capitals on the night of December 18 with instructions to convey that the United States would have trouble comprehending a negative reply. It began by saying that president was writing as a friend and as the leader of a neutral nation trying to determine how best to protect its interests. It explained that his query and Germany's had no connection. He was not writing to propose peace or offer mediation, he said; he merely wanted each nation at war to state the terms it considered essential for a lasting peace. He said he felt justified in asking because all of the belligerents seemed to have the same general goals: national security, the right to govern themselves as they saw fit, freedom to develop their trade. Each had promised to protect the rights of small states, and each had expressed an interest in a league of nations. He urged the belligerents to state their aims soon, lest civilization be damaged beyond repair.

David Lloyd George, England's new prime minister, responded unofficially but unequivocally, showing his displeasure by lumping America's offer with Germany's to give Wilson a taste of how it felt to be put on the same moral plane as the kaiser. The Allies would reply jointly to the United States, Lloyd George told the House of Commons, but in the interim he wished the American government to know that it had erred in saying that the Allies had not stated their war aims. The aims had been stated repeatedly, he said: evacuation of the occupied territories, reparations, and a guarantee that the acts of aggression that started the war would not be repeated. For the Germans, who had summarily declared victory and asked the Allies to confer, the prime minister had a question: "What are the proposals?" To confer without the slightest hint of Germany's intentions was, he said, "to put our heads into a noose with the rope end in the hands of Germany." Lloyd George went on, quoting Abraham Lincoln under similar conditions: "We accepted this war for an object, a worthy object, and the war will end when that object is attained." In Paris, the once and future premier Georges Clemenceau could hardly believe that Wilson had put all the belligerents in the same class. The president's idea that the objects on both sides seemed the same was "almost blasphemous," Clemenceau wrote. "The moral side of the war has escaped President Wilson."

The note was published in the United States on December 21, and when the newspapermen appeared at the State Department for their morning briefing, they wanted to know what had prompted it. It had been sent because of the president's growing concern that the rights of the United States were being seriously eroded by both sets of belligerents, Lansing said. "I mean by that we are growing nearer the verge of war ourselves and therefore we are entitled to know exactly what each belligerent seeks in order that we may regulate our conduct in the future." He continued, but the reporters had their headline: "U.S. Near Verge of War."

Called to the White House to explain himself, Lansing said he that he had been trying to depict the realities of the moment and that newsmen had leapt to the wrong conclusion. Wilson asked him to issue a statement correcting the misinterpretation. Lansing said he would go that far but would not retract his words. Wilson accepted, reluctantly. Lansing was at least as annoyed as Wilson, because Wilson had privately admitted the realities to him more than once. In his clarification, Lansing expressed regret, but only for using words that were open to misinterpretation.

Despite the "clarification," Lansing was unrepentant. "I do not think we can continue this uncertain state much longer," he wrote Wilson on the day of the ruckus. German submarines were now attacking merchant ships without warning almost every day, and the loss of American life continued. Berlin had obviously concluded that the United States was afraid to act.

Wilson's admirers have accused Lansing of trying to sabotage Wilson's peace effort, citing the fact that the secretary had met with Spring Rice and Jusserand just after the note was sent and had assured both of them that Wilson would not harm the Allies. But that was hardly a promise to help them, and Lansing urged both ambassadors to tell their governments to honor the president's request for a list of war aims.

The conversation at the State Department had left the French ambassador's head spinning. He tried to sort it out for the Quai d'Orsay, but his rambling dispatch merely confirms the confusion created by a president who could not yet bring himself to act and a secretary of state who could no longer mount a convincing defense of inaction. Only a few weeks before equating the Allies with the Central Powers, the president had invited Jusserand and his wife to join him and the first lady at ceremonies making the Statue of Liberty part of the National Park Service. At the banquet following the ceremonies, the ambassador read a short statement from the president of France, who said that the statue had been presented to the United States "to honor liberty and the heroes fallen in her cause," the same cause for which the French people were now fighting. The guests applauded, stomped, and waved their handkerchiefs, Jusserand wrote. "When the applause subsided, there was a new wave of enthusiasm when the band played the Marseillaise, and everybody sang."

Once the crowd was seated again, Jusserand said to Edith Wilson, "Voilà! This is the kind of neutrality I like."

"Me too," she said.

Wilson spoke last, pleasing Jusserand with his talk of the common ideals of France and the United States and his thought that "One republic must love another republic. . . . There is a common pulse in us all." For his fellow citizens, Wilson raised a question worth pondering. When he looked at the Statue of Liberty, he said, he wondered if the American people were worthy of such a symbol. "I wonder if we remember the sacrifices, the mutual concessions, the righteous yielding of selfish right that is signified by the word and the conception of liberty. . . . The spirit of the world rises with the sacrifice of men. The spirit of the world rises as men forget to be selfish and unite to be great." To Ambassador Jusserand, it sounded as if President Wilson was declaring an end to American neutrality.

How to reconcile the Wilson who had spoken so affectingly of liberty and sacrifice on December 2 with the Wilson who sent the note of December 18? Ambassador Spring Rice had given up. The president was growing ever more isolated, he wrote London. "He lives enveloped in mystery, and there are strange stories of the difficulty which is encountered by anyone even in the highest position who desires to have access to him." The British embassy now regarded the White House "rather as Vesuvius is regarded in Naples, that is, as a mysterious source of unexpected explosions."

But Spring Rice thought he understood the political currents in which the president was forced to swim, and he urged Britain to bear them in mind as it pondered its response to the note. "I must insist again that the American people as a whole are not interested in the sea, are not very sensitive on the point of national honor, and are absolutely bent on keeping out of the war," he wrote the Foreign Office. "As someone said to me the other day, the Statue of Liberty is an image of gilded bronze, hollow inside, with its back turned to Europe."

In short order, Germany declined Wilson's request, and the Allies declined Germany's request as well as Wilson's. Wilson was undaunted. Three days into the new year, he insisted that the United States would remain at peace. "We are the only one of the great white nations that is free from war today, and it would be a crime against civilization for us to go in," he told House.

By January 10, the day the Allied rejection arrived, Wilson was deep into his next peace project, an address in which he would describe the kind of peace that the United States would be willing to defend. He would deliver it in the Senate but had a much larger audience in mind: the peoples of the warring nations. To ensure that his message reached them, he would send it in advance to American embassies for distribution to their newspapers on the day he spoke. House came to Washington on January 11 and pronounced the speech "a noble document."

In the course of his conversation with House, Wilson mentioned that he had come close to asking for Lansing's resignation after the "verge of war" gaffe. House did not ask (or at least did not record) the reasons for the stay of execution, but they are easily guessed. Lansing's resignation would have told the world that the Wilson administration was not of one mind on its foreign policy, and coming on top of Bryan's resignation, it might suggest that the most serious problem in U.S. foreign relations was the president. At the end of their day together, the president and the colonel set aside their unhappiness with Lansing, changed into their evening clothes, and went off to a dinner in Wilson's honor at Lansing's home.

Serving as Wilson's secretary of state brought Lansing little joy. The president treated him like a clerk, the diplomatic corps knew that he did not enjoy the president's confidence, and when he sent along ideas that did not square with the president's, the president often denied him the basic courtesy of a reply. But Lansing did not resign, although he had two perfectly respectable excuses: the transition from Wilson's first term to his second—often a time for cabinet changes—and his own health. In 1916, Lansing learned that he had diabetes, a condition for which there was not yet an effective treatment, and he had been ill for much of the year. Lansing left no account of his reasons for staying on, but three possibilities come to mind. Given his strong sense of duty and his belief that the United States was on the verge of war, desertion would have been repugnant to him. He also firmly believed that democracy would perish unless the Allies won, and he could do more for their cause as a secretary of state than as an ex-secretary of state. Nor would he have wanted to miss an opportunity to play a part in the greatest clash of arms the world had ever seen.

The day after the dinner party, Wilson shared the draft of his address with Lansing for the first time. Lansing thought it unseemly for a president of the United States to appeal to the citizens of other countries over the heads of their governments, but he kept the thought to himself. He expressed a worry about only one phrase, "peace without victory," which he thought would offend the Allied governments. Wilson disagreed.

Wilson aimed to take Washington by surprise, and he succeeded. Tumulty did not know of his plans until a reporter telephoned him late on the morning of January 22 to inquire about the address the president was scheduled to make at one o'clock. Word of Wilson's address flew across Washington, and by the time he was escorted down the aisle by Senator Stone, Stone's colleagues were in their seats, and members of the House were standing four deep along the walls. Edith Wilson and Helen Bones sat in the president's box, "smiling tensely," according to one observer.

After shaking hands and taking his place behind the clerk's desk, Wilson began reading from the sheaf of small notepaper in his hand. His voice was low but audible, his diction precise. First came a rather sunny interpretation of the responses to his request for war aims. Noting the willingness of the Central Powers to confer with the Allies and the Allies' willingness to provide a general list of peace terms, the president said, "We are that much nearer a definite discussion of the peace which shall end the present war . . . that much nearer the discussion of the international concert which must thereafter hold the world at peace."

Wilson had come to the Senate, he said, "because I thought that I owed it to you, as the council associated with me in the final determination of our international obligations, to disclose to you without reserve the thought and purpose that have been taking form in my mind." At his next sentence—"It is inconceivable that the people of the United States should play no part in that great enterprise"—one of the reporters present noted a small but definite atmospheric disturbance. Wilson, showing no sign that he had felt it, carried his thought even further. Through their government, Americans would "add their authority and their power to the authority and force of other nations to guarantee peace and justice throughout the world."

It seemed to Wilson that the stability of the postwar world hung on the world's answer to a single question: "Is the present war a struggle for a just and secure peace, or only for a new balance of power?" For him, there was only one right answer: "There must be, not a balance of power, but a community of power; not organized rivalries, but an organized common peace." He believed that such a peace was within reach and proceeded to lay out the terms he had in mind.

First was the necessity of "a peace without victory. . . . Victory would mean peace forced upon the loser, a victor's terms imposed upon the vanquished." Accepted under duress, it would not be permanent. Nor could there be a lasting peace until every nation, regardless of its power, had the same rights as every other nation. And every nation would have to accept the principle that "governments derive all their just powers from the consent of the governed, and that no right anywhere exists to hand peoples about from sovereignty to sovereignty as if they were property." Enforcing the peace would require an international armed force so powerful that "no nation, no probable combination of nations could face or withstand it." He also called for a restoration of freedom of the seas and a global arms limitation agreement. Wilson finished by expressing his belief that he had voiced the feelings of the people of the United States and his hope that he had also spoken for friends of humanity everywhere.

The applause was begun by a Republican who often crossed swords with the president, Senator Robert La Follette of Wisconsin, and when asked to comment on the address, he said, "We have just passed through a very important hour in the life of the world." La Follette was correct. Wilson had shared his understanding of the causes of the world's ills: militarism, imperialistic aggrandizement, and a world order dictated by the Great Powers. As a cure he had proposed a worldwide community of self-governing equals, all of them committed to keeping the peace so that each could live without fear of outside aggression and without the need for large armies and navies.

The French praised Wilson for "a new declaration of rights that would find a profound echo in the soul of France" but balked at "peace without victory" because it made no distinction between the assailant and the assailed. (The journalist David Lawrence wished that Wilson had thought to say "peace without revenge," and Walter Page, who read the speech before it was delivered, had suggested "peace without conquest.") The British felt much the same as the French. Berlin dismissed Wilson as a "political romantic," and Vienna took his talk of self-government to mean that he wanted to dismember the Austro-Hungarian Empire. The kaiser, celebrating his fifty-sixth birthday, sounded a call for more war: "The unshakable will to victory of the German people, who are prepared for every sacrifice of blood and treasure, will, I trust God, preserve the Fatherland from the ruin contemplated by its enemies and will force by the sword the peace necessary for the blessed development of the people."

In the United States, Theodore Roosevelt scoffed that peace without victory was the natural ideal of a man who was too proud to fight. Roosevelt's friend Lodge soon rose in the Senate to offer a critique that was measured but no less scalding. Perhaps the warring world *ought* to believe in the superiority of peace without victory, Lodge said, but it did not, "and we must deal with things as they are."

Lodge found it easy to subscribe to Wilson's ideal of a world in which every government ruled with the consent of the governed, but he wondered just how the ideal might be put into practice. Who would compel governments that were not democratic to change their ways? And how, in light of its own history, could the United States insist? In any debate of the idea, Americans might find themselves up against people asking whether the United States had secured its territory by a vote of the people. And if the world wanted to create a league with the power to enforce the decisions it made, it had better anticipate the consequences, Lodge said. "Everything here depends upon the details." All would go well as long as quarreling parties agreed to abide by the decisions of the league, but what would happen when one of them refused? The league would call its member nations to send troops and members would find themselves involved in a war. Lodge had other questions: How many troops? Who would command them? And why would any nation bind itself to go to war at the command of other nations?

Admitting that he had once been attracted to such a league, Lodge said he had changed his mind because he could see no way around the difficulties. In place of Wilson's grand vision, Lodge offered three modest proposals: Fortify the United States, which still did not have an army and navy capable of repelling an invasion by a major power. Work for arms limitation. Assist with the restoration of the rule of international law. However meager his suggestions might seem, Lodge said, they were practical, reasonable, and sure to do substantial good. It does not appear that Wilson read Lodge's critique, and Lodge would later hear that Wilson's daughter Jessie had said at a dinner party in Boston that "Father doesn't read any criticisms—they make him nervous."

In the last week of January, as Wilson continued his desperate search for a way to end the war, Lansing was ever more certain that war was imminent. Just after the "peace without victory" speech, the secretary heard that a senior official at the German embassy, on learning that an acquaintance had just sailed for Europe, had burst out, "For God's sake, why did you let her go? You know she ought not to go now." Lansing deduced that Germany was about to resume its unrestricted submarine warfare, a suspicion that proved correct. The German admirals had finally persuaded the kaiser that the U-boats were essential to victory. The submarines, to be turned loose on February 1, were to destroy every cargo ship sailing to and from Britain.

On January 31, Bernstorff telephoned Lansing to request a meeting at four o'clock. He arrived late, and although he moved with the usual spring in his step, his smile seemed forced. He sat in the easy chair next to Lansing's desk, took out some papers, and explained that he had been instructed to share them. They were translations of several documents, the crucial one being an announcement that Germany would resume unrestricted submarine warfare on February 1. It blamed Germany's decision on the Allies, who had spurned Germany's peace offer. Determined to starve Germany with their illegal blockade and continue their war on the battlefield, the Allies were prolonging the world's agony, the note said, so the Imperial Government of Germany had acted, unable to neglect any means that might end the war. Another document explained that the U-boats would be tasked with preventing all merchant ships, including those owned by neutrals, from reaching or leaving Allied countries. Another spelled out the latitudes and longitudes of the war zone and promised to allow one American passenger ship each week to sail safely to Falmouth as long as it kept to a prescribed route and bore prescribed markings.

When Lansing finished reading, Bernstorff said, "I am sorry to have to bring about this situation, but my government could do nothing else."

The United States would be unable to accept that argument, Lansing said.

"Of course, of course, I understand that," Bernstorff replied. "I know it is very serious, very, and I deeply regret that it is necessary."

Lansing assured Bernstorff that he did not hold him personally responsible, an opening Bernstorff seized in a bid for credit for the efforts he had made to preserve peace. Lansing did not indulge him. That Germany would give the United States only hours' notice of its hostile intention was indefensible, he said. Lansing brought the interview to an end. Bernstorff rose, and the two shook hands. The ambassador's eyes misted as he said good-bye.

Next Lansing summoned his deputy, Frank Polk, and Lester Woolsey, the assistant solicitor, to read the documents and share their reactions. Both thought the situation called for an immediate break with Germany. Wilson was not available when Lansing phoned him, so a State Department aide carried the papers over to the White House and asked Ike Hoover, the head usher, to give them to Wilson as soon as possible. It was after eight o'clock when Wilson read them, and Lansing was soon in the president's study, where they talked for nearly two hours about the government's next step. Lansing reminded Wilson that the United States had vowed in the *Sussex* pledge to sever relations if Germany resumed all-out submarine warfare. Wilson hesitated. He was deeply incensed by the German decision, Lansing wrote, but "said that he was not yet sure what course we must pursue and must think it over."

Lansing argued that if the United States did not keep its word to break with Germany for abandoning its pledge, Americans might well lose the respect of the rest of the world. Wilson was unmoved. He was willing to bear any amount of opprobrium, he said, if he thought the world would benefit from continued American diplomatic ties to Germany. He would not authorize a break unless he was convinced that it was, from every vantage point, the wisest course to take. Lansing replied that national greatness came from national character and that a nation that did not live up to its word could not be great. In the end they agreed that Lansing should prepare a draft of a note outlining Germany's breach of faith and breaking relations. But, Wilson emphasized, the draft was only to be a basis for further discussion.

In New York, House had spent January 31 waiting for a courier to deliver a letter from Bernstorff, and as the afternoon wore on, one of House's English contacts in Washington telephoned to say that the German and Austrian embassies had been open all night and were unusually busy all day. House's source guessed that they were planning to "do something" to the ninety-one German ships interned in U.S. ports. House passed the word to the collector of the Port of New York, but it was too late. At ten o'clock that morning, Bernstorff had given the order to wreck the engines of all ninety-one ships.

House took the overnight train to Washington, went directly to the White House, and had breakfast by himself. Wilson joined him soon afterward, looking depressed, House told his diary. "The president said he felt as if the world had suddenly reversed itself; that after going from east to west, it had begun to go from west to east and that he could not get his balance." Throughout the day, Wilson was agitated and despondent, and House had no luck in cheering him up. Wilson sat listlessly at times, paced his study, rearranged his books. Brooks, the president's valet, went in for a moment and told Agent Starling, the Secret Service man on duty in the corridor, "They're just sitting around looking sad." The president wondered if he should convene the cabinet. House thought not, as it was scheduled to meet the next day. With no more to discuss and nothing to do, they passed the time at the White House pool table.

Lansing arrived at noon to discuss whether it would be better to send Bernstorff home forthwith or wait for a German act of aggression against the United States. To Lansing's relief, Wilson leaned toward immediate action. But he insisted that the severing of relations would not lead to war if he could help it. Once again he argued that the United States had to remain neutral in order to save Europe when the fighting ended. When he described Germany as "a madman that should be curbed," House asked if it was fair to expect the Allies to do all the curbing. "He noticeably winced," House wrote. But Wilson stood by his conviction that it would be better, if possible, not to go to war.

House returned to New York that afternoon, and Lansing spent the evening drafting the note severing relations with Germany. It was largely a review of Germany's broken promises, and he made no attempt to be polite. He thought of it as an indictment and, he said, "it was to go to the president and I wanted him to know exactly how I felt." He wrote of "wanton slaughter," "premeditated barbarism," and "crimes without mercy and apparently without remorse." Unburdened of anger he had long suppressed, Lansing was able to write a second letter in his usual dispassionate style. As he saw it, the administration had two choices, both necessitating a break. And after the break, the government could either warn American ships away from the new German war zone or the president could ask Congress for a declaration of war. Lansing strongly preferred the latter course. "It amounts to a frank declaration that an outlaw government is an enemy of mankind," he wrote Wilson. He thought it would inspire other neutrals to follow suit and hasten the end of the war. He also believed that it would give the United States a prominent role in the peace negotiations, and that, he wrote, would give "tremendous moral weight to the cause of human liberty and the suppression of absolutism."

The cabinet met at two-thirty on Friday, February 2, and the president asked only one question: "Shall I break off diplomatic relations with Germany?" McAdoo argued for a prompt, strong response. Baker and Daniels were attracted to restraint and the long view. Houston, like Lansing, believed that fundamental rights were at stake. "If we acquiesce, we ought not to pose as a nation or as a free people," he said.

"Very well," Wilson said. "What is the concrete suggestion? What shall I propose? I must go to Congress. What shall I say?" Houston urged him to break with Germany first and plan his next moves later.

Wilson closed the cabinet meeting with a reading of Lansing's draft of the note severing relations with Germany but did not say what he planned to do. The cabinet left at 4:45, and Wilson went straight to the Capitol for a conference with Senator Stone in the rooms of the Committee on Foreign Relations. The Senate had already adjourned for the day, but Stone sent the pages off to find members who had not yet gone home and ask them to wait in the President's Room. Wilson asked each man whether he thought the United States should sever relations immediately or wait for an act of aggression against Americans. Fourteen of sixteen favored an immediate break.

The president left the senators as he had left his cabinet—in the dark about his next move.

On Saturday morning, Wilson sent for Lansing and told him that he was ready to make the break. Lansing returned to the State Department to put Bernstorff's dismissal and Gerard's recall in motion, Tumulty arranged for the president to address a joint session of Congress, and Wilson put the last touches on his remarks.

At twelve-thirty, his usual lunch hour, Lester Woolsey left his office at the State Department and headed to a café, where he ordered a plate of beans. He was soon joined by three newspapermen who had tailed him on the chance that he might be out on other business. He was, and after lunch he allowed them to walk with him to the German embassy, where at 1:52 he handed Count Bernstorff the embassy's passports and a copy of the president's speech.

On Capitol Hill, the president was calmly explaining why he thought that the United States had no honorable choice but to break with Germany. He hoped that the Germans would not attack neutral ships, but if they did, he said, he would return to Congress to ask for the authority to use any means necessary to protect American merchant vessels on the high seas.

23

Decision

F riday, March 23, found Senator Henry Fountain Ashurst in a solemn mood. That was not the stuff of headlines, but it was notable because Ashurst counted himself the least solemn member of the U.S. Senate. Proud son of pioneers who had brought him into the world in a covered wagon and raised him in a log cabin, Ashurst left school at thirteen to work on the family ranch. Possessed by the idea that he might one day hold a seat in the U.S. Senate, he continued his education on his own, studying the dictionary, reading the great works of literature, and training his voice by giving speeches while running uphill. He joined the Democratic Party of the Arizona Territory, won election to both houses of the territorial legislature, and realized his life's ambition in 1912, when Arizona became a state and sent him to Washington. He was thirty-nine. Handsome, affable, and amusing, he affected the dress of senators past—batwing collar, spade-tail coat, striped trousers, and pince-nez dangling from a long black cord. Ashurst's love of orating matched Woodrow Wilson's, and he rarely passed up a chance to show off his vocabulary or his vast store of literary allusions. The long black cord and the pince-nez were twirled round and round, propeller-like, as he held forth. They called him "Five-Syllable Henry" and "the Silver-Tongued Sunbeam of the Painted Desert."

The weeks since the break with Germany had stunned Senator Ashurst into something akin to plain speaking, at least in his diary. "The incredible has become the commonplace," he wrote. "From inability to respond to each new amazement, the human mind now accepts multitudinous world-staggering events as matters of course. One day's news of these times will fill volumes for future investigators, historians, and poets. We are too near these stupendous destinies to catch their meaning."

First had come a shipping crisis. As threatened, the U-boats began executing their new orders on February 1 and within three weeks sank 128 ships, forty of them flying neutral flags. Two were American, but the more significant fact was that only five American cargo ships had sailed, because American shipping companies were now unwilling to risk a crossing. Harbors on the Atlantic seaboard were clogged with ships. Mountains of cargo rose on the piers, and freight trains were backed up for miles around the ports. In ten days, exports from New York shrank by 98 percent. Germany had paralyzed American trade.

Shipowners turned to Washington for help, and on February 8, Lansing informed them of their legal right to arm their vessels for self-defense. But with no suitable guns or trained gunners, the right was useless. For the next two weeks, as hundreds of cargo ships waited, Wilson and his cabinet worked their way to a solution: the government would authorize the navy to lend guns and gunners to the shipping companies.

In a speech at the Capitol on Monday, February 26, Wilson had asked for a law to meet the emergency. Mindful that Congress would adjourn on March 4 and not reconvene for months, he also asked for authority to deal with crises that might arise during the recess. The Constitution implied that he already had such powers, but given the uncertainties of the moment, he wished to feel that he had Congress behind him. He was not contemplating war, he said. What he wanted, in addition to the authority and the funds to equip American ships for self-defense, was the latitude to use any other methods needed to protect Americans who were making peaceful use of the seas. He closed with a move that had marred several of his recent speeches, a suggestion that those who differed with him were deficient in patriotism: "I cannot imagine any man with American principles at his heart hesitating to defend these things."

The president's allies in Congress introduced the Armed Ship Bill that afternoon, but the next day Wilson learned of a German plot that destroyed all hope of keeping the United States out of the world war. In a telegram sent six weeks before, Arthur Zimmermann, Germany's foreign secretary, had given his minister to Mexico an astonishing order: if the United States declared war on Germany, the minister was to persuade President Carranza to attack the United States—with the help of Japan if possible. Zimmermann promised that Germany would fund the venture and help Mexico regain the 500,000 square miles of territory the United States seized in the Mexican-American War of 1848.

The Zimmermann telegram had reached Mexico City by a circuitous route. The German Foreign Office put it into cipher and cabled it to Ambassador Bernstorff in Washington, who sent it by Western Union to his man in Mexico. Washington learned of it from the British, who had intercepted and decoded the cable, then passed it along to the American ambassador to Britain, Walter Hines Page, who sent it straight to the State Department. Secretary Lansing was out of town when it arrived, so Frank Polk walked it over to the White House. Wilson was so outraged that he wanted to expose the plot at once, but Polk persuaded him to talk with Lansing first.

By the time the president and his secretary of state sat down together, on February 27, Lansing had learned that the State Department had unwittingly played a part in the episode. Sometime in 1916, Bernstorff had romanced House into helping him secure a privilege he never should have had: use of the State Department's wires to communicate, in cipher, with Berlin. The British had cut Germany's transatlantic cable at the beginning of the war, forcing the Germans to send their diplomatic dispatches to other points in Europe for transmission to the United States. The process was slow and cumbersome, and the colonel had been seduced by the ambassador's argument that use of the American cable would expedite his efforts to preserve the peace between Germany and the United States. A German embassy courier left coded messages at the State Department, which cabled them to the American embassy in Berlin, which forwarded them to the Wilhelmstrasse. Cables from the Wilhelmstrasse traveled the same path in reverse.

From time to time Lansing had expressed uneasiness with the arrangement, and when Bernstorff complained to House about Lansing's attitude, House asked Wilson to intervene. Wilson decided that the Germans could continue using the wire if they promised to use it only for dispatches that contained nothing unneutral. Using the U.S. Department of State to transmit an order to incite a war between Mexico and the United States was unneutral in the extreme.

"Good Lord!" Wilson said as Lansing walked him through the maze. "Good Lord!" He wanted to inform the newspapers immediately, but Lansing explained that it would be unwise to act until they found a way around one more complication: if Germany knew how the United States had learned of the plot, it would know that Britain had cracked the German code. Lansing suggested sharing the gist of the telegram with a trusted journalist but not sharing the source. Zimmermann's scheme was so outlandish that Lansing knew he would be asked about the source, and he planned to say that it had to remain confidential. Wilson gave his assent.

The next afternoon, Wilson spent an hour with a delegation from a coalition of peace organizations, the Emergency Peace Federation. The visitors admired the ideals Wilson had set forth in his "peace without victory" speech, and they thought that Wilson might avoid going to war by making a direct appeal to the German people. Wilson listened, but the Zimmermann telegram had killed his desire for peace overtures. One of the visitors, Jane Addams, was startled to hear him say that he would have no say in the peacemaking unless the United States entered the war.

For more than a year, House, Page, and Lansing had been making the same point, but Wilson had stuck to his conviction that only a nation unstained by war would have the moral authority to procure a just peace. The visiting pacifists were apparently the first to hear Wilson argue the opposite: there would be no just peace unless the United States went to war. For a man of another temperament, the about-face might have furnished a memorable lesson in the limitations of moral authority in world affairs, but if the situation prompted any reflections of that sort, Wilson did not record them.

On February 28 Lansing paraphrased the Zimmermann telegram for an Associated Press reporter and held his breath. The idea that Germany would form an alliance with Mexico and Japan to make war on the United States was so preposterous that Lansing expected Zimmermann to deny it and challenge the United States to produce proof. But Zimmermann readily admitted sending the message and asked why anyone should be surprised. In his mind, it went without saying that if the United States declared war on Germany, Germany would retaliate.

On March 1, the day the newspapers published the Associated Press story, Senator Lodge introduced a resolution calling on the president to vouch for the authenticity of the telegram. In truth, Lodge had no doubts about it, but he realized that if he could wring a verification from Wilson, Wilson would find it difficult to go on defending U.S. neutrality. The White

House and the State Department quickly confirmed that the telegram was genuine.*

The House reacted to the news of the German plot by voting 403 to 13 in favor of the Armed Ship Bill, and the Senate voted unanimously to consider the House bill, but the discussion began when the Sixty-fourth Congress was only twenty-six hours away from its mandated hour of adjournment, noon on March 4. The Senate's pacifists took the floor and ran out the clock, preventing any version of such a bill from coming to a vote. The Armed Ship Bill was dead, at least for the moment.

Wilson's first term also expired at noon, and because March 4, 1917, fell on a Sunday, he had decided on a two-part inauguration, a private swearing-in on Sunday to fulfill the constitutional requirement and the customary public celebration on Monday. At ten-thirty on Sunday morning, in a hard rain, he and his wife were driven to the Capitol and escorted to the President's Room, where a number of bills awaited his signature. Aware of the battle raging just across the hall in the Senate chamber, he did his best to ignore it. A reporter shuttling between the chamber and the President's Room reported that Wilson seemed "chipper and lively . . . full of vigor and swing."

At 12:04, with his hand on the Bible, Wilson took the oath of office before his wife, his cabinet, and a sprinkling of political associates. The Bible lay open to the Forty-sixth Psalm, which begins, "God is our refuge and strength, a very present help in trouble." In the sixth verse the heathens rage, and in the eighth the Lord "maketh wars to cease unto the ends of the earth." The Wilsons were back at the White House by twelve-thirty, and according to Colonel House, the president came in denouncing the senators who had blocked the vote. House urged him to tell the public what had happened and explain the consequences. Wilson appreciated the suggestion and promised to act on it later in the week. House thought he should seize the moment,

---

* The telegram was real, but Zimmermann's offer was not. Soon after Americans learned of his telegram, Zimmermann confided to his colleagues that Germany had no intention of helping Mexico regain its lost territory and no faith that Japan would join such an alliance. He said he was simply trying to lure Mexico into attacking the United States "as quickly as possible, thus preventing American troops from being sent to the European continent." (Friedrich Katz, *The Secret War in Mexico,* [Chicago: University of Chicago Press, 1981], 352–53.)

and Wilson gave in, shutting himself up for the afternoon to write a statement for the press. He talked it over with House before dinner and after dinner consulted McAdoo, Burleson, and Tumulty. With their approval, it went off to the wire services.

Washington went to bed thinking that Monday would be a day of celebration but awoke to find the honoree in a terrible mood. His statement appeared on the *Post*'s front page under a headline eight columns wide. "A little group of willful men, representing no opinion but their own, have rendered the great government of the United States helpless and contemptible," Wilson had written. In a moment when action was sorely needed, they had made action impossible, and unless the Senate's rules were changed to limit debate, an extraordinary session of Congress would be pointless, because the paralysis of the Senate would remain.

In spite of the president's fury, the inaugural show had to go on, and in its way it was as unsettling as the filibuster. J. Fred Essary of the *Baltimore Sun*, a veteran Washington correspondent and a member of the committee in charge of the 1917 inauguration, would write that the capital had not witnessed a ceremony as fraught with "uncertainty, uneasiness, and foreboding" since the second inauguration of Abraham Lincoln. The Wilsons traveled to the Capitol in a horse-drawn carriage protected by thirty-two Secret Service men augmented by columns of cavalry and mounted police. Armed National Guardsmen lined both sides of Pennsylvania Avenue. Sharpshooters kept a lookout from the rooftops. The crowds who had come out to see the president were thick with plainclothesmen.

It seemed to the reporters covering the extravaganza that Washington had never seen so many flags, and they were right. The inaugural subcommittee on street decorations had set itself one goal—"promote patriotism"—and had pursued it in every corner of the capital. Civic groups urged their members to fly the flag. Automobile dealerships and parking garages posted large signs asking motorists to decorate their cars with flags and, while they were at it, to encourage friends and neighbors to display the flag. The city's schoolteachers were given a "fly the flag" letter to read to their pupils. The committee even persuaded women's suffrage groups to furl their banners for the day, "leaving none but Old Glory flying in the breeze."

Chief Justice Edward Douglass White administered the oath again, for the benefit of the crowd, and Edith stood at Woodrow's side, a place no previous first lady had claimed at an inauguration. The sun shone brightly, but the wind blew hard. The temperature was just above freezing. Wilson, in silk hat and Chesterfield coat, looked elegant and commanding, but his inaugural address was a disappointment. For one thing, he was speaking into the wind, which made his words inaudible to the thousands gathered on the lawn. For another, much of the address was borrowed from his speeches of the last year. The one moving moment came last, in a sentence that read like a prayer for himself and the country: "The shadows that now lie dark upon our path will soon be dispelled, and we shall walk with the light all about us if we be but true to ourselves—to ourselves as we have wished to be known in the councils of the world and in the thought of all those who love liberty and justice and the right exalted."

The Wilsons rode back to the White House through the sea of flags, but the mystic influence of the Stars and Stripes along Pennsylvania Avenue on March 5, 1917, produced none of the exuberance of the Democratic convention at St. Louis. This was a subdued show of patriotism, perhaps because of the stinging wind, perhaps because the president and first lady were barely visible behind the mounted police and the Secret Servicemen. Thomas W. Brahany, a member of the president's office staff, suggested another possibility: "This is not a time for wild cheering. The country is in a serious state of mind."

In the evening the family and Colonel House had a quiet dinner then gathered in the oval sitting room upstairs to view the fireworks over the Mall. Most of the group watched from the main windows, but Woodrow and Edith invited the colonel to join them at a side window. House was touched to see Woodrow holding Edith's hand and leaning his face against hers.

By the next morning it was clear that the country sided with the president in the controversy over the filibuster. La Follette was hanged in effigy on the campus of the University of Illinois, and the town fathers of Wheeling, West Virginia, announced that they had canceled the speech he was scheduled to give later in the week. But the dozen senators who had held out against the Armed Ship Bill vehemently objected to Wilson's aspersions. Their opposition had not been selfish or willful or unpatriotic, they said; they were convinced that arming the ships would lead to war.

Wilson regretted giving in to his pique but was too proud (and perhaps too hurt) to apologize. In its closing days the Sixty-fourth Congress had rejected his request for broad and unspecified powers, thwarted his effort to arm the merchant fleet, and left the Senate no time to consider a long list of other major bills passed by the House. Now he would have to call for an extra session, which he had hoped to avoid. On March 7, Wilson did what he had so often done when the world turned against him: he took to his bed, staying in the family quarters for ten days. Cabinet meetings were postponed. Correspondence piled up on his desk downstairs. Appointments were canceled. A cold, said Dr. Grayson.

Woodrow clung to Edith, and for the first time she played a visible role in his work. At his request, she wrote a note to Lansing, asking him to review and comment on some documents from Daniels. Before the month was out, she went with Woodrow to a meeting with Daniels and one with Lansing. She was not making decisions or acting in his stead, but he seemed to need the comfort of her presence. On March 9 he asked the attorney general, Thomas Watt Gregory, whether a president could arm the ships without the approval of Congress. When Gregory assured him that he could, Wilson asked Lansing and Daniels to draw up the proper procedures and, Edith wrote, "They replied in long memoranda which I read to the president as he lay in bed." On March 12, he gave the order.

In her diary on March 13, Edith noted that "W. did not get up until lunch-time; he still feels wretched." On March 14: "Still raining. W. in bed until one, but seemed better." The White House usher's diary for the same day adds that there were no callers and that after joining the family for lunch, the president again retreated. On March 15, Edith reported that Woodrow was cheered by the news that the Russian people had forced Czar Nicholas II to abdicate, liberating themselves after 350 years under the Romanovs and promising to establish a democratic government.

Since the beginning of the war, it had galled Wilson to hear Britain and France speak of fighting a war against autocracy when their principal ally, Russia, lived under the heel of an autocrat as reprehensible as the kaiser. At a stroke, the Russian Revolution removed Wilson's objection and ensured that he could support the Allies without a troubled conscience. In 1913 Wilson had been the first head of state to grant recognition to the Republic of China, and in 1917 he became the first to recognize the provisional government of Russia.

The final blow to Wilson's hopes for continued neutrality landed on March 18, when the Germans torpedoed three American ships. Still, Wilson resisted. He summoned Lansing the next day to discuss the attacks, but he seemed to want the secretary of state to confirm that the United States could do no more than arm its ships. Lansing told Wilson that war was inevitable and the sooner the United States admitted it, the taller it would stand in the eyes of the world. Lansing hoped that Wilson would come around to his view but sensed that he resented abandoning the neutrality he had worked so hard to preserve. Depressed and anxious, Lansing dashed off a plea to

Colonel House: "If you agree with me that we should act now, will you not please put your shoulder to the wheel?"

A few hours after seeing Lansing, Wilson unburdened himself in an off-the-record conversation with Frank I. Cobb, editor of the *New York World*. Although he had defended the order to arm the ships in his talk with Lansing, he admitted to Cobb that it was not going to work. Armed or unarmed, ships in the war zone were going to be torpedoed. He also confessed that he could no longer think of an alternative to war. He was hoping that Cobb might be able to see a way out. Cobb could not.

Wilson asked Cobb to consider the consequences of going to war. "It would mean that we should lose our heads along with the rest and stop weighing right and wrong," Wilson said. "It would mean that a majority of the people in this hemisphere would go war-mad, quit thinking and devote their energies to destruction." The Allies would win, and Germany would be forced to accept a punitive peace. It would mean the end of civil liberties in the United States. "To fight you must be brutal and ruthless, and the spirit of ruthless brutality will enter into the very fiber of our national life, infecting Congress, the courts, the policeman on the beat, the man in the street," Wilson said. "If there is any alternative, for God's sake, let's take it."

Lansing brooded all day about Wilson's indecision and late that night wrote him a long letter. He began on bended knee, saying he agreed with Wilson's judgment that the latest submarine attacks on American ships were not sufficient cause for declaring war. But, he added, an armed American ship was bound to clash soon with a submarine, and after that, the United States would find it impossible to "maintain the fiction that peace exists." He admitted that his argument made little sense unless one accepted the inevitability of war, but if he was right, the United States had much to gain by declaring war as soon as possible. It would hearten the Allies. It would strengthen the new Russian government and encourage the budding democratic insurgency in Germany, opportunities that might disappear if the United States delayed. And, he said, "prompt, vigorous and definite action in favor of Democracy and against Absolutism" would increase American influence at the peace negotiations after the war, when Germany would need "a merciful and unselfish foe" and the world would need reordering.

Lansing's letter went to the White House the next morning, and at the cabinet meeting that afternoon he was surprised by Wilson's serenity. The president shook hands with everyone on his way into the room and after a few pleasantries said he wanted the cabinet's advice on dealing with Germany. All were in favor of asking the Sixty-fifth Congress to begin its extraordinary session on April 2, two weeks earlier than planned, to expedite the declaration of war.

But the cabinet disagreed on what should happen after that. McAdoo, doubtful that the United States could raise an army large enough to end the war, proposed that Washington concentrate on financing the Allies. Houston concurred but added the thought that the U.S. Navy might prove useful to the Allies. Baker, the pacifist who had become secretary of war, was now as militant as any of the generals on his staff. He advocated raising a large army on the grounds that news of the American decision to train hundreds of thousands, perhaps millions, of soldiers, would force the Central Powers to realize that they were beaten.

Lansing recited the arguments he had been making to Wilson and added his belief that the American people were longing for strong leadership, ready to fight, and likely to be confused if the government wavered. Furthermore, he said, the war had to be a war for democracy, a point he made with such force that the president asked him to lower his voice lest it be heard in the corridor. When Wilson said he did not see how he could ask Congress for a declaration of war in the name of an abstraction, Lansing suggested that Wilson could propose a war against the inhumanity of German autocracy and remind Congress of Germany's broken promises and its conspiracies against the United States. "Possibly," Wilson said. Lansing pressed. Not everyone would agree that the two hundred Americans lost to submarine attacks justified a war, but the idea that autocracies like Germany had to be stopped because they threatened the United States and every other democracy would, he said, "appeal to every liberty-loving man the world over."

Eventually Wilson called on Daniels. Left fatherless and destitute by the Civil War, he had been a pacifist all his life. His eyes filled with tears, and his voice trembled as he said that now that war was unavoidable, Congress ought to be summoned as soon as possible. The account of the cabinet meeting in his diary is brief and makes no mention of his own distress. But unlike Lansing, who had taken the president's composure at face value, Daniels could see Wilson's anguish, and it pained him. "President was solemn, very sad!" he wrote.

After hearing from the rest of the cabinet, Wilson said, "Well, gentlemen, I think that there is no doubt as to what your advice is. I thank you." He was no more forthcoming with the fifty White House reporters waiting for news of the cabinet meeting. When they protested to his office, he issued a one-line statement as exasperating as his silence: "The international situation was thoroughly discussed in all its phases."

Next morning, on his way out to golf with Grayson, Wilson gave his staff the text of the proclamation calling for an extraordinary session of Congress to begin at noon on April 2 "to receive a communication concerning grave matters of national policy." For readers wondering what the grave matters might be, *The Washington Post* explained: "the United States and the German empire are about to go to war."

Wilson and Grayson did not play golf. They rode around the countryside for several hours. When they returned, Wilson dropped by his office to sign the proclamation, then went upstairs. "Apparently he is not in a working mood these days," a White House aide told his diary. "He spends nearly all his time with Mrs. Wilson, reading, playing pool or visiting." As soon as the newspapermen read the proclamation, they wanted to know what the president planned to say, and they pestered his staff until one of them went upstairs to ask Wilson if he would grant them a few minutes. He would not.

Wilson fell prey to every kind of anxiety in the two weeks before his address to Congress. The cabinet saw a self-righteous version of it at a meeting on March 27, when McAdoo suggested removing the German crews from the ships they had disabled. McAdoo feared that when war was declared, the Germans would dynamite the ships, doing considerable damage to the ports. Wilson said firmly that the United States would not do anything that looked grasping or self-interested. When McAdoo raised the issue again a few days later, Wilson was even more adamant. As Daniels put it in his diary, "President said it offended him to see people covet these ships. America must set an example of splendid conduct in war." McAdoo's instinct was to protect the ports, which would be crucial in wartime. Wilson's reaction seemed a page torn from a code of chivalry, irrational in an age of total war.

House happened to be on hand after the cabinet's first discussion of the German crews, and he was not surprised when Wilson complained of a headache. Eager to soothe, House told his friend that managing the war would not prove as difficult as challenges he had already met but that this challenge conflicted with the kind of man he was: "too refined, too civilized, too intellectual, too cultivated not to see the incongruity and absurdity of war." War required "a man of coarser fiber," House said. The flattery seemed to please Wilson but did not convince him that he could succeed. He said he did not feel fit to be a war president. House assured him that everything he would have to do had already been done by the Allied leaders. Wilson took heart.

On March 30, Wilson began writing his communication on grave matters, and at the cabinet meeting that afternoon, he stood and put himself through a series of physical exercises, explaining that he was stiff from writing all morning. Wilson had often complained of a stiff arm after hours of writing, and it was his writing arm that was temporarily paralyzed in the two strokes at Princeton, but this is the first report of tension throughout his body.

To stretch his muscles and relax his mind, Wilson remained faithful to his golf regimen, going out almost every morning with his wife or with Grayson. He spent the morning of March 31 on the links with Edith, lunched with her, then told the household staff that he was going to his study and wanted quiet. Hoover, the head usher, sent a subordinate to close the study door. Wilson lit into him. He did not want the door *closed,* he said. He wanted *quiet.* "I have never known him to be more peevish," Hoover told a member of Wilson's office staff. "He is out of sorts." Wilson's anxiety was also apparent to Starling, who would remember the president "with a melancholy, preoccupied air. When he spoke his voice was soft, as if the whole world were a sickroom through which he was tiptoeing. I was sorry for him."

On Sunday morning, April 1, Woodrow and Edith went to church, and that afternoon he finished his speech. April 2 was given over to golf with Edith and an afternoon of killing time with her and House as they waited for Congress to come to order and inform the president that it was ready to receive his communication.

Sometime during the afternoon Wilson read his speech to House, who thought it excellent and in his diary did not hesitate to compliment himself: "it contains all that I have been urging upon him since the war began." When House asked Wilson why he had not shared a draft with the cabinet, Wilson said they would have picked it to pieces.

Wilson's decision to keep the speech to himself was a lapse of judgment as well as a measure of his anxiety. The speech was sure to be the most consequential Wilson had ever given, for the country and perhaps the world. At the very least it ought to have been vetted by the secretary of state, and Wilson would have risked nothing by showing a draft to the whole cabinet. He would have had the benefit of their counsel, could have declined their suggestions, and might well have been given a warm bath of reassurance. But he was apparently too distraught to submit to any kind of review, even a review he was free to ignore.

At about three o'clock the White House learned that Congress would be ready to receive the president at eight-thirty. Dinner, shared with Edith, Margaret, cousin Helen, and the colonel, was a quiet affair with conversation of the sort the president liked with his meals. "We talked of everything excepting the matter in hand," House noted in his diary. The Wilsons, accompanied by Grayson, left for the Capitol at 8:20 in a limousine protected by the Secret Service, mounted cavalry, and a motorcycle escort. The Capitol dome, illuminated and heavily patrolled, glowed through the mist of a light rain.

Members of the House were already in their seats. The senators, almost all of them wearing or carrying small American flags, had marched in together. The justices of the Supreme Court had been ushered to an improvised first row of chairs. And for the first time in memory, the diplomatic corps was seated on the House floor rather than in the galleries. At 8:32, when the speaker of the House announced the president, the Supreme Court rose to applaud and the rest of the room followed.

Wilson customarily allowed himself a gesture now and then as he delivered a speech, but on this evening he scarcely moved. He held his manuscript in both hands and rested an arm on the clerk's desk, as if to steady himself. He began with a review of Germany's offenses, particularly "the cruel and unmanly business" of a submarine war with no restrictions. The United States could not submit to it, he said. "The wrongs against which we now array ourselves are no common wrongs; they cut to the very roots of human life." He was well into the speech before he made his request of Congress:

> With a profound sense of the solemn and even tragical character of the step I am taking and of the grave responsibilities which it involves, but in unhesitating obedience to what I deem my constitutional duty, I advise that the Congress declare the recent course of the Imperial German Government to be in fact nothing less than war against the government and people of the United States; that it formally accept the status of belligerent which has thus been thrust upon it, and that it take immediate steps not only to put the country in a more thorough state of defense but also to exert all its power and employ all its resources to bring the Government of the German Empire to terms and end the war.

He outlined the necessities: close cooperation with the Allies, continued production of their matériel, industrial mobilization, immediate improvements in the navy, and an army of at least 500,000 men "who should, in my opinion, be chosen upon the principle of universal liability to service." (He could not bring himself to say "conscription.") He also asked Congress to fund the war mainly with new taxes rather than loans so that the cost would not be passed on to future generations.

The United States had no quarrel with the German people, Wilson said. Its quarrel was with the German autocracy. No autocracy could be trusted to honor the principles of a partnership of the world's democracies. He spoke briefly of the Russian Revolution and his joy that "the great, generous Russian people," having overthrown their autocracy, had added their "majesty and might to the forces that are fighting for freedom in the world."

Wilson's peroration was the most stirring rhetoric heard in the United States since the days of Lincoln:

The world must be made safe for democracy. . . . We desire no conquest, no dominion. We seek no indemnities for ourselves, no material compensation for the sacrifices we shall freely make. We are but one of the champions of the rights of mankind. We shall be satisfied when those rights have been made as secure as the faith and the freedom of nations can make them.

It is a fearful thing to lead this great peaceful people into war, into the most terrible and disastrous of all wars, civilization itself seeming to be in the balance. But the right is more precious than peace, and we shall fight for the things which we have always carried nearest our hearts—for democracy, for the right of those who submit to authority to have a voice in their own governments, for the rights and liberties of small nations, for a universal dominion of right by such a concert of free peoples as shall bring peace and safety to all nations and make the world itself at last free. To such a task we can dedicate ourselves and our fortunes, everything that we are and everything that we have, with the pride of those who know that the day has come when America is privileged to spend her blood and her might for the principles that gave her birth and happiness and the peace which she has treasured. God helping her, she can do no other.

The speech was followed by a silence of several seconds that to Robert Lansing felt like several minutes—"the finest tribute ever paid to eloquence," he wrote. Then nearly everyone rose and applauded and cheered. As Wilson left the chamber, Lodge took his hand and said, "Mr. Wilson, you have expressed in the loftiest manner possible the sentiments of the American people."

Wilson had taken Lansing's advice to go to war as a champion of democracy, but only after the U-boats and the Zimmermann telegram made it impossible to go on defending neutrality, after the Russian revolutionaries relieved him of his qualms about the Allies, and after he accepted that he would have no role in shaping the postwar world unless the United States entered the war. But he was sickened by the prospect of sending troops into the hell of the Western Front, where millions had died and no one knew when the killing would end. When Wilson left the Capitol, his face was ashen, his step leaden. Tumulty would remember Wilson saying to him after the speech, "Think what it was they were applauding. My message today was a message of death for our young men."

Quickly but not without debate Congress approved the war resolution with votes of 82 to 6 in the Senate and 373 to 50 in the House. The senators opposed included Robert La Follette, who addressed himself to Wilson: "The poor, sir, who are the ones called upon to rot in the trenches, have no organized power, but oh, Mr. President, at some time they will be heard."

A congressional courier delivered the resolution to the White House at one o'clock in the afternoon on April 6, Good Friday. In 134 words it indicted Germany for repeated acts of war against the American people and their government, asserted that those acts had created a state of war between the United States and Germany, formally declared the United States at war, and authorized the president to use the army, navy, and resources of the United States "to carry on war against the Imperial German Government; and to bring the conflict to a successful termination." The president was having lunch with his wife and a cousin when the messenger arrived, and they immediately went to Ike Hoover's office, where Wilson added his signature to those of the speaker of the House and the president of the Senate. With that, the United States was at war. Hoover pressed a button to notify the Navy Department, and an aide telephoned the executive offices to alert the newspaper reporters who were standing by. There would be no statement from the president.

"Step by step the president had been pursued and brought to bay," Winston Churchill would write in his history of the Great War. "By slow merciless degrees, against his dearest hopes, against his gravest doubts, against his deepest inclinations, in stultification of all he had said and done and left undone in thirty months of carnage, he was forced to give the signal he dreaded and abhorred." Churchill went on to excoriate him for not entering the war two years earlier, after the attack on the *Lusitania,* and to wonder how much agony and ruin might have been prevented if Woodrow Wilson had not told his countrymen that there is such a thing as being too proud to fight. Theodore Roosevelt, Robert Lansing, and many other influential Northeasterners had similar convictions, but until the Zimmermann telegram came to light, most Americans did not. Musing on the moment in his diary, Senator Ashurst predicted that "When the excitement of these days is forgotten, the impartial historian will say that W.W. valiantly strove to avert war." That he had.

24

The Associate

Emotionally, morally, and politically, the decision to lead the country into war was the most wrenching of Wilson's life. Once past it, though, he was resolute and clearheaded, determined to pour the full might of the United States into the war, and certain that he could avoid entanglements with the Allies. Rather than join them, the United States would fight as an Associated Power, aligned with their aim of defeating Germany but not bound by their treaties with one another.

The Allies met Wilson's decision for war with high praise and its customary sequel, supplication. By the spring of 1917, they were desperate for American help—at sea, in their land war, and on the financial front. As soon as the United States declared war, Britain, France, Italy, and Russia asked to send delegations to Washington. Wilson gave his consent, but not without trepidation. The British were coming first, and while he understood the importance of connecting His Majesty's generals, admirals, and technical experts with their American opposites, he feared that the newspapers of William Randolph Hearst and other Anglophobes would paint the mission as a British attempt to seize control of the U.S. war effort. Spring Rice alerted London and urged the envoys to tread lightly.

Arthur Balfour, Britain's new foreign secretary and head of its delegation to the United States, had his first audience with Wilson and Lansing on April 23. The president emphasized the U.S. government's commitment to the war in spite of his decision to stand apart from the Allies. As he explained to Balfour, he was planning for the day when one or another of the Allies would have a treaty dispute, and if that happened, the Associate, having no vested interest in the outcome, might prove useful as an umpire. Balfour noticed that the American war effort had barely begun, but he believed that Wilson understood the magnitude of the challenges.

Balfour was invited for a quiet family dinner at the White House, and House met with him in advance to go over the territorial "adjustments" the Allies expected to make after the war. Balfour's idea was that he and House could identify the ones on which the United States and Britain were likely to agree, then House could brief the president for an after-dinner discussion. As Balfour was speaking of Trieste, on the northern end of the Adriatic, it became apparent that he was headed down a path that House wanted Wilson to avoid, a path into a thicket of secret Allied treaties. Trieste was part of the Austro-Hungarian Empire, but Balfour was saying that it would go to Italy after the war.

House foresaw trouble and asked the difficult question: what did the Allies' treaties actually say about the division of spoils? Balfour admitted that the treaty with the Italians promised them virtually everything they wanted, including control of much of the eastern coast of the Adriatic. The new territory had been Italy's price for entering the war. Wilson deplored that sort of bargain, because it took no account of the wishes of the inhabitants. It is not clear from House's diary whether he made the point aloud, but Balfour sensed his disapproval and, House wrote, "spoke with regret of the spectacle of great nations sitting down and dividing the spoils of war or, as he termed it, 'dividing up the bearskin before the bear was killed.' I asked him if he did not think it proper for the Allies to give these treaties to the president for his confidential information." Balfour agreed to share them.

Still wary, House asked another question: would it not be best for the United States and Britain to avoid such agreements so that when the peacemaking came they could stand together against the greed of other nations? Agreeable to a fault, Balfour endorsed the idea. But he did not promise that Britain would make peace in the spirit of selflessness advocated by Woodrow

Wilson, and he wriggled out of the colonel's grasp with an extravagant compliment: "I like to confer with you. I like your mind. It is so clear and direct."

Balfour and House had supper with the Wilsons on April 30. Edith Wilson, who often felt unsure of herself in rarefied company, found Balfour accessible and appreciative. He was also tall, handsome, and sympathetic. Nearly seventy, he was an Eton and Cambridge product who had drifted into government through his family's connections and wafted all the way up to prime minister, succeeding an uncle who resigned to make way for him. Voted out after four years, Balfour could have left politics, which he did not relish. (He never thought about them in bed, he said. His passions were philosophy, tennis, and golf.) But he stayed on, and when Lloyd George was elected prime minister in 1916, Balfour replaced Sir Edward Grey as foreign secretary. Politicians who agreed on little else agreed that Balfour was a useful man.

Wilson seemed unable to relax and enjoy his guest. "To my mind, he was not at his best because of an apparent eagerness to excel," House told his diary. The president jabbered away about the value of studying the classics, history, architecture. As planned, the after-dinner talk centered on the shape of the postwar world, and House was distressed to hear Wilson agree with Balfour's idea of putting the Dardanelles under some kind of international governance as a way of guaranteeing that all nations would have access to the waters linking the Black Sea and the Mediterranean. House observed that such a move might well elicit demands to internationalize the Suez and Panama canals. They got the point, he wrote in his diary, but they insisted that the Dardanelles were different. The colonel noted the tendency of statesmen to regard their own interests as exceptions to the rules they applied to everyone else.

What the colonel did not note, although he had been told of it during his 1915 meetings in Europe, was that the Asian side of the Dardanelles and the city of Constantinople had been promised to Russia. The Ottoman sultan had cast his lot with the kaiser, and the Allies privately agreed that when they finished off the kaiser, they would help themselves to the Ottoman Empire, which included Turkey and most of the modern Middle East. Another of the secret treaties gave Romania a big slice of Hungary, and still another bestowed upon Japan two prizes she had long coveted: a foothold on the Chinese mainland (a swath of Shantung, which was occupied by the Germans under a concession from China) and a sprinkling of German islands in the Pacific. The fifth and last of the secret pacts, signed early in 1917, promised that Alsace-Lorraine would be returned to France and the Polish provinces conquered by the German army would revert to Russia. Wilson and Lansing knew next to nothing of these secret agreements until after the United States committed itself to war.

The discussions of territorial adjustments had allowed Balfour to take soundings that might prove useful when the fighting ended, but in the spring of 1917 he and his colleagues had more pressing concerns. They had been sent to Washington to gauge the Americans' readiness for war, channel their surging patriotism toward decisions that would benefit Britain, and above all, secure ships and loans. The British quickly made their way to the Treasury, where they confessed the dire state of their finances. McAdoo would remember the visitors as "war-weary, jangled, nervous." He had already persuaded Congress to pass the Emergency Loan Act, which put $7 billion at the Treasury's disposal, $3 billion of it for the Allies. He gave the British mission a check for $200 million, and another $100 million went to the French.

In meetings with Secretary Daniels and his staff, the Royal Navy's representatives confided that the U-boats were annihilating Britain's merchant fleet. By the Admiralty's calculations, Britain would be done for by November unless the U-boats were driven from the seas. Daniels sent six American destroyers speeding across the Atlantic to begin hunting submarines. The British asked for more, and the ranking admiral of the French mission seconded their request. "Ships and ships and then more ships," Daniels noted in his diary. Dozens were soon on their way. When the British recommended that the interned German ships be repaired and put to work, the administration could report that the project was well under way. The ships had been seized as soon as the United States declared war, the crews were interned, and six of the ninety-one vessels went into service while the British and French were in Washington. The rest would be carrying troops and cargo by the end of the summer.

The French mission had just embarked when General Robert Nivelle, the new commander of the French armies, launched an elaborate attack to blast a wide hole in the German line and end thirty months of stasis on the Western Front. The fighting, which was supposed to be over in two days, dragged on for twelve and the Nivelle Offensive would go down in history as one of the greatest military disasters of all time. The French suffered 187,000 casualties, and the fury of the survivors set off a mutiny that ultimately spread to more than half the army's infantry divisions at the front. The troops were still willing to defend the line but regarded further offensives as suicidal.

The French delegates to Washington smiled bravely, and thanks largely to the most celebrated member of their party, Marshal Joseph Joffre, they drew enthusiastic crowds wherever they went. Marshal Joffre, hero of the Marne: the newspapers never said one without the other. In the first weeks of the war, he had held the Germans at the Marne, stopping their race to Paris and depriving Germany of the quick victory promised by the kaiser. The reporters who followed him during his stay in the United States rarely mentioned that the hero of the Marne had just been relieved of his command. Frustrated by the long stalemate, the government had replaced him with Nivelle. The end of the offensive marked the end of Nivelle's command, and France was forced to search for yet another marshal.

Joffre had come to the United States to ask for men, men, and more men—immediately. By 1917, France had lost more than two million soldiers, a figure that included the dead, the permanently maimed, and prisoners of war. The British who came to Washington proposed that 500,000 American recruits be rushed to England for nine weeks of training, after which they would fill out British battalions winnowed by casualties. The British did not rule out an independent American force, but their plan would put Americans at the front long before troops could be trained in the United States. The French War Ministry had conceived a similar plan, but Joffre intuited that the Associate would resist. It was one thing for France and Britain to amalgamate troops from their colonies, but Joffre could not imagine that a world power would allow its citizens to be absorbed "like poor relations in the ranks of some other army and fight under a foreign flag." He decided to approach the U.S. Army with offers of autonomy as well as training, equipment, and advisors. Joffre was acting on his own authority. His government had asked him only to press for the speedy delivery of "a symbolic American corps, even if very weak" in the interest of raising French morale.

After meetings with the War Department, Joffre sat down with Wilson at the White House. Wilson was at his best, and Joffre understood that he and his British counterpart were competing for American troops. The president opened with a broad question: how should the U.S. Army be used in the war? The old marshal asked for an American division as soon as possible. "When the American flag flies beside the French flag and the English flag, the effect on morale will be considerable," he said.

Wilson asked how long it would take to prepare the division for combat. Joffre replied that with a month's training in France, the Americans would be ready to take over one of the quieter sectors at the front. Wilson assumed that Joffre was requesting a division of soldiers already in the army, not a division made up of raw recruits, but he inquired all the same. "Just so," Joffre said. "The essential thing will be to complete their training by instructing them in the specialties that modern war demands and that we can teach them right behind our front."

In making their case for sending men to England, the British had told Wilson that French ports were jammed, but when he asked Joffre about the problem, the marshal offered a simple solution: ports farther down the coast, where there was less traffic.

Wilson was pleased to hear that Joffre wanted trained soldiers. The question of sending volunteers had been raised by Theodore Roosevelt, who yearned to go to France at the head of a volunteer division that he had been planning since the attack on the *Lusitania*. Roosevelt had exchanged several letters with the War Department and had paid a call on Wilson but was still awaiting a decision. Wilson had no intention of giving Roosevelt an opportunity to turn himself into a war hero and a frontrunner for the Republican Party's next presidential nomination. Now Wilson could take cover behind the hero of the Marne.

Joffre did Wilson an even greater service. The French mission was billeted at the home of Henry White, a former American ambassador to France, and its visit coincided with the congressional debate over the Selective Service Act. A newspaper poll taken just after the U.S. declaration of war showed formidable opposition in both the House and the Senate. Joffre agreed to be the guest of honor at a series of dinner parties that White hosted for congressmen and senators determined not to draft Americans to serve in foreign armies. With the help of an interpreter, Joffre explained that France wanted the Americans to fight under their own flag, and he endorsed the administration's conclusion that a draft was the only way to raise an army large enough to win the war that would make the world safe for democracy. In mid-May, when both houses of Congress passed the draft legislation by overwhelming majorities, Joffre was thrilled.

The British did not object to the idea of hurrying an American division to France but assumed that United States would form its principal military partnership with Britain, if only because Americans and Englishmen spoke the same language. But Washington proved to be more concerned with *égalité* than *fraternité*. Since the U.S. Navy's primary partnership would be with Britain, Baker thought it advisable to make France the main partner with the U.S. Army. The United States did not want either ally to have the upper hand.

Wilson privately promised Balfour that there would be one and a half million American soldiers on the Western Front in 1918, but first he would send a division to France. On May 2 the War Department telegraphed General John J. Pershing at Fort Sam Houston in San Antonio, where he had stayed after bringing the Punitive Expedition home from Mexico in early February. The telegram said that the United States would probably send troops and if it did, "you will be in command of the entire force."

Pershing had been angling for the job. From the Mexican desert, he filed a successful application for promotion from brigadier to major general, the rank held by the officers sure to be on the War Department's short list for Europe. Pershing's chief rival for the European command was likely to be Major General Leonard Wood. A graduate of Harvard Medical School, Wood had joined the army as a surgeon, won a Congressional Medal of Honor during the Indian Wars, and topped off his experience with a celebrated memoir, *Chasing Geronimo.* As a colonel in the Spanish-American War he commanded a brigade that included Theodore Roosevelt's Rough Riders, then stayed on in Cuba as military governor of Santiago. In 1902 President Roosevelt appointed him to lead the U.S. Army in the Philippines. William Howard Taft's service as governor general of the Philippines overlapped with Wood's command, and when Taft became president, he selected Wood as the army's chief of staff.

And then came Woodrow Wilson. In the spring of 1913, during the crisis with Japan over the Alien Land Law in California, someone in the high reaches of the army or navy leaked word that the navy was sending the fleet to the Pacific in case of war with Japan. The leak appeared to come from Wood's office, and Wood lost his position as chief of staff. He was given the command of the army's Eastern Department and banished to the fort on Governors Island in New York Harbor. The War Department approved Wood's plan to establish officers' training camps (forerunner of the Reserve Officers' Training Corps), and while Wilson tolerated the camps, he found himself increasingly irritated by Wood's hawkishness. In January 1917, when the Senate Military Affairs Committee asked Wood to comment on the strength of the nation's defenses, Wood gave a critique of the War Department so intemperate that he destroyed whatever chance he might have had for a European command.

Baker summoned Pershing to Washington with the idea of sending him and a small staff to France at once. An expeditionary force of about twelve thousand experienced soldiers would follow as soon as it could be assembled, and while they were being trained by the French, Pershing would share his observations and recommendations with the War Department. Wilson approved, and Baker saw Pershing on May 10. As Pershing told the story in his memoir, the secretary had given him only two orders: "one to go to France and the other to come home. In the meantime your authority will be supreme." In fact, Pershing went off with a six-point set of orders, which he himself had drawn up. The fifth point delineated a sharp boundary between the Associate and the Allies: "you are directed to cooperate with the forces of the other countries . . . but in doing so the underlying idea must be kept in view that the forces of the United States are a separate and distinct component of the combined forces, the identity of which must be preserved." Both Pershing and Wilson believed that if American troops were folded into the French and British armies, the United States would not get full credit for its contributions on the battlefield.

Conferring with the Allies got the American war effort off to a good start, but in the rush for ships, troops, and financing, there had been little time to discuss the fallout of the Russian Revolution. On April 10, three weeks after the czar's abdication, House had learned that the provisional government's leaders were seriously divided on the question of whether Russia should carry on its fight in the world war, which had produced two million casualties and untold misery and privation on the home front. House's informants, one from England and the other from France, suggested that the United States send a high-level mission to Russia to deliver the message that if the new government made a separate peace with Germany, it would forfeit the goodwill and financial support of the United States.

The idea of sending a mission to Russia appealed to Wilson on several counts: A sprawling new republic of 200 million citizens would do a great deal to make the world safe for democracy. An official visit by representatives of the world's most powerful democracy would undoubtedly impress the Russian people. And the visitors could assess the strength of the new government and Russia's capacity to continue waging the war on the Eastern Front.

McAdoo had the excellent idea that the mission be headed by Elihu Root. Wilson was an intensely partisan president, and the selection of a prominent Republican would assure the Republicans that the administration planned to wage a bipartisan war. Root was also superbly equipped for the assignment—a former senator, secretary of state, and secretary of war as well as a respected authority on international law and a longtime champion of international arbitration.

Root received his presidential summons just after exhorting fellow Republicans to show their patriotism by giving their full support to the president during the war. "We must have no criticism now," he told the Republican Club of New York City. Root found little to admire in Wilson or his New Freedom, but having publicly made the case for standing with the president, he could hardly refuse a presidential request. "You have no idea how I hate it," he wrote Taft, "but it is just like our boys going into the war: there can be no question about doing it."

Root's companions, selected by Lansing and Wilson, included upstanding representatives of American business and finance, labor, the army, the Socialist Party, and the YMCA. They spent five weeks in Petrograd, listening, encouraging, and cajoling. The Russian leaders got the point: no fight, no loan. Although there was nothing unusual about a loan with strings attached, in this instance the United States was asking the impossible. The provisional government needed broad popular support in order to survive, yet nothing in Russia was more unpopular than the war. The new leaders assured the visiting Americans that Russia would not make a separate peace, but Root was skeptical. The war had gone on much longer than expected, Russia was on the verge of bankruptcy, the railway system had collapsed, and the new government faced the opposition of officials in sympathy with Germany. It was rumored that some of these officials were being paid by the Germans.

Along with dozens of other radicals, Vladimir Lenin, who had been in exile in Switzerland, was returned to Russia in April with German assistance. German soldiers on the Eastern Front began fraternizing with the Russians on the other side of the line, spreading the word that the war was not theirs but the czar's, and that with the czar gone, there was no point in continuing the fight. The argument for continuing was that a peace with Germany would be temporary and that when Germany launched its next invasion, Russia, having deserted her Allies, would find herself standing alone. Sound as the argument was, it lacked the appeal of immediate peace, and it required a leap of faith. What if the Allies lost the war?

A few weeks after filing their report, Root and three other members of the mission went to Washington to see Wilson. One of them, the mission's secretary, remembered Wilson as well informed on Russia but ill at ease with Root. The secretary was neither the first nor the last to notice Wilson's discomfort in the presence of formidable public figures. Wilson had nothing to fear from Root, who at seventy-two was out of politics. Both men were passionate about using international institutions to prevent war. But Wilson had had nothing to fear from Balfour, either. What was it? Envy? Competitiveness? Dread of not measuring up?

House, aware of his friend's anxiety and of the bewilderment and ill will it caused, had asked Edith Wilson to use her influence with her husband to broaden his political mind and urge him to consult leading Republicans from time to time. But when he told her that Wilson was undiplomatic, she agreed and said that she was even worse. Both of them shrank from cultivating people they did not like.

Wilson had treated Pershing with the same indifference. Pershing was about to lead the largest army in American history into the most deadly war the world had ever seen, yet when he was taken to the White House to meet the president, the president showed almost no curiosity about him. Baker had suggested putting Pershing in charge, Wilson had given his consent, and that was that. Wilson would involve himself in military affairs as needed but preferred to concentrate on the problem that had absorbed him since the beginning of the war: peace.

25

––––– • • • • • • • • • –––––

The Right Men

Through a combination of executive orders and new laws passed swiftly by Congress, Wilson soon had all the power and organizational machinery he thought he would need to help the Allies win the war. The laws covered the raising of an army, war finance, espionage, control of the nation's food and energy supplies, and restrictions on exports. A day after the declaration of war, Wilson issued Executive Order 2587A, authorizing the heads of federal agencies to fire a civil servant when there were grounds for believing that his continued employment "would be inimical to the public welfare by reason of his conduct, sympathies, or utterances, or because of other reasons growing out of the war." No explanation was required, and the order was kept secret. It is not known how many civil servants were dismissed, but 868 applicants were denied the opportunity to take civil service exams because of questions about their loyalty. Other executive orders put the government in control of areas Wilson deemed crucial to the success of the war, from labor to censorship and propaganda to telegraph and railway lines.

In 1925, looking back on the U.S. contributions to victory, Franklin D. Roosevelt credited the Wilson administration rather than the patriotism and hard work of the American people. "If Wilson and his cabinet ever get historical praise for anything it should be for the very remarkable leadership and direction of public opinion which resulted in the grand effort," he wrote. "It was carefully thought out, the right men . . . were called in, and, in other words, the American organization for war was created *from the top down,* NOT *from the bottom up.* This is most important." Nearly all of the right men were Democrats and acolytes of Woodrow Wilson. They admired his idealism, shared his devotion to the public interest, and dared to hope— as he hoped—that the United States would lead the world to a lasting peace.

As commander in chief, Wilson was ultimately responsible for 4.8 million men in uniform, the largest armed force the United States had ever assembled. But he spent little time with generals or admirals. He did his fighting with the aid of a small band of civilians in Washington, some from his cabinet, the rest appointed for the duration of the war. All were given enormous power, and most had sense enough not to flaunt it. Edicts were few. Officials relied instead on publicity campaigns exhorting citizens to cooperate with government in the interest of winning the war and showing the world that choice, the essence of democracy, was more potent than force.

Even the draft, which is first and last a form of governmental coercion, was given an air of voluntarism. It was brought into being by a new law, the Selective Service Act, which allowed local draft boards composed of civilians to decide whether a man would render more service as a soldier or as a worker in a war-related job. And that, Wilson told the country, was "a new thing and a landmark in our progress. . . . It is in no sense a conscription of the unwilling. It is, rather, selection from a nation which has volunteered in mass."

In the weeks leading up to the declaration of war, Wilson and Baker had envisioned calling for volunteers first and then instituting a draft. But a few days before his war speech to Congress, Wilson scrapped the call for volunteers. He and Baker would maintain that the change was made for practical reasons: conscription would yield more predictable results than a call for volunteers, and once registration was complete, the system would be as manageable as a spigot—turned on when troops were needed and adjusted up or down as casualties or battle plans demanded. England had learned the hard way (and the United States had absorbed the lesson) that when skilled workers volunteered for the battlefield, factory production often suffered.

The Senate needed only two weeks to pass the administration's bill, but the debate in the House dragged on for weeks. Wilson stood fast, refusing all requests for compromise. In a tirade that lasted for more than an hour, the Speaker of the House, Champ Clark, said that he prayed that his son, who had just enlisted, would fight shoulder to shoulder with other volunteers, "not by the side of the slackers and loafers." Some congressmen insisted that conscription had no place in a democracy. Others predicted that the riots sure to follow the passage of a draft law would give heart to the enemy.

The most vehement opposition came from the Southern bloc. Ordinarily, Hubert Dent of Alabama, chairman of the House Committee on Military Affairs, would have been the bill's sponsor, but Dent refused to serve. His fellow Alabamian George Huddleston took to the floor to warn against sinister forces plotting to militarize the United States. Although none of the Southerners dared to give a speech stating the region's real objection to the draft, a few confided it to the army's chief of staff, who shared it with a friend: "they do not like the idea of looking forward five or six years by which time their entire male Negro population will have been trained to arms."

The bill's passage in the House was also delayed by Theodore Roosevelt, who was determined to raise a volunteer force and take it to France despite the fact that Secretary Baker had already rejected the idea. Weeks of jockeying by Roosevelt's friends led Congress to amend the Selective Service Act, empowering Wilson to raise such a force if he wanted one. He did not.

Roosevelt would insist that Wilson had excluded him for political reasons, and Wilson would pretend that he had not. While politics was not the only factor in the president's decision, Wilson rarely made a move without considering its likely effects on the Democratic Party, and he and other Democrats feared that Roosevelt would parlay his service on the Western Front into another presidential nomination.

The draft began on June 5, when men between the ages of twenty-one and thirty were to present themselves at their local polling places to register with their draft boards. Baker, fearing a reprise of the violent resistance to the military officers in charge of the Civil War draft, wanted civilians and local government front and center in raising the millions of American soldiers needed for the war. He also wanted the whole country to treat Registration Day as a patriotic occasion, and with that in mind he called on governors and mayors to organize festivities and urge young men to heed the call. Not that they had a choice. Failure to register was punishable by as much as a year in prison.

The Department of Justice deputized thousands of temporary marshals to stand guard at polling places, but Registration Day proved uneventful. The country's major newspapers reported only four arrests and four antidraft demonstrations. Nearly everywhere the turnout was greater than expected. The state-by-state tallies were awaited as eagerly as presidential election returns, and the final count, 10,264,896, was hailed as the first American victory of the world war.

White planters in the South had opposed the conscription of African Americans on the ground that it would leave them shorthanded in the fields, but the army insisted that its needs took precedence. The first two calls to register for the draft drew a total of 2,290,527 African Americans. But black soldiers quickly learned that answering the call to duty did not guarantee equal treatment in the army. Draft board officials were told to tear off the bottom left-hand corner of any registration form filled out by a black applicant, a step taken with the idea of creating a segregated army. On the day the Selective Service Act was signed, the secretary of war informed the president that the army had plans for a separate training camp, at Fort Dubuque, Iowa, for black soldiers. Secretary Baker went on to say that Howard University, the Hampton Institute, and the Tuskegee Institute were cooperating with the War Department in establishing the camp. Many African Americans hoped that by rising to the defense of their country in wartime, they would inspire the government to eliminate the obstacles to racial equality once peace was restored.

In all, there were three Registration Days, bringing the rolls to 23,900,000 men. Of the 6,400,000 selected for military service, the army took 2,700,000. Another 1,500,000 enlisted, bringing the total number of soldiers in the U.S. Army during the war to 4,200,000, half of whom served in France.

The job of carrying the troops across the Atlantic fell to Secretary Josephus Daniels of the navy, and as the United States entered the war, President Wilson might have been the only one in Washington who believed that Daniels would rise to the challenge. Daniels had been under attack for years—rebuked by Republicans for his pacifism and his initial resistance to the defense buildup, reviled by big business for opening government-run factories to make the navy's gunpowder and armor plate, and resented for banning alcohol from the captain's table and for enabling enlisted men to acquire the knowledge necessary for an officer's commission. Colonel House, fearing that the attacks might cost Wilson the election of 1916, had urged him to fire Daniels. When Wilson refused, one of the publicity men at his campaign headquarters was put to work writing *Wilson and the Issues,* a book-length hosanna to the president. The author, George Creel, later confessed that nine of the book's ten chapters were padding for the one aimed at raising the stock of Josephus Daniels.

Daniels counted himself a champion of the common man, by which he meant the common white man. Willingly, even eagerly, he forced the U.S. Navy to abandon its elitism but showed no interest in ending its virtual exclusion of blacks, who were rarely allowed to serve anywhere but the galley.

To the ambitious young men who worked for him in Washington, Daniels seemed less a modernizer than an old-time Southerner. Day in, day out, he wore a bow tie, shirt with a soft collar, and broad-brimmed hat. His suits were white in summer, black in winter. On foot, in conversation, and in making up his mind, he seemed allergic to speed. Although cordial, he said little, a trait so rare in official circles that it raised questions about his brainpower. But he listened attentively and was a close student of reports prepared by his staff. Subordinates who complained of his procrastination learned that he often waited as a hunter waits, on the alert for the first good moment to bag a senator essential to the success of his next endeavor. Wilson had confidence in the secretary's judgment and no doubt appreciated his loyalty, which was absolute.

The pacifism of Josephus Daniels brought no end of criticism, and the critics seemed not to notice that he set it aside whenever Wilson ordered a military intervention. At Veracruz in 1914, in Haiti in 1915, and in the Dominican Republic in 1916, the navy and the marines (not yet a separate branch of the armed services) had been in the vanguard. The Punitive Expedition had been an army affair, but naval flotillas patrolled Mexico's east and west coasts. Daniels had backed these operations to the full in the belief that unless the United States kept order in the region, it would be vulnerable to the depredations of one imperial power or another. But on March 20, 1917, when Wilson asked each cabinet member to say whether he thought the United States should or should not enter the war, Daniels had been the last to speak and the only one who seemed reluctant to say yes.

Despite his aversion to armed conflict, Daniels had closely followed the world war at sea from the beginning. In the spring of 1917, with their armies still deadlocked on the Western Front, the duel between the British blockade of the North Sea and the U-boat campaign in the waters off Britain appeared to hold the key to final victory. When the United States entered the war, the U-boats were sinking the merchant ships sailing to and from Britain twice as fast as they could be replaced. The Germans were betting that their submarines could win the war before the U.S. Army showed up in force on the Western Front, and Daniels was determined to prove them wrong. At the urging of the British, he suspended a program to build large battle cruisers and focused instead on turning out scores of destroyers and sub-chasers capable of thwarting the U-boats.

No wartime accomplishment of the U.S. Navy pleased Daniels more than the transport of two million American soldiers to France without the loss of a single ship. Convoyed by destroyers as soon as they reached waters menaced by U-boats, the troopships traveled in packs and kept up a zigzag course, making it virtually impossible for a submarine to put itself in position and carry out the preparations needed for a good shot. Merchant ships were also convoyed, keeping losses to one-half of one percent.

Wilson put a globetrotting American engineer named Herbert Hoover in charge of the food supply. Born on an Iowa farm in 1874, Hoover had been orphaned at nine and handed from relative to relative until he finished high school. With the help of a tutor, he managed to get into a new college that charged no tuition, Leland Stanford Junior University in California. To support himself he worked in an office on campus and started a laundry service for students. He graduated in 1895 with a major in geology. After working briefly as a mining engineer in California, he went to Australia as an employee of a British mining concern. The company gave him a raft of assignments in Asia, and in 1902 he decided to settle in London and hire himself out as a mining consultant. In his quiet hours he wrote a textbook that became a perennial bestseller, *Principles of Mining*. He was a canny investor as well. By the time he turned forty, in 1914, he was a millionaire many times over.

Hoover spent the first weeks of the world war as a volunteer at the U.S. embassy in London, helping thousands of stranded American tourists find a way home. He also helped to start a private relief effort to save Belgium from starvation. He donated huge sums to the cause, raised millions more, and as chairman of the organization was soon purchasing $5 million worth of food and medicine each month and managing a fleet of three dozen relief ships. Ambassador Page, an early admirer, wrote Wilson that Hoover was "a simple, modest, energetic man who began his career in California and will end it in Heaven."

As soon as the United States declared war, Hoover sailed home. On May 3 he had an audience in New York with Colonel House, and House wrote Wilson to recommend that Hoover, not Secretary Houston of the Department of Agriculture, be entrusted with the challenge of keeping Americans well fed while increasing food exports to Europe. Hoover had one condition: he wanted absolute authority. House advised Wilson to grant it, explaining that Hoover was "the kind of man that has to have complete control in order to do the thing well."

The president took the colonel's advice and also submitted a bill asking

Congress for the power to control two vital commodities, food and fuel, during the war. When it became apparent that the bill would not be passed without a long fight, Wilson moved ahead without Congress. He put Hoover to work as food administrator and trusted that the Food Administration would follow. Hoover would not be a dictator, Wilson promised. His enormous powers would be exercised only where "some small and selfish minority proves unwilling to put the nation's interests above personal advantage."

Skeptics wondered why the food supply needed any controls at all. American farmers had been feeding their fellow citizens and rounding out the supplies of the Allies and neutrals since the outbreak of the war. But after a lean wheat harvest in 1916, silos were nearly empty, and food prices were headed for the stratosphere. In February 1917, mothers who could not feed their families had taken to the streets in New York and several other cities to protest. Grain reserves in Europe were also dangerously low.

Hoover had three ideas for keeping hunger at bay. The first was to set the price of wheat, the most critical foodstuff, at a point high enough to spur farmers to plant fencepost to fencepost. He also proposed to monopolize the wheat trade through a government-owned grain corporation. With total control of the market, Hoover said, he could prevent hoarding and speculation and end the frenzied international bidding that had driven up the price. Radical as these measures were, they paled beside his third idea. Rather than impose rationing, he wanted to persuade Americans to change their eating habits. He was convinced that if they would voluntarily substitute other grains for wheat and trade their beef and pork for fish and fowl, no one in the United States would go hungry and he could fill the Allies' orders as well.

With Wilson's approval, Hoover reached into every kitchen of the country. Housewives and restaurateurs were asked to become members of the Food Administration and sign a pledge to follow its directives as far as their circumstances allowed. Edith Wilson signed on and, like millions of housewives across the country, complied with Hoover's request to display her membership placard in a front window.

The most remarkable aspect of the idea to ask Americans to change their menus was that it had occurred to Herbert Hoover, a man so unrelievedly pessimistic that Wilson soon came to dread their meetings. Yet Hoover was also confident that he could beguile his fellow Americans into Meatless Mondays and Wheatless Wednesdays, heaping their plates with vegetables, and trying peculiar new foods called "peanut butter" and "cottage cheese."

Hoover succeeded by delegating the charm offensive to a handful of the advertising and public relations men who volunteered in Washington during the war. Taking every opportunity to lionize Hoover so that the public would do as he asked, they peddled the story of the rags-to-riches orphan who became "the almoner of starving Belgium." By the war's end, it would have been hard to find a newspaper reader who did not know that Hoover and his chief aides were serving the government without pay. The publicists supplied an endless stream of statistics illustrating his point that small sacrifices added up, and they persuaded magazines and newspapers to publish recipes (sometimes whole cookbooks) for new dishes. Americans grumbled about having to "Hooverize" their dining, but they did it. Seven of ten households took the Food Administration's pledge.

A nerd and a technocrat before those words entered the language, Herbert Hoover focused intently on whatever had his attention—so intently that he was once observed chewing his way through an entire cigar without thinking to light it. To figure out how to feed the United States, the Allies, and the neutrals, he pored over the Department of Agriculture's statistics, discovered that wheat was the crux of the problem and made wheat the crux of the solution. He let the American people think of themselves as the heroes of his story, and perhaps they were. They made their sacrifices voluntarily, every day for more than a year. Herbert Hoover's Food Administration was one of the home front's greatest successes.

The winter of 1917–1918 was one of the coldest in decades, and by Christmas, the newspapers were full of stories of babies freezing to death in their cribs, frostbitten soldiers in training camps, and shivering city dwellers forced out of their apartment houses and into neighborhood missions and police stations—all for want of coal. There was plenty of coal coming out of the mines, but the carrying capacity of the railroads had been strained to the limit by the demands of the army and navy.

On December 26, Wilson took control of the railroads. For the rest of the war, they would be run by the brand new Railroad Administration, the management of which he added to McAdoo's responsibilities at the Treasury. After weeks of discussion, the two had concluded that the temporary consolidation of hundreds of competing railways into a common national service was the only way to end the chaos, and neither of them could think of an entity other than the federal government capable of running the operation impartially. To the astonishment of many, the railroads did not protest. "On the contrary," McAdoo wrote, "their attitude was distinctly one of relief. . . . They were, speaking frankly, at their wits' end."

The blizzards and subzero temperatures continued, and the coal crisis worsened until January 14, when McAdoo set shipping priorities for the railroads: coal for consumers and public utilities first, food second, and transatlantic ships third. A few days later, the federal government ordered a weeklong shutdown of all factories east of the Mississippi to be followed by ten weeks of five workdays instead of the customary six. Wilson hesitated, fearing that if the plan failed, the coal crisis would be worse than ever. He consented only because no one could think of another solution. In the end, the gamble worked. The railroads were untangled, and the nation's furnaces were fired in an orderly fashion. But the success came at a steep price: billions in lost wages, billions more in lost production.

The Senate's inquiry into the coal fiasco was one of five congressional investigations of the administration's war effort under way as 1918 began. After giving Wilson all the power he had sought in the first months of the war, after voting unprecedented sums for the mobilization, and after waiting for progress that always seemed to be just around the corner, Congress had run out of patience. The most wide-ranging investigation, by the Senate Committee on Military Affairs, had exposed confusion, delays, mistakes, and shortages of practically every necessity of war, from boots and uniforms to arms and ammunition. While the army's procurement officers debated the relative merits of this weapon and that, soldiers were training with wooden rifles and hauling log cannons around their artillery ranges. "Broomstick preparedness," Theodore Roosevelt called it in one of a series of newspaper columns on the chaos in the War Department. Worst of all, waves of disease were sweeping through the training camps. Housed in unheated barracks or damp tents, recruits were vulnerable to meningitis, diphtheria, scarlet fever, and more.

On January 10, after a month of listening to scores of witnesses, the Senate Committee on Military Affairs, chaired by George E. Chamberlain, an Oregon Democrat, summoned Secretary Baker to testify. The questions were brusque, and throughout the three-day interrogation, it was clear that committee members were less interested in explanations than in forcing his resignation. Baker got no credit for all that had gone right: a massive buildup in the rank and file from 200,000 to 1,400,000 men, the commissioning and training of 100,000 new officers, and the construction of sixteen large training camps where hundreds of thousands of recruits had been readied for France. He owned the mistakes but pointed out that many had been corrected. Asked about sickness among the troops, he noted that the death rate had been three times higher in the camps where the army trained soldiers for the Spanish-American War.

Above all, Chamberlain wanted to solve the problems uncovered by his investigation, and he proposed to do it by shifting the management of the war from the president and his secretaries of war and navy to a director of munitions and a three-man war cabinet composed of distinguished outsiders. He and Wilson discussed the idea after Baker's first day of testimony, and the senator could not have been surprised to find the president adamantly opposed. The creation of a war cabinet would tell the country, in the plainest possible terms, that Woodrow Wilson had failed as a war president. Wilson tried to dissuade Chamberlain, but his arguments were vague, and by January 18, Chamberlain had moved his bill through his committee. A day later, at a luncheon in New York, he told a large audience filled with Republicans that "The military establishment of America has fallen down; there is no use to be optimistic about a thing that does not exist; it almost stopped functioning. Why? Because of inefficiency in every department of the Government of the United States."

Wilson sent Chamberlain a frosty note to ask whether he had been correctly quoted. Chamberlain confirmed the quotation but asked Wilson to consider it in the context of his whole speech, which made the point that the current problems were the consequence of a long history of American neglect of military affairs. "All present understood the criticism," Chamberlain wrote, "and you will note that ex-President Roosevelt in his speech shortly following mine made substantially the same criticism of conditions during the Spanish-American War." Chamberlain closed with an offer to meet at any time to review the testimony given at his committee hearings.

Wilson did not want another meeting. He wanted to kill the war cabinet idea, and he struck his first blow in a statement denouncing Chamberlain's speech as "an astonishing and absolutely unjustifiable distortion of the truth" and praising Baker as one of the ablest public officials he had ever known. (Baker had privately offered to resign after Chamberlain's speech, but Wilson would not hear of it.) The president also summoned his Senate stalwarts and asked them to throw their all into the fight against Chamberlain. Although willing, they were pessimistic about the president's chances.

Senator William J. Stone of Missouri, chairman of the Committee on Foreign Relations, tried to help with a long-winded speech accusing congressional Republicans of playing politics with the war and of hoodwinking Chamberlain into doing their dirty work. Lodge reminded Stone that the Republicans had strongly supported the president's war measures.

Chamberlain defended himself against the president's accusations and suggested that Wilson was underinformed. For three hours he illustrated his point by reading from testimony from his committee hearings. The president, meanwhile, was spending the day in his bedroom, felled by a bad cold. The pattern—political crisis, physical illness, seclusion—was familiar.

Chamberlain now had the upper hand, but Wilson was determined not to go down in history as the president who had led his country into a war only to fail as commander in chief. After sizing up the fight, he concluded that Baker would have to redeem himself and that the White House could trump Chamberlain only by proposing its own bill and persuading a hostile Congress to pass it. A few days later, speaking from an outline scrawled on a single sheet of paper, Baker testified again, holding forth for more than four hours. At one point Chamberlain asked the secretary why his earlier testimony had been so much less candid. Baker explained that he had not wanted to give Germany any information it did not already have, and for that reason, he said, he would not disclose how many American troops were in France. But he did reveal that 500,000 more were ready to go whenever there were ships to take them.

While frank about the War Department's errors and false starts, Baker also reminded the committee that the challenges of the war were unprecedented in kind and scope. He had consulted the experts, he said, but they often disagreed. And once in France, the United States faced immense obstacles. The building of barracks, for example, began not with deliveries of wood to a construction site but with the felling of trees and the milling of lumber.

Wilson made his legislative move a week later, asking Senator Lee S. Overman, a North Carolina Democrat who chaired the Judiciary Committee, for the power to reorganize the executive branch and reallocate money as he saw fit. When Overman introduced the bill, the Senate flew into a rage. More than a few of its members said that if they were to give the president such power, they might as well abdicate.

Overman's fight to move the bill through his committee lasted six weeks and was so bitter that he thought he should wait a bit before taking it to the Senate floor. It needed to "soak," he explained to Wilson. "Let the senators consider it and talk about it in the cloakroom, and I think we will stand a better chance." Once on the floor, the bill set off a debate that dragged on for another three weeks, with one side swearing that the bill would give the president more power than the kaiser and the other swearing that the bill's defeat would help the kaiser by keeping the president in shackles.

The impasse ended on April 24, when Chamberlain announced that he would drop his own bill and support the president's. He urged his colleagues to join him, and by then even the Republicans were inclined to let Wilson have his way. With one man in charge of the war effort and free to carry out the task as he saw fit, there would be no plausible alibis for inaction and no one else to blame for mistakes. The Overman Act, passed by wide margins in both houses, enabled the president to reorganize any agency of the executive branch, fire and transfer officials, and move funds from one agency to another as long as they were used for the purpose originally specified by Congress. The new powers were vast but temporary—set to expire six months after the war's end.

Chamberlain had convened his hearings in December 1917, Overman's advocacy of the president's bill began in February, and it took until May 1918 to put the new law on the books. As Wilson waited for it, he appointed Bernard M. Baruch as chairman of the War Industries Board, which had been created to coordinate the government's purchases of all the goods and commodities needed for the war. The appointment was a bold move on several counts. Baruch was a Wall Street speculator with no administrative experience, the business establishment loathed government interference in private enterprise, and Baruch would have more power to interfere than any federal official had ever had.

Wilson took the risk because he believed that the War Industries Board needed an autocrat and that Baruch would make a good one. He had been watching Baruch closely and relying on his advice for more than a year. Baruch had moved to Washington early in 1917, at Wilson's request, to serve on the advisory commission of a lethargic body known as the Council of National Defense. Frustrated by the dithering, Baruch moved ahead on his own. Responsible for the purchase of minerals and raw materials, an area he knew well from his investing, he contacted the two most powerful copper barons of the United States and talked them into selling their ore to the government for less than half the market price. He rested his case on two points. The first was that they were going to make millions anyway, because of massive government spending. The second was that business ought to cooperate in order to show the world that American soldiers were not being asked to fight a war for the rich. The two copper men quickly granted Baruch's request. Other copper companies had no choice but to follow suit. Baruch publicly praised the industry for coming around without a fight.

Wilson unchained the War Industries Board from the Council of National Defense and gave Baruch carte blanche to "guide and assist" the armed forces in allocating contracts, taking control of strategic materials, and accelerating production and delivery schedules. Once Baruch told an industrialist or a general what to do, his dictum could not be appealed except to the president, who nearly always sided with his own men.

Baruch took over the War Industries Board only eight months before the war ended, but he and his lieutenants managed to minimize delays, create order, and conserve untold tons of raw materials. Under Baruch's leadership, munitions and other matériel soon began rolling smoothly off the assembly lines. But it would have taken a miracle to transport all of it to France; the United States never came close to building or borrowing the number of ships needed to fully equip Pershing's army. American soldiers did much of their fighting with arms purchased from the British and the French. The Allies could not keep pace with the demand as the United States scaled up its forces in France. In the words of one judicious historian of the American war effort, "Only the armistice saved the day."

In May 1918, weary of congressional investigations, Wilson asked Charles Evans Hughes to conduct an independent inquiry into the most expensive disaster of the war effort, a billion-dollar aircraft program that had yet to send a single plane to France. Hughes, who had returned to the practice of law after losing the presidential election of 1916, suspected that Wilson had turned to him in order to counter the charge that the White House was running a partisan war, and that was undoubtedly true. But Hughes was also the right man for the probe. As a Republican, he would have no motive to whitewash his findings, he was as rectitudinous as Wilson, and he had risen to national prominence as an investigator of financial scandals. With a team from the Department of Justice, Hughes soon amassed mountains of data and testimony from nearly three hundred witnesses. Their findings, which ran to seventeen thousand pages, boiled down to a simple conclusion: the aviation industry was guilty not of fraud but of colossal ineptitude. The news was disheartening, but it removed the taint of scandal.

William Howard Taft was also drafted in the spring of 1918, for service on the National War Labor Board, a court of last resort for labor disputes. Abandoning his usual practice of putting one man in charge of a new agency, Wilson appointed two, a Democrat and a Republican. The Democrat was Frank P. Walsh, a genial lawyer of liberal persuasions and an old hand at industrial relations. The Republican spot went to Taft, the man Wilson had turned out of the White House in 1912. By all accounts, Taft fully embraced his new role and after a tour of Southern textile mills, he showed labor more sympathy than he had ever done in the past. He ordered the mill owners to double, in some cases triple, their wages. His conservative Republican friends could scarcely believe it when he championed the eight-hour day, the right to unionize, collective bargaining, equal pay for women, and a living wage. No one was more surprised than Taft. All he could think to say about his change of heart was that he had come into "curiously agreeable relations" with the labor representatives on the board.

Quickest and most energetic of the president's men was his son-in-law, William Gibbs McAdoo, who had begun preparing the Treasury for war months before Wilson made up his mind to fight. As a first step McAdoo reread his books on the financing of the Civil War, hoping to find advice and inspiration. Recalling the exercise years later, he wrote, "I did not get much . . . except a pretty clear idea of what not to do." Lincoln's treasury secretary, Salmon P. Chase, had relied on a hodgepodge of expedients born of desperation and had neglected to tap the North's patriotic fervor. "This was a fundamental error," McAdoo thought. "Any great war must necessarily be a popular movement. It is a kind of crusade; and, like all crusades, it sweeps along on a powerful stream of romanticism."

McAdoo tried to estimate the war's cost in advance, but there was no telling how long the war would last, and each new set of financial projections from the army and navy was higher than the last. Ideally, expenses would be met as they were incurred, with tax increases, but it soon became clear that taxes alone would not suffice. The government would also have to borrow, and it fell to McAdoo to find the golden mean. He settled on one-third taxes, two-thirds loans.

By the time Congress declared war, McAdoo had drawn up a bill calling for the largest issue of government securities in the history of the world, a $7 billion package of bonds and short-term notes. He understood that the huge numbers would stagger the congressional imagination but believed that the public interest would be better served by divulging the stupendousness of the undertaking sooner rather than later. McAdoo had a well-deserved reputation for cussing, and when he told the House Ways and Means Committee that the United States would have to lend billions to the Allies in addition to funding its own war, the committee's chairman was floored by the amount of profanity it took to make the simple point that strengthening the Allies would save American lives. But McAdoo received the authority he needed without delay.

That hurdle crossed, McAdoo immediately faced another: the Treasury had never gone to the investing public with a bond offering of even $1 billion. He rejected the obvious alternative, a series of smaller offerings, because he knew that before the ink dried on one set of bonds, he would have to issue another. And another. Also, he wanted to send a big, bold message to Berlin and thought that a war financed in "driblets" would make the United States look weak. In the circumstances, $1 billion seemed like

a driblet, but if he aimed too high, the offering might fail for lack of investors. And that, he thought, would be as demoralizing as a major military
defeat. After consulting some of the country's best financiers, he settled on
$2 billion—an informed guess but still a guess.

McAdoo faced a similar challenge in setting the interest rate on the bonds.
Priced too high, they would inflate the cost of the war; priced too low, they
might go unsold. Both he and Wilson regarded the war as a people's war, a
war for democracy, and McAdoo wanted ordinary citizens, not just the rich,
to buy the bonds. His idea, he wrote, was to build "a financial front which
would rest on the same inspiration as the military front of the army. . . . A man
who could not serve in the trenches in France might nevertheless serve in the
financial trenches at home." McAdoo fixed the price at 3-1/2 percent at a time
when bonds returned an average of 4 percent. He sweetened the offer by ex-
empting the bonds from income tax and promising that if future issues carried
a higher interest rate, bondholders could convert the old ones into the new.

Finally, McAdoo had to figure out how to sell his bonds to a public that
did not know a bond from a stock and regarded both with suspicion. For
this end of the work, William Gibbs McAdoo was superbly equipped. He
was a showman by nature and a salesman by experience, having raised huge
sums to build the first railway tunnels under the Hudson River. He was
good-humored and tenacious, and at six feet, six inches tall had no trouble commanding an audience. He liked people, and people generally liked
him. The notable exception was his father-in-law, who benefited immensely
from McAdoo's exuberance and tenacity but clearly disliked competing for
attention at family gatherings.

Before taking his new product to market, McAdoo gave it a catchy name:
the Liberty Loan. Newspapers, brochures, and advertisements explained that
when a family bought a piece of the Liberty Loan in the form of a Liberty bond,
it was lending money to the U.S. government, not speculating on Wall Street.
The bonds were safe, they earned a solid return, and if a bondholder needed
his money before the bond matured, he could cash it at the corner bank or
the nearest post office. To attract the masses, the Treasury sold the bonds in
denominations as small as $50 and allowed purchases on the installment plan.

Launched on May 2, the Liberty Loan appeared to be an instant success.
Orders flowed into the Treasury at the rate of $1 million an hour on May 3
and swelled to $20 million an hour on May 4. Three days in, when the Trea-
sury announced that $300 million of the bond issue had been sold, the press
rejoiced and speculated that it would be fully subscribed well before the offering closed, on June 15. McAdoo was not ready to celebrate. Nearly all of

the early buyers were big financial institutions, corporations, and wealthy individuals, and he worried that the positive reports in the newspapers would lead ordinary Americans to think that the job was done. He asked Wilson to issue a proclamation urging all citizens to subscribe, and Wilson responded with a $10,000 subscription and a short note that he allowed McAdoo to share with reporters.

Overnight the Treasury began a marketing campaign on a scale never before attempted by the federal government. After the war, when McAdoo boasted that the Treasury had reached nearly every home in the country, he was not exaggerating. He used all the techniques known to the advertising men of the day, from parades and rallies to posters and pamphlets. Post offices began canceling stamps with a message exhorting citizens to buy Liberty bonds, ads for the bonds appeared on mail trucks, and every postman sported a small ad in his hat band. McAdoo created a National Women's Liberty Loan Committee headed by his wife. Women's clubs across the country acted as sales agents. The Boy Scouts of America, 300,000 strong, made a house-to-house canvass on behalf of the bonds. Department stores sold the bonds to employees and shoppers alike, and factories shut down assembly lines so that workers could hear Liberty Loan speeches and make purchases. The Treasury's advertising men appealed to every group it could think of, except blacks. The editors of the *Afro-American* in Baltimore noted the lapse but urged their readers to buy Liberty bonds anyway, "in order that we may measure up to the standard of good citizenship."

Not wanting a penny of the $2 billion loan to go unsold, McAdoo made sure that it was oversubscribed. He stumped the country as if he were running for president, explaining how the bonds worked and why the money was needed. Somewhere in his travels, the Liberty Loan became known as the First Liberty Loan. Oversubscribed by $1 billion, it attracted four million investors. With a few months to prepare for the Second Liberty Loan, McAdoo was able to mount a sales campaign that would do even more to capitalize on the emotion of the people. By the time the second loan went to market, 150,000 American soldiers were in Europe, and hundreds of thousands more were in training camps. McAdoo took it as axiomatic that the parents of soldiers in France would not hesitate to buy the bonds if the need for the money was well explained. In all, his four Liberty Loans, two in 1917 and two in 1918, raised nearly $17 billion, $7 billion of which was lent to the Allies. The government spent $24.3 billion during the two fiscal years that began July 1, 1917, about one third from taxes and two thirds from borrowing. McAdoo had guessed right.

But neither McAdoo nor his successor, who raised another $4.5 billion in a 1919 Victory Loan, accurately reckoned the total bill for of the war. A decade later, the Treasury put the cost at $37.5 billion, which included the principal and ten years' worth of interest on the Allied loans. The Allies borrowed a total of $9.5 billion from the United States, and by 1930 they owed $11.3 billion. McAdoo became the scapegoat. When his critics said that the loans had been gifts in disguise, he pointed out that the Allies had signed loan agreements. With the entire world mired in the Great Depression, he understood that European exchequers could not simply hand over the money. Still, it galled him to hear Europeans refer to Uncle Shylock and complain about American greed. He was angry enough to devote a chapter of his memoir to the Allied loans, and while he managed not to swear, he damned them all: "It is well, in considering these baseless aspersions, to remember that the United States is the only nation arrayed against Germany that did not seek or receive indemnities or colonies when the war was over."

Wilson's management of the war was not perfect, and his decision to champion U.S. neutrality until the last possible moment forced his lieutenants into a mad scramble when war was declared. Most of them had given serious thought to the actions they would have to take in the event of war, but Wilson's refusal to allow them to make any visible move suggesting an abandonment of neutrality caused innumerable delays. American forces ultimately proved vital in curbing the U-boats and ending the stalemate on the Western Front, and Wilson was hailed in London, Paris, and Rome as the leader who saved the world from the kaiser. If the Allies had lost, Woodrow Wilson would have been remembered as one of the worst presidents in American history. But luck was with him. The Americans arrived just in time. The credit for that belongs to Robert Lansing, who had persuaded Wilson to make war in the name of democracy, the only rationale the president could stomach. Newton D. Baker amassed an army of more than four million in a year's time. Josephus Daniels proved nimble and shrewd in deploying the navy. Bernard Baruch and Herbert Hoover gave industry and agriculture their marching orders and kept them on the march. William G. McAdoo figured out how to fund the American war effort and simultaneously stave off the insolvency of the Allies. As chief executive of the mobilization, Wilson deserves credit for two things: talking the war Congress into a vast but temporary expansion of presidential power and making excellent use of the right men.

26

·············

One White-Hot Mass Instinct

The United States had been at war with Germany and Austria for only a week when Wilson took aim at the enemies within: spies and saboteurs, pacifists and protesters, and others suspected of disloyalty. This war, for the hearts and minds of the American people, would be waged by the Justice Department, the Post Office, and a new agency called the Committee on Public Information (CPI). Though the name seemed to promise that the committee would keep the public informed, the CPI's real missions were censorship and propaganda. Wilson established the CPI with an executive order signed on April 13, 1917.

At the suggestion of Josephus Daniels, Wilson gave the chairmanship of the CPI to George Creel. Energetic, imaginative, and persuasive, Creel had made himself useful during Wilson's reelection campaign, and he had suggested himself for the job of censor if the United States entered the war. "I know I could fill it better than anybody else," he told Daniels. "I know the newspaper game, I can write, I have executive ability, and I think I have the vision."

Creel's first big task was to assure the press that the administration favored "expression, not suppression" and to voice his belief that most of the censoring would be done by the newspapers themselves. In a preliminary statement to the press, he stressed the importance of the free flow of information in a democracy and said he had no wish to censor anything but news that would help the German army—news of troop movements, for example.

When the press grumbled, Creel decided to concentrate on his duties as propagandist in chief. Like Wilson, he was certain that the survival of civilization depended upon America's success on the battlefield. Writing after the war, Creel said that in the spring of 1917, Americans had not been of one mind about the war. As he remembered it, millions were angry, full of ethnic prejudices, and unsure what to believe—a situation "that could not be permitted to endure. What we had to have was no mere surface unity, but a passionate belief in the justice of America's cause that should weld the people of the United States into one white-hot mass instinct," a nation united by a "*war-will,* the will-to-win."

To Creel, the CPI was not a ministry of propaganda but "a vast enterprise in salesmanship," an undertaking that emphasized the positive and "the simple, straightforward presentation of facts." The latter claim became the subject of debate, but no one challenged his description of the CPI's reach: "There was no part of the great war machinery that we did not touch, no medium of appeal that we did not employ. The printed word, the spoken word, the motion picture, the telegraph, the cable, the wireless, the poster, the sign-board—all these were used in our campaign to make our own people and all other peoples understand the cause."

The CPI was run on a shoestring by a small paid staff and a massive army of volunteers—150,000 in all. In some ways it resembled a government bureaucracy, with offices to help the foreign-born, answer queries from the public, and sustain the morale of the troops. In other respects it was like a media conglomerate, with divisions for news, syndicated features, advertising, film, and public speaking; subdivisions for still photographs, pictorial publicity (posters and cartoons), and film distribution. At Wilson's insistence, the CPI also published the *Official Bulletin,* an executive branch approximation of the *Congressional Record.*

Creel flooded the country with information. At one point newspapers were receiving six pounds of CPI material a day. Nearly all war "news" was announced by the government through the CPI, and editors eager to show their patriotism published reams of it verbatim. From grumbling about Creel's censorship, the press moved on to grumbling that he was monopolizing the news. The CPI also produced movies, collaborated with movie studios, and distributed American films abroad. Creel and his movie brigade dramatized American ideals, captured everyday life in the United States, showed off the army and navy, and assured families that their boys were well cared for. More inclusive than McAdoo, Creel authorized the making of one film about black soldiers and another featuring the contributions of blacks on the home front.

The bulk of the CPI's publicity was propaganda of the cheerleading variety: salutes to America's wartime achievements and celebrations of American ideals. But the president's second Flag Day address, on June 14, 1917, brought a sharp increase in propaganda calculated to spread fear and outrage. While American liberals worried about the consequences of unthinking patriotism, Wilson and his cabinet sensed that the public was still unenthusiastic about the war and unconvinced of the dangers they faced. There had been no attack on American soil, and once it became clear that Mexico and Japan would not accept the German government's invitation to invade the United States, many Americans doubted that Germany posed an imminent threat. Fear, hatred of the enemy, war-will—all had to be manufactured.

Speaking in a downpour at the Washington Monument, the president noted that the United States was about to carry the Stars and Stripes into battle and call untold numbers of men to "die beneath it on fields of blood far away." And for what? he asked. His answer took the form of an unsparing indictment of Germany—for its acts of aggression against the United States, its militarism, and its quest for world domination. The Imperial German Government was now the only villain on Wilson's horizon, and its villainy had left the United States to choose sides. It had done so and, he said, "Woe be to the man or group of men that seeks to stand in our way."

Germany's defeat would enable George Creel to boast that the CPI had been instrumental in winning the war, and boast he did, in an official report to the president and a long book, *How We Advertised America: The First Telling of the Amazing Story of the Committee on Public Information That Carried the Gospel of Americanism to Every Corner of the Globe.* Neither acknowledged that in the course of fusing the country into a white-hot mass, the CPI filled Americans with a hatred for all things German and led self-appointed guardians of patriotism to harass thousands of pacifists, socialists, and German immigrants who had chosen not to become citizens. Even the most casual expression of qualms about the war could result in a beating and the humiliation of being made to kiss the flag in public. People who declined to buy Liberty bonds sometimes awoke to find their homes streaked with yellow paint. Several Mennonite churches, which preached pacifism, were set ablaze. The University of Texas fired every German alien on its staff. Wilson privately deplored such actions but declined to protest until the war was almost over. He never acknowledged the part that his Flag Day speech had played in legitimizing the animosity.

The day after the speech, Wilson signed the Espionage Act, which invested the postmaster general and the attorney general with enormous power to stifle dissent. The new law made it a crime to "cause or attempt to cause" insubordination or resistance in the armed forces or to obstruct recruiting or enlistment. Offenders were subject to fines of as much as $10,000 and prison sentences of up to twenty years. The postmaster general was soon given even more power, under the Trading with the Enemy Act, which required editors of American newspapers published in foreign languages to furnish the Post Office with an English translation of every article they wished to print about the U.S. government or any nation involved in the war. The financial burden was so onerous that many of the papers suspended publication.

Postmaster General Albert S. Burleson moved against the heretics as soon as the Espionage Act took effect. He had no authority to shut them down, but he could bar printed matter from the mails and could revoke second-class mailing permits, which gave newspapers and magazines a heavily discounted postage rate. One of his first targets was *The Milwaukee Leader,* a socialist paper that decried war. Its editor, Victor Berger, was a former member of the U.S. House of Representatives, and in the *Leader* he had criticized Wilson's decision to abandon neutrality, accused Congress of being no more than a rubber stamp for the president, and argued that the United States was fighting to make the world safe for capitalism. He had also voiced his objections to the idea of conscription, although he stopped short of advocating resistance to the draft.

When the Post Office informed the *Leader* that it was obstructing the war effort, Berger reminded Burleson that Americans had a long and honorable tradition of opposing war. Burleson was unmoved. After a hearing conducted by a postal official, he withdrew the *Leader*'s second-class mailing privileges, a move that octupled the paper's postage expenses. Forced to increase its subscription rates, the *Leader* quickly discovered that thousands of readers were unwilling or unable to pay.

Protests streamed into the White House, and when Wilson forwarded one of them to Burleson, Burleson responded by sharing a transcript of the hearing, which contained excerpts from the *Leader* that in his mind demonstrated the paper's subversive character. "I am afraid you will be shocked," Wilson replied, "but I must say that I do not find this hearing very convincing." Burleson pointed out that he was not ordering any paper to cease publication. Publishers denied the second-class mailing rate or access to the mails were free to deliver their papers by other means, and those who felt unjustly treated by the government could seek redress in the courts. Wilson retreated.

Burleson also moved quickly against *The Masses,* which billed itself as a magazine of revolutionary opinion. Based in Greenwich Village, it published the leading radicals of the day. Wilson had scant regard for socialism, but he saw the editor of *The Masses,* Max Eastman, as well intentioned, and he urged Burleson to take a broad view. "Let them blow off some steam," he said. Burleson, a master of doubletalk, answered that he did not object to steam but either had to enforce the Espionage Act or resign. Wilson did not press him to reconsider, nor did he protest when the August 1917 issue of *The Masses* was barred from the mails because of four cartoons and a poem that seemed to Burleson to promote "insubordination, disloyalty, mutiny or refusal of duty in the military or naval forces." After a long legal battle, *The Masses* folded.

In all, Burleson censored seventy-five small papers either by withdrawing their second-class permits or barring them from the mails. Forty-five were socialist organs, opposed to all wars on principle. Most of the rest were papers published in German or Gaelic. As Eastman noted, Burleson aimed nearly all of his attacks at "helpless small-fry." Other small-fry got the point and muzzled themselves. Along with most mainstream newspapers, they waved the flag on every conceivable occasion and all but abandoned the defense of free speech. Far from the public-spirited voluntary censorship that Creel had envisioned, it was a supine concession to Burleson's power.

As Burleson and postmasters across the country combed printed matter for signs of disloyalty, the attorney general of the United States, Thomas Watt Gregory, rounded up spies, saboteurs, and subversives real and imagined. Gregory had had no more preparation for war than anyone else in Wilson's cabinet. He was an antitrust lawyer and, like Burleson, a Texan and an associate of Colonel House. In the 1890s, when House helped one Democrat after another into the Texas governorship, Gregory steered the governors toward policies friendly to big business, the mainstay of his legal practice. It was House who persuaded Gregory to back Wilson in 1912 and House who suggested that Wilson put him in the cabinet. Gregory had taken over the Justice Department in 1914, when Wilson's first attorney general went to the Supreme Court.

Moving as quickly as Burleson, Gregory opened his war for national unity with a series of sensational trials involving German agents and well-known American radicals. Emma Goldman and Alexander Berkman—lovers, anarchists, and vocal opponents of conscription—were arrested on the day Wilson signed the Espionage Act. Saboteurs conspiring to dynamite factories, bridges, and ships were convicted, as was a ring of German agents caught raising an army of Hindu immigrants to return to India and lead a revolt against British rule. At the end of 1917 Attorney General Gregory proudly reported that every one of his espionage and sabotage cases had resulted in at least one conviction. He hoped that the verdicts would serve as a deterrent, but in case would-be traitors missed the point, he made it explicit in a speech: "May God have mercy on them, for they need expect none from an outraged people and an avenging government."

In fact, the avenging government was drowning in work. The country had been scared out of its wits by the propaganda of the CPI and a preposterous but persistent rumor that as many as 300,000 foreign agents were on the loose in the United States. Every day brought hundreds of reports of suspicious characters, all of which required some degree of investigation. Gregory established a War Emergency Division and quintupled the staff of his Bureau of Investigation, and in anticipation of the war's demands, he made the surprising decision to accept an offer of help from a forty-two-year-old advertising man named Albert M. Briggs. Founder and head of a voluntary organization called the American Protective League (APL), Briggs had recruited 250,000 members in no time by appealing to the cloak-and-dagger fantasies of middle-aged businessmen. For seventy-five cents, a man who joined the APL would be enrolled in its Secret Service Division and receive an impressive badge. The men who joined were much like Briggs: middle-class, too old for the army but eager to serve, and titillated by the thought of chasing spies.

Alert to the risks of unleashing a vast counterespionage force composed of amateurs, Gregory wrote several precautions into his agreement with Briggs. He provided a modicum of supervision by linking the APL's six hundred chapters to Justice Department field offices, and he confined the league to surveillance work. APL members were to investigate suspicious characters and report to their field offices, nothing more. Gregory also blurred the nature of the relationship between the Justice Department and the APL, allowing the league to maintain its independence even as he declared that it would operate under his department's direction. The equivocation enabled him to back the league when it served his purposes but disavow it if necessary.

The first serious complaint about the APL came from one of Gregory's cabinet colleagues, William Gibbs McAdoo. As treasury secretary, McAdoo was in charge of the real Secret Service, and as he told Gregory, the APL's Secret Service Division and its badges would make for "misunderstanding, confusion, and even fraud." When McAdoo shared his concerns with Wilson, Wilson registered an even deeper objection. "It seems to me," he wrote Gregory, "that it would be very dangerous to have such an organization operating in the United States." Gregory assured the president that the league was an upstanding group of patriots doing excellent work at no expense to the government. Wilson let it go. Gregory was to have as much latitude as Burleson.

Respectful to Wilson, Gregory was positively surly with McAdoo. The badges of the Secret Service and the Secret Service Division were nothing alike, he said, and Briggs had told him that new badges would cost thousands of dollars. "I know of no authority I have to instruct this organization to destroy these badges," Gregory went on, "and on account of the efficient work they are doing and the tremendous importance of having good citizens of the class involved cooperate with the government in the manner in which these people are doing, I should hesitate to issue such instructions even if I had the power."

Neither argument held a drop of water. Few citizens had ever seen a Secret Service badge, and the idea that the attorney general would have no say over the matter was preposterous. Clearly, Gregory wanted the public to be confused about the APL's authority. Otherwise he would not have countenanced the Secret Service Division or its badges, nor would he have allowed Briggs to establish an Investigation Bureau, which was sure to be mixed up with the Justice Department's Bureau of Investigation.

The spat dragged on for months before McAdoo cornered Gregory with the obvious: "if I were a German spy, I should want nothing better than the opportunity of joining this organization, getting one of its 'Secret Service' badges, and carrying on my nefarious activities." Gregory surrendered, banning the phrase "Secret Service Division" from the APL's printed materials and ordering that no new Secret Service Division badges be issued.*

But there was no order to turn in the old ones, and APL members continued to use them to intimidate bankers and others into sharing confidential information, crash political meetings, and bluff their way into office

---

* The confusion between the Secret Service Division and the Secret Service literally followed Briggs to the grave. His obituary in *The New York Times* (March 6, 1932) stated that he had worked for the Secret Service during the war.

buildings after hours in order to photograph the files of persons of interest. After the war the APL claimed that it had conducted three million investigations, yet it had failed to turn up even one spy. Although Gregory had misgivings about the League, he always praised it in public. In a report written at the end of the war, he boasted that the country had never been so thoroughly policed.

But thorough policing did not ensure the public order, and the war brought on an epidemic of mob justice. On July 12, 1917, a vigilante force of two thousand armed men rounded up 1,186 striking copper miners in Bisbee, Arizona, herded them into boxcars, and shipped them to New Mexico, where they were left boxed up in the desert sun without food or water. When the news reached the White House that evening, Wilson was at the theater, and Tumulty decided to consult the secretary of war instead of the attorney general. Tumulty's choice probably saved the miners' lives. Rather than ponder the question of whether federal or state authorities should intervene, Secretary Baker simply sent the cavalry to the rescue.

Wilson deplored the incident but rather than press Gregory on the matter, he appointed a commission to investigate, mediate, and advise. When the commission recommended that the vigilante leaders and the mine owners who had paid them be indicted by the Justice Department, Gregory declined to charge the mine owners, the preparation of the case against the vigilantes proceeded at a snail's pace, and a federal judge eventually quashed the indictment.

For Gregory, Bisbee was not about civil liberties but about the power of strikers to sabotage the war effort. Most of the Bisbee miners belonged to the country's most radical labor union, the Industrial Workers of the World (IWW), which was philosophically opposed to war and frank in its ambition to abolish capitalism. The IWW had been involved in more than a hundred strikes since its founding in 1905 and had often been accused (though never convicted) of industrial sabotage. By 1917 it had powerful enemies who were determined to use the war and the Bisbee strike to crush the IWW. Rumors took wing: the strike was said to be the work of German provocateurs, and the strikers were said to be bad citizens, brazenly exploiting the war for selfish purposes.

The White House, the Capitol, and the Justice Department were flooded with demands for action against the IWW, and in early August, in the midst of a strike at copper and zinc mines in Montana, a posse of masked men hauled an IWW leader out of bed in the middle of the night and lynched him. Washington professed shock, but by that point Gregory was well launched on a plan to liquidate the IWW. With Wilson's approval and the help of the APL, the Justice Department had piled up evidence for a mass trial of IWW leaders. At three o'clock on the afternoon of September 5, federal agents raided IWW offices in thirty-three cities, seizing files and making arrests. A few weeks later 166 IWW leaders were charged with conspiring to obstruct the draft and disrupt the production and transportation of war supplies. Ninety-nine defendants went to trial, and it took the jury less than an hour to convict them on all counts.

Gregory had hoped that the IWW trial would end mob rule by showing the vigilantes that the federal government had the subversives under control. The pundits got the point, but the vigilantes did not. In Tulsa, a masked mob took seventeen union members to a spot outside town, where they were stripped, tied to trees, whipped raw, tarred and feathered, and sent packing. Elsewhere, vigilantes continued to rough up German aliens, radicals, pacifists, and anyone else whose patriotism seemed less than white-hot. The problem grew steadily worse, in part because the vigilantes were rarely punished. Juries were afraid to bring in a verdict of guilty—afraid of retribution and of being seen as opponents of the war.

Gregory could think of only one remedy: a law that would give him and Burleson even more power than they had under the Espionage Act. He got it in the spring of 1918 by capitalizing on two disturbing events: Russia's exit from the war and a lynching in Illinois. With the realization that 350,000 German troops in Russia would soon be transferred to the Western Front, American super-patriotism swelled into outright paranoia. One of the first victims of this new phase of the war was a young German alien, Robert Paul Prager, a baker's assistant in Collinsville, Illinois. He was lynched on April 5, and when the facts were in, it was clear to the attorney general and the president that Prager had not been guilty of anything. Far from opposing the war or sympathizing with Germany, he had tried to join the U.S. Navy, but was turned down because of a glass eye. Nevertheless, Prager's killers were speedily acquitted.

The drive to fuse Americans into a white-hot mass instinct of war-will had perverted a wholesome love of country into hatred of everything deemed un-American. Wilson shook his head in dismay when high schools stopped teaching German and German music disappeared from concert programs, but he did nothing to discourage such practices.

George Creel, who had not foreseen where the CPI's "savage Hun" propaganda might lead, blamed the war madness and the lynch mobs on the newspapers. "The press, from which we had the right to expect help, failed us miserably," he wrote years later. "One alien speaking disrespectfully of the flag could be sure of front-page notice, but ten thousand aliens could gather in a great patriotic demonstration without earning an agate line." Upset by Prager's death, Creel had gone to see Wilson at once, and as he remembered it, Wilson's "public denunciation of the mob spirit sobered the people as a whole, if not the super-patriots." But Creel's memory failed him. Wilson did not raise his voice against the mobs for months.

Capitalizing on the outrage over Prager's death, Gregory asked Congress to strengthen the Espionage Act so that the federal government, not the states, would have jurisdiction over allegations of disloyalty. He understood that his remedy would be seen as drastic, but without it, he said, the lynching would continue and the result would be "a condition of lawlessness from which we will suffer for a hundred years." Under the amended law, it would be illegal to display enemy flags, make false statements intended to hamper U.S. forces or help the enemy, encourage disruptions of industrial production, discourage the sale of Liberty bonds, and publicly utter any word or deed favoring the enemy or opposing the cause of the United States. Most drastic of all, the amendment would ban "any disloyal, profane, scurrilous, or abusive language about the form of the United States government, or the Constitution of the United States, or the military or naval forces of the United States."

In the Senate, those in favor of the new provisions argued that in a time when American soldiers were risking their lives for the Constitution, it was not unreasonable to ask for total devotion on the home front. Opponents could hardly believe their ears. If the new measures were passed, Americans who voiced any negative opinion about the government or the conduct of the war risked fines of up to $10,000 and twenty years in prison. California's new Republican senator, Hiram W. Johnson, was equally perturbed. He appreciated that the country was at war, he said, "But good God, Mr. President, when did it become war upon the American people?" In the end, yeas outnumbered nays by nearly two to one in the Senate, and the House recorded only one nay, from Meyer London of New York, a member of the Socialist Party. Wilson signed the amendments (commonly known as the Sedition Act) on May 16, 1918.

The new strictures did nothing to curb the vigilantes, and the Justice Department was soon swamped with reports of sedition, sometimes 1,500 a day. The U.S. attorney for the Northern District of Ohio, Edwin Wertz, immediately tried to do to the Socialist Party what Gregory had done to the IWW. Wertz informed the Justice Department in June that he wanted to press charges against the party's leader, Eugene V. Debs, for remarks he had made in the course of an address to the party's state convention in Canton.

Most of the speech was a fond look at the Socialist Party's role in American politics and a call to continue standing up to "the political twins of the master class"—the Republicans and the Democrats. But he also lashed out against war profiteers and blamed their "gold-dust lackeys" in government for prosecuting Socialists who dared to protest the war. "The truth has always been dangerous to the rule of the rogue, the exploiter, the robber," he said. "So the truth must be ruthlessly suppressed." Debs reminded his listeners that the people never had a voice in declaring war. "If war is right, let it be declared by the people," he said. "You who have your lives to lose, you certainly above all others have the right to decide the momentous issue of war or peace."

The head of the Justice Department's War Emergency Division told Wertz that the case against Debs struck him as flimsy, but Wertz could not resist the chance to put the country's leading Socialist behind bars. So Debs was arrested in July and soon found guilty of three charges: obstructing the draft; attempting to incite "insubordination, disloyalty, mutiny, and refusal of duty in the military and naval forces"; and using language "intended to incite, provoke, and encourage resistance to the United States and to promote the cause of the enemy." He was sentenced to three concurrent ten-year sentences.

Summing up his war against subversives in a letter to Wilson, Gregory wrote that he had had to walk a narrow path between super-patriots who wished to prosecute any criticism of the government and free speech extremists who objected to any prosecution of dissent. "The fact that our course is not satisfactory to either side is one of the best evidences that we are about right," Gregory said. But when his Justice Department boasted that it won half of its espionage and sedition cases (1,055 of 2,168), civil libertarians cited the conviction rate as evidence that half of the accused had been prosecuted for no good reason. Soon after the war's end, Gregory asked Wilson to commute more than a hundred sentences, explaining that injustices had occurred because of "intense patriotism and aroused emotion on the part of the jurors." Wilson gave his consent. Debs was not on Gregory's list.

There had been a time—July 4, 1902, to be precise—when Woodrow Wilson publicly declared that American patriotism flourished on "the right of every man to speak his real conviction and to conform to the opinion of nobody." The flag that Americans honored on their holidays had "started in a kick, in a rebellion, in a dissent," he said, "and if a man living under that flag has not the right to dissent, there is no flag that floats in the world under which men can utter their difference from the majority of their fellow men. That flag is the flag of freedom of opinion."

Although Wilson never explained the gulf between his old reverence for free speech and his willingness to let Burleson and Gregory silence dissent that posed no real threat to the Republic, the reasons are easily divined. In his run for a second term, Wilson had allowed his campaign to imply that the man who had kept the country out of war would continue to do so. When he sought a declaration of war only one month into his new term, millions of Americans felt betrayed. Wilson understood that, but he also understood that his war could not be won unless it became their war, too. In his war address, he had predicted that only a malignant few would stand in the way of a great nation fighting unselfishly to make the world safe for democracy. But he also fired a warning: "If there should be disloyalty, it will be dealt with a firm hand of stern repression."

With few exceptions, Wilson stood by as the firm hand carried out an unprecedented assault on the civil liberties of those who opposed the war. Creel's super-patriotism set off a wave of terror, and Gregory's Sedition Act made it worse. Freedom of speech was no longer a right but a privilege to be affirmed or denied by the federal government. Freedom from unreasonable search and seizure ceased to exist. Burleson, Gregory, and Creel would escape largely unscathed. Wilson would not. He is still remembered as the president who repressed dissent more often and more harshly than any other occupant of the White House.

27

Over Here, Over There

In the fall of 1917, as Wilson tended the home front, Colonel House headed to Europe. Once again he would serve as Wilson's personal envoy, but for the first time he was traveling as head of a delegation, the American equivalent of the European missions that had come to Washington in the spring. Determined to speed the transport of American troops to Europe, the British offered the visitors every comfort. House was put up in a handsome home on loan from a duke.

The Royal Navy was finally sinking U-boats faster than they could be replaced, but the Allied armies had had a devastating year. Hoping to end the standoff on the Western Front, the French and the British launched massive offensives in the spring and summer. Their ground gains were negligible, their casualties appalling—in the range of 500,000. House and his entourage reached London on the heels of two more catastrophes. The Austrian army had just plowed through the Italian line at Caporetto, inflicting 40,000 casualties and taking 265,000 prisoners. Fifteen hundred miles to the north, in Petrograd, the Bolsheviks overthrew the provisional government of Russia and announced that Russia would leave the war. On its first full day in office, the new regime issued a decree calling on all the peoples and governments at war to open negotiations for a peace without territorial annexations or financial indemnities.

The Allies responded to the Italian disaster by creating the Supreme War Council and devising a unified military strategy. Heretofore, each country had planned its own operations. General Pershing supported the change, as did General Tasker H. Bliss, who was traveling with House and would soon give up his post as the army's chief of staff in order to represent the United States in the new council.

The Italians regrouped, but even if the Allies managed to hang on, casualties were likely to be high, and nearly every able-bodied Frenchman and Briton had already been called up. In Berlin, as in London and Paris, all eyes were on the Americans, and the question was whether Germany could destroy the Allies before the Americans' long-promised million-man army was ready to fight.

The danger was acute, Pershing wrote Washington at the end of November 1917. With their reinforcements from the Russian front, the Germans would outnumber the Allies by five to three on the Western Front. A German offensive would further thin the Allied ranks, he wrote, "and the longer the war continues the greater will the demands on America become." If the Allies and the United States did not find more ships to carry American troops to France, the war would probably be lost.

Bliss agreed with Pershing. Neither the president nor the secretary of war disagreed with the generals, but the United States and Britain would haggle for months over which ships would be diverted for troop transport, which troops would be sent first, and where the Americans would serve. Pershing was still determined to build an army as independent as those of the French and the British, and he wanted his 27,000-man divisions to travel intact, train intact, and fight intact. The French and British begged Pershing for the troops they needed most, battalions of infantry and artillery. The Allies promised to give the Americans a few weeks of instruction and experience, then return them to the American Expeditionary Force (AEF). When House and his delegation got to France, Georges Clemenceau, the new premier, warned the colonel that if the American troops did not study with the French army, they would learn the hard way, at the hands of the Germans.

Wilson had authorized Pershing to put his troops into the Allied lines if he thought it necessary, but Pershing refused for a host of reasons, all of them hypothetical: The American people would not like their soldiers fighting under foreign flags. The popular disapproval would stir political opposition to the administration's conduct of the war. German propagandists would ridicule the world's largest democracy for putting its troops into armies fighting for monarchs and colonial empires. Moving battalions from one army to another and back would slow the work of fine-tuning the operations of the AEF. National differences in military methods would sow confusion.

Pershing also feared that if his infantrymen and machine-gunners went into French or British lines, he would never get them back. The writer John Dos Passos, who drove a field ambulance and served as an army medic during the war, explained why: "None of the Allies wanted an independent American army; what they wanted was American cannon fodder."

House understood the Allies' desperation, but during his travels in England and France he seemed more concerned with peace than war. While the Allied governments wondered how their armies could survive the next German onslaught, House was dreaming of peace and imagining that if the right words could be found, he could hasten the war's end. In meetings with Lloyd George, Clemenceau, and others, he campaigned for a high-minded joint statement assuring the world that they were fighting not for selfish interests but for the end of militarism and a future in which all nations would have the right to live as they saw fit, as long as they did not threaten the world's peace. The French told him that it was premature to speak of peace. As Clemenceau would soon put it, "My home policy: I wage war; my foreign policy: I wage war. All the time I wage war."

The colonel decided to urge the president to make the declaration on his own. In House's mind, Wilson was the ideal spokesman for a just peace because the United States was the only Great Power not hoping for spoils of war. Still, the Allies' rejection stung, and his diary grew increasingly critical of their conduct of the war. On December 1, at the first meeting of the Supreme War Council, he watched in frustration as Britain and France quarreled over whose general ought to be in charge of the unified command. For House, the quarrel summed up the central military problem of the war: the German army was not inherently superior, but it was better organized and more methodical.

But even as the colonel privately lambasted the Allied leaders for putting national interests ahead of their urgent common need, he followed their example. When Lloyd George suggested that the United States join the Allies in appointing a permanent representative to the political wing of the Supreme War Council, House declined, not wanting to drag the United States into squabbles that might jeopardize the independence it enjoyed as an Associate. Bliss readily agreed when House suggested that they attend the council's meeting as observers, gathering information but taking no positions.

The colonel sailed home on December 8 with mixed feelings about his mission. The Allies had showered him with praise. But his dealings with the Allied leaders had left him discouraged. "The armies and navies are fighting with courage and tenacity," he told his diary, ". . . but what is lacking is some great executive mind at the head to bring together these elements of strength and make them as great a force against the Germans as is necessary to win the war." House believed that the great executive mind belonged to Woodrow Wilson.

On December 17, two days after reaching the United States, the colonel was at the White House, hoping to talk the president into making the declaration that the Allies had spurned. Wilson agreed at once. "I never knew a man who did things so casually," House marveled in his diary. "We did not discuss this matter more than ten or fifteen minutes when he decided he would take the action."

But there was nothing casual about Wilson's decision. He had refused to recognize the Bolsheviks' government and had been fretting about their leaders for weeks. He thoroughly disapproved of their communism, their coup, their seizure of American property in Russia, and their renunciation of the treaties and the debts of their predecessors. Russia and Germany had just signed an armistice, and Wilson shared the Allies' worry that Germany's Eastern armies would reach the Western Front before the AEF was ready to fight. He could not singlehandedly speed American troops to France, but he could give an address aimed at rousing the conscience of the world and persuading the Russians to stand by the Allies.

The president asked the colonel for a memorandum on the issues most likely to arise when the Allies and the United States sat down to discuss their peace terms. House knew that the Allies' secret treaties about the spoils of war would figure in any peace talks, and he offered to list these and other issues off the top of his head. Wilson, wanting details and recommendations in hand, asked House to get them from the Inquiry, a study group organized to collect and analyze information for Wilson's eventual use at a peace conference. House was the nominal head of the Inquiry, and he had delegated its management to his brother-in-law, Sidney Mezes, president of City College in New York.

House summoned the Inquiry's secretary, Walter Lippmann of *The New Republic,* and explained that Wilson wanted material for an address that would lay out general terms for a lasting peace and try to persuade Russia to return to the war. Years later, describing the task, Lippmann said that he and his colleagues were asked to "take the secret treaties, analyze the parts which were tolerable, and separate them from those which we regarded as intolerable, and then develop an American position which conceded as much to the Allies as it could, but took away the poison. Each point was constructed for that purpose. It was all keyed upon the secret treaties." By working around the clock, the Inquiry team completed its assignment in three days.

The colonel carried the memorandum to Washington two days before Christmas, but Wilson was preoccupied with the Senate's investigation of the war effort, the coal shortage, and the emergency nationalization of the railroads. Wilson faced every challenge without flinching and was keeping himself in good physical shape on the golf course, but the pressures were sometimes unbearable. In early December, for example, he was undone by the congressional reaction to his State of the Union speech. "[W]asn't it horrible?" he asked a young aide after the speech. "All those congressmen and senators applauding every wretched little warlike thing I had to say, ignoring all the things for which I really care. I hate this war! I hate all war, and the only thing I really care about on earth is the peace I am going to make at the end of it." By the end of his protest, Wilson was in tears.

Surrounded by his family, Wilson rested during the Christmas holidays and was in good spirits when House returned to Washington, on Friday, January 4. The negotiations for a permanent peace between Russia and Germany had broken down, fueling Wilson's hope of inspiring the Russians to return to the battlefield. The colonel reached the White House after dinner, and he and the president pored over the Inquiry's memorandum and a thick stack of supporting material until nearly midnight.

On Saturday morning, the two picked up where they had left off. "We actually got down to work at half past ten and finished remaking the map of the world, as we would have it, at half-past twelve o'clock," House boasted in his diary. On Sunday, the president refined the ideas in a shorthand draft and converted the shorthand to typescript. On Monday Lansing reviewed the speech. On Tuesday Woodrow and Edith started the day with a round of golf, and at ten-thirty he asked his office to notify Congress that he wished to speak to a joint session at twelve-thirty. Speaker Clark and Vice President Marshall had to scramble to draw up the resolution necessary for a presidential address and secure its approval before Wilson arrived.

The novelty of Wilson's presidential addresses to Congress had worn off by the time he delivered his Fourteen Points speech, and newspaper correspondents no longer bothered to set the scene or comment on the president's demeanor. They still listened closely to his words, however, and on this day, January 8, 1918, they were astounded. Woodrow Wilson remapped the world, proposed a world order that rested on the equality of all nations rather than the power of a few, committed the United States to the preservation of peace, and presented America's war aims.

The chief end of the American program, he said, was peace. To secure it, he proposed six ideas that he believed would revolutionize the conduct of world affairs: "open covenants of peace, openly arrived at"; freedom of the seas even in wartime; free trade for nations committed to world peace; armies and navies large enough for self-defense but no more; an adjudication of colonial claims that would give due consideration to the interests of the subject populations; and an association of nations charged with preserving the territorial integrity and political independence of all member states. There followed eight territorial proposals. While there was no mention of secret treaties, Wilson made sure that none of his proposals conflicted with the terms the Allies had worked out among themselves.

As for postwar Germany, Wilson said, the United States had no wish to interfere with her legitimate exercise of political power or block her trade if it joined the other peace-loving nations of the world in "covenants of justice and law and fair dealing. We wish her only to accept a place of equality . . . instead of a place of mastery."

Wilson's peroration emphasized the underpinnings of the Fourteen Points: "justice to all peoples and nationalities, and their right to live on equal terms of liberty and safety with one another, whether they be strong or weak. Unless this principle be made its foundation no part of the structure of international justice can stand. The people of the United States could act upon no other principle; and to the vindication of this principle they are ready to devote their lives, their honor, and everything that they possess."

The Fourteen Points address won the applause of Republicans, Democrats, and internationalists of both parties. Even Theodore Roosevelt pronounced himself pleased. The most perceptive praise appeared in the *New-York Tribune*, a paper that rarely endorsed any emanation from Wilson. The editors likened the speech to the Emancipation Proclamation and predicted that it would become "one of the great documents in American history and one of the permanent contributions of America to world liberty." Wilson had not only drawn a new map of the world, the *Tribune* said; he had also written its constitution. The *Tribune* also noted that he had broken with the tradition of American isolation: "He has carried the United States back to Europe; he has established an American world policy and ideal of international policy throughout the civilized world. . . . He has made us prouder of being Americans, because he has made America mean something more than it ever did before for us and for the world."

The day after the speech, Ambassador Spring Rice made his last visit to the White House. His thyroid imbalance had grown steadily worse, and he was being replaced. Despite his malady and despite his occasional quarrels with the State Department, Spring Rice had endeared himself to many in the capital, and no one was better at explaining Washington to London and vice versa. His instruction continued to the last. When London failed to compliment the president on his Fourteen Points, the ambassador gently reproved his superiors in a cable saying, "I gather that the president would have been glad of an expression of opinion from H.M. Government about his speech." London explained that H.M. Government could not oblige because Lloyd George's war aims did not exactly match Wilson's. On the eve of his departure from Washington, Spring Rice stole a moment to forward a compliment from Lord Balfour, the foreign secretary—a gesture obviously intended to keep Britain in good standing with the president. Four weeks later, Spring Rice died of a heart attack.

To judge by the London press, Wilson's standing with the British had never been higher, and even as the Senate bared the shortcomings of the War Department, the president continued to assure the Allies that the AEF was coming and would help them win the war. But huge obstacles remained. For lack of training camps, the vast majority of the AEF was still awaiting instruction. For lack of weapons, the instruction was woefully inadequate. For lack of ships, most of the troops who *had* completed their training were stranded in the United States. As for the 177,000 American soldiers in France at the end of 1917, only a handful had ever seen combat. None had had sufficient training in the ways of war on the Western Front.

In a February 3 meeting at the White House, Sir William Wiseman of the British embassy tried to persuade the president and the secretary of war to do what Pershing would not: temporarily assign troops to the Allied armies. Wilson resisted. But he was less adamant than Pershing had been, and he confided that he was not standing in Pershing's way.

The American strategy of professing military cooperation while withholding it had no practical consequences during the winter, when the fighting was in abeyance, but the stakes rose considerably in early March, when Russia and Germany signed the Treaty of Brest-Litovsk. The Bolsheviks had surrendered one million square miles of territory along with a vast cache of war matériel: guns and ammunition, grain and oil, and enough locomotives and trucks to carry it all away. In a single stroke, the treaty paved the way for

Germany's subjugation of Russia, ended the crippling shortages caused by the British blockade, and freed 350,000 German soldiers for duty in France.

Meanwhile, on the Western Front, the Germans were moving into position to play what they called "the last card," an all-out offensive designed to win the war before the great influx of American troops. The German General Staff had calculated that if Germany did not defeat the Allies in the first half of 1918, its forces would be outnumbered. Secretary Baker arrived in Paris on March 10 for a tour of American military operations and visits to the headquarters of the Allied armies. On the morning of March 21, as he and Pershing motored over to Compiègne for lunch with General Henri Philippe Pétain, they heard the fire from Germany's heavy guns build and build until there was no lull between shots. To one of the Americans in Baker's party it sounded like "ten thousand breakers on an uneven shore, a roar that was so widespread that it seemed to extend beyond the curve of the earth." The German offensive had begun.

Within forty-eight hours, the British government cabled its new ambassador in Washington, Lord Reading, and begged him to impress upon the president that the battles now in progress might well decide the war. The Germans had struck first against the British, who were strung out along a hundred miles at the northwestern end of the front. Casualties were heavy, they would worsen, and Britain no longer had enough men to replace the dead and wounded. Nor would the British army be able to spare troops to move eastward to assist the French, who were certain to be hit as soon as the Germans exhausted the British. Reading was instructed to ask Wilson to rush American infantrymen to France. The situation was critical, the cable said, "and if America delays now she may be too late."

At the White House, Reading and his aide Sir William Wiseman found Wilson in shock. He had been warned of the all-out offensive, but recent reports of rising antiwar sentiment in Germany had encouraged him to think that the kaiser and his generals were losing their hold on the government. Reading and Wiseman left the White House with radically different impressions of Wilson's intentions. Reading reported to Lloyd George that Wilson was anxious to do all he could. But according to Wiseman, Wilson had insisted that the United States was already doing its utmost. Wiseman warned London against pressing him too hard: "we must have his cordial personal cooperation if we are to secure the last ounce of American effort. Expediency demands that we should help the president in order that he will help us."

The Supreme War Council met the emergency by promoting General Ferdinand Foch of France to Marshal and giving him command of the coalition's armies. Pershing favored the idea but still refused to compromise

THE WESTERN FRONT
March 20 to November 11, 1918

Front Line, March 20
Front Line, November 11
German offensives in 1918
Army Group boundaries

the independence of the AEF. Bliss, who believed that the crisis trumped Pershing's ideal, turned to Baker, who told Pershing that the time had come to put the AEF into action. Wilson concurred.

On March 28, Pershing made a brilliant surrender. He presented himself at Foch's headquarters and begged, in French, for a place in the fight—as if the Allies had been keeping him out of it. "I have come to say to you that the American people would hold it a great honor for our troops were they engaged in the present battle," he said. "I ask it of you in my name and in that of the American people. There is at this moment no other question than that of fighting. Infantry, artillery, aviation—all that we have—are yours to dispose of as you will."

Wilson agreed to send 120,000 infantrymen and machine gunners to France in April but left it to Pershing to decide how long they would spend in French and British lines. Lloyd George thanked Wilson in one breath and used the next to urge Reading to keep pressing the White House. Although the Allies had survived the first wave of the offensive, there would be more. "In the circumstances," the prime minister wrote, "everything depends upon your going beyond ordinary province of ambassador and exercising personal supervision of carrying out of pledge."

Pershing has often been portrayed as the least cooperative of the coalition's generals, but he was no more protective of his country's interests than his British and French counterparts, Douglas Haig and Henri Pétain. It was Haig, not Pershing, who was to blame for the querulous period between the Supreme War Council's call for a commander of all Allied Forces and the agreement to give the job to Foch. Committed to defending the French and Belgian ports closest to England, Haig feared being abandoned by the French if the Germans came within reach of Paris. The dispute was ended by limiting Foch's powers. He could coordinate the strategy of the armies on the Western Front, but the French, British, Italian, and American commanders retained the right to make their own tactical decisions and the right to appeal Foch's directives.

After consulting the Allies, Pershing sent his entire First Division west from Lorraine to Picardy, the scene of the fighting, but by the time it settled in near Beauvais, the assault had ended. The Germans had stopped after tearing a sixty-mile-wide hole in the British lines and driving a wedge through the territory where the French and British armies overlapped. Outmanned three to one, the British suffered horrendous losses (164,000 dead and wounded, 90,000 captured).

The Allies had managed to stop the offensive ten miles short of Amiens, a railway hub vital to their supply lines. As costly as the battle had been for the French and British, it stunned the Germans, who had not expected such fierce resistance. The Germans had also run into the wall that plagued nearly every offensive of the world war: the same storms of artillery fire that opened the way for the infantry left a morass of mud and craters. Soldiers on foot could make their way through, but the wheeled vehicles carrying their supplies could not.

Believing that the Germans would have another go at Amiens, the Allies strengthened their positions accordingly, but the Germans struck far to the north, in Flanders, in hopes of sweeping the British into the sea. Haig's Special Order of the Day for April 11 would be remembered by Britons for generations: "Every position must be held to the last man; there must be no retirement. With our backs to the wall, and believing in the justice of our cause, each one of us must fight to the end."

Secretary Baker was on the Atlantic, heading back to the United States, when Lloyd George armed Ambassador Reading for his next skirmish with the administration. "We can do no more than we have done," he wrote. "It rests with America to win or lose the decisive battle of the war. But if it is to be won America will have to move as she has never moved before and the president must overrule at once the narrow obstinacy which would put obstacles in the way of using American infantry in the only way in which it can be used to save the situation. If she fails, disaster is inevitable. I want you to get that into the president's mind."

Through their ambassadors, France and Britain pressed Wilson for more than the agreed-upon 120,000 infantrymen and machine gunners, and when they failed, Wiseman appealed to House. A State Department official took Reading to the War Department, and on May 10 Baker decided to let Pershing and Foch work out an agreement.

The AEF began to make itself felt at the end of May, when one of the First Division's infantry regiments stormed a hilltop held by the Germans at Cantigny. The Germans counterattacked multiple times ("I thought they would never cease," wrote the division's commander, General Robert Lee Bullard), but after five weeks, they gave up. Although small, the AEF's victory was strategically and psychologically important. The hilltop offered an excellent view of the German lines to the north and west, and the American performance under withering fire convinced both the Allies and the Germans that Pershing's troops would, as Bullard put it, "fight and stick." The French bestowed lavish congratulations and medals, and the German troops who lost Cantigny were bitterly denounced by their superiors.

The fight for Cantigny had barely begun when General Erich Ludendorff launched a third offensive, along the Chemin des Dames, a ridge east of Soissons. AEF intelligence officers had warned of such an attack, but the French discounted the report and were caught off guard. Ludendorff had seen the maneuver as a prelude to a larger offensive against the British in Flanders: by luring the Chemin des Dames troops eastward, he wanted to make it impossible for them to reinforce the British. But after an easy ten-mile advance in a single day, he abandoned his Flanders plan and stayed on the path of no resistance. In five days, the Germans rolled thirty miles, all the way to Château-Thierry on the Marne. From there it was a straight run across open ground to Paris, fifty-odd miles away. Ludendorff decided to consolidate his gains near the Marne in the hope that a serious threat to Paris would force the French to surrender.

There were 722,000 American troops in France when the attack on the Chemin des Dames began, on May 27. Foch ordered five American divisions into quiet sectors held by the French in order to free experienced French troops to defend the Marne. Pershing, in response to a plea from Pétain, ordered the AEF's Second and Third Divisions in the same direction. But at a meeting of the Supreme War Council in early June, Pershing protested the Allies' request for infantry and more infantry. Foch threatened to take his case to the White House. Pershing was uncowed. "Refer it to the president and be damned," he said. "He will simply refer it back to me."

While the Supreme War Council debated at Versailles, a French officer near Château-Thierry wrote that as he and his countrymen watched endless columns of Americans moving toward the Marne, "We all had the impression that we were about to see a wonderful transfusion of blood. Life was coming in floods to reanimate the dying body of France." The AEF's Third Division arranged itself along the river's south bank at Château-Thierry, where it blew up the main bridge and helped the French beat back every German attempt to cross on makeshift bridges. The Second's fighting in and around Château-Thierry delivered the AEF's first major victory. By coming to the aid of the French, the Americans had forced the Germans to retreat from the Marne. Winston Churchill captured the essence of the moment in his history of the war: "Half trained, half organized, with only their courage, their numbers and their magnificent youth behind their weapons, they were to buy their experience at a bitter price. But this they were quite ready to do." Their dead and wounded numbered ten thousand.

Americans would come to think of the AEF's victories on the Marne in June 1918 as the turning point of the war. In a sense they were. Ludendorff's armies would never again be so close to Paris. And while the battles were minuscule compared to the engagements at Verdun and on the Somme, the

Germans understood the stakes. Ludendorff believed that by crushing the Second and Third Divisions on their first big outing, he could destroy the AEF itself. He was still optimistic after Château-Thierry, but at least one German officer on the scene felt a shift in the balance of military power. The Europeans in the field were sick of war, but the troops of the Second Division were young, strong, and brave to the point of recklessness, he wrote.

By the Fourth of July, the United States had fulfilled its promise of a million-man army in France, and a million more would arrive before the war's end. France celebrated by giving the country a holiday and renaming a major Parisian thoroughfare for President Wilson. Three thousand American soldiers paraded along the Seine, cheered at every step by Parisians on the curbs, in windows, in trees, and on rooftops. At a luncheon hosted by the American Chamber of Commerce in Paris, Captain André Tardieu, then serving as French high commissioner to the United States, catalogued the Americans' wartime accomplishments: U.S. Navy destroyers and torpedo boats had helped the Royal Navy chase the U-boats from the seas. The ranks of the U.S. Army had grown from 200,000 to 2,500,000. Merchant shipping capacity had more than doubled. Through the U.S. Treasury, the American people had taken on a debt of billions to help the Allies and fund their own war effort. "All that the war has demanded America has accepted," Tardieu said; "all that it has represented she has understood, and all that is required for victory she has given."

28

So Many Problems Per Diem

Wilson spent his Fourth of July as the leading man in a patriotic extravaganza staged by George Creel. Meant to show off the unity of a country whose citizens hailed from every slice of the globe, the day began at the Navy Yard, where the president and first lady welcomed an assortment of diplomats and leaders of ethnic communities aboard the *Mayflower* for a cruise to Mount Vernon. Once ashore, the honored guests filed past Washington's tomb, laying wreaths as the Irish-born tenor John McCormack pumped out verse after verse of "The Star-Spangled Banner." The immigrants' designated speaker, a Belgian by birth, mentioned that he and his companions hailed from thirty-three nations but were "Americans all." Behind them, he said, were millions more, "pledging themselves to the cause of this country and of the free nations with which she is joined." For proof, he said, one had only to acknowledge the variety of names on the casualty lists.

In a speech that contained not a word about immigrants, Wilson spoke of the war as the global equivalent of the American Revolution, and voiced the hope that the United States and its friends in other nations would secure for all peoples what Washington and his compatriots had won for Americans: the right to govern themselves.

The only overpowered and suffering people Wilson mentioned at Mount Vernon were the Russians, who had gone from the miseries of living under Czar Nicholas II to the tyranny of Lenin and Bolshevism. Lenin's decision to leave the war had thrown the Allies into a panic, and for months they had been begging the United States for troops to be used in two small military interventions in Russia—one in the northwest, near Archangel and Murmansk, the other in Siberia, six thousand miles to the east. At first the Allies aimed to block the Germans' transfer of troops and matériel to the West, but when Ludendorff's spring offensives inflicted hundreds of thousands of fresh casualties on French and British forces on the Western Front, Russia grew ever more alluring. Rationales multiplied, hopes waxed fantastical. With a few thousand well-placed troops, the Allies imagined that they could rally the Russian people to rise up against the Bolsheviks, reconstitute the Eastern Front, stave off the kaiser's subjugation of Russia, and win the world war in the East if it could not be won in the West.

While they were at it, the Allies planned to connect with the so-called Czech Legion, some seventy thousand Czechs and Slovaks who had fought for Russia in hopes of defeating the Austro-Hungarian Empire and establishing a state of their own. On some days the Allies hoped to help the legionnaires move to Russian ports for transfer to the Western Front; on others they wanted to use the legion to keep Russian railways out of German hands. And then there was Japan, a short cruise away from the Siberian port of Vladivostok, where thousands of tons of weapons, munitions, and strategic raw materials were stockpiled. The Allies wanted Japan to handle the Siberian intervention and were willing to allow Japan to reward itself with a swath of Asiatic Russia.

Wilson and his War Department saw both ventures as distractions from the AEF's task on the Western Front. He also thoroughly disapproved of the Allies' willingness to let Japan install itself in Russia. Nor did he buy the Allies' assertion that the interventions would help the Russian people at a time when they could not help themselves. Chastened by his failed attempts to restore order in revolutionary Mexico, Wilson now believed in letting new governments "work out their own salvation, even though they wallow in anarchy for a while."

Wilson had resisted the Allies' Russian pleas for months, but when it became clear that Japan wished to go into Siberia on its own, he found himself in a corner: if he intervened, he would be accused of infringing upon Russian sovereignty, but if he stood by while Japan did as it pleased, all of Asia would be at risk. A few days after the excursion to Mount Vernon, Wilson wrote House that he was "sweating blood over the question of what is right and feasible *(possible)* to do in Russia. It goes to pieces like quicksilver under my touch." He reported himself "very tired, for there never were so many problems per diem, it seems to me, as there are now." Perhaps to reassure House, perhaps to reassure himself, he added, "I am well. *We* are well."

Edith was indeed well. She spent her afternoons at an old Washington railway depot that had been turned into a Red Cross canteen. Troop trains pulled in, and the volunteers dispensed sandwiches and coffee along with good cheer. Edith enjoyed the work except for the wilting summer heat, which rumpled her uniform and left her feeling well below first lady standards. She bore the trial with good humor, and to judge by her own account, was pleased to be of service. Woodrow, still deeply in love, sometimes turned up at the end of her shift to take her home. He seemed especially pleased when there were troops on hand. As Edith remembered it, he was always glad to see them, and numerous photographs and firsthand accounts bear her out.

Such pleasures were fleeting. By the middle of July, after the Japanese ambassador promised the United States that his government would not compromise Russia's territorial integrity or interfere in her politics, Wilson offered the Allies a few thousand American soldiers, but not for a military intervention. U.S. troops would guard military stores, help the Czech Legion to the Western Front, and render whatever aid the Russians found acceptable as they organized their defenses against the Germans. He reserved the right to withdraw the troops, and he held out the possibility of a venture more to his liking, an American mission to Siberia.

Wilson's decision simultaneously pleased the Allies and affirmed his independence from them, but it won him no applause. Americans inspired by Wilson's vision of a world free of Great Power aggression were particularly disappointed. To Oswald Garrison Villard of *The Nation,* Wilson's one foot in, one foot out approach seemed the height of hypocrisy: "The president has assured us that it is to be only a little intervention, and we are to forgive it or approve it on grounds of its littleness."

However justifiable the interventions might have been in the bleak days after Russia's exit from the war, they were irrelevant by the time Wilson acted. On the very day that he made his offer to the Allies, General Ludendorff concluded that Germany could not win the war on the Western Front. All of the general's gains in the spring had been achieved by surprise, but on July 15, when he attacked Reims, the surprise was on him. German soldiers captured by the French had given away his plans, and the French and the Americans were ready for him. Called off on July 17, the advance on Reims would be the Germans' last.

Ludendorff clung to the hope that God would not desert the German army but thought it prudent to inform the kaiser that the army was finished. Wilhelm, profoundly upset, began referring to himself as a defeated warlord and asking his retainers to treat him gently. That night, unable to sleep, he lay awake in the grip of a humiliating vision of himself reviewing an endless parade of royal cousins, ministers, and generals, all taunting him as they marched past. Ludendorff was no less distraught. One of his officers proposed a retreat to the Hindenburg Line, a chain of well-fortified positions that stretched on for a hundred miles. The southern tip of the line was only thirty miles from Reims, but Ludendorff seemed paralyzed, and his troops were deserting and surrendering by the thousands. On August 8, a 75,000-man British force broke the German line near Amiens. The Germans started the day with 37,000 men and ended with 10,000. Nearly half the men lost had handed themselves over to the enemy.

Ludendorff would remember August 8 as "the black day of the German army." The British would immortalize it as the start of the Hundred Days Offensive, the drive that ended the war. By relentless, tightly coordinated fire from planes, tanks, and infantry, the British at Amiens had overwhelmed the German defenses. It was a new way of waging war, and the exhausted Germans never adjusted to it. It also marked the end of trench warfare. From Amiens till the end, the fighting would be done on the move, with the Germans in retreat and the Allies and the AEF at their heels.

Ludendorff raged, and the object of his rage was the German people, who were turning against the war in large numbers. A psychologist advised him to get more sleep and to sing German folk songs when he rose each morning. On August 13, Ludendorff and the rest of the High Command, along with the chancellor and the foreign secretary, appeared before the kaiser at the German General Headquarters at Spa. The foreign secretary, Paul von Hintze, was given permission to begin a confidential exploration of peace with the head of a neutral state, Queen Wilhelmina of the Netherlands, as intermediary. Emperor Charles I of Austria and his foreign minister reached Spa the next day and disclosed their desire to ask the enemy for peace. The Germans urged them to wait, believing that the Central Powers would have more bargaining power if they put up a stiff fight. Hintze was given the unpleasant task of returning to Berlin and assuring party leaders that there was no reason to doubt the army's final triumph. "We shall be vanquished only when we doubt that we shall win," he said.

While the Germans and Austrians parleyed at Spa, the president of the United States was on his way to the seaside town of Magnolia, Massachusetts, where he and Colonel House discussed the eventual peace conference. Wilson planned to attend as head of an American commission that he would appoint, but he was not ready to decide who would go with him. House told him (not for the first time) that he would have to appoint at least one Republican and supposed that the country would expect it to be Taft, Roosevelt, or Root. Wilson summarily rejected all three.

The two friends also had a troubling conversation about Wilson's great dream for the postwar world, a league of nations. At the president's request, the colonel had drafted a covenant for the league, Wilson had edited it, and they now felt that they had a substantive plan, which Wilson wanted to keep under lock and key until the peace conference. Both the colonel and the president hoped that the covenant would be written into the peace treaty, but they differed sharply on a crucial point. Like many Republicans and most European leaders willing to entertain the idea of an international peacekeeping league, House believed that the world's major powers would not join a league in which every nation had an equal say in matters of war and peace. The difficulty, House said, was that the world had fifty-odd nations, but only a dozen were capable of contributing large numbers of troops and substantial financing in the event of another world war. And whenever a major issue came to a vote, the forty-odd small nations could easily thwart the wishes of the big ones.

The problem had been publicly pointed out numerous times by Roosevelt, Taft, and others, but from House's account it appears that Wilson had never before taken it seriously. At first he dissented ("quite warmly," according to House), saying that such a view contradicted his highly public advocacy for a world order based on the equality of all nations. After seeing the colonel's point, Wilson wondered if it might be possible to reach equality in a gradual way, forming a league of big nations first and expanding it later. House acquiesced, betting that his view, not Wilson's, would be sustained by the Great Powers at the peace conference.

The conversation did not speak well of either man. Wilson clearly understood that Republicans would raise objections to U.S. participation in a league of nations, yet he was unwilling to take up the problems with them, and House was all too willing to let the Allies curb Wilson's lofty ambitions.

House's diary entries for their days together at Magnolia are strangely silent on the forthcoming congressional elections. At a meeting of party leaders in June, the Democrats had decided to campaign on the idea that it would be unpatriotic to vote against the president and his party during a war. From "He Kept Us Out of War" the party had moved on to "Win the War with Wilson" and "Stand by the President." The AEF's victories at the Marne, suggested that Wilson would indeed win the war and that it would be foolhardy to desert him.

The Republicans immediately took note. In a July 3 fundraising letter, they pointed out that the president's war legislation had received more support from the GOP than from his own party. They also predicted that the next session of Congress would have to manage the economic transition from war to peace. The nation's prosperity would hinge on the decisions made by Congress, the letter said, and unless "Republican principles" were adopted, the country was likely to tumble into a recession. The principles they had in mind were a return to the days of high tariffs, minimal regulation of business, and no income tax.

Wilson had gone to Congress in May to ask for tax increases to meet the soaring cost of the war and to make a case for passing them sooner rather than later. He left the details to Congress but suggested that the government's need could be met with higher taxes on war profits, high incomes, and luxuries. Aware that voters were inclined to punish congressmen and senators who raised taxes on the eve of an election, Wilson appealed to their patriotism. "These are days when duty stands stark and naked and even with closed eyes we know it is there," he said. The United States was not only in the middle of a war, it was at the peak of it. "There can be no pause or intermission," he said. The duty of the hour was plain, and it must be met without selfishness or fear. "Politics is adjourned."

Spokesmen for the House Ways and Means Committee and Senate Finance Committee promised that Congress would do its duty, but it did not. The House did not approve a tax bill until September, and the Senate's objections to it would delay final passage until three months after the election.

Lodge stayed on the sidelines until late August, when he was elected minority leader of the Senate. The Senate was about to approve a bill authorizing another military draft, and Lodge used the occasion to make a speech that began with an endorsement of the bill and moved on to questions of war and peace. Ever since Wilson's "peace without victory" speech of January 1917, Lodge had worried that the president would make a premature and overly generous peace. Now that the Germans were losing, the United States would have to decide what it meant by peace, Lodge said. It was insufficient to say that it wanted a just and righteous peace; on that point Americans were agreed. "But what is a just and righteous peace? What are the conditions that would make it so? What is the irreducible minimum? We intend to make the world safe for democracy. But what exactly do we mean by democracy?" The United States and the Allies were fighting for security, independence, self-government, the sanctity of treaties, and general disarmament, but exactly how were these demands to be satisfied? "Broadly speaking," Lodge said, "there is only one way . . . and that is by reducing Germany to a condition where by no possibility can she precipitate another war for universal conquest."

Lodge's list of essentials began with territorial adjustments similar to those in the Fourteen Points, but he omitted the president's calls for a league of nations, free trade, and freedom of the seas. He also made demands that Wilson had not: financial reparations and a dictated peace rather than a negotiated one. "When Germany is beaten to her knees and the world is made safe by the arrangements which I have suggested, then, and not before, we shall have the just and righteous peace for which we fight."

Wilson undoubtedly found the speech distasteful, but he did not reply. And at that point, after more than a year of "Kill the Hun" propaganda from George Creel's office, the American public was feeling no more merciful than Henry Cabot Lodge.

A day after Lodge delivered his peace program, *The New York Times* reported a rumor that if the Republicans got behind the idea of a constitutional amendment giving women the right to vote, he would support the measure. Many of his party's progressives, including his friend Roosevelt, believed that supporting the amendment would help them win votes in November.

Wilson had reached the same conclusion. Early in 1918, after years of favoring a state-by-state approach to women's suffrage, he decided to join the drive for an amendment. Wilson described his change of heart as a "conversion" and said it had come to him "with an overwhelming command." But his timing suggests that the command was less spiritual than political. He declared himself on the eve of a House vote on a resolution endorsing the constitutional amendment that Susan B. Anthony had drawn up forty-three years before: "The right of citizens of the United States to vote shall not be denied or abridged by the United States or by any State on account of sex."

On January 9, after conferring with the House suffrage committee, Wilson urged that the resolution be passed "as an act of right and justice to the women of the country and of the world." The resolution needed 274 votes to pass, and the vote was 274 to 136, the necessary two-thirds majority but without one vote more than necessary. The slim victory in the House lengthened the odds against it in the Senate, and the Democratic senator in charge of the resolution, Andrieus A. Jones of New Mexico, decided not to bring it to the floor until he had the votes. Five months later, when his polling showed that he was close, Wilson began pleading with the undecided as well as the frankly opposed. The American people wanted a suffrage amendment, he said, and if the Democratic-controlled Senate did not give it to them, the people might elect a Republican Congress.

When Jones introduced the suffrage resolution on Thursday, September 26, it set off a five-hour debate that showed the Senate at its least edifying. Duncan U. Fletcher, a Florida Democrat, opined that a constitutional amendment on suffrage would do violence to states' rights. John Sharp Williams of Mississippi wanted the word "white" inserted before "citizens," a change that Thomas W. Hardwick of Georgia endorsed with more passion than logic. The Negro vote had caused no end of problems in the South, Hardwick said, and giving the vote to Negro women was bound to make things worse. "I predict that after this war the Negro question in this country is going to be one of the most difficult ones. You will have colored soldiers coming home from France, where they have been fighting and you will want them to vote. . . . It is in the hysteria of war that this suffrage amendment has been forced upon us. In other times it would be quickly voted down. Now men are afraid to do it."

McAdoo telephoned the White House to urge Wilson to go before the Senate and make one last appeal. When Wilson said that the Senate would resent his interference, McAdoo countered that the United States was fighting a war for democracy but denying a fundamental democratic right to women. He also argued that whatever the Senate's vote, Wilson's address would make a powerful impression on the American people, who might be moved to elect enough pro-amendment senators to ensure its swift passage in the next session. At five o'clock that afternoon Edith let McAdoo know that Woodrow was writing the speech.

Wilson spoke at one o'clock the next day, September 30. Clearly peeved, he said he had assumed that the Senate would consent to putting a suffrage amendment before the country because no disputable principle was involved. Both parties were pledged to equal suffrage, and the war had rendered the state-by-state method obsolete. If the United States wished to lead the peoples of the world to democracy, it had to behave accordingly. If it did not, he said, the rest of the world "will cease to believe in us." Enfranchising women as soon as possible was both a necessity and a matter of simple justice, Wilson said. "We have made partners of the women in this war; shall we admit them only to a partnership of suffering and sacrifice and toil and not to a partnership of privilege and right?"

On Tuesday, October 1, the resolution was defeated by two votes. "No Vote Changed by Wilson's Plea," *The Atlanta Constitution* gloated. Republicans gloated, too; of the thirty-one votes against the amendment, Republicans had cast only ten. The congressional elections were only a month away, and the vote gave Republicans fresh evidence for their argument that they were the party who stood by the president on every wartime legislative measure he considered important.

A delegation of suffragists from all forty-eight states called at the White House two days after the speech to thank Wilson for all he had done. Still angry with his opponents in the Senate, he told his visitors that some men refused to learn. "I have to restrain myself from intellectual contempt," he said. "That is a sin, I am afraid, and being a good Presbyterian, I am trying to refrain from it." He explained that his conversion to their cause had come from "listening to the heart of the world." In the flood of pleas coming to him from abroad, he said, he felt an undercurrent of democratic longing, "a great voice" that would be dangerous to ignore. Inspired by that voice, Wilson would come to care less and less about the voice of the Senate.

The illiberal wing of the Democratic Party pained the president, and with world opinion moving in a liberal direction, he thought that Americans would have to form a new political party in order to keep up. But in at least one matter, race, Wilson himself was still ignoring the most progressive opinion of the day. Although he had not authorized the segregation of the civil service that began at the outset of his presidency, he had let it stand. In 1915 he outraged liberal opinion with a White House screening of the virulently racist *Birth of a Nation.* No explanation or apology followed, although he privately told Tumulty that he considered the film "very unfortunate."

When the United States entered the war, many black spokesmen exhorted their young followers to join up and do their utmost. As W. E. B. Du Bois of the NAACP put it, "If this is OUR country, then this is OUR war." Another NAACP official, James Weldon Johnson, framed his counsel as a prediction: the black soldier would do his duty to his country "not stupidly, not led by any silly sentiment, not blindly, but with his eyes wide open." And then he would demand that his country do its duty by him.

The 370,000 blacks who served in the AEF were treated no better than black civilians. The Army had long practiced segregation, and Secretary Baker decided not to take on the task of arbitrating "the so-called race question." Blacks and whites served in the same division, but black troops were assigned to black battalions and housed in segregated quarters. And although black soldiers had served in combat since the Civil War, the army's initial plans for the world war envisioned blacks as stevedores and laborers. Pressed by the NAACP, the War Department created a camp to train black officers and approved the creation of two black divisions, both of which fought in France.

In the violent summer of 1917, a summer filled with lynchings and riots, a clash between black soldiers and police in Houston left four soldiers and twelve civilians dead. In the rush to placate white Southern opinion, the army court-martialed and hanged thirteen of the soldiers arrested in the rioting. Their cases did not reach Washington for review by the army's judge advocate general until three months after the soldiers had been executed. African Americans across the country were outraged. The army's provost marshal decreed that no more death sentences would be carried out without presidential review and approval. Of the sixteen additional death sentences meted out to black troops, Wilson let six stand and commuted ten to life imprisonment, explaining that he saw no compelling evidence of their involvement in the civilian deaths. The ten joined fifty-three other black soldiers who had been sent to prison for life after the Houston riot.

Black citizens had little reason to support the Democratic Party in the midterm elections of 1918. Most still lived in the South, where their efforts to vote were routinely obstructed by white supremacists, but between 1910 and 1918, hundreds of thousands of blacks had moved to the North and the West in search of better jobs and, they hoped, less racial prejudice. A report prepared by two black clergymen at Tumulty's request claimed that there were now 600,000 black voters outside the South and estimated that they could be the deciding factor in at least ten of the congressional contests of 1918.

In July, Wilson issued a public denunciation of lynching, a step no previous president had been bold enough to take. But he seemed to understand that he had failed the black citizens of the United States. When Creel asked him to receive a group of black editors meeting in Washington, he declined, saying that whenever he met such delegations, they went away dissatisfied. On October 1, possibly at the urging of the Democratic campaign committee, he did see a delegation from the National Race Congress of the United States of America in a meeting that was brief and carefully choreographed. The delegates had a long list of concerns for him to consider, but the concerns were not to be part of the discussion. They were put on paper and left with his office. The group's spokesman was assigned the role of paying a few compliments and asking the president to raise his voice against "un-American, undemocratic" practices.

Wilson asked them to temper their expectations. "We all have to be patient with one another," he said. "Human nature doesn't make giant strides in a single generation. . . . I have a very modest estimate of my own power to hasten the process, but you may be sure that everything I can do will be accomplished." In theory he could have abolished segregation in the civil service with an executive order, but every Southern Democrat in Congress would have turned against him. Had he been willing to weather a smaller storm, he could have found an occasion, perhaps in a speech or one of his State of the Union addresses, to connect black yearnings for political equality with the democratic yearnings he sensed in the rest of the world. He had drawn the parallel when he asked the Senate to support the women's suffrage amendment, but he never made the same argument on behalf of black America.

On September 14, after an unbroken and seemingly unbreakable string of victories by the American and Allied armies, the Austrian government sent all the belligerents a request for a preliminary discussion of peace. The cable arrived in Washington at 6:20 p.m. on September 16, and Lansing dispatched Wilson's rejection twenty-five minutes later. The United States had repeatedly stated its terms for peace, Wilson said, and saw no point in meeting to discuss other proposals. Paris and London also said no.

Wilson had enunciated the American terms on four occasions in 1918. In January he presented his Fourteen Points. In April he said that Germany's insistence on ending the war by force compelled the United States to fight back with "Force, Force to the utmost, Force without stint or limit." On the Fourth of July he called for the destruction of every militarily aggressive autocracy, an international association to maintain peace, and government with the consent of the governed.

At the end of September he covered the ground once more. To help McAdoo get the fourth Liberty Loan off to a good start, he agreed to speak at the Metropolitan Opera House, but with his first sentence—"I am not here to promote the loan"—he gave himself leave to take up the large questions raised by the war. Were the militarists to be allowed to go on determining the fortunes of peoples they had no right to rule? Were strong nations to be free to wrong weak ones? Would the peace of the world be left to chance and shifting alliances rather than to a permanent community of nations pledged to protect common rights? The war had forced these issues upon the world, he said, and they must be settled for all time "with a full and unequivocal acceptance of the principle that the interest of the weakest is as sacred as the interest of the strongest." There could be no bargain with the governments of the Central Powers. "They observe no covenants, accept no principle but force and their own interest," he said. "We cannot 'come to terms' with them. They have made it impossible." Wilson reiterated several of his Fourteen Points, affirming his desire to replace the outsized sway of a handful of Great Powers with a world order in which all nations were equal. What the world required, he said, was a peace that secured all peoples and made another global war impossible.

The audience cheered Wilson's rebukes of Germany but showed no reaction to his insistence on impartial justice for all. It seemed to House that most of Wilson's speech at the opera house went over the heads of the crowd, and the *New-York Tribune* sensed a fair amount of "mist" in the president's message. But Wilson had an uncharacteristically exuberant reaction to his performance. He was, House wrote, "flushed with excitement and altogether pleased with the day's effort."

September 27 had in fact been a memorable day. The Allies had accepted their first surrender, from the government of Bulgaria, and the AEF had just recaptured one hundred square miles of territory for France in the Meuse-Argonne. The drive against the Germans' last lines of defense had begun. The drive was only a few days old when Ludendorff informed the chief of the German General Staff, Paul von Hindenburg, that the army could not go on. On Sunday, September 29, the two of them met with Wilhelm and Hintze at Spa and demanded an immediate armistice. The kaiser took the news quietly, but Hintze, who had told the German people to expect victory, feared that a sudden announcement of defeat might topple the government. He persuaded the kaiser and the generals to arrange an immediate, orderly transition of power. On Monday, Chancellor Georg von Hertling resigned, and the kaiser announced that the German people would henceforth have a larger say in the national government. On Tuesday, Prince Maximilian von Baden, a liberal, disliked by the military caste, replaced Hertling. On Wednesday, the Reichstag was told that Germany could not win the war. On Thursday, Max dispatched a peace note to Wilson. Asking for an immediate armistice, he vowed that Germany was willing to negotiate on the basis of the Fourteen Points and the president's subsequent peace addresses. Austria immediately followed Germany's lead.

Max sent his proposal on October 3, and by the time it reached Wilson, on October 6, the gist of it had appeared in the newspapers. As Wilson pondered his reply, senators of both parties were damning the German request as abhorrent, unthinkable, and preposterous.

Lloyd George and Clemenceau, together at a Supreme War Council meeting when Max's note came to light, waited anxiously for word of Wilson's intentions. House suggested that Wilson consult them, but Wilson was determined to proceed on his own. He decided that however long the correspondence went on, the American side of it would hew to one principle: "If the Germans are beaten, they will accept any terms; and if they are not beaten, we don't want them to accept any terms." On October 8, Wilson notified Berlin that he could not recommend an armistice to the Allies unless the Central Powers immediately agreed to withdraw their forces from the invaded territories.

Before Berlin made its next move, Wilson learned that his note had displeased the Allies. The armistice they had in mind would require more than withdrawals, and its terms would be devised by Allied military experts, not by the president of the United States. Within hours, Wilson was assuring Ambassador Jusserand that he had no intention of making a proposal for an armistice but made it clear that the United States, after sending an army of two million men to France, must be part of the armistice discussion.

As the notes were being exchanged, Wilson also held talks with Sir William Wiseman and Sir Eric Geddes, a member of the war cabinet who happened to be in Washington. Geddes wrote London that Wilson was cordial and committed to the war but "outstandingly fearful" that the military advisors would draw up an armistice too humiliating for Germany to accept. What he wanted, he said, was for the Allies and Associates "to end this war as finely as we began and show the world that we are the better fellow."

The president and first lady spent Columbus Day in New York, where he marched in a Liberty Loan parade. Afterward, as they dined at the Waldorf with Colonel and Mrs. House, Tumulty came in with a message from Military Intelligence: the Germans had accepted the president's terms. All three men wondered if the message was correct. During the evening, Tumulty confirmed the report with the State Department and *The Washington Post,* but they had no additional information and there was still no official text. The next day, a Sunday, the Wilsons returned to Washington, taking House with them. On Monday morning, when the president finally received the official text, he saw that Military Intelligence had picked up only half the message. The Germans had indeed affirmed their acceptance of the American terms. But they had also asked Wilson to form a commission with representatives from both sides for a discussion of the withdrawals. "I never saw him more disturbed," House told his diary. ". . . It reminded him, he said, of a maze. If one went in at the right entrance, he reached the center, but if one took the wrong turning, it was necessary to go out again and do it over."

Five hundred passengers on an Irish ship had just lost their lives in a U-boat attack, and House suggested a demand for a cessation of all atrocities. With that useful idea in hand, Wilson quickly found his way through the maze. He and House collaborated on a draft, they summoned Lansing, Baker, and Daniels to review it, and then off it went. Wilson told the Germans that the terms of the armistice would be set by the American and Allied military advisors, who would insist on maintaining the present military supremacy of their armies. The United States would not consider an armistice if Germany continued to sink passenger ships or kept up its wanton destruction as it retreated from Belgium and France. On all of these points, he said, he was confident that the Allies would agree with him. In parting he directed the Germans' attention to his earlier call for the defeat of "every arbitrary power anywhere."

As House and Wilson were writing the note to the Germans, Wilson decided that the colonel should leave for Europe at once to serve as his representative to the Supreme War Council and elsewhere. When House left for his train, Wilson said he had not given him any instructions, because he believed that the colonel would know what to do for him. In his diary, House reveled in Wilson's trust: "The president certainly gives me the broadest powers. It virtually puts me in his place in Europe."

House was at sea when Wilson received the next note from Berlin. The Germans, having nothing else to propose, protested Wilson's lecture on their inhumanity and assured the world that their new government represented the people. On October 23 Wilson replied that he was forwarding the U.S. and German correspondence to the Allies. But, he added, "it does not appear that the heart of the present difficulty has been reached." The German people still had no means of controlling their military, and if the United States should have to deal with the previous regime, it would feel obliged to demand "not peace negotiations but surrender."

Throughout the exchange of notes, Wilson took a firm stand with the Germans, but Republicans told voters that he was on the wrong track. Roosevelt, speaking at a Liberty Loan rally, insisted that the United States had no business discussing peace with anyone but the Allies. He would end the war by fighting, not writing, he said, and the end he wanted was unconditional surrender. Roosevelt stayed on the attack even after Wilson left the armistice to the generals.

For some time Wilson had been considering the possibility of asking the country to vote Democratic in the congressional elections, which were now only ten days away. Edith was not keen on the idea, fearing that it would simply expose his pique with his Republican critics. But in October, as the Democrats' electoral prospects flagged and the Republican criticism of Wilson's leadership grew more vitriolic, he could not resist drafting the appeal he had in mind. He shared it with two trusted members of the Democratic campaign committee on October 20. Both advised him to soften his tone, but neither questioned the wisdom of making such a plea.

A few days later, after dinner with Edith, Woodrow went to his study to type out the final version. Edith came in just as he finished, and he read it aloud. "My Fellow Countrymen," he began. "The congressional elections are at hand. . . . If you have approved of my leadership and wish me to continue to be your unembarrassed spokesman in affairs at home and abroad, I earnestly beg that you will express yourselves unmistakably to that effect by returning a Democratic majority to both the Senate and the House of Representatives." A Republican Congress would divide the leadership, he said. "The leaders of the minority in the present Congress have unquestionably been pro-war, but they have been anti-administration. . . . In ordinary times divided counsels can be endured without permanent hurt to the country. But these are not ordinary times."

"I would not send it out," Edith said. "It is not a dignified thing to do." Woodrow said he had to go forward, because he had promised "them" (presumably the Democratic campaign committee) that he would.

Wilson's appeal for a Democratic Congress was the most damaging political blunder he had ever made. It freed the Republicans to tear him to pieces, and they set to work before the day was out. Their leaders in the House and the Senate pointed out that President Wilson was willing to let Republicans buy Liberty bonds, pay higher taxes, and die for their country but unwilling to let them have a hand in governing the country. Who was Woodrow Wilson to say that this was no time for divided counsels? Roosevelt asked his fellow Americans. The Constitution required the president to work with Congress no matter which party had the majority. Heading into the last week of the campaign, the GOP chairman issued his own appeal to the country: "Mr. Wilson forces the Republican Party to lie down or fight. I say fight! Answer with your votes!"

On November 5, the president lost his majorities in both houses of

Congress. In a letter written just after the election, Lodge told an English friend that "the feeling that beat him, which was apparent from one end of the country to the other, was that the people did not mean to have a dictatorship." Few American elections have had more momentous consequences than the congressional elections of 1918. Faced with a Republican Congress for the first time, Wilson would fail at virtually everything he hoped to accomplish during his last two years in office.

"For the political disaster which overtook his party on Election Day Mr. Wilson has only himself to blame," *The Nation* declared. "Deep chagrin and humiliation should be his, for the blow to liberalism is grave indeed." In his desperation to prevent a resurgence of reactionaries and isolationists, Wilson had actually brought it into being. The source of the trouble was Wilson himself, *The Nation* said. For six long years, he had "imposed his will upon his party and upon Congress as no president has ever imposed it before. The congressional cloak-rooms might murmur and rebel as they pleased, but prior to the war they were powerless before his prestige, his political skill, and his superior ability." Once the United States was at war, he sought and acquired even more power, and it exacerbated his antipathies, his stubbornness, and his desire to act alone.

29

Defiance

The election results gave Wilson a momentary twinge, but he voiced no regret over his appeal to voters, and he shrugged off the defeat as a natural reaction to a long period of progressive reform. Nor was he visibly troubled by the Republicans' claim that the vote amounted to a repudiation of his leadership. He was still president, he would be president for another twenty-seven months, and the president, as he never tired of saying, was the only public servant elected by all the people.

Wilson's refusal to reckon with the consequences of the election would exact a high price, but he was momentarily spared by events in Europe, where the war was rushing to an end. On November 9, the kaiser's generals persuaded him to go into exile in order to prevent a revolution in Germany. Before he could abdicate, he was deposed, and before the sun came up again, he and his entourage had left the German army's Belgian stronghold at Spa for a Dutch village near Maastricht.

As the kaiser's exit was being arranged, the Allies allowed a small motorcade from the new German government to travel across Allied territory to the French city of Compiègne to hear the Allied proposition for an armistice.* Among other things, it required Germany to evacuate its occupied territories, make reparations, surrender or disable most warships and aircraft and heavy artillery, and cancel its confiscatory peace treaty with Russia. Prisoners of war and captured merchant vessels were to be returned, and the British blockade would remain in place. The German envoys were also informed that the offer of an armistice would expire at the eleventh hour of the eleventh day of the eleventh month.

The White House learned of the signing a few hours after the fact, at 3:00 a.m. Washington time. Recalling the moment in her memoir, Edith wrote that she and Woodrow "stood mute—unable to grasp the full significance of the words." The president declared a holiday for federal employees and spent the morning in his study, writing the address he would deliver to Congress that afternoon.

Millions of Americans took to the streets, hollering with joy and banging cowbells, gongs, and garbage can lids. They fired pistols into the air, waved flags, threw confetti, sang, wept, and marched behind makeshift bands. Church bells rang, and factory whistles were cocked open to blow nonstop. Effigies of the kaiser were dragged through the streets and hanged. Soldiers in uniform were carried aloft.

The president was cheered by a throng outside the Capitol, and the cheering inside the House chamber began as soon as he was announced. The New York Times correspondent, expecting Wilson to show signs of strain, seemed relieved to report that he was "the personification of physical vigor." But he was not in a celebratory mood. After a somber recitation of the terms of the Armistice, he offered a somber assessment of the state of the world. The military autocracy of Germany had been destroyed, and the victors had committed themselves to a peace that he said would "satisfy the longing of the whole world for disinterested justice." With the British blockade in mind, he said, "Hunger does not breed reform; it breeds madness and all the ugly distempers that make an ordered life impossible." He assured the vanquished

---

* An armistice is more formal and generally longer lasting than a ceasefire or a truce. Typically an armistice is negotiated by the warring parties. But sometimes, as in 1918, it is dictated by the victors. Armistices aim to prevent hostilities during the months often required to formulate and agree upon a peace treaty. A war does not officially come to an end until the enemies sign the treaty.

that the victors had hearts as well as minds and that they had resolved unanimously to do everything possible to supply the defeated peoples with food and other necessities. The future, he said, would belong to those who showed themselves friends of mankind through their example and assistance. But he frankly admitted that he did not know what would happen next.

The Allies' unanimous support of the kind of peace Wilson described had been secured only at the last minute, in a tense week of negotiations in Paris between Colonel House and the leaders of Britain, France, and Italy. In late October, a few days after Germany agreed to make peace on the basis of Wilson's program, House began pressing the Allies to follow suit. When they balked, House took a firm stand. If their peace conditions did not square with Wilson's, he said, Wilson would probably go to Congress and ask whether the United States should continue to stand with the Allies.

Panicked by the prospect of a U.S. withdrawal, the Allied leaders agreed to the Fourteen Points with two reservations. Lloyd George would not consent to Wilson's demand for absolute freedom of the seas. The most he would give was a promise of further discussion. Clemenceau inserted a clause entitling the Allies to make claims for reparations, a term not used in the Fourteen Points. "If I do not hear from you to the contrary, I shall assume that you accept the situation as it now is," House wrote Wilson. "This I strongly advise."

Wilson agreed and directed Lansing to notify the Germans of the U.S. acceptance and add a clarification on the matter of reparations: the Fourteen Points had called for the restoration as well as the evacuation of Germany's occupied territories, and the Allies wanted it understood that "restoration" meant compensation for all damage done to their civilian populations and their property during the war.

In a note to Wilson, House praised his hard-won agreement and speculated that the prime ministers had no idea how far they had committed themselves to the American peace program. But in agreeing to continue the discussion of freedom of the seas, Lloyd George had conceded nothing, and in establishing the Allies' claim to reparations without setting any limits, Clemenceau had opened the door to financial demands far in excess of actual damages.

If the colonel's triumph was not as grand as he made it out to be, it was, without a doubt, significant. After the United States entered the war, Wilson had shared the Allies' wholehearted commitment to victory but had blazed his own trail in the matter of peace. While the Allies' notions of peace were thought out with an emphasis on national interests and a division of the spoils, Wilson had been working for a peace that would benefit all nations.

He had an unshakable faith in the idea that what was best for the world would be best for the United States. He dreamed of going to the peace talks and saying, "Gentlemen, I am here to say for the United States that I don't want anything out of this. And I am here to see that you don't get anything out of it." In gaining the Allies' endorsement of the Fourteen Points, House had forced them to consider American desires alongside their own; had House failed, Wilson's ideals would have counted for nothing.

A day after his speech to Congress, Wilson informed the cabinet that he intended to go to Europe for the peacemaking. Lansing begged him to stay in Washington, arguing that the Fourteen Points had made him the hope of the world and that he could virtually dictate the terms of the peace if he kept out of the quarrels sure to erupt among the Allies. Wilson's face "assumed that harsh, obstinate expression which indicates resentment at unacceptable advice," Lansing wrote after the meeting. "He said nothing, but looked volumes."

From Paris, House reported that Clemenceau opposed Wilson's coming for a different reason: the French, the British, and the Italians would be represented by their prime ministers, and Wilson, as a head of state, would outrank them. The British had the same objection, House added. The colonel wished that the president would leave the peacemaking to him and McAdoo and Hoover, but he contented himself with a smaller suggestion: announce a decision to take part in the preliminary talks on the treaty but say nothing about staying for the peace conference itself. "That can be determined later," House said.

Wilson took the advice but suspected that the British and the French were probably less concerned about titles than about the possibility that he would rally the smaller nations against them. He was right. Lloyd George, foreseeing the hero's welcome awaiting the president in Europe, blanched at the thought that Wilson would galvanize world opinion in favor of a peace more generous than the one the Allied governments had in mind.

The debate on the wisdom of Wilson's decision proceeded politely until the end of November, when the White House announced the names of the five men who would represent the United States at the peace conference: President Wilson, Secretary of State Lansing, Colonel House, General Bliss, and Henry White, a retired career diplomat who had been ambassador to France and Italy. The press release was given out on a Friday night, a ploy often used to bury bad news. Washington immediately noticed and immediately took umbrage.

Republicans felt insulted yet again. Yes, Henry White was a Republican, but he was inconsequential in party circles and virtually unknown to the American public. Party leaders had not expected Wilson to name Lodge or Roosevelt, his fiercest critics, but they were incensed that he had overlooked Taft and Root. Both were widely respected, experienced in foreign affairs and international law, and ardent in their desire for a postwar association of nations. The Senate, the body responsible for ratifying treaties, was also irritated. President McKinley had appointed three senators to the commission that negotiated the peace after the Spanish-American War, but Wilson had not selected one. In choosing four compliant men, Wilson was saying that he was the only American peace commissioner who mattered.

Three days later, when the president delivered his State of the Union address to Congress, his stock fell again. "Republicans had said they would give him an ice bath and they were sullen and quiet," Josephus Daniels told his diary. "It was the most unhandsome performance—churlish." The president took his humiliation in silence.

After a lengthy review of domestic issues, Wilson spoke briefly about his trip, acknowledging that his absence would inconvenience the country. But, he said, the Allies wanted his counsel, and he wanted to give it, in the interest of a lasting peace. More than fifty thousand Americans had fought and died for the ideals in the Fourteen Points, which were the ideals of the United States. "It is now my duty to play my full part in making good what they offered their life's blood to obtain," he said. "I can think of no call to service which could transcend this." He asked for their support.

Roosevelt responded with his umpteenth complaint about the vagueness of the Fourteen Points and warned Wilson not to try to play referee between the Allies and the Central Powers. "It is our business to stand by our Allies," he wrote. Taft, the only sympathetic Republican of any prominence, announced that he was for Wilson's trip and against sniping at the president while he was abroad.

Wilson sailed for France on December 4 aboard the USS *George Washington*, one of the German liners repurposed and renamed by the U.S. Navy during the war. Among the 113 members of the president's party were Edith Wilson and her social secretary, Dr. Grayson, Secretary Lansing, Ambassador White, George Creel, Jimmie Starling and seven other Secret Service agents, two stenographers, the chief usher of the White House, a handful of servants, a trio of reporters from American wire services, and twenty-three members of the Inquiry. Since its founding in the fall of 1917, the Inquiry had worked largely in secret, compiling facts for American use at the peace conference. Numbingly thorough, the 150 scholars assigned to the project amassed so many maps, books, bibliographies, articles, reports, and statistics that three army trucks were needed to deliver them to the *George Washington.*

The Wilsons were no more hospitable at sea than on land, although they were often seen walking the decks and watching the movies shown nightly in the ship's main dining room. On Grayson's orders, Wilson spent most of his time resting. He held few meetings, and by all accounts was still in a defiant mood. With the Republicans out of his way for the time being, he was girding himself for a showdown with the Allies. Four days out, he summoned the reporters to discuss a wireless message from Colonel House, who had just learned that the Allied prime ministers were bent on squeezing every last pfennig out of Germany.

"I am absolutely opposed to this," Wilson told the reporters. If the peacemakers delivered a treaty filled with spoliation, it would go down in history as a scourge. If the Allies insisted on egregious financial or territorial demands, he would withdraw from the conference. Wilson was also put out with the British for promising to continue the discussion of the freedom of the seas and simultaneously promising the people of Britain that His Majesty's government would never relinquish its naval supremacy. If the British did not abandon the idea of controlling the seas, Wilson told the reporters, he would vow to build a navy even larger than Britain's.

At one of the movie screenings, William C. Bullitt, the State Department's brash young advisor on Russian affairs, took a seat next to Wilson and told him that he ought to convene the Inquiry men and share his thoughts on the policies he meant to pursue at the peace conference. Because they had no idea what the president planned to do in Paris, Bullitt explained, they were growing cynical.

Wilson saw ten of the Inquiry scholars the next day, and he was at his best—frank, engaging, warm, and good-natured. The gathering was less conversation than lecture, with Wilson behind a desk and his listeners seated in a semicircle before him. He talked for an hour. Of the League of Nations, he said he pictured a council of representatives from member states, watching the world and proposing a course of action if war seemed imminent. If the world war had shown anything, it was that any war could quickly engulf the world, he said. Would-be disturbers of the peace would be kept in line with a threat of an economic boycott—no international trade, no trains or ships crossing the border, no telephone or telegraph links to other countries.

The president also gave the Inquiry a long description of his general approach to the conference, beginning with his oft-stated idea that the United States would be the only nation present not seeking material gain from the war. Throughout the negotiations, he said, the only American question would be, "Is it just?" He was confident that Europe would heed the wishes of the United States for two reasons: a just peace was the surest way to prevent the discontent that fueled the spread of Bolshevism, and it would be unjust to ignore the U.S. contributions to victory. "It is not too much to say that at Château-Thierry we saved the world, and I do not intend to let those Europeans forget it," Wilson said. It *was* too much to say that the AEF had saved the world at Château-Thierry, but the sheer size of the American army in the summer of 1918 (two million men in the field and two million more in training) had forced the Germans to abandon their hope of winning the war.

The Inquiry men were thrilled by the president's last remarks: "You are, in truth, my advisers, for when I ask information, I will have no way of checking it, and must act on it unquestioningly. We shall be deluged with claims plausibly presented, and it will be your job to establish the justice or injustice of these claims, so that my position may be taken intelligently." What he wanted was simple, he said. "Tell me what's right and I'll fight for it."

Sensing that the Paris mission would be the riskiest of his career, Robert Lansing had been trying for two months to get Wilson to divulge his plan for the League of Nations and for making peace. Just after the Armistice, Lansing sent him a list of thirty-three questions. Which nations would come to the conference? Would all the belligerents attend? What voice should provisional governments have? What instructions should be given to the American commissioners? And so on. Obviously hoping to make the exercise an easy one, Lansing confined himself to mechanics and left space between the questions for the president's answers. Wilson did not reply.

As Lansing submitted his questions, he gave some thought to the role of the peacemakers and concluded that they would have to succeed at two monumental tasks: devising a treaty that would last and constructing a new political foundation for the world. In place of the old balance of power, which had been destroyed in the fall of the German, Austro-Hungarian, Russian, and Ottoman empires, he envisioned a world order resting firmly on justice "between nations, between society and its members, and between individuals. It is international, social, and industrial justice."

On that he and Woodrow Wilson agreed. But Wilson placed his hopes for a just world on the Allies' acceptance of the Fourteen Points, and Lansing had little confidence that the unity would hold. The Allies had come together to defeat the Central Powers, but now that the danger had passed, Lansing wrote a friend, "the tendency will be to fly apart. Conflicting interests will come into play."

Lansing boarded the *George Washington* in an anxious frame of mind. At sea he had time to read for pleasure and catch up on his sleep, and he and his wife thoroughly enjoyed their meals in the dignitaries' dining room. But he was hardly relaxed. Wilson had only an hour's talk with him and White about the League, and while White was pleased to find that Wilson had no rigid ideas on the workings of the new organization, Lansing felt as frustrated as ever. When he tried to point out some of the hazards, Wilson said brusquely that arrangements could be made to obviate the risks. With the American landing in France only five days away, the question was, when would Wilson be ready to make any arrangements, even provisional arrangements, for negotiating any of the issues sure to arise at the peace conference?

Lansing was not the only baffled member of the presidential party. The spell that Wilson cast over the Inquiry men wore off in a day or two, leaving most of them wondering how the president would be able to put his ideals into practice. Wilson unburdened himself to George Creel on an evening walk around the deck. "It is to America that the whole world turns today, not only with its wrongs, but with its hopes and grievances," Wilson said. "The hungry expect us to feed them, the roofless look to us for shelter, the sick of heart and body depend upon us for cure. All of these expectations have in them the quality of terrible urgency. There must be no delay. It has been so always. People will endure their tyrants for years, but they tear their deliverers to pieces if a millennium is not created immediately. Yet you know, and I know, that these ancient wrongs, these present unhappinesses, are not to be remedied in a day or with a wave of the hand. What I seem to see—with all my heart I hope that I am wrong—is a tragedy of disappointment."

30

·········

Final Triumph

The *George Washington* arrived in France on Wilson's day of days, Friday the 13th. The cheering, which began as soon as the president came into view, went on for weeks. Millions (two million in Paris alone) came out to see him. Londoners were delighted to see him on their front pages with George V, and delighted again when they noticed that only one leg of the presidential trousers had a cuff. The English public allegedly took the mismatch as a sign that the great idealist had no time for minutiae.

Thousands heard his speeches. Thousands more knelt along railway tracks to offer prayers as he passed. In Italy, wounded soldiers tried to kiss his clothes, and civilians showered the streets with handbills proclaiming him God of Peace, Savior of Humanity, Moses from Across the Atlantic. Europeans said they had never before seen such adulation. Nor had Wilson, who beamed and bowed and tipped his silk hat times without number.

Carried away by a stupendous ovation in Milan, he stood on a balcony and blew kisses to the crowd.

In October, as the war hurtled to an end, the Allies were expecting to draw up a treaty as soon as the American peace commissioners could get to Europe. Wilson scheduled his departure accordingly, but just after his plans were set, the British called a national election for December 14. Tallying the votes would consume another two weeks. Three more would pass before the formal opening of the peace conference. With no news to report, the hundreds of foreign journalists encamped in Paris wrote about the cold, grim city, where a walk in any direction brought them face-to-face with uncountable amputees in uniform, uncountable women in black, and ugly heaps of artillery pieces captured from the Germans. Watching the influx of supplicants from four continents—"men with patriarchal beards and scimitar-shaped noses," men in fezzes and sugarloaf hats and miters, men in business suits—a correspondent for the *Daily Telegraph* of London realized that Paris was about to become "the clearing-house of the Fates, where the accounts of a whole epoch, the deeds and misdeeds of an exhausted civilization, were to be balanced and squared."

Reporters filed innumerable stories on the Wilsons' quarters on the rue de Monceau. Lent to them by Prince Joachim Murat, whose ancestors included Napoleon Bonaparte as well as George Washington, the Hôtel Murat was not a hotel but a small palace filled with antique furniture, paintings, sculptures, and tapestries. Brocade and bibelots abounded. Edith was pleased to have three sumptuous drawing rooms and seventeen servants in scarlet knee breeches and long-tailed coats. An English journalist who toured the palace seemed relieved that the president's bedroom was vast and mostly empty, offering the honored guest plenty of space to walk about as he thought.

Wilson filled the blank weeks with travel, speechmaking, and meetings arranged by Colonel House, who had been in Paris for months. As usual, House had been cultivating politicians and other men of influence. Georges Clemenceau, the French premier, was an early catch. "I can talk to him frankly, and he talks that way with me," Clemenceau told a friend. The premier and the colonel would remain friends for life.

By nature sympathetic and eager to please, House made friends easily and took it on faith that a leader who made himself congenial could accomplish more than one who did not. No one had tried harder than House to turn his social gifts to the advantage of his unsociable friend in the White House. Knowing that the shape of the postwar world would be determined largely by Britain, France, and the United States, House brought Clemenceau and Wilson together on Wilson's second day in Paris. In separate conversations beforehand, the colonel instructed both men to stick to pleasantries. Given the stakes of the peace conference, serious differences were inevitable, and House wanted the two leaders to appreciate each other before the swords were drawn. After the meeting, both statesmen professed delight—a good omen, House thought.

Clemenceau had strayed beyond the chitchat at one point to say that he no longer opposed Wilson's participation in the peace conference. House, having already persuaded Wilson that he would have more influence if he returned to Washington soon after the formal opening of the proceedings, was disappointed. When Wilson decided to stay, House thought it a big mistake, as did David Lloyd George. It seemed to the prime minister that an occasional White House cable intimating that the president would not sign a treaty containing this or that would make it easier for the French and British to persuade their citizens to accept Wilson's terms.

Clemenceau agreed with Lloyd George, and that was why he wanted Wilson to stay in Paris. As he confided to a friend, Wilson in the White House would be "Zeus on Mount Olympus. He could keep us all dangling while he makes up his mind." Wilson in Paris would be more easily swayed than Wilson in Washington, and Clemenceau, anticipating serious quarrels with Britain, hoped that he could persuade the United States to side with France.

A few days after the chat at the Murat, Clemenceau told the British ambassador to France, Lord Derby, that he did not expect much trouble from Wilson, but Derby called on Colonel House for further reassurance. House blithely promised to talk the president out of positions that Britain found objectionable. Although Wilson had not yet discovered House's duplicity, he assumed that the Allies were not always candid with him and that he had to demonstrate that he would not be their pawn. Just after meeting Clemenceau, Wilson accepted invitations to visit England and Italy. Apparently caught off guard, Clemenceau requested that he postpone the trip to England. Wilson refused. He also declined French invitations to tour the battlefields, suspecting that France was trying to harden him against Germany. "I don't want to see the devastated regions," he told one of his callers. "As a boy, I saw the country through which Sherman marched to the sea. The pathway lay right through my people's properties. I know what happened, and I know the bitterness and hatreds which were engendered. I don't want to get mad over here, because I think there ought to be *one* person at that peace table who isn't mad." He would visit the front in a party of his own and on his own timetable. Stunned, the French took his refusal as indifference to their suffering.

The Wilsons left Paris on Christmas Eve and spent Christmas Day far from the devastation, at the field headquarters of General Pershing, who presented him with his first look at the Americans who had fought in France. Ten thousand men marched in review and stood in formation as Wilson promised to give his all to realize the ideals for which they had fought. From there, the president and his entourage moved on to England, where Lloyd George's reelection was confirmed on December 28.

After that, in the blank weeks before the peace conference, the president's tour dominated the headlines. He used his speeches to state and re-state the case for a new international organization committed to keeping the peace. In the first address, given in London, he declared that the statesmen charged with rebuilding the world would have to put it on an entirely new foundation. Rather than form military alliances that pitted one bloc of states against another, as the old balance of power had done, he proposed to bring the world into a single alliance, a league of nations built on moral force and goodwill. The superiority of moral force, an old theme with him, figured in nearly every speech on his tour. "It is moral force that is irresistible," he told the citizens of Carlisle, who had gathered to hear him in a Presbyterian church where his grandfather Woodrow had served. "It is moral force as much as physical that has defeated the effort to subdue the world. Words have cut as deep as the sword." In Manchester he warned that if the peace conference produced only a new balance of power, the United States would back away: "she will join no combination of power which is not the combi-nation of all of us. She is not interested merely in the peace of Europe, but in the peace of the world."

Clemenceau returned fire in a rousing speech to the Chamber of Dep-uties. "America is very far from Germany, but France is very near," he said, "and I have preoccupations which do not affect President Wilson as they do a man who has seen the Germans for four years in his country." Clemenceau vowed not to abandon the balance of power. Nor would he willingly give up the military and naval partnership forged by the victors, including the United States. If his fellow deputies wished to chart a different course, he said, they should choose a new premier before the peace conference. Now nearly eighty, Clemenceau nodded off during meetings, and his ministers grumbled that he was growing "unmethodical," but he was still *Le Tigre,* a title bestowed decades earlier for his ferocity in debate. Amid wild cheers the deputies voted three to one to tie themselves to the Tiger's tail.

In a less defiant hour of his life, Woodrow Wilson might have paused to consider the balance of personal power he would face at the peace confer-ence. The deputies had given Clemenceau carte blanche, British voters had given Lloyd George's coalition a victory, and both leaders understood that the new Republican majorities in both houses of Congress meant that Wilson no longer spoke for the majority of his fellow Americans. But Wilson expressed no apprehension. Even before meeting Clemenceau, he had written him off (privately) as "an old man, too old to comprehend new ideas." Lloyd George he regarded as "a second-rate politician." When Colonel House gently pointed out the political realities, Wilson smiled and told him, "Men die, but ideas live." Seeing himself as the spokesman of humanity, Wilson was sure that his vision would prevail.

But the Europeans were skeptical, and many Americans—admirers as well as critics—considered a peace treaty more urgent than a covenant establishing something as experimental as a league of nations. With Germany edging toward anarchy and Bolshevism spreading across Europe, any delay in the peacemaking seemed an unnecessary risk. All the same, Wilson prevailed—at least in the short term. France, Britain, and Italy bowed to his demand for a league covenant out of fear, hope, and need: fear that if they did not back Wilson the U.S. Senate would reject the peace treaty, hope that if they supported his great dream he would prove accommodating when their wishes were on the table, and their acute need for financial assistance from the United States.

Well before the peacemaking began, however, Henry Cabot Lodge gave a speech warning the Allies that if Wilson brought home a treaty as vague as the Fourteen Points, the Senate might well reject it. Sir Edward Grey, now a private citizen, was so alarmed by Lodge's threat that he advised his old friend House to urge Wilson to proceed with caution. But the idea that the Senate would reject the treaty struck Wilson as beyond preposterous.

While the Allied governments hoped that the president was right, they did not share his certitude. Nor did Robert Lansing. Even before Lodge's speech, the secretary of state was writing himself a memo on the most high-flown phrases in the Fourteen Points. When Wilson spoke of national self-determination, what unit did he have in mind? A race? A territory? Freedom of the seas sounded attractive, but what exactly was it? More than once Lansing had asked for a definition only to be brushed aside by Wilson. Of open covenants, openly arrived at, Lansing declared it "silly" to pretend that diplomatic negotiations could be conducted like town meetings. True, Wilson had explained that he was merely calling for the disclosure of treaties after they were made, but most Americans, including many members of the press, were expecting him to force Old World diplomats to do their work in the open. Lansing feared that Wilson would be accused of hypocrisy for holding confidential meetings with the Allies, and he was. There were more than two hundred such meetings in Paris, and the press would pummel Wilson repeatedly for breaking a promise that had thrilled the world.

The day after Lodge's speech appeared in the papers, Lansing was so upset by the possibility of a treaty defeat in the Senate that he sent Wilson a memo intended to help him snuff the Republican opposition. Marked "Secret and Urgent," it dealt with one of Wilson's most cherished ideas for the League of Nations covenant, a pledge by all members to come to the defense of any member under attack. On the *George Washington,* Lansing had tried to explain why the Senate would strenuously object, but Wilson had cut him off. In the memo Lansing pointed out three problems with the requirement: it would, at least in theory, oblige the United States to send troops whenever a League member was invaded; it would infringe on the right of Congress to declare war; and it raised the specter of European intervention in hostilities between the nations of the Western Hemisphere, a development that would end the protections afforded by the Monroe Doctrine. Declaring himself "earnestly in favor" of the president's wish to secure the world against war, Lansing suggested that Wilson turn his idea inside out: instead of committing every League member to send troops each time one of them was invaded, it could simply require all members to pledge not to make war on each other. Wilson never replied to Lansing's plea.

Lansing continued to fret about the extravagance of Wilson's promises, particularly the promise of national self-determination. As he saw it, "The phrase is simply loaded with dynamite. It will raise hopes which can never be realized. It will, I fear, cost thousands of lives. In the end it is bound to be discredited, to be called the dream of an idealist who failed to realize the danger until too late."

Back in Paris on January 7, Wilson finally paid a call on the other American peace commissioners, who had been deposited in an office on the first floor of the Hôtel de Crillon and left to fend for themselves. Secretary Lansing and Ambassador White had nothing to do and no instructions from Wilson. General Bliss had put himself to work, gathering military statistics that would be useful to the president. Delegations and teams of experts from the Allied and Associated Powers were streaming into Paris, and Bliss wondered what he was supposed to say if an envoy from another government asked for the American point of view on some subject.

Colonel House, embarrassed by the president's neglect of their fellow commissioners, encouraged Lansing to begin work on a skeletal version of the peace treaty. The secretary of state summoned two American lawyers who had come to Paris for the peace conference, and they quickly drew up an outline of conference topics as well as a list of positions aligned with Wilson's goal of making a just peace. As the skeleton neared completion, House gave Lansing a copy of Wilson's draft of the League's covenant, which Lansing had wanted to see for months. Lansing passed it along to the lawyers, who revised it and added it to their draft.

The colonel took the president to the Crillon a few days later, Lansing proudly presented the skeleton, and Wilson angrily demanded to know who had authorized it. He did not want lawyers drafting the treaty, he said. Humiliated, Lansing wanted to resign but stayed on, unwilling to embarrass the president at a delicate moment in the world's affairs. House could have rescued Lansing by disclosing that he had suggested the revision, but he said nothing. Worse, he admitted in his diary that he had recommended the treaty exercise to the idle commissioners simply to keep them occupied.

The Paris Peace Conference flickered to life on January 12, a dank Sunday, with a select gathering of delegates from the members of the Supreme War Council: Britain, France, Italy, and the United States. At Britain's suggestion, Japan would join them the next day. The head of each delegation brought a second, usually his chief of foreign affairs, and the body became known as the Council of Ten.* At last Robert Lansing had a place at the table. Over the next month, the Ten would meet daily, sometimes twice a day, to set policies and agendas.

The Ten accredited thirty-two delegations to the conference, twenty-seven from the Allied and Associated Powers plus a delegation from each of the five dominions of the British Empire. Not all of the accredited states had fought in the war, but all had severed relations with Germany. Germany and its allies were not invited. The victors, after negotiating among themselves, would present their terms to the vanquished.

---

* In 1921, rebutting the charge that the fate of the postwar world had been decreed by four fallible men ill prepared for their task, a future premier of France named André Tardieu pointed out that the treaty was the product of six months of study by 58 expert commissions that held 1,646 meetings and conducted 26 local investigations on behalf of the Council of Ten. Tardieu's tabulations show that the Ten met 72 times and often broke into smaller groups for additional work: the Five (foreign ministers) held 39 meetings, and the Big Four (Clemenceau, Lloyd George, Vittorio Orlando, and Wilson) convened 145 times. (André Tardieu, *The Truth About the Treaty* [Indianapolis: Bobbs-Merrill, 1921], 97.) The decisions were made largely by the Big Four, and, when Orlando returned to Italy, by the Big Three.

The Ten met at the Quai d'Orsay behind the soundproof double doors to the office of Stephen Pichon, the French foreign minister. The Ten would later admit a rotating cast of representatives of smaller nations, scholars, and experts, but on the first day they sat at a large oak table before a marble fireplace that had been blazing long enough to warm the room to the point of suffocation. Grayson opened a window, prompting Lloyd George to muse that they might be breathing the first fresh air let into the room since the age of Louis XIV.

For nearly a week, the Ten discussed procedural matters, the chaos in Russia, and the Armistice, which had to be renewed from time to time. To judge by the minutes, the Japanese rarely spoke. The Europeans did most of the talking, addressing almost every issue that arose and advancing their national interests whenever possible. The French came to the table with demands for security from German aggression and for punitive as well as actual damages for the ruin of France. Among other things, Britain sought control over the disposition of Germany's colonies and a large say in reconfiguring the Middle East, where the demise of the Ottoman Empire had left a political void. The Italians intended to collect on the promises made in the secret treaty that brought them into the war: new territory to the north of Italy and along the eastern shore of the Adriatic. Japan was waiting for an opportune moment to make a bid for Germany's Pacific colonies and a permanent foothold in China. The United States wanted a just and lasting peace, and Wilson insisted that it could not be had until the League of Nations was brought into being, because he said, it was "key to the whole settlement."

The European leaders had become acquainted during the war, and their Foreign Offices had interacted for centuries. But the United States had seldom figured in their geopolitical calculations before the war, and Lloyd George and Clemenceau knew Wilson only through his ambassadors and from the dispatches of their own envoys in Washington. Presented with the man himself, they were somewhat baffled. One American journalist at the peace conference recalled Clemenceau studying the president "as if he were a new and disconcerting species. He thought Wilson had the Messiah complex." When Lloyd George watched Clemenceau watching Wilson, he saw an old dog casting a wary eye on an unfamiliar dog that had wandered into the farmyard: "He listened with eyes and ears lest Wilson should by a phrase commit the conference to some proposition which weakened the settlement from the French standpoint. If Wilson ended his allocution without doing any perceptible harm, Clemenceau's stern face temporarily relaxed, and he expressed his relief with a deep sigh."

Lloyd George would come to like Wilson but at first had the feeling that the president regarded himself as a missionary come to save the heathens. "He was apt to address us in that vein, beginning with a few simple and elementary truths about right being more important than might, and justice being more eternal than force," Lloyd George wrote in his memoir of the peace conference. "No doubt Europe needed the lesson, but the president forgot that the Allies had fought for nearly five years for international right and fair play. . . . They were therefore impatient at having little sermonettes delivered to them."

At one point Wilson startled Lloyd George by observing that organized religion had yet to devise practical solutions to the problems of the world. Christ had articulated the ideal, he said, but He had offered no instruction on how to attain it. "That is the reason why I am proposing a practical scheme to carry out His aims," he told his fellow statesmen. And at that remark, Lloyd George wrote, "Clemenceau slowly opened his dark eyes to their widest dimensions and swept them round the assembly to see how the Christians gathered round the table enjoyed this exposure of the futility of their master."

But if any of the men present thought that Wilson was saying that he intended to outshine the Lord, they were mistaken. Like faithful Christians through the ages, Wilson regarded himself as one of the Lord's servants. He claimed no special relationship with God, no divine understanding. He was simply a believer who drew strength from believing in an all-knowing, all-powerful, beneficent God. As he had told a group of religious leaders in England, "I think one would go crazy if he did not believe in Providence. It [life] would be a maze without a clue."

Wilson was first and last a man of principle, and he tried hard to live up to the exacting standards he set for himself and for the United States. But the popular acclaim for his high-minded vision for the postwar world seems to have exacerbated his moral vanity. He had nothing but contempt for Republicans who questioned the wisdom of his internationalism. He saw Clemenceau's constant advocacy of French interests as selfish and myopic. As for Lloyd George, Wilson found him magnetic and was amused by his boyishness in the meetings of the Big Four, where he often addressed himself to Clemenceau alone and then turned to smile at Wilson and Prime Minister Vittorio Orlando—"as if he expects us to applaud and agree with him," Wilson told Grayson. Wilson could have admired Lloyd George's uncanny ability to intuit the psychological needs of others, his spontaneity, and his genius for argument, but the president, looking down his nose, saw a cunning lawyer for the unsavory cause of empire and a politician who changed positions with every twitch of British public opinion.

Wilson's opposites considered him visionary and woefully ignorant of European affairs. While he should (and could) have been better informed on the hard choices facing Europe in the aftermath of the war, it is worth pointing out that the Europeans found him ignorant mainly when his views did not coincide with theirs. In the Council of Ten, he showed none of the spitefulness that often marred his dealings with political opponents at home. Apart from the sermonettes, he was cordial, forthcoming, and able to disagree without pique. His questions were courteously if plainly put. Why did the five British dominions need separate delegations? he asked at one of the Ten's first meetings. Because each dominion was autonomous, Lloyd George replied. Wilson predicted that the arrangement would magnify the suspicion that the Great Powers were trying to run the world. Lloyd George shot back that the Great Powers had run the war. But that was war, Wilson said. Peace, particularly this peace, was different, because it would make a settlement affecting the entire world, and the small nations were bound to be dissatisfied unless they played a substantive role in the proceedings. Still, the only change Wilson proposed was cosmetic: he suggested that the Ten refer to their meetings as informal conversations rather than conferences.

Without question the Council of Ten was imperfect and unrepresentative, but it was hardly free to act without reference to the rest of the world. Nearly every challenge it faced quickly became tangled in a web of conflicting demands and the needs of other nations. In the first discussion of renewing the Armistice, for example, Wilson suggested that if it proved necessary to introduce any changes, they should be made under clauses already in the Armistice. Otherwise, he said, the victors would be open to the charge that they were imposing terms that went beyond the original agreement. But when the Ten met the next day, Marshal Foch presented a new clause requiring Germany to secure its gold reserves and guard the presses that printed its banknotes. The clause had nothing to do with keeping the peace. It aimed to ensure that Germany's gold did not disappear from the Reichsbank before Germany paid the reparations bill that France intended to submit. Pichon, foreseeing a calamity if the German people found out that the victors were seizing control of Germany's finances, urged that the new clause be kept secret. Wilson, champion of open covenants, agreed to the secrecy.

All of the Ten understood that starvation was rampant in the defeated countries, and none had a need for a sermonette on the link between hunger and revolution. But the Allies would not be hurried. Britain argued about whose ships would carry the foodstuffs, and France did not want Germany to buy food with money that ought to go toward reparations. Wilson pointed out that if the Allies did not find a way to feed the Germans, they would be unable to pay any damages at all.

On January 17 the Council of Ten invited all of the delegations to meet at three o'clock the next afternoon for the first plenary of the Paris Peace Conference. The weather was foul—cold, with a vertical river of rain—and the plenary was something of an anticlimax. The *Chicago Tribune* ran its story on an inside page under the headline "Peacemaking Has the Thrills of an Inquest." The journalists, relegated to the arches that ran along one wall of the Salle de l'Horloge (the Clock Room), reported that the delegates were seated in sixty-nine chairs arranged around the inner and outer faces of a horseshoe-shaped table covered with green baize. Clemenceau, flanked by Wilson and Lloyd George, presided from a table at the head of the room. Behind them, over the mantel, stood a colossal sculpture of Marianne, symbol of the French Republic, looking invincible and ready to leap from her post at the first whiff of a threat to France.

For the Americans, whose public architecture was inspired by the simplicity of ancient Athens and Rome, the cherubs around the frieze, the massive chandeliers, and the predominance of red, black, and gilt suggested the great theaters of Broadway. But what might it mean to meet in a room that was a statement of the glory of France? And who would be able to ignore French demands while seated beneath the looming Marianne? If the reporters from the United States wondered, they did not say so to their readers.

Nor did they catch the drift of the opening speeches delivered by President Raymond Poincaré and Premier Clemenceau. Overly impressed by the nods to Wilson's ideals, the American press either missed or chose to downplay the French leaders' insistence on holding their enemies accountable. Poincaré said that true justice demanded "restitution and reparation for the peoples and individuals who have been despoiled or maltreated. . . . It pursues a twofold object—to render to each his due and not to encourage crime through leaving it unpunished." He reminded the delegates that on this day in 1871, in the Hall of Mirrors at Versailles, France had signed a treaty surrendering Alsace-Lorraine, the price it had been forced to pay to end the Franco-Prussian War. The Germans had used the occasion to proclaim the birth of the German Empire. "Born in injustice, it has ended in opprobrium," Poincaré said. "You are assembled in order to repair the evil that has been done and to prevent a recurrence of it."

Clemenceau, too, made a case for imposing a financial penalty on Germany in addition to collecting reparations, but he was less concerned with punishing Germany than with weakening it to a point where it could not launch another war. Preoccupied with the security of France, he begged the states represented in Paris to stand together and to embrace the League of Nations. "It is in yourselves," he said, "it is for you to make it live; and for that it must be in our hearts. As I have said to President Wilson, there must be no sacrifice which we are not ready to accept." To the American journalists, it sounded as if the Tiger had forsaken the balance of power for Wilson's internationalism. He had not. He wanted a military alliance of the Great Powers in addition to the League, wanted it as badly as Wilson wanted the League, and would persist until he got it.

Clemenceau invited all delegations to submit memoranda on any subject to the secretary of the conference, announced that the next plenary would begin with a discussion of the League, and adjourned the meeting. Lansing would later rank Clemenceau as the strongest leader at the peace conference, but his first impression was unfavorable. The meeting reminded him of ward politics in the United States, where a party boss who found himself in the minority could prevail anyway, simply by keeping a tight rein on the meeting.

At the second plenary, on January 25, Clemenceau called for the appointment of five commissions, one of them on the League of Nations. In stating the case for the League, Wilson said it would maintain peace in the long term and in the short term could prove invaluable by taking up disarmament and other questions requiring months and months of study. Anticipating that some of the decisions made in Paris might require modification, he urged the conference to create an institution and processes capable of making the adjustments deemed necessary in the interest of a just peace.

Lloyd George and others praised Wilson's speech and commended the League of Nations to the conference, and then, Lansing wrote, "the beargarden broke loose." The Belgian foreign minister asked who would serve on the commission. Clemenceau replied that each of the Great Powers had designated two delegates and would allow five more delegates selected by other powers. One after another, the peeved rose to object, and a Brazilian envoy stated the situation with cutting simplicity: "It is with some surprise that I constantly hear it said, 'This has been decided, that has been decided.' Who has taken a decision? We are a sovereign assembly, a sovereign court. It seems to me that the proper body to take a decision is the conference itself."

Clemenceau waited out the abuse, then delivered a jeremiad. The Council of Ten had decided on the five commissions in the same way it decided to call the Paris Peace Conference, he said. The Great Powers, having made the largest sacrifices in the war, might well have devised a peace of their own. But they had summoned all of the Allied and Associated Powers, "not to impose our will upon them . . . but to ask for their help." He said that the world would not care whose representatives sat on which commission. "It will ask us for results, ask us what we have done for the League of Nations."

Here was Georges Clemenceau, firm believer in the supremacy of military force, proselytizing for the League of Nations, the epitome of moral force, with all the fervor of Woodrow Wilson. There had been no sudden conversion. The boss of the global ward meeting had merely struck a pose in order to do the very thing he claimed not to be doing: impose the will of the Great Powers on the rest of the world. Clemenceau followed his speech with a deft turning of the tables, asking the plenary to adopt the resolutions creating the five commissions as well as a proposal for a meeting at which delegates of nations with a stake in any of the five issues could elect representatives to the new bodies. Offered a voice and a vote, the delegates could scarcely refuse. The measures were quickly approved, and the meeting was adjourned.

Wilson now had what he wanted most: a commission to write the covenant that would create the League and the Council of Ten's promise that the covenant would be part of the treaty. Victories in hand, he was at last willing to make his pilgrimage to the battlefields. The presidential party set out at eight o'clock the next morning, in a motorcade of seven cars. They went first to Château-Thierry and Belleau Wood, stopping to inspect a trench where the U.S. marines had awaited their order to advance. Nearby, at the Americans' temporary military cemetery, Wilson took off his hat and stood in silence, staring at row after row of wooden crosses. He and Edith had called on wounded Americans hospitalized in Paris, but the visit to the cemetery put him face-to-face with the American dead of the world war for the first time. After lunch they motored through forty miles of rubble and blackened terrain to the immense ruin of Reims. A thriving metropolis of 250,000 before the war, Reims in 1919 was home to only 3,000, many of them living in the wine caves under the city. The cardinal of Reims, frail and old, gave the presidential party a tour of what remained of the cathedral. Edith would recall his red-gloved hand pointing skyward and a light snow falling through great holes in the roof. The president listened attentively but made no comment.

Traveling back to Paris that night, Wilson was pensive and depressed. Perhaps he was seeing red, just as he had feared, and struggling to control his rage against the Germans. Perhaps he was remembering the black scars of Sherman's March. Certainly he was exhausted. He realized that he would be expected to comment on his day among the ruins, but he could muster only a sentence: "No one can put into words the impressions received amid such scenes of desolation and ruin." He gave it to Grayson to give to the papers. Criticized for not visiting the front soon after he arrived, Wilson would now be criticized for the paltriness of his response to the devastation.

At least two visitors who saw Wilson that week were alarmed by his fatigue and afraid that he would break down. Now, as chair of the League of Nations commission, he would have to do even more. Most of the commission's meetings would take place at night, after he had put in a long day with the Council of Ten. Lloyd George and Clemenceau had decided not to chair any commissions for fear of overextending themselves, but Wilson, bound heart and soul to the League, apparently never questioned the necessity of bearing a double load. The commission worked late into the night and on some days met more than once. Fortunately, its labors were compressed into eleven days, a feat made possible by years of British spadework and the round-the-clock efforts of uncountable lawyers, Inquiry scholars, and technical advisors.

Despite the high speed of their deliberations, the members of the League commission found time to quarrel. Britain firmly refused to countenance any provision for freedom of the seas. France fought for the creation of an international army. Wilson's notion that territorial boundaries set by the Paris Peace Conference could be adjusted later by the League was rejected for fear that the agitation for further adjustments would be endless. Thirteen of the fourteen nations represented on the commission, including the United States, favored a clause granting equal status to all races, but the idea was abandoned after the British argued that it interfered with the right of nations to govern their internal affairs as they saw fit.

Many of the twenty-six articles in the covenant outlined the general procedures of the League and gave it a rudimentary structure: a Secretariat, a Body of Delegates from all member states, and an Executive Council of nine, with a representative from each of the five Great Powers and four from other states. The Great Powers had permanent seats in the council; the League would select the others and set the length of their membership. Watching from the sidelines, Lansing saw that the "Big Fellows" were "running the whole show. . . . The small nations have no more voice in settling the destinies of the world than they had a hundred years ago." Wilson's notion of the equality of all nations would survive only as a myth.

In a significant break with the past, Article XXII prevented the victors from laying permanent claim to vast swaths of territory that had been part of one or another of the four empires toppled by the war. Wilson, determined to prevent the customary division of the spoils, fell for a proposal by Jan Smuts, an Oxford-educated South African general who helped the British refine their ideas for the League of Nations. "Europe is being liquidated, and the League of Nations must be the heir to this great estate," Smuts had written just after the war's end. "The peoples left behind by the decomposition of Russia, Austria, and Turkey are mostly untrained politically; many of them are either incapable of or deficient in power of self-government; they are mostly destitute and will require much nursing towards economic and political independence." A Great Powers scramble for territory while Europe lay bleeding from every pore would be madness, Smuts argued. He suggested putting the territories into a trusteeship overseen by the League with day-to-day governance entrusted to so-called mandatory powers—League members willing to undertake the task.

The French had resisted, wanting outright possession of several former German colonies in Africa. Wilson protested that if the French had their way, it would be said that the Great Powers had preyed upon the most powerless peoples of the earth and only then formed a League of Nations. Lloyd George kept the mandates alive with a proposal to divide them into three categories. The former Ottoman territories, well along the road to self-government, would be designated as "A" mandates and allowed to choose their own mandatory powers. The "B" mandates, former German colonies in Africa, were to be governed humanely and to stand on an equal economic footing with the states in the League of Nations. The "C mandates," South West Africa and former German colonies in the Pacific, would be governed by the laws of the mandatory powers and prepared for self-rule.

To Lansing, Article XXII was a division of the spoils cleverly disguised as magnanimity. Wilson had not asked the Allies why they were willing to settle for temporary authority over the territories in question, a lapse that Lansing attributed to Wilson's high-mindedness and a mistaken belief that the Allies shared his feeling of protectiveness toward new states. It had not occurred to Wilson that the motive for the mandates was financial: if the Allies had insisted on permanent control rather than temporary mandates, Germany would have been in a strong position to argue that the value of its former possessions should be subtracted from the reparations bill.

Article X, one of Wilson's most cherished ideas, pledged every League member to protect all members from external aggression. In case of such aggression (or even the threat of it) the Executive Council was supposed to "advise upon the means by which the obligation shall be fulfilled." The key feature of Article X was not that it required all League members to spring to the defense of any member under attack; it was the requirement that the Executive Council *advise* the members on how to carry out their pledge to defend one another. To Lord Robert Cecil, a staunch advocate of the League, the fact that Article X was merely advisory suggested that the pledge of mutual defense was an illusion. "Do any of us really mean it?" he asked at a meeting of the League commission. Wilson let the question hang in the air. The French, quick to see that a League member might well reject the Executive Council's advice to take up arms, acceded to Wilson's wishes but strengthened their resolve to win greater security for France by other means.

The provision on disarmament was also advisory, and the article empowering the League to create an international court of arbitration stopped short of making arbitration compulsory. In place of open covenants, openly arrived at was a requirement that all League members register their future international agreements with the League. As for the omission of freedom of the seas, Wilson laughed it off in his next meeting with reporters. The joke was on him, he said. Historically, freedom of the seas was a right asserted by neutrals in wartime, but if the League realized its dream of preserving the peace, there would be no neutrals because there would be no war.

Wilson planned to leave for the United States on February 14 to tend to domestic affairs for a few weeks, and at a Council of Ten meeting on February 13, he reported that the covenant would be completed that night. He asked to present it in a plenary the next afternoon. Clemenceau, apparently taken by surprise, wondered whether the Ten should consider it first. Wilson replied that it should go first to the plenary, whose vote had authorized the League commission. Lord Balfour, Britain's foreign secretary, backed him up, pointing out that Wilson would speak only as chairman of a commission, so nothing that he said would commit the Great Powers in any way. Clemenceau, who clearly dreaded the possibility of a debate that might slip out of his control, said he hoped that the gathering could be adjourned as soon as Wilson had made his presentation. Wilson said he did not see how the delegates could be denied a chance to speak. He reminded Clemenceau that there was nothing to lose, because no vote would be taken.

Next morning, Wilson went to see House, who would head the American peace delegation while Wilson was away. Hoping to assure the president that the peace conference would not come to a standstill, House said he thought he could "button up everything during the next four weeks." Wilson, fearing that House would make compromises in the interest of speed, looked alarmed. House backpedaled, explaining that he was thinking of his efforts as groundwork for decisions to be made by Wilson when he returned. It seemed to House that Wilson was pleased by the idea, but the colonel took the precaution of pointing out that the United States had been compromising all along. Although House tactfully refrained from reciting the specifics, Wilson had given up on freedom of the seas, stopped fighting for the equality of nations, and pushed for more secrecy than any other member of the Council of Ten. Finished with their private business, they sent for Lansing, Bliss, and White, and Wilson spent an hour telling them about the covenant. Lansing, still hurt by his exclusion from all business related to the League, was in a cold fury. "Not having studied it I reserve opinion as to its excellence," he told his diary.

Despite the short notice and bad weather, nearly all of the accredited delegates attended the February 14 plenary. Edith Wilson, making her first appearance at the conference, sat with Grayson in an alcove near the back of the Salle de l'Horloge. Clemenceau began by asking the delegates to approve the minutes of the two previous plenaries, the delegates obliged, and without ceremony Clemenceau recognized the president of the United States. Wilson gave an undramatic reading of the covenant followed by an equally understated explication. The covenant was the work of men from fourteen nations, all of whom had assented to it, he said. The unity was crucial, for the success of the League would depend mainly on "one great force . . . the moral force of the public opinion of the world." And if the world's moral force did not avail, physical force would be brought to bear. "But that is the last resort," Wilson said, "because this is intended as a constitution of peace, not as a league of war." He characterized the simplicity of the covenant as a great virtue. Inherently flexible, the League would be able to exert as much or as little power as it thought necessary in a given set of circumstances. But for all the covenant's elasticity, it was not vague, Wilson said. "It is a definite guarantee of peace. It is a definite guarantee by word against aggression. It is a definite guarantee against the things which have just come near bringing the whole structure of civilization into ruin."

To Wickham Steed of the *Daily Mail*, it seemed that the air filled with "a sense that something new, something irrevocable had been done." It was impossible to listen to the proceedings without feeling that the affairs of the world had been raised to new heights, he thought. The world had been elevated, "if only for an instant, to a higher plane, on which the organized moral consciousness of peoples, the publicity of international engagements, and of government by the consent . . . of the governed, became prospective realities."

Even Lansing was impressed. Scanning the Salle de l'Horloge as Wilson spoke, he could see that the delegates were deeply affected. Wilson's dignity, earnestness, and logic "won the admiration of all," Lansing wrote.

Lord Cecil spoke next, expressing his pleasure that the covenant was being disclosed to the world, a move that would enable peoples everywhere to comment and offer advice on it. Prime Minister Orlando of Italy described the covenant as a fitting monument to the fallen. A few dissonant notes followed. Léon Bourgeois, a member of the French delegation, announced that France reserved the right to propose changes. Baron Makino Nobuaki of Japan reiterated the point on behalf of his country. Rustem Haidar, the envoy from the Arabian kingdom of Hejaz, inquired about the word "mandate." "What does it mean?" he asked. "We do not exactly know." Not unreasonably he accused the Great Powers of making a secret compact to dispose of the nations of the Middle East.

When Clemenceau had had enough, he turned a question about when the delegates would discuss the covenant into an opportunity to bring the plenary to a close. The covenant had been deposited with the secretary of the conference and could be examined and discussed by any delegation at any time, he said. He promised that a plenary discussion would be held soon after the preliminary examination had been completed. With that, he adjourned the meeting, leaving everyone to wonder what a "preliminary examination" was and when it would end.

It was nearly seven o'clock. Wilson, surrounded by delegates wanting to shake his hand, worked his way free, and he and Edith headed to the Hôtel Murat. He was exhausted but deeply satisfied, telling Edith, "It will be sweet to go home, even for a few days, with the feeling that I have kept the faith with the people, particularly with these boys"—the young men who had served in the war. At nine o'clock they left for Gare des Invalides, where a red carpet lined with palms and evergreens stretched from the curb to their train. Clemenceau and the French cabinet had come to see him off, as had the British ambassador, and a number of Americans, including Colonel House. Wilson took House's hand, put an arm around him, and gave him a warm good-bye. To his diary House reported that his friend "looked happy, as well indeed he should."

31

Storm Warning

In a cable dispatched on his last day in Paris, Wilson asked Tumulty to arrange a White House dinner with the members of the Senate and House committees on foreign affairs. House had suggested the dinner, Wilson had reluctantly agreed, and the invitation had all the charm of an arrest warrant. There was no sense that the host looked forward to seeing his guests, no hint of the pleasure he would take in sharing his experiences abroad, no flattering suggestion that he might need their advice. They were told to turn up at eight o'clock on February 26, asked not to debate the League's covenant before then, and informed that debate would prove superfluous because there was "a good and sufficient reason for the phraseology and substance of each article."

The Wilsons left for Brest that night, and the next morning the *George Washington* set sail for Boston. The original itinerary called for a New York landing without ceremony in order to speed Wilson to his duties in

Washington. But in early January, just after Lodge gave a long speech critical of the League, it occurred to Tumulty that Wilson's enemies could use the lack of fanfare as evidence of his waning influence in the United States. Picturing a Boston arrival with a public celebration and a presidential speech, Tumulty predicted in a telegram that it "would make ovation inevitable throughout New England and center attack on Lodge."

A few days before landing, Wilson notified Tumulty that he did not want an elaborate reception in Boston. He was willing to speak informally, he said—on the pier, perhaps, or at the train station. Not possible, Tumulty replied. Arrangements had been made, and an eleventh-hour change "would be open to mischievous misconstruction." Wilson finally confessed his fear that an extravaganza in Boston would antagonize Congress. Tumulty held firm.

As radiograms flew back and forth between the *George Washington* and the White House, the Wilsons lunched with David Francis, the former U.S. ambassador to Russia, and Franklin and Eleanor Roosevelt. When Francis volunteered his opinion that Americans would support the League of Nations, Wilson, perhaps with his new worries in mind, replied, "The failure of the United States to back it would break the heart of the world."

Eleanor Roosevelt was impressed by the depth of feeling in Wilson's remark but otherwise found him a puzzle. She could scarcely believe his indifference to the entertainments staged for him by the crew and was shocked by his admission over lunch that he had not read a newspaper since the beginning of the war. He relied on Tumulty to clip the essential articles for him, he said. Wilson's approach was efficient and perhaps necessary, but it was not customary among the public men of Wilson's day, and Eleanor Roosevelt was not alone in wondering how a president could govern without reading the news. She did not inquire, but he had recently explained to the first lady's social secretary, Edith Benham, that he felt that the newspapers spoke for the moneyed classes rather than the general public, so he gathered his impressions from other sources. He also reminded her that he had saturated himself in American political history. Benham, who wanted to understand how he got from a welter of impressions to the fully formed ideas expressed in his speeches, asked, "Don't you go deeper than that?" Wilson reflected for a moment, then said that he felt so imbued with American thought that when a new idea occurred to him, he just tried to voice it in a way that resonated with the people.

On February 24 Boston gave Wilson an exuberant welcome, with twenty-one-gun salutes, ear-splitting boat whistles, and daredevil aviators somersaulting across the sky. A few days earlier, Clemenceau had been shot in an assassination attempt, prompting Boston to assign thousands of policemen and armed soldiers to the president's route. Their presence did nothing to dampen the celebration. Set against the flags rippling on every storefront, the men in blue and khaki registered as one more salute to the president.

At the city's largest auditorium, Wilson declared that the United States had a responsibility to do more than sign a conventional peace treaty. Apparently afraid to utter the words "League of Nations" or "covenant" on Lodge's home ground, he spoke of guaranteeing the peace "by the united forces of the civilized world" and of the "utter blackness that would fall on the world" if America stood aside.

Headlines labeled the speech "defiant," and the editors of *The New York Times* called it "a threat aimed at the Senate." Lodge complained about it (privately) for months. He resented being attacked in his own backyard, but even more he resented Wilson's hypocrisy. As he put it in a letter to a friend, it might be acceptable "under the modern fashion" for a president to speak out after asking others to remain silent, but it violated the code of conduct he had learned in his youth.

Wilson reached Washington on February 25 and planned to stay until March 4, the last day of the Sixty-fifth Congress. Waiting for him was a note from a friendly Democratic senator, Thomas J. Walsh of Montana, who urged him to confer with a half-dozen members of Congress sympathetic to the League of Nations. Together, Walsh said, they could scrutinize the covenant clause by clause, as they did with bills in committee. Reminding Wilson that they had used the same approach to polish the Federal Reserve bill, Walsh said that a collaborative effort would make the covenant's language more precise and address the most serious objections raised by its congressional critics. Wilson declined, pleading a lack of time and confessing that it would prove virtually impossible to revise the covenant agreed upon in Paris.

The following evening, thirty-four members of the House and Senate committees on foreign affairs complied with their summons to the White House. (There were three absentees: a Democratic congressman who was ill and two Republican senators, William E. Borah of Idaho and Albert B. Fall of New Mexico, who found themselves implacably at odds with Wilson's internationalism.) Lodge's notes on the evening describe the dinner as "very pleasant" but omit the fact that he was given the honor of sitting next to the first lady. His courtesy led her to think that he would eventually support the League and enabled him to suppress his annoyance as she gushed about his hometown's enthusiastic reception of her husband. Later he could not resist telling a fellow Republican, Senator Frank B. Brandegee of Connecticut, that Edith Wilson's fingernails were "black with dirt."

After dinner, the guests were ushered into the East Room and seated in a semicircle facing the president, who announced that he would be happy to answer their questions about the covenant. Lodge gave him high marks in goodwill but did not think that Wilson grasped the covenant's impact on American foreign policy. Brandegee, who took the lead in quizzing Wilson, failed to elicit anything but shibboleths. "I feel as if I had been wandering with Alice in Wonderland and had tea with the Mad Hatter," he told the *New York Sun*.

Years later, Edith Wilson would reveal that Woodrow had ended the conversation by inviting his guests to send him their suggestions on the covenant. She missed the hollowness of asking for improvements to a document said to be beyond revision, and neither she nor her husband seemed to catch the subtlety of Lodge's last remarks of the evening. The president had pulled the senator aside to promise that he would do his best for the United States at the peace conference and to ask whether Lodge thought that the covenant as it stood would be approved by the Senate. Lodge replied that if the Committee on Foreign Relations approved it, it would undoubtedly be ratified. According to Edith's account, Woodrow had responded, "Very well then, I consider that, armed with your approval, I can go back and work feeling that you and your associates are behind me." Lodge nodded. But a nod can signal comprehension rather than agreement, and Wilson had missed the import of Lodge's "if."

Although there is no transcript of the evening's discussion of the covenant, it is known that the senators and congressmen present were most concerned about Article X, which authorized the Executive Council of the League to call on members for troops whenever they were needed to defend a member from foreign aggression. From interviews with several of the guests, the *New-York Tribune*'s Washington correspondent cleverly distilled Wilson's other comments into fourteen points. Among them: Joining the League would require some surrender of sovereignty, but Wilson claimed that every treaty had that effect. The League's recommendations on the size of each member's defense establishment would be purely advisory. The League's success would depend on the good faith of its members. The League could not prevent all wars. The current draft of the covenant would be approved by the peace conference, and it would be incorporated in the treaty. A day after giving the president his say, the *Tribune* compiled the reactions of the guests, which came down to one point: Wilson had failed to win over the skeptics, not all of whom were Republican.

On February 27, Wilson went up to the Capitol to offer his help with the raft of bills awaiting passage before the end of the session. Republicans, claiming that the dillydallying of the Democrats had caused the logjam, demanded that the president call an extraordinary session to take care of the unfinished business. Wilson refused. Barring an emergency, he said, he would wait until his final return from Paris to ask for a special session. Twice during his presidency Wilson had asked for such sessions, once to pass the Federal Reserve Act and once for war legislation. Calling extra sessions was a presidential power, and when Wilson declined to exercise it in March 1919, Washington understood that he was denying his Senate opponents the opportunity to use their dignified chamber as a stage for a sustained attack on his great cause while he was away.

With time running out, Lodge made two provocative moves. The first, on the morning of February 28, was a long speech to an overflow crowd in the Senate. He reminded the president that Democrats were not the only champions of world peace. "Everybody hates war," he said. Walking his listeners through the covenant, Lodge praised some articles and pointed out the hazards he saw in others. He was not advocating a wholesale rejection of the covenant, he said. What he wanted was careful debate of every article—by the Senate, the press, and the American people.

Lodge's argument rested on the wholesome assumption that when a great political issue is thoroughly examined, the people and their elected representatives will make intelligent decisions. As a student at Princeton, Woodrow Wilson had cherished the same assumption and honed his verbal talents in hopes of someday making a name for himself in the debates of the Senate. A few years later, in *Congressional Government,* he lamented that the tradition of public debate in the Capitol had given way to unsavory bargaining in committee rooms, where self-interest mattered more than the good of the Republic. As president, Wilson could rely more on oratory than debate, and he grew ever more impatient with Lansing and others who felt obliged to argue with him. But Lodge's call for free and full discussion invoked a democratic ideal that Wilson could not easily disown.

Meeting with the Democratic National Committee later in the day, Wilson tried to appear unconcerned about Lodge's speech, but it quickly became apparent that he had no intention of trying to win Republicans to his cause. He implored the Democratic leaders to expose the Republicans' shortsightedness and urged them to send speakers on tour to make the case for U.S. participation in the League of Nations. "[T]he civilized world cannot afford to have us lose this fight," he said. "I tried to state in Boston what it would mean to the people of the world if the people of the United States did not support this great ideal . . . but I was not able to speak when I tried to fully express my thoughts. I tell you, frankly, I choked up; I could not do it. The thing reaches the depth of tragedy."

Faced with a tragedy, Wilson was also faced with a choice: he could try to win over his opponents, or he could try to annihilate them. Certain that he owned the high ground, he chose annihilation. Put on your war paint, he told the Democrats. Not for the party but for the good of the country and the world. "[G]et the true American pattern of war paint and a real hatchet and go out on the war path and get a collection of scalps that has never been excelled in the history of American warfare."

Lodge's second move, made in collaboration with Brandegee, was a frontal assault on the covenant. They spent March 2 and 3 drafting a resolution declaring that the present draft ought not to be accepted by the United States, that the American delegation in Paris ought to focus on making peace with Germany, and that the covenant ought to be removed from the treaty and considered after the peace was made. Rather than submit the resolution on their own, Lodge and Brandegee decided to make it a round-robin, with signatures from as many Republican senators as possible.

Until the round-robin, the American public knew that some senators opposed the League of Nations, but Lodge's maneuver showed that the president lacked the two-thirds majority required to ratify a treaty. With thirty-nine of the Senate's ninety-six members against any treaty containing the current draft of the covenant, Wilson had fifty-seven votes. He needed sixty-four. The round-robin was not a lethal blow to Wilson's hopes. It was merely a tally of Republican opinion in the Senate as of March 3, 1919. But it did make clear that no matter how many battles Woodrow Wilson won in Paris, he would be defeated at home unless he convinced sixty-four senators that U.S. participation in the League of Nations would serve American interests better than the policies laid down by George Washington and James Monroe.

Wilson left Washington on March 4 and headed for New York, where he would show off a formidable new ally in the fight for the League, William Howard Taft. Former president, respected Republican, and longtime advocate of international arbitration and a world court, Taft had agreed to join Wilson onstage at the Metropolitan Opera House and speak in favor of the League of Nations and the covenant. For four years, Taft had led the League to Enforce Peace (LEP), which advocated a global peacekeeping organization consisting mainly of a world court and an international army. Disputes between nations would be adjudicated by the court and, if necessary, enforced by the army. In early February Taft and several other prominent Americans had set off on a four-week speaking tour to promote the LEP across the country, but as soon as they read the Paris covenant, they threw their support behind Wilson and the League of Nations. As Taft explained to his wife, "It is a real League with *cinch* and *clinch* in it. It does not quite come up to the League to Enforce Peace program but it is very near it."

Convinced that the League was essential and that the covenant did belong in the peace treaty, Taft accepted Wilson's invitation and braced himself for abuse from the Republicans who were leading the attack on Wilson. "It is hard for me to be patient with that kind of partisanship," he wrote one of his sons. "It is not only narrow but it is blind; but whatever they say I am going ahead as I think it wise." Still, he was bothered by Wilson's unwillingness to court the Senate and a sense that Wilson wanted all the credit for the covenant and the League.

The sight of a Democratic president and a Republican ex-president walking onstage arm in arm brought the audience to its feet and set off a long roar of applause. Taft spoke first, pronouncing the covenant indispensable to the treaty, arguing that the work of preserving peace in Europe was vital to the security of the United States, and contesting the claim that the League would be a super-state capable of overriding the sovereignty of its members. The covenant, he said, put the people of the world in sight of the Promised Land, and the president deserved the support of every American.

Wilson, looking pale and drawn, launched his speech by taking a cue from the popular wartime tune "Over There," which the Marine Band played just before he spoke. "I accept the intimation of the air just played," he said. "I will not come back 'till it's over, over there.'" And as soon as he reached the other side of the water, he said, he would report that an overwhelming majority of Americans favored the League of Nations. (Opinion polls had shown this to be true.)

He professed to be amazed—"not alarmed, but amazed"—by the "comprehensive ignorance" of certain Americans. How could they be so out of touch with the currents of the world? The world wanted and needed the League of Nations, the world would have it, and those who stood against the tide would be swept away, he said. He accused his opponents of partisanship, of indifference to the hopes of the world, of betraying the boys in khaki. "And do you suppose that, having felt that crusading spirit of those youngsters who went over there . . . I am going to permit myself for one moment to slacken in my effort to be worthy of them and their cause?" He vowed again not to come back until it was over over there and said that his work in Paris would end only when the world was assured of lasting peace. "And when that treaty comes back," he said, "gentlemen on this side will find the covenant not only in it, but so many threads of the treaty tied to the covenant that you cannot dissect the covenant from the treaty without destroying the whole vital structure."

A disappointed Taft wrote a friend that Wilson's speech at the Metropolitan Opera had the same flaws as all his other speeches. "He never answers any argument at all. He usually defies his opponent in many different ways, and makes a number of taking apothegms and epigrams, states a few high ideals and lets it go at that." But Taft had no thought of abandoning the president. He hoped that Wilson would revise the covenant, and he guessed that the Allies would cooperate in securing the changes Wilson needed to eliminate the major hurdles to ratification. If that happened, Taft thought, "the Senate will have to take the burden of postponing peace in order to defeat the covenant, [and] I don't think they will be so anxious to rush into the breach."

32

·····················

The Fog of Peace

The *George Washington* landed in France under a bright moon on March 13, 1919. Wilson's train left for Paris at eleven o'clock, and among the miles and miles of American soldiers posted along the tracks, Edith Benham spotted a muscular sentry silhouetted against the moon—a veritable poster of America protecting the future of Europe, she thought.

Pretty as it was, the picture misled. Wilson was heading into what has been called "the dark period" of the peace conference, when most of the decisions fell far short of the ideals of the Fourteen Points. In the consuming, ultimately futile effort to bring about a just and lasting peace, he would fall ill twice. He would also lose sight of the fact that while he was away, influential Republicans who opposed American membership in the League of Nations were turning the country against the idea. Political isolation had served the United States well, the critics said. They acknowledged that while Wilson made an inspiring case for internationalism, he could not prove that it would work.

Colonel House had come out from Paris to meet the president but was dreading their reunion. He had not fared well while Wilson was away, and when they conferred in the morning, their talk went so badly that House's diary mentions only one portion of it, a testy exchange about the White House evening with Lodge and his colleagues. Wilson was blunt: "Your dinner to the Senate Committee on Foreign Relations was a failure." House countered that it had exposed the dishonesty of those who accused the president of conducting foreign affairs without the advice and consent of the Senate. Wilson conceded the point, but when House nattered on about the favorable public impression made by the occasion, Wilson made no reply that House cared to include in his diary.

Accounts by Wilson's other intimates emphasized his consternation at the colonel's news from Paris. Edith Wilson, who saw her husband just after the meeting, wrote that he seemed ten years older, and his jaw was set in that way it had when he was making a superhuman effort to control himself. House, he explained, had "given away everything I had won before we left Paris. He has compromised on every side, and so I have to start all over again and this time it will be harder."

Ray Stannard Baker, press secretary of the American peace commission, noticed the new chill between the president and the colonel. Edith Wilson felt that House had betrayed her husband, but Baker blamed the backsliding on House's middling intellect, excessive optimism, and outsized desire not to disappoint. "He liked and sympathized with people and hated to decide against them," Baker wrote; "he wanted to get them all together, use soft words, and assure them that there were no real differences."

There were enormous differences—between the United States and the Allies, among the Allies, and among the Great Powers and the rest of the world. For one thing, news reports of the friction at the White House dinner had emboldened Lloyd George and Clemenceau to take up Lodge's idea of detaching the League's covenant from the treaty. The British hoped that the excision would ensure American ratification of the treaty, and the French, fixated on securing their country against another war with Germany, had so little faith in the League that they did not care whether it was written into the treaty or not. House had put up no fight for Wilson's position.

Nor had the colonel protested a French proposition that was anathema to Wilson, the expropriation of thousands of square miles of western Germany to serve as a barrier to another German invasion. House had promised to send Wilson a French memorandum on the subject, but he did not follow through. Nor did he reveal that he had endorsed it in a discussion with one of Clemenceau's advisors. House's cables to Washington had hinted at various disagreements, but he told his diary that he was saving the full report for the reunion. Because House had ingratiated himself with nearly every notable at the peace conference, Wilson had to continue using his services in Paris, but the door that had always been open to the colonel began to close. Wilson immediately stopped confiding in him.

For the rest of their stay in Paris, the Wilsons lived at 11 Place des États-Unis as guests of the French government. Lloyd George and Balfour lived across the street, on rue Nitot, and Clemenceau's home was a short drive away, on rue Benjamin Franklin. French officials, still on edge from the attempt on Clemenceau's life, filled a house near Wilson and Lloyd George with gendarmes. The Wilsons found their new quarters less imposing than the Hôtel Murat, although Edith's bathroom was the ne plus ultra of luxury: gold faucets, huge sunken tub, and walls painted with life-size apple trees in bloom. In the center of the ceiling, where the tree branches met, hung a chandelier shaped like a bough and ornamented with tiny sculptures of birds and butterflies. The artist had painted pink petals here and there in the tub inviting the bather to imagine they had fluttered down from the trees. The president's bathroom had a green tub, half of which was set into the wall, and overhead was a puzzling little balcony. Edith Benham joked that it was for the musicians who would be called in to serenade the president as he scrubbed.

The Wilsons' private quarters were on the ground floor. The president's suite overlooked the garden at the back of the house, and the first lady's looked out toward the street. Above the wall that screened the house from the sidewalk, she had a view of Lloyd George's upper stories. Wilson's second-floor study was handsomely paneled in dark wood and hung with masterpieces—a Rembrandt, a Delacroix, a few Goyas. Three large windows let in an abundance of light, and in four comfortable armchairs arranged in a semicircle before the hearth, Wilson, Clemenceau, Lloyd George, and Orlando would make the decisions that reordered the world. The room appeared to have a single entrance, but one day Ray Baker saw the president disappear through a trompe l'oeil bookcase.

The first lady would remember the president setting to work in the new house "without an hour's delay . . . to win back what had been surrendered by Colonel House." The next day Wilson issued a written denial of the rumors about the covenant. He reminded the world that the decision to fuse the two had been made by a plenary session of the peace conference and was therefore "of final force." Rather than attack those who had conspired against him, he merely reiterated the reasons for the plenary's decision, the main one being that the covenant belonged in the treaty because the treaty would be enforced by the League.

The French immediately denied Wilson's denial. And so, wrote the *Washington Post*'s correspondent, "the familiar impenetrable fog of mystery again descends upon the proceedings at Paris." Wilson had it out with Clemenceau, Lloyd George, and Orlando, and the fog seemed to lift when the French foreign minister claimed to have been misunderstood and Lord Cecil told newsmen that the British delegation supported the president. But when Lloyd George took exception to Cecil's pronouncement, the fog rolled back in. Worried about the treaty's fate in the U.S. Senate, Lloyd George wanted the question of inclusion left unanswered in the hope that he and Clemenceau would be able to convince Wilson that exclusion was the wiser course.

With Wilson's return, the Great Powers were eager to draft the rest of the treaty, and for the next seven weeks, Wilson labored under enormous strain, debating the Allies by day and devoting many a night to the final draft of the covenant. The revising began with a pleasant surprise: after saying at the White House dinner that the Allies were sure to resist changes, he found them in a receptive mood. The League commission had received a sheaf of proposed amendments, a development that made it easy for him to take up suggestions from William Howard Taft and Senator Gilbert M. Hitchcock, the ranking Democrat on the Committee on Foreign Relations. Both men were trying to clear the path to ratification by helping Wilson meet the most serious American objections to the draft he had shared in Washington.

Wilson seized the moment and won several critical amendments. On several points, the president faced stiff opposition. France was peeved by Wilson's insertion of a promise that the League would respect the Monroe Doctrine, the "Keep Out" sign posted on the Western Hemisphere by the United States in 1823. Although the French appreciated that a failure to mention the Doctrine would probably doom the treaty in the United States, they noted the absurdity of granting special status to the foreign policy of a single state. They worried too that some future American administration, one without Wilson's sense of global responsibility, might invoke Monroe as a reason for not coming to the defense of Europe. Britain decided to support Wilson. France, forced to give in, retaliated by renewing its demands for an international army. Wilson beat it back.

To defeat the Japanese, who wanted the covenant's preamble to affirm the principle of racial equality, Wilson needed the aid of Lord Cecil. Wilson had no sympathy with the idea, nor did the U.S. Senate. Southern senators would have seen it as a threat to white supremacy, and the many states in the Far West had laws discriminating against Asians. The prime minister of Australia was virulently anti-Japanese, and England's support of racial equality would have prompted the black, brown, and yellow subjects of the British Empire to demand independence. Cecil acknowledged the nobility of Japan's idea but said he thought it best for the world, at least for the moment, not to mention race or religion in the covenant. Cecil's defense of the status quo echoed the arguments that Wilson made whenever black leaders or white progressives challenged his administration's segregation of the civil service and its general indifference to racial injustice.

The issue came to a head at the League of Nations commission's final meeting, on April 11. After reaching agreement on changes to a dozen of the articles of the covenant, the commission turned to the preamble. Baron Makino Nobuaki, Japan's foreign minister and chief of its delegation in Paris, made an eloquent plea for the addition of a clause affirming the equality of all races and warned that League members who felt slighted might be unwilling to send troops to defend those who considered themselves superior.

Cecil declared himself personally sympathetic but unable to endorse the principle because of his government's belief that it infringed upon Britain's sovereignty. The Japanese countered that they wanted nothing more than assurance that all League members would be treated equally in world affairs. They also indicated that they might refuse to join the League if the covenant failed to recognize the equality of all races.

At that point, Prime Minister Orlando of Italy spoke up in favor of the idea and was quickly joined by the prime ministers of Greece and Czechoslovakia, the two French members of the commission, and the Chinese representative. The commissioners approved the Japanese amendment by a vote of eleven to six, with Wilson and House abstaining. And then, say the minutes of the meeting, "President Wilson declared that the amendment was not adopted inasmuch as it had not received the unanimous approval of the commission." When a French commissioner protested, Wilson replied that the group's decisions had to be unanimous. Makino requested that the vote be recorded and announced that he would reintroduce the issue at the next suitable opportunity.

On March 24, the Council of Ten was whittled to a Council of Four—Clemenceau, Lloyd George, Orlando, and Wilson. Lansing and the other foreign secretaries plus Makino of Japan would meet as the Council of Five and deal with matters handed to them by the Four. Rarely consulted by Wilson and now relegated to the wings of the stage in Paris, Lansing deprecated the Four as "unsystematic . . . loose . . . inexpert." Henry White, Lansing's fellow peace commissioner, would come to believe that Lloyd George and Clemenceau broke up the Council of Ten because they sensed that Wilson would be more manageable alone than he was in the company of his secretary of state.

It was House who had proposed the Council of Four, and Wilson endorsed it on the assumption that four men could move more swiftly than ten. Speed was crucial. More than 160 million Europeans were on the brink of starvation, and the new states under construction on the ruins of the old empires were ill equipped to cope with food riots, shortages of coal and other necessities, labor strikes, disruptions of trade, and a resurgence of ethnic conflict. The Four were also in a state of near desperation about the spread of Bolshevism. The Bolsheviks had just taken control of Hungary and gained a foothold in the German state of Bavaria. While the Four often disagreed, they were united in their belief that Bolshevism was as great a menace to world peace as militarism had been. At the first meeting of the Four, Wilson declared that they were in a "race between peace and anarchy" and requested that they take up the thorniest issues first. With those resolved, he said, the rest of their work would go quickly.

They started with reparations. Before the Armistice, Germany had agreed to pay for damage done to civilians and their property, but by the time the victors assembled in Paris, Clemenceau and Lloyd George had promised their electorates every last mark that could be wrested from the government in Berlin. On top of compensation for actual damages, they now demanded pensions for their soldiers and war widows as well as the costs of waging the war. As one historian has written, "Their basic argument was simply: winner takes all."

Clemenceau had an additional motive. When he looked at Germany, he saw a country stronger than France, more populous, unscarred by war, industrially intact. What good was a victory over an aggressor who could easily rise again? Reducing such an enemy to penury seemed a necessity to the French. Calculated by Clemenceau's financial experts, the Allied bill totaled $200 billion. Lloyd George's experts filed an estimate of $120 billion. The British wanted to include pensions and war costs, because the British Isles had suffered virtually no property damage during the war. If the Germans were required to pay only for the repair of physical damages, Britain would get nothing.

Wilson's financial advisors, who adamantly opposed the inclusion of any costs beyond reparations, proposed a sum of $30 billion after concluding that Germany could pay no more. For months, Wilson had stood with his advisors and at one point told the Allies that it would be dishonorable to change the terms just because they had the power to do so. He understood that Lloyd George and Clemenceau were inflating the price for political reasons: both had led their constituents to believe that no tax increases would be necessary to pay for the war. At the first few meetings of the Four, Wilson continued his campaign for reparations only and warned that if they set the price too high, Germany might refuse to make peace.

Lloyd George ended the impasse in two brilliant moves. First he embraced an American proposal to establish a reparations commission, which would be given two years to set the amount and the payment schedule. He also asked General Jan Smuts, whom Wilson admired, to compose a memo aimed at persuading the president to take a broader view of reparations. Written on March 31, it argued that if French farmers who lived in the path of destruction deserved compensation for their economic losses, so did disabled war veterans and war widows.

The next day Wilson informed his financial advisors that he would support Smuts's idea. When they noted that he was breaking promises made to the Germans in the Armistice agreement and that his new position led logically to the inclusion of all war costs, he said, "I don't give a damn for logic." Nor did he worry about the plan to present the Germans with a treaty demanding reparations without stating the price. He took it on faith that the reparations commission soon to be appointed would make a clear-eyed assessment of Germany's finances and ignore the exorbitant French and British claims. As for what the term "reparations" might encompass, Wilson had decided he did not care. What did it matter if one of the Allies used its share for pensions and another allocated its funds to rebuilding?

Wilson, accustomed to acting on his own in the realm of foreign relations, clearly disliked thrashing things out in the Council of Four. Orlando rarely spoke unless Italy's interests were at stake, but the strain of matching wits with the agile Lloyd George and the single-minded Clemenceau was almost unbearable to Wilson. On March 28, only five days into the council's discussions, Wilson wondered aloud if he should return to the United States. At issue in that moment was Germany's Saar Basin, on the northern edge of Alsace-Lorraine. It was rich in coal, it had belonged to France during Napoleon's reign, and France wanted it back. With the Saar's coal, the French said, they could simultaneously rebuild their own steel industry and hurt Germany's.

Wilson vehemently opposed French ambitions in the Saar because he opposed annexation in principle and because the vast majority of the region's 650,000 inhabitants were German. When Clemenceau accused him of being

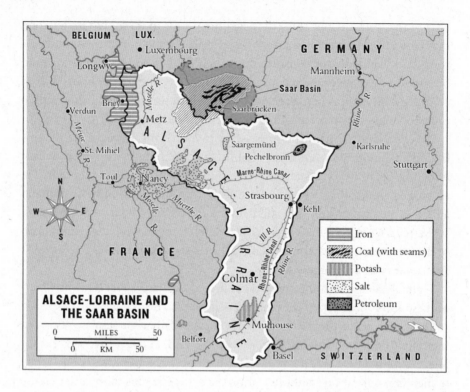

ALSACE-LORRAINE AND
THE SAAR BASIN

pro-German, Wilson was so incensed that he again raised the possibility of going home. The Four broke for lunch, and when they returned to their armchairs in Wilson's study, Wilson rose and delivered a sermon. If they did their work in a high-minded fashion, their names would be forever honored, he said, but if they crushed Germany, the world would turn against them. Angered by Wilson's self-righteousness, Clemenceau started to rise, and Wilson told him to sit down and listen. Clemenceau obeyed, and by the time the sermon ended, the Tiger thought it better to purr than to growl. According to one account, he took Wilson's hand and said, "You are a good man, and a great one." In private, though, he continued to seethe. When an aide suggested a tête-à-tête with Wilson about the Saar, Clemenceau threw up his hands. "Talk with Wilson! How can I talk to a fellow who thinks himself the first man in two thousand years to know anything about peace on earth?"

The principals were saved by their advisors, who collaborated with less heat and more light. After a few days of quiet work, they presented a compromise giving the Saar's coal to France for fifteen years and establishing an arbitration commission to handle disputes arising from the new arrangement. When the fifteen years were up, the inhabitants of the Saar would vote on whether to unite with France or Germany. All that remained was to choose which of the two nations would govern the Saar in the interim.

Wilson was pleased by the thought that the people of the Saar would eventually decide their political future, but he worried that allowing France or Germany to govern the territory for fifteen years would tilt the final vote in favor of the country in charge. To eliminate the problem, he said, they could let the League of Nations govern the Saar. Why not let France govern under a mandate from the League? Clemenceau asked. Wilson replied that he was striving for a mutually satisfactory solution; just as Clemenceau had to please France, he had to please the United States. Lloyd George took Wilson's side, and Clemenceau eventually gave in. The agreement would be hailed as a victory for Wilson's ideals, but it was also a gain for the old balance of power. Lloyd George had supported it because he did not want France to become the superpower of postwar Europe.

Though valuable for its coal, the Saar was too small to protect France against another German invasion. For that France wanted the Rhineland, ten thousand square miles of territory between the Rhine River and Germany's borders with Belgium, Luxembourg, and France. Knowing that Wilson would balk at an outright annexation, the French proposed turning the territory into an independent neutral state, the so-called Rhenish Republic. Unfortunately, the new state the French had in mind was neither independent nor republican. It would be occupied by Allied troops and live under French control. Lloyd George vigorously opposed the idea, arguing that severing the Rhineland from Germany would repeat the error the Germans had made when they helped themselves to Alsace-Lorraine. The resentment would be so lasting and deep that it might precipitate a second world war. Wilson concurred, adding that the French plan would deprive the citizens of the Rhenish Republic of the right to determine their own form of government.

Certain that France would not let go of the idea unless it had some other bulwark against Germany, Wilson and Lloyd George made a startling offer: a military alliance in the form of a treaty promising that the United States and Great Britain would come immediately to the defense of France in the event of a German attack. Clemenceau had often spoken of his wish to preserve the alliance that had defeated Germany, and Lloyd George and Wilson were offering to grant his wish if he persuaded his government to give up the idea of the Rhenish Republic.

Clemenceau was open to the idea but first had to overcome the opposition of his generals and the French political right, which would have been happy to chop Germany to pieces. Despite his age, despite his fatigue, despite

THE POSTWAR ALLIED OCCUPATION OF THE RHINELAND

Occupied zone   Demilitarized zone

0   MILES   100
0   KM   100

frequent paroxysms of coughing caused by the assassin's bullet lodged in his chest, Clemenceau took on his French foes and fought until they abandoned their phony republic in the Rhineland. They agreed to the military alliance and to German retention of the Rhineland as long as the peace treaty required Germany never to fortify it. They also demanded a demilitarized zone thirty miles wide and a fifteen-year Allied occupation of three strategic bridgeheads. The costs of the occupation were to be borne by Germany.

When Clemenceau took the proposition back to the Council of Four, Lloyd George and Wilson objected to the length of the occupation, and Lloyd George observed that the expense might leave Germany short of funds for reparations. No, said Clemenceau, the presence of a large armed force on German soil, ready and able to advance to Berlin, would spur the Germans to keep up their payments. Both Lloyd George and Wilson made clear that their countries' military presence in the Rhineland would be minimal. Clemenceau shrugged. All he wanted, he said, was "one battalion and a flag." As long as he could claim that the occupation was an international project, he could defend himself and France against charges of revenge.

Wilson's critics wondered why he imagined that the Senate would consent to an alliance binding the United States to take part in a European war. Wilson did not explain himself, and his admirers praised him for preventing the covert annexation of the Rhineland and predicted that the United States and Britain would not have to send troops, because Germany, knowing that it would face the armed might of three powerful nations, would never again march on France. Wilson and Lloyd George had also left themselves a broad escape route: the agreement would not take effect if either the United States or Britain rejected it.

The Saar and Rhineland conflicts raged alongside an equally fierce struggle over crime and punishment. Lloyd George had campaigned for reelection amid cries of "Hang the Kaiser!" and one of the first plenaries in Paris established a commission to fix the blame for the war, investigate war crimes, and make arrangements to bring the accused to trial. The commission concluded that all enemy offenders, including heads of state, were liable to criminal prosecution. It proposed that the accused be tried by a panel of judges from the victorious nations.

When the Four considered the question on April 2, Lloyd George remarked that holding high officials accountable would reduce the risk of future wars. But the two American members of the Commission on Responsibilities, Robert Lansing and James Brown Scott, an authority on international law, had dissented, and Wilson agreed with them. Making a spirited fight against war trials, Wilson said that it would be difficult to determine the extent of the kaiser's culpability and manifestly unjust to try the accused before a tribunal composed entirely of enemies. He also pointed out the unfairness of arraigning a sovereign when sovereigns had traditionally enjoyed immunity from prosecution. To him, the honorable course was to establish the principle of liability first and hold it in reserve for future offenses against international law. He too wanted Germany condemned by history, he said, but he did not want history to condemn the peacemakers for abusing their power.

Lloyd George observed that history might condemn them for weakness if they let the malefactors go unpunished. Stung, Wilson swore that he felt the horrors of the war keenly—so keenly, he said, that "I struggle constantly against emotion, and I am compelled to put pressure on myself to keep my judgment sound." Fed up with Wilson's pieties, Clemenceau snarled that nothing could be done without emotion. "Was not Jesus Christ driven by passion on the day when he drove the merchants from the temple?" Without waiting for Wilson to defend the Lord, Lloyd George declared that the world would scoff if the peace treaty offered no more than a promise to try the war criminals of the future. Wilson hung on. "I want us to act, ourselves, in a manner which satisfies our conscience."

For Wilson, "conscience" was an absolute. He understood the forces that drove politicians onto the low road, but he had always been repelled by men in high office who refused the dictates of conscience when faced with a great moral question. He also assumed that all nations would benefit from a peace that satisfied the world's conscience, an assumption not shared by Georges Clemenceau. A veteran of the Franco-Prussian War, Clemenceau could not forgive Germany for its annexation of Alsace-Lorraine in 1871 or its attack on France in 1914. Lofty principles, the League of Nations, global cooperation for global good—none of these meant as much to Clemenceau as the security of France.

Wilson left the meeting profoundly upset. "I have never seen him so irritated, so thoroughly in a rage," Edith Benham told her diary. Over lunch, he fumed about the lack of progress and confided that he had sent Clemenceau an ultimatum: if the Big Four did not soon draft a peace based on the Fourteen Points, he would leave Paris, and the United States would negotiate its own peace with Germany. Still distraught when Ray Baker came to 11 Place des États-Unis for his nightly briefing, Wilson revealed that he was contemplating a bolt if the impasse lasted another week. Wilson also shared the thought with House, who passed the word to André Tardieu, a member of Clemenceau's inner circle. Once again House undercut his chief. Instead of telling Tardieu the truth, House said that Wilson might have to leave because of urgent business in Washington.

At the next morning's session there was no talk of trying the kaiser, and the afternoon meeting had barely begun when Wilson was felled by a searing headache, intense abdominal pain, a violent cough, and a fever of 103°. Grayson ordered him to bed, where he stayed for four days, a victim of an unidentified respiratory virus.

Told that the president had a cold, Lansing had his doubts. He suspected fatigue and anxiety, and privately, Grayson suspected the same. A few days before sending Wilson to bed to recover, Grayson wrote his wife that the president was "showing the strain of the overwork considerably. . . . I shall be happy to get him home soon. He is showing his age more than ever." Lansing too felt the strain. Shut out of the deliberations, he was deeply unhappy and thought again of resigning but could not bring himself to desert.

"Not a word comes out of the Council," he wrote a friend in the State Department. "They sit in as thick a cloud as that which shrouded Mount Sinai when Moses received the tablets of the law."

Unable to see Wilson that evening, Baker called on House, who was stretched out on a chaise longue, dictating his diary to his secretary. "I found him tonight quite cheerful: quite optimistic," Baker wrote. "Told me that if he had it to do he could make peace in an hour!" Baker went home deeply troubled. There was House, the dilettante with nothing serious at stake, while Wilson—"gray, grim, lonely there on the hill—fights a losing battle against heavy odds. He can escape no responsibility and must go to his punishment not only for his own mistakes and weaknesses of temperament but for the greed and selfishness of the world. I do not love him—but beyond any other man I admire and respect him."

The colonel ran afoul of Edith Wilson at about the same time that Baker wrote him off. The president's return to Paris and the creation of the Council of Four had raised expectations for a speedy end to the peacemaking, and when the discussions dragged on with no discernible results, reporters went to House for explanations. House gave away no secrets, but the information he shared and his intimacy with the principals left two impressions: he was the mainstay of the American delegation, and the most significant U.S. contributions to peace had been made while Wilson was in Washington. The articles enraged Edith Wilson. One afternoon when she found herself alone with the colonel, who was waiting for the president, she read aloud an article she found particularly obnoxious and said she knew that he too would resent it. After listening for a bit, House turned crimson and fled without seeing the president. He occasionally returned to the house on official business but was never again allowed to see Edith Wilson.

By Sunday, April 6, Wilson's temperature had dropped to 99°, and he told Grayson that he was going to send his colleagues, and the world, a message by summoning the *George Washington* to France. He wanted it on hand in order to sail home at once if he withdrew from the peace conference. Ready to issue the order, he asked Grayson for permission to hold a bedside meeting with Lansing, Bliss, and White. Grayson feared a setback but gave his consent when Wilson said that he would find it salubrious to unburden himself. The president spent two hours with his fellow peace commissioners, slept well, and early the next morning announced that the *George Washington* would soon cross the Atlantic. When the reporters called Lansing, he simply confirmed the announcement, but when they called House, he remarked that many orders were issued for public effect, with no thought that they would be carried out.

House was as wrong as he was disloyal. Baker, who met with Wilson that evening, found him melancholy but resolute. "I shall never forget the utter sadness of the president's response as he stood there by his desk, his face gaunt from his recent illness," Baker recalled. Wilson regretted having to stand alone but could see no other way, he said. "The time has come to bring this thing to a head."

The patient was well enough on the afternoon of April 8 to hold a Big Four meeting in his bedroom. When the group resumed its discussion of trying the kaiser and his associates, Wilson tried to end it by suggesting that the evidence needed to secure convictions had probably been destroyed. Lloyd George adroitly homed in on a point already proven: Germany's violation of the treaties protecting the neutrality of Belgium and Luxembourg. He professed not to care whether the man who broke that pact and unleashed the war stood trial or was banished to a remote island; the point was to ensure that he would never again harm the world.

Clemenceau insisted that the kaiser be brought to trial, because Germany's crimes were so egregious that the conscience of the world would not accept less. Wilson, unimpressed by the genuflection to conscience, reverted to the legal argument: there was no precedent for such a trial. Lloyd George and Clemenceau asked the president if he meant that the kaiser should go unpunished. Wilson said that he favored a stern punishment but did not want the victors to forsake established principles of law. Nor did he think it wise to exalt the culprit by summoning him before the loftiest tribunal they could devise. He also pointed out that they had no way to force Holland to deliver the kaiser. Lloyd George suggested that they could deny Holland admission to the League of Nations.

For reasons that are not clear, Wilson dropped his opposition. In the end, the Treaty of Versailles arraigned the kaiser and called for a trial before a special tribunal of five judges, one from each of the Great Powers. Germany's former chancellor, Theobald von Bethmann Hollweg, tried to spare Wilhelm with an eleventh-hour offer to stand trial himself, explaining to Clemenceau that the German constitution made the chancellor responsible for the kaiser's political acts. Bethmann's argument did not carry, and the five Great Powers asked the Dutch government to extradite the kaiser. Holland declined. Wilhelm, his future now settled, purchased a medieval castle near the Dutch village of Doorn, and there he remained. He lived until 1941, long enough to see Germany start World War II, a development that filled him with joy. As Hitler flattened one enemy after another, including France, the kaiser boasted that the victories were the work of generals who had been young officers under his command in World War I. Holland never sought membership in the League of Nations.

At last able to see an end to their deliberations, the Council of Four summoned the Germans to appear at Versailles on April 25. Only two big vexations remained: the territorial claims of Italy and Japan. In a secret 1915 pact known as the Treaty of London, the Allies had coaxed Italy into the war by promising that if they won, Italy's spoils would include the South Tyrol, the port of Trieste and, on the eastern shore of the Adriatic, a generous stretch of Yugoslavia's Dalmatian coast. There were rewards elsewhere as well, including a protectorate over Albania and pieces of Germany's colonies in Africa. Having promised the moon during the war, Britain and France felt obliged to deliver at the peace conference.

From first to last, Wilson bungled the Italian case. Soon after his first arrival in Paris, he agreed that Italy could have the South Tyrol. The decision lengthened Italy's line of defense along the Alps, but it also put some 200,000 Austrians and Germans under Italian rule, an outcome at odds with Wilson's

THE ITALIAN DISPUTE
Proposed Italian gains

call for national self-determination. According to Colonel House, Wilson regretted the mistake but, having given his word, felt obliged to keep it.

Emboldened by the concession, Italy dared to hope for even more than the Treaty of London had promised. In particular, it wanted the eastern Adriatic port of Fiume, an enclave of 24,000 Italians in a region inhabited by 500,000 Slavs newly liberated from the Austro-Hungarian Empire. The Slavs (Croats, Serbs, and Slovenes) had already united to form the new state of Yugoslavia, whose delegates to the peace conference were demanding the entire Dalmatian coast, including Fiume. The Italians claimed that they needed the coast to protect themselves from a Slavic invasion, an argument the Yugoslavs considered preposterous. The Adriatic gave Italy a barrier nearly a hundred miles wide, and the Dalmatian coast was part of the Yugoslavian landmass. The Yugoslavs had an equally commanding argument for keeping Fiume: the port was indispensable to the commerce of the landlocked Slavic countries to the east.

The Italians' champion in Paris was Prime Minister Orlando, a handsome man with clear eyes, smooth skin, and a ready smile. Lansing liked him and admired the precision of his thought but pegged him as the least influential of the Big Four, in part because he was the only one who spoke no English. Forced to rely on an interpreter, Orlando spoke only when necessary. In hopes of a quid pro quo, he made himself agreeable on issues crucial to France and Britain, and he crossed Wilson only once, to side with the Japanese in their fight for recognition of racial equality. But as Orlando smiled and waited for an opportune moment to press his claims, Italian nationalists were stirring up a popular frenzy for Fiume, insisting that it was a lost province. For decades before the world war, it had been a largely autonomous entity under Hungarian rule, and with the demise of the Austro-Hungarian Empire, Italians insisted that Fiume be returned to Italy. *"Italia irredenta!"* the patriots cried. "Italy unredeemed!" They vowed to do the redeeming if the peace conference did not.

Clemenceau and Lloyd George refused. To them, it was an open-and-shut case: Fiume was not mentioned in the Allies' secret wartime Treaty of London, therefore Italy could not have it. Wilson agreed. But he also protested the demand for even a square inch of the Dalmatian coast, holding that the region's inhabitants were overwhelmingly Slavic and that Italian security did not require possession of either Fiume or Dalmatia. Orlando threatened to leave Paris if he did not get Fiume.

The Big Four went round and round for days, and when Lloyd George ruefully observed that he could think of no solution, Orlando walked to a window and wept. Lloyd George proceeded delicately, praising Italy for committing itself to the war and acknowledging the difficulty of its new challenges. He also expressed sympathy for Italy's foreign minister, Baron Sidney Sonnino, who said he was overwhelmed by the guilt he felt for ushering Italy into a war that had brought nothing but ruin. He repeated that Italy was only trying to close the door to a Slavic invasion. Wilson, who regarded the Italians as overemotional, insisted that such annexations would open the door to endless trouble.

Sonnino was in the middle of a rebuttal when Clemenceau lobbed a grenade in the form of a telegram just in from the German government: a German delegation would appear at Versailles on the night of April 25 to receive the text of the peace treaty and would depart immediately for home. In other words, the Germans wished to come and go under cover of darkness. On hearing the official titles of the emissaries, Lloyd George realized that they were underlings and protested against dealing with mere "messengers." Together the Four drafted a demand for envoys fully authorized to deal with the treaty and sign it in the name of the German people.

In the morning, Lloyd George and Clemenceau called on Orlando and Sonnino, who warned that Italian nationalists would start a revolution unless the peace conference devised a proposal acceptable to the Italian people. Next Clemenceau and Lloyd George went to see Wilson, who said he had figured out how to end the standoff he had created: he would issue a statement. He had already drafted it, and when he read it aloud, Lloyd George pronounced it fine in the manner of a father telling a bad boy that he is a good boy in hopes of persuading him not to jump off the roof. He advised Wilson to pocket the statement for the moment. Clemenceau agreed. Wilson protested.

"It will set off a tempest in Italy," Lloyd George warned. "Everything will be topsy-turvy." Wilson would not let go and finally admitted why: the rumors being fed to the press made him look unreasonable. He wanted to clear the air and make his case before the Italians made theirs. "I would let them be," Lloyd George counseled. Clemenceau suggested that Wilson wait for forty-eight hours and then decide whether the circumstances still warranted a pronouncement.

Wilson waited, nothing changed, he gave out his statement on April 23, and everything went topsy-turvy. Orlando accused him of appealing to the Italian people over the heads of their government and announced that he was going home to ask Parliament for a vote of confidence. Clemenceau wanted to know when he was coming back. The Germans were now scheduled to arrive on April 29, and if Italy was absent, Clemenceau feared that Germany would try to exploit the rift among the Allies.

Orlando offered to make the point to the Italian Parliament but refused several pleas to set a date for his return. He left Paris and entered Rome in triumph. The Italian people, who in January had welcomed Wilson with an enthusiasm verging on hysteria, now denounced him. A sign on a Roman street recently named in his honor was painted over with "Long live Fiume!" He was called out as a hypocrite for making huge concessions to Britain and France while humiliating Italy.

The British had led Wilson to expect that Lloyd George and Clemenceau would publicly state their objections to the Italians' demand for Fiume, but at the last minute they reneged. Wilson had to take the heat alone. When he asked Lloyd George and Clemenceau about their silence, they tried to cajole him into believing that he had made the case for all of them. The ploy left him "white with anger," according to his wife.

By turning his fury on Lloyd George and Clemenceau, Wilson absolved himself of all blame for a crisis that threatened to wreck the peace conference. He was as hard and unrepentant as he had been after urging his fellow Americans not to give their votes to Republicans in the midterm election just before the Armistice. He was also about to crack from the strain. When he got up on the morning of April 28, his right arm was trembling so badly that he had trouble shaving. He also found it difficult to sign letters. Decades later, the editors of *The Papers of Woodrow Wilson* noticed the deterioration in his penmanship and asked several medical experts to study the record of Wilson's life in the spring of 1919 and offer their opinions on the state of his health. The physicians were not of one mind, but their investigations raised the possibility that Wilson suffered two small strokes, one on this day and one in early April, coinciding with his respiratory infection.

Neither episode paralyzed Wilson's right arm—the most visible symptom of his strokes in the 1890s—and later in the day he presided without difficulty at the plenary called to approve the revised covenant of the League of Nations. With sleet pelting the windows of the Clock Room, Wilson simply catalogued the revisions and moved that they be adopted. Makino rose to say that although the Japanese were disappointed by the lack of recognition of racial equality, Japan would approve the covenant and carry its fight to the halls of the League of Nations. Among the other objectors was the progressive French statesman Léon Bourgeois, who said that while France would not try to block the approval of the covenant, it would reserve the right to seek changes in the articles vital to French security. As soon as the dissents ended, Clemenceau announced that the covenant had been unanimously adopted and adjourned the meeting.

American newspapers praised Wilson for meeting the objections of critics at home and for founding a global institution designed to maintain world peace. Taft offered his compliments and said that it gave the world a clear choice: settle differences in the League of Nations or commit suicide by war.

Wilson barely noticed. He was exhausted, and except for the covenant, the peace taking shape in Paris bore only a faint resemblance to the Fourteen Points. As he wrote his daughter Jessie on the day of the plenary, "The plot constantly thickens over here, and anxieties rather exceed satisfactions in number, but on the whole we are groping our way towards a solution which will have fewer bad elements in it, I believe, than I at one time feared."

The day that followed was one of the most suspenseful of the peace conference. Orlando received sweeping votes of confidence from both houses of the Italian Parliament. Lloyd George dispatched an envoy to Rome in hopes of enticing Orlando back to Paris, and President Poincaré sent a message about the importance of French and Italian unity. Orlando did not yield. The Italian people were still insisting on the annexation of Fiume, he said, and he could not sign the treaty unless they got their way.

That night, two olive-drab trains still bearing the crest of the kaiser, drew into Vaucresson, an out-of-the-way stop on a branch line west of Paris. As the *Manchester Guardian*'s correspondent explained, Vaucresson had "no special merits that one knows of save its inaccessibility to a Paris mob." When the Germans had disembarked, the local prefect stepped forward, bowed stiffly, and recited a chilly welcome composed at the Quai d'Orsay. A tall, distinguished-looking German in light gray, the apparent leader of the group, removed his hat for the reading, which took less than a minute. The tall man was Count Ulrich von Brockdorff-Rantzau, the foreign minister. He offered a few words of thanks, and in a move obviously arranged in advance, his secretary told the newspapermen, "Words fail me to describe my feelings as I crossed your devastated regions. I hope the peace which we are about to sign will give satisfaction to all the nations which participated in the war." The French had forced the German trains to cross the wasteland at a crawl.

After a day of settling in, the German diplomats exchanged credentials with a delegation from the Allied and Associated Powers. The transaction, in the Trianon Palace Hotel at Versailles, took only five minutes but was clearly an ordeal for Brockdorff-Rantzau. His face went white, and throughout he seemed on the verge of fainting. The newspapers referred to the encounter as the opening of peace negotiations between Germany and her enemies, a characterization that must have surprised the victors. They had no intention of negotiating. Despite Wilson's speeches about a just and lasting peace, despite an armistice agreement based on his vision of a new world in which right would trump might, the peace being drawn up in Paris was a victors' peace. The Germans would be allowed to review it and reply, but would be offered only one choice: take it or leave it.

On the same day, Wilson, Clemenceau, and Lloyd George settled the last major issue on their agenda, a quarrel between the Republic of China and the Japanese Empire over rights to a hundred-square-mile swatch of the Chinese province of Shantung. The quarrel had a tangled history, beginning with an economic concession reluctantly granted by China to Germany in 1898. Two weeks into the world war, Japan captured Shantung's major port (Tsingtao) and the German naval base on Kiaochow Bay. The Japanese victory was a huge gain for the Allies, foreclosing the possibility of a German conquest of Asia. It also gave Japan a beachhead on the Chinese mainland, complete with rich deposits of coal and iron, a railway to Peking, and the right to station troops in the region.

The government of the young Chinese Republic was far from robust, and during the war, the Japanese had forced Peking to bow to a series of measures that tightened their control of the Shantung Peninsula. The Japanese had also secretly promised military and naval assistance to the British and the French in exchange for German territory in Asia in the event of an Allied victory. At the peace conference, Clemenceau and Lloyd George stood ready to honor the promises, allowing the Japanese to retain their economic privileges in Shantung and giving them Germany's Pacific island colonies north of the equator. Wilson resisted. He had been the first head of state to recognize the new Republic of China, in 1913, and he saw Japanese imperial ambitions as a threat to China's fledgling democracy, to peace in the Far East, and to American security in the Pacific.

In January, both the Japanese and the Chinese had presented their briefs. Japan had cited written agreements with China and made a strong legal case for its claims, while China pleaded for rights it considered "fundamental and transcendent . . . the rights of political sovereignty and territorial integrity." Delivered by V. K. Wellington Koo, a thirty-one-year-old American-educated diplomat who was Peking's minister in Washington, the Chinese brief dovetailed with the Fourteen Points and with established principles of international relations: by every criterion—race, language, religion, culture, and history—Shantung's people were Chinese. The bay, port, and railhead were vital to China's defense and commerce. The agreements with Germany and Japan had been signed under duress. Koo also pointed out that China had not granted Germany the right to transfer its lease to another power; if the peace conference permitted Japan to succeed Germany in Shantung, it would add one wrong to another.

Lansing, who rarely enthused, told his diary that Koo had "simply overwhelmed the Japanese with his argument." Clemenceau too admired the speech, privately calling Koo "a young Chinese cat, Parisian of speech and dress, absorbed in the pleasure of patting and pawing the mouse." But the mouse, Clemenceau added, had been "reserved for the Japanese," and France and Great Britain felt obliged to help them get it.

The quarrel over Shantung had been set aside for months as the Four dealt with other matters, but at the end of April, with the arrival of the Germans and the urgent need to send the peace treaty to the printer, they had to render a decision. The dispute disturbed Wilson more than any other controversy in Paris. It kept him awake, and on April 30 Grayson cabled Tumulty that the days were "terrible for the president physically and otherwise."

Wilson the idealist sympathized with China and resented being ensnared by still more secret treaties. But he did not see how the victors could arraign Germany for violating its treaty promises and at the same time break their treaty with Japan. "I admit those were unfortunate agreements," he told Koo at a meeting with Lloyd George and Clemenceau. "But they were signed to save the world and China from German domination." Lloyd George put the matter even more plainly: "It is impossible for us to say to the Japanese: 'We were happy to find you in time of war; but now, good-by.'"

The Japanese compounded Wilson's anxieties by threatening to withdraw from the peace conference unless their Chinese claim was honored. Lansing believed that the Japanese were bluffing, Lloyd George believed that they were in earnest, and Wilson believed Lloyd George. "They are not bluffers," Wilson told Ray Baker, "and they will go home unless we give them what they should not have." If the Japanese followed the Italians out the door and declined to sign the treaty, Wilson went on, Germany might also decline. And that, said Wilson, would merely encourage Japan to penetrate more deeply into Shantung. In his view, the only hope for world peace was "to keep the world together, get the League of Nations with Japan in it, and then try to secure justice for the Chinese."

Ultimately Wilson joined Clemenceau and Lloyd George in awarding the German rights in Shantung to Japan. And in an agreement not written into the treaty, Japan promised to return the Shantung Peninsula to Chinese sovereignty and to withdraw its troops from Shantung "at the earliest possible time." Refusing to be party to a secret agreement, Wilson persuaded the Japanese to disclose their pledges in a newspaper interview. "I suppose it could be called an even break," he told Grayson. "It is the best that could be accomplished out of a dirty past."

Believing that the Japanese *were* bluffers, Lansing was heartsick over the Shantung decision. He poured his feelings into a letter to a State Department colleague, a letter "blue enough to be written on blue paper with indigo ink," he wrote. He also joined Bliss and White in a written protest to Wilson. And in yet another memo to himself, he voiced thoughts he did not share with the president: "Frankly, my policy would have been to say to the Japanese: 'If you do not give back to China what Germany stole from her, we don't want you in the League of Nations.' If the Japanese had taken offense, I would have welcomed it, for we would have been well rid of a government with such imperial designs. But she would not have gone. She would have submitted."

The Chinese understood exactly what had happened. As one of their delegates told a French journalist, "Japan is strong and China is weak; it is easier to sacrifice the latter than to offend the former." Wellington Koo, bitterly disappointed, said that China had been betrayed in the house of its only friend. He informed House that he would not sign the peace treaty unless Peking insisted. The colonel tried to persuade him that if he signed, he would be a hero when Japan delivered on its promise to leave Shantung.

"But I'll be a dead hero," Koo answered. "If I sign the treaty—even under orders from Peking—I shall not have what you in New York call a Chinaman's chance. . . . I am too young to die. I hope they will not make me sign. It would be my death sentence."

On May 4, the day the treaty went to the printer, thousands of Chinese students massed in Tiananmen Square to denounce their ineffectual government, its delegates to the peace conference, and the United States. The May Fourth Movement, as it came to be known, marked a turn away from the West and gave rise to the Chinese Communist Party.

There was also a backlash in the United States. Wilson's minister to China resigned in protest, and many warm supporters of Wilson's new world order never forgave him for "the shame of Shantung." Wilson remained confident that he could convince the American people that he had made the right choice.

The president of the United States had insisted to the prime minister of Great Britain and the premier of France that they could not have their peace treaty unless he got his League. But after they paid his price, he was obliged to pay theirs, compromising again and again, for without the treaty, there would be no League. Solely to spare Lloyd George and Clemenceau the wrath of their electorates, Wilson agreed to demand the kaiser's trial and force Germany to sign a blank check for reparations. With an assist from Lloyd George, Wilson prevented the creation of a bogus republic in the Rhineland, but he also committed American troops to the occupation demanded by the French. In dealing with the Italians, he confused the world by standing for self-determination in Fiume but not in the South Tyrol. In the dispute over Shantung, he abandoned self-determination altogether, bowing to the Great Power politics he abhorred.

Wilson would put a good face on the Four's decisions, but Lansing could not. Writing an old friend on May 5, he blamed the defects on Wilson's willingness to confer with the Allies in secret: "In this form of negotiation, which involves intrigue and deception and continual bargaining, the president has been no match for Lloyd George and Clemenceau, especially since they would arrange a course of action before going into conference. The result is that the president has been outplayed and persuaded to do a lot of things he would six months ago have flatly refused to do." The British and French had given Wilson a League of Nations, but it was hardly a league of equals. With their permanent majority on the Executive Council, the Great Powers would always dominate. "The distressing thing," Lansing wrote, "is that the high principles upon which we announced our intention to negotiate peace have simply been shot to pieces to gain unanimous support for the League of Nations. . . . We have the great powers dictating a peace, a victor's peace; we have them organizing a League ruled by them; we have a treaty drafted by them, of which the lesser powers do not even know the terms, nor will they, except in the form of a summary, until the German delegates receive the text. . . . I wonder what verdict history will pass upon this epoch-making Congress of the Nations."

33

. . . .

Settling the Accounts

M ay 7, the fourth anniversary of the sinking of the *Lusitania,* was a brilliant, breezy day at Versailles. The cherry and chestnut trees had flowered, and the grand dining hall of the Trianon Palace Hotel was awash in sunlight. At two-thirty, eighty delegates from the Allied and Associated Powers began taking their places. Just after three o'clock, the room's double doors were flung open, and the French Foreign Ministry's chief usher, in black livery with knee breeches and silk stockings, marched in to deliver his line: *"Messieurs, les plénipotentiares allemands!"* The delegates rose as the German foreign minister, Count Ulrich von Brockdorff-Rantzau, and his fellow envoys filed in, bowed, and took their seats. The victors had not wanted the Germans to feel like criminals summoned for an indictment, but the comparison was unavoidable. There were only six of them, and they had been placed at a small table at the bottom of a long room crowded with their enemies. At the opposite end sat the men who had rendered the judgments written into the treaty: Clemenceau, Wilson, and Lloyd George.

Clemenceau rose again and coldly told the Germans where things stood: "The hour has come to settle our accounts. You asked us for peace. We are disposed to grant it to you." As the secretary general of the peace conference handed the treaty to Brockdorff-Rantzau, Clemenceau pointedly called it the Second Peace of Versailles, the first being the humiliating treaty that had sundered Alsace-Lorraine from France after the Franco-Prussian War. This second peace, said Clemenceau, "has been too dearly bought by the peoples represented here for us not to be unanimously resolved to secure by every means in our power all the legitimate satisfactions which are our due." There would be no negotiations, no oral exchanges. If the Germans wished to comment, they would have to do so in writing, within fifteen days.

After an interpreter repeated Clemenceau's speech in English and German, Brockdorff-Rantzau raised his hand, and Clemenceau ceded the floor. The count remained in his chair to deliver his address, alienating his listeners from the start. Clemenceau went red in the face. Wilson and Lloyd George considered the lapse a deliberate insult, but the journalists, transfixed by Brockdorff-Rantzau, saw a man struggling to keep his composure. He fiddled with his monocle, his face was ashen, his legs trembled, and his voice seemed not entirely under control. The delegation's secretary later explained that the count was afraid he would collapse if he stood, but another of their colleagues said he had stayed in his chair to avoid looking like a prisoner in the dock.

The count began straightforwardly, acknowledging Germany's defeat and the urgent need for peace. But his real audience was in Berlin, and he quickly turned defiant: "We know the force of the hatred which confronts us here, and we have heard the passionate demand that the victors should both make us pay as vanquished and punish us as guilty." His delegation would not seek the complete exoneration of Germany, Brockdorff-Rantzau said, "but we emphatically combat the idea that Germany, whose people were convinced that they were waging a defensive war, should alone be laden with the guilt." In a voice rising with anger, he reminded his enemies of their refusal to end the blockade after the Armistice. The thousands of civilians who starved "were killed with cold deliberation, after victory had been won and assured to our adversaries," he said. "Think of that when you speak of guilt and atonement."

Brockdorff-Rantzau had already heard about many parts of the treaty, and he warned the victors that they would not get away with abandoning the terms of the pre-Armistice agreement. Germany stood alone at Versailles, he said, but "we are not defenseless. You yourselves have brought us an ally: Justice, which was guaranteed to us by the agreement relating to the bases of peace. . . . President Wilson's principles therefore became binding upon both belligerent parties—upon you as well as upon us."

The German had to be translated twice, into French and English, a process that lengthened his performance to forty minutes and filled Lloyd George with an urge to stride down the room and slug Brockdorff-Rantzau. The prime minister stayed put but snapped an ivory paper knife in half. The president of the United States privately dismissed the speech as "stupid."

Almost lost in the news of the day were three other events of note. The first was the return of the Italians. Orlando had surprised the Big Three at their eleven o'clock meeting, ambling into Wilson's study and taking his usual seat as if there had been no angry departure and no long absence. He and Sonnino had come back to stand with the Allies at Versailles and to re-sume the campaign for Fiume. The second was the public disclosure of the military guarantee that Wilson and Lloyd George had given Clemenceau. Three Republican senators immediately poured ice water on the plan, but Wilson calmly explained that the agreement merely expedited the response the United States would make to fulfill its obligations as a member of the League. The last was the news that Wilson would tour the United States to explain the treaty and the League to the American people.

The German envoys stayed up all night, translating and typing, and by dawn they knew exactly how far their foes had gone. The treaty demanded the sur-render of one eighth of Germany's territory and one tenth of its population. It forced the Germans to demobilize, disarm, and destroy numerous forti-fications. They were expected to replace, "ton for ton, and class for class," the cargo ships and fishing vessels they had destroyed. Their colonies would become wards of the British Empire, France, Japan, and Belgium. The kaiser would be tried. While the reparations total had not yet been fixed, $5 billion would come due in the next two years. On top of the requirement to give up the Saar and its coal mines for fifteen years, Germany was ordered to deliver millions of tons of coal to France, Belgium, and Italy. To ensure that the terms of the treaty would be carried out, Germany would have to submit to a fifteen-year military occupation of the Rhineland. Worst of all, Germany was held responsible for the war and for all the damage and losses inflicted by the Central Powers.

The victors had cast Imperial Germany as history's greatest villain and written their treaty accordingly. Perhaps Germany ought not to have been surprised, but it was. In the German telling, the people of Germany had rallied round the kaiser to defend their country against Russian aggression. Germany had defeated Russia, fought to a draw on the Western Front, and agreed to an armistice before it was beaten on the battlefield. And on the very day of the kaiser's abdication, the German people had traded their monarchy for a republic. Brockdorff-Rantzau's vehemence at the Trianon was a reminder of Germany's pride in the war, and it raised a harrowing question: what if the Germans refused to sign the treaty?

The day after the encounter at Versailles, Wilson attended his first horse race, at Longchamp, with Grayson and the two Ediths. Grayson noticed that Wilson enjoyed sitting in the sunshine and watching the crowd as much as he enjoyed the races, but Benham noticed that the crowd barely applauded when the president and his party made their exit. The chill was undoubtedly a reaction to the denunciations of the treaty in the morning papers. By French lights, the peace was too soft, and the high-minded Wilson was a ready scapegoat.

While Wilson was sunning himself, Lansing was at the Crillon, reading all 440 articles of the treaty, an exercise that left him thoroughly depressed. He saw the peace conference as the climactic battle of the world war, a clash between the old nationalism of the Great Powers and the new internationalism of Woodrow Wilson—between the self-interest of nation-states and the lasting peace that might be achieved by compromise and collaboration in the League of Nations. Self-interest had triumphed with a vengeance, and Lansing did not believe that the peace made in Paris would hold. It was humiliating, unduly punitive, and impossible to carry out.

Nor did Lansing share Wilson's faith in the League of Nations. The organization's ultimate authority was vested in the nine-member Executive Council, where each of the five Great Powers had a permanent seat as well as veto power. What chance did the weak have against these new masters? Lansing wondered. They had given the League an aura of idealism, but it was essentially an alliance of the five great military powers—Britain, France, Italy, Japan, and the United States. Justice had been given a backseat to force. A day later, Lansing informed Wilson that he and his wife were heading to London for a holiday. Without a rest, he said, "I am afraid that I will break down."

Other reactions soon followed. Saying that the treaty meant death for

Germany, Chancellor Philipp Scheidemann decreed a week of national mourning. In Britain, the treaty was damned as too lenient in some quarters, too severe in others. Socialists in Europe and the United States deplored it, as did many American liberals. In a single editorial *The Nation* called it "madness," "an international crime," and "a moral collapse." The world had expected a rigorous peace, *The Nation* said. "But it was not prepared for a peace of undisguised vengeance, for a peace which openly flouts some of the plainest dictates of reason and humanity, repudiates every generous word that Mr. Wilson has ever uttered regarding Germany, flies in the face of accepted principles of law and economics, and makes the very name of democracy a reproach." Many Americans disagreed. Taught to hate the Hun by George Creel's ministry of propaganda, the people of the United States were generally pleased by the stiff punishment.

The treaty set off a wave of defections from the ranks of Americans working for the peace commission in Paris. Eight aides submitted letters of resignation. Some believed that the treaty would drive the Germans to revenge. Others thought it abandoned American ideals or ran counter to the long-term interests of the United States or dishonored those who had given their lives to make the world safe for democracy. The most outspoken of the disaffected was twenty-eight-year-old William C. Bullitt, the State Department's Russia specialist. Vain, cocky, and as moralistic as Woodrow Wilson, Bullitt had been in a pout since March, when Lansing sent him on a secret mission to Moscow, where he was supposed to study Russia's political and economic conditions for the American peace commission. Bullitt had larger ambitions, and in a meeting with Lenin and his foreign minister, he presented proposals for negotiating an end to the civil war that had broken out in Russia and for bringing home the Allied and American troops sent to Russia in 1918. The Bolsheviks offered proposals of their own, and Bullitt returned to Paris with grand expectations. Wilson, preoccupied with other matters, declined to see him, and Lloyd George, whose aides had helped with the proposals, dropped Bullitt as soon as a London newspaper exposed the undercover mission and railed against any rapprochement with the Bolsheviks. Bullitt felt betrayed and, after reading the treaty, disgusted. He resigned, wrote a blistering letter to Wilson, and announced his departure for the Riviera. There, he said, he would "lie on the sand and watch the world go to hell."

As the German delegation labored over the response due on May 22, Brockdorff-Rantzau filed several short protests with the Big Four, probably to test their unity and resolve. The Three yielded nothing and were soon weighing the merits of reinstating a total blockade if Germany refused to sign.* On the eve of their deadline, the Germans requested an extension, explaining that they needed the time for more consultation with experts in Berlin. The Big Four gave them an extra week. Ray Baker was as well informed as anyone in Paris, but even he could not figure out whether the Germans would sign, and he feared that Wilson would collapse under the strain. Just before the deadline, Baker found the president exhausted and suffering from a facial twitch so strong that it pulled down the bottom of one eyelid. His penmanship had gone jittery again, and he sometimes had trouble remembering the day's deliberations with Lloyd George and Clemenceau.

The German reply was delivered to the secretary general of the peace conference shortly after noon on May 29. Running to nearly 150 pages, it proposed a drastic revision for two reasons: the Treaty of Versailles scarcely resembled the Wilsonian principles that both sides had accepted as the basis of peace, and it exacted a price far greater than Germany could pay.

"We hoped for the peace of justice that had been promised to us," Brockdorff-Rantzau wrote. "We were aghast when we read in that document the demands made upon us by the victorious violence of our enemies. The more deeply we penetrated into the spirit of this treaty, the more convinced we became of the impossibility of carrying it out." Taking away territory and peoples that had been part of Germany for centuries was a flagrant violation of Wilson's principle of national self-determination. The expropriation of Germany's colonies contradicted the fifth of Wilson's Fourteen Points, which called for an open, impartial adjudication of colonial claims. To attain peace, Germany was willing to disarm, cede Alsace-Lorraine and other territory, pay enormous reparations, commit herself to reconstruction, and more, Brockdorff-Rantzau wrote. But with the wholesale confiscation of German assets—merchant fleet, foreign securities, foreign businesses, and colonies—Germany could not meet the financial terms imposed by the

---

* In January the Allies had agreed to permit deliveries of food, but the deliveries were delayed until March because of quarrels over whose ships would transport it. The Allies had wanted German vessels to do the job. Germany resisted, fearing that its unarmed ships would be easy prey for the Royal Navy if the Armistice did not hold. The first post-blockade food shipments came from the United States, in American ships. (Sally Marks, "Mistakes and Myths: The Allies, Germany, and the Versailles Treaty, 1918–1921," *Journal of Modern History* 85, no. 3 [Sept. 2013]: 650–51.)

treaty. The count's letter also vehemently objected to Germany's exclusion from the League of Nations, insisted on face-to-face negotiations, and demanded an impartial investigation of the question of Germany's war guilt. The treaty was a death sentence, and Germany would not sign.

Now it was the Big Four's turn to reply and Germany's turn to wait.

Wilson passed the next afternoon in the town of Suresnes, on the outskirts of Paris. It was Memorial Day, and he had been asked to speak at the dedication of one of the first permanent American military cemeteries of the world war. Laid out on a hillside crowned by a fortress, the burial ground had a view of Paris shimmering in the distance, but its most striking feature in the spring of 1919 was the straw laid over the raw, brown dirt of the graves. The 1,500 white crosses sprouting from the earth looked like what they were, a crop of death. Edith Benham tried to convince herself that Suresnes would be lovely in time.

Still hoping to convince the French that he felt the depths of their suffering, Wilson did his best to link the sacrifices of two nations devoted to liberty. The Americans buried in France were in a foreign soil but not an alien one, he said. "They are at home, sleeping with the spirits of those who thought the same thoughts and entertained the same aspirations." All had died for a great cause, Wilson said, "and they have left us to see to it that that cause shall not be betrayed, whether in war or in peace. . . . So it is our duty to take and maintain the safeguards which will see to it that the mothers of America and the mothers of France and England and Italy and Belgium and all the other suffering nations should never be called upon for this sacrifice again. This can be done. It must be done. And it will be done. . . . The League of Nations is the covenant of governments that these men shall not have died in vain."

For the Americans present, Wilson drew a parallel between the troops who had fought for the preservation of the Union in the American Civil War and those who had just fought for the freedom and unity of the world. And to the League's opponents he sent a warning: "I look for the time when every man who now puts his counsel against the service of mankind under the League of Nations will be just as ashamed of it as if he now regretted the union of the states."

Ray Baker had wondered when Wilson would engage his enemies at home, and with the address at Suresnes, the battle was joined. As for the enemies, they immediately declared that they would not tolerate such abuse, that Congress had declared war not to create a League of Nations but to defend American rights trampled by Germany, and that Wilson's call for membership in a league sure to compromise American sovereignty was an insult to the war dead.

The Wilsons had a quiet weekend. Edith was recovering from a foot infection, and Dr. Grayson had urged her to stay off her feet. At Suresnes, she had listened from the car, and after dinner the two of them retired to her suite, where she rested and he indulged in a favorite pastime, solitaire. It was the perfect game for Wilson, who enjoyed his work most when he could do it alone. He understood the necessity of cooperation in politics and in Paris often spoke of the importance of teamwork, but group effort gave him no pleasure. From the beginning of his presidency, he delegated the courting of congressmen and senators to more sociable men—Tumulty, Burleson, McAdoo, and the oleaginous House. When circumstance forced Wilson to do the asking, he did not ask as one man to another, much less as a man in need. He asked from the mountaintop of the presidency, summoning carefully chosen members of Congress to the White House or using the Capitol as a stage for an address to the nation. Wilson's arguments on these occasions often left the impression that congressmen and senators who failed to cooperate with the president would be guilty of betraying the American people.

Strained to the limit in Paris, Wilson increasingly sought refuge in the company of his wife and physician, who devoted themselves to his well-being. There is no sign that Edith worried about Wilson's growing isolation, but Grayson mentioned it to him. Unfortunately, the doctor spoke so obliquely that Wilson seemed not to understand that he was being given a hint. He merely agreed that Grayson had accurately perceived an aspect of his character.

Lloyd George's weekend provoked the most serious crisis of the peace conference. British opinion had been turning against the idea of a harsh treaty, and the prime minister was deluged with pleas for a softer peace. Fearing that Germany would not sign and that he would be turned out of office if he ignored the calls for moderation, he held four meetings with cabinet ministers, his advisors at the peace conference, and delegates from the British dominions. As he put it to one of his aides, the time had come to decide whether the world was to have a "hell-peace" or a "heaven-peace."

General Jan Smuts made the argument: an exorbitant reparations bill would kill the goose that was supposed to lay the golden eggs. The long occupation of the Rhineland was dangerously provocative and, in light of the British and American pledges to defend France, superfluous. The clause empowering any of the victors to demand that Germany surrender any suspected war criminal at any time, along with the evidence to be used in his trial, was outrageous in its sweep. Smuts contended that the Germans were right to reject a treaty that violated the Wilsonian principles accepted by both sides before the Armistice. He warned that ending the war in the way that Germany had begun it, with a breach of a solemn international agreement, would be a wrong even worse than the original "because of all that has happened since August 1914 and the fierce light which has been concentrated on this very point."

In the end, Lloyd George was not for heaven or hell but for what Winston Churchill, now secretary of state for war, called a "split-the-difference" peace. The prime minister asked for and received a unanimous mandate to press for a handful of changes, including Germany's admission to the League of Nations once the German government proved that it was making an earnest effort to carry out its treaty obligations.

Wilson maintained the appearance of calm, writing Smuts a friendly note to say that the peacemakers would be willing to reconsider some of their conclusions. But by June 2, when the Big Four resumed their discussions, the lines had been drawn: Lloyd George wanted concessions, Clemenceau would not hear of changing a comma, and Wilson would not referee. Lloyd George took them to the brink. If the British demands were not met and Germany refused to sign, he said, Britain would oppose a resumption of either the fighting or the blockade.

The crisis drove Wilson to convene the only meeting he ever held with the American Commission to Negotiate Peace and its three dozen technical advisors. When they gathered in Lansing's office on June 3, Wilson genially explained that he had come not to talk but to hear their thoughts on the new British demands. The financial advisors argued again for putting a price on reparations. Without it, they said, Germany would be unable to obtain the credit needed to revive its industrial life, and without that, there would be no money for reparations.

House said little, perhaps fearing that he would give himself away. In private meetings with Lloyd George and Robert Cecil, he had told the British, Yes, you are right: the treaty is too severe. But he had told the French that they were right: the treaty should not be altered in any major way. Admitting the duplicity in his diary, he blamed it on Wilson, Lloyd George, and Clemenceau, all of whom had ignored his pleas for a less draconian peace.

To Wilson, the essential question was not how or whether to modify the treaty but how to resolve the eleventh-hour crisis without dividing the

Great Powers. He was willing to eliminate any flagrant injustice but dead set against making revisions solely to win Germany's acceptance.

One of the advisors interjected that some of his British counterparts blamed Wilson for giving in too easily to Lloyd George and Clemenceau. Wilson kept his composure. He had made concessions, but he firmly believed that they had been necessary to preserve the peacemakers' unity against Germany. And he took it on faith that the mistakes made in Paris would soon be corrected by the League of Nations.

Lloyd George's sparring with Wilson and Clemenceau yielded only one significant change to the treaty, permission for the two million inhabitants of Upper Silesia to decide whether they wished to be part of Germany or Poland. Both Wilson and Clemenceau were furious with Lloyd George's last-minute demands, Clemenceau because they would come at the expense of France and Wilson because of a fear that any concession would trigger unending calls for more. Clemenceau, asked to shorten the fifteen-year occupation of the Rhineland, retorted that he would not even consider a reduction to fourteen years and three hundred sixty-four days. Wilson decided to stand with Clemenceau, forcing Lloyd George to choose between giving in or going home. He gave in for unity's sake, just as Wilson had done.

The victors' reply, delivered to the Germans at 6:45 p.m. on Monday, June 16, ran to eighty pages but came down to a few stern points. The first had been made by President Poincaré at the opening session of the peace conference: Germany would have justice, but there would be justice for all—the dead and wounded, the orphaned and bereaved, the millions whose property and livelihood had been destroyed. Next came a flat denial of the German accusation that the Treaty of Versailles violated the Wilsonian principles written into the pre-Armistice agreement. The victors also denied that the treaty would crush Germany. Praise for Germany's decision to transform itself into a republic came wrapped in a surly reminder that the German people had supported the kaiser until the moment they realized that the war was lost. As for immediate membership in the League of Nations, the victors claimed that it was "impossible to expect the free nations of the world to sit down immediately with those by whom they have been so grievously wronged." Apart from minor adjustments, the treaty must be accepted or rejected as it stood, the victors said. And rejection would mean that the Armistice was at an end and Germany's enemies would take whatever steps they considered necessary to enforce their terms.

Ellen Louise Axson, a Presbyterian minister's daughter, met Woodrow Wilson, a Presbyterian minister's son, in 1883. They married two years later.

Professor Woodrow Wilson, circa 1889.

Woodrow and Ellen at Prospect House, official home of the president of Princeton University. Wilson was installed in 1902 and resigned in 1910, after losing two major battles with the university's board of trustees. He was elected governor of New Jersey a few weeks after resigning.

4

Mary Allen Hulbert Peck met Wilson in Bermuda, where he sometimes took a respite from his duties at Princeton. Estranged from her husband, she was vivacious, intelligent, and sympathetic. When she and Woodrow became friends, Ellen suspected an affair. Both Woodrow and Mary denied it. The available evidence supports their denial, but his political enemies floated the gossip in hopes of derailing his 1912 and 1916 presidential campaigns.

5

Governor Woodrow Wilson of New Jersey and his family, at Sea Girt, New Jersey, in the summer of 1912, when he received the Democratic Party's presidential nomination. (Behind Woodrow and Ellen, left to right: Jessie, Nell, and Margaret.)

6

Wilson's running mate, Governor Thomas Riley Marshall of Indiana, was chosen by party leaders with their eyes on Indiana's fifteen electoral votes.

7

Ellen and Woodrow Wilson leaving Princeton for Washington on March 3, 1913, the day before his inauguration.

8

Wilson's most trusted advisors: his wife, Ellen (*left*); his secretary and chief aide, Joseph P. Tumulty; his minister without portfolio, Edward M. House (*bottom left*); and his physician, Captain Cary T. Grayson (*bottom right*).

9

10

11

12

Wilson had cool relationships with the four cabinet members he needed most. Postmaster General Albert S. Burleson (*top left*) and Treasury Secretary William G. McAdoo shepherded the president's legislation through Congress. Determined to act as his own secretary of state, Wilson was relieved when William Jennings Bryan (*bottom left*) resigned in 1915. Five years later, Wilson fired Bryan's successor, Robert Lansing (*bottom right*), accusing him of disloyalty.

13

14

15

The United States was a neutral in the world war until 1917, but soon after the war began, in 1914, the U.S. government and the Great Powers found themselves at odds on a host of issues. Wilson involved himself in critical situations, but most problems were addressed by the secretary of state in consultation with the key ambassadors: Cecil Spring Rice of Great Britain (*top left*), Jean Jules Jusserand of France (*top right*), Johann-Heinrich von Bernstorff of Germany (*bottom left*), and Konstantin Dumba of Austria-Hungary (*bottom right*).

In March 1915, seven months after the death of Ellen Wilson, Woodrow was introduced to Edith Bolling Galt, a Washington widow sixteen years his junior. Adventurous and glamorous, she was the first woman in the capital to own an electric car. He proposed in May, their engagement was announced in October (a few days before they were photographed at a World Series game), and they married in December.

21

22

When Wilson's reelection campaign adopted the slogan "He kept us out of war" in 1916, many voters thought it meant that he would keep country out of the world war—a promise he never made. Above all, he feared that a German U-boat attack with substantial American casualties would sweep the United States into war. It almost happened a month before the 1916 election, when the U-53 (above) sank nine merchant ships off the New England coast. But none of the ships was American, the raid took place just outside U.S. waters, the U-53's commander allowed the crews to evacuate, and all hands were rescued.

"He kept us out of war" referred to war with Mexico, where a long revolution had caused widespread losses of American lives and property. In March 1916, after the rebel leader Pancho Villa stormed into New Mexico and killed more than fifty Americans, Wilson authorized a five-thousand-man "punitive expedition" into Mexico under the command of General John J. Pershing. The mission: capture Villa and defeat his army. Villa remained at large.

25

April 2, 1917. Telling a joint session of Congress that "the world must be made safe for democracy," Wilson asked for a declaration of war against Germany.

26

27

Like Wilson, Secretary of War Newton D. Baker (*left*) and Secretary of the Navy Josephus Daniels (*right*) were pacifists.

28

Wilson was a frequent target of protest by women who wanted the right to vote, African Americans in search of equal rights, and citizens who opposed U.S. involvement in the world war. Eugene V. Debs, leader of the Socialist Party of America (*bottom left*), went to prison for obstructing the draft. William Monroe Trotter (*bottom right*) of the National Equal Rights League pressed Wilson to end his administration's segregation of the civil service.

29

30

As the U.S. commander on the Western Front, General Pershing fought one war on the battlefield and another with French and British commanders who wanted to put American troops into their lines. Pershing cooperated with the Allied armies but fielded an independent force—with Wilson's blessing—to ensure that U.S. military contributions were plain to all.

Wilson visited with American troops near Chaumont, France, on Christmas Day, 1918.

The Big Four of the Paris Peace Conference of 1919 (*left to right*): David Lloyd George, Vittorio Orlando, Georges Clemenceau, and Woodrow Wilson.

(*Left*) Baron Nobuaki Makino, Japan's chief negotiator at the peace conference. Wilson blocked the Japanese delegation's efforts to include a clause on racial equality in the covenant of the League of Nations. (*Right*) V. K. Wellington Koo, the thirty-one-year-old leader of the Chinese delegation to the peace conference. During the war, Japan captured Germany's leasehold in the Chinese province of Shantung. Afterward, China wanted the peacemakers to restore its sovereignty over the region. At Wilson's urging, the Japanese promised an exit in the future but balked at putting their pledge in the Treaty of Versailles. Bitterly disappointed, the Chinese refused to sign the treaty.

Hoping that public pressure would force the Senate to approve the Treaty of Versailles and American membership in the League of Nations, Wilson left Washington on September 3, 1919, for a cross-country speaking tour on behalf of the League.

On September 26, Wilson collapsed under the strains of high blood pressure, the treaty fight, and his speaking schedule. Forced to abandon the tour, he headed home, managing a faint smile for the crowd at Washington's Union Station.

On October 2, 1919, Wilson had a stroke that permanently paralyzed his left side and rendered him nearly blind. Dr. Grayson and Edith Wilson orchestrated an elaborate cover-up of the seriousness of his physical condition. Eight months later the Wilsons posed for this photograph in hopes of convincing a skeptical Congress and the public that the president was in good health, of sound mind, and on the job. Wilson was still seriously impaired. His adamant refusal to consider Republican modifications to the Treaty of Versailles contributed significantly to its defeat in the Senate. As a result, the United States never entered the League of Nations, which Wilson had given his all to establish.

40

Believing himself much healthier than he was, Wilson made a covert bid for the Democratic presidential nomination in 1920. He sent his new secretary of state, Bainbridge Colby (*left*), to the party's national convention with instructions to wait for a deadlock and then put Wilson's hat in the ring. Party leaders who got wind of the scheme convinced Colby that nominating Wilson for a third term would ensure the Democrats' defeat. The eventual nominees for president and vice president, Governor James M. Cox of Ohio (*left*) and Franklin D. Roosevelt, assistant secretary of the navy, visited Wilson at the White House a few days later.

Wilson rode in Warren G. Harding's inaugural procession to the Capitol on March 4, 1921, but did not stay for the ceremony. Clockwise from left: Wilson, Harding, Senator Philander C. Knox of Pennsylvania, and Representative Joseph G. Cannon of Illinois.

Woodrow and Edith Wilson took part in the funeral procession for the American Unknown Soldier, whose coffin was carried through the streets of Washington to Arlington National Cemetery on November 11, 1921. Unable to negotiate the stairs at Arlington's amphitheater, Wilson left the procession near the White House. A crowd of five hundred admirers fell in behind his carriage and followed him to the house where he lived after his presidency, at 2340 S Street.

43

Dr. Grayson (*left*) speaking with reporters at Wilson's front door on February 2, 1924, the day before Wilson's death.

Brockdorff-Rantzau left for Germany that night and for the next ten days the world gaped in disbelief as one disturbance followed another. The count was delivered safely to his train, but the twenty-two automobiles in his entourage traveled in a hail of bricks thrown by French hooligans. By June 17, when the Germans reached Weimar, Brockdorff-Rantzau had studied the reply and was unwilling to bow to the terms. He tried to persuade the German cabinet to bide its time and bank on the groundswell of British resistance to the treaty. He believed that the protest would split the Great Powers and force them to negotiate with Germany. Against him in the cabinet was a contingent with a formidable list of reasons for signing: peace, order, the resumption of business as usual and with it the return of prosperity. The count's opponents also argued that a failure to sign would mean more war, a total blockade, and the aggravation of tensions already threatening to provoke a civil war. Seven cabinet ministers voted for signing, seven against.

On June 18 the victors let it be known that Marshal Foch was touring the Allied encampments on the Rhine, where 600,000 troops—French, British, American, and Belgian—were preparing to march on Berlin if the German government rejected the treaty.

On June 19 Vittorio Orlando was forced out as prime minister by a parliament tired of waiting for Paris to reach a decision on Italy's claims to Fiume and Dalmatia. Baron Sonnino succeeded Orlando as head of the Italian delegation to the peace conference.

At two o'clock in the morning on June 20, the chancellor of Germany resigned. Still in favor of rejecting the treaty, he and his allies were now outnumbered. When the chancellor stepped down, Brockdorff-Rantzau and the rest of the cabinet went with him. Wilson went to the Crillon to tell his fellow peace commissioners that he was confident that the new German government would sign and to urge them to project the same confidence.

On June 21, hundreds of miles to the north, Vice Admiral Ludwig von Reuter ordered the scuttling of seventy-four German warships interned by the British at Scapa Flow, in the Orkney Islands. Fifty-two of them were on their way to the bottom before the Royal Navy reached the scene. Publicly the Admiralty denounced the sabotage as a violation of the Armistice, but privately it exulted. Under the treaty, the vessels were to have been parceled out among the victors. Reuter had spared Britain the unpleasant task of sharing the ships with rival navies.

That evening, the new chancellor, Gustav Bauer, sent word to the German delegation at Versailles that his government was ready to sign the treaty but could not accept the clauses blaming the war on Germany and forcing the surrender of German officials for trial. The note was forwarded to Clemenceau, who dispatched copies to Wilson and Lloyd George on the morning of June 22. They met at five o'clock and sent the Germans a stiff reply: the Allied and Associated Powers would accept no reservations. Germany must accept or reject the whole by 7:00 p.m. on June 23. If Germany refused to sign, Marshal Foch would order his armies to advance.

The morning of June 23 began with a German request for an extension, a request promptly denied. The next news—unofficial—came at four after the British intercepted a German message indicating Germany would sign because it had no choice. Cannons boomed, sirens wailed, and the streets were soon packed with men and women shouting their joy. Clemenceau ordered Foch to stand down, and Wilson, who had been indoors all day, headed out for a drive. He was cheered again and again by the crowds in the streets, an experience he had not had since his first days in Paris.

Three days passed before the Germans appointed new plenipotentiaries. No one wanted to bear the stigma of signing the treaty, but the duty fell to one official in no position to resist, Hermann Müller, the new foreign minister, and to another whose department had been rendered superfluous by the demise of the German Empire, Johannes Bell, minister of colonial affairs. They reached Versailles at three o'clock in the morning on June 27.

With the signing set for the following afternoon, Wilson seized the moment to meet with reporters at the Crillon. All things considered, he told them, the Treaty of Versailles was "a wonderful success." It was rough on Germany, he admitted, but Germany had wronged the world. The war and the treaty had liberated more than a hundred million people from imperial rule, bringing nine new nations into the world.* It banned wars of conquest. It declared that all nations were equal. And it had established the League of Nations to keep the world's peace by taking on those who would disturb it. It was, said Wilson, "a colossal peace."

Was he proud of it? a reporter asked.

"Yes," he said, "I am proud of it." Still, he was anticipating a fight with

---

* The nine nations created by the Treaty of Versailles: Austria, Czechoslovakia, Estonia, Finland, Hungary, Latvia, Lithuania, Poland, and Yugoslavia. In addition, the Ottoman Empire became known as Turkey.

the Senate, and he fired the first shot: "The American people have been misled, not to say lied to, about the treaty."

Which parts?

"Pretty nearly every part—especially about the League of Nations." Asked how closely the treaty conformed to the Fourteen Points, Wilson gave a cagey answer: "more closely than I had a right to expect."

While it was true that Wilson's agenda was not entirely abandoned by the peace conference, it had been cut to the bone. "Open covenants, openly arrived at" survived as "open covenants," meaning that diplomats could go on negotiating in secret but would have to register their signed international agreements with the League of Nations. With Britain's flat refusal to consider freedom of the seas, it disappeared from the agenda. In place of universal disarmament there was German disarmament. Germany's colonial possessions were disposed of by fiat, not by the "free, open-minded, and absolutely impartial adjustment" urged in the Fourteen Points and promised in the pre-Armistice agreement.

In calling for national self-determination, Wilson had imagined that drawing national boundaries along ethnic lines would eliminate a major cause of war, but the Council of Four had allowed political and strategic aims to trump ethnic considerations in Shantung, Poland, and elsewhere. Most notably, the treaty prohibited the union of Germany and the new state of Austria despite the fact that Austria was inhabited almost entirely by Germans. As for the quarrel over Fiume and Dalmatia, Wilson, Clemenceau, and Lloyd George had given up. The failure to reach an agreement had forced Orlando out of office on June 21, and Italy and Yugoslavia would fight over Fiume for years. The unfinished business also included Russia, where a bloody civil war made it impossible for the peacemakers to tell who represented the Russian people. Nor could anyone say what would emerge from the new mandate system set up to govern the millions who lived in Germany's colonies and the Middle Eastern territories of the defunct Ottoman Empire.

Still, Wilson had reason to be proud. Among other things, he and Lloyd George forced France to settle for less than it wanted in the Saar Valley. Thanks to Wilson, the reparations bill would be a small fraction of the sums initially demanded by France and Britain. Neither Wilson nor Lloyd George wanted the occupation of the Rhineland, but they acquiesced because it was a decided improvement over the original French plan to sever the territory from Germany and turn it into a buffer state.

For all their differences, the Big Four had maintained the united front necessary to impose their peace on Germany, and all would be subjected to criticism by constituents unhappy with the outcome. The question of whether Wilson could have accomplished more at the peace conference invites more questions: What else might he have won, and how might he have won it? Having cast the United States as the white knight who had fought selflessly to rescue the world from autocracy and war, he did not go to Paris in search of money or territory. He took for granted that Americans would fare well in a peaceful world with free markets, and he believed that the treaty and the League of Nations put such a world within reach. He might have made American financial assistance contingent on Allied acceptance of universal disarmament and other ideals. But he declined to use that club. He also ignored one of the fundamentals of negotiation: every compromise presents an opportunity to press for something in return.

Wilson was made for oratory, not negotiation, and as Walter Lippmann observed, "a closed conference was, of course, the most unfavorable terrain for the exercise of Mr. Wilson's virtues. If there is one thing you cannot do to an old salt like M. Clemenceau it is to intoxicate him with visions and eloquence. That inimitable old man has none of the qualities of a crowd; as an audience he must be thoroughly disconcerting; and as a debater he will drive through a generalization like a tank through a rosebush."

The treaty was signed on June 28, the fifth anniversary of an event inextricably linked to the outbreak of the world war: the assassinations of the heir to the throne of the Austro-Hungarian Empire, the Archduke Franz Ferdinand, and his wife, Sophie, Duchess of Hohenberg. Between the assassinations and the formalities at Versailles, four empires, including the one Franz Ferdinand did not live to inherit, disappeared. Twenty-three nations and a long list of colonies mobilized 65 million men and pitched them into the most hellish battles in history. The death tolls were unprecedented: seventeen million, nearly half of them civilians.

That the signing occurred on the anniversary of the assassinations was pure coincidence, but there was nothing accidental about the site chosen for the occasion. In 1871 Chancellor Otto von Bismarck had proclaimed the birth of the German Empire in the Hall of Mirrors at the Palace of Versailles, and in 1919 France would have the satisfaction of burying it on the same spot. Clemenceau did not hide his glee. "It is a great day for France," he told Lansing before the ceremony. Lansing replied that it was a great day for the world, but he softened the retort by extending his hand. Clemenceau, not to be one-upped on his day of glory, said, "No, give me both your hands. That is the way France and America should greet each other today."

Outside the palace, France had mounted a military spectacle, lining the approach to Versailles with twenty thousand of its soldiers—cavalrymen bearing long lances decked with streamers and behind them a double row of poilus standing shoulder to shoulder. On the staircase in front of the palace stood the elite Garde Républicaine in gleaming black boots, white breeches, dark blue jackets, drawn sabers, and silver helmets. Inside, the Hall of Mirrors was so crowded with the delegations, their guests, and four hundred members of the press that almost no one but the principals had more than a sliver of a view. The most unsettling sight in Lansing's field of vision was a contingent of twenty French soldiers, all of them hideously disfigured by the war. Cadres of American and British soldiers were also present, along with a group of elderly French veterans of the Franco-Prussian War.

Müller and Bell and their three colleagues were waiting in the wings. When they were ushered into the Hall of Mirrors at three o'clock, no one rose. The Germans were seated among their enemies, between the delegations of Japan and Brazil. Clemenceau stood and in thirty seconds rasped out the purpose of the gathering. As he spoke of Germany's obligation to honor the treaty, Müller nodded. Lansing was pained by Clemenceau's severity and by the sight of the Germans. "They were nervous and unquestionably felt deeply the humiliation which they . . . had to bear," he wrote.

Two French officials escorted Müller and Bell to a Louis XV table where the treaty lay open to the page for their signatures. After hastily writing their names, they were ushered back to their seats. The news was announced by cannon fire from a nearby fort. The American delegation went next, with Wilson in the lead. He signed his first name with ease but had trouble with his last, a difficulty he attributed to excitement rather than his neurological troubles. As House approached the table, his wife got to her feet, startling Edith Wilson. "Please," Mrs. House said, "just let me stand long enough to see my lamb sign." In the space of thirty-seven minutes, all signatures had been entered. Clemenceau spoke again, for perhaps ten seconds: "The signature of the conditions of peace between the Allies and the Associated Powers and the German Empire is now an accomplished fact and the proceedings are thus closed."

Awed by the majesty of Versailles and the military pomp, several American reporters portrayed the occasion as a brilliant pageant, but a French observer found it "brief, dry, and ungenerous." Clemenceau, Lloyd George, and Wilson were all smiles as they came out onto the terrace at the rear of the palace, and the thousands who had turned up to see them shouted "Vive

Clemenceau!" "Vive Lloyd George!" and "Vive Wilson!" But many of the Americans and the British who served their governments at the peace conference were as heartsick as Lansing. General Smuts had signed but issued a statement protesting the harshness of the treaty and calling on the British Empire and the United States to spare no effort in repairing the war's damage to Europe. Like Wilson, Smuts counted on the League to correct the errors made in Paris.

Three days before the ceremony at Versailles, Wellington Koo had tried to persuade Wilson that China should be allowed to sign with reservations on the articles pertaining to Shantung. Wilson turned him down, explaining that he was going to insist that the U.S. Senate accept the treaty whole. Rebuffed, Koo notified Clemenceau that the Chinese delegation would abstain from signing, and he issued a statement saying that the treaty denied justice to China. Koo spent June 28—"a day of sorrow," he called it—wandering the streets of Paris alone.

The Wilsons left Paris as quickly as decorum permitted. They made a brief appearance at President Poincaré's reception at the Élysée Palace, hurried through dinner at home, and spent a few minutes with Lloyd George, who dropped by to congratulate the president on the treaty and on the new closeness of Britain and the United States. At Gare des Invalides by 9:45 p.m., the Wilsons walked the red carpet one last time and said farewell to Poincaré, Clemenceau, and the rest of the French cabinet. When Clemenceau said, "I feel as though I were losing one of the best friends I ever had," Wilson beamed. The League of Nations would have been stillborn without Clemenceau's support, and Clemenceau had backed it despite serious doubts about its value. Clemenceau was even more indebted to Wilson—for his concessions to France, the new military alliance with the United States and Britain, and his decision to stand with France rather than Britain in the last Allied battle of the peace conference.

House too had come to say bon voyage and urge Wilson to treat the Senate cordially. "House," Wilson replied, "I have found one can never get anything in this life that is worthwhile without fighting for it." House retreated into platitudes about fighting as a last resort and compromise as the cornerstone of civilization. If Wilson offered a further thought, House did not record it. The two men never spoke to each other again.

Also on the platform were Secretary and Mrs. Lansing. Wilson had shown Lansing no more respect in Paris than in Washington, but Lansing's courtesy never flagged. He and his wife had briefly excused themselves from a dinner hosted by the president of Poland in order to send the Wilsons off with good wishes. Despite his troubles with Wilson and his anguish over

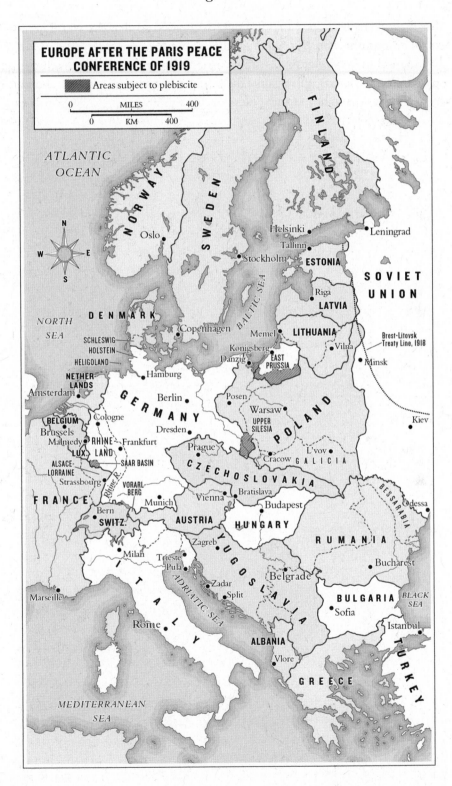

**EUROPE AFTER THE PARIS PEACE
CONFERENCE OF 1919**

Areas subject to plebiscite

0   MILES   400

0   KM   400

ATLANTIC
OCEAN

N
W   E
S

NORWAY

SWEDEN

FINLAND

Oslo

Helsinki

Leningrad

Tallinn

Stockholm

ESTONIA

SOVIET
UNION

BALTIC SEA

Riga

LATVIA

NORTH
SEA

DENMARK

Copenhagen

Memel

LITHUANIA

Brest-Litovsk
Treaty Line, 1918

SCHLESWIG
HOLSTEIN
HELIGOLAND

Königsberg

Danzig

EAST
PRUSSIA

Vilna

Minsk

NETHER-
LANDS

Hamburg

Berlin

Posen

Amsterdam

GERMANY

Warsaw

POLAND

Kiev

BELGIUM

Cologne

Dresden

UPPER
SILESIA

Brussels

Malmedy

RHINE
LAND

Frankfurt

Prague

L'vov

LUX.

Prague

Cracow

GALICIA

ALSACE-
LORRAINE

SAAR BASIN

CZECHOSLOVAKIA

Strassbourg

Rhine R.

VORARL-
BERG

Vienna

Bratislava

BESSARABIA

FRANCE

Munich

AUSTRIA

Budapest

Odessa

Bern

SWITZ.

HUNGARY

RUMANIA

Milan

Zagreb

Trieste

Pula

YUGOSLAVIA

Belgrade

Bucharest

Marseille

ITALY

ADRIATIC SEA

Zadar

Split

BULGARIA

BLACK
SEA

Rome

Sofia

Istanbul

ALBANIA

Vlore

TURKEY

GREECE

MEDITERRANEAN
SEA

the treaty, Lansing hoped that it would be ratified so that the world could move beyond the war. But when he considered the opposition that Wilson would meet in Washington, Lansing worried. Congress was filled with men who felt only "vicious spite against the president," he wrote a friend, and the president was going home with "blood in his eye."

34

·········

Stroking the Cat the Wrong Way

As the presidential train rolled out of Gare des Invalides, Edith and Woodrow Wilson stood at a window and watched Paris fade into the summer night. For a time they were lost in separate thoughts, and when she finally turned his way, he said, "Well, little girl, it is finished, and, as no one is satisfied, it makes me hope we have made a just peace. But it is all on the lap of the gods."

So far the gods had been kind to Wilson, granting his wish for the League of Nations and carrying him safely through the grueling work of the peace conference. Grayson was enormously grateful, and his relief was complete when he and the Wilsons boarded the *George Washington* to head for home. Ten days at sea offered the First Patient a chance to relax and recover his strength. Or so Grayson hoped. In his diary the doctor did not confess to anxiety about the president's health during the voyage, but the facts recorded there leave no doubt that Wilson was physically and mentally depleted. He slept in, napped often, and had an uncharacteristically hard time composing the speech he would give when he submitted the treaty. Unaware that his arterial disease was affecting his mind, he blamed his struggle on the complexity of the material as well as his low regard for the audience, which would be filled with antagonists. As he told Grayson, it was "impossible to reason out of a man something that had not been reasoned into him."

Wilson completed the address on the morning of the Fourth of July. A day later, still fretting over the speech, he summoned several advisors, read his draft aloud, and invited suggestions. A long discussion produced a handful of small changes. Of the three advisors who wrote about the meeting in their diaries, not one praised the speech. A fourth, Bernard Baruch, waited for a private moment to urge Wilson to seize the day. Put your critics on the defensive, or they will put you there, Baruch advised. He wanted Wilson to make an unassailable case for the League and explain how membership would serve the United States. But before the end of the voyage, Baruch could see that Wilson did not feel up to the fight he faced. On a walk around the deck, the financier found the president alone at the rail, staring at the sea. When he looked up, he said, "You know, Baruch, only a god could perform what is expected of me."

On July 8 hundreds of thousands of New Yorkers jammed the streets to greet the president, and thousands more cheered his energetic speech at Carnegie Hall. He looked in the pink, and the warm reception appeared to revive his morale. Speaking of his commitment to the peace made in Paris, he vowed to give his all to see that it endured.

Wilson began by giving up his prized seclusion and inviting twenty-eight senators (twenty-four of them Republican) for individual conferences at the White House. All but two accepted. He also invited the members of the Senate's Committee on Foreign Relations. And on July 10 he held his first White House press conference in two and a half years. He did not answer every question the press corps asked, but he made himself clear on Article X, which was already raising senatorial hackles.* If the League's Executive Council advised member states to take action against an aggressor, Wilson said, every nation would decide for itself whether it wished to do so. In the

---

* The text of Article X: "Members of the League undertake to respect and preserve as against external aggression the territorial integrity and existing political independence of all Members of the League. In case of such aggression or in case of any threat or danger of such aggression the Council shall advise upon the means by which this obligation shall be fulfilled."

case of the United States, the decision to go to war would be made as it had always been made, by Congress. By the time he came home from Paris, he had no doubts about the rightness of the covenant (Articles I through XXVI of the treaty) and no room for the doubts of others. He was absolutely sure that the covenant would transform the world. For the first time in history, the nations of the world would be organized for peace rather than war and small states would have protection from aggression by the strong.

Wilson had persuaded himself that ratification was inevitable. For one thing, the Senate had always ratified peace treaties. He also assumed that any changes made to the treaty would require a two-thirds majority, and a two-thirds majority would be impossible to muster because his party still held nearly half the seats in the Senate. And even if the Republicans could achieve the impossible, it seemed to Wilson that they would not dare go that route, because every change would have to be submitted to the treaty's other signatories, a process that would cause an unconscionable delay in making peace with Germany.

Unfortunately, all of these calculations were wrong. The leaders of the Senate in 1919 felt no obligation to honor the historical pattern. Ratification required a two-thirds majority, but treaty reservations needed only a simple majority. And not every change would require the approval of the other parties to the treaty. Amendments needed it, but reservations did not. As the assistant solicitor of the State Department explained, reservations merely notified the other signatories of the U.S. government's position on the issues in question.

The president's arrival in the Senate Chamber set off long waves of cheers and applause, but as he waited for the ovation to subside, he could see that the Republicans were sitting in silence. Wilson began promisingly, placing himself at the disposal of the senators and their Committee on Foreign Relations. He spoke as if he assumed that the Senate shared his desire for a speedy ratification of the treaty as it stood. Ignoring Baruch's advice, he devoted most of his thirty-seven minutes to the scope and purpose of the treaty. From time to time he stumbled over his words, and at some points he could not be heard in the galleries.

Only in the final minutes did Wilson reach the heights of his finest speeches. On the battlefield and in the peacemaking, the United States had won the confidence of the world, he said. "There can be no question of our ceasing to be a world power. The only question is whether we can refuse the moral leadership that is offered us, whether we shall accept or reject the confidence of the world. . . . The stage is set, the destiny disclosed."

Most Republicans agreed with Senator Frank B. Brandegee of Connecticut, who complained that Wilson had offered only soap bubbles and soufflé. Most Democrats praised the speech as a stirring call to a new duty. But one Democrat, Senator Henry Fountain Ashurst, told his diary that the lack of detail left him "petrified with surprise." It was "as if the head of a great corporation, after committing his company to enormous undertakings . . . should arise before the board of directors and tonefully read Longfellow's 'Psalm of Life.'" Ashurst was also alarmed by the Republicans' delight in Wilson's poor performance and by the president's physical condition. As Wilson deposited the treaty on the rostrum, Ashurst noticed "a contraction of the back of his neck and a transparency of his ears; infallible indicia of a man whose vitality is gone." (The editors of *The Papers of Woodrow Wilson* speculate that the contraction and the verbal stumbles might have been symptoms of a headache. The translucency of his ears signified inadequate blood flow to the head.) Ashurst was no physician, but his layman's observations were dead-on. The president had gone into a serious physical decline, and his oratorical power—his greatest political gift—had gone with him.

For the next six weeks, Wilson divided his attention between the treaty and a host of domestic problems. The country had not made a smooth transition from war to peace, and much of the federal government's business had been put on hold while he was abroad. By the summer of 1919, the woes included runaway inflation, a recession, labor unrest, race riots, and the so-called Red Scare, which set off a Justice Department witch hunt for anarchists and for radicals who shared Lenin's dream of a worldwide revolution. The hunt had begun in the spring, with the discovery of a plot to send letter bombs to three dozen well-known businessmen and public officials. On the night of June 2, eight bombs had gone off in eight cities, one of them at the home of the attorney general of the United States, A. Mitchell Palmer. Palmer and his family escaped unharmed, but the house was badly damaged and the explosion shattered windows up and down the block. The bomber, a man of Italian extraction who sympathized with the revolutionaries but had no known ties to radical groups, was found in pieces on the street.

Palmer immediately added an intelligence division to the Justice Department's Bureau of Investigation and put twenty-four-year-old J. Edgar Hoover in charge. Over the next two years, Hoover and his agents amassed files on sixty thousand radical aliens and arrested ten thousand men and women suspected of advocating violence against the U.S. government. The attorney general reported that 90 percent of the communist and anarchist agitation was traceable to aliens. He was hoping for mass deportations under the Immigration Act passed during the war.

Each of the race riots (there were twenty) began with an act of white violence against blacks. Washington offered no redress. Palmer's Justice Department was alarmed not by violence against blacks but by the supposed dangers of black radicalism. Hoover maintained that white radicals "looked upon Negroes as particularly fertile ground" for the spreading of doctrines at odds with the Justice Department's notion of true Americanism. Hoover made his case in a report that reprinted page after page of disillusioned commentary from the black press, concluding that there was "a dangerous spirit of defiance and vengeance among the Negro leaders, and, to an ever-increasing extent, among their followers."

The Wilson administration appeared oblivious to it, but the commentary also showed that African Americans were bitterly disappointed when they found that their fight to make the world safe for democracy had not made America safe for them. *Challenge,* a black monthly, painted a bleak picture: "We are ignored by the president and lawmakers. When we ask for a full man's share, they cry 'Insolent.' When we shoot down the mobist that would burn our properties and destroy our lives, they shout 'Bolshevist.' When a white man comes to our side armed with the sword of righteousness and square dealing, they howl 'Nigger lover and bastard.' If we take our grievances to Congress they are pigeonholed. . . . We are abandoned, cast off, maligned, shackled, shoved down the hill toward Golgotha in 'the land of the free and the home of the brave.' "

Palmer figured in yet another postwar contretemps with American progressives, the continued imprisonment of those who had protested the war. Just before leaving Paris, Wilson had asked Tumulty to speak to Palmer about reprieves for Americans jailed for their antiwar speeches and writings, saying that he thought it would be "a very serious mistake to continue to detain anyone merely for the expression of opinion." When Tumulty shared Wilson's concern with Palmer, Palmer said that no one had been convicted simply for voicing an opinion. Palmer's claim was debatable, and Wilson tried again, after hearing from prominent liberals urging the release of the war's best-known protester, the Socialist Party leader, Eugene V. Debs. Palmer temporized, and Debs would remain in prison for the rest of Wilson's presidency.

By early August, Wilson was mired in an economic crisis. Since the war's end, thousands of factories had closed or sharply curtailed production. Unemployment was on the rise, veterans could not find work, and the cost of living, which had marched steadily upward during the war, continued to climb. Wilson went to the Capitol on August 8 to promise that his administration prosecute all who conspired to control supplies and prices. He also exhorted producers, wholesalers, and retailers to deal fairly with customers, and he predicted that "the more extreme leaders of organized labor" would soon realize that the strikes they had in mind would not solve their problems.

But government action and the forces of supply and demand could not effect a complete cure, Wilson said. Referring obliquely to the ratification of the treaty, he said that the world was waiting to know when it would have peace and what kind of peace it would be. "Politically, economically, socially the world is on the operating table, and it has not been possible to administer any anesthetic," he said. Until peace was firmly established, business could not make intelligent plans and governments could not provide sound direction to economic affairs.

Members of both parties found much to praise in Wilson's program, though some Republicans resented his suggestion that the Senate was dragging its feet on the treaty. Lodge noted that the treaty, which had been seven months in the making, had come to the Senate only four weeks before and the Committee on Foreign Relations was still waiting for the president to submit documents crucial to the committee's deliberations. (Wilson forwarded a few and explained why he could not furnish more: many were still in Paris, and many were confidential.) Lodge neglected to tell reporters that he had frittered away two weeks by reading the treaty aloud to the committee. Toward the end of this marathon, Lodge was the only one in the room.

On July 31 Lodge had convened hearings that would drag on for six weeks. Scrutiny was justifiable in light of the treaty's departures from the American tradition of standing apart from conflicts outside the Western Hemisphere, but Lodge was also stalling to give the treaty's opponents time to prepare for their war on Wilson. Nearly all of the treaty's opponents were Republican, and some Democrats suspected that the critics were less interested in improving the treaty than in using it to discredit Wilson and recapture the White House in 1920.

There were broad grounds for such suspicions. Since February, Lodge had been speaking out against American membership in the League of Nations, arguing that it would compromise American sovereignty and draw the United States into uncountable wars. And he recognized that if he made a frontal assault on the League, he would find himself at odds with the vast majority of Americans, who thought of it as humanity's best hope for preventing another world war. A poll of 1,377 American newspaper editors, conducted as the League of Nations commission was putting the last touches on the covenant, found 87 percent in favor.

Lodge understood that his fellow citizens were drawn to the notion of eternal peace, but he was determined to convince them that Wilson's League of Nations would be bad for the United States. When a like-minded senator asked him how they could defeat an idea as popular as the League, Lodge laid out his strategy in a two-hour disquisition that came down to one word: reservations. Observing Wilson's hypersensitivity to any criticism of the League, Lodge deduced that the president would have no tolerance for reservations and guessed that he would rather destroy the treaty than consent to any changes in the League covenant. With that insight, Lodge had his strategy: he would defeat the treaty by loading it up with reservations.

The senator had found the president's Achilles' heel.

Ratification required sixty-four of the Senate's ninety-six votes, but as things stood in the summer of 1919, Wilson could count on only sixty-one. Foes as well as friends warned him that the treaty would be rejected unless he agreed to a handful of reservations, and Ambassador Jusserand assured him that France and Britain would accept the kinds of reservations the Republicans had in mind. To Jusserand's astonishment, Wilson replied that he would "consent to nothing. The Senate must take its medicine." Wilson seemed to believe that he would prevail because he was right.

Wilson's refusal to bend has been attributed to everything from his stubbornness and outsized pride in the League of Nations to his deteriorating health and a fear that accepting one reservation would trigger demands for more. Wilson laid his refusal to the urgent need for peace in Europe. Pointing to a proliferation of pro-League editorials, letters to the editor, and polls of newspaper readers, some of his allies encouraged him to hold fast, but others, including Tumulty and McAdoo, soon realized that Wilson could gain command of the fight only if he showed a willingness to consider reservations on the articles most troubling to the Senate.

Wilson occasionally claimed to be open to talks with his most reasonable opponents, the so-called Mild Reservationists, but he balked when Lansing warned that if he did not strike a bargain with them, they would join forces with the senators demanding strong reservations. "[H]is face took on that stubborn and pugnacious expression which comes whenever anyone tells him a fact which interferes with his plans," Lansing wrote in a note on the meeting. ". . . The way I see it, the president is 'riding to a fall' and a pretty bad one too."

The next day Lodge attacked the treaty, calling for five reservations and savagely mocking Wilson's internationalism. He wanted to clarify the terms of withdrawal from the League (Article I); spell out that Congress, not the League, would decide when to use force abroad (Articles X and XI); state explicitly that only the U.S. government would set policy on its domestic issues (Article XV); and exempt the Monroe Doctrine from interpretation by the League (Article XXI).

As for internationalism, Lodge called it a sorry substitute for nationalism. Nationalism was not the same as isolationism, he said. He did not want the United States to become a hermit, but he saw a vast difference between "bearing a due responsibility in world affairs and plunging the United States into every controversy and conflict on the face of the globe." Although Wilson had explained that the United States would never commit troops without the consent of Congress, Lodge objected to the very idea of responding to such a call from a foreign body. Americans did not need foreigners to tell them when or where to exert military force, he said.

Lodge went on, equating all internationalism with the Bolsheviks' drive for world domination and ridiculing Wilson's vision of a peaceful international order maintained by the League of Nations. "We are told that we shall 'break the heart of the world' if we do not take this league just as it stands," Lodge said. But visions were merely rhetorical tricks, "as unreal and short-lived as the steam or canvas clouds, the angels suspended on wires, and the artificial lights of the stage. They pass with the moment of effect and are shabby and tawdry in the daylight. Let us at least be real." To Lodge, the notion that the League deserved support because of its ideals was pure cant. "We too have our ideals, even if we differ from those who have tried to establish a monopoly of idealism. Our first ideal is to our country, and we see her in the future, as in the past, giving service to all her people and to the world . . . of her own free will." A stupendous ovation followed, and when Senator John Sharp Williams of Mississippi accused Lodge of showing off, the crowd in the galleries hissed.

Wilson replied that he did not understand those who drew a distinction between nationalism and internationalism. To his way of thinking, "The greatest nationalist is the man who wants his nation to be the greatest nation, and the greatest nation is the nation which penetrates to the heart of its duty and mission among the nations of the world." Wilson took for granted that the nation which carried out its duty to the world would have more power and influence than could ever be attained by force or wealth. Sadly, Wilson did not voice the thought for weeks and then offered it only as an aside.

To beat back Wilson's foes, Senator Hitchcock, the ranking Democrat on the Committee on Foreign Relations, immediately demanded that the treaty be reported out of committee and sent to the Senate floor for debate. Furious with Lodge's temporizing, Hitchcock said it was pointless for the hearings to continue when every member of the committee had already decided how he would vote.

Lodge, master of the game, took immediate action, but it was action calculated to prolong the hearings while appearing to hasten them. He asked Wilson to meet with the Committee on Foreign Relations. Wilson granted the request, and as Lodge prepared for the session, he wrote a friend that he and his colleagues were going to the White House only in search of facts. "We shall not inquire as to his views, because we do not care what his views are," Lodge said. "We have heard them stated many times and are wearied by his chatter about 'voices in the air' and 'visions' and 'lights on the path' and the 'dawn of a new day.'"

Sixteen of the seventeen members of the Committee on Foreign Relations were shown into the East Room at ten o'clock on August 19. Wilson opened the session by reading a statement addressing their principal concerns. Much of it was a recitation of his oft-stated reasons for expeditious ratification of the treaty as it was. He added that he was not dead set against reservations but insisted that they be put into a separate document. Only if they were separate, he said, would they not require the approval of others. (Lodge and Senator Philander C. Knox of Pennsylvania, a former secretary of state, would correct him, to no avail.) Wilson professed bafflement over some senators' confusion as to the meaning of certain articles pertaining to the League of Nations. He reminded the visitors that suggestions made by members of Congress during his winter visit to the United States had been adopted.

For three and a half hours, the president and the senators went round and round, devoting more time to the military obligations that might arise from Article X than to any other subject. Wilson had already described the obligations as moral rather than legal, and Senator Warren G. Harding of Ohio raised a basic question: if League members had only a moral obligation to commit troops, what good was Article X? Wilson was taken aback. Harding persisted. Suppose a League member was under attack and every other member said, Well, this is only a moral obligation, and we don't think this situation merits our participation. What then? Harding asked.

It was a matter of "national good conscience," Wilson said. "When I speak of a legal obligation, I mean one that specifically binds you to do a particular thing. . . . Now a moral obligation is of course superior to a legal obligation and, if I may say so, has a greater binding force; only there always remains in the moral obligation the right to exercise one's judgment." Harding went on. ("To clear my slow mind," he explained.) What would happen, he asked, if a Balkan state attacked Italy and the League recommended that members send troops? "We would be our own judges," Wilson replied. He was trying to assure the senators that the United States would decide, case by case, whether or not to take up arms, but he had not come close to dispelling the confusion over what, if anything, a moral obligation entailed.

Senator William E. Borah of Idaho inquired whether the second treaty that Wilson had submitted, the one promising that the United States and Britain would rush to the defense of France in the event of another German invasion, imposed a moral obligation or a legal obligation. Moral, Wilson replied. He was mistaken, but no one bothered to correct him. Lodge had already stuffed the treaty into a pigeonhole from which it would never emerge. In a book published after Wilson's death, Lodge maintained that even a discussion in committee would have been pointless, as few senators would have supported any agreement binding the United States to go to war.

When the senators mentioned that Lansing had told the committee that Japan would have signed the peace treaty even if Shantung had been returned to China, Wilson said the minutes from the Council of Four's deliberations showed otherwise. But the senators would have to take him at his word, he said, because the minutes were confidential. They would also have to take on faith—as he had—that Japan would restore China's sovereignty as soon as practicable. Lodge did not take it on faith, and on August 23 proposed an amendment to immediately restore China's sovereignty over the Shantung Peninsula. The vote in the committee was nine to eight, with all but one of the Republicans favoring the change and every Democrat against it. Discussing the vote with Lansing, Wilson said that if the Republicans wanted war, he would "give them a bellyful." Before the week was out, the White House announced that Wilson would spend most of September on the road, explaining the treaty and the League to his fellow citizens across the country. Following the fight from London, James Bryce, who had known Wilson for decades, wondered why he persisted in "stroking the cat the wrong way."

Afraid that the president was not up to the strains of barnstorming, Edith Wilson and Cary Grayson begged him to wage his fight from the White House. Wilson insisted on going for the sake of peace and for the American soldiers who had believed him when he said that they were going to war to end all war. If he did not fight wholeheartedly for the treaty, he told his wife, "I will be a slacker and never be able to look those boys in the eye."

Tumulty drew up a schedule calling for a four-week run of ten thousand miles, with fifty speeches in twenty-one states. As Grayson noted, "The president was endeavoring to do in less than one month what no one else, not even William Jennings Bryan, the noted transcontinental tourist, had ever attempted in less than sixty days."

Though Wilson had not given a memorable speech since his European travels in January, he still had faith in his oratorical powers and in oratory itself. Oratory had carried him into the governorship of New Jersey, helped him win the White House twice, and persuaded Congress to enact an unprecedented number of major economic reforms. His allies, remembering his successful 1916 tour to win the country's support for expanding the army and navy, now hoped that he would be able to turn the general goodwill toward the League into a roar the Senate could not resist.

But this time Wilson was swimming against a strong Republican current, and neither his mind nor his body was up to the task he had set for himself. His coronary artery disease, which had progressed beyond the point where a good night's sleep could cure his fatigue, had also begun to cloud his judgment. With a clearer head, he might have ruled out the tour on the basis of an observation he had made in his last scholarly book, *Constitutional Government in the United States*: when congressional opposition drove a president to take his case to the people, he would stand a greater chance of success against a truculent House than a truculent Senate. Facing reelection every two years, congressmen were more susceptible to public pressure than senators, who held their seats for six years.

To say that Wilson's illness affected his judgment is not to say that he was now mentally incompetent. Though less swift and agile than it had been, his mind was still capable of complex thought. If his memory had holes, it was still prodigious. He remained commanding onstage. And strange as it sounds, the growing stubbornness that pained his allies in Washington would be an asset on tour. While they feared that obstinacy would doom his great cause, his audiences would see a man aglow with high ideals, conviction, and hope.

Wilson set out on the night of September 3. The first lady and Grayson and Tumulty went with him, as did his valet, Edith's maid, a porter, two cooks, three stenographers, a Secret Service detail, and a large contingent of reporters, photographers, and newsreel men. The president and his party traveled at the end of the train in the Mayflower, a car with a sitting room, kitchen, office, and four bedrooms. The Wilsons used two bedrooms and gave the others to Grayson and Tumulty.

The president had not had time to prepare even one speech, yet he mustered the energy to mix his ideas afresh for every audience. From Columbus to Seattle, down the length of the Pacific Coast and then north and east through the Rockies, Wilson found a dozen ways to say that he had come to explain the treaty, not debate it. In St. Louis and elsewhere he pointed out the economic consequences of delaying ratification: uncertainty was bad for business, and the United States was falling behind its rivals in rebuilding trade with Germany. He admitted the treaty's imperfections but character-ized them as minor when set against the magnitude of the settlement. It was one of the world's great charters of liberty, he said, because the victorious Great Powers had taken an unprecedented step: they made a solemn cove-nant to protect the weak. He confessed his disappointment in the Shantung decision. He conceded that the League of Nations would not prevent all wars but argued that some insurance was better than none. More than once he detailed the ruinous costs, human and financial, of the world war. After reciting the grim statistics for an audience of businessmen in San Francisco, he said that the peacemakers in Paris had given the world nothing less than an alternative to war.

Wilson was at his most eloquent in pleading for American membership in the League of Nations. Calling it the climax of the grand drama that had begun with the Declaration of Independence and the founding of a govern-ment based on the consent of the governed, he said he could not believe that the American people of 1919 would refuse to complete the revolution they had begun in 1776. Pointing out that the world war had liberated millions from imperial subjection and given life to a host of democracies, he asked what true American would not want these new democracies to thrive. And who could fail to see that the League's protection against international ag-gression was critical to their survival? Arguing the case in Oregon, Wilson said that the United States had sent its army to Europe to beat back the advances of the Central Powers, and the army had succeeded. But what "is the use clearing the table if you are going to put nothing on it?" he asked. The destructive work of war had to be followed by the constructive work of peace.

From first to last, Wilson asserted that if the United States left the job unfinished, "we are of all men the most unfaithful." Such rhetoric was up-lifting, but Wilson never got around to telling his fellow citizens why they should believe it or why his unadulterated treaty would serve the United States better than a treaty with the reservations proposed by his critics. In place of rebuttals, he had only insults for "the gentlemen" who questioned the wisdom of a treaty without reservations. The slight irritated senators of both parties, and a steadfast Wilson supporter alerted Tumulty that the president's speeches were having no effect on Capitol Hill "except perhaps to stiffen opposition."

But Wilson continued to stroke the cat the wrong way. What were the gentlemen afraid of? he taunted. Had the gentlemen not read the covenant, or could they not understand plain English? The time had come to "put up or shut up," Wilson said. "If the gentlemen who don't like what was done at

Paris think that they can do something better, I beg that they will hold their convention soon and do it now."

Wilson seldom asked anything of the audiences on his tour, and when he did exhort, he spoke as a clergyman might: "let us—every one of us— bind ourselves in a solemn league and covenant of our own that we will redeem this expectation of the world . . . so that men shall always say that American soldiers saved Europe and American citizens saved the world." There was no call to action, no suggestion for sympathizers who wished to further the cause. The crowds were receptive, but few of his listeners went home and wrote their senators.

Senators hostile to the League were not idle during Wilson's tour. They gave numerous speeches on the Senate floor, and the most vociferous traveled in Wilson's wake to warn that the League of Nations would injure the United States. A week after Wilson left Washington, Lodge counted forty-nine Republicans and six Democrats against ratifying the treaty as it stood. Sixteen of them, the so-called Irreconcilables, vowed to vote against the treaty in any form. Far more numerous were the Reservationists (Mild and Strong). All of the Reservationists claimed to want to ratify the treaty but only after attaching their conditions. While differing on many points, they unanimously opposed Article X. They could not picture a day when Congress would vote to send troops to assist Japan in a dispute with China, for example. Nor could they imagine the United States taking up arms to help the British quell an uprising in Ireland. They found it hard to believe that any nation would heed a call for military assistance unless its own interests were threatened. And that being so, the hope offered by Article X was an illusion, the Reservationists said.

On September 10 the Committee on Foreign Relations forwarded the treaty to the full Senate along with transcripts of the committee's hearings to date, the reservations, and a blistering six-page report authored by Lodge. Writing on behalf of the majority of the committee, he denied Wilson's continuing accusations of delay, denounced his case against reservations, and damned the League.

Lodge's reservation to Article X was not a reservation at all; it frankly declared that the United States would not abide by it. Talking about his handiwork with a newspaper reporter, Lodge boasted, "I mean to kill Article X or kill the treaty." The final slap at Wilson was a demand that the reservations be part of the resolution of ratification.

A day later, Senator Hitchcock, Wilson's chief advocate for an unchanged treaty, submitted the committee's minority report. Rather than reply point by point to Lodge, Hitchcock called for swift ratification of the existing treaty and catalogued the virtues of the League: it would—for the first time in history—organize the nations of the world for peace rather than war, it had comprehensive plans for universal disarmament, it established machinery for the peaceful resolution of disputes, and it would strive to spare the world the horror of war and the ruinous expense of large armies and navies.

Caught in the middle was William Howard Taft. He had embraced the League of Nations and recruited prominent members of his League to Enforce Peace on behalf of Wilson's league. After reading Lodge's report, Taft wrote a friend that "Never in the history of all American citizenship have we had such an egregious exhibition of blind, selfish, conceited, unwise opportunism and real Prussianism as Lodge has given. The tone is flippant, cheaply sarcastic and brutal." At the same time, Taft feared that Wilson's tour was hurting his cause. He could scarcely believe that the president was speaking so contemptuously of men whose votes he needed, and Wilson's insistence on a treaty without reservations struck Taft as suicidal. He could also foresee that Wilson's decision to ignore the Mild Reservationists would drive them into the arms of the most reactionary Republicans.

With the treaty now on the floor of the Senate, the battle lines were drawn, and it was clear that Wilson's forces were outnumbered. This could not have surprised the president, but he was completely unprepared for the testimony of a witness who appeared at the final session of the Committee on Foreign Relations hearings, on September 12. William C. Bullitt, the young aide who had showily resigned from the staff of the American peace commission in Paris, read part of a memorandum composed just after his exit interview with Lansing. When Bullitt mentioned his moral compunctions about the treaty, Lansing had confided that he too regarded many of its provisions as "thoroughly bad." According to Bullitt's notes of the conversation, Lansing had said, "I consider that the League of Nations at present is entirely useless. The great powers have simply gone ahead and arranged the world to suit themselves." Lansing had also mused that if the Senate and the American people fully grasped the consequences of the treaty, it would not be ratified.

Lansing's candor, which made Wilson look like a dunce, was front-page news across the country. In a telegram to the president, Lansing admitted sharing his concerns with Bullitt. But, Lansing said, he had also described the problems as "probably unavoidable," given the conflicting aims of the Great Powers. He also said he had told Bullitt that nothing ought to stand in the way of a speedy peace. Lansing offered to make a public statement if

Wilson thought it would aid their cause, and he expressed deep regret that he had ever had any conversation with that "disloyal young man."

Lansing's telegram caught up with Wilson on Sunday, September 21, when the Wilsons were looking forward to a quiet day at their hotel in Los Angeles. Exhausted by nearly three weeks on the road and coughing fits that interfered with his sleep, plagued by headaches so intense and persistent that he could hardly eat, the president was in terrible shape—gaunt, easily agitated, and empty of nearly every strength but his formidable will. After reading the telegram, Wilson said, "Think of it! This from a man whom I raised from the level of a subordinate to the great office of secretary of state of the United States. My God!" He wanted to fire Lansing but felt he could not do so while he was on the road.

Although Grayson witnessed the outburst, his diary makes no mention of it. But what he did record was alarming: Wilson had turned white, flecks of saliva appeared at the corners of his mouth, and his mouth trembled. Those symptoms in combination with the others suggested that a stroke might be imminent. Hoping to calm his patient, Grayson changed the subject and tried to amuse him. He also began thinking about how to persuade Wilson to abandon the rest of the tour.

Coming on top of Lodge's unremitting campaign against the League, the revelation of Lansing's disloyalty seems to have hardened Wilson's resolve to win the fight on his own terms. The Senate had homed in on Article X, and Wilson followed suit. In Reno, recalling the courage and endurance of American soldiers in France, he told his audience that the Americans were legendary for their refusal to retreat. Now some gentlemen wanted to turn tail, he said, but he believed that the American people would insist on continuing the march toward the League. Forward was the only choice, he said, for no other direction led to peace.

In Salt Lake City, Wilson went further. Senators from both parties were trying to draft a compromise reservation to Article X—a version less drastic than the one put forward by Lodge—and after reading the latest iteration aloud, Wilson called it a knife in the heart of the covenant. Without the original Article X, he said, "the whole treaty falls to the ground." Ridiculing the gentlemen's fear that the United States would be dragged into foreign wars in every quarter of the globe, he said, "If you want to put out a fire in Utah, you don't send to Oklahoma for the fire engine."

The next day, at Cheyenne, Wilson was anxious, drained and, said Grayson, "suffering a great deal." But when Edith suggested that they rest for a few days, Woodrow refused, saying that the people were with him, and it would be a dereliction of duty to cancel any speeches. Picking up where he had left off in Salt Lake City, Wilson told the citizens of Cheyenne about the heroism of the American soldiers at Belleau Wood and the Argonne. *They* had had no reservations about their service, he said. "They never thought of saying, 'We are going to do this much of the job and then scuttle and leave you to do the rest.' . . . And I am not going to turn back any more than they did. I am going to keep my face just as they kept their face—forward towards the enemy." Vowing not to surrender, he issued a warning: if the Senate attached a reservation to Article X, he would regard it as a repudiation of the entire treaty. In Denver on September 25, Wilson pushed even harder, challenging the Senate to hold an up-or-down vote on the treaty as it was.

Later in the day, as he was about to speak at Pueblo, Wilson stumbled. Jimmie Starling of the Secret Service put a hand on his arm, and Wilson allowed it to stay. He needed it to climb the stairs to the platform. Standing close behind him in case he collapsed, Starling noticed that Wilson spoke with difficulty, mumbling, pausing, and saying certain words as if for the first time. It seemed to Starling that every phrase was an effort for his whole body.

Wilson defended his hard line by reminding his listeners that he had come home in the middle of the peace conference, met with the Senate and House committees on foreign affairs, and taken their suggestions back to Paris, where they were written into the League covenant. "What more could I have done?" he asked. Telling of his visit to the American military cemetery at Suresnes, Wilson said that he wished the gentlemen opposing the peace for which American troops had died could visit the cemetery and feel what he had felt, "the moral obligation that rests upon us not to go back on those boys, but to see the thing through, to see it through to the end and make good their redemption of the world."

At the end of the speech Wilson took shelter in his faith in the idealism of his fellow Americans and in the promise of the Twenty-third Psalm. He believed that men would see the light. "There is one thing that the American people always rise to and extend their hand to, and that is the truth of justice and of liberty and of peace," he said. "We have accepted that truth, and we are going to be led by it, and it is going to lead us, and through us, the world, out into pastures of quietness and peace such as the world never dreamed of before." In the supreme test of his religious faith, Wilson's father had waged an enormous struggle with his doubts about God's love after losing a political quarrel at the seminary where he taught. Joseph Wilson had emerged victorious by refusing to give in to his doubts. Woodrow Wilson clung to his faith in the better angels of humankind, and even as the nonbelievers in the Senate gathered their forces against him, he continued to hope that they would see the light.

Soon after the train left Pueblo for Wichita, Wilson complained of another severe headache. Grayson ordered an unscheduled stop in order to take the president and first lady for a walk. Starling, who followed them, would remember Wilson in the slowest of trudges, his feet moving "as if they were weighted and shackled." Refreshed by the exercise and the mountain air, Wilson ate heartily for once and retired early, hoping that a long sleep would end the headache. But in the middle of the night he roused Edith to report that the pain was unbearable. His face twitched, he struggled for breath, and he was agitated and nauseated. When Grayson was summoned, he told Wilson that it was time to give up the tour and go home. Wilson protested, and it took Grayson hours to get him to sleep. Watching over him, Edith sensed that life would never be the same. Reconstructing that night two decades later, she wrote, "[S]omething had broken inside me; from that hour on, I would have to wear a mask—not only to the public but to the one I loved best in the world; for he must never know how ill he was, and I must carry on."

Woodrow woke at seven and announced that he had to get ready for the day's engagements in Wichita. Edith, sure that he could not make another speech, saw him to his room and sat down with Grayson and Tumulty to cancel the rest of the tour. In the middle of their conversation, Wilson came in, freshly dressed and shaved but looking "piteously ill" to his wife. When the conspirators suggested a vacation, Wilson said no. When they urged it, he said no. Grayson argued that carrying on might prove fatal. "No, no, no," Wilson said. "I must keep on." Not until Edith declared the tour over did he give in. He looked at Tumulty and said, "My dear boy, this has never happened to me before. I felt it coming on yesterday. I do not know what to do." He turned away and began to cry.

Just after nine o'clock, Tumulty gathered the press corps and in a shaky voice read Grayson's official statement canceling the trip because of the president's "nervous exhaustion." "His condition is not alarming," the statement read, "but it will be necessary for his recovery that he have rest and quiet for a considerable time."

35

·········

Paralyzed

The tracks were cleared, and with a separate engine leading the way, the presidential special started for Washington. As the last of seven cars, the *Mayflower* caught the sway of the whole train, adding considerably to Wilson's suffering. Grayson twice ordered the engineer to slow down. When the president was awake, the first lady did a fine imitation of their quiet evenings at home—making small talk, knitting, and generally trying, she said, "to go on as though the structure of our life did not lie in ruin around us."

Forty-nine agonizing hours after leaving Wichita, the Wilsons were back in the White House. Unable to work or even read because of the pain in his head, Woodrow spent the rest of the day pacing. Over the next few days he began feeling somewhat better, but at 8:50 a.m. on October 2, Edith Wilson phoned Ike Hoover, the chief usher, to say that the president was seriously ill and she wanted Grayson. After sending a car for the doctor, Hoover raced upstairs to offer his assistance. Finding the doors locked, he waited in the hall for Grayson, who was shown in and reappeared ten minutes later. Throwing his arms in the air, he said, "My God, the president is paralyzed." Hoover never again heard anyone in Wilson's inner circle use the word "paralyzed." The most serious case of presidential disability, along with a White House cover-up of unprecedented magnitude, had begun.

Hoover had a close look at the president that afternoon while helping to rearrange furniture in the Lincoln Bedroom. He would remember Wilson stretched out on the bed, "just gone as far as one could judge from appearances." Wilson had had a major stroke caused by a blood clot in the right half of his brain. His left arm and leg were paralyzed, much of his vision was destroyed, and the impaired muscles on the left side of his face made it difficult for him to swallow. He had collapsed in his bathroom, hitting his head as he sank to the floor. Edith heard a groan, went to his aid, and found him unconscious.

Vice President Thomas Riley Marshall, first in the line of presidential succession, rushed to the White House as soon as he learned of Wilson's collapse but was turned away. A man who felt several sizes too small for the vice presidency, Marshall was afraid of becoming president and terrified at the prospect of having to take the office without any preparation. Wilson ignored him for five and a half years after taking office, and the inattention would undoubtedly have continued if Wilson had not decided to go to the Paris Peace Conference. When Republicans complained that his absence would leave the United States without a president, Wilson designated Marshall "acting president" and asked him to chair cabinet meetings for the duration. Marshall played the part, but only for a few weeks, because the cabinet secretaries paid him no more attention than Wilson had.

Lansing, who was in New York when Wilson was stricken, returned to Washington that evening and telephoned Grayson, who would only say that the president was in bad condition. Next morning Lansing went to see Tumulty, who took him into the Cabinet Room and revealed that Wilson was gravely ill. "In what way?" Lansing asked. Apparently torn between a promise of secrecy and a sense that the facts ought to be disclosed, Tumulty resorted to pantomime, drawing an imaginary line down the length of his left arm. Lansing understood: paralysis of the left side. Tumulty summoned Grayson, who described the president's illness as nervous exhaustion requiring complete rest. Grayson said nothing about a stroke but admitted that if the president recovered, it would probably be months before he could resume his duties.

Lansing raised the idea of invoking the Constitution and calling on Marshall to serve as president while Wilson was incapacitated. Losing his temper, Tumulty said he did not need a tutorial from Lansing on the Constitution.* And just who, he wanted to know, would certify to the president's disability? When Lansing advised a statement by Tumulty or Grayson, Tumulty declared that he would not be a party to any attempt to oust the president. Grayson took the same position. Tumulty added that if anyone outside the White House tried to prove that Wilson was not up to his duties, "Grayson and I would stand together and repudiate it."

Two days after the stroke, Grayson and the other doctors called in to treat the president realized that the paralysis would be permanent and decided that the public should be told. But Grayson's notes of the discussion say that "in view of the wishes of _____ this was deferred." He filled in the blank a few sentences later, after explaining that despite the new prognosis, "I thought it was wise to issue general statements only. Further, Mrs. Wilson, the president's wife, was absolutely opposed to any other course." The many official bulletins that he and Tumulty prepared for the press over the next four months were deliberately vague and contained no mention of paralysis or a stroke.

Deeply upset by Wilson's illness, Tumulty had seen Lansing's overture as yet another betrayal of Wilson. But Lansing had not gone to the White House with nefarious intent. As secretary of state, he outranked every member of the cabinet but the president and wanted to ensure that Wilson's illness did not paralyze the executive branch. Undeterred by Tumulty's outburst, he told Newton Baker, the secretary of war, that Wilson was paralyzed, and asked if a cabinet meeting was in order. Baker thought it was.

---

* The pertinent passage, part of Article II, reads: "In case of the Removal of the President from Office, or of his Death, Resignation, or Inability to discharge the Powers and Duties of the said Office, the Same shall devolve on the Vice President." The Twenty-fifth Amendment to the Constitution, ratified in 1967, supersedes the original and is much more comprehensive, covering succession to the presidency, the appointment of a vice president to fill the vacancy created when a vice president moves up to president, and the procedure to be followed when a president is temporarily disabled. The amendment was prompted by the assassination of John F. Kennedy, which left the office of president in vulnerable hands: the new president, Lyndon Johnson, had suffered a heart attack some years prior, and next in line were the seventy-one-year-old speaker of the House and the eighty-six-year-old president pro tempore of the Senate. The history of the Twenty-fifth Amendment is well told in Birch Bayh, *One Heartbeat Away* (Indianapolis: Bobbs-Merrill, 1968).

On Monday morning, every cabinet secretary attended a meeting convened by Lansing. The first order of business was an interrogation of Grayson. What was the exact nature of the president's trouble? Lansing asked. How long would he be sick? Was his mind clear or not? After months of concealing the decline in Wilson's health, Grayson easily fielded the questions and went so far as to put Lansing on notice. The president was improving though not yet up to conducting business, Grayson said, and his mind was not only clear but active—so active, in fact, that he had been "very much annoyed" when told of the cabinet meeting, and he had demanded to know why and by whom it had been called.

Lansing was taken aback by the report of the president's anger, and Secretary Baker rescued him by suggesting that Grayson tell the president that the cabinet secretaries had come together as a mark of their affection for their chief, that they were looking out for his interests, and that the government was running smoothly. The cabinet approved the idea, and after Grayson was excused, there followed a long discussion of whether to take action under the disability clause. Lansing favored the idea, but the rest of the group was inclined to wait and see.

There were many reasons not to act. Congress could legislate on its own, and the bills it passed would automatically become law if the president failed to sign them within ten days. Also, the question of who would declare the president disabled had no clear answer. To some, the cabinet seemed a logical choice, if only because of a tradition in place since 1821: five presidents had died in office, and in every case the secretary of state, acting for the cabinet, had notified the vice president of his succession to the presidency. The cabinet had never ruled on a case of presidential disability. What if the secretaries disagreed on whether Wilson was too sick to perform his duties?

On Capitol Hill, there was a thought that Congress should arrange the transfer of authority from a disabled president to a vice president, because members of Congress were elected officials and cabinet members were not. Yet another camp held that the decision should be made by the Supreme Court. With no clear path to follow, no substantive information on the president's condition, and a vice president dreading the prospect of assuming the presidency, Washington was reduced to watchful waiting.

Neither Grayson nor Tumulty would hear of removing Wilson from the presidency, but they soon shared the big secret of the sickroom—the stroke—with trusted outsiders. Grayson told Breckinridge Long, third assistant secretary of state, that the president's life might hang in the balance for weeks. Though Wilson's blood pressure was returning to normal, he was very weak, and some of his veins were worrisomely thin. Fearing that the smallest upset might have disastrous consequences, Grayson had even banned newspapers from the sickroom. Long shared the information with Lansing.

Tumulty briefed J. Fred Essary of *The Baltimore Sun* and asked him to brief the vice president. Explaining the need to delegate the task, Tumulty claimed that no one from the White House could talk to Marshall even un-officially for fear that the conversation would be seized upon as proof of the president's inability to govern. Tumulty did not reveal that Wilson *was* un-able to govern. Nor did he say that any White House approach to Marshall would have been vetoed by Edith Wilson, who feared that the vice president would capitulate to the Senate's demand for treaty reservations, the very thing her husband had repudiated on his speaking tour. Immediately after seeing Tumulty, Essary went to the Capitol and informed the vice president that the president might die at any moment. Stunned, Marshall bowed his head, fell into a silence, and could not climb out. Essary thought it best to leave, but he looked back from the door and saw Marshall, hands clasped, still staring at his desk.

Though the cover-up at the White House cannot be excused, it can be explained. The president's three guardians were in shock. They put the in-terests of the patient first. They hoped that he would soon be well. And because the disability clause of the Constitution was vague and untried, they were in unknown territory. But there *was* a recent precedent for a temporary transfer of power, and the guardians were aware of it: Wilson's designation of Marshall as acting president during the Paris Peace Conference. With the "acting president" model in mind, Tumulty or Lansing could have asked the attorney general about the possibility of devising a temporary transfer of power on grounds of temporary disability. If the framers of the Constitution had not envisioned such a solution, neither had they ruled it out. But it does not appear that the idea was ever considered.

Edith Wilson's memoir gives a markedly different account of the crisis. Writing twenty years after the fact and still seething at accusations that she had promoted herself to de facto president, she told her readers that she was writing as if she "had taken the oath to tell the truth, the whole truth, and nothing but the truth—so help me God." As she remembered it, she wanted the doctors to be frank about the president's possibilities for recovery so that she could "be honest with the people." She also claimed that she had been open to a Marshall presidency. Had she forgotten? Was she lying? Or were Tumulty and Grayson lying when they blamed her for the cover-up?

According to Edith, the doctors said that because Wilson's mind was clear and because he had begun to gain ground, recovery was possible as long as he was kept free of every problem while Nature repaired the damage done by the stroke. Edith said she pointed out that every matter that came to the president was a problem. And she claimed that she asked whether it would make more sense for Marshall to take the reins so that the patient would get the undisturbed rest he needed. Did Tumulty and Grayson lie? Did Edith's memory fail her? Or was this another coat of whitewash?

Francis X. Dercum, a distinguished neurologist called in by Grayson, supposedly suggested an alternative to Marshall in conversation with Edith: "Have everything come to you; weigh the importance of each matter, and see if it is possible by consultations with the respective heads of the departments to solve them without the guidance of your husband. In this way you can save him a great deal. But always keep in mind that every time you take him a new anxiety or problem to excite him, you are turning a knife in an open wound. His nerves are crying out for rest, and any excitement is torture to him."

Edith wrote that she resisted the proposal until Dercum suggested that the president's resignation would injure the country and the patient. As Edith remembered it, Dercum said that the president had "staked his life and made his promise to the world to do all in his power to get the treaty ratified and make the League of Nations complete. If he resigns, the greatest incentive to recovery is gone; and as his mind is clear as crystal he can still do more with even a maimed body than anyone else." Dercum allegedly reminded her that after five years of talking with him about public affairs, she was well equipped to serve as his go-between.

Writing in the 1980s, the neuropsychiatrist Edwin Weinstein took a skeptical view of Edith's reconstruction of her conversation with Dercum. Weinstein pointed out that Dercum's voice sounds just like Edith's. Also, Dercum was fully aware that Wilson's recovery would be slight, and in such circumstances, Weinstein wrote, it was "extremely unlikely" that a doctor would have taken on the responsibility of suggesting that Wilson was up to the demands of the presidency. Many of the records in the case were buried in Grayson's papers until 1991, but once these documents were uncovered, it was clear that Wilson had no intention of leaving office until the end of his term and that he and his wife were determined to conceal the facts of his condition.

About one point there is no doubt: Edith went to work as Woodrow's assistant, studying requests and reports from government officials and preparing digests of matters she deemed essential for his consideration. "I, myself, never made a single decision regarding the disposition of public affairs," she wrote. "The only decision that was mine was what was important and what was not, and the *very* important decision of when to present matters to my husband." But if Edith Wilson was not setting policy or taking action as the nation's chief executive, she did wield more power than anyone else in the White House for the final seventeen months of her husband's presidency. With his wife as gatekeeper and with the cooperation of Grayson and Tumulty, Woodrow Wilson continued to be President Wilson. The gate was high, it rarely opened, and business was anything but usual at the White House.

On occasion Grayson also served as a go-between. Just after the cabinet meeting convened by Lansing, the War Department heard from General William S. Graves, commander of the U.S. forces sent to Siberia in 1918. The end of the world war and the start of Russia's civil war had left Siberia and the Allied mission in chaos, but the Americans stayed on and took up the humanitarian task of protecting rail shipments of food. In the fall of 1919 they found themselves caught between a Bolshevik advance and a Japanese drive to seize control of the Siberian coast. General Graves wanted to know what his government expected him to do. Baker discussed the situation with Lansing and Josephus Daniels of the Navy Department, and when all agreed on the need for a presidential decision, they enlisted Grayson as messenger. The problem, which had been building for months, did not catch Wilson by surprise or overtax his weary mind. He asked Lansing to request an immediate Japanese response to a recent American communiqué expressing concern about Japanese intentions in Siberia.

Minuscule as the president's role was, Grayson made the most of it. On October 11—only nine days after the stroke—he issued a bulletin saying that the doctors considered the president's progress encouraging and that although his recovery would be very slow, he had already taken care of some official business. For good measure, Grayson gave his fellow Americans a peek into the sickroom, revealing that a Victrola had been installed for the patient's pleasure and that the first lady often read him poetry and light prose. With a few deft strokes, Grayson had sketched a picture of a president who was ailing but well tended and able to carry out his duties.

Though Grayson has been thrashed for his part in the cover-up, he was a man in an impossible position—a physician who happened to be an admiral, torn between the tradition of doctor-patient confidentiality and his oath as a naval officer to uphold the Constitution. But however conflicted Grayson might have felt, he quickly came down on the side of confidentiality. He fended off all challengers, including friends as devoted to Wilson as Baruch and Daniels. Two weeks after the stroke, when Baruch suggested that it was time to share the facts with the public, Grayson professed to agree but said that he and the other doctors were waiting until they felt they could give a definitive prognosis. (In fact, the prognosis had been reached forty-eight hours after the stroke.) Six weeks later, when Daniels repeated Baruch's suggestion, Grayson again agreed but offered a different excuse: "I am forbidden to speak of it. The president and Mrs. Wilson have made me make a promise to that effect."

The first attempt to scale the wall of secrecy surrounding the stroke was made by a freshman senator, George H. Moses of New Hampshire. A Republican strongly opposed to the entire Treaty of Versailles, Moses wrote a friend back home that Wilson was "a very sick man. He suffered some kind of cerebral lesion. . . . His condition is such that while this lesion is healing, he is absolutely unable to undergo any experience which requires concentration of mind . . . . Of course, he may get well—that is, he may live, but if he does he will not be any material force or factor in anything."

Although Moses had hit the mark, Dercum and Grayson immediately attacked the senator's credibility. Many absurd rumors were making the rounds, Dercum said, and the one passed along by Moses was "nonsensical beyond discussion." When Grayson was asked to comment, he coolly asked whether Senator Moses was a physician. Told that he was not, Grayson said that the senator "must have information that I do not possess."

Suspecting that there was more to the story, *The New York Times* noted the swelling chorus of demands for specifics. Grayson parried by telling a group of reporters that Wilson's mind was as clear as ever and that he was capable of conducting business but still needed a long rest. If he and the other doctors were to ease their restrictions, they might regret it, he said, and "when I have the care of the president's life in my hands, I consider it my duty to take no chances whatsoever." He promised that nothing would be withheld from the public if the president's health took a critical downturn.

The critical downturn came on the same day, October 14, with a swollen prostate gland that blocked the flow of urine and caused a dangerously high fever. At least one of Wilson's doctors argued that without surgery, he would die within two hours. Others, led by Grayson, insisted that Wilson was so weak that the surgery might kill him. The doctors left the decision to Edith, who sided with Grayson. His bulletin for the day falsely reported that the president's overall condition was good. Fortunately, several days of hot compresses eliminated the constriction, and the fever abated. But the American people were never told that their president had spent several days on the brink of death or that the setback had undone the slight recovery he had made since the stroke.

Ike Hoover would remember Wilson lying helpless for weeks. Once a day he was lifted out of bed and deposited in an armchair but had to be propped up to remain in place. After a time he could sign documents, although even that seemed to wear him out. A month after the stroke, when he was placed in a wheelchair, he was too weak to sit up. The chair was adjusted so that his legs could be stretched out straight, a posture that held him upright. "If ever there was a man in bad shape he was," Hoover wrote. "There was no comparison with the president who went to Paris and before. He was changed in every way and everyone about him recognized and understood it to be so."

In her memoir, Edith Wilson tried to cast doubt on Hoover's account by challenging a few of its details, but the thrust of his observations was corroborated decades later by Bert E. Park, a neurosurgeon and student of medical history. A study of the records of Wilson's stroke brought Park to a blunt conclusion: "Wilson was seriously disabled, both in a medical and Constitutional sense, despite Grayson's and other doctors' assertions to the contrary." Given Wilson's heart trouble and his history of small strokes, a major stroke was inevitable and, said Park, "neither Wilson's thought processes nor his conduct in office would ever be the same again."

36

Altogether an Unfortunate Mess

oodrow Wilson was paralyzed, but the government was not. Congress passed a raft of bills that became law without him. The Supreme Court, designed to operate at a remove from the Capitol and the White House, rolled on. Inevitably there were delays in the executive branch, but by the time of the stroke, the cabinet secretaries were almost as autonomous as the justices. They had been managing domestic affairs largely on their own for almost a year, while Wilson concentrated on the peace.

Even the battle over the treaty went on without a pause. Only two days after his collapse in Wichita, Wilson lost his most influential Republican ally, William Howard Taft. Finally convinced that the Senate would reject a treaty without reservations, Taft publicly urged Wilson to compromise. With the peace of the whole world at stake, Taft argued, it was unacceptable for the president to say, "I won't play because I can't have my way."

Colonel House, who had stayed in Europe to help organize the League of Nations, returned to New York in mid-October and soon wrote the White House to volunteer his services. When the first lady proved unreceptive, he boldly dispatched one of his former aides in Paris, Stephen Bonsal, to Henry Cabot Lodge. An old friend of the Lodge family, Bonsal was given a warm welcome, and Lodge seemed open to a compromise with the president. The senator took a copy of the treaty, penciled in the changes he wanted to see in the League covenant, and agreed that Bonsal could deliver them to Colonel House, who would forward them to the White House.

As Lodge reviewed the alterations with him, Bonsal noticed that they were much less strident than the fourteen reservations now attached to the treaty.* He also realized that Lodge's suggested phrasing barely differed from the phrasing in the covenant. But when Bonsal mused aloud that Lodge's latest additions to the original Article X went without saying, Lodge had a dry retort: "If it goes without saying, there is no harm in saying it— and much advantage." Lodge also voiced his skepticism about the staying power of the League and his fear that if it broke down, the United States would be drawn into the world's chaos. Nevertheless, Lodge entrusted his marked-up treaty to Bonsal, who raced to the post office and mailed it to House.

Thrilled, the colonel passed the word to Wilson. There was no reply, and when Lodge made no further move, Bonsal guessed that the senator's pride had been wounded by the president's apparent refusal of an olive branch. In his diary Bonsal blamed Wilson's gatekeepers: "the president is kept a prisoner . . . and all the efforts of House and his friends to establish relations with our stricken leader have failed. Lodge may well think that . . . the president has snubbed him; on the other hand, the olive branch may never have reached him—altogether an unfortunate mess."

House undoubtedly relished the prospect of saving the treaty, the president, and the world, and Bonsal seemed to think that a great opportunity had been

---

* The Lodge reservations affirmed U.S. sovereignty in many matters, including membership, American representation in the League, the Monroe Doctrine, war, disarmament, immigration, and the conduct of foreign policy. Many Republicans had contributed ideas to the reservations, and Lodge arranged them in fourteen parts, a jab at Wilson's Fourteen Points. These reservations and others are laid out and discussed in Thomas A. Bailey, *Wilson and the Peacemakers: Woodrow Wilson and the Great Betrayal* (New York: Macmillan, 1947), 387–94, and Henry Cabot Lodge, *The Senate and the League of Nations* (New York: Charles Scribner's Sons, 1925), 178–226.

missed. But the colonel erred in supposing that Wilson was looking for an alternative to his rigid stance. Even on his sickbed Wilson was determined to prevail, and the victory he envisioned required the opposition to yield. Certain that he was right—morally right—he held his adversaries in contempt.

As the vote on the treaty neared, Bernard Baruch and other friends urged Wilson to compromise. So did Gilbert M. Hitchcock, leader of the president's fight for ratification without reservations. He was an excellent man for the job. Son of Nebraska's first congressman, he had cut his teeth on politics. As a young man, he studied law and then took up publishing, making his newspaper, the *Omaha World-Herald,* into one of the country's best. A progressive Democrat in a state that often voted Republican, Hitchcock was elected three times to the House of Representatives and was serving his second term in the Senate. He was well liked and often praised for his courage, political finesse, and powers of persuasion.

But he was not a favorite of the White House. He and Wilson had clashed publicly on several occasions, and in the summer of 1919, when Hitchcock decided to take a vacation just after Wilson's return from Europe, reports of a "lack of warmth" between the two men made the front page. It was big news because Hitchcock was the acting minority leader of the Senate. Had Wilson not been sidelined, he would have led his ratification battle and consulted Hitchcock as needed. Now bedridden, Wilson was stuck with Hitchcock.

And Hitchcock was stuck with Wilson. Like Lansing, Hitchcock thought that Wilson had blundered by spurning the Republicans who had tried to interest him in mild reservations. To the senator as well as to the secretary of state, it seemed that Wilson was denying the first law of political mathematics: ratification would require sixty-four votes, and he would get them only if twenty-four Republicans voted with the forty Democrats. But Wilson was unavailable during September and October, and during those months, the Strong Reservationists (out to minimize U.S. involvement in world affairs) and the Irreconcilables (against the treaty in any form) had persuaded the country that the treaty was riddled with flaws and that the League menaced the independence of the United States.

Hitchcock sensed that he was leading a lost cause, but despite his apprehensions and his lukewarm relationship with Wilson, he proved a steadfast ally as the treaty moved toward a vote. He called at the White House a few days after the stroke to tell Tumulty that forty Democratic senators were ready to do whatever the president asked of them. He also stood foursquare behind Grayson's efforts to downplay the seriousness of the president's physical condition. Wilson thawed too. Hitchcock was the first elected official allowed into the sickroom.

The senator was shocked by the president's appearance. Overnight, he "had become an old man," Hitchcock would write. "As he lay in bed slightly propped up by pillows, with the useless arm concealed beneath the cover I beheld an emaciated old man with a thin white beard." (Wilson had grown it to conceal the left side of his mouth, which drooped because of the facial muscles weakened by the stroke.) The president was alert and resolute but taken aback when Hitchcock reported that the treaty could not win ratification in its original form. When Wilson asked how many votes he could get for a treaty without reservations, Hitchcock put the maximum at forty-five—far short of the necessary sixty-four. Wilson groaned and asked, "Is it possible, is it possible?"

In mid-November, four days before the vote, Hitchcock met with Edith Wilson and told her that the treaty would be beaten unless the Democrats accepted Lodge's reservations. Edith excused herself and went off to beg her husband to bow to reality. "For my sake," she pleaded. Taking her hand, he said, "Little girl, don't you desert me; that I cannot stand." He insisted that he had no moral right to alter a treaty he had signed without giving the other signatories the same opportunity. "Better a thousand times to go down fighting than to dip your colors to dishonorable compromise," he said. Edith, apparently unaware that reservations did not require the Allies' approval, could not continue the argument. On rejoining Hitchcock, she said that she would never again ask her husband to change his mind about the treaty.

A few days later Hitchcock tried again, writing the president indirectly, through the first lady. With the vote imminent, he had to have definite word of the president's position, he explained. Did Wilson really want the friends of the treaty to reject Lodge's resolution of ratification, with its fourteen reservations? In a note on the back of Hitchcock's envelope, Edith Wilson confirmed that the president favored rejection.

Two days before the vote, Hitchcock was again allowed into the sickroom, and for more than an hour gently tried to put Wilson on the path to compromise. Wilson was not only unyielding, he vowed to take revenge against senators who voted against him. When Hitchcock asked for his thoughts on the consequences of the treaty's defeat, Wilson predicted that the United States would incur the contempt of the world. But he seemed to prefer contempt to Lodge's reservations, and he vowed to take revenge. "I am a sick man, lying in this bed," he said, "but I am going to debate this issue with these gentlemen in their respective states whenever they come up for reelection if I have breath enough in my body to carry on the fight. I shall do this even if I have to give my life to it. And I will get their political scalps when the truth is known to the people."

It must have taken courage to argue with an invalid at high risk for another stroke, but Hitchcock admitted his willingness to compromise with the Republicans on certain points. Wilson tried to show that he too was a man of compromise, willing to accept clarifying reservations but unwilling to make substantive changes. Hitchcock noted that compromise would be essential. "Let Lodge compromise," Wilson snapped.

Hitchcock agreed that Lodge would also have to bend, but, he said, "we might well hold out the olive branch."

"Let Lodge hold out the olive branch," Wilson said. Perhaps he had forgotten the offer Lodge tendered through Bonsal and House, or perhaps Edith had not shown it to him.

On his way out, Hitchcock said he hoped that their talk had not been too tiring. Wilson assured him that it was invigorating. In a moment alone with Grayson, who had sat in on the meeting, Hitchcock said he would "give anything if the Democrats, in fact, all the Senate, could see the attitude that man took this morning."

Perhaps inspired by Wilson's high spirits, Grayson allowed his patient to venture outdoors later in the day, a first since the stroke. Taken to the lawn near the South Portico of the White House, he was rolled about in his wheelchair for more than an hour, after which the press was informed that the outing was one more milestone on the president's journey toward recovery. There was another such outing the following day, and Grayson let it be known that the cabinet, then meeting in the White House, could see the president as he and his companions moved about the grounds. It is not known if any cabinet members saw him, but Grayson's remark subtly implied that the president's caretakers had nothing to hide.

Hitchcock allowed himself to think that the president's fight could be won, although not on the first try. To hearten fellow Democrats, he drafted a message from the president, urging rejection of Lodge's resolution of ratification because it was, in effect, a defeat of the treaty. The letter went on to explain that after the vote, the door would probably be open for a compromise resolution that would make ratification possible.

Wilson reviewed the draft and made two fateful changes, replacing the word "defeat" with "nullification" and deleting the mention of compromise. Both revisions were sure to anger nearly every member of the Senate. "Nullification" carried echoes of the nineteenth-century Constitutional crisis precipitated by South Carolina's move to invalidate certain federal laws. In using the word, Wilson was accusing his opponents of flouting a higher authority.

The ferocity of Wilson's opposition to the Lodge reservations has been variously ascribed to his hatred of Lodge, his innate stubbornness, and the psychological inflexibility that often afflicts stroke patients. All three factors seem to have played a part. Wilson's stubbornness had always been pronounced, but it had served him well in his fights with Congress before the war. Unfortunately, his successes nurtured a sense of invincibility that ultimately worked against him. By 1918 he was regularly ignoring advice that could have spared him the debacles of the last years of his presidency. He had refused to listen when his wife and Colonel House warned that his letter urging Americans to vote Democratic in the midterm elections would backfire. He had refused to appoint prominent Republicans to the American peace delegation. He had refused Lansing's suggestions for a League covenant better aligned with traditional American diplomacy. Jealously guarding his Constitutional prerogative to conduct foreign policy on his own, he had not even communicated with the Senate while he was in Paris. And when he came home to a huge fight, he had ignored all counsel to stay in Washington and negotiate.

On November 18, the day before the vote, Stephen Bonsal called on Hitchcock and found him close to despair. As he told Bonsal, most Democrats favored ratification even on Lodge's terms, because they saw peace as the only way to steady a deeply unsettled world. Russia was still in the throes of a bloody civil war. The new government of Germany faced threats of Bolshevism, fascism, and hyperinflation. An Italian poet and war hero, Gabriele D'Annunzio, had raised a small army of super-patriots and seized control of Fiume. The British Empire was struggling to suppress independence movements in Ireland, India, and elsewhere, and Japan was waging the same battle against its restive subjects in Korea. Hitchcock agreed that the president's purism was out of place in such a world, but he felt obliged to carry out the president's instructions. "His honor is at stake," Hitchcock explained. "He feels he would be dishonored if he failed to live up to the pledges he made to his fellow delegates in Paris."

Hitchcock also confided that he found Lodge as mulish as Wilson. After several futile attempts to negotiate with him, Hitchcock concluded that the problem was not the treaty but Lodge's hatred of Wilson. Watching Wilson and Lodge from the sidelines, Taft pronounced both men guilty of putting "their personal prestige and the saving of their ugly faces above the welfare of the country and the world."

That evening Hitchcock made one last effort to interest the president in a compromise at some point in the future. Anticipating the defeat of both versions of the treaty—Lodge's with reservations and Wilson's without—Hitchcock wrote that he then would make a motion to keep the matter of ratification before the Senate. To underscore the necessity of concessions, Hitchcock enclosed a recent letter from Senator Thomas J. Walsh of Montana, a Democrat who urged his party to rethink its opposition to Lodge's evisceration of Article X. The League could institute a boycott or use other means to deal with disturbers of the peace, Walsh said. Hitchcock, aware that the first lady might keep his letter and Walsh's from her husband, tried to ensure that at least one point got through: "I would like to say to the president that many Democrats hold the same view that Senator Walsh expresses."

"Breakfasted early and went direct to the Capitol," Senator Henry Fountain Ashurst told his diary on November 19. "The breeze from my motor-car stirred the dead leaves strewn about, and I knew that President Wilson's treaty would soon be as dead as those leaves." At ten-thirty he and his fellow Democrats listened as Hitchcock read Wilson's call to reject the treaty with Lodge's reservations. Hitchcock passed the letter around, and Ashurst noticed that it was signed with a rubber-stamp facsimile of the president's signature, another indicator of the seriousness of his disability. Wilson's writing arm—his right—was not paralyzed, but it had lost much of its strength.

The full Senate came to order at noon. Within minutes, Lodge read Wilson's letter aloud, adding tartly that "comment is superfluous, and I shall make none." It is not clear who leaked the letter, but Democrats were upset by the leak and Republicans were outraged by the content. Long frustrated by the president's intransigence, they felt wounded anew by his charge of nullification. Ashurst heard sotto voce swearing from the Mild Reservationists, who had been hoping that Wilson would bow to reality.

For the first time in history, the Senate opened its doors to a treaty debate, and the crowd, too large for the galleries, stretched far down the corridor. After months of senatorial speechifying on every jot and tittle of the covenant, Ashurst wondered why he and his colleagues were being subjected to more. "For God's sake!" he shouted. "Let us all keep our mouths shut and vote, vote, and only vote."

Ashurst was applauded but outflanked. There would be another five and a half hours of oratory, much of it overheated. The low point was the diatribe of Lawrence Y. Sherman of Illinois, who said that the collective security promised by Article X made the League "an international homicide club." Close behind was Frank Brandegee of Connecticut, who predicted that when the League faced its first international crisis, it would "blow up, just like an automobile tire when it is pumped too hard, and those who are riding in the vehicle will have to make other arrangements."

The afternoon's finest address came from William E. Borah of Idaho, a Republican and an Irreconcilable. Borah had been objecting to membership in an association of nations since the United States entered the world war, and the Paris Peace Conference had barely come to order when he rose in the Senate to say that "If the Savior of Mankind would revisit the earth and declare for a League of Nations, I would be opposed to it."

Surprisingly, Borah's opposition did not pierce Wilson's thin skin, perhaps because the president recognized the senator as a kindred spirit. Borah too was a moralist. He loathed compromise. He excelled at oratory and had an outsized faith in its power. He preferred solitude to the camaraderie of his fellow politicians. Senator Borah also had a virtue not possessed by Senator Lodge: he refrained from attacking the president when he attacked the League.

On November 19, Borah poured out his fears and hopes for two hours. With or without reservations, the treaty would not have his vote, he said. As he saw it, ratification of either version would imperil American democracy. The Senate's approval would put the United States into the League of Nations, which automatically thrust America into Europe's affairs. And the beginning of that involvement would mark the end of George Washington's principle of "no entangling alliances," the bedrock of U.S. foreign policy for 150 years. Borah also argued that the peace made at Versailles was bound to fall apart because it was fundamentally unjust.

Worse, the United States would have a permanent seat on the League's decision-making body, the Executive Council, which was dominated by the great imperial powers. The fact that the council could not act without unanimous consent was no consolation to Borah. There remained a deeper problem, he said, and he could see no way around it: "You cannot yoke a government whose fundamental maxim is that of liberty to a government whose first law is that of force and hope to preserve the former," he said. "These things are in eternal war, and one must ultimately destroy the other." Revolted by the thought of making the United States an accomplice to the overlords, he implored the Senate to cleave to the democracy created by the Founding Fathers.

In his closing argument, Hitchcock ripped into the Republicans who had mocked the president's dream of a world organized for peace, and he reminded the Senate that an association of nations had been one of the war aims of the United States. Despite his conviction that ratification would require a compromise on Article X, Hitchcock defended Wilson's insistence on the original, predicting that the Allies would feel abandoned if America shirked the military obligations that they had assumed. Hitchcock even stood up for Wilson's use of the word "nullification." "How can we think otherwise?" he asked. Pointing out that the reservations had been framed entirely by Republicans, including some of the Irreconcilables, Hitchcock said that self-respecting Democrats could not accept terms dictated by senators who were bent on the defeat of the treaty.

The voting started at five-thirty, and Lodge's resolution of ratification, with its fourteen reservations, went down with 39 ayes and 55 nays. The ayes came from Lodge and the Reservationists who had lined up behind him. Hitchcock swiftly made a motion to adjourn, expecting that he and his allies would be permitted to present a new resolution in the morning. He had discussed the motion with Lodge and believed that Lodge would cooperate, but either Hitchcock had misunderstood or Lodge had changed his mind.

A long parliamentary boxing match followed, and Lodge won every round. As ten o'clock neared, the other senator from Massachusetts, Democrat David I. Walsh, broke ranks with his party and moved that the Senate vote again on Lodge's resolution of ratification. Lodge happily gave his consent. Coming from a Democrat, the call for a second vote meant that when it failed again—which it did—it would be plain that the president's own party had killed his treaty. As soon as the votes were in, Lodge plucked another Senate rule out of the air: when a second vote confirmed the results of the first, the contest was over. "The Senate has therefore taken final action," Lodge said.

Senator Oscar Underwood, Democrat of Alabama, observed that the Senate had merely finished with Lodge's resolution, not with the treaty. Underwood called for a vote on ratification without reservations. Lodge assented, secure in the knowledge that this proposition—Wilson's proposition—would also fail to win the necessary 64 votes. The roll was called once again, producing 53 nays and 38 ayes. At that point, Senator Claude A. Swanson, Democrat of Virginia, collared Lodge and said, "For God's sake, can't something be done to save the treaty?"

Lodge was glacial. "Senator, the door is closed. You have done it yourselves." He was equally curt with the Democrat Duncan Fletcher, who moved that the Senate apprise the president of the votes. There was no need, Lodge said. "I am sure that the president will take official notice of the action of the Senate." Such communiqués were routine, but Lodge had come to the floor armed with a precedent for *not* informing the White House of a treaty's defeat. When he trotted it out, Fletcher appealed to Marshall. No match for Lodge in a contest over Senate rules, the vice president allowed Lodge's argument to stand. Blocking the message to the White House was a small thing, but it smacked of kicking a man when he was down. More than any other incident of the treaty fight, this slight showed the depths of Lodge's hostility to Wilson.

Eleven o'clock had come and gone, but Lodge introduced one more piece of business, a resolution proposing that the United States make its own peace with Germany. Needing only a simple majority, Lodge got it, and the resolution was referred to the Committee on Foreign Relations for deliberation. To Hitchcock's astonishment, Lodge then called for an adjournment *sine die*—without a fixed day for its next meeting.

A small group of Republicans, Borah and Lodge among them, went off to celebrate at the home of Alice Roosevelt Longworth, a passionate Irreconcilable. The wife of Senator Warren G. Harding scrambled eggs for a midnight supper, and there was jubilation all around. A stranger to Washington might have wondered why the Reservationists, who professed to want the treaty, were as jolly as the Irreconcilables. The answer was that most if not all of them were like Lodge—Irreconcilables who found it expedient to masquerade as Reservationists.

When the *Chicago Tribune*'s correspondent asked Lodge who killed the treaty, he indicted the Democrats. When Hitchcock was asked, he objected to the question. "The treaty is not dead," he said. "The president can resubmit it at the next session of Congress." Trying to put the setback in a positive light, he noted that the Democrats had held firm while the Republicans, who "counted on being able to ram down the throats of the friends of the treaty a resolution of ratification framed by its enemies . . . could not do it."

The press blamed Lodge's strategy of "rule or ruin" and Wilson's vanity. The *New-York Tribune* begged "sane men of both parties" to come together and save the treaty. On the one hand, the *Tribune* said, "the president's assumption that his word shall be accepted as law must be smashed, and on the other hand, everything that is not required to preserve the Constitution and our national independence must be stricken from the reservations."

From her exchanges with Hitchcock, Edith Wilson undoubtedly knew that the treaty would go down to defeat. But when the news arrived, she could hardly bear to tell Woodrow. As she remembered it, he listened, thought for a moment, and said, "All the more reason I must get well and try to bring this country to a sense of its great opportunity and greater responsibility." He did not blame himself for obstructing the path to ratification.

Despite his banishment, Colonel House still wanted to help. On November 24 he sent two notes to the White House, one to the first lady and one to the president. He told Edith that although he hesitated to intrude while the president was unwell, he felt a sense of urgency about the treaty. Objectionable reservations could be adjusted later, and the important thing now was to make sure that the president's great work would live, he said. "His place in history hangs in the balance." In the note to Wilson, House advised public silence, another try at ratification when the Senate reconvened, and an understanding with Hitchcock that the treaty should be ratified "in some form." A few days later, House wrote again. He was not counseling surrender, he said, but nearly everyone close to the struggle believed that the treaty could not be ratified without substantial reservations. He pointed out that Wilson did not have to agree to the reservations; he could simply accept the Senate's vote. "I feel as certain as I ever did of anything that your attitude would receive universal approval," House wrote. "On the one hand your loyalty to our Allies will be commended and, on the other, your willingness to accept reservations rather than have the treaty killed will be regarded as the act of a great man."

House's suggestions offered Wilson an honorable way out of the impasse he had created, but the colonel's letters went unanswered. Suspecting that they had gone no further than Edith Wilson, House would never again volunteer advice to the White House.

Hitchcock continued to insist that the treaty was still alive, writing Wilson that the vote had produced only a deadlock. When the Senate reconvened, he said, "we will have eighty-one senators who favor or pretend to favor ratification in some form." That gave him a margin of seventeen votes over the sixty-four required, and he was confident that a new resolution of ratification could succeed. Next Hitchcock reported that he had canvassed the Republicans and found a consensus for a reasonable compromise—one that would satisfy the Republicans but "still leave the League in good working order."

Wilson put the treaty on hold and turned his attention to his seventh annual report on the state of the Union, due on December 2. He had delivered the first six in person but in 1919 was in no condition to compose the message much less give a speech. His voice was weak, and he sometimes burst into tears for no apparent reason (a common occurrence among stroke patients). Wilson's mind was often sharp, but when he tried to read or write he could not concentrate for more than a few minutes.

The task of writing the message fell to Tumulty, who stitched together material supplied by cabinet members and gave the prose a Wilsonian feel with phrases and ideas borrowed from the president's speeches. Unable to read the draft on his own because of his eyesight, Wilson asked Edith to read it to him and pencil in the changes he wanted to make. Most important, he deleted references to the treaty. Essentially a catalogue of the year's achievements with a few recommendations for the year ahead, Tumulty's creation resembled Wilson's previous State of the Union messages, but it drew scoffs from Republican senators who suspected the White House of hiding the truth about the president's health. George Moses, the first to disclose the rumor that Wilson had had a stroke, called the text "a very poor piece of literary mechanics, considering its putative authorship." Albert Fall of New Mexico wondered just when Wilson had written it.

The critics were immediately answered by "persons close to the White House," claiming that the serious stage of Wilson's illness had passed, his penmanship had improved, and he was able to do more work with each passing day. But the bulletin failed to quiet the skeptics. On December 4, an agitated Tumulty telephoned Lansing to report that the Committee on Foreign Relations had instructed Senators Fall and Hitchcock to ask for a meeting with the president, ostensibly to discuss an escalating crisis with Mexico. William O. Jenkins, an American entrepreneur who also held a post at the U.S. consulate in Puebla, had been kidnapped by rebels and released, only to be clapped into jail by the Mexican government. Venustiano Carranza was still president, but the revolution ground on, and his deputies were insisting that Jenkins had staged the kidnapping in order to undermine public confidence in Carranza. Tumulty understood that the Jenkins episode was simply a pretext for a close look at the patient, and he feared that the visit would end with Fall declaring that Wilson was too ill to remain in office. Tumulty wanted Lansing to give him a good excuse for turning the senators away. Perhaps Lansing could not think of one, or perhaps he was trying to avoid being a party to the cover-up, but he was no help. He pointed out that if Wilson was as well as the official bulletins made him out to be, the senators' request was not unreasonable.

When Grayson told Wilson that Fall and Hitchcock wanted to see him about Mexico, Wilson immediately grasped that the senators were coming on "a smelling expedition." Relishing the challenge, he asked Grayson to invite them for two-thirty that afternoon and threw himself into setting the stage for their visit. He ordered the lights turned up in every part of the room except near his bed. He asked that his papers be stacked on the nightstand next to his good arm. He had himself shaved and helped into a sweater, which made him look like a perfectly healthy man who had just awakened from a nap.

Edith, cast in the role of secretary, was outfitted with a tablet in one hand and a pencil in the other, props signaling that she was a supporting character rather than a co-star. (In her memoir, she explained that the props also allowed her to avoid shaking hands with Fall, whose frequent cries for military intervention in Mexico disgusted the president. Wilson had ample reason to think that Fall favored intervention solely to protect the mining interests of Americans who paid handsomely for his legal advice.)

When Fall and Hitchcock arrived, Grayson played his part to perfection. He said that he had ordered the president into bed in order to conserve his energy, an explanation suggesting that the president would have preferred to be in a chair. In fact, Wilson was still too weak to sit upright on his own. When Fall asked how long they might stay, Grayson left the decision to the visitors.

Tumulty played the press secretary devoted to the public's right to know. He allowed reporters onto the grounds of the White House for the first time since the stroke and stationed them on the main portico, where they would be able to interview the senators as they left. Like Grayson, he was crossing his fingers and praying that the president would turn in a bravura performance.

Upstairs, Grayson ushered the senators into the president's bedroom. Fall opened the conversation with an arresting if dubious pronouncement: "I hope you consider me sincere. I have been praying for you, Sir."

In a flash Wilson asked, "Which way, Senator?"

Fall laughed.

Wilson, who had been briefed on the friction with Mexico, acquitted himself well, and as implausible as it sounds, the Jenkins crisis came to an end in the middle of the meeting. As if in a play, an aide entered the room and beckoned Grayson to the telephone. Exit Grayson. Lansing was on the other end of the line, reporting that the Mexican government had just released Jenkins. Enter Grayson, delivering the good news.

Toward the end of their forty-five minutes together, Wilson told the senators that he expected to be on his feet soon and was looking forward to visiting the Capitol. With a touch of sarcasm, he asked Fall to pass the word to Moses.

The newsmen on the portico heard glowing reports from Fall as well as Hitchcock. Hitchcock, who had also seen the president two weeks earlier, said that he had improved considerably since their last meeting. Fall, taken in by Wilson's stagecraft, reported that he had seen the president using both hands, something he was physically unable to do. Fall described Wilson's speech as "somewhat thick" but, he added, "I could understand every word that he said."

Believing that Wilson was more disabled than he appeared to Fall, Lansing wished that White House would come clean. In a memo to himself on the day of the smelling expedition, he wrote, "I think that the American people are entitled to know and the cabinet ought to know the truth. It is not a matter of invading the privacy of an individual. It is not Woodrow Wilson but the president of the United States who is ill. His family and his physicians have no right to shroud the whole affair in mystery as they have done. I would not blame Congress if they instituted an investigation to ascertain the facts."

The facts that Lansing craved would not come to light for more than sixty years. The editors of *The Papers of Woodrow Wilson* left few stones unturned, but they did not see the papers of Francis X. Dercum, the Philadelphia neurologist who examined Wilson frequently after the stroke, until the 1980s, when a neurologist named Steven Lomazow acquired Dercum's papers and shared them with the editors. In the files were two letters to Dercum from R. A. Rogers, a physical therapist sent to the White House a few days after the smelling expedition. Clearly reluctant to let anyone else in on the concealment, Grayson kept Rogers at bay for days. Not until Rogers threatened to leave did Grayson relent.

Both Woodrow and Edith liked Rogers, and the First Patient gamely submitted to a new regimen of baths, massages, and exercises. Writing Dercum after the first day of therapy, Rogers reported that the president was "pleased to think that there could be something more to be done for him." But Rogers also reported that Wilson was still far from well. He had frequent dizzy spells even in bed, he was forgetful, he occasionally suffered from double vision, his muscles were weak, and he had virtually no stamina. He was also nervous and unable to sleep when he wanted. He still could not sit up in a chair for a meal. His stomach troubles—the "turmoil in Central America" that he described the first time he consulted Grayson—were still with him. And when his digestion was off, his irritability increased.

No doubt Grayson was aware of these symptoms, but he rarely if ever mentioned them in his diary once he began to trumpet Wilson's progress. On December 13, with Rogers supporting his left side, Wilson stood on his right leg for the first time, and "White House officials" immediately announced that Wilson had been walking around his room—a gross exaggeration. *The Washington Post* took the announcement at face value and informed the world that the rumors of a paralyzed leg were false. But Wilson's leg *was* paralyzed, permanently.

On December 15, prompted by a rumor that Republican leaders were hoping that he would soon make a move to end the deadlock on the treaty, Wilson broke his silence on the subject. The White House issued a statement saying that the president had "no compromise or concession of any kind in mind" and firmly believed that the Republicans should continue to bear the responsibility for the fate of the treaty and the state of the world.

Senators of both parties were dumbfounded, and Democrats who had supported Wilson's position out of party loyalty began talking about desertion. Hitchcock's most recent exchanges with Wilson had given him the impression that he should collaborate with the Mild Reservationists on a new resolution of ratification—one that would simultaneously honor Wilson's ideals and alleviate the greatest fears of the Strong Reservationists. Evidently too peeved to contact Wilson after the statement, Hitchcock sent for Tumulty and asked him to find out what Wilson wanted. The reply came from Edith Wilson, who said that the president was "clear in the conviction that it would be a serious mistake for him (or for our side) to *propose* anything. Any proposition must come from those who prevented the ratification of the treaty."

Defying Wilson's wishes, Senator Underwood submitted a proposal for a bipartisan committee to draft a new resolution of ratification. Lodge, who could be as stubborn as Wilson, refused to consider the idea. Underwood persisted, begging him and Hitchcock to show some Christmas spirit and assure the country that both parties were willing to cooperate on the treaty. Underwood was still talking when Lodge got to his feet. "I do not think just on the eve of adjournment that this can be disposed of," he said. "I cannot give my consent." Angered by Lodge's pettiness, the Mild Reservationists vowed that if he did not get out of their way, they would ignore his leadership. That night, when the Senate adjourned for the holidays, Republicans were in revolt against Lodge, Democrats were in revolt against Wilson, and the spirit of the Prince of Peace was nowhere to be found in Washington.

37

Breaking the Heart of the World

The Wilsons had a quiet Christmas—no guests, no tree. The president signed a bill and spent the morning outdoors in his wheelchair, savoring the sunshine in the White House garden. At noon he and Edith dined in his room, after which he rested and she went out to deliver gifts to friends.

A few days later, in an item about a family gathering at the White House to celebrate the president's sixty-third birthday, *The New York Times* noted that he had spent his sixty-second at Buckingham Palace. It was a jolting reminder of all that had been lost since the days when millions crowded the streets of London and Paris and Rome to cheer Woodrow Wilson. He felt the losses keenly. "It would probably have been better if I had died last fall," he told Grayson. Grayson urged him to resign. Wilson was inclined to take the advice, but according to Grayson, they were overruled by the first lady.

Wilson's fight for the treaty resumed in early January, when Tumulty tried to convince him that reservations were the price of ratification. Rarely allowed to see the president after the stroke, Tumulty was reduced to sending memos upstairs and waiting, usually in vain, for a reply. Edith Wilson had never liked him, and unless he got an answer, Tumulty could not tell if she shared his missives with her husband or set them aside. On this occasion, there was no personal reply, just an ornery repetition of Wilson's promise to accept clarifying reservations and reject substantive changes. He made the point in a public message to Democrats gathered for the party's annual Jackson Day Dinner and added that if the Senate decided against him, the American people ought to make the next election "a great and solemn referendum" on the League of Nations.

Publicly, Henry Cabot Lodge complained that the president had conceded nothing, but privately the senator rejoiced. Without reservations, the treaty was going to die, and the dagger was in Wilson's hand, not his. Certain that he was right, Lodge bided his time and cheerfully met with a bipartisan committee still searching for a path to ratification. The Irreconcilables, furious with him for running the risk that the two parties would come to terms, hauled him out of a meeting, dragged him to another room, and threatened to choose a new majority leader. The bipartisan committee never met again.

Wilson's cause was further damaged by two thunderbolts from across the Atlantic. The first was the American publication of an English bestseller, *The Economic Consequences of the Peace,* by a thirty-six-year-old former British treasury official, John Maynard Keynes. As an advisor at the peace conference, Keynes had tried to persuade the Big Four that the reparations bill they planned to deliver to Germany was so excessive that it might provoke another war. Instead, Keynes said, the victors ought to set a realistic price and forget about collecting on their war debts. By his calculations, such a program would speed Europe's return to prosperity, and prosperity would increase the likelihood of a lasting peace. When the Big Four rejected his ideas, Keynes resigned and batted out his book. Part exposé and part call to action, *The Economic Consequences of the Peace* contained a series of savage character sketches suggesting that the Treaty of Versailles was the sum total of the defects of Georges Clemenceau, David Lloyd George, and Woodrow Wilson. (Vittorio Orlando barely figured in the tale.) In the United States the book reinforced the suspicion that Wilson's sternest critics were right: the president had botched it in Paris.

Noting that the Treaty of Versailles barely resembled Wilson's promise of a just and generous peace, Keynes asked, "What weakness or misfortune had led to so extraordinary, so unlooked-for a betrayal?" Keynes was not the first to think that Wilson had been outplayed by Clemenceau and Lloyd George, but he was the first to say publicly what Secretary Lansing had long said in private: Wilson was a terrible negotiator. Keynes saw him as "a blind and deaf Don Quixote," a well-intentioned man who had mastered none of the arts of the council chamber. Puzzled by Wilson's habit of making concessions without seeking a quid pro quo, Keynes speculated that the president's pride in his decision to forgo the spoils of war did him in. As soon as Clemenceau and Lloyd George realized that Wilson was ruled by his conscience, they began slathering their self-interested demands with altruism.

Keynes had been part of the posse that cornered Lloyd George in the last weeks of the peace conference and reported that the British public now favored a peace less harsh than the one just presented to Germany. After hearing them out, Lloyd George tried to enlist Wilson's help in lobbying the French for softer terms. Alas, Keynes wrote, Lloyd George found that "it was harder to de-bamboozle this old Presbyterian than it had been to bamboozle him. . . . Thus in the last act the president stood for stubbornness and a refusal of conciliation."

Years later, Bernard Baruch, who had witnessed Lloyd George's importuning, offered another explanation for Wilson's stiffness. As Baruch remembered it, Wilson had listened to Lloyd George's plea and burst out, "Mr. Prime Minister, you make me sick!" Then Wilson told him off for changing his mind after months of rejecting softer terms and for shifting ground at the last minute, when any crack in Allied unity might embolden Germany to reject the treaty. Keynes also neglected to mention that Clemenceau and Lloyd George had not bested Wilson in every round. Wilson persuaded them to slash the price they initially set for reparations, and he forced France to abandon its scheme for a phony republic in the Rhineland. Keynes also glossed over the challenge inherent in the Council of Four's commitment to unanimous decisions. If it was true that Wilson surrendered more than he might have, it was also true that he rarely gave in without a ferocious fight.

Herbert Hoover, who spent much of 1919 organizing an international drive to relieve a famine spreading across Eastern Europe, agreed with Keynes on the likely economic repercussions of the treaty but strongly protested Keynes's critique of Wilson's performance. To Hoover, the president's losses in Paris were minor and of interest mainly because they showed the gulf between a world dominated by a handful of overreaching, overaggressive Great Powers and Wilson's vision of a new world order, a community of all nations dedicated to peace. Much more significant than Wilson's failings, Hoover wrote, were his role in establishing the League of Nations, his championship of the twenty-one new democracies emerging from the wreckage of the old empires, and his support of famine relief. Thanks largely to Wilson, the U.S. government put up $100 million and the American people raised another $100 million, preventing the starvation of millions.

Although relatively few Americans read *The Economic Consequences of the Peace* when it appeared in the United States, Keynes's flaying of Wilson was widely quoted in newspapers and magazines. Weary of the ratification fight and still resentful of the secrecy of the Big Four's negotiations, many Americans thought that Keynes was revealing the quintessential Wilson—obstinate and so enamored of his own loftiness that he could be fooled by men who played to it. The Irreconcilables were especially taken with Keynes's portrait, and one of them, Senator Borah, publicly posed an unsettling question: if the great Woodrow Wilson was so easily gulled, how would lesser American envoys fare in the cut and thrust of the League of Nations?

The other thunderbolt was hurled by Sir Edward Grey, Britain's former foreign secretary. Called out of retirement and sent to the United States as special ambassador in September 1919, Grey was supposed to allay American fears of the League of Nations and persuade the United States that its participation in the League was essential to world peace. Grey arrived on the day Wilson broke down near Wichita, and the two men never met. Grey's requests to see the president were declined on grounds of the president's illness, but Lansing suspected that Grey was being snubbed because of an off-color joke attributed to a military aide at the British embassy. As the joke had it, Edith Galt was so startled by Woodrow Wilson's proposal of marriage that she nearly fell out of bed. It was said that the same aide had spoken of Edith as a social climber and hinted that she had offered hush money to Mary Hulbert. The stories had begun making the rounds before Grey's arrival, and when he was informed of the president's displeasure, he was expected to send the officer back to England. With no proof of the man's guilt, Grey let him stay.

Frustrated by the president's inaccessibility, Grey nevertheless held confidential talks with Lansing and with leading senators of both parties, offering assurance that Britain would accept the Lodge reservations. (France was flashing the same signal.) Unable to do more in Washington, Grey returned to Britain in January 1920 and wrote a long letter to the *Times* of London, ostensibly to explain to his fellow Britons that joining the League of Nations would be a huge departure for the United States, which had always shunned alliances. "Hence this desire for some qualification and reservation," he wrote. He urged his countrymen to take an understanding view of the reservations and argued that American ratification with strings attached would do more than no ratification to ensure a lasting peace. Without the United States in the League, he said, "the old order of things will revive, the old consequences will recur, there will again be some great catastrophe of war." Newspapers in the United States quickly reprinted Grey's letter, and Americans understood that Lord Grey was telling them that Britain was prepared to live with the reservations Senator Lodge had in mind.

In Washington, Grey's revelation came as a relief to nearly everyone but Wilson, who considered it foreign interference in American affairs. Had Grey pulled such a stunt while still in the United States, Wilson said, he would have insisted that Britain recall him. Wilson made his remarks in a statement prepared for the press, but someone (probably Tumulty) wisely put it aside. Unwilling to let the matter rest, Wilson ordered Lansing to find out whether Grey's unofficial move had official support. The governments of Britain and France had quietly given their blessings to Grey's project, but neither government was willing to admit it to the United States.

Next Wilson lit into Lansing. Was it true, Wilson asked him, that he had been holding cabinet meetings? Saying that "custom and precedent" dictated that only the president could convene the cabinet, Wilson declared that meetings called by anyone else would be a serious breach. "I have therefore taken the liberty of writing you to ask you this question, and I am sure you will be glad to answer."

It was a peculiar query, as Lansing had sent the president a summary of nearly every one of the two dozen cabinet meetings since the stroke. Before answering, Lansing purged himself in a confidential rant against Wilson's "mania," "lack of mental balance," and "exaggerated ego" and finished with an exultation: "Thank God, I shall soon be a free man!" Taking out a fresh sheet of paper, Lansing wrote the president that the cabinet had met—informally—to discuss business that could not be postponed, and that he had done his best to see that the administration's policies were carried out. He closed with an offer to submit his resignation.

Wilson replied that he was "much disappointed" by Lansing's rationale and would indeed appreciate the resignation, which, he said, would "afford me an opportunity to select someone whose mind would more willingly go along with mine." Lansing's letter of resignation began and ended politely, but after years of seething in silence, he let Wilson have it: "I confess that I have been surprised and disappointed at the frequent disapproval of my suggestions, but I have never failed to follow your decisions, however difficult it made the conduct of our foreign affairs." On Friday, February 13, one of his doubly auspicious days, Wilson informed Lansing that his resignation was effective immediately.

Wilson was dead wrong to accuse his secretary of state of encroaching upon the powers of the president. Faced with Tumulty's threat to block any effort to remove Wilson from office, Lansing had committed himself to a constructive alternative—damage control. The unofficial cabinet meetings had been a boon to Wilson. They prevented the wheels of the executive branch from seizing up. They reinforced the illusion that the paralyzed president was still in command. And they minimized the chances of a congressional investigation that surely would have exposed the cover-up and forced him out of office. Here was irony piled upon irony: Lansing, an honorable public servant trying to carry out his Constitutional responsibilities, had been stymied by Tumulty, whose personal devotion to the president ruled out any possibility of arranging for the vice president to succeed the president. Then Lansing, who strongly disapproved of the conspiracy to conceal the seriousness of the president's illness, became a co-conspirator because he could not see a way around it. Finally, after putting the needs of the executive branch ahead of his Constitutional concerns, Lansing had been sacked for usurpation.

In the middle of this trying winter, Ray Stannard Baker, Wilson's press secretary in Paris, went to the White House to offer his services on behalf of ratification. Baker had already written a series of pro-League articles for a newspaper syndicate and turned them into an adulatory book, *What Wilson Did at Paris*. With another treaty vote in the offing, he wanted to do even more. In a talk with Edith Wilson, he pointed out that the American people were growing impatient because they saw little difference between the original covenant and the version with reservations. "I know," she replied, "but the president still has in mind the reception he got in the West, and he believes the people are with him."

"That is the trouble!" Baker wailed in his diary. "He has been ill since last October and cannot know what is going on. He sees almost nobody: and hears almost no direct news." On his next visit to Washington, Baker spoke with several of Wilson's admirers, all of whom were as pained as he was by the president's unwillingness to yield. "The poor president!" Baker lamented in private. "So nearly friendless a man. . . . There is something indescribably tragic in the sight of this sick man, now willing to kill his own child rather than to have it misborn in the world! It is the old old tragedy of a man's dearest desire thwarted by the defects of his own temperament, and his own physical weakness."

The Senate took up the treaty again on February 9. The new resolution of ratification consisted of slightly modified versions of Lodge's fourteen reservations plus a fifteenth endorsing Ireland's aspirations to independence. Wilson had just made a nod toward compromise in a letter to Senator Hitchcock, but all hope for a real change of heart vanished on March 8, in another letter to Hitchcock. Homing in on Article X, Wilson called his version a moral victory even greater than the military victory over Germany and said that if he did not give his all to preserve it, he would not be able to look American soldiers in the eye.

The letter won the president no new allies, and when the vote came, on March 19, he lost twenty-one of the Democrats who had sided with him in November. The galleries were packed, and the mood was funereal. With eighty-four senators on the floor, fifty-six yeas were required for a two-thirds majority. (Had all ninety-six senators been in the chamber, sixty-four votes would have been needed.) The twelve not present had taken advantage of a congressional rule allowing members to pair their votes, in effect canceling each other out.

The last chance for ratification hung on the vote of Hitchcock himself. As minority leader, he had waged two exhausting fights, one in support of Wilson's position and one in a futile effort to get Wilson to see the obvious: nine-tenths of the loaf was better than none. Hitchcock's name came early in the roll of Democrats, and if he parted company with Wilson, other Democrats would see that they were being given permission to do the same. But Hitchcock could not bring himself to abandon Wilson, and the final count—49 yeas, 35 nays—was 7 shy of two-thirds. Hitchcock came to think of his vote as the greatest mistake of his life. Mourning the outcome—"America's isolation is now a reality"—*The New York Times* laid the blame on Lodge. The senator knew better than to gloat about the demise of the treaty, and some historians have argued that he hoped the reservations would save the treaty. For eight tense months, he had wooed the Reservationists, both Mild and Strong, and they were persuaded that he wanted the treaty as much as he did. But he had also wooed the Irreconcilables, and they were equally certain that the reservations were simply a device to prevent ratification.

Even Lodge's intimates were left wondering about his aim. On the night of the vote, he told Corinne Roosevelt Robinson, sister of his late friend Theodore, "Just as I expected to get my Democrats to vote with my Republicans on going into the League, a hand came out of the White House and drew back those Democrats, and prevented our going into the League with reservations." But his daughter swore that he "hated and feared the Wilson league, and his heart was really with the irreconcilables . . . and when it was finally defeated he was like a man from whom a great burden was lifted."

The newspapers either blamed Wilson or professed bafflement at his decision to bar the United States from the League rather than make concessions that most Americans considered prudent. Others blamed Hitchcock for not giving up on Wilson and rallying the Democrats to vote for the reservations. In that case, the treaty would have been ratified, and it would have fallen to Wilson to accept or reject the Senate's decision. Senator Irvine Lenroot of Wisconsin, a Mild Reservationist, was the only one who came close to a plausible explanation for Wilson's ineffable resistance. Recalling Wilson's remark that the failure to ratify would break the heart of the world, Lenroot wondered whether the president had changed his mind or his mind had changed him.

Wilson's mind had indeed changed him. After the stroke, he was locked in the past—in warm memories of roaring crowds, in haunting thoughts of the war dead, in the belief that compromise would violate his promises, and in the conviction that substantive reservations were a dishonorable attempt to evade American responsibilities in a dangerous new world. Wilson had not lost his mind, but the pragmatism that had once tempered his idealism was gone. In a letter to a friend, Lodge ascribed the defeat of the treaty to Wilson's selfishness, which, he said, "goes beyond what I have ever seen in any human being." By "selfishness," Lodge undoubtedly meant Wilson's possessiveness about the League and his moral vanity, which often led him to regard himself as more principled than his opponents. Lodge's judgment was not inaccurate, but it was incomplete. There was one more culprit— brain damage. He could carry on an intelligent conversation, but tasks that required long stretches of concentration were beyond him, as was reading. One of his early strokes had blinded him in one eye, and the final stroke had reduced the vision in the other eye by half.

Wilson emerged from the League fight with his honor intact but seemed unable to grasp that it had been purchased at the expense of the United States and the world. The Senate's defeat of the treaty meant that the United States and Germany were still at war. It also deprived the League of its greatest champion. And it deprived the United States of an unparalleled opportunity to build international support for American ideals and policies. With a seat in the councils of the League, U.S. envoys would have had a finger on the pulse of the world, a potentially valuable addition to the intelligence flowing into the State Department from embassies and consulates.

A strong League might not have been able to prevent World War II, but the odds were even longer against a weak League, and without the United States, the world's strongest, richest democracy, the League was undernourished from the start.

Despite Wilson's insistence to the contrary, the Lodge reservations did not mutilate the covenant. In the opinion of David Hunter Miller, an American lawyer who went to Paris with Wilson and labored over the phrasing and ramifications of every article in the covenant, the reservations "were of a wholly minor character, they left [the League's] structure intact, and they would have interfered with its workings not at all."

The animosity between Lodge and Wilson also played a part in the defeat of the treaty. At the most primitive level, Lodge hated the covenant because it was Wilson's, and Wilson hated the reservations because they were Lodge's. But Lodge's strategy offered a possibility for saving the treaty. Wilson's all-or-nothing strategy did not. In the end, it was Wilson who broke the heart of the world.

38

Best of the Second-Raters

Edith waited till morning to tell Woodrow of the vote. As she remembered it, he took the news calmly, sure that he would be vindicated by history. But she was writing years after the fact. Grayson, writing in the moment, found the president "very blue and depressed," wishing to go back to bed and stay there.

Wilson's fighting spirit revived a few days later, when Tumulty sent a memo urging him to announce that he would not run for a third term. Wilson ignored it and fumed that he would not hand the party back to William Jennings Bryan. Nor could he imagine declining a nomination he had not been offered. But if the voting at the Democratic National Convention reached an impasse and the party turned to him, he would then feel free to accept, he told Grayson. Wilson did not ask if he could withstand the strains of a presidential campaign, and Grayson remained silent for fear of depressing him.

Wilson was now able to walk slowly, with a cane, for short distances but still needed a wheelchair to reach other parts of the White House. He had also resumed taking automobile rides, although he had to be lifted into the car and propped in a corner in order to remain upright. Jimmie Starling and his Secret Service colleagues did the lifting and, Starling wrote, "conspired in every way to give him solace." Among other things, they recruited friends to stand at the White House gate and cheer when Wilson returned from a spin. Assuming the gatherings were spontaneous, Wilson was moved to tears.

Summoned to the president's room at 2:00 a.m. on April 13, Grayson found his patient agitated and wide awake. For two hours he rambled on about the hypocrisy of the Senate, his break with Colonel House, and the question of resigning. Aware of his inefficiency, Wilson said that he did not want his pride to stand in the way of his duty. When he asked for Grayson's thoughts, the doctor suggested calling a cabinet meeting, believing that it would do Wilson good to confer with his advisors and see that he was still useful to the country.

A day later the cabinet assembled in Wilson's study for its first meeting with him in more than seven months. As an aide announced each arrival, at least one cabinet member silently wondered why, and no explanation was offered. Few outside the sickroom knew that the stroke had severely damaged Wilson's vision. David F. Houston, now secretary of the treasury, was devastated by the president's old and haggard face, his useless left arm, and the drooping jaw and faint voice. More cabinet meetings followed, but Wilson often showed more interest in the past than in the pending business of the executive branch. He sometimes spoke bitterly of the senators who had killed the treaty, oblivious to his own role in its demise. When Albert S. Burleson, the postmaster general, urged him to resubmit it with reservations he considered acceptable, Wilson said that he had forced the Allies to agree to his terms and could not ask them to do more. The willingness of Britain and France to live with the American reservations seemed immaterial to him.

The Senate's rejection of the treaty meant that the United States was still technically at war with Germany, and absent a formal peace, the two countries could not renew diplomatic ties or resume normal commercial relations. Nor could the United States file claims for lives and property lost to U-boat attacks during the neutrality period. Taking matters into its own hands, Congress declared the war against Germany at an end in a joint resolution approved May 27. Wilson vetoed it immediately, enraged by the idea of making peace without the Allies and by the fact that Congress was willing to make a peace that did not require Germany to right the wrongs it had committed. Congressional leaders could not find the votes to override the veto, and Republicans went on complaining that the most serious obstacle to world peace was Woodrow Wilson.

Both parties would soon hold their national conventions and choose their presidential nominees, and neither party had a clear frontrunner. The Republican short list included Senator Hiram Johnson of California; General Leonard Wood, a stand-in for his late friend Theodore Roosevelt; and the popular governor of Illinois, Frank Lowden, one of the last American politicians born in a log cabin. Among the dark horses were Calvin Coolidge, the law-and-order governor of Massachusetts, and Senator Warren Gamaliel Harding of Ohio, a former small-town newspaper publisher with little to show for his five years in Washington. As a fond Senate colleague put it after Harding's death, "The simple fact is that my dear old friend just did not like to work." Harding liked golf and poker, smoking and drinking, parties and female companionship. Wilson, stunned by the interest in Harding, asked, "How can he lead when he does not know where he is going?"

The Democrats' early favorites were Wilson's son-in-law, William G. McAdoo, the former treasury secretary; A. Mitchell Palmer, the current attorney general; and William Jennings Bryan, the old war horse. And the Democrats too had an Ohio newspaper publisher, Governor James M. Cox. Wilson found fault with all of them. He felt betrayed by Bryan, who had come out for treaty reservations. Palmer did not want the election to be a great and solemn referendum on the League. Cox struck him as small beer. "Dear Mac" got things done, but Wilson worried that he was insufficiently reflective for the presidency.

As the spring wore on, Wilson convinced himself that the election had to be a referendum on the League and that he was the one to lead the fight. In early June he jotted down the questions he would ask the voters: Did they wish him to serve for another term? Did they approve of his conduct of the war? Did they want the Treaty of Versailles ratified and the United States in the League? He also made a list of potential cabinet members.

Tumulty knew nothing of the lists but feared the worst because of Wilson's silence on the matter of his candidacy. In desperation he confided in a friendly reporter, Louis Seibold of the *New York World,* and together they drew up questions for a newspaper interview—the first since the stroke. The interview would be a coup for Seibold, and he agreed to help Tumulty by asking Wilson about the American tradition of leaving the presidency after two terms and about his plans for life after the White House. The interview request, along with questions, went upstairs to Edith Wilson on June 12.

Wilson agreed to see Seibold a few days later but rejected many of the questions, and the first lady informed Tumulty that the article had to be a hymn of praise. Tumulty read the order and told her to go to hell—in a note for his files.

Seibold's visit was staged even more carefully than the encounter with the smelling expedition. It was al fresco, on the South Portico, where the air was rich with the scent of roses and the grounds were at their lushest. The president, seated at a small table, was wearing a gray suit and a Panama hat broad enough to shade most of his face. His wife, crisp in white linen, stood with a hand on the back of his chair. He started to rise, she blocked the move, and he settled for a handshake. Seibold seemed pleased that Wilson's grip was firm and that he declared himself capable of more than his keepers would allow.

The play produced for Seibold had three acts: an hour of watching Wilson take care of correspondence, an hour and fifteen minutes of watching a Western with the Wilsons, an intermission of an unspecified length, and lunch. Seibold's three and a half hours at the White House yielded a hymn of thanksgiving as well as the requisite praise. Wilson's face showed the strain of his ordeal, but his eyes were bright and alert. He limped, but the limp was slight. He needed a cane, yes, but it was reed-thin. He moved slowly but without evident discomfort and without dragging his left leg. (In fact, Wilson used the strength of his right side to swing his left leg forward, a move that Seibold mistakenly took as proof that the leg was not paralyzed.) No, he could not get into an automobile on his own, but he needed only slight assistance, an assertion that must have surprised the aides who strained to hoist the president in and out of the car. There was no mention of the drag in Wilson's speech.

Seibold returned the next day for an hour's talk on politics. The Republicans had just nominated the affable nonentity Warren Harding. As Senator Brandegee explained, "There ain't any first-raters this year. . . . We've got a lot of second-raters, and Warren Harding is the best of the second-raters."

When Seibold asked Wilson for his thoughts on the convention, Wilson dryly remarked that the nominee matched his party's reactionary platform. Besides rolling back twenty years of progressive reform, the Republicans seemed intent on making the election a referendum on Woodrow Wilson. The platform denounced him as "unconstitutional and dictatorial," declared that he had been as unprepared for peace as he was for war, and accused him of pursuing a foreign policy that was "humiliating to America and irritating to other nations."

"I suppose I should feel flattered over being made the issue," Wilson said. As he saw it, the insults were meant to cloud the great and solemn issue and confuse the American people. Did Wilson have an opinion on the type of man the Democrats should nominate? Seibold asked. Wilson reminded him that there was to be no discussion of the Democratic field. As the interview was coming to a close, Seibold tried again, and Wilson again demurred.

Seibold's long report, widely reprinted after its June 18 publication in the *World*, left most Americans with the impression that their president's mind was as sharp as ever and that his body (apart from the limp) was in good shape. There was nothing in the article about Wilson's plans for life after the White House. Tumulty had gambled and lost.

By refusing to sideline himself, Wilson had signaled that he was available, and the Democrats found themselves in a fix. They could not openly disown the president, but they could not indulge him, either—because of his health and because they did not feel the Democrats could win if they flouted the two-term tradition. Reading Seibold en route to the party's convention in San Francisco, the bosses of Tammany Hall told a reporter that they would lead the fight against Wilson's nomination. The boss of Illinois vowed to join them.

The first casualty of Wilson's unwillingness to step aside was William Gibbs McAdoo, who could hardly run against his own father-in-law. It is easy to imagine that Wilson's caginess set off a streak of Dear Mac's wall-blistering profanity, but in a statement issued on the heels of Seibold's story, McAdoo said only that he did not wish his name placed before the convention. He had left the Treasury in order to rehabilitate his personal finances, he explained, and had not yet completed the task. McAdoo called his decision irrevocable, but Wilson noticed that he had not explicitly promised to decline the nomination. Insiders understood that McAdoo still yearned for the nomination but could no longer pursue it openly.

Discussing the Democratic platform with Wilson a day later, Senator Carter Glass of Virginia expressed regret that Wilson was not in shape to lead the fight for the League. If Glass was fishing for a renunciation, he did not get it. Wilson remained silent. Tumulty and Grayson collared the senator on his way out of the White House and escorted him to Union Station, where Grayson begged him—for the third time in ten days—to prevent a Wilson stampede at the convention. "If anything comes up, save the life and fame of this great man," Grayson said. Grayson was even more direct with a party official named Robert W. Woolley: "No matter what others may tell you, no matter what you may read about the president being on the road to recovery, I tell you that he is permanently ill physically, is gradually weakening mentally, and can't recover. He couldn't possibly survive the campaign." Woolley assured him that the president would be honored but not nominated.

Aware that Glass was not the only influential Democrat who opposed his candidacy, Wilson enlisted his new secretary of state, the man he thought of as "the flower of his cabinet," Bainbridge Colby. New to Washington and not a member of the Democratic establishment, Colby was probably the only one Wilson could have trusted to represent him at the convention. Wilson had him accredited as a delegate from the District of Columbia and invited him to the White House for a talk on June 20. Wilson believed that a deadlock was inevitable. A dozen men were going to San Francisco in hopes of receiving the nomination, but only one-quarter of the delegates had pledged themselves to anyone, and a candidate needed two-thirds of the votes to carry the convention. Wilson asked Colby to stay in touch with him and wait for the deadlock. They would conceal their dealings from Tumulty by wiring each other in code.

When the convention opened, on Monday, June 28, the unveiling of an enormous photograph of Wilson touched off the kind of long, heartfelt demonstration feared by the party's leaders. Delegates whooped and marched for twenty minutes and would have gone on and on had not someone thrown a switch that turned off the auditorium's brightest lights. Colby told a reporter that the fervor for Wilson was so intense that a motion to suspend the rules and nominate the president by acclamation would have carried at any moment.

On Friday, as the balloting got under way, the chairman of the Democratic Party somehow learned of Wilson's machinations, and on Saturday the convention's leaders confronted Colby. The tongue-lashings, which included the accusation that he did not have the president's best interests at heart, left him feeling like a criminal.

Colby's contrition was short-lived. McAdoo and Palmer had been leading the field, but after twenty-two rounds of balloting, both men stalled. It seemed to Colby that Wilson was still the sentimental favorite, and he told Wilson that without definite orders to the contrary, he would seize the first moment to move for a suspension of the rules and nomination by acclamation.

On Sunday, Ray Stannard Baker telephoned Tumulty from San Francisco to alert him to Colby's plan and to report that Wilson was aware of it. Tumulty dashed off a memo to the first lady, a warning that the plan would fail. The Democrats opposed to a third term for Wilson were numerous enough to defeat a motion to suspend the rules, and when they did, Tumulty said, Wilson would suffer a public humiliation at the hands of his own party. Tumulty also pointed out that if Colby's plan were exposed, the malevolent would say that the president's friends "had connived to bring about a deadlock and that the purpose from the first was to nominate the president."

Colby folded later in the day, the balloting dragged on, and on the forty-fourth round, at 1:40 a.m. on July 6, the Democrats bestowed their nomination on James M. Cox, governor of Ohio. A farm boy who had taken up journalism and built a modest fortune as a newspaper publisher, Cox was fifty years old and in splendid physical shape from the hours he devoted to hunting, fishing, and golf. His personal history included a divorce, but he was so upright and steady that the people of Ohio refused to be scandalized. They had twice elected him to the House of Representatives and given him three terms as governor. A middle-of-the-road progressive, he favored a League of Nations covenant with reservations, and he enforced the Prohibition laws because he was governor, not because he was a temperance man. (In the battle between the "drys" and "wets," he was classified as "moist.") The Democrats hoped that Cox would attract moderates of both parties, carry the crucial state of Ohio, persuade Congress to exempt beer and wine from Prohibition, and honor the triumphs of Woodrow Wilson without promising to perpetuate his regime.

After telephoning Cox in Ohio and getting some sleep, the leaders of the convention named his running mate—Franklin D. Roosevelt, assistant secretary of the navy. With FDR, the Democratic ticket got the aura of the Roosevelt name, a shot at the forty-five electoral votes of his home state of New York, and a big infusion of charisma. FDR was one of the most attractive candidates in the history of American politics: young (thirty-eight), tall (six-foot-two), handsome, and personable. He had not done especially well in his single term as a state senator, but he had learned to give a memorable speech and to guard his independence. Despite eight years in the Wilson administration, he carried no Wilson baggage.

Within hours of FDR's nomination, a reporter tracked down his mother and asked for a comment. "He's a fine boy," she said, "and I shall certainly vote for him." The boy did not have to be told that his place was in the backseat. He was in San Francisco as a delegate and could have been present for his nomination but had had the sense to disappear beforehand in order not to upstage the absent Cox.

Wilson wired his congratulations to both nominees and on July 18 received them at the White House. Watching from a distance as an aide rolled the president's wheelchair onto the portico, Roosevelt was shocked. This Wilson—almost inert, his left arm concealed by a shawl—was a husk of the man Roosevelt had known before the stroke. Cox's eyes filled as he stepped forward to shake the president's hand and praise his fight for the League. "Mr. Cox," Wilson replied, "that fight can still be won." Cox declared that the Democrats' campaign would be "a million percent with you, and your administration, and that means the League of Nations." Wilson, clearly in low spirits, could muster only a few words of thanks: "I am very grateful. I am very grateful."

The convention had been unsettling for Wilson. Twice while it was in progress he summoned Grayson in the middle of the night to report that he could hardly breathe. In the weeks after the convention, Wilson complained that everyone, including his wife and doctor, had lost interest in him because they considered him a hopeless case. He was so depressed that he scarcely noticed when the Nineteenth Amendment, giving all American women the right to vote, was ratified by Tennessee, last of the thirty-six states needed to make it the law of the land. Although slow to abandon the state-by-state approach to suffrage, he had decided in 1918 to put the power and prestige of his office behind the amendment. He understood that the victory was historic, but apart from congratulating the Tennessee legislature, he did nothing to mark the occasion.

Harding spent most of the next few months on the front porch of his home in Marion, Ohio, attacking Wilson's record and vowing to lead the country in the direction of something he called "normalcy." He was not aiming for a return to the old order, he said, but for "a regular steady order of things. I mean normal procedure, the natural way, without excess." The statement implied that Woodrow Wilson's presidency had been abnormal, unnatural, and excessive. Early in the campaign Harding sometimes claimed to favor America's entry into the League of Nations but he was soon touting nationalism over internationalism. The United States had no need to go adventuring abroad, he said. There was enough work to do at home, and doing it well would set an example for the rest of the world. Future generations would wonder how a banality like "normalcy" inspired anyone to go to the polls, but inspiration was not wanted in 1920. As a veteran political correspondent put it, "The country was tired of the high thinking and rather plain spiritual living of Woodrow Wilson. It desired the man in the White House to cause it no more moral overstrain than does the man you meet in the Pullman smoking compartment."

Wilson spoke out only a few times during the campaign. He reminded voters on October 3 that the election ought to be a referendum on the League. On October 27 he gave his first speech since the stroke, to an audience of fifteen prominent Republicans and independents who favored League membership. They moved in close to his wheelchair and strained to catch his words, which called on the American people to complete the great moral task they had undertaken on entering the war. If the United States did not join the League, he said, the war would have been fought in vain. "The whole future moral force of right in the world depends upon the United States . . . and it would be pitiful indeed if, after so many great free peoples had entered the great League, we should hold aloof. I suggest that the candidacy of every candidate for whatever office be tested by this question: Shall we or shall we not redeem the great moral obligations of the United States?" At several points he seemed to choke back tears.

Those who noticed that Wilson did not mention Cox in either pronouncement correctly surmised that the president was irritated by Cox's openness to treaty reservations, even on Article X. Tumulty, fearing that a rift between Wilson and Cox would hurt the Democrats at the polls, persuaded the president to write an open letter praising Cox's governorship and his campaign. This time around, the president made no mention of the League. Despite Tumulty's attempt to paper over the differences, it was clear that Cox was a disappointment to Wilson and Wilson was a millstone for Cox.

"Tomorrow the dirty job," H. L. Mencken wrote on the eve of the election. "I shall be on my knees all night, praying for strength to vote for Gamaliel." Mencken admired nothing about Harding, whom he saw as a "blank cartridge," but he preferred Harding to Cox, whom he saw as a man endlessly willing to change his mind to please the crowd. It seemed to Mencken that presidential politics had taken a sharp turn for the worse. In a country with more than 100 million citizens, a candidate for president could meet no more than a sliver of the electorate, leaving the rest to form their impressions from the newspapers. Force of character, force of ideas—both had been subsumed by the blandness required of each candidate as he tried to persuade the masses that only he would serve all the people all the time. "The presidency tends, year by year, to go to such men," Mencken wrote. "As democracy is perfected, the office represents, more and more closely, the soul of the people. We move toward a lofty ideal. On some great and glorious day the plain folks of the land will reach their heart's desire at last, and the White House will be adorned by a downright moron." But all of this took the reader "far from Gamaliel, and the eve of his annunciation," Mencken wrote. "Unless all signs fail, he will be elected tomorrow by a colossal plurality. The solemn and holy referendum will thrust upon us, certainly for four years and maybe for eight, a ruler with the high ideals of a lodge joiner and the general intellectual lift and punch of a mackerel."

Mencken was right. On November 2, Harding's fifty-fifth birthday, the men and women of the United States gave him the greatest landslide in a hundred years: 60 percent of the popular vote, 76 percent of the electoral vote. Of the 26 million votes cast, 16 million went to Harding, 9 million to Cox. Nearly a million votes were bestowed upon the Socialist Eugene Debs, who made his run from a federal penitentiary, where he was serving his sentence for protesting the draft. In every state, the Republicans received a larger share of the vote in 1920 than in 1916. They also widened their majorities in Congress, picking up sixty-four seats in the House and ten in the Senate. The Democrats did not even carry the whole of their supposedly solid South.

"The American people wanted a change, and they have voted for a change," said the *New York World*. "They did not know what kind of change they wanted, and they do not know today what kind of change they have voted for." *The Nation* observed that the country was "absolutely through with Woodrow Wilson," and in his diary Colonel House explained why: "Another Samson has pulled a temple down upon himself."

Lodge privately boasted that he and his fellow Republicans had "torn up Wilsonism by the roots" and advised Harding to ditch the League and make a fresh start in foreign policy. Needing no persuasion, Harding would see to it that the United States turned its back on the League and on Wilson's vision of a world order committed to democracy, free trade, and collective security.

To the relief of his caretakers, Wilson received the election news serenely, although he could not make himself congratulate the victor. Friends who wrote to assure Wilson that Americans still cherished his ideas need not have bothered; he was sure that he was right about the League, sure that his ideals would be realized. Ellen Wilson's brother Stockton, who was visiting the White House, marveled at the president's appearance, his high spirits, and his equanimity.

The buoyancy did not last. When asked again to pardon Debs, Wilson could hardly contain his wrath. "I should never be able to look into the faces of the mothers of this country who sent their boys to the other side," he told Tumulty. Wilson knew that he would be denounced by champions of free speech but did not care.

Ray Stannard Baker, who paid Wilson a visit at the end of November, found him deeply depressed. "It was dreadful," Baker told his diary. "I cannot get over it yet. A broken, ruined old man, shuffling along, his left arm inert, the fingers drawn up like a claw, the left side of his face sagging frightfully. His voice is not human: it gurgles in his throat, sounds like that of an automaton. And yet his mind seems as alert as ever." Baker and Grayson joined the Wilsons to watch newsreels of their first intoxicating days in Europe. "There we were," Baker wrote, "sailing grandly into the harbor at Brest, the ships beflagged, the soldiers marshalled upon the quai and flying machines skimming through the air. There was the president himself, smiling upon the bridge, very erect, very tall, lifting his hat to shouting crowds. By magic we are transported to Paris. There he was again, this time with the president of France, driving down the most famous avenue in the world, bowing right and left." Wilson watched in silence. When the show ended, an aide came forward in the darkness and planted a foot next to one of Wilson's feet to prevent a slip when he rose. He got up and limped from the room without a word to his companions.

A week later Wilson spent a few minutes in the Blue Room with a delegation from the House and Senate, come to give official notice that Congress was again in session. Wilson leaned on his cane the whole time, explaining that he could not yet do without his "third leg." In fact, he could stand on his own for a bit, but he had decided not to shake hands with any of the visitors in order to avoid shaking the hand of one of them in particular, Senator Lodge.

A few shafts of sunlight penetrated the gloom. The League of Nations met for the first time, in Geneva, and on opening day unanimously approved a tribute to Wilson. He sent his thanks and his hope for the League's success. Wilson also managed to compose his eighth and last State of the Union message to Congress, probably the most complex intellectual task he had set himself since the stroke. Like his previous annual messages, it made legislative recommendations, but this time he had only a handful. He used the occasion for a farewell couched as a confession of faith. Uppermost in his mind, he said, was a sentence of Abraham Lincoln's: "Let us have faith that right makes might, and in that faith let us dare to do our duty as we understand it."

To Wilson, faith in the power of right was the essence of the American experiment, as crucial to the country's founding as to its success. And with that faith, he said, came the hope of a new order "in which reason and right would take precedence over covetousness and force." He was certain that this faith had won the war and certain that only this faith would lift the postwar world out of its chaos and despair. He took it as axiomatic that the American faith had given birth to an American mission—the mission to champion democracy by living up to its ideals at home and by standing for right in international affairs. To do otherwise, he said, would be to cast aside the great gift of the men who had struggled against long odds and formidable adversaries to bring American democracy into being.

Without mentioning the treaty, the League, or even peace, Wilson had offered a blueprint for American foreign policy in the next chapter of the world's history. He presented it as an inevitable, indispensable extension of the American past and the surest way to make the world safe for democracy. And in asking the United States to stand with the right and the just in international affairs, he sent up one last flare for his ideals, which had inspired a world devastated by war to strive for lasting peace. Wilson's confession of faith was a fitting farewell for a president whose belief in the force of American ideals was abiding as his faith in God.

December also brought a Nobel Peace Prize, shared with Léon Bourgeois, for their work in creating the League of Nations. The prize carried an award of $29,000, a welcome addition to Wilson's life savings of $250,000. Presidential pensions did not yet exist, and Wilson, facing retirement with uncertain prospects for generating income, fretted about his finances.

After weighing the merits of several cities, the Wilsons had decided to stay on in Washington, partly because Edith had lived there for decades and partly because of the Library of Congress, which Woodrow considered essential to a book he had long wanted to write, on government. Wilson was about to become the first ex-president to remain in Washington.

Months of searching finally turned up the perfect house, four stories of dignified red brick and limestone, at 2340 S Street. The owner spontaneously volunteered to sell when he learned of the Wilsons' interest, but Edith feared that he had acted on a whim and would change his mind. On the sly Woodrow recruited her brother to approach the owner again, and Woodrow surprised her with the deed just before Christmas. With a nudge from Grayson, ten of Wilson's friends put up $100,000 of the $150,000 purchase price. Almost new, the house had every modern convenience, and workmen were soon adding the vital missing parts—an elevator and more bookcases. Five of his Princeton chums also pooled $3,500 to buy him the White House limousine he liked best—the fanciest model of one of the fanciest automobiles on the market, a Pierce-Arrow Series 51.

Shortly before leaving the White House, Woodrow gave Edith another gift, the dedication page for his next book. It was for her, he wrote, because it was "a book in which I have tried to interpret life, the life of a nation, and she has shown me the full meaning of life." There would be no book, but she kept the page and reproduced it in her memoir. Wilson also imagined that he would be able to practice law and asked Bainbridge Colby if they could open a firm together. Recognizing the folly of the idea, Edith urged Colby to ignore it, but Colby went ahead and on Wilson's last day in office, Tumulty told the press about the founding of Wilson & Colby.

The final hour of Wilson's presidency began in the Blue Room, where he and the first lady received Warren and Florence Harding at eleven o'clock before going up to the Capitol for the inauguration. Tradition called for the president and president-elect to scale the front steps of the Capitol together, but Grayson had walked all the stairs and corridors the inaugural party would be expected to take on inauguration day and declared them beyond Wilson's powers. Harding left the car to make the ascent alone, and the car deposited Wilson at the Senate's freight elevator. On the main floor he was seen leaning heavily on his cane and limping the fifty feet to the President's Room to sign the last bills of the Sixty-sixth Congress. Harding was there to greet him, as were the members of the cabinet and a host of congressional Democrats.

Among the reporters on hand was Wilson's old Princeton student David Lawrence, who was moved to pity by the sight of the president sinking awkwardly into the chair at the desk. "For a moment the president had appeared as the decrepit figure so often pictured since his physical collapse . . . and then again as he sat at his desk and signed bills with a firm hand and a steady pen, his eyes burned with the fire of the soldier who never surrenders," Lawrence wrote. "Warren Harding stood over him, bending low and almost paternally beside the man whose arduous labors in the presidential office had caused his physical, if not political, overthrow." Lawrence was close enough to hear Harding tell Wilson that he would understand if Wilson did not feel up to going outdoors for the inaugural ceremony. "I guess I had better not try it," Wilson said.

The first bill presented for Wilson's signature authorized additional funds for hospitals caring for disabled veterans. Between signatures, Wilson shook hands with members of Congress who had come to pay their respects, and at one point he greeted General Pershing, at the Capitol to serve as marshal of the inaugural parade. Pershing, who had watched Wilson hobble to the desk, reported to his sister that he had never witnessed a spectacle more "pitiable and tragic."

Wilson was about to leave when he found himself face-to-face with a group led by Senator Lodge. Wilson flushed, and for an instant Tumulty feared that the president would give full rein to his animosity. But Wilson looked Lodge in the eye as the senator delivered his official message: "This committee begs to inform you that the two Houses have completed their work and are prepared to receive any further communications from you." Wilson was as brusque as Lodge. "I have no further communication," he said. "I would be glad if you would inform both Houses and thank them for their courtesy. Good morning, sir."

The moment was the last skirmish in one of the greatest feuds in American political history, and with his cold "Good morning, sir," Wilson fired the last shot.

By 11:55 a.m., the President's Room had emptied and the east porch of the Capitol was filling up with dignitaries. "Then it was," Lawrence wrote, "that Woodrow Wilson, with halting step and downcast head, his left shoulder stooped but his eyes turned upward endeavoring to smile, trying to the end to exhibit a fighting spirit and an attitude of no surrender, passed out of official life."

39

. . . .

Swimming Upstream

I n the three years that remained to Woodrow Wilson, the task of keeping him alive and relatively content fell to a company of seven. He had
the undivided attention of his wife, the full-time secretarial help of her
brother John Randolph Bolling, and the daily ministrations of Dr. Grayson.
(Still on active duty, Admiral Grayson was posted to S Street by President
Harding.) Also in attendance were a night nurse who doubled as a masseur,
as well as a chauffeur and two servants—Isaac Scott and his wife, Mary
Scott.

To minimize the disorientation of the move, Edith arranged Woodrow's
new bedroom on the same plan as the one he had used in the White House
after the stroke. As she explained in her memoir, "Every article was in the
relative position it had occupied at the White House; all the little things:
footrests, easy chairs with large casters to move without effort, pillows, the
small tables conveniently placed to hold books and papers, reading lights,

etc. etc.; and last of all the extraordinarily large bed that had been made to order." It was a replica of Lincoln's four-poster. A patriotic banner and a wartime poster that Wilson especially liked were hung on the walls, and on the mantel stood the empty brass shell from the first shot fired in France by the American army.

Edith's tenderness, great as it was, did not keep Woodrow from falling into a slump. Depleted and morose, he was beset by a host of physical maladies, including digestive upsets, which in his case were often triggered by emotional distress. To Ray Stannard Baker, who saw him often in the spring of 1921, Wilson looked totally lost and "inconceivably old, gray, worn, tired." Baker found Wilson's mind clear but ablaze with anger: "He feels himself bitterly misunderstood and unjustly attacked."

The press was giving his presidency mixed reviews. As expected, the *New York World* showered him with compliments: No other American had made as much world history. He had inspired the first moral revolution in modern international relations. Even without his war victory, he would outrank every other president since Lincoln because of his economic reforms. *The Baltimore Sun* credited him with resurrecting the Democratic Party and making it a powerful instrument of progressive reform. But the *Sun* also mourned the fall that began with Wilson's ill-considered demand for a Democratic victory in the midterm elections of 1918 and ended with the disastrous treaty fight, leaving the American people in a thoroughly disillusioned state. The *Chicago Tribune* damned Wilson for overreaching: "He tried to do something which is beyond the intelligence and wisdom of any man. He tried by word to correct all the ills of government, accumulated in centuries, sharpened by national instincts and animosities, in all lands, and he failed thereby to correct any of them or to preserve the rights of the United States." With a touch of asperity, the *Afro-American* of Baltimore mused that "[p]erchance the times were not as ripe for action as they were for preachment. If so, Mr. Wilson was fully justified in leaving the nation's 'Race Problem' precisely where he found it—unsolved, tantalizing and strife-provoking."

The first memoir by a cabinet member was Robert Lansing's. In bookstores three weeks after Wilson left office, *The Peace Negotiations* bared the secretary of state's disagreements with the president over Article X, Shantung, and the secrecy of the Council of Four. Lansing stated Wilson's positions respectfully then tore them to pieces, sharing the protests he had made at the time and the stands he would have taken to avoid the mistakes he thought Wilson had made.

Wilson had no intention of reading Lansing's book and was sure that it would be dismissed as the rant of a man with a score to settle. In fact, *The Peace Negotiations* caused a sensation. Several chapters were widely syndicated, and the newspapers devoted multiple columns to choice anecdotes and summaries of Lansing's main points. The book's success would spur Lansing to write two more memoirs of his years as secretary of state.

Wilson's caretakers protected him from most of the unfavorable press, but he had a general awareness of it, and the very thought of someone who had crossed him was enough to set off a tirade. During his last year in the White House, Wilson had sometimes despaired, but he had also comforted himself with recollections of life before the stroke, dreams of physical recovery, and his faith in the League of Nations. By the time he and Edith moved to S Street, his recovery had stalled. His ego received a further blow on April 12, when Harding announced that the United States would stand by its decision to stay out of the League. Now powerless stand by politically as well as physically, Wilson sulked and, on his worst days, raged. On a 1921 visit to S Street, Sir Maurice Hankey, secretary to the British cabinet, heard a long, bitter soliloquy on the treachery of his old opponents, the American abandonment of the League, and France's capitulation to her militarists. "I left with the feeling that he was a terribly pathetic figure," Hankey wrote Lloyd George.

Longing for meaningful work but unable to sustain his efforts, Wilson visited the Washington offices of Wilson & Colby only once. Nearly every client of interest to Colby struck Wilson as beneath the dignity of an ex-president, and when Wilson grasped that he was more hindrance than help, the partnership was amicably dissolved. Another try at writing a book was quickly abandoned. With enormous effort, he managed to write a short opinion piece, "The Road Away from Revolution," that appeared in *The Atlantic Monthly,* but only after an overhaul by George Creel and Stockton Axson. Although Wilson rarely complained about his lot, there came a day when he told a visitor, "I am tired of swimming upstream."

Edith and Grayson refused to give up, and Wilson eventually adopted a routine that gave him a degree of satisfaction and did not overtax his energy. He breakfasted and read the papers with Edith, and then, still in his dressing gown, took the lift downstairs to tend to the mail. Only a handful of letters received a personal reply.

Correspondence done, Wilson exercised, pacing up and down the main corridor on the ground floor. Then he returned to his bedroom. He usually stayed in his dressing gown until the afternoon, when he sometimes received visitors and always went out for an automobile ride with Edith. They left S Street around three o'clock and, at Woodrow's request, traveled the same route every day. In the evening they sometimes watched movies at home, and Edith sometimes read to him. Every Saturday night they went to B. F. Keith's High-Class Vaudeville Theatre, a pleasure they had shared before the stroke. His arrivals and departures always brought the audience to its feet and sparked a round of cheers. Once the Saturday night pattern was established, crowds gathered outside and applauded as his Pierce-Arrow came and went.

By the end of June, Wilson's pallor had disappeared, his voice was appreciably stronger, and his mood had taken an upswing. Unlike most Washingtonians, he thrived in the heat, and for the first time in his life he was not wary of public adulation. He relished the waves from pedestrians who recognized his automobile, and the silent tributes of the crowds that often stood across the street from his new home. He was also pleased to learn that a small group of admirers had begun raising $1 million to endow the Woodrow Wilson Foundation. It would promote his ideals and annually award a $25,000 prize to recognize notable contributions to peace, justice, or democracy. Cleveland Dodge and Wilson's other affluent friends put up most of the money. The rest came from Woodrow Wilson clubs on college campuses and from unsolicited donations, often from parents who had lost sons in the war and fervently believed that the League of Nations was the only hope for humankind.

Much of the work of organizing the foundation was done by Franklin Roosevelt, who had returned to New York and the practice of law when Wilson left office. As assistant secretary of the navy, Roosevelt had often clashed with Secretary Daniels and President Wilson, and in 1919, he had given further offense by inviting Sir Edward Grey, persona non grata at the White House, to Christmas dinner. Roosevelt was disinclined to explain his new devotion to the former president, but his motive is easily guessed: he was angling for Wilson's blessing on his next political race, whatever it might be.

After a June visit with Wilson, Roosevelt drafted a prospectus for the foundation and left for his family's retreat on Campobello Island, in Nova Scotia. On August 10, FDR was stricken with infantile paralysis and would never walk again. He was forty-one. Wilson occasionally sent notes of encouragement. Roosevelt, unsure of his political prospects but unwilling to give up the idea of holding office again, threw himself into civic and charitable work that could be done from home. Every newspaper mention of his name would remind the public that he was still at work.

Wilson too was nursing political ambitions. In June he told a delegation of Princeton students that he planned to take an active part in keeping his ideals before the American people. Three months later, when Harding submitted the peace treaty with Germany for ratification, Wilson worked behind the scenes to defeat it. Still convinced that a peace made without the Allies would disgrace the United States, he persuaded Senator Carter Glass to try to unite the Democrats against it. Word of Wilson's involvement leaked out, and the Democrats refused the overtures from Glass. When the treaty passed by a wide margin, Wilson privately denounced its supporters as "the most partisan, prejudiced, ignorant, and unpatriotic group that ever misled the Senate of the United States."

Overlooking Wilson's plot against the treaty, the affable President Harding invited him to join the presidential party for an Armistice Day procession from the Capitol to Arlington National Cemetery, where the American Unknown Soldier would be interred. Everything was agreeable to Wilson until he learned that just past the White House, Harding and the other dignitaries marching on foot would board automobiles for the rest of the journey. Wilson was informed that he could follow in his carriage and then make his way into the amphitheater to the box reserved for his party. Knowing that he would not be able to manage the stairs, Wilson asked to watch from his carriage. Back came the news that the secretary of war had decided that Wilson's carriage should leave the procession altogether once it passed the White House. Harding struggled to explain: "I fear a note of inharmony would be suggested if one formerly in authority accompanied the procession to the cemetery when those who constitute the great body of the official division of the procession are dropping out." Harding seemed to be trying not to confess his fear of being upstaged by the sight of the Unknown Soldier and his crippled commander in chief ascending the cemetery hill together.

Furious, Wilson dictated a statement explaining why he would not take part in the procession. But before releasing it to the press, he asked the advice of Louis Seibold of the *New York World*, who persuaded him to accept the War Department's terms and maintain a dignified silence.

Wilson took the advice, and come Armistice Day, he and his wife set off early in a rented carriage to find their place in the line of march. A traffic jam near the Capitol cost them their spot near the front of the procession, and the officer in charge worked them into line at the end, an improvisation that gave a pleasing symmetry to the cortege: The caisson bearing the coffin of the Unknown Soldier came first. Just behind, marching shoulder to shoulder, were President Harding and General Pershing. And finally, after blocks and blocks filled with government officials, came the commander in chief of the army that had turned the tide against Germany.

Along the line there had been scatterings of applause as the procession came into view, but Harding and Pershing had signaled for quiet, the tribute they thought most fitting for the Unknown Soldier. By the time Wilson appeared, decorum had run out. As the *World* put it, "[T]he pale face of the man who gave his health and strength to uphold the same ideals for which the Unknown Soldier died seemingly unleashed the pent-up emotions of the watchers." Wilson kept a solemn face but acknowledged the applause now and then with a restrained tip of his silk hat.

As directed, the former president's carriage left the procession just beyond the White House and headed for S Street. A sizable contingent fell in behind to escort the Wilsons home, where a crowd of twenty thousand packed the streets. Front and center was an automobile carrying three disabled veterans, and Wilson limped over to pay his respects before going inside. Asked to disperse, the crowd stayed put and continued to cheer. The Wilsons acknowledged the tribute from an upstairs window and before long came outside again. An admirer leapt onto the running board of the veterans' car and delivered a speech congratulating Woodrow Wilson, "a wounded soldier of the war," on his recovery and promising that his dream of a world without war would never die. With the help of his cane and his servant Isaac Scott, Wilson went out to say that he wished his voice were strong enough for a full expression of the gratitude he felt. When someone shouted "Long live the best man in the world!" he reached for his wife's hand. Both of them were in tears. Wilson rounded out his Armistice Day experience with a one-sentence note to Seibold: "Your counsel saved me from a very stupid blunder, and I thank you with all my heart."

Although Wilson returned to the silence advised by his friends, he continued to carp in private about the new administration. He was particularly irked by its Conference on the Limitation of Armament (soon known as the Washington Naval Conference), which opened the day after the Unknown

Soldier was laid to rest. The world's first arms control meeting, it was also the first summit meeting held in the United States—a gathering of nine friendly nations: Belgium, China, France, Great Britain, Italy, Japan, the Netherlands, Portugal, and the United States.

Invited to attend the opening session, Wilson had sent his regrets, citing his convalescence. It was just as well. After the ovation due a former president, he would have had to listen to Harding insult Wilsonian idealism by saying that the conference had not been called to remake humankind. Secretary of State Charles Evans Hughes followed suit, pointedly ignoring the disarmament plans in the works at the League of Nations.

As the presiding officer of the conference, Hughes was in a position to seize the initiative, and he went straight to the point. The new naval arms race had to be stopped, and the only sure way to stop it was to stop it now, he said. Next he told the visiting admirals that he expected them to shrink their navies. They were to stop building new battleships for ten years, and they were to scuttle some of their existing warships as well as some of their ships under construction. He had also devised a formula for the size of the three largest navies—a ratio of 5:5:3, with the United States and Great Britain limited to 500,000 tons of ships and Japan to 300,000. The ceiling for France and Italy was set at 1.75. Then Hughes announced that to fit his 5:5:3 scheme, the United States would scrap thirty capital ships and Britain and Japan would scrap thirty-six more. Vast sums of public money would be saved, he said, and because the cuts were mutual, no one would be left at a disadvantage.

Through three months of hard bargaining, Hughes's audacious terms remained largely intact, and he brokered four naval treaties plus several agreements protecting the independence of China. None would hold for the ages, but they gave the world a ten-year respite from the arms race at sea. Journalists spoke of the conference as "the Republican Versailles." In a swipe at Wilson's globalism, Senator Lodge attributed the success of Hughes's conference to its limited scope, calling it "a great lesson for all the nations." But *The Kansas City Post* spoke for many when it pointed out the irony: "The naval holiday plan of Secretary Hughes is a triumph for Woodrow Wilson and the ideals for which he was crucified."

Wilson rejected all comparisons between the League of Nations and Hughes's patchwork. It seemed to him that the new agreements bore an unsettling resemblance to the old balance-of-power alliances, which overnight had fanned a regional dispute into a world war.

As the Washington Naval Conference neared its end, Wilson broke his long silence on public affairs. On January 15, 1922, after a fundraising event for the Woodrow Wilson Foundation, five thousand people marched to S Street. Wilson went out to greet them, and for the first time since the stroke, his voice was strong enough to reach well into the crowd. Without mentioning Harding or Hughes, he said, "There can be no doubt as to the vitality of the League of Nations. It will take care of itself. Those that don't regard it will have to look out for themselves. I have no anxiety for it." The cheers went on and on. He took a step toward the crowd, hoping to shake hands, but Edith held him back.

Edith's restraint was prudent in light of Woodrow's physical condition, but his eagerness for the crowd's embrace was much more than a spontaneous reaction to the excitement of the moment. He was longing to return to politics, and he had deceived himself into thinking that a comeback was possible. From the summer of 1921 until his death, he devoted more of his limited energy to politics than to any other pursuit. A journalist who knew Wilson well observed that he never stopped thinking of himself as "the spiritual leader of a cause only temporarily lost . . . never completely abandoned the hope that he might again become the standard bearer of his party."

Wilson began with a secret project that became known as "The Document," a declaration of progressive principles for Democrats in a world undone by the Great War. He asked a few trusted associates to help him expand and refine it but did not trust them enough to reveal that he planned to use it as a platform for a presidential run in 1924. By the spring of 1922, he was so consumed by the idea that he should have the next Democratic presidential nomination that when he and Joe Tumulty had a misunderstanding over the party's future, Tumulty was banished from S Street. The trouble started when Tumulty asked Wilson for a message to be read at the Democratic Party's Jefferson Day Dinner in New York. Tumulty was the honoree, and after ten years of unstinting service, he certainly deserved a public nod from his old chief. But when there was no word from Wilson, Tumulty, extrapolating from a recent chat on S Street, composed a message for the occasion and attached Wilson's name to it. That was presumptuous, to be sure, but it was also something Tumulty had been expected to do innumerable times as Wilson's chief of staff. Had Wilson not been in the grip of the delusion that he could run for president again, he might not have objected to the platitude that Tumulty had supplied for the occasion: "Say to the Democrats of New York that I am ready to support any man who stands for the salvation of America, and the salvation of America is justice to all classes."

But when the reporters interpreted the message as Wilson's endorsement of the evening's main speaker, James M. Cox, Wilson could not forgive Tumulty's trespass. Tumulty's apologies were not accepted, and he had to endure the further humiliation of having his misdeed exposed by Wilson in a letter to *The New York Times*. Though the letter did not mention Tumulty, Wilson stated categorically that he had not sent or authorized any message to the dinner.

Tumulty, who worshipped Wilson, was never allowed to see him again. He blamed Edith Wilson, and his suspicions were well founded. She had always disliked him, and no one else in her memoir—not even Lodge or Lansing or House—is treated as harshly as he is. Decades later, Tumulty wept as he told the story of his last visit to S Street. On doctor's orders, Wilson regularly drank a bit of Scotch, which in his day was often prescribed as a blood thinner. Whiskey was hard to get once Prohibition became law, but a number of Wilson's acquaintances kept him supplied. One night, Tumulty learned of a new cache of Black & White Scotch—Wilson's favorite—and he ventured out in a blizzard to make his purchase. With no trolley or taxi in sight, he trudged through snow and sleet, and his eyes were nearly frozen shut by the time he reached S Street. When he rang the bell and was ushered in, Edith called down from upstairs, "If that is Mr. Tumulty, take what he has and bring it upstairs." Then came the weak voice of Woodrow Wilson: "Is that you, Tumulty? Come right up." Edith insisted otherwise, and Tumulty was shown out.

As Wilson's secret pursuit of the Democrats' next presidential nomination continued, those who knew him best realized what he had in mind. When Ray Stannard Baker figured it out, he marveled in his diary, "The sheer spirit of the man! Here he is, paralyzed, blind in one eye, an invalid, 66 years old and sees himself leading a campaign in 1924!"

In a June talk with Homer Cummings, one of the party's leaders, Wilson described the man the Democrats ought to nominate: someone of vision and great character, a man who would boldly take the lead in solving the problems of the day. Wilson was describing himself, of course, but Cummings artfully replied that such men were in short supply. Wilson insisted that if the call were issued, "the right kind of men" would come forward. Cummings said that it would depend on who called them and mused that the situation might require a summons from Wilson. The conversation ended there, with Wilson in a corner. Coveting the nomination himself, he was not about to urge anyone else to seek it.

Come November 7, the Democrats did not win control of Congress, but they added seventy-seven seats in the House and six in the Senate. Wilson took heart, and when a crowd of five thousand made a second Armistice Day pilgrimage to S Street, he gave a speech attacking the Senate for its failure to ratify the Treaty of Versailles. The rejection of the treaty had left the United States out of the positive work of securing world peace, he said. "The future is in our hands, and if we are not equal to it, the shame will be ours."

The New York Times reported that "Mr. Wilson was very happy. There could be no question about that." Mr. Wilson was also in excellent form, bright-eyed, speaking without notes, and jauntily tucking the head of his cane into a coat pocket to show that he could stand on his own.

Mr. Wilson was still happy three weeks later, when Georges Clemenceau paid him a visit. Clemenceau, now eighty-one and out of office, was in the United States on a lecture tour. Edith Wilson would remember the reunion as jolly, but Clemenceau was so shaken by the sight of the paralyzed former president that he left after fifteen minutes and asked his Washington host to excuse him from dinner that evening.

Mr. Wilson's happiness evaporated on December 13, when the *Washington Evening Star* published an editorial clearly intended to knock him out of the next presidential race. Official Washington had interpreted his Armistice Day speech as a bid for the leadership of the Democratic Party, and liberals were hoping that the Democratic gains in Congress portended a revival of Wilson's ideals and another drive for U.S. membership in the League of Nations. Nearly all of the newspapermen who had covered both of Wilson's Armistice Day appearances commented on his physical vigor, but the *Star* did not buy it. Improved as his condition might be, the *Star* said, surely he was not up to the strains of a national campaign, much less the demands of the presidency. Wilson complained to a friend that the editorial was intended "to create as much prejudice and jealousy against me as possible," and in a note to his daughter Nell, he cast himself as the object of "political persecution." Woodrow Wilson had often scorned his enemies, but he had not been inclined to think of himself as persecuted. Very likely the editorial stung because it challenged his belief that he was up to another four years as president.

By December 28, his sixty-sixth birthday, Wilson had recovered his good cheer and his confidence. He told Grayson that Americans would send a Democrat to the White House in the next election and that the victory would be even more sweeping than Harding's. He and his collaborators continued to work on "The Document," and the press continued to suggest that the recent improvement in his health had rekindled his political ambition. In June 1923 a friendly Washington correspondent, R. V. Oulahan of *The New York Times,* took on the *Star* and others who doubted Wilson's physical fitness. In a long piece about the former president's life on S Street, Oulahan wrote that "the current of his life flows easily and serenely." After setting the scene, Oulahan tried to clear up the public confusion about the state of Wilson's health. People who saw him hoisted into and out of his automobile at Keith's went home with the impression that he was "a hopeless cripple," Oulahan wrote. But he had made an extraordinary recovery from the helplessness that followed his stroke, and mentally, "he is the Woodrow Wilson of the stirring days prior to September 1919." Oulahan claimed that Wilson's left arm and hand had recovered a bit of their usefulness, that he could walk without a cane, and that he could get into and out of his automobile on his own but accepted assistance "for caution's sake."

The reporter was mistaken. Wilson's left side was still useless. He could stand without his cane, but walking more than a step or two without it heightened the risk of being toppled by the deadweight of his left side. As for entering and exiting the car, he might have needed less help in 1923 than in 1920, and he apparently believed that he could manage it on his own, but there is no eyewitness report of his having done so. Oulahan also reported that Wilson needed much less medical care than in the past. Grayson, who used to be in constant attendance, was now just a frequent caller, and there was no longer a day nurse. But there had been no day nurse since the White House.

Oulahan compiled a long list of visitors to S Street—nearly all of them political associates—and reported that they came bearing the latest political intelligence. Ducking the rumors of Wilson's desire for another presidential nomination, Oulahan settled for saying that the former president was intensely interested in the question of who would head the ticket but unwilling to commit himself to any of the aspirants.

Wilson had not yet told anyone that he wanted the nomination, and he was virtually alone in believing that the Democrats could recapture the White House by mounting another fight for the League. Remembering 1920 and suspecting that he might try again in 1924, party leaders trembled with every favorable report on his health but could not summon the nerve to confront him.

To the evidence for the argument that fact is stranger than fiction must be added one of the most peculiar coincidences in American presidential history: in the summer of 1923, Woodrow Wilson's successor in the White House had a stroke. Aware that he was sick and in need of a rest, Harding had decided to take a cruise to Alaska, where the abundance of natural resources had triggered a fierce Republican quarrel over what was to be done with the riches. Harding also needed a respite from a series of financial scandals involving government officials. Though not personally implicated, he was being seared by the press for surrounding himself with scoundrels. Making speeches as his train headed west would give him a chance to make other headlines, and he was not anticipating any strain. "I like to go out into the country and 'bloviate,'" he said. At Tacoma he would board a naval vessel, cruise up to Alaska and back, travel down the West Coast by train to San Diego, and go home by way of the Panama Canal. Harding left Washington on June 20 (in robust health, according to the newspapers). He felt worse and worse as the trip progressed, caught pneumonia in late July, and on August 2, in San Francisco, had an instantly fatal stroke.

A few days later the Wilsons and Dr. Grayson boarded the Pierce-Arrow and drove to the White House, where they would join the procession of automobiles escorting Harding's body to the Capitol. An enterprising reporter who had spotted the Wilsons waiting in their car during the funeral service inside the White House asked Grayson how Wilson was feeling. The doctor was quick to say that Wilson's hour in the broiling sun had not had any ill effects, and he could not resist adding that the former president was even stronger now than he had been a year ago. He omitted the fact that Wilson had not wanted to be part of the cortege without his doctor at his side. Grayson had been about to leave town to join his wife and children on vacation when the new president, Calvin Coolidge, asked him to accompany the Wilsons. Coolidge had not thought of this on his own; he had acted on a request from Wilson.

At the end of August, with the blessings of her husband and his doctor, Edith Wilson took her first holiday since the stroke, joining friends at the seaside in Massachusetts. She wrote her "Dearest One" often, sending love and detailing the pleasures of her carefree days. Pecking away one-handed on his typewriter, he wrote "My Lovely Sweetheart," professing to be happy on account of her happiness but also lamenting her absence. Grayson, in need of respite himself, decided to eat and sleep on S Street but spend his days working at the Naval Dispensary. He was astounded to find that even his limited hours with Wilson were exhausting. "I have had a real job on my hands night and day," he wrote his wife. The experience gave him his first full appreciation of the grueling pace of Edith's life for the last four years.

Edith came home refreshed but unprepared for the sight of her husband. Four years of watching him fight for his life and rebuild his strength had convinced her that apart from his paralysis, he was perfectly well. But after ten days away, the face she saw did not match the image she had taken with her. Looking at him on September 6, 1923, she understood that a serious decline had begun.

Apparently oblivious to the true state of his health, Wilson soon asked to see George Brennan, chairman of the Democratic Party of Illinois, and revealed that he was willing to be drafted for the presidential nomination if his health permitted. Startled, Brennan asked what he should say if a reporter inquired about their conversation. "Tell them anything you want to," Wilson replied. Brennan shared the revelation, but it raised only the smallest flutter in the papers—an indication, perhaps, that the press had come to share the *Star*'s opinion that Wilson was not well enough for another term in the White House.

After that, Wilson went silent for nearly two months. Lloyd George, who called on October 25, was told to keep his visit short. "Physically he was a wreck," Lloyd George would write. Wilson was cordial, but he was also enraged by the thought of a nonentity like Coolidge in the White House and still angry about the deviousness of certain French officials at the peace conference. The fulminating gave Lloyd George a glimpse of "the old Wilson with his personal hatreds unquenched . . . this extraordinary mixture of real greatness thwarted by much littleness."

Wilson spent the day before Armistice Day in bed with a pounding headache. He had promised to give a radio address—his first—that evening, and he kept his promise in spite of blurred vision and a bad case of nerves. Still in his dressing gown, he went to down to his library, where the broadcasters had set up their equipment. He stood at the microphone, and Edith sat nearby, with a copy of his remarks—in case he needed prompting. At 8:30 p.m. he began speaking to the country. His daughter Margaret, who listened with friends in New York, wired love and congratulations to her father: YOUR SPEECH WAS A WONDER. EVERY WORD WAS CLEAR AND EASILY HEARD.

In a sense the speech *was* a wonder, four minutes of brimstone deploring the "sullen and selfish isolation" of the United States. There was no trace of the Woodrow Wilson who had thrilled the world and filled his audiences with hope and asking that they join in the great work of making the world safe for democracy. Instead he scolded his countrymen for marring their great military victory by abandoning their responsibilities for peace. "This must always be a source of deep mortification to us," he said. He saw only one way to correct this "fatal error" and fulfill the promise of Armistice Day: find the will to lead and to make the right prevail. "Thus, and only thus, can we return to the true traditions of America."

The annual Armistice Day pilgrimage up the hill to 2340 S Street drew a crowd that stretched for five blocks. Those nearest the house saw a frail and struggling Wilson, on his feet but leaning against a pillar for support. Deeply moved by a tribute from his friend Senator Glass, he had trouble composing himself, and his voice broke several times as he thanked the crowd and asked them to transfer their tribute to the soldiers who had won their war and to General Pershing. After only a minute, he stopped and murmured, "That's about all I can do." Recovering a bit as the crowd applauded, he raised a hand for silence and added that he had no anxiety about the eventual triumph of his principles. "I have seen fools resist Providence before and I have seen the destruction, as will come upon these again—utter destruction and contempt. That we shall prevail is as sure as that God reigns. Thank you." Most news accounts noted his frailty. Some mentioned that the police had barred photographers from taking pictures at the event. On whose orders the reports did not say.

Wilson was dying, but he had not lost his will to lead his errant people into the League or his conviction that they would follow. In December, admitting that he was not well enough for the fight, he was still hopeful that his health would improve. "I must get well and help," he told a visitor. Another caller found Wilson reliving the horrors of the world war and declaring that such a war must never be repeated. Remembering those who had damned the League as too idealistic, his blood boiled. "The world is *run* by ideals," he said. "Only the fool thinks otherwise."

In January he agreed to a ceremonial visit from the Democratic National Committee. He received them in his library, remaining seated as scores of committee members filed past to shake his hand and say hello. Those who had known him before the stroke were aghast. White-haired, pale, and stooped even in his armchair, he seemed a ghost of the Woodrow Wilson they remembered. But a few days later, in a last burst of energy, he touched up "The Document" and made notes for two speeches. One he meant to give when he accepted the presidential nomination. The other was his next inaugural address.

As the end approached, Grayson issued a stream of bulletins for the newsmen keeping vigil in a vacant lot across from 2340 S Street. At 11:20 a.m. on Sunday, February 3, 1924, he went out to announce that Wilson had died five minutes before. In tears, Grayson explained that Wilson's end had been peaceful, with his heart weakening until it simply gave out. He gave the underlying causes of death as arteriosclerosis and the stroke, the immediate cause as exhaustion induced by a serious digestive disturbance. Grayson shared Wilson's last sentence ("I am ready") and his last word ("Edith").

Edith declined President Coolidge's offers to arrange for Wilson's body to lie in state at the Capitol Rotunda and for burial at Arlington. She wanted a small private service at home. Joe Tumulty was not on the guest list, an omission discovered and set right at the last minute by her son-in-law William Gibbs McAdoo. Colonel House waited for an invitation that never came. When Edith learned that the Senate had designated Henry Cabot Lodge as its official representative, she sent him a note pointing out that the funeral was not official, asking him not to attend. Although Lodge replied courteously, the newspapers were told that because of a cold, his doctor had ordered him to stay home.

Wilson was laid out in the library, in an open casket. Fearing that she would break down during the service, Edith posted herself on the landing, where she sobbed uncontrollably. At the end of the short Presbyterian liturgy, eight decorated war veterans carried the coffin to the hearse, and Edith, heavily veiled, walked to the car on her brother Randolph's arm. The cortege set off for the burial service, at the National Cathedral, with the Tumultys' car last in line.

After the brief Episcopal Ritual for the Burial of the Dead, all but one of the mourners left, and Wilson's body was lowered into the crypt. It was Grayson who had stayed behind to see that his old commander in chief was properly laid to rest. With the cathedral still in the early stages of construction, the earthly remains of Woodrow Wilson would have to wait until 1956, the centennial of his birth, for a permanent resting place—a sarcophagus in a chapel along the south face of the nave. The remains of his presidency have yet to find repose.

Epilogue

The Wilsonian Century

A few weeks before the end of the war, Senator Henry Fountain Ashurst called at the White House and tried to persuade Wilson to demand an unconditional surrender from Germany. Wilson's talk of a just peace was raising fears that he would be too generous to the enemy, Ashurst explained; Americans needed assurance that he would hold the Germans to account.

"Senator," Wilson replied, "it would relieve a great many people of anxiety if they did not start with the assumption that I am a damned fool." He asked Ashurst to take the floor of the Senate and declare that the American people had no reason to fear. The president had no intention of letting the Germans off scot-free, nor did the generals who would dictate the terms of the Armistice. Wilson also reported that with Germany's defeat in the offing, he was thinking well beyond the end of the war. He was, he said, "playing for a hundred years hence."

Wilson was playing for the whole world as well. Against long odds, he persuaded the victors to adopt his new world order, at the center of which was the League of Nations, a global alliance committed to peace. Senator J. William Fulbright, an Arkansas Democrat who chaired the Committee on Foreign Relations from 1959 to 1974, called it "the one great new idea of the century in the field of international relations." The League was designed to prevent war by standing up to threats of international aggression—with discussion if possible, sanctions if necessary, and a collective military response if all else failed. Wilson was not fool enough to believe that there would never be another war, but he did believe that peace would bring prosperity, that prosperity would nurture Europe's nine new democracies, and that the spread of democracy would make war less likely.

Wilson also believed that the United States could—and should—do more than any other nation to make the new world order a success. The United States was in a position to do more because of its unrivaled economic strength and because its government, however imperfect, was the most democratic on earth. Wilson assumed that longings for the democracy, liberty, and justice won in the American Revolution were universal and that Americans had a mission to share them with the rest of the world.

Unhappily for Wilson, the war had left many Americans wanting less foreign involvement, not more. He fought hard to change their minds, but he lost, and his liberal internationalism died four deaths—three in the Senate and one in the landslide that put the provincial Warren G. Harding in the White House. Harding had promised to put America first and return the country to "normalcy."

Eight years before, on the eve of his own inauguration, Wilson had mused to a friend that it would be "the irony of fate" if foreign relations dominated his presidency. Fate had an even greater irony in store: despite the fact that Wilson's fellow citizens rejected his idealistic internationalism, it remained at the heart of American debates on foreign policy for almost a hundred years after his conversation with Ashurst.

Harding had scarcely settled in when mainstream Republicans began looking for alternatives to Wilson's internationalism, which they found vague and too sweeping. The question the Republicans were trying to answer was not "Should the United States be an internationalist or an isolationist power?" It was "What kind of internationalism would best serve American national interests?" Under the Republican presidents in office from 1921 to 1933 (Harding, Calvin Coolidge, and Herbert Hoover) the party's internationalists pursued several items on Wilson's agenda: the economic recovery of Europe, disarmament, and the establishment of a world court. Even Harding, who refused to reopen the question of U.S. membership in the League of Nations, allowed unofficial American observers to sit in on most of the League's conferences on arms and on trade. The observers were also permitted to advise and assist in matters that were more humanitarian than political (curbing the opium trade, for example).

In 1921, Harding's secretary of state, Charles Evans Hughes, chaired the world's first disarmament conference. And in 1928, Republicans showed as much daring as Wilson in their search for a formal means of safeguarding the peace, offering the world a chance to outlaw war. Crafted by Coolidge's secretary of state, Frank Kellogg, and his French counterpart, Aristide Briand, the Pact of Paris required signatories to submit their international disputes to arbitration. Sixty-two nations took the pledge. In form, the pact was a defeat for the League, but in spirit it was thoroughly Wilsonian. Kellogg and Briand (like Wilson) received a Nobel Peace Prize.

The outbreak of World War II seemed to prove that Wilson in particular and internationalism in general were colossal failures. But President Franklin D. Roosevelt saw Wilson's plan for a new world order as a first draft worthy of revision. In 1943 the Allies agreed to establish a new global organization, the United Nations. Many of the aspirations in its charter were taken straight from the League's covenant, and the decision to base the new organization in New York signaled the American intention to take the lead in stabilizing the postwar world—the course that Wilson had wanted to follow.

Determined to avoid Wilson's mistakes, FDR cultivated bipartisan support for his plans. He also made certain that the U.N.'s charter would be separate from the peace treaty. And when he concluded that the League had been asked to shoulder too many responsibilities, he proposed that the U.N. be supplemented by other organizations. The suggestion led to the creation of the International Monetary Fund (1944), the World Bank (1945), the North Atlantic Treaty Organization (1949), and many more.

Roosevelt died in April 1945, two months before the delegates of fifty nations gathered in San Francisco to sign the U.N. charter. The new president, Harry S. Truman, spoke at the ceremony, paying tribute to Roosevelt and sounding a decidedly Wilsonian note in calling for self-restraint. The most powerful nations had no right to dominate the world, Truman said; they had a duty to use their power to lead the world to peace and justice.

Six weeks later, Truman authorized the use of the deadliest weapon the world had ever seen. The atomic bombs dropped on Hiroshima and Nagasaki killed more than 100,000 Japanese instantly, and 200,000 more would die later of radiation poison and other injuries inflicted in the bombings. The vast majority were civilians. Japan surrendered within days, and Truman would always maintain that the bombings had saved the United States from having to invade Japan, a project that might have upped American casualties by tens of thousands.

There is no way to know what Wilson would have made of the decision to drop the bombs, but it seems safe to say that after arguing in vain against the punitive peace made in Paris, he would have endorsed the Marshall Plan. Named for Secretary of State George C. Marshall, it epitomized Wilson's conviction that if a nation did the morally right thing it would turn out to be the practical thing as well. As the beneficiaries of the Marshall Plan, most Western Europeans found American democracy more attractive than Soviet communism.

With its emphasis on containing the spread of communism after World War II, the diplomacy of the United States took on a hard edge, but Wilson's idealism remained a staple of American Cold War rhetoric. When John F. Kennedy put the Soviet Union on notice in his inaugural address, he did it in a tone as lofty as Wilson's declaration that the world must be made safe for democracy: "Let every nation know, whether it wishes us well or ill, that we shall pay any price, bear any burden, meet any hardship, support any friend, oppose any foe, in order to assure the survival and the success of liberty." But the willingness to pay any price led Kennedy and his advisors to plunge the United States into the long, unwinnable war against communism in Vietnam. Protest of the war destroyed the presidency of Kennedy's succesor, Lyndon B. Johnson, and brought about the election of Richard M. Nixon.

Nixon was a realist who did not put much stock in visions of world community. But even as he escalated the war in Vietnam and carpet-bombed Cambodia, he wrapped himself in the mantle of the great idealist in American foreign relations. In a 1969 address from the Oval Office, he said, "Fifty years ago, in this room and at this very desk, President Woodrow Wilson spoke words which caught the imagination of a war-weary world. He said, 'This is the war to end war.'" (Wilson had never used the desk, nor had he ever given a major speech in his office.) Nixon went on to say that he was not promising that the war in Vietnam would end war but had embarked on a path that would bring the United States "closer to that great goal to which Woodrow Wilson and every American president in our history has been dedicated—the goal of a just and lasting peace." On another occasion Nixon predicted that Wilson would be remembered "not as a man who tried and failed, but as one of those Americans who saw the truth before his time." By following Wilson's example, Nixon went on, "by not fearing to be idealists ourselves, we shall make the world safe for free men to live in peace." Set against Nixon's deeds, such words invited cynicism. His secretary of state, Henry A. Kissinger, tried to resolve the contradiction by explaining that Nixon understood the value of international cooperation but was skeptical of relying on the global community when national security was at stake.

Long an outspoken foe of communism, Nixon stunned the world in 1972 with trips to the Soviet Union and China. In Moscow he negotiated an arms control agreement, and in China he made the first moves to restore diplomatic ties severed in 1949, when the communists came to power. By courting both countries, he hoped to win their help in pressuring North Vietnam to negotiate an end to the war. At the same time, he was betting that the new friendship with China would cause the Soviets to think twice before seeking more territory by conquest. He made admiring mentions of Wilson in speeches to the Russians and the Chinese, but his divide-and-conquer strategy was a classic example of the balance-of-power realism that Wilson despised.

In 1990, after the collapse of the Soviet Union, President George H. W. Bush announced the end of the Cold War in deliberately Wilsonian terms, saying that humanity stood at the threshold of "a new world order," with an opportunity "to achieve the universal aspirations of mankind—peace and security, freedom, and the rule of law." Wilson's ghost reappeared the following year, when Bush sought and won the U.N. Security Council's approval for a multilateral war against Iraq after its invasion of Kuwait. The coalition of thirty-four nations was hailed as a prime example of the collective security advocated by Woodrow Wilson. After Iraq had been driven out of Kuwait, Bush echoed Wilson again, speaking of the war as a mission rooted in shared interests and shared ideals. And the ideals, Bush said, were boldly and clearly American.

Bill Clinton was the first president born after the creation of the United Nations and the first to enter office after the Cold War. Like Wilson, he was beset by a succession of foreign crises: the first terrorist attack on the World Trade Center, genocide in Rwanda, and Serbian aggression in Bosnia and Kosovo. Clinton was an internationalist, but he was an internationalist sobered by the morass of Vietnam. Unwilling to pay any price or bear any burden, he declined to send troops to support the U.N.'s forces in Rwanda. Condemned for his inaction, he expressed his regret on numerous occasions and took the lead in orchestrating NATO's response to Serbia's ethnic cleansing in the Balkans.

Clinton and his advisors shied away from calling themselves Wilsonians unless they preceded the term with modifiers such as *neo* and *pragmatic*. As Strobe Talbott, Clinton's deputy secretary of state, explained, "we were often on the defensive against critics who used *Wilsonian* pejoratively, as a synonym for naïve." Clinton practiced a tempered internationalism. His presidency coincided with the acceleration of climate change, globalization, and terrorism, all of which posed serious threats to national and international interests. He was willing to address such challenges, but not alone.

The first all-out American assault on the international order envisioned by Woodrow Wilson and realized by FDR came from Clinton's successor, George W. Bush, who entered the White House in 2001. His world was not a community but a battleground where the forces of good and evil were locked in perpetual struggle. The terrorist attacks of September 11, 2001, confirmed this view and led him to adopt a foreign policy that divided the world into two hostile camps. "Either you are with us, or you are with the terrorists," he declared nine days after the attacks. "From this day forward, any nation that continues to harbor or support terrorism will be regarded by the United States as a hostile regime." He claimed a right to "pre-emptive" war, and he declared that U.S. forces were prepared to act without the approval of the international community. He also rejected Wilson's idea that liberty was America's gift to the world. It was, said Bush, "God's gift to humanity."

But even as Bush marched the United States down the path to wars in Afghanistan and Iraq, his supporters hailed him as an heir to Woodrow Wilson. Bush was out to "finish the job that Woodrow Wilson started," wrote the diplomatic historian John Gaddis. "The world, quite literally, is to be made safe for democracy, even those parts of it, like the Muslim Middle East, that have so far resisted that tendency." Wilson might have agreed before his chastening in revolutionary Mexico, but by the time revolutionary Russia descended into chaos, he thought it better to let revolutionaries work out their own destiny.

Reflecting on the catastrophes that followed in Afghanistan and Iraq, Tony Smith, an authority on Wilsonianism, noted that Bush and his supporters had appropriated Wilson's rhetoric to camouflage "change as continuity in American practice, war as peace, a bid for world supremacy as a continuation of American exceptionalism exercised for the common good." In Smith's judgment, Bush pursued "an aggressively imperialistic aim that threatened to discredit the United States as a champion of world stability, the role that Wilson had seen for it in 1919."

Barack Obama, who had no interest in Bush's pursuit of world domination, put a high priority on avoiding what he called "stupid" mistakes. But Obama's rejection of his predecessor's overambition did not herald a return to the broad internationalism of Wilson or Roosevelt. Like Clinton and the first President Bush, Obama was a proponent of multilateralism, seeing it as a brake on the hubris built into Americans' image of themselves as exceptional. He shared Wilson's view that American power imposed a responsibility to address threats to world order, but he also shared Clinton's idea that the United States was unable to bear any burden or pay any price.

In 2018, as Woodrow Wilson's hundred years came to an end, the peaceful world order of his dreams was nowhere in sight. Nationalism and autocracy were on the rise, and democracy was under attack in some of the most democratic countries on earth, including the United States. In its 2017 survey of political rights and civil liberties around the world, Freedom House, a nonpartisan advocate of human rights and democratic change, noted a disturbing new trend: setbacks to democracy were concentrated in countries ranked as Free (as opposed to Partly Free or Not Free) in the organization's ratings system. The pronounced nationalism of the new U.S. president raised questions about the stability of the global order in place since the end of World War II, as did Britain's vote to leave the European Union and the growing popularity of xenophobic political candidates in Europe. The authors of the report glumly concluded that it was "no longer possible to speak with confidence about the long-term durability of the EU; the incorporation of democracy and human rights priorities into American foreign policy; the resilience of democratic institutions in central Europe, Brazil, or South Africa; or even the expectation that [atrocities] will draw international criticism from democratic governments and U.N. human rights bodies."

Despite the setbacks, the world of the twenty-first century is still more democratic than it was before Wilson threw his moral force against imperialism, militarism, and autocracy. And he turned out to be right about the central fact of life in a world of global markets, global finance, instant communication, and the possibility of instant annihilation: withdrawal is impossible.

Acknowledgments

First thanks to my editor, Alice Mayhew, whose questions and comments on a work in progress elevate every page of every draft. My gratitude for her judgment, care, and thoughtfulness is immense.

I am also grateful to Alice's colleagues at Simon & Schuster: assistant editor Stuart Roberts; the jacket designer, Lauren Peters Collaer; the book designer, Lewelin Polanco; the production team, Lisa Erwin, Lisa Healy, and Kristen Lemire; deputy director of publicity Julia Prosser and her associates, senior publicist Elizabeth Gay and publicity assistant Lauren Carsley; and marketing manager Stephen Bedford. The copy editor that Simon & Schuster chose for the book, Fred Chase, and the cartographer, David G. Lindroth, did extraordinary work. My one regret is that of all these contributions, only the visual ones can be seen by the reader. The invisible work is equally beautiful and vital, and as I held the first bound version for the first time, I was reminded again of my good fortune in having so much skill, taste, and energy brought to bear on my words.

Kris Dahl of ICM Partners is the ideal literary agent and perfect ally. She excels at finding the great story buried in a broad subject, and there is no better person to have at your side when things do not go according to plan. I am also indebted to her associates (present and former): Tamara Kawar, Caroline Eisenmann, Laura Neely, and Montana Wojczuk.

The sources of the book's photographs are listed on pages 599-601, but three people who gave me a hand with them deserve special thanks here. Barry P. Fitzgerald shared two from the collection of his grandfather, Edward N. Jackson, who photographed Wilson for the U.S. Army Signal Corps. Dick Lehr, author of *The Birth of a Movement: How* Birth of a Nation *Ignited the Battle for Civil Rights,* came to the rescue when I needed a high-resolution image of W. Monroe Trotter. Jim Nickelson, a master photographic printmaker, got all the images into good shape and good order for publication.

A biographer's happiest days are probably the ones spent in libraries. At that early stage, the biography is perfect because it exists only as a series of shimmering possibilities, and the biographer can fantasize that every one of them will be realized in prose so magnificent that readers will give thanks for having lived to see such a book. I owe special thanks to three experts in the libraries at Columbia University: Jennifer B. Lee of the Rare Book and Manuscript Library, Bob Scott of the Digital Humanities Center, and Mary Marshall Clark of the Oral History Research Office. I am also grateful to Daniel Linke and his colleagues at the Seeley G. Mudd Library at Princeton University, Jeff Flannery in the Manuscript Division of the Library of Congress, and Peter Drummey of the Massachusetts Historical Society. At the Woodrow Wilson Presidential Library and Museum in Staunton, Virginia, Robin von Seldeneck, chief executive officer, gave me a warm welcome, and several members of her staff—Andrew Phillips, Mark Peterson, Jacque Frankfort, and Danna Faulds—have gone to great lengths to share manuscripts and photographs pertinent to my book. Thanks also to Thomas Sayre, a descendant of Woodrow Wilson, for permission to read the library's Jessie Wilson Sayre Papers.

In the early stages of the writing, I spent four months as a public policy scholar in the Division of United States Studies at the Woodrow Wilson Center for International Scholars in Washington, D.C. For many courtesies, favors, and good company there, I thank Philippa Strum, Lee Hamilton, Michael Van Dusen, and Janet Spikes. At the suggestion of my fellow author Sylvia Nasar, Peter Goddard, then director of the Institute for Advanced Study at Princeton, gave me a spot as a director's summer visitor. Many thanks to them and to Linda Cooper, my guide to the daily workings of the institute.

Another early gift came from Professor Anders Stephanson of Columbia University, who allowed me to audit his course on American diplomatic history in the twentieth century. His lectures and readings grounded me in the subject and greatly informed my subsequent reading on Wilson's conduct of foreign policy. The experience of studying American history with someone who grew up outside the United States was equally instructive.

Anders is a native of Sweden and received much of his formal education there and in Britain. His perspectives on leaders and events often brought me up short, making me realize that many of my ideas about the United States on the international stage rested on assumptions not shared by the rest of the world. I have thanked him silently many times in the years since I took notes in his classroom, and I am glad to have this opportunity to thank him here.

In the School of the Arts at Columbia, my fellow nonfiction faculty members Lis Harris, Margo Jefferson, Richard Locke, Phillip Lopate, and the late Michael Janeway listened kindly to my endless ruminations on Woodrow Wilson and furthered my progress with intelligent questions and perceptive observations. Richard played an additional role, applying his considerable editorial gifts to several knotty parts of the book. With his help, the knots were untangled, extraneous threads went into the wastebasket, and the threads that remained were seamlessly rewoven. My appreciation for these interventions is boundless.

I would also like to thank Dean Carol Becker, Associate Dean Jana Wright, and Timothy Donnelly (then chair of the Writing Program), and Bill Wadsworth (director of academic administration) for their support during a long siege of medical bad luck. They did everything possible to make sure that I was one of those rare patients with nothing to think about except getting well. Which I did. Five times.

Several of my former students ventured bravely into the dust and disintegration of century-old books, endured the hostility of microfilm and microfiche, and took on temperamental databases to assist in hunting, gathering, and verification: Adina Kay-Gross, Nika Knight Beauchamp, Meghan Flaherty Maguire, Alicia Oltuski, and Sophia Wetzig. Michael R. Shea was my first secretary of transportation, getting me and a large cargo of files and books to and from the Institute for Advanced Study. I thank them all for excellent work and good cheer throughout.

The preparation of a biographical manuscript entails an inordinate amount of typing, checking, and chasing after details. Most of that work fell to my former student (now fellow author) Sarah Perry, who arrived on the scene just after I broke a shoulder. Sarah proved to be a first-rate researcher, meticulous tracker of details, and perfect companion for someone who has lost the use of a dominant arm. I hired her, but there is no way to compensate her for the thoughtfulness or remarkable skill set she brought to the job. A few years on a roller derby team had taught her how to tend to all manner of broken bones. Months after the break, when I still had only minimal use of the arm, she agreed to serve as my second secretary of transportation, driving me down to the Woodrow Wilson Presidential Library and back. I still marvel at my luck in finding the one person with all the qualities necessary to see me through the most vexatious stretch of a most vexatious year: a good editorial mind, historical curiosity, a passion for order, computer savvy, stamina, and unending kindness.

Many thanks to the generous friends who read and commented on all or part of various drafts: Nancy Baker, Kathleen Dalton, Barb Draper, Mathea Falco and Peter Tarnoff, Valerie Seiling Jacobs, Jerry Jellison, John Judis, Jill Norgren, Bridget Potter, Philippa Strum, and Strobe Talbott. In the last sprint toward publication, Deborah Weisgall and Throop Wilder suspended their regular lives and devoted two weeks to the first page proofs in order to prune the mistakes, repetitions, and infelicities that often elude an author whose eye is no longer fresh. Marilyn Chapman gave the same care and scrutiny to the endnotes and bibliography.

By a stroke of good luck, I happened to meet John Milton Cooper, Jr., the world's greatest authority on Woodrow Wilson, just as I began work on the book. I had long admired his scholarship and his prose, and I have now read all of his Wilson books to pieces. His *Woodrow Wilson* sets a high bar for judiciousness and, barring the discovery of significant new sources, *Breaking the Heart of the World,* his account of the fight over the ratification of the Treaty of Versailles, will stand for all time. Our conversations and email exchanges have been invaluable, and his generosity is an equally great gift.

I have also benefited from the friendship and insights of Phyllis Lee Levin, whose *Edith and Woodrow* is one of the shrewdest, most eloquent books in the Wilson literature. I am grateful, too, to Thomas J. Knock, for a long and enlightening talk about the presidential election of 1916. His book *To End All Wars: Woodrow Wilson and the Quest for a New World Order* is indispensable to any study of Wilson's internationalism.

The squad mentioned in the dedication has my unending thanks. To have their affection and attention for a year with five surgeries, a hundred post-operative treatments, and uncountable visits to doctors and lab technicians leaves a person believing—as Woodrow Wilson did—that that humankind has a greater capacity for goodness than history and headlines suggest. If I am ever asked to devise a new world order, I will start by calling in the squad.

Notes

KEY TO FREQUENTLY USED SOURCES

	EMH Diary, EMH Papers, EMH Papers. Edward Mandell House Papers, Manuscripts and Archives, Yale University
FO	Foreign Office (National Archives, Kew, United Kingdom)
FRUS	Department of State. *Papers Relating to the Foreign Relations of the United States.* Washington, D.C.: U.S. Government Printing Office, 1861–.
IPCH	Charles Seymour, *The Intimate Papers of Colonel House.* 4 vols. Boston: Houghton Mifflin, 1926.
MAE	Ministère des Affaires étrangères et européennes (Ministry of Foreign and European Affairs, Diplomatic Archives, La Courneuve, France).
PWW	Arthur S. Link, ed., *The Papers of Woodrow Wilson.* 69 vols. Princeton: Princeton University Press, 1996–1994.
WHU	White House Usher's Diary (March 4, 1913–March 4, 1921), Library of Congress
WWLL	Ray Stannard Baker, *Woodrow Wilson: Life and Letters.* 8 vols. Potomac edition. New York: Charles Scribner's Sons, 1946.
WWWS	Ray Stannard Baker, *Woodrow Wilson and the World Settlement.* 3 vols. Garden City, N.Y. Doubleday, Page, 1922.

KEY TO FREQUENTLY USED NAMES

| CPA | Chandler P. Anderson |
| CTG | Cary Travers Grayson |

EAW   Ellen Axson Wilson
EBW   Edith Bolling (Galt) Wilson
EMH   Edward M. House
EWM   Eleanor Wilson McAdoo
HAW   Henry A. White
HCL   Henry Cabot Lodge
JPT   Joseph P. Tumulty
JWS   Jessie Wilson Sayre
MAH   Mary Allen (Peck) Hulbert
NDB   Newton Diehl Baker
RL   Robert Lansing
RSB   Ray Stannard Baker
TR   Theodore Roosevelt
WGM   William Gibbs McAdoo
WHT   William Howard Taft
WHU   White House Usher (Irwin Hood Hoover)
WJB   William Jennings Bryan
WW   Woodrow Wilson

MANUSCRIPTS AND ARCHIVES

Chandler P. Anderson Diary, Library of Congress
Newton Diehl Baker Papers, Library of Congress
Ray Stannard Baker Papers, Library of Congress
Ray Stannard Baker Papers, Seeley G. Mudd Library, Princeton University
Bernard Mannes Baruch Papers, Woodrow Wilson Collection, Seeley G. Mudd
    Library, Princeton University
Henry W. Bragdon Papers, Woodrow Wilson Collection, Seeley G. Mudd Library,
    Princeton University
Albert Sidney Burleson Papers, Library of Congress
Gilbert Close Papers, Seeley G. Mudd, Library, Princeton University
Cary Travers Grayson Papers, Woodrow Wilson Presidential Library
William Hard Papers, Seeley G. Mudd Library, Princeton University
Edward Mandell House Papers, Manuscripts and Archives, Yale University
Charles Evans Hughes Papers, Rare Book and Manuscript Library, Columbia University
    versity
Jean Jules Jusserand, Papiers Jusserand, Ministère des Affaires étrangères et eu-
    ropéennes
James Kerney Collection, Seeley G. Mudd Library, Princeton University
Albert Richard Lamb Papers, Seeley G. Mudd Library, Princeton University
Robert Lansing Papers, Library of Congress

Robert Lansing Papers, Seeley G. Mudd Library, Princeton University*

Walter Lippmann Papers, Manuscripts and Archives, Yale University

Walter Lippmann, Reminiscences, Rare Book and Manuscript Library, Columbia University

Henry Cabot Lodge Papers, Massachusetts Historical Society

Breckinridge Long Papers, Library of Congress

Sidney Edward Mezes Papers, Reminiscences, Rare Book and Manuscript Library, Columbia University

John Bassett Moore Papers, Library of Congress

John Lord O'Brian, Reminiscences, Rare Book and Manuscript Library, Columbia University

Walter Hines Page Papers, Houghton Library, Harvard University

Alice Paul, Reminiscences, Rare Book and Manuscript Library, Columbia University

Jessie Wilson Sayre Papers, Seeley G. Mudd Library, Princeton University

Jessie Wilson Sayre Papers, Woodrow Wilson Presidential Library

James Thompson Shotwell, Reminiscences, Rare Book and Manuscript Library, Columbia University

William Howard Taft Papers, Library of Congress

Norman Mattoon Thomas, Reminiscences, Rare Book and Manuscript Library, Columbia University

Joseph Patrick Tumulty Papers, Library of Congress

Oswald Garrison Villard Papers, Houghton Library, Harvard University

James Wolcott Wadsworth, Reminiscences, Rare Book and Manuscript Library, Columbia University

Hugh C. Wallace Papers, Seeley G. Mudd Library, Princeton University

Henry White Papers, Library of Congress

William Allen White Papers, Library of Congress

Edith Bolling (Galt) Wilson Papers, Library of Congress

Woodrow Wilson Papers, Library of Congress

Woodrow Wilson Collection, Seeley G. Mudd Library, Princeton University

CHAPTER 1: *Son of the South*

1   *Thomas Woodrow Wilson: WWLL: Youth*, 14–16, 23–24. Jessie's given name was Janet, but in the family she was called Jessie and Jeanie. *PWW*, 1:1.

1   *Before his second birthday:* John Mulder, "Joseph Ruggles Wilson: Southern Presbyterian Patriarch," *Journal of Presbyterian History* 52 (1974): 249–50.

---

* There are three collections of Robert Lansing Papers: the two cited here and *The Lansing Papers,* 2 vol. (Washington, D.C.: U.S. Government Printing Office, 1939–40).

1   *In the autumn of 1860:* WWLL: Youth, 28.

2   *Torched:* John Hope Franklin, *Reconstruction after the Civil War,* 2nd ed. (Chicago: University of Chicago Press, 1994), 2.

2   *Tommy grew up:* Weinstein, *Woodrow Wilson,* 8–12; Mulder, "Joseph Ruggles Wilson," 254, 257.

2   *Joseph Wilson's Presbyterianism:* WWLL: Youth, 83–84.

2   *Joseph Sr. graduated:* Mulder, "Joseph Ruggles Wilson," 247.

2   *The Wilsons prized:* Weinstein, *Woodrow Wilson,* 13.

3   *Tommy was odd man out:* George and George, *Woodrow Wilson and Colonel House,* 7–11; Weinstein, *Woodrow Wilson,* 14–18; P. G. Aron, *Dyslexia and Hyperlexia: Diagnosis and Management of Developmental Reading Disabilities* (Boston: Kluwer Academic Publishers, 1989), 3–4. One in ten children, most of them boys, is afflicted with dyslexia, which results from a delay in the development of certain parts of the brain. The lag puts the right and left lobes in a competition that sets off something akin to static in the signaling system that governs reading, spelling, and mathematics. Weinstein based his diagnosis on Wilson's adult letters, with their uncertain spelling and their mentions of his slow reading, his inability to master a foreign language, and his difficulty with mathematics.

3   *Joseph suspected:* Walworth, *Woodrow Wilson,* 1:10.

3   *The adult Woodrow Wilson:* WWLL: Youth, 38–39.

3   *Jessie rarely figured:* PWW, 5:322; Weinstein, *Woodrow Wilson,* 11–12.

3   *Yet she must have been more:* WWLL: Youth, 35.

3   *Tommy's adolescence:* PWW, 1:20–21, 24–25, 28.

3   *All his life:* PWW, 3:522.

3   *At sixteen:* WWLL: Youth, 57.

3   *The last of his invented selves:* PWW, 1:54–56.

4   *He turned in:* PWW, 1:67n.

4   *But in his second semester:* PWW, 6:693–96.

4   *Tom's need:* Weinstein, *Woodrow Wilson,* 7–8; PWW, 1:50n2, 235.

4   *it appealed to Tom:* John Grier Hibben, "Princeton College and Patriotism," Forum 22:2 (Oct. 1896): 222.

4   *shorthand:* PWW, 1:57–63.

5   *"an old young man":* WWLL: Youth, 78.

5   *He grimly lashed himself:* Mulder, "Joseph Ruggles Wilson," 257–58. Dr. Wilson's continuing struggle is evident in several of the sermons he gave over the next few years in Wilmington, passages of which are quoted by Mulder.

5   *As undergraduates, Wilson and Talcott:* PWW, 2:500.

5   *Tom competed:* WWLL: Youth, 92.

5   *He also labored:* PWW, 1:137, 2:147–48.

5   *Tom's wish:* PWW, 1:166.

5   *At a stalemate:* WWLL: Youth, 104.

5   *Aware of Tom's overreaching:* PWW, 1:332.

6   *Unenthusiastic:* Maynard, *Woodrow Wilson,* 24.

6   *"I have made a discovery":* Axson, *"Brother Woodrow,"* 15.

6   *Instead he devoured:* WWLL: Youth, 86–88.

6   *As a Southerner:* Maynard, *Woodrow Wilson,* 10.

6   *"Tommy dear":* PWW, 1:228–33.

6   *Tom kept his fists at his side:* PWW, 1:143.

6   *That was true:* The literacy figures are for 1870. National Center for Education Statistics, http://nces.ed.gov/naal/lit_history.asp, accessed May 21, 2015.

6   *Tom's antipathy:* PWW, 1:479–81.

7   *Making friends:* George and George, 16; *WWLL: Youth,* 98–103.

7   *"Cabinet Government in the United States":* PWW, 1:493–510.

7   *The young author's prescription:* Walter Bagehot, *The English Constitution* (Garden City, N.Y.: Dolphin Books, n.d.), 71–72.

7   *Weakness produced deadlock:* Ibid., 83.

8   *The review paid:* Frank Luther Mott, *A History of American Magazines* (Cambridge: Harvard University Press, 1938), 3:16–17, 35. The *International Review's* international side consisted of translations of works by French and German authors.

8   *Wilson spent his mite:* WWLL: Youth, 139n1.

8   *"There's no college life here":* PWW, 1:656.

8   *The object of his affections:* WWLL: Youth, 129–30.

8   *He later explained:* WWLL: Youth, 137; Maynard, *Woodrow Wilson,* 29.

9   *When he proposed:* Walworth, *Woodrow Wilson,* 1:29–30.

9   *Deeply pained:* PWW, 2:106–8.

9   *Two months later:* PWW, 2:82, 128.

9   *Henry W. Grady:* Edwin Du Bois Shurter, ed., *The Complete Orations and Speeches of Henry W. Grady.* n.p., South-west Publishing Company, [1910], 18.

9   *Woodrow Wilson had expressed:* PWW, 2:82.

9   *With another fledgling lawyer:* WWLL: Youth, 140–43.

9   *He was still living:* PWW, 2:145

9   *"It is hardly like you":* PWW, 2:135–36, 303–4.

10   *After only a few months:* WWLL: Youth, 144–48.

10   *Wilson's speech won compliments:* Atlanta Constitution, Sept. 24, 1882; U.S. Congress, House of Representatives, *Report of Tariff Commission,* 2:1294–97, 47th Cong., 2nd Sess., 1882.

10   *he continued:* PWW, 2:19–25, 119–25, 306–11.

10   *"I am unfit for practice":* PWW, 2:343–44.

10   *Law had been a stepping-stone:* PWW, 2:499–500.

11   *Bridges sympathized:* PWW, 2:347.

11   *All doors:* Maynard, *Woodrow Wilson,* 28; PWW, 2:335.

11   *With his fantasies:* PWW, 2:10.

11   *Ellen Louise Axson:* WWLL: Youth, 161–62; PWW, 2:468.

11   *"a new and altogether delightful":* PWW, 2:465–69.

12 *Both Woodrow and Ellen:* Walworth, *Woodrow Wilson,* 1:37–38.

12 *Telling a friend: PWW,* 3:27.

CHAPTER 2: *When a Man Comes to Himself*

13 *Preoccupied: PWW,* 2:457.

13 *The reason: PWW,* 2:479–80.

14 *"How very fortunate": PWW,* 2:494.

14 *"what no American has ever contributed": PWW,* 2:499–505.

14 *Woodrow guessed: PWW,* 2:517.

14 *More political science than history:* WW, *Congressional Government* 28, 53.

14 *Presidents had exercised:* Ibid., 47–48.

15 *It seemed to Wilson:* Ibid., 77.

15 *Congress had grown powerful:* Ibid., 31, 57, 69, 71.

15 *"How is the schoolmaster":* Ibid., 185–86.

15 *Once again, Wilson declared:* Ibid., 144.

15 *"Each session of the Lords and Commons":* Ibid., 92, 94.

15 *Public speaking "sets my mind": PWW,* 3:484.

16 *"One feels no sacrifice": PWW,* 3:553.

16 *"The question is, What next?": PWW,* 3:506–7.

16 *Contemplating his future:* EWM, ed., *The Priceless Gift,* 117–19.

16 *Wilson lasted two years:* WWLL: *Youth,* 235–37.

16 *Ellen, however, was skeptical: PWW,* 3:494–95.

16 *Woodrow admitted: PWW,* 3:498–500.

16 *Her father:* Axson, *"Brother Woodrow,"* 2.

17 *Encouraged by her teachers:* Weinstein, *Woodrow Wilson,* 73–79.

17 *The couple honeymooned:* WWLL: *Youth,* 239; Heckscher, *Woodrow Wilson,* 79.

17 *Woodrow worried that his salary:* EWM, *The Woodrow Wilsons,* 40.

17 *Wilson had been at Bryn Mawr:* Heckscher, *Woodrow Wilson,* 84–85.

17 *With Renick's help:* Bragdon, *Woodrow Wilson,* 158.

17 *but no one offered:* Walworth, *Woodrow Wilson,* 1:47.

17 *"Thirty-one years old":* WWLL: *Youth,* 289.

17 *The post returned him:* Only 15 of Wesleyan's 215 students were women. Bragdon, *Woodrow Wilson,* 163.

18 *In 1890:* WWLL: *Princeton,* 2–9.

18 *salary of $3,000: PWW,* 6:523.

18 *"the baby, the little baby":* WWLL: *Princeton,* 317.

18 *Woodrow thoroughly enjoyed: PWW,* 6:559–60.

19 Harper's Weekly *paid generously:* WWLL: *Princeton,* 126n5.

19 *As his reputation grew: PWW,* 8:69, 73.

19 *During a lonely stay in Baltimore: PWW,* 8:460.

19 *"Never blame me": PWW,* 9:208.

19 *"Love's Playmate": PWW,* 9:195–96.

19   *Ellen rarely responded in kind: PWW,* 10:175.

19   *"Yes, sir, I do want 'all of you'": PWW,* 10:178.

19   *"country-bred":* Weinstein, *Woodrow Wilson,* 150.

19   *"All his life he dreaded": WWLL: Governor,* 209.

19   *To one of his women friends: PWW,* 12:272.

20   *One said that with women:* Interviews with Madge Axson Elliott, Mrs. George M. Harper, David F. Magie, and Lyman P. Powell. Henry W. Bragdon Papers.

20   *Wilson's closest friend:* Maynard, *Woodrow Wilson,* 53.

20   *Only half in jest: PWW,* 8:633–34.

20   *Several fingertips:* Weinstein, *Woodrow Wilson,* 141–42.

20   *Although his arm: WWLL: Princeton,* 31, 33.

20   *"Really, this out-of-door life": PWW,* 9:532.

21   *The serenity: PWW,* 9:528.

21   *Cambridge: PWW,* 9:521.

21   *Oxford: PWW,* 9:537–38.

21   *He read the proofs: PWW,* 10:3–4.

21   *"Princeton in the Nation's Service": PWW,* 10:11–31.

21   *With his right arm:* Maynard, *Woodrow Wilson,* 43–44; *PWW,* 10:36n1, 124n3.

21   *Wilson tried to conserve:* Maynard, *Woodrow Wilson,* 53.

21   *Though his salary, now $4,300: PWW,* 10:497.

22   *When one of his friends:* Maynard, *Woodrow Wilson,* 53–54.

22   *Beyond drawing: PWW,* 10:497.

22   *In 1898, Cleveland Dodge: WWLL: Princeton,* 40.

22   *"a vulgar, commonplace empire":* Robert L. Beisner, *Twelve Against Empire: The Anti-Imperialists of 1898–1900* (Chicago: University of Chicago Press, 1985), 152.

22   *if America rejected: New York Times,* Jan. 25, 1899.

22   *"the thing is done": PWW,* 10:575–76.

23   *The West would try:* WW, "Democracy and Efficiency," *PWW,* 12:6–20.

23   *"a false self-confidence": PWW,* 12:13.

23   *"When foreign affairs play a prominent part":* WW, *Congressional Government,* 22–23.

23   *"How I hate business": PWW,* 11:197.

23   *"I have done what I could": PWW,* 11:205.

23   *"a very keen sense":* Maynard, *Woodrow Wilson,* 54–55.

24   *Only when a man:* WW, *When a Man Comes to Himself* (New York: Harper & Brothers, 1915), 2, 6, 13–15, 36. *When a Man Comes to Himself,* first published as a magazine article and then as a book, was immensely popular for many years. Seeing it as a source of wise counsel, fathers often gave it to their sons. It made a lifelong impression on Hubert Humphrey, Jr., whose copy was given to him by his father. Humphrey, who spent twenty-five years in public office, as mayor of Minneapolis, U.S. senator, and vice president, kept his copy of Wilson's little book on his desk. (Richard Meryman, "Hubert Humphrey Talks His Self-Portrait," *Life* 65, no. 13 [Sept. 27, 1968]: 22B.)

24 *Woodrow Wilson's first taste of power:* Bragdon, *Woodrow Wilson*, 277.

24 *Accepting the office:* PWW, 14:70–71.

25 *"like a new prime minister":* PWW, 14:27.

25 *"Princeton for the Nation's Service":* PWW, 14:170–85.

25 *"[I]t has quite taken":* PWW, 14:347–48.

25 *He won praise:* Alexander Leitch, *A Princeton Companion* (Princeton: Princeton University Press, 1978), 512–16.

25 *Special dispensations:* Maynard, *Woodrow Wilson*, 69.

25 *"companions and coaches":* PWW, 14:274.

26 *And then, on May 28, 1906:* PWW, 16:412n1.

26 *"Of course 50-year-old arteries":* Weinstein, *Woodrow Wilson*, 165–66.

26 *When the trustees urged:* EWM, *The Woodrow Wilsons*, 94.

26 *Woodrow was soon tramping:* PWW, 16:432.

26 *He went to Edinburgh:* PWW, 16:446.

26 *"an awful thing":* PWW, 16:429–30; EWM, ed., *The Priceless Gift*, 243.

26 *Woodrow also agreed:* Weinstein, *Woodrow Wilson*, 168.

26 *The streamlining:* The controversy over the quadrangles is covered in *WWLL: Princeton*, 213–74, and Link, *Wilson: The Road to the White House*, 46–57.

26 *Outside the classroom:* Maynard, *Woodrow Wilson*, 114.

27 *"the most agreeable and aristocratic country club":* PWW, 17:35.

27 *"Do I understand?"* RSB, *WWLL*, 2:256-57.

27 *Wilson took one more do-or-die stand:* On the fight over the graduate school, see *WWLL: Princeton*, 275–357, and Link, *Wilson: The Road to the White House*, 59–88.

27 *In his inaugural address:* PWW, 14:183.

28 *"I seem to have come to the end":* PWW, 19:620.

28 *"We have beaten the living":* WWLL: Princeton, 346.

CHAPTER 3: *Ascent*

30 *"We now expect":* Bragdon, *Woodrow Wilson*, 386–87.

30 *Aware of the politicos' interest:* Ibid., 388, 391.

30 *"I never saw him excited":* EWM, *The Woodrow Wilsons*, 108.

30 *September 15:* Kerney, *The Political Education of Woodrow Wilson*, vii–x.

31 *His audiences liked him:* PWW, 23:4.

31 *His coat-tails:* Blum, *Joe Tumulty and the Wilson Era*, 24.

31 *Nationwide:* O'Toole, *When Trumpets Call*, 110.

31 *President Taft:* Ibid., 112.

31 *To Wilson it seemed:* PWW, 22:216.

31 *Wilson's victory:* Bragdon, *Woodrow Wilson*, 404.

31 *"The first evening":* EWM, *The Woodrow Wilsons*, 115–17.

32 *in those days, senators were elected:* The procedure is spelled out in Article I, Section 3 of the U.S. Constitution. The rule, intended to create a feeling of solidarity

between state and national governments, had two unforeseen consequences: men of means who aspired to the Senate found it relatively easy to bribe their way in, and long deadlocks became common. By 1910, New Jersey and several other states had elasticized the Constitution by allowing the people to vote— unofficially—for senator, after which the legislature officially elected the people's choice. But direct election of senators did not become the law of the land until the Seventeenth Amendment to the Constitution was ratified, in 1913. (Mark Graber, University of Maryland, email to author, May 18, 2009.)

32   *Big Jim Smith:* Bragdon, *Woodrow Wilson,* 398; *PWW,* 26:46–48; Blum, *Woodrow Wilson and the Politics of Morality,* 45–49; Blum, *Joe Tumulty and the Wilson Era,* 48–49.

32   *Insisting that he had been elected:* PWW, 22:46–48; Blum, *Woodrow Wilson and the Politics of Morality,* 45–49; Blum, *Joe Tumulty and the Wilson Era,* 48–49.

32   *"the country is not Democratic":* Literary Digest 41, no. 21 (Nov. 19, 1910): 915.

32   *He feared:* JPT, *Woodrow Wilson as I Know Him,* 80–81.

32   *Soon after his inauguration:* Blum, *Woodrow Wilson and the Politics of Morality,* 42–50.

33   *Bryan accepted:* WWLL: *Governor,* 209–10; EWM, ed., *The Priceless Gift,* 266.

33   *William F. McCombs:* Frank Parker Stockbridge, "How Woodrow Wilson Won His Nomination," *Current History* 20, no. 4 (July 1924): 561–72.

33   *In May:* PWW, 23:129.

33   *But in an interview:* PWW, 23:61–62.

33   *"the control of our politics":* PWW, 23:7.

33   *After the* Los Angeles Times: PWW, 23:41.

33   *In a speech to college students:* PWW, 23:94.

34   *On occasion:* PWW, 23:24–25, 69, 106.

34   *"grants that government":* PWW, 23:3–4.

34   *"You must let the people":* PWW, 23:57.

34   *as a lifelong student:* PWW, 23:93.

34   *"What pleases me":* PWW, 23:11.

34   *He was startled:* PWW, 23:49–50.

34   *"almost amusing":* PWW, 23:80.

34   *"wicked pleasure":* EWM, *The Woodrow Wilsons,* 126–27.

34   *Informed by Ellen:* PWW, 23:127.

34   *The state treasurer:* New York Times, May 25 and July 7, 1911.

34   *In July the family left:* Trenton Times, July 15, 1911.

34   *Governor's Cottage:* EWM, *The Woodrow Wilsons,* 127–33.

35   *"how full the place is":* PWW, 23:425.

35   *To relax:* Ibid., July 30, 1911.

35   *"My right eye":* Don Van Natta, Jr., *First Off the Tee* (New York: PublicAffairs, 2003), 138.

35   *The cottage had its drawbacks:* EWM, *The Woodrow Wilsons,* 127–33.

35   *"Sometimes . . . my whole life":* PWW, 23:239–40.

36   *It was whispered:* Phyllis Lee Levin, *Edith and Woodrow,* 128–29.

36   *"daintily puffing":* EWM, *The Woodrow Wilsons,* 131.

36   *Nell had found a house:* Ibid., 127, 138; *PWW,* 24:74.

36   *"You can't do anything":* New York Times, Nov. 4, 1911.

36   *some wondered:* Ibid., Nov. 9, 1911.

36   *"Absolutely false":* Ibid., April 12, 1912.

37   *The news that Mary Peck: New York Times* and *New-York Tribune,* Dec. 9, 1911.
     The insight about the placement on the front page is from Phyllis Lee Levin,
     Edith and Woodrow, 131.

37   *Woodrow sent a reassuring letter: PWW,* 23:606.

37   *"It would cost me dear": PWW,* 24:44.

37   *"Would that we could":* Link, *Wilson: The Road to the White House,* 352–54.

37   *When the letter appeared: New York Times,* Jan. 9, 1912.

37   *The letter had come to light: Washington Post,* Jan. 8, 1912.

37   *With the Democrats poised: New York Times,* Jan. 21, 1912.

38   *Bryan's face: Washington Post,* Jan. 11, 1912.

38   *Wilson gave an adroit performance: PWW,* 24:9–16.

38   *Champ Clark: Atlanta Constitution,* Jan. 9, 1912.

38   *The political banquets:* Bryan's speech is covered in *The Boston Globe,* Jan. 9, 1912.

CHAPTER 4: *Against All Odds*

40   *As the electioneering began:* "McCombs, the Original Wilson Man," *Current Lit-
     erature* 53, no. 6 (Dec. 1912): 637–38; Frank Parker Stockbridge, "How Wood-
     row Wilson Won His Nomination," *Current History* 20, no. 4 (July 1924): 568;
     McCombs, *Making Woodrow Wilson President,* 24, 34–35.

41   *Recalling the energy and optimism:* White, *Autobiography,* 487–88.

41   *Oratory would always be:* WWLL: *Governor,* 279.

41   *Wilson also reasoned: PWW,* 24:249.

42   *Wilson suspected: PWW,* 24:248, 299.

42   *but when told he needed:* Link, *Wilson: The Road to the White House,* 405–6.

42   *he hastened: PWW,* 24:287.

42   *Hoping to win the Illinois primary: PWW,* 24:305–6.

42   *He was stunned: Trenton Times,* April 10, 1912.

42   *"Willingness":* Evans Woollen, "The Direct-Primary Experiment," *Atlantic* 110
     (July 1912): 41–45. Woollen's article assessed state and local primaries, which
     were widespread by 1912. On the first presidential primary season, see George
     Kibbe Turner, "Manufacturing Public Opinion," *McClure's* 39, no. 3 (July
     1912): 316–27; "Presidential Primaries," *Outlook* 101, no. 2 (May 11, 1912):
     56–58; and "Defects of the Presidential Primary, *Nation* 94, no. 2449 (June 6,
     1912): 556.

42   *"Possibly the people will wake up later": PWW,* 24:398.

42   *"He intimated it":* McCombs, *Making Woodrow Wilson President,* 103.

42   *After two more losses:* Atlanta Constitution, May 4, 1912; *PWW*, 24:385, 398.

43   *Toward the end of May:* PWW, 24:413–28.

43   *Had wages kept pace:* O'Toole, *When Trumpets Call,* 207.

44   *The gentlemen:* New York Times, May 24, 1912.

44   *Wilson carried:* Trenton Times, April 4, 1912

44   *South Dakota:* Lewis L. Gould, *Four Hats in the Ring: The 1912 Election and the Birth of Modern American Politics* (Lawrence: University Press of Kansas, 2008), 189.

44   *"Just between you and me":* PWW, 24:466–67.

44   *"sometimes when I see":* PWW, 24:402.

45   *The newspapermen:* Philadelphia Inquirer, June 24, 1912; EWM, *The Woodrow Wilsons,* 154.

45   *He did not dread:* PWW, 24:481–82.

45   *Wilson's managers:* New York Times, June 24 and 25, 1912; New-York Tribune, June 24, 1912.

46   *McAdoo found Bryan:* WGM, Crowded Years, 134–36.

46   *After the seventeenth ballot:* New York Times, June 30, 1912.

46   *Delegates trapped:* Charles Moreau Harger, "The Two National Conventions," Independent 73, no. 3318 (July 4, 1912): 15.

46   *Many ran out of money:* New York Times, July 2, 1912.

46   *After seven days:* Los Angeles Times, July 2, 1912.

47   *To one reporter:* White, *The Autobiography of William Allen White,* 478–80.

47   *Whether he was secretly scheming:* Arthur Link presents considerable evidence for the view that Bryan wanted the nomination (*Wilson: The Road to the White House,* 431–65), while Bryan's memoirs, which were completed by his wife after his death, aver that he declined all her suggestions to run in 1912. Before Baltimore, he had made no effort to get it, and when she urged him to try, he said that it would be better for the Democrats to choose someone else. After Roosevelt quit the GOP and formed his own party, Mary Bryan again urged her husband to push for the nomination. He told her that a late bid would be unfair to his competitors, who had been working long and hard for the prize. When the convention was deadlocked ballot after ballot and Mary tried one last time, he told her that he would take the nomination only if the convention could not agree on another candidate and the party turned to him "as one upon whom the different factions can unite. This condition is not probable." (Coletta, *William Jennings Bryan,* 2:74–75.) What is incontestable is that Bryan did a great deal at the convention to try to create that condition.

47   *Bryan knew that once roused:* WJB, *A Tale of Two Conventions,* 152.

47   *Next came Arkansas:* Link, *Wilson: The Road to the White House,* 446.

47   *McAdoo found:* WGM, Crowded Years, 140–41.

47   *Most favored Wilson:* Ibid., 142; New York Times, June 17, 1912.

47   *With that in mind:* Link, "A Letter from One of Wilson's Managers," *American Historical Review* 50 (July 1945): 769–71.

48   *"So, McCombs, you feel it is hopeless?":* WWLL: *Governor,* 351; JPT, *Woodrow Wilson as I Know Him,* 120–21.

48   *When he joined the family:* WGM, *Crowded Years,* 155.

48   *Clark had peaked:* Ibid., 154–55.

48   *Clark's strength diminished:* WGM, *Crowded Years,* 151–52; Link, *Wilson: The Road to the White House,* 449–50.

48   *"I shall withhold my vote":* WJB, *A Tale of Two Conventions,* 193–97.

48   *Bryan's move:* Coletta, *William Jennings Bryan,* 2:69.

48   *Bryan refused: New York Times,* July 1, 1912.

48   *When Bryan's switch:* Ibid.

48   *Twenty reporters shouting the news:* PWW, 24:516–17.

49   *McCombs claimed:* McCombs, *Making Woodrow Wilson President,* 162–63.

49   *White's informant:* White, *Woodrow Wilson,* 260–61.

49   *Forty-five minutes:* WW, 24:522–28; *New York Times,* July 3, 1912.

50   *"Papa was excited, too": Washington Post,* July 7, 1912.

50   *Thomas Riley Marshall:* PWW, 24:527n8, 528; WWLL: *Governor,* 362; *New York Times,* July 3, 1912.

50   *The New York Times, long suspicious: New York Times,* July 2 and July 3, 1912. The *New-York Tribune* (July 3, 1912) also contended that Wilson was nominated in spite of Bryan.

CHAPTER 5: *A New Freedom*

51   IT IS BETTER TO BE SAFE THAN SORRY: PWW, 25:426–27.

51   *Woodrow Wilson promised:* WW, *The New Freedom* (Garden City: Doubleday, Page, 1913), 30–31.

51   *"Prosperity?":* PWW, 25:9.

52   *"I think I might as well give up":* Pringle, *The Life and Times of William Howard Taft,* 2:817–18.

52   *"The country will have none of him":* PWW, 25:55–56.

52   *"I haven't a Bull Moose's strength":* PWW, 25:113.

52   *But McCombs and McAdoo:* WWLL: *Governor,* 375–76; Link, *Wilson: The Road to the White House,* 487.

52   *Wilson made more than seventy:* Link, *Wilson: The Road to the White House,* 517.

52   *They saw a rather plain fellow:* PWW, 24:573.

53   *Many who met him:* PWW, 22:218.

53   *"the hand he gave me":* White, *The Autobiography of William Allen White,* 479.

53   *He had studied elocution:* WGM, *Crowded Years,* 518–19.

53   *Edmund Wilson: The Shores of Light* (New York: Farrar, Straus & Young, 1952), 305.

53   *"the greatest power granted unto man":* PWW, 2:104.

53   *"a sort of sensitive dial":* PWW, 6:670–71.

53   *"There are men to be moved":* PWW, 6:650.

54   *"We naturally ask ourselves":* PWW, 25:10.

54 *He would raze:* PWW, 25:73, 75.

54 *Wilson accused the monopolists:* PWW, 25:322.

54 *"afraid to venture out":* WW, *The New Freedom,* 259–60.

54 *At the Dedham Polo Club:* John T. Morse, Jr., to HCL, Feb. 13, 1916, HCL Papers.

54 *By the time Brandeis:* Irving Katz, "Henry Lee Higginson vs. Louis Dembitz Brandeis: A Collision Between Tradition and Reform," *New England Quarterly* 41, no. 1 (1968): 72.

55 *Roosevelt's way:* Strum, *Louis D. Brandeis, Justice for the People,* 197.

55 *"thralldom of monopoly":* PWW, 25:370.

55 *the strangulating grip:* PWW, 25:189.

55 *"have set us in a straitjacket":* PWW, 25:374.

55 *By October:* PWW, 25:327. Wilson first used the term "New Freedom" in a speech on October 3, 1912.

55 *"revived and clothed":* WW, *The New Freedom,* vii.

55 *"absolutely free opportunity":* Ibid., 14–15.

55 *"a queer kind of Toryism":* Boston Daily Globe, Sept. 10, 1912.

55 *"leave unchecked":* O'Toole, *When Trumpets Call,* 209.

55 *"The minute you are taken care of":* PWW, 25:73–75.

56 *"That old man with the burning eyes":* Salvatore, *Eugene V. Debs,* 225.

56 *"Too many black people":* Afro-American (Baltimore), July 13, 1912.

56 *"The poverty of the colored man":* Ibid., Aug. 12, 1912.

56 *Wilson assured Bishop Alexander Walters:* PWW, 25:448–49.

56 *"a friend of Governor and Mrs. Woodrow Wilson":* New-York Tribune, July 10, 1912.

57 *One of Roosevelt's confidants:* White, *Woodrow Wilson,* 268–69.

57 *"It at once came into my mind":* PWW, 25:284–85.

57 *Finding nothing unseemly:* White, *Woodrow Wilson,* 268–69.

57 *Roosevelt's candidacy was threatened:* O'Toole, *When Trumpets Call,* 217–19.

57 *William Jennings Bryan:* Ibid., 220.

58 *Taft's campaign was a misery:* Ibid., 222.

58 *On Election Day:* WWLL: Governor, 400–401, 407–10; PWW, 25:517–21; *Washington Post* and *Chicago Tribune,* Nov. 6, 1912; EWM, *The Woodrow Wilsons,* 180–81; Walworth, *Woodrow Wilson,* 1:252.

59 *William Gladstone:* H. C. F. Bell, *Woodrow Wilson and the People* (Garden City, N.Y.: Doubleday, Doran, 1945), 88.

59 *Taft and Roosevelt wired:* PWW, 25:521.

59 *No incumbent president had ever fared worse:* This assertion is based on election returns from 1872 onward; many of the statistics for earlier elections are questionable.

59 *Ever since 1912:* The four closest Wilson-Roosevelt contests (decided by a margin of less than 5 percent of the popular vote) were in Illinois, Maine, Indiana, and North Dakota.

60 *"an irony of fate":* Harley Notter, *The Origins of the Foreign Policy of Woodrow Wilson* (Russell & Russell, 1965), 145.

61   *When he resigned from Princeton: PWW,* 20:125, 133.

61   *"We have no compromises": PWW,* 20:146.

CHAPTER 6: *A President Begins*

62   *Sworn in: PWW,* 24:148–52.

63   *there was no inaugural ball: PWW,* 27:59–61.

63   *President Franklin Pierce and his wife:* The Pierces had had three boys and with the death of their twelve-year-old son—in a railway accident—had lost them all.

63   *the new first lady thought it vulgar:* Jonathan Daniels, *The End of Innocence* (Philadelphia: J. B. Lippincott, 1954), 85.

63   *Small wonder:* Irwin Hood Hoover, *Forty-Two Years in the White House,* 58; EWM, *The Woodrow Wilsons,* 211.

63   *Come morning: WWLL: President,* 13–14.

63   *Wilson's break with custom: PWW,* 27:153.

63   *"Seekers After Pie": The State* (Columbia, S.C.), March 6, 1913.

63   *"cold nose":* Lane and Wall, eds., *Letters of Franklin K. Lane,* 133–34.

63   *"no mark of the recruit":* Houston, *Eight Years with Wilson's Cabinet,* 1:35.

64   *At noon: WWLL: President,* 17–19.

64   *Wilson had never owned an automobile:* Ibid., 5, 19.

64   *Riding in a car:* Kerney, *The Political Education of Woodrow Wilson,* 235.

64   *Back in his office by five-thirty: WWLL: President,* 19–20.

64   *Once that prickly business was done:* Ibid., 17–20.

64   *Taft had warned Wilson:* EWM, *The Woodrow Wilsons,* 208.

64   *"They either grow or they swell":* Ibid., 256.

64   *At times he feared: PWW,* 27:200.

65   *"at the beck and call of others": PWW,* 27:490.

65   *To be alone:* Saunders, *Ellen Axson Wilson,* 240–42.

65   *"When I saw him":* EWM, *The Woodrow Wilsons,* 166, 223–24, 240–41.

65   *The White House valet:* Seale, *The President's House,* 2:772–73.

65   *The White House handed over to the Wilsons:* Ibid., 2:756–59, 770–77.

65   *With her painter's eye:* EWM, *The Woodrow Wilsons,* 237.

66   *Her rose garden:* Margaret Truman, *The President's House: A First Daughter Shares the History and Secrets of the World's Most Famous Home* (New York: Ballantine, 2003).

66   *Before coming to Washington: Washington Post,* May 24, July 20, and Oct. 26, 1913. By one estimate, there were sixteen thousand people living in three thousand hovels in the alleys. The history of Washington's alleys is well documented in two scholarly articles by James Borchert: "The Rise and Fall of Washington's Inhabited Alleys: 1852–1972," *Records of the Columbia Historical Society, Washington, D.C.* (1971/1972), 267–88, and "Builders and Owners of Alley Dwellings in Washington, D.C., 1877–1892," *Records of the Columbia Historical Society, Washington, D.C.* (1952), 345–58.

66   *Margaret: Washington Post,* Dec. 1 and 22, 1913.

66   *Jessie:* JWS to Alice Appenzeller, Oct. 22, 1912, Jessie Wilson Sayre Papers, Princeton

66   *Nell:* EWM, *The Woodrow Wilsons,* 235.

66   *Woodrows and Wilsons and Axsons:* Saunders, *Ellen Axson Wilson,* 241.

66   *Belle believed that:* EWM, *The Woodrow Wilsons,* 228–29.

66   *Belle was one of the first:* Seale, *The President's House,* 2:772.

67   *Joseph Patrick Tumulty:* JPT, *Woodrow Wilson as I Know Him;* Blum, *Joe Tumulty and the Wilson Era,* 6, 55–67; Seale, *The President's House,* 2:780–81.

67   *Set up in a room adjacent to the Oval Office:* Truman, *The President's House,* 160.

67   *Captain Cary T. Grayson:* CTG, *Woodrow Wilson,* 2–3.

68   *"While I am not ill":* Houston, *Eight Years with Wilson's Cabinet,* 1:46–47.

68   *Wilson had total confidence:* Link, "Dr. Grayson's Predicament," *Proceedings of the American Philosophical Society* 138, no. 4 (Dec. 1994): 487–94.

68   *A cannier politician:* CTG, *Woodrow Wilson,* 47.

68   *He delegated: Chicago Tribune,* April 10, 1954.

68   *Edward Mandell House:* IPCH, 1:37.

68   *House watched Wilson's ascent: PWW,* 23:458.

69   *"He is not the biggest man":* IPCH, 1:46.

69   *When Wilson offered: PWW,* 27:163–64.

69   *Wilson found the presidency:* WW, *Constitutional Government in the United States,* 68–72.

70   *As he explained in a 1911 interview: PWW,* 23:278.

70   *Within days of his inauguration:* Link, *Wilson: The New Freedom,* 152.

70   *(Wilson suspected):* Josephus Daniels, *The Wilson Era,* 1:100–101.

70   *Wilson's request was granted: New York Times,* April 8, 1913.

70   *Washingtonians curious:* Details of Wilson's first congressional address are from *Boston Globe* and *Chicago Tribune,* April 9, 1913; EWM, *The Woodrow Wilsons,* 246–48.

70   *His family attended: PWW,* 27:268–69.

71   *Wilson began by saying: PWW,* 27:268–72.

71   *Wilson returned to the Capitol: Chicago Tribune,* April 10, 1913.

71   *His listeners replied: New York World* and *New-York Tribune,* April 10, 1913.

71   *Two days later:* Wilson's institutionalizing of the White House press conference also led to the founding of the White House Correspondents' Association, which ensured that the reporters present were in fact reporters. It also established a process for dealing with complaints from and against reporters. (Truman, *The President's House,* 330.)

72   *"You have got to write": PWW,* 27:210–13.

72   *The president's iconoclastic week: PWW,* 27:294–97.

72   *He had dominated the headlines: Boston Globe,* April 9, 1913.

72   *Reporters soon discovered:* Hilderbrand, *Power and the People,* 99–104.

CHAPTER 7: *Lines of Accommodation*

73　*"wet nurses":* EWM, *The Woodrow Wilsons,* 282–83.

74　*It fell to Burleson: WWLL: President,* 44–47.

74　*On May 8:* Ibid., 113, 116; *New York Times,* May 8, 1913.

74　*Wilson staged:* Link, *Wilson: The New Freedom,* 177–97.

75　*Once again: New-York Tribune,* June 24, 1913; *PWW,* 27:570–73.

75　*On June 20: New York Times,* June 21, 1913.

75　*Cornish:* Albert Shaw, "The New 'Summer White House,'" *American Review of Reviews* 48 (July–Dec. 1913): 46–48.

75　*But after he lectured: Boston Globe,* June 30, 1913.

75　*Although the House:* Link, *Wilson: The New Freedom,* 220; *Washington Post,* July 2, 1913.

75　*Bryan tried to shepherd: New York Times,* July 2, 1913.

75　*At the end of July: Chicago Tribune,* July 27, 1913.

75　*Burleson helped:* CPA Diary, CPA Papers.

75　*"great, very great": PWW,* 28:84

76　*Why, he wondered: PWW,* 28:336–38.

76　*Going well beyond:* Weinstein, *Woodrow Wilson,* 250; CTG Papers, July 23, 1913.

76　*"lovely fellows": PWW,* 28:161.

76　*The neuritis: PWW,* 27:298; CTG Papers, Aug. 13, 14, and 18, 1913.

76　*"the thickest disruptive charge":* Samuel Howard Monell, *High Frequency Electric Currents in Medicine and Dentistry* (n.p.: William R. Jenkins, 1910), 307–9.

76　*"Indeed, dear, I must go!": PWW,* 28:109.

76　*He longed for her, too: PWW,* 28:113–14.

76　*Those who earned less than $3,000:* Frank Burdick, "Woodrow Wilson and the Underwood Tariff," *Mid-America* 50–51 (Oct. 1968): 277–79, 284; W. Elliot Brownlee, "Wilson's Reform of Economic Structure: Progressive Liberalism and the Corporation," in Cooper, ed., *Reconsidering Woodrow Wilson,* 62–63.

76　*Printed on gilt-edged parchment: New York Times,* Oct. 4, 1913; *PWW,* 28: 351–52.

77　*The optimists: PWW,* 28:301, *WWLL: President,* 197.

77　*He called a few friendly senators: New York Times,* Oct. 8, 1913.

77　*Black voters:* Link, *Wilson: The New Freedom,* 243–54.

78　*An NAACP investigation: Chicago Defender,* Sept. 20, 1913; *PWW,* 28:60, 164, 402–8.

78　*Black civil servants were shunted:* Christine Lunardini, "William Monroe Trotter's Meetings with Woodrow Wilson, 1913–1914," *Journal of Negro History* 64, no. 3 (Summer 1979): 251n1.

78　*A freshman congressman: Washington Post,* July 17, 1913.

78　*Senator James K. Vardaman:* Ibid., May 4, 1913.

79　*When NAACP leaders decided: PWW,* 28:60–61.

79   *Distressed by the prospect: PWW,* 28:65.

79   *"Never before has the Federal Government": PWW,* 28:163–65.

79   *As soon as the protest: PWW,* 27:442.

79   *Now he told Villard: PWW,* 28:202.

79   *Infuriated: PWW,* 28:239-40.

79   *In the hour he spent with Wilson:* Oswald Garrison Villard, "Woodrow Wilson and the Negro," *Crisis,* December 1938, 384–85; Villard, *Fighting Years,* 239.

79   *Showing no sympathy: PWW,* 28:342–45.

79   *Wilson had replied: PWW,* 28:352–53.

80   *Shortly after Villard left:* CTG, *Woodrow Wilson,* 2–3; CTG Diary, CTG Papers, March 22–27, March 30–April 3, April 26–27, and Dec. 3–16, 1913; *PWW,* 27:298, 395; 29:23.

80   *Edwin A. Weinstein:* Weinstein, *Woodrow Wilson,* 250–52.

80   *In December Wilson suffered: PWW,* 29:33–34.

80   *"The men who have fought": PWW,* 29:63–66.

CHAPTER 8: *Our Detached and Distant Situation*

82   *The Federal Reserve Act: Chicago Tribune* and *Boston Globe,* Dec. 24, 1913.

82   *"few flowers": PWW,* 29:23.

83   *The most dangerous: FRUS, 1913,* 732.

83   *Virtually everyone:* Samuel Flagg Bemis, *The Latin American Policy of the United States* (New York: Harcourt, Brace, 1943), 172.

83   *But a revolution next door:* Link, *Wilson: The New Freedom,* 349.

83   *nearly all of whom:* Collectively, American investments in Mexico exceeded $1 billion. Gene Z. Hanrahan, *The Bad Yankee: American Entrepreneurs and Financiers in Mexico* (Chapel Hill, N.C.: Documentary Publications, 1985), 2, Appendix D, 381.

83   *By the time Wilson took office:* Henry Lane Wilson, *Diplomatic Episodes in Mexico, Belgium and Chile,* 247–48.

83   *Wilson made: PWW,* 27:172–73.

83   *While most Americans applauded: Los Angeles Times,* March 14, 1913.

83   *John Bassett Moore:* J. B. Moore to WW, May 14, 1913, John Bassett Moore Papers, Library of Congress.

83   *The U.S. ambassador to Mexico: FRUS, 1913,* 799-800.

84   *"Nations as well as individuals":* Felix Gilbert, *To the Farewell Address,* 138.

84   *The great departure:* Buehrig, *Woodrow Wilson and the Balance of Power,* 3–17.

85   *The U.S. Department of State in 1913:* Rachel West, *The Department of State on the Eve of the First World War* (Athens: University of Georgia Press, 1978).

85   *"I must have the best men": WWLL: President,* 23.

85   *Charles W. Eliot:* R. S. Baker, memorandum of conversation with Charles W. Eliot, May 22, 1925, RSB Papers, Box 1, Princeton.

85   *Walter Hines Page:* Link, *Wilson: The New Freedom,* 100–101.

85   *Paris was the post:* McCombs, *Making Woodrow Wilson President,* 221, 308.

86   *"cooling-off treaties":* New York Times, New-York Tribune, Washington Post, April 24 and 25, 1913; *FRUS, 1913,* 8–9.

86   *The scheme:* James Bryce to Edward Grey, April 24, 1913, FO 881/10472.

86   *and within six weeks: FRUS, 1913,* 9–10.

86   *Wilson came to the presidency:* Eugene P. Trani, "Woodrow Wilson, China, and the Missionaries, 1913–1921," *Journal of Presbyterian History* 49, no. 4 (Winter 1971): 328–51.

86   *Sun Yat-sen: PWW* 26:576.

86   *a pair of bankers: FRUS, 1913,* 88; Chernow, *The House of Morgan,* 137.

87   *As a pacifist:* Houston, *Eight Years with Wilson's Cabinet,* 1:44-45; *FRUS, 1913,* 170–71.

87   *If Wilson and Bryan: FRUS, 1913,* 150–51, 163–71.

88   *The success of Japanese farmers: PWW,* 24:351–53.

88   *Candidate Wilson: PWW,* 24:382–83.

88   *The news of California's intention: Los Angeles Times,* April 18, 1913.

88   THE TIDE MUST BE CHECKED: *PWW,* 27:265.

88   *He had spoken:* Josephus Daniels, *The Wilson Era,* 1:161.

88   *The government of Japan viewed: Washington Post,* April 23, 1913.

88   *Hoping to calm Tokyo: FRUS, 1913,* 625.

88   *Alien Land Act: PWW,* 27:396. Thomas A. Bailey, "California, Japan, and the Alien Land Legislation of 1913," *Pacific Historical Review* 1 (1932): 36–59, gives a useful overview. Valuable contemporary accounts are Walter V. Woehlke, "White and Yellow in California," *Outlook* 104 (May 10, 1913): 61–65, and Kiyoshi K. Kawakami, "The Japanese on Our Farms," *Forum* 50 (July 1913): 82–93. The connections between Japan's internal political crisis and the California dispute are detailed in Jun Furuya, "Gentlemen's Disagreement: The Controversy Between the United States and Japan over the California Alien Land Law of 1913" (PhD diss., Princeton University, 1989), 190–317.

88   *All that remained: FRUS, 1913,* 627–28.

88   *"We have accomplished the big thing": New York Times,* May 4, 1913.

88   *"painful disappointment": FRUS, 1913,* 629–32, 641.

88   *When Chinda protested again:* J. B. Moore, memo, May 1, 1913, John Bassett Moore Papers.

88   *In Tokyo: Washington Post,* June 19, 1913; *Los Angeles Times,* May 30, 1913.

88   *Another called for an end: New-York Tribune,* June 29, 1913.

89   *In Washington the Joint Board:* Cronon, ed., *The Cabinet Diaries of Josephus Daniels,* 60–64.

89   *At a cabinet meeting:* Houston, *Eight Years with Wilson's Cabinet,* 1:66.

89   *When Garrison insisted:* Josephus Daniels, *The Wilson Era,* 1:164–67.

CHAPTER 9: *Moral Force*

90 *"I propose to teach":* Hendrick, *The Life and Letters of Walter H. Page,* 1:205.

91 *Wilson's armed interventions closer to home:* Herring, *From Colony to Superpower,* 386–90.

91 *"He is a man-eater":* Edwin Emerson, "Victoriano Huerta: The Strong Man of Mexico," *Fortnightly Review* 94, no. 563 (Nov. 1913): 845–45, 856–57.

91 *Huerta drank constantly:* Quirk, *An Affair of Honor,* 39; O'Shaughnessy, *A Diplomat's Wife in Mexico,* 12.

91 *He openly referred:* Katz, *The Secret War in Mexico,* 119–20.

91 *"What to do with Mexico":* Cronon, ed., *The Cabinet Diaries of Josephus Daniels,* 42–43.

92 *Henry Lane Wilson:* FRUS, *1913,* 768–76.

92 *"the prize amateur nation":* JPT, *Woodrow Wilson as I Know Him,* 298.

92 *The first of the emissaries:* PWW, 27:335.

92 *Hale's first report:* PWW, 27:536–52; Hill, *Emissaries to a Revolution: Woodrow Wilson's Executive Agents in Mexico* (Baton Rouge: Louisiana State University Press, 1974).

92 *Deducing that Hale was a spy:* WWLL: *President,* 254–55; PWW, 28:7, 17–22; Henry Lane Wilson, *Diplomatic Episodes in Mexico, Belgium and Chile,* 318–20, 329.

93 *Responsibility for the embassy:* FRUS, *1913,* 812.

93 *On August 4:* New York Times, Aug. 5, 1913.

93 *After a two-hour talk:* Washington Post and Chicago Tribune, Aug. 10, 1913.

93 *After an extravagant profession:* PWW, 28:110–11.

93 *Nonplussed:* HCL to William Sturgis Bigelow, Aug. 30, 1913, HCL Papers.

94 *On Thursday:* PWW, 28:168–75.

94 *"Hard day on P.":* CTG Diary, CTG Papers, Aug. 18, 1913.

94 *That was no trivial matter:* See, for example, Frank Billings and J. H. Salisbury, eds., *General Medicine, Series 1913* (Chicago: Year Book Publishers), 1:209.

94 *At an impasse:* O'Shaughnessy, *A Diplomat's Wife in Mexico,* 250–51.

94 *In hopes of putting:* PWW, 28:227–31.

95 *Congress honored:* New York Times, Aug. 28, 1913.

95 *But Lodge had no faith:* HCL to Cecil Spring Rice, Aug. 13, 1913, HCL Papers.

95 *Occasionally Wilson sought advice:* PWW, 28:212–15; J. B. Moore, memoranda, Aug. 13 and 22 and Nov. 10, 1913, John Bassett Moore Papers, Library of Congress; Coletta, *William Jennings Bryan,* 2:150n12.

95 *Sure that Huerta intended to steal the election:* PWW, 28:399.

95 *Come election day:* FRUS, *1913,* 850, 866; Katz, *The Secret War in Mexico,* 171–72, 218.

95 *"You hear of 'concessions' to foreign capitalists":* PWW, 28:448–52.

96 *The French ambassador:* J. B. Moore, memorandum, Nov. 9, 1913, John Bassett Moore Papers, Library of Congress.

96   *The British wondered: Manchester Guardian,* Oct. 28, 1913.

96   *The Germans accused Wilson: New York Times,* Nov. 1, 1913.

96   *Wilson had seemed a tower of confidence: PWW,* 28:483–84.

96   *Wilson asked Nelson O'Shaughnessy: PWW,* 28:482–83.

96   *Lind heard about O'Shaughnessy's talks:* Hill, *Emissaries to a Revolution,* 102–4.

97   *Lind had no such instructions: Washington Post,* Dec. 3, 1913.

97   *Wilson summoned Moore:* Hill, *Emissaries to a Revolution,* 106.

97   *On December 2: PWW,* 29:3–11.

98   *"the imperialism of idealism":* William Appleman Williams, *The Tragedy of American Diplomacy,* 53.

CHAPTER 10: *A Psychological Moment*

99   *"Sometimes I get desperately tired": PWW,* 29:345–47.

100 *He still did not feel: PWW,* 29: 361–66.

101 *"Watchful waiting": Washington Post,* March 2, 1914.

101 *Wilson doubted: PWW,* 29:218.

101 *In the hope: PWW,* 29:180–84.

101 *Lind pressed Wilson for more: PWW,* 29:328, 359.

101 *The trouble began:* Quirk, *An Affair of Honor,* 8.

101 *The men from the* Dolphin: *FRUS, 1914,* 448, 452; Josephus Daniels, *The Wilson Era,* 1:186–87.

102 *Huerta made his case:* O'Shaughnessy, *A Diplomat's Wife in Mexico,* 260–62.

102 *On the same day: FRUS, 1914,* 453–55.

102 *It had been six weeks: PWW,* 29:391, 395, 439.

102 *"ill will and contempt": PWW,* 29:434.

102 *On Tuesday: PWW,* 29:438–39; *FRUS, 1914,* 463–66.

102 *Nor, frankly:* Quirk, *An Affair of Honor,* 8–9.

103 *He expected no casualties: FRUS, 1914,* 477.

103 *By Saturday: FRUS, 1914,* 468–72.

103 *On Monday:* Houston, *Eight Years with Wilson's Cabinet,* 1:11; Josephus Daniels, *The Wilson Era,* 1:189.

103 *Next he briefed: PWW,* 29:468–70.

103 *At two o'clock:* HCL, *The Senate and the League of Nations,* 13–14; *FRUS, 1914,* 477.

104 *At three o'clock: PWW,* 29:471–74.

104 *Within hours: New York Times* and *Boston Globe,* April 21, 1914.

104 *At two-thirty on Tuesday morning:* JPT, *Woodrow Wilson as I Know Him,* 151–52.

105 *Daniels wired:* Josephus Daniels, *The Wilson Era,* 1:193.

105 *American sailors and marines: FRUS, 1914,* 481; Quirk, *An Affair of Honor,* 95.

105 *The USS* Utah: Quirk, *An Affair of Honor,* 98.

105 *The German cruiser* Dresden: *FRUS, 1914,* 480; Josephus Daniels, *The Wilson Era,* 1:201; Doerries, *Imperial Challenge,* 36–37, 257n119; Katz, *The Secret War in Mexico,* 234–40.

105 *In minutes, the Germans:* Quirk, *An Affair of Honor,* 89.

105 *In Mexico City, O'Shaughnessy saw Huerta:* O'Shaughnessy, *A Diplomat's Wife in Mexico,* 287–91.

105 *Five battleships:* Quirk, *An Affair of Honor,* 99–102.

105 *Nineteen American sailors:* HCL, *The Senate and the League of Nations,* 17.

105 *"preternaturally pale":* WWLL: President, 330.

106 *Carranza did not hesitate:* PWW, 29:483–85.

106 *the seizure of the port:* New York Evening Post, April 22, 1914.

106 *"We found Mr. Wilson":* HCL, *The Senate and the League of Nations,* 17–18.

106 *Luckily for Wilson:* FRUS, 1914, 487-91

106 *Within hours of Huerta's decision:* PWW, 29:515–24.

107 *The ABC Powers:* FRUS, 1914, 496, 505.

107 *The* Ypiranga: *Washington Post,* May 24, 1914.

108 *The United States had assumed:* Doerries, *Imperial Challenge,* 36–37, 257n119; Katz, *The Secret War in Mexico,* 234–40.

CHAPTER 11: *Departures*

109 *On May 7:* EWM, *The Woodrow Wilsons,* 260, 284–87; WGM, *Crowded Years,* 276.

109 *The father managed:* Axson, *"Brother Woodrow,"* 219; PWW, 29:345–47, 371–72, 30:12–13.

110 *Wilson had no evident wish:* Axson, *"Brother Woodrow,"* 218–19; EMH Diary, EMH Papers, Sept. 24, 1914.

110 *After the invasion:* PWW, 30:39–42; FRUS, 1914, 513.

110 *Haunted by the deaths:* EWM, *The Woodrow Wilsons,* 289.

110 *At the Navy Yard:* Josephus Daniels, *The Wilson Era,* 1:198–99; New York Times and New-York Tribune, May 12, 1914. The dead numbered nineteen, but there were only seventeen coffins. Two of the men died after the *Montana's* departure from Mexico.

110 *The commander in chief:* PWW, 30:13–15.

111 *From Brooklyn:* PWW, 30:21–23.

112 *Britain claimed that in 1901:* PWW, 29:34–35.

112 *Page hoped:* Hendrick, *The Life and Letters of Walter H. Page,* 1:270–72.

112 *The Great Adventure:* IPCH, 1:235–85.

113 *As a guest at the U.S. embassy:* Gerard, *My Four Years in Germany,* 77–79.

113 *"jingoism run stark mad":* PWW, 30:108–9.

113 *House let Tirpitz know:* EMH Diary, EMH Papers, May 26, 1914.

113 *Gerard took House:* Ibid., June 1, 1914; PWW, 30:139–40.

114 *"Every nation in Europe":* Hendrick, *The Life and Letters of Walter H. Page,* 1:295.

114 *"I told the kaiser":* EMH Diary, EMH Papers, June 1, 1914; PWW, 30:139–40.

114 *In Paris:* PWW, 30:189–90; EMH Diary, EMH Papers, June 9, 1914.

114 *In London:* PWW, 30:189–90.

115 *"The idea, then":* EMH Diary, EMH Papers, June 27, 1914.

115 *House made one more attempt:* EMH Diary, EMH Papers, June 24 and 27, 1914.

116 *"I feel we have gone a long way":* EMH Diary, EMH Papers, July 3, 1914.

116 *"The kaiser does not want war":* Boston Globe, July 30, 1914.

116 *"I clearly foreshadowed":* EMH Diary, EMH Papers, Aug. 6, 1914.

116 *"just think how near we came":* Hendrick, *The Life and Letters of Walter H. Page,* 1:300.

117 *From Washington came a sympathetic note: PWW,* 30:336.

CHAPTER 12: *The General Wreck*

119 *On August 3: FRUS, 1914, Supplement,* 547–51.

120 *The president also asked reporters: PWW,* 30:331–32. The European incidents of lawlessness are reported in Grew, *Turbulent Era,* 1:130–40; *New York Times,* July 31–Aug. 4, 1914; *Times* (London), Aug. 1 and 4, 1914.

120 *Thousands of American tourists: PWW,* 30:365; T. Bentley Mott, *Myron T. Herrick, Friend of France* (Garden City: Doubleday, Doran, 1929), 127.

120 *When Holland declared:* Gerard, *My Four Years in Germany,* 110.

120 *"Crazy men": PWW,* 30:367.

120 *On August 4: PWW,* 30:342.

120 *Ellen's failure to recover: WWLL: President,* 475–77.

120 *Then the diagnosis was revised:* CTG, *Woodrow Wilson,* 33–35.

120 *"We sat all day waiting":* EWM, *The Woodrow Wilsons,* 299.

121 *"we are still hoping": PWW,* 30:352.

121 *On the same day: WWLL: President,* 478–79; EWM, *The Woodrow Wilsons,* 299–300.

121 *"I must not give way":* Walworth, *Woodrow Wilson,* 1:400. Ellen Wilson was the third and last presidential wife to die in the White House. Letitia Tyler was the first, in 1842, and Caroline Harrison died there in 1892.

121 *The coffin traveled: PWW,* 30:373–75; Saunders, *Ellen Axson Wilson,* 279.

121 *"I want to think":* CTG, *Woodrow Wilson,* 35–36.

121 *"I never understood before": PWW,* 30:437.

121 *He blamed: PWW,* 30:375.

121 *Twenty-one of Bryan's cooling-off treaties: PWW,* 30:378. Details of the discussion and ratification of the cooling-off treaties from *FRUS, 1914, Supplement,* 4n1, 11, 71–72; *Washington Post,* Aug. 14, 1914; *Christian Science Monitor,* Aug. 5, 1914; and *New York Times,* Aug. 19, 1914.

122 *The value of exports: New York Times,* Aug. 26, 1914.

122 *Imports also plummeted: PWW,* 30:467–68.

123 *McAdoo proposed:* WGM, *Crowded Years,* 294–96.

123 *Although Congress quickly approved: New York Times,* Sept. 3, 1914.

123 *"Money is the worst of all contrabands": PWW,* 30:372–73; *WWLL: Neutrality,* 174–76.

123 *But a sale of munitions: PWW,* 31:442.

123 *"You owe it to the country": PWW,* 30:385.

124 *"my great safety": PWW,* 30:395.

124 *"In God's gracious arrangement": PWW*, 31:3–4.

124 *On August 18: PWW*, 30:393–94. The idea of asking the public to take neutrality seriously came from Lansing: *FRUS, The Lansing Papers, 1914–1920*, 1:151–52.

124 *Within days of his appeal: Baltimore Sun*, Aug. 24, 1914.

125 *House did not mention: PWW*, 30:461–67.

125 *The worst of these depredations:* E. Alexander Powell, *Fighting in Flanders* (New York: Charles Scribner's Sons, 1914), 87.

125 *Five days later:* Hugh Gibson, "Through the Louvain Inferno," *World's Work* 34, no. 6 (October 1917): 640–49. See also Leon van der Essen, "Belgian Judicial Report on the Sacking of Louvain," in Charles F. Horne, ed., *Source Records of the Great War: National Alumni*, 1924, 2:150–64.

125 *Wilson predicted: PWW*, 30:463.

125 *House, too, was in despair: PWW*, 30:432–33.

125 *There were demands: PWW*, 30:387.

126 *Ambassador Jusserand wondered: Washington Post*, Aug. 28, 1914.

126 *"What is our duty?": Baltimore Sun*, Aug. 29, 1914.

CHAPTER 13: *At Sea*

127 *"that passage in the Scriptures": PWW*, 30:456–57.

128 *"a world pest": PWW*, 31:21–22.

128 *Count Johann Heinrich von Bernstorff:* Doerries, *Imperial Challenge*, 39–41; *New York Times*, Aug. 26, 1914.

128 *The British and French ambassadors:* Young, *An American by Degrees*, 76.

128 *Spring Rice was distressed:* Gwynn, ed., *The Letters and Friendships of Sir Cecil Spring Rice*, 2:228.

128 *Spring Rice met with Wilson: PWW*, 30:472; Gwynn, ed., *The Letters and Friendships of Sir Cecil Spring Rice*, 2:218–23.

129 *Spring Rice should have been:* For contemporary medical and psychological views of hyperthyroidism, see James J. Walsh, *Psychotherapy* (New York: D. Appleton, 1912), 500–507; George W. Crile, "A New Principle in the Treatment of Graves' Disease," *The Lancet—Clinic*, April 1, 1911, 332ff.

129 *He was also suspect:* Gwynn, ed., *The Letters and Friendships of Sir Cecil Spring Rice*, 2:215.

129 *Jusserand, who was also fond of Roosevelt:* Biographical details from "Jules Jusserand," *Les Affaires Étrangères et Le Corps Diplomatique Français*, Tome II, 1870–1980 (Paris: Editions du Centre de la Recherche Scientifique, 1984), 280–86.

129 *Robert Lansing ranked Jusserand first:* Daniel M. Smith, *Robert Lansing and American Neutrality*, 73.

130 *("his favorite spot"):* Spring Rice to HCL, Sept. 25, 1914, HCL Papers.

130 *Jusserand nevertheless waged: PWW*, 31:347–49; *Washington Post*, Aug. 28, 1914; *FRUS, 1914, Supplement*, 489–91; *FRUS, The Lansing Papers*, 1:136–37, 140; Link, *Wilson: The Struggle for Neutrality*, 132–36.

130 *So began the U.S. investment:* Bailey, *A Diplomatic History of the American People,* 622.

130 *Stakes were high:* Elihu Root, "The Real Significance of the Declaration of London," in Scott, ed., *The Declaration of London,* 1–2.

130 *Sir Edward Grey would remember:* Grey, *Twenty-five Years,* 2:107, 110.

130 *The defense of America's neutral rights fell to Robert Lansing:* Biographical details in Daniel M. Smith, *Robert Lansing and American Neutrality,* 1–9; RL to E. B. Bryan, June 3, 1915; RL to Maxwell Blake, Aug. 9, 1917; RL to David Fairchild, Dec. 11, 1916, RL Papers, Library of Congress.

131 *"Not much power this morning":* CPA Diary, Jan. 19, 1918, CPA Papers.

131 *ideals had no place in foreign policy:* Daniel M. Smith, *Robert Lansing and American Neutrality,* 62.

131 *Copper:* FRUS, 1914, Supplement, 280–83, 338–39, 344–46; *PWW,* 31:110–11.

132 *An enterprising Swede:* Grey, *Twenty-five Years,* 2:113.

132 *The State Department instructed Page: PWW,* 31:166.

132 *Spring Rice understood the American pique and begged Grey:* Gwynn, ed., *The Letters and Friendships of Sir Cecil Spring Rice,* 2:237–38.

132 *Spring Rice also worked: FRUS, 1914, Supplement,* 233–35; *PWW,* 31:194-95.

132 *In the war's first year:* RL, *War Memoirs of Robert Lansing, Secretary of State,* 112; Link, *Wilson: The Struggle for Neutrality,* 117; *PWW,* 31:197–204.

132 *The commodity in question: FRUS, 1914, Supplement,* 290; *World Almanac,* 1914, 217; *Wall Street Journal,* Aug. 5 and Oct. 23, 1914; *WWLL: Neutrality 1914–1915,* 105; *PWW,* 31:126–27.

133 *Although the crisis would pass: Washington Post,* Nov. 3, 1914; May, *The World War and American Isolation,* 23–25; Link, *Wilson: The Struggle for Neutrality,* 91–92, 130–31; Grey, *Twenty-five Years,* 2:115–16.

133 *The war forced Wilson: PWW,* 31:168–74.

133 *Extrapolating: New-York Tribune,* Nov. 5, 1914.

133 *Wilson took some comfort: PWW,* 31:289–90.

133 *People were not stupid: PWW,* 31:265.

133 *"it was useless": PWW,* 31:274–75.

133 *The problem of segregation:* Biographical details from John A. Wagner, "Trotter, William Monroe (1872–1934)," in *Race and Racism in the United States: An Encyclopedia of the American Mosaic,* edited by Charles A. Gallagher and Cameron D. Lippard (Westport, Conn.: Greenwood, 2014), 3:1255–56; and W. E. B. Du Bois, "William Monroe Trotter," *Crisis,* 41, no. 5, (May 1934), 134.

134 *"I assure you": PWW,* 28:491–98.

134 *The situation did not improve:* There is a transcript of the meeting in *PWW,* 31:298–308. On Wilson's anger with himself for losing his temper, see *PWW,* 31:309n2.

135 *This time he asked Grayson:* The details of Wilson's trip to New York are from EMH Diary, EMH Papers, Nov. 14, 1914.

CHAPTER 14: *Moonshine*

136   *The Federal Reserve's regional banks:* PWW, 31:32.

136   *"All the elasticity":* PWW, 31:454–55.

137   *"I am laying plans":* EMH Diary, EMH Papers, Sept. 5, 1914.

137   *House spent Saturday evening:* PWW, 31:5–6.

137   *Years after his visit:* Dumba, *Memoirs of a Diplomat,* 213.

137   *A worldly man:* On Dumba's life and diplomatic career, see William D. God-sey, *Aristocratic Redoubt: The Austro-Hungarian Foreign Office on the Eve of the First World War* (West Lafayette, Ind.: Purdue University Press, 1999), 30, 37, 87; and "Doctor Dumba: The Rejected Austro-Hungarian Ambassador in Washington," *Current Opinion* 9 (July–Dec. 1915): 237–38.

138   *Dumba arrived:* Dumba, *Memoirs of a Diplomat,* 191–92.

138   *Perhaps it was mere coincidence: New York Times,* Aug. 27, 1914.

138   *When the dinner conversation turned to the war:* Link, *Wilson: The Struggle for Neutrality,* 196–97.

138   *Excited by the thought:* Oscar S. Straus, *Under Four Administrations* (Boston: Houghton Mifflin, 1922), 379–85.

139   *Bryan called Wilson:* PWW, 31:15.

139   *"Bernstorff is less clever":* EMH Diary, EMH Papers, Sept. 9, 1914.

139   *Bernstorff admitted as much:* PWW, 31:9–10; Link, *Wilson: The Struggle for Neutrality,* 196–99.

139   *Born in London:* Bernstorff's biographical details are drawn from J. H. Bernstorff, "As Between Ambassadors," *Living Age,* Feb. 24, 1915, 316–19; "The New German Ambassador in Washington," *Current Literature* 46, no. 2 (Feb. 1909): 151; "Bernstorff: The Most Conspicuous Member of the Diplomatic Corps," *Current Opinion* 59, no. 1 (July 1915): 1919.

140   *By the middle of September 1914:* PWW, 31:15, 37; Doerries, *Imperial Challenge,* 86–87.

140   *It was the Battle of the Marne:* Doerries, *Imperial Challenge,* 94.

140   *Unwilling to accept:* PWW, 31:55, 60–61, 76–77.

140   *"neither of us could quite figure out":* PWW, 31:94.

141   *"It is adorned":* Gwynn, ed., *The Letters and Friendships of Sir Cecil Spring Rice,* 2:240–41.

141   *The argument made no sense to Bryan:* PWW, 31:378–79.

141   *House was unreceptive:* PWW, 31:384–85.

142   *He finally shared it:* PWW, 31:458–60.

142   *Two days into the new year:* EMH Diary, EMH Papers, Jan. 4, 1915.

142   *After three months of shuttling:* PWW, 31:522.

143   *With Wilson's consent:* PWW, 32:17–18n1.

143   *By House's watch:* PWW, 32:61.

143   *The next day House outlined:* PWW, 32:64–65; Spring Rice to Grey, Jan. 8, 1915, FO 800/85, and Jan. 14, 1915, FO 800/851.

144 *The colonel finished his wearying day: PWW,* 32:65.

144 *"The president's eyes were moist":* Ibid., Jan. 25, 1915.

145 *"channel of confidential communication": PWW,* 32:157–58.

145 *Colonel and Mrs. House:* EMH Diary, EMH Papers, Feb. 5, 1915.

145 *While the* Lusitania *was at sea: FRUS, 1915, Supplement,* 96–97.

145 *"England wants to starve us":* "Germany's Submarine Blockade of England," *Literary Digest,* 50, no. 7 (Feb. 13, 1915): 304.

145 *The idea of using submarines:* On Arthur Conan Doyle and the German submarine strategy, see Holger H. Herwig, "Total Rhetoric, Limited War: Germany's U-Boat Campaign, 1917–1918," in Roger Chickering and Stig Förster, eds., *Great War, Total War* (Cambridge, England: Cambridge University Press, 2000), 191. The story, "Danger! Being the Log of Captain John Sirius," which appeared in *The Strand* in July 1914, was actually Conan Doyle's second on the subject. The first, a Sherlock Holmes tale called "The Bruce-Partington Plans," was published in 1908. Conan Doyle also warned of the dangers of submarines in "England and the Next War," a nonfiction piece published in *The Fortnightly Review* in 1913. John Llenberg, Daniel Stashower, and Charles Foley, *Arthur Conan Doyle: A Life in Letters* (New York: Penguin, 2007), 550, 552, 597–98.

146 *Britain was more relieved than alarmed:* Link, *Wilson: The Struggle for Neutrality,* 335.

146 *"strict accountability": PWW,* 32:209.

146 *Repelled by the idea: PWW,* 32:260–62.

147 *As directed: PWW,* 32:265; RSB, *WWLL, Neutrality,* 258; Cooper, *Walter Hines Page: The Southerner as American,* 301-2; *IPCH,* 1:445; *FRUS, 1915, Supplement,* 118–20, 127–30.

147 *"no one who did not sit here daily": PWW,* 32:232–33.

147 *He was also anxious: PWW,* 32:265.

147 *"does not so much desire": PWW,* 32:265–68.

147 *"in admirable shape": PWW,* 32:349–50.

147 *Page informed the president: PWW,* 32:357–63.

148 *House went to Berlin by way of Paris: PWW,* 32:372–73; EMH Diary, EMH Papers, March 12, 13, 14, 1915.

148 *"If I can establish": PWW,* 32:377–78.

148 *He had a fresh idea: IPCH,* 1:369–70.

149 *freedom of the seas: IPCH,* 1:407–8.

149 *House reached Berlin:* EMH Diary, EMH Papers, March 19, 24, and 27, 1915; *PWW,* 32:422, 438–42, 455–56, 504–7.

150 *On March 28: PWW,* 32:438–41; EMH Diary, EMH Papers, April 19, 1915.

150 *"It is a dangerous thing to inflame a people": IPCH,* 1:404.

150 *"[S]omething is sure to crack": PWW,* 32:403.

150 *"I had but little difficulty":* EMH Diary, EMH Papers, April 30, 1915.

150 *Buying time:* Link, *The Struggle for Neutrality,* 230

151 *"The ingenious loophole":* Hendrick, *The Life and Letters of Walter H. Page,* 2:414. From Berlin, Ambassador Gerard also wrote House about the German government's skepticism about the notion of "freedom of the land." (*IPCH,* 2:13.)

CHAPTER 15: *Strict Accountability*

153 *"strict accountability":* RL to WJB, May 5, 1915, RL Papers, Library of Congress.

153 *"We have been doing":* WWLL: Neutrality, 257.

153 *Wilson was in no haste:* PWW, 33:37–41.

153 *The violations that had begun:* Carnegie Endowment for International Peace, Division of International Law, "Violation of the Laws and Customs of War," published for the Endowment by Oxford University at the Clarendon Press, 1919, 17–18.

153 *Bernstorff had no worries:* Bernstorff, *My Three Years in America,* 134–38.

153 *The* Lusitania's *captain:* Diana Preston, *Lusitania: An Epic Tragedy* (New York: Walker, 2002), 45, 49, 62, 66–67, 178–79.

154 *The* Times *of London:* May 2, 1915.

154 *so far, 99.7 percent:* Times (London), May 10, 1915.

154 *Five days into the voyage:* David Masters, *The Submarine War* (New York: Henry Holt, 1935), 178–79.

154 *Watching from the deck:* Thomas A. Bailey and Paul B. Ryan, *The Lusitania Disaster: An Episode in Modern Warfare and Diplomacy* (New York: Free Press, 1975), 150–52.

154 *The American embassy in London:* Hendrick, *The Life and Letters of Walter Hines Page,* 2:12; EMH Diary, EMH Papers, May 7, 1915.

154 *a reporter intercepted Bryan:* Link, *Wilson: The Struggle for Neutrality,* 379.

154 *A White House secretary:* WHU Diary, May 7, 1915.

154 *Bryan, coming home from a dinner party:* WJB, *The Memoirs of William Jennings Bryan,* 2:421.

155 *He soon learned:* Preston, *Lusitania,* 134.

155 *The day after the disaster:* FRUS, 1915, Supplement, 385–86.

155 *Wilson ignored them:* Villard, *Fighting Years,* 258.

155 *"very earnestly, but very calmly":* PWW, 33:154n1.

155 *When Tumulty tried:* JPT, *Woodrow Wilson as I Know Him,* 232–34.

155 *"As our main interest is to preserve":* Spring Rice to Foreign Office, May 8 and 9, 1915, FO 115/1998.

155 *Bernstorff maintained:* FRUS, 1915, Supplement, 387; Bernstorff, *My Three Years in America,* 145.

156 *The coincidence:* Gerard, *Face to Face with Kaiserism,* 42.

156 *The German admiralty's written orders:* Bailey and Ryan, *The Lusitania Disaster,* 117-18,

156 *Bernstorff regarded:* Villard, *Fighting Years,* 268–69.

156 *From Berlin, Gerard forwarded:* FRUS, 1915, Supplement, 389.

156 *"the scene of war is no golf links":* Bailey and Ryan, *The Lusitania Disaster,* 231.

156 *Wilson emerged briefly:* Villard, *Fighting Years,* 258.

156 *On Monday he kept:* Starling and Sugrue, *Starling of the White House,* 46.

157 *The uproar: PWW,* 33:174–78.

157 *From London, House and Page cabled:* EMH Diary, EMH Papers, May 13, 1915; *FRUS, 1915, Supplement,* 397.

157 *In Berlin: FRUS, 1915, Supplement,* 396.

157 *As secretary of state:* WJB, *The Memoirs of William Jennings Bryan,* 2:399–400; *PWW,* 33:186–87, 192–95.

158 *On May 17, Dumba called on Bryan:* Bernstorff, *My Three Years in America,* 155–56; *FRUS, 1915, Supplement,* 407–9; Link, *Wilson: The Struggle for Neutrality,* 400–401; *PWW,* 33:212–13, 248n1.

158 *"we earn as a nation":* Hagedorn, ed., *The Works of Theodore Roosevelt,* 18:378–79.

158 *an end to the British blockade: PWW,* 33:197–98, 205.

159 *Grey seemed generally amenable:* EMH Diary, EMH Papers, May 19, 1915.

159 *House's decision to press for the bargain:* See ibid. and *PWW,* 33:253–54.

159 *Germany in no need of food: FRUS, 1915, Supplement,* 415. On wartime hunger in Germany, see Charles Paul Vincent, *The Politics of Hunger: The Allied Blockade of Germany* (Athens: Ohio University Press, 1985), 6–7; Gerard, *Face to Face with Kaiserism,* 61, 63; Chickering, *Imperial Germany and the Great War, 1914–1918,* 41–43.

159 *The president wanted: PWW,* 33:283–84.

160 *"let the odium of rejection fall on England": PWW,* 33:284

160 *The German reply: FRUS, 1915, Supplement,* 419; 422; Bailey and Ryan, *The Lusitania Disaster,* 251–53.

160 *There was indeed an order: PWW,* 33:327–28.

160 *Germany blamed the disaster: FRUS, 1915, Supplement,* 420; Coletta, *William Jennings Bryan,* 2:333–34. For reactions to the German reply, see *Wall Street Journal,* June 2, 1915.

160 *Wilson typed out his reply: WWLL: Neutrality,* 351.

160 *Bryan, who came in a bit late:* Houston, *Eight Years with Wilson's Cabinet,* 1:132–39.

161 *Bryan did not retreat:* Coletta, *William Jennings Bryan,* 2:331.

161 *Bryan replied:* The letters that Wilson and Bryan exchanged in the days before Bryan's resignation are in *PWW,* 33:309–12, 321–26, 342–43.

161 *Wilson let Bryan know:* My account of the events preceding Bryan's resignation is based on WJB, *The Memoirs of William Jennings Bryan,* 2:419–24; Coletta, *William Jennings Bryan,* 2:329–42; WGM, *Crowded Years,* 346.

161 *And as a pacifist: FRUS, 1915, Supplement,* 436–38.

161 *Wilson consulted Tumulty and Secretary Houston:* Houston, *Eight Years with Wilson's Cabinet,* 1:140–41.

161 *Bryan resigned in a letter: PWW,* 33:375–76.

162 *"I sincerely deplore it": PWW,* 33:376.

162 *In the days leading up to Bryan's departure:* Link, *Wilson: The Struggle for Neutrality,* 424.

162 *"always painful":* PWW, 33:377–78.

162 *Bryan was also wounded:* Coletta, *William Jennings Bryan,* 2:356.

162 *The two had run into each other:* Jusserand recounted his conversation with Bryan in *Le Sentiment Américain pendant la Guerre,* 38. WHU (June 9, 1915) notes that Jusserand had come to introduce his new military attaché to the president.

162 *"as we know all too well":* Jusserand to Paris, June 10, 1915, Papiers Jusserand.

162 *No other secretary of state:* Jusserand to Paris, June 14, 1915, Papiers Jusserand.

162 *"When I think how aggravating I have been":* Gwynn, ed., *The Letters and Friendships of Sir Cecil Spring Rice,* 2:272–74.

163 *"I go out into the dark":* Houston, *Eight Years with Wilson's Cabinet,* 1:146.

CHAPTER 16: *Haven*

164 *The question of who would succeed Bryan:* PWW, 33:397, 409.

164 *"he will be barred":* EMH Diary, EMH Papers, EMH Papers, June 14, 1915.

164 *"I have a feeling":* PWW, 33:449.

165 *Unlike Theodore Roosevelt:* Irwin Hood Hoover, *Forty-two Years in the White House,* 31.

165 *the White House usher's diary:* WHU Diary, March 4, 1913–March 4, 1921.

165 *"I have never had any patience":* PWW, 34:241.

166 *Spring Rice admired:* Spring Rice to Grey, June 25, 1915, FO 800/85.

166 *"very competent":* Jusserand, *Le Sentiment Américain pendant la Guerre,* 39.

166 *Apart from the headaches:* PWW, 33:234–35; 34:192, 413–14.

166 *Edith Bolling Galt:* Phyllis Lee Levin, *Edith and Woodrow,* 51–52.

166 *"Her every characteristic":* Irwin Hood Hoover, *Forty-two Years in the White House,* 1–8, 13–16.

167 *The seventh of eleven children:* EBW, *My Memoir,* 1–8, 13–16.

167 *Alexander's cousin Norman:* Ibid., 17–18, 20, 22–23; Kristie Miller, *Ellen and Edith,* 101–5; Phyllis Lee Levin, *Edith and Woodrow,* 64–70.

167 *Edith Galt's road:* EBW, *My Memoir,* 29, 56.

167 *On March 23, Edith returned:* Phyllis Lee Levin, *Edith and Woodrow,* 54; EBW, *My Memoir,* 19–20.

168 *"So I went":* EBW, *My Memoir,* 57–58.

168 *"Oh, you can't love me":* Ibid., 60–61.

169 *Well after midnight:* PWW, 33:109–10.

169 *"I know that you may be my haven":* PWW, 33:132.

169 *"I need you":* PWW, 33:137–38.

169 *Wilson spoke on May 17:* PWW, 33:209-11; Jusserand to Paris, May 18, 1915, Papiers Jusserand.

169 *The fleet set sail:* New York Times and Washington Post, May 19, 1915.

170 *The official explanation:* New York Times, May 20, 1915.

170 *"Instead of golden sunlight":* PWW, 33:228.

170 *In the month after their trip:* WHU Diary, May 21–June 19, 1915; Irwin Hood Hoover, *Forty-two Years in the White House,* 61.

170 *"My only message is this":* PWW, 33:278–79.

170 *"but my love seems inadequate":* PWW, 33:285.

170 *"I have been blind":* PWW, 33:284.

170 *"very full":* PWW, 33:286.

171 *"You made me so happy":* PWW, 33:286–87.

171 *Tumulty stayed behind:* PWW, 33:470.

171 *Edith's curiosity about Woodrow's work:* PWW, 34:78.

171 *Woodrow assured her:* PWW, 34:210, 212; Phyllis Lee Levin, *Edith and Woodrow,* 100.

171 *The first was an engagement:* PWW, 33:458n1.

171 *three small* Washington Post *items:* July 5, 11, and 30, 1915.

172 *"as we sped down the driveway":* EBW, *My Memoir,* 73–74.

CHAPTER 17: *Dodging Trouble*

173 *Tender letters:* PWW, 34:72–77, 90–91, 126–27.

173 *The day after:* PWW, 34:76.

174 *"Dear Tiger":* PWW, 34:480.

174 *Woodrow missed:* PWW, 34:118.

174 *He kept her up to date:* PWW, 34:91, 124.

174 *"I felt so queer":* PWW, 34:194–195.

174 *The tallies made:* "Summing Up a Year of Slaughter," *Literary Digest* 51, no. 7 (Aug. 14, 1915): 281–85; *Washington Post,* Aug. 8, 1915.

174 *The kaiser took the occasion: Boston Globe,* Aug. 1, 1915.

174 *In an exchange of telegrams: Times* (London), Aug. 5, 1915.

174 *The Russians: Baltimore Sun,* Aug. 2, 1915; *New York Times,* Aug. 1, 1915.

174 *Pope Benedict XV:* "Pope Benedict's Anniversary Plea for Peace," *Current History* 2, no. 6 (Sept. 1915): 1022–24.

174 *Enraged: FRUS, 1915, Supplement,* 52–53; *Nation* 101, no. 2617 (Aug. 26, 1915): 254.

174 *To the English author H. G. Wells:* H. G. Wells, "Civilization at the Breaking Point," *New York Times,* May 27, 1915.

174 *Woodrow Wilson had had similar thoughts: WWLL: Neutrality,* 73–74.

175 *"At the end":* PWW, 34:202.

175 *Insisting once again: FRUS, 1915, Supplement,* 480–82.

175 *The kaiser covered his copy:* Link, *Wilson: The Struggle for Neutrality,* 448–49.

175 *On August 19:* Ibid., 565; "The Attack on the Arabic," *Literary Digest* 51, no. 9 (Aug. 28, 1915): 387.

175 *In a plaintive letter:* PWW, 34:271–72.

175   *"In view of what has been said":* PWW, 34:298–99.

175   *When* Arabic *survivors reported:* "The Attack on the Arabic," 387.

176   *On September 1:* Link, *Wilson: The Struggle for Neutrality,* 585.

176   *With that, the crisis seemed to be over:* PWW, 34:407.

176   *The first was set:* FRUS, 1915, Supplement, 932–33; FRUS, The Lansing Papers, 1:81–82.

176   *Lansing informed:* FRUS, 1915, Supplement, 933–34, 941; PWW, 34:503.

176   *Dumba's covert operation:* Dumba's contributions to the Central Powers' espionage and sabotage are detailed in Václav Horcicka, "On the Brink of War: The Crisis Year of 1915 in Relations Between the US and Austria-Hungary," *Diplomacy and Statecraft* 19 (2008):187–209.

176   *Huerta, who had been living in Spain:* Fascinated by the ex-dictator, reporters often sought him out after his arrival in the United States. My account of his activities in New York is based on newspaper stories in the *Washington Post* (April 13 and May 3, 1915), *Chicago Tribune* (April 13, 1915), *Los Angeles Times* (April 26, 1915), *Christian Science Monitor* (May 6, 1915), *New York Times* (May 14, 1915), and *New-York Tribune* (June 11, 1915).

177   *When Huerta appealed to the German embassy:* PWW, 34:56.

177   *"Did you ever hear anything more amazing?":* PWW, 34:74.

177   *Rintelen lasted only a few months:* Link, *Wilson: The Struggle for Neutrality,* 562.

177   *And before they were deported:* John Price Jones and Paul Merrick Hollister, *The German Secret Service in America* (Boston: Small, Maynard, 1918), 60–70, 155, 157–62.

177   *As the one who approved:* Ibid., 1–19; Horcicka, "On the Brink of War: The Crisis Year of 1915 in Relations Between the US and Austria-Hungary," 198–99.

177   *With no hard evidence:* RL, Confidential Memoranda, Oct. 10, 1915, RL Papers, Princeton.

177   *The second wildfire: Wall Street Journal,* Aug. 26, 1915; "The Cotton-Contraband Controversy," *Literary Digest* 51, no. 8 (Aug. 21, 1915): 341–42.

177   *Weeks before the change:* FRUS, 1915, Supplement, 192–93.

177   *When Bernstorff's spies:* PWW, 34:123.

178   *"What crude blunderers they are!":* PWW, 34:142.

178   *Secretary McAdoo lost no time:* PWW, 34:275–80, 421–23.

178   *Wilson acquiesced:* PWW, 34:329.

178   *"The government has no power":* PWW, 34:503–4.

179   *By the time:* American private lending to the Allies is well covered in Kathleen Burk, "The Diplomacy of Finance: British Financial Missions to the United States, 1914–1918," *The Historical Journal* 22, no. 2 (June 1979): 351–72; John Milton Cooper, Jr., "The Command of Gold Reversed: American Loans to Britain, 1915–1917," *Pacific Historical Review* 45, no. 2 (May 1976): 209–30; Richard W. Van Alstyne, "Private American Loans to the Allies, 1914–1916," *Pacific Historical Review* 2, no. 2 (June 1933): 180–93.

179   *Bryan protested: New York Times,* Sept. 21, 1915.

179 *Senator Robert M. La Follette:* Ibid., Sept. 20, 1915.

179 *Others who opposed:* John W. Burgess: "Effects of the Half-Billion-Dollar Loan on America's Future," *Current Opinion* 59, no. 5 (Nov. 1915): 304.

179 *A senator: Washington Post,* Sept. 17, 1915; *Wall Street Journal,* Sept. 18, 1915.

179 *Colonel House would soon complain:* EMH Diary, EMH Papers, Nov. 22, 1915.

179 *The* Hesperian: *FRUS, 1915, Supplement,* 533–35.

180 *"We are not trying to keep out of trouble": PWW,* 35:49.

180 *But he knew: PWW,* 34:473–74.

180 *"My chief puzzle": PWW,* 34:493.

180 *"I have never seen a man": PWW,* 34:508.

180 *Twenty-seven years old: PWW,* 31:514; Phyllis Lee Levin, *Edith and Woodrow,* 135.

181 *When she mentioned the difficulty: PWW,* 34:412–13, 469.

181 *Over lunch: PWW,* 34:507–8.

181 *Dr. Grayson delivered the message:* EBW, *My Memoir,* 75–77.

181 *Woodrow, made physically ill:* Starling and Sugrue, *Starling of the White House,* 52.

181 *"Thank God there is such a* woman": *PWW,* 34:492.

181 *"A new chapter": PWW,* 34:494.

181 *Years later, after Wilson left office:* Dean Mathey, a Princeton trustee, told the story to Henry W. Bragdon, who interviewed many of Wilson's associates for his biography, *Woodrow Wilson: The Academic Years.* Mathey attributed it to Gene Watson, a reporter for *Munsey's Magazine.* According to Mathey, Watson spoke with Mary Hulbert in 1923, after he was shown the correspondence between her and Wilson, which she tried unsuccessfully to publish. Bragdon did not use the story in his book but preserved it in his interview files. Henry W. Bragdon Papers.

181 *After his death:* Mary Allen Hulbert, "The Woodrow Wilson I Knew," *Liberty* 1, no. 40 (Feb. 7, 1925): 23–26.

182 *To Agent Starling:* Starling and Sugrue, *Starling of the White House,* 52–53, 55–56.

182 *Woodrow and Edith were married:* Irwin Hood Hoover, *Forty-two Years in the White House,* 75; Starling and Sugrue, *Starling of the White House,* 61–62.

CHAPTER 18: *The World Is on Fire*

184 *A British liner: PWW,* 35:41920.

184 *"The man who, without rattling a sword":* Knock, *To End All Wars,* 61.

184 *Surprisingly: PWW,* 35:422.

185 *The Wilsons reached the White House:* WHU Diary, Jan. 4, 1916; EBW, *My Memoir,* 89–90.

185 *By ten o'clock: PWW,* 35:424.

185 *Her house would soon go up for sale:* EBW, *My Memoir,* 89.

185 *Mrs. Wilson would have none of the leisure:* Ibid., 89–91.

185 *At her White House debut: Washington Post,* Jan. 15, 1916; *Baltimore Sun,* Jan. 22, 1916; *New York Times,* Jan. 22 and 26, 1916.

186 *Two weeks after: PWW,* 35:492–94.

186 *The reports were not reassuring:* Lindley M. Garrison, "An Outline of the Proposed Military Policy," Nov. 1, 1915, Garrison Papers, Princeton; "America Unready," *Literary Digest* 50, no. 23 (June 5, 1915): 1314–16; "The Atlantic Fleet in 1915: Letter from the Secretary of the Navy," 64th Cong., 1st Sess., Senate, Document No. 251, Jan. 25, 1916.

186 *With recommendations: PWW,* 35:298–300, 305–6.

186 *Most Americans cast:* "Outline for Debate," *Literary Digest* 52, no. 9 (Feb. 26, 1916): 509–10.

186 *The Southern wing:* Link, *Wilson: Confusions and Crises,* 46–47, 51.

186 *"joyriding with the jingoes": Chicago Tribune,* Feb. 19, 1916; Knock, *To End All Wars,* 61.

187 *Tumulty advised Wilson: PWW,* 35:492-94; Blum, *Joe Tumulty and the Wilson Era,* 102–5.

187 *On his first outing: PWW,* 36:8–11.

187 *In a show of nonpartisanship: New York Times,* Jan. 31, 1916.

187 *Those afraid: PWW,* 36:27, 29.

187 *"The world is on fire": PWW,* 36:31–32.

187 *From the rear platform: PWW,* 36:54, 56–57, 76, 80.

187 *At Kansas City: PWW,* 36:104–5, 109–10.

188 *Topeka: New-York Tribune,* Feb. 3, 1916.

188 *More than 100,000 people:* Crowd estimates varied from 250,000 (*Christian Science Monitor,* Feb. 4, 1916) to 1,000,000 (*New York Times,* Feb. 4, 1916).

188 *"gained in every way": New-York Tribune,* Feb. 4, 1916.

188 *The first casualties:* Millis, *Road to War,* 256; *WWLL: Facing War,* 31–37.

188 *"I never go to bed without realizing":* White, *Woodrow Wilson,* 290.

189 *Questions from the twelve reporters:* Rodney Bean, "President Among the People," *World's Work* 31, no. 6 (April 1916): 610–12.

189 *Wilson never mastered: PWW,* 50:xvii–xx.

189 *"Deliver me from a man":* Starling and Sugrue, *Starling of the White House,* 52–53.

189 *For months Sir Edward Grey: IPCH,* 2:88-89.

190 *It was said of Colonel House: IPCH,* 1:93

190 *"master-stroke of diplomacy": IPCH,* 2:85.

190 *"It has occurred to me": IPCH,* 2:90–91.

190 *Wilson inserted a "probably": PWW,* 35:80–82.

191 *"what to say in London": PWW,* 35:382.

191 *The United States was concerned: PWW,* 35:387–88.

191 *House moved from capital to capital:* After House's visit to Paris, Paul Cambon, French ambassador to Britain and brother of the secretary general of the French Foreign Ministry, wrote his son, "At bottom, I think House came

simply to demand that the English and French press save his president by not embarrassing him at the opening of the campaign for the presidency. Wilson, puritan, professor, disinterested, detached to all appearances, is no more than a candidate whose policy consists of pussyfooting in order not to lose a vote." (Paul Cambon, *Correspondance, 1870–1924* [Paris: B. Grasset, 1940–46], 3:99.) The British had concluded as much a year earlier. When Sir Francis Bertie, His Majesty's ambassador to France, met the colonel in Paris in 1915, he wrote in his diary, "He [House] is, I understand, looking around to see what opportunity the president may find for proposing peace, and so securing the German vote for a second presidential election." (Lady Algernon Gordon Lennox, ed., *The Diary of Lord Bertie of Thame* [London: Hodder & Stoughton, 1924], 1:130.)

191 *"the Empty House"*: Link, *Wilson: Confusions and Crises*, 129.

191 *"His mind"*: Devlin, *Too Proud to Fight*, 462.

191 *"and give a blessing"*: Hendrick, *The Life and Letters of Walter H. Page*, 2:222–23.

191 *House had been in London*: EMH Diary, EMH Papers, Jan. 15, 1916; Grey, *Twenty-five Years*, 2:129–30.

191 *As Page reminded House*: EMH Diary, EMH Papers, Jan. 7, 1916.

192 *"we should be ready"*: PWW, 35:488.

192 *In Berlin*: Doerries, *Imperial Challenge*, 136; "President Wilson's Peace-Plan," *Literary Digest* 52, no. 24 (June 10, 1916): 1685.

192 *Arthur Zimmermann*: Grew, *Turbulent Era*, 1:220; FRUS, *1916, Supplement*, 153.

192 *House, taking the praise at face value*: EMH Diary, EMH Papers, Jan. 29, 1916.

192 *In Paris*: EMH Diary, EMH Papers, Jan. 11, 1916; Link, *Wilson: Confusions and Crises*, 123; PWW, 36:126n.

193 *During his final talk*: Recording the promises he had made in France, House took the unusual step of underscoring his words: "In the event the Allies are successful during the next few months I promised that the President would not intervene. In the event they are losing ground, I promised the President would intervene." EMH Diary, EMH Papers, Feb. 7, 1916; PWW, 36:138.

193 *"Then you would wipe out Turkey?"*: EMH Diary, EMH Papers, Feb. 7 and 14, 1916; PWW, 36:148–50.

193 *On his way back to London*: EMH Diary, EMH Papers, Feb. 8, 1916.

193 *In Boulogne*: EMH Diary, EMH Papers, Feb. 2, 1916; PWW, 36:147–51.

193 *"I wish I had"*: EMH Diary, EMH Papers, Jan. 19, 1916.

193 *He also complained*: EMH Diary, EMH Papers, Jan. 10, 14, and 15, 1916.

194 *Nor did the colonel trust*: Devlin, *Too Proud to Fight*, 436.

194 *The enlargement of the cast*: Cooper, *Walter Hines Page*, 326–28; EMH Diary, EMH Papers, Jan. 19, 1916.

194 *Shocked to learn*: Hendrick, *The Life and Letters of Walter H. Page*, 281–82; EMH Diary, EMH Papers, Feb. 9 and 11, 1916.

194 *"I do not believe"*: PWW, 36:181–82.

194 *the House-Grey Memorandum*: PWW, 36:180n2.

195 *House reported to the White House*: PWW, 36:262–63.

195 *Wilson made only one change:* PWW, 36:266. Devlin, *Too Proud to Fight,* 436–37, reproduces the text of the memorandum with Wilson's "probably."

195 *Some historians have taken:* A. J. P. Taylor, *The Struggle for the Mastery of Europe* (New York: Oxford University Press, 1954), 554n1.

195 *while others have argued:* Bailey, *A Diplomatic History of the American People,* 636.

196 *He told Spring Rice and Jusserand:* Link, *Wilson: Confusions and Crises,* 137–38; Jusserand to Paris, March 31, 1916, Papiers Jusserand.

196 *"The life I am leading":* EMH Diary, EMH Papers, March 10, 1916.

CHAPTER 19: *Stumbling in the Dark*

197 *"red-letter days":* EBW, *My Memoir,* 95–96.

198 *Among the items:* C. H. Cramer, *Newton D. Baker: A Biography* (Cleveland: World, 1961), 23, 77–81.

198 *"Would you accept":* PWW, 36:251.

198 *Wilson saw Baker at ten o'clock: Washington Post,* March 9, 1916.

198 *Baker surrendered:* Palmer, *Newton D. Baker,* 1:25.

198 *Secretary Daniels: Washington Post,* March 10, 1916.

198 *Asked to choose one:* Palmer, *Newton D. Baker,* 1:9.

198 *Pancho Villa:* PWW, 36:280n1.

199 *The Mexican Revolution:* Robert Lansing, July 11, 1915, Confidential Memoranda, RL Papers, Princeton; Katz, *The Secret War in Mexico,* 328–29.

199 *punitive expedition:* Ellery C. Stowell, *Intervention in International Law* (Washington, D.C.: John Byrne, 1921), 41–42.

199 *On March 15: New York Times,* March 16, 1916. In his official report on the expedition, Pershing wrote that he left Columbus with 4,800 men plus 192 officers. (Walter Johnson, ed., *Selected Letters of William Allen White,* 204–5.)

199 *Within two weeks:* Palmer, *Newton D. Baker,* 1:15–18.

199 *Carranza was deeply unhappy:* FRUS, *1916,* 493, 505–9, 513, 521–22, 530.

199 *and on April 12:* FRUS, *1916,* 520–21, 526; Welsome, *The General and the Jaguar,* 213–19.

199 *Villa was still on the loose:* Welsome, *The General and the Jaguar,* 223.

199 *Some of Wilson's cabinet members:* PWW, 36:424-25

199 *Germany had ordered U-boat commanders:* Link, *Wilson: Confusions and Crises,* 227. The decision was made on February 29 and took effect about two weeks later. (Fischer, *Germany's Aims in the First World War,* 287.)

199 *On March 24:* The *Sussex* crisis is comprehensively treated in Link, *Wilson: Confusions and Crises,* 222–29; FRUS, *1916, Supplement,* 215, 218–21, 227–29.

201 *Lansing wanted to set conditions:* PWW, 36:371–73.

201 *"My impressions":* PWW, 36:381–82.

201 *House, who was recuperating:* EMH Diary, EMH Papers, March 20. 1916.

201 *Like Lansing:* Ibid., March 27, 1916.

201 *"He does not seem to realize":* PWW, 36:375.

201 *and Wilson still dreamed:* RL, *War Memoirs of Robert Lansing, Secretary of State,* 137.

201 *He asked House to ask Grey:* PWW, 36:421.

201 *Grey not only rejected:* PWW, 36:511–12.

201 *On April 2:* EMH Diary, EMH Papers, April 2, 1916.

201 *and he now saw cabinet meetings:* EMH Diary, EMH Papers, April 11, 1916.

201 *"Weave the world together":* WWLL: *Facing War,* 239.

202 *House and Lansing had to persevere:* PWW, 36:421–22.

202 *House went home that night and returned on April 11:* PWW, 36:459–63.

202 *"practically an ultimatum":* Los Angeles Times, April 20, 1916.

202 *unless the German government:* FRUS, 1916, Supplement, 232–34.

202 *Lansing was immovable:* RL Papers, 1:552–53.

202 *The message went to Ambassador Gerard:* FRUS, 1916, Supplement, 232–34.

202 *At ten the next morning:* New-York Tribune, April 20, 1916.

203 *"The Government of the United States":* PWW, 36:506–10.

203 *In residence:* Görlitz, ed., *The Kaiser and His Court,* 153–54.

203 *On April 27:* Gerard, *My Four Years in Germany,* 324–46; Grew, *Turbulent Era,* 1:221–41; PWW, 36:613–16.

204 *The State Department had given Gerard:* The Lansing Papers, 1:540–43.

204 *The standoff ended:* PWW, 36:621–26.

204 *Washington promptly rejected:* PWW, 649–51.

204 *"The two countries are stumbling in the dark":* New Republic 7, no. 80 (May 13, 1916): 25.

204 *Colonel House proposed:* IPCH, 2:255–56.

204 *Bernstorff agreed:* Bernstorff, *My Three Years in America,* 257–58.

204 *By the Germans' reckoning:* Katz, *The Secret War in Mexico,* 338.

204 *On May 2:* FRUS, 1916, 523, 527–29, 533–40, 543–45, 547.

205 *"It seems to me":* PWW, 37:57–58; Thomas A. Bailey, "The United States and the Blacklist During the Great War," *Journal of Modern History* 6, no. 1 (March 1934): 15–16.

205 *A crowd of two thousand:* WWLL: *Facing War,* 235.

205 *League to Enforce Peace:* Jessup, *Elihu Root,* 2:376.

205 *"Probably it will be impossible":* HCL, *The Senate and the League of Nations,* 131–32.

205 *"We are participants":* PWW, 37:113–16.

206 The New Republic *hoped:* "Mr. Wilson's Great Utterance," *New Republic* 7, no. 83 (June 3, 1916): 102–4.

CHAPTER 20: *The Mystic Influence of the Stars and Stripes*

207 *Wilson sailed on:* Link, *Wilson: The New Freedom,* 10–15, 212, 434–38.

208 *But Hughes, sequestered on the bench:* Pusey, *Charles Evans Hughes,* 1:323–25.

208 *By four o'clock:* PWW, 37:186.

208 *"weak and vacillating":* New York Times, June 11, 1916.

208 *Like Woodrow Wilson: New York Times,* Aug. 28, 1948.

209 *To one of his Washington neighbors:* Slayden, *Washington Wife,* 279.

209 *Flag Day: PWW,* 37:122–23. June 14 had been chosen because it was the date in 1777 when the Continental Congress decided that the flag of the United States would consist of thirteen red and white stripes and a blue field with a white star for each state. A few states and cities had been honoring the day for years, but Wilson was the first president to call for a national observance, which became law in 1949.

209 *Walter Lippmann:* "The Issues of 1916," *New Republic* 7, no. 83 (June 3, 1916): 107.

209 *"Flag Day was Wilson Day": Washington Post,* June 15, 1916.

209 *Watching her husband:* EBW, *My Memoir,* 101.

210 *After lunch: PWW,* 37:221–25.

210 *And sometime during the day:* J. Bruce Kremer (comp.), *Official Report of the Proceedings of the Democratic National Convention* (June 14–16, 1916), 122–23. The plank was telegraphed to St. Louis on June 14. (*New-York Tribune,* June 15, 1916.)

211 *"We stand for":* Kremer, *Official Report of the Proceedings of the Democratic National Convention,* 14.

212 *"I can't keep the country out of war": WWLL: Facing War,* 258.

212 *The* New York Times *reporter: New York Times,* June 15, 1916. See also E. Neal Claussen, " 'He Kept Us Out of War': Martin H. Glynn's Keynote," *Quarterly Journal of Speech* 52, no. 1 (1966): 23–32.

212 *Next up:* Kremer, *Official Report of the Proceedings of the Democratic National Convention,* 88–90.

213 *Spent:* Link, *Wilson: Campaigns for Progressivism and Peace,* 47; Kremer, *Official Report of the Proceedings of the Democratic National Convention,* 98–99.

213 *The convention moved on:* Kremer, *Official Report of the Proceedings of the Democratic National Convention,* 100–101, 107.

213 *The sordid plank:* Ibid., 122–23.

213 *The platform contained the usual boasts:* Ibid., 128.

213 *Wilson's draft: PWW,* 37:200n3.

213 *The members:* Kremer, *Official Report of the Proceedings of the Democratic National Convention,* 128.

213 *"the splendid diplomatic victories":* Ibid., 130.

213 *"President Wilson has had his day":* "Woodrow Wilson," *New Republic* 7, no. 86 (June 24, 1916): 185–87.

CHAPTER 21: *By a Whisker*

216 *Reasoning that Hughes: IPCH,* 2:358.

216 *Hughes was said to be a progressive:* Walter Johnson, ed., *Selected Letters of William Allen White,* 170–71.

216 *In one of his appeals: PWW,* 38:131.

216 *It was true: WWLL: Facing War,* 263n1.

216 *Although the new party: PWW,* 38:304–5.

216 *Wilson immediately mobilized:* R. B. Johnson, "The Punitive Expedition," 599, 602.

216 *On June 21:* Welsome, *The General and the Jaguar,* 270–78.

216 *"The break": PWW,* 37:281.

217 *Lodge was disturbed:* HCL, *The Senate and the League of Nations,* 22.

217 *The first good news: PWW,* 37:332–36.

217 *The Mexicans soon proposed: FRUS, 1916,* 599–600; Knight, *The Mexican Revolution,* 2:352–53.

218 *a blacklist: PWW,* 37:466–67.

218 *Hughes offered a long critique: New York Times,* Aug. 1, 1916.

218 *The speech was a dud:* Charles Evans Hughes to HCL, Aug. 4, 1916, HCL Papers.

218 *Hughes suffered more serious wounds:* Pusey, *Charles Evans Hughes,* 1:335–49; "Hiram Johnson, the California Progressives, and the Hughes Campaign of 1916," *Pacific Historical Review* 31, no. 4 (Nov. 1962): 410.

219 *Wilson began rising at five:* EBW, *My Memoir,* 102.

219 *Apart from a long bout of indigestion:* Weinstein, *Woodrow Wilson,* 305–6.

219 *"Cities will be cut off": PWW,* 38:96–101.

219 *Shadow Lawn:* EMH Diary, EMH Papers, June 22, 1916; EBW, *My Memoir,* 103–4.

219 *The president recited: PWW,* 38:126–39.

220 *Campaign donations:* Link, *Wilson: Campaigns for Progressivism and Peace,* 99–100.

220 *and Hughes lit into Wilson: Washington Post,* Sept. 5, 1916.

220 *Wilson parried: PWW,* 38:217.

220 *Edith, who was resolutely old-fashioned:* Kristie Miller, *Ellen and Edith,* 127.

220 *Woodrow had not only authored:* Christine A. Lunardini and Thomas J. Knock, "Woodrow Wilson and Woman Suffrage: A New Look," *Political Science Quarterly* 95, no. 4 (Winter 1980–1981): 661.

220 *But in early August: New York Times,* Aug. 2, 1916.

220 *there were ninety-one:* Lunardini and Knock, "Woodrow Wilson and Woman Suffrage: A New Look," 661–62.

220 *But Wilson held back: PWW,* 37:529.

221 *In hopes of persuading: PWW,* 38:161–64.

221 *The optimists: PWW,* 38:170, 173–74.

222 *Wilson also suffered:* Link, *Wilson: Campaigns for Progressivism and Peace,* 97; *PWW,* 38:176.

222 *Mary Allen Hulbert: Washington Post,* April 18, 1999; Kristie Miller, *Ellen and Edith,* 141–42 and 302n31.

222 *Wilson's tribulations:* Oswald Garrison Villard, "The Mystery of Woodrow Wilson," *North American Review* 204, no. 730 (Sept. 1916): 362–72. The magazine was owned and edited by another Wilson ally-turned-antagonist, George Harvey.

222 *"It is a matter of frequent comment"*: Creel, *Wilson and the Issues*, 160–61.

222 *Creel was not entirely wrong*: Creel wrote the book at high speed in the midst of carrying out a long list of other campaign chores. See Creel, *Rebel at Large*, 153.

223 *The Democrats put William Jennings Bryan*: PWW, 38:280, 372.

223 *Omaha: Baltimore Sun*, Oct. 6, 1916; PWW, 38:531, 541.

224 *The combination*: Knock, *To End All Wars*, 93–95.

224 *Hughes rejected: New York Times*, Oct. 27, 1916.

224 *Sometimes he talked over the heads: New York Times*, Oct. 10, 1916.

224 *After proudly committing*: Ibid., Sept. 9, 1916.

224 *Theodore Roosevelt spent a month*: Pusey, *Charles Evans Hughes*, 1:364.

224 *"the bearded iceberg"*: Morison and Blum, eds., *Letters of Theodore Roosevelt*, 8:1055, 1078, 1115.

225 *Hughes grew increasingly irritated*: PWW, 38:349.

225 *The last foreign crisis*: Wellington Long, "The Cruise of the *U-53*," *U.S. Naval Institute Proceedings*, October 1966, 91–92.

225 *Wilson met twice*: Link, *Wilson: Campaigns for Progressivism and Peace*, 113–14.

225 *When Ambassador Jusserand*: PWW, 38:409.

225 *The British found it galling*: Long, "The Cruise of the *U-53*," 94.

226 *Ambassador Page asked*: FRUS, 1916, *Supplement*, 780–83.

226 *Roosevelt, blaming: New York Times*, Oct. 19, 1916.

226 *"and if it is wrong"*: PWW, 38:306.

226 *Infuriated by such extrapolations: New York Times*, Oct. 16, 1916.

226 *"I am a man of peace": New-York Tribune*, Oct. 15, 1916.

226 *In the last days of October: Baltimore Sun*, Oct. 28, 1916; *New York Times*, Oct. 27, 1916.

226 *the Democrats were loudly predicting: Washington Post*, Oct. 23 and 28, 1916; *Chicago Tribune*, Nov. 4, 1916.

227 *Black voters felt abandoned*: Moorfield Storey, "President Wilson's Administration," *Yale Review* 5, no. 3 (April 1916): 464–65; *Afro-American* (Baltimore), Nov. 4, 1916.

227 *Hughes had met: Afro-American* (Baltimore), Oct. 28, 1916; Lewis, *W. E. B. Du Bois*, 522–23.

227 *At Madison Square Garden*: PWW, 38:597–602.

227 *Roosevelt lamented: New-York Tribune*, Nov. 4, 1916.

228 *The Democrats made one last appeal*: WWLL: *Facing War*, 294.

228 *In his turn: New York Times*, Nov. 5, 1916.

228 *Wilson had the last word*: PWW, 38:608–15.

228 *"Again and again"*: PWW, 38:617–18; RL, *War Memoirs of Robert Lansing, Secretary of State*, 164; Link, *Wilson: Campaigns for Progressivism and Peace*, 154–55.

229 *"It required 16 men": Trenton Evening Times*, Nov. 7, 1916.

229 *Hughes, who was at the Astor Hotel*: "Why Wilson Won," *Literary Digest* 53 (Nov. 18, 1916): 1313; Pusey, *Charles Evans Hughes*, 1:360.

229 *Nor was Joe Tumulty*: JPT, *Woodrow Wilson as I Know Him*, 217–18.

230 *At five the next morning:* Starling and Sugrue, *Starling of the White House,* 76–78.

230 *The* World *hailed it: New York World,* Nov. 9, 1916.

230 *"we can settle down in soberness": PWW,* 38:626.

230 *The popular vote:* S.D. Lovell, *The Presidential Election of 1916.* Carbondale: Southern Illinois University Press, 60–61, 111, 156.

230 *Jeannette Rankin:* "Woman's Hand in the Election," *Literary Digest* 53 (Nov. 18, 1916): 1315. Among the suffrage states, only Oregon and Illinois voted for Hughes.

231 *To an English friend:* HCL to James Bryce, Dec. 21, 1916, HCL Papers.

231 *"yellow":* Walter Johnson, ed., *Selected Letters of William Allen White,* 172–74.

231 *"What we're electing":* Steel, *Walter Lippmann and the American Century,* 105–6.

CHAPTER 22: *Verge of War*

232 *Edith and Woodrow:* EBW, *My Memoir,* 119; *PWW,* 38:649, 40:170; *WWLL: Facing War,* 368.

232 *Just before the election: WWLL: Facing War,* 301, 364; *PWW,* 38:607–8; "The German Submarine Record," *Current History* 5, no. 6 (March 1917): 996.

233 *The kaiser still sided: PWW,* 40:141–46.

233 *Wilson, fearing the worst: PWW,* 38:645–47.

233 *"was unusually late": PWW,* 38:656–57.

234 *The president slept all afternoon:* EBW, *My Memoir,* 120–21.

234 *House mentioned: PWW,* 38:656–60.

234 *his 1916 State of the Union address: PWW,* 40:155–59.

234 *Sending his regrets to House: PWW,* 40:62.

234 *Excused from his trip: PWW,* 40:67–70.

235 *Knowing that Wilson's request was pointless: PWW,* 40:190–91.

235 *Wilson replied on Saturday: PWW,* 40:197–200.

235 *On Sunday:* "The President's Attitude Toward Great Britain and Its Dangers," September 1916, Confidential Memoranda, RL Papers, Princeton; *PWW,* 40:209.

235 *Chancellor Bethmann Hollweg:* Görlitz, ed., *The Kaiser and His Court,* 222; *FRUS, 1916, Supplement,* 94.

236 *"Having made up his mind":* RL, *War Memoirs of Robert Lansing, Secretary of State,* 183–84.

236 *The note went off: FRUS, 1916, Supplement,* 97–99.

236 *David Lloyd George:* Scott, ed., *The Declaration of London,* 16–20.

236 *Georges Clemenceau: New York Times,* Dec. 23 and 24, 1916.

237 *"I mean by that":* Ibid., Dec. 22, 1916.

237 *Called to the White House:* RL, *War Memoirs of Robert Lansing, Secretary of State,* 186–88.

237 *"I do not think we can continue this uncertain state": PWW,* 40:313–14.

237 *Wilson's admirers:* e.g., Link, *Wilson: Campaigns for Progressivism and Peace,* 223–24.

237 *He tried to sort it out:* Jusserand to Paris, Dec. 21, 1916, Papiers Jusserand.

237 *Statue of Liberty: Washington Post,* Dec. 3, 1916.

238 *The guests applauded:* Jusserand, *Le Sentiment Américain pendant la Guerre,* 83–84.

238 *Wilson spoke last: PWW,* 40:119–21.

238 *To Ambassador Jusserand, it sounded:* Jusserand, *Le Sentiment Américain pendant la Guerre,* 85.

238 *"He lives enveloped in mystery":* Gwynn, ed., *Letters and Friendships of Sir Cecil Spring Rice,* 2:368

238 *In short order: PWW,* 40:331, 439–41.

238 *Wilson was undaunted:* RL, *War Memoirs of Robert Lansing, Secretary of State,* 193.

238 *"We are the only one": PWW,* 40:409.

239 *By January 10: PWW,* 41:55.

239 *"a noble document": PWW,* 40:445.

239 *In the course of his conversation with House: PWW,* 40:445.

239 *Serving as Wilson's secretary of state:* Gwynn, ed., *Letters and Friendships of Sir Cecil Spring Rice,* 2:366.

239 *diabetes:* Thomas Henry Hartig, "Robert Lansing: An Interpretive Biography" (PhD diss., Ohio State University, 1974), Appendix B: Robert Lansing's Health, 337–41.

239 *Lansing thought it unseemly:* RL, *War Memoirs of Robert Lansing, Secretary of State,* 193–94; *PWW,* 40:447.

240 *Tumulty did not know of his plans:* Towne, *Senator William J. Stone and the Politics of Compromise,* 201.

240 *Word of Wilson's address:* Except where otherwise noted, the account of Wilson's speech and the reaction to it is based on the coverage and commentary in the *New York Times, New-York Tribune,* and *Washington Post,* Jan. 23 and 24, 1917. The text of Wilson's speech is in *PWW,* 40:533–39.

241 *The French praised Wilson: Baltimore Sun,* Jan. 24, 1917.

241 *"peace without revenge":* Lawrence, *The True Story of Woodrow Wilson,* 190.

241 *"peace without conquest": PWW,* 40:531–32.

241 *The British felt:* Scott, ed., *The Declaration of London,* 58.

241 *Berlin dismissed: Chicago Tribune,* Jan. 30, 1917.

241 *Vienna took his talk: New York Times,* Jan. 30, 1917.

241 *"The unshakable will to victory":* Ibid., Jan. 28, 1917.

241 *Theodore Roosevelt scoffed:* Ibid., Jan. 29, 1917.

241 *Perhaps the warring world ought to believe:* HCL, *War Addresses, 1915–1917,* 252–55, 264–71, 276–78; Widenor, *Henry Cabot Lodge and the Search for an American Foreign Policy,* 257–58, 276–78.

242 *"Father doesn't read any criticisms":* William Sturgis Bigelow to HCL, Feb. 28, 1918, HCL Papers.

242 *"For God's sake":* RL, *War Memoirs of Robert Lansing, Secretary of State,* 206–9.

242 *The German admirals:* May, *The World War and American Isolation, 1914–1917,* 414; Görlitz, ed., *The Kaiser and His Court,* 229–31.

242 *On January 31:* PWW, 41:74–79.

243 *When Lansing finished reading:* RL, *War Memoirs of Robert Lansing, Secretary of State*, 209–12.

243 *Next Lansing summoned:* Ibid., 212–13.

244 *At ten o'clock:* "The Crisis in American Ports," *Current History* 5, no. 6 (March 1917): 997.

244 *House took the overnight train:* PWW, 41:86–89; RL, *War Memoirs of Robert Lansing, Secretary of State*, 214.

244 *"They're just sitting around looking sad":* Starling and Sugrue, *Starling of the White House*, 79.

245 *and Lansing spent the evening:* RL, *War Memoirs of Robert Lansing, Secretary of State*, 214–15.

245 *He wrote of "wanton slaughter":* PWW, 41:96–99.

245 *"It amounts to a frank declaration":* PWW, 41:99–100.

245 *The cabinet met at two-thirty:* Houston, *Eight Years with Wilson's Cabinet*, 1:229–30.

245 *Wilson closed the cabinet meeting:* PWW, 41:116.

245 *Wilson went straight to the Capitol:* Towne, *Senator William J. Stone and the Politics of Compromise*, 205–7.

246 *The president left the senators: Baltimore Sun*, Feb. 3, 1917.

246 *On Saturday morning:* Link, *Wilson: Campaigns for Progressivism and Peace*, 299.

246 *At twelve-thirty: Washington Post*, Feb. 4, 1917.

246 *On Capitol Hill:* PWW, 41:108–12; *New York Times*, Feb. 4, 1917.

CHAPTER 23: *Decision*

247 *Friday, March 23:* Sparks, ed., *A Many Colored Toga*, 60; biographical details from obituaries published June 1, 1962, in the *New York Times, Los Angeles Times,* and *Chicago Tribune*.

248 *First had come:* Justus D. Doenecke, *Nothing Less Than War: A New History of America's Entry into World War I* (Lexington: University Press of Kentucky, 2011), 257–58.

248 *Harbors on the Atlantic seaboard: Baltimore Sun*, Feb. 17, 1917; *Washington Post*, Feb. 15, 1917.

248 *Shipowners turned to Washington:* RL, *War Memoirs of Robert Lansing, Secretary of State*, 223–24.

248 *In a speech at the Capitol:* PWW, 41:283–87.

249 *The Zimmermann telegram:* Except where otherwise noted, this account is based on RL, "Memorandum on the Message of Zimmermann to the German Minister to Mexico," March 4, 1917, Private Memoranda, RL Papers, Library of Congress. For the text of the Zimmermann telegram, see *FRUS, 1917, Supplement 1, 147*.

249 *Wilson was so outraged:* Tuchman, *The Zimmermann Telegram*, 163–64.

249 *use of the State Department's wires:* Ibid., 126–32, 161, 238–39; Katz, *The Secret War in Mexico*, 373.

249 *A German embassy courier:* Hendrick, *The Life and Letters of Walter H. Page*, 3:339–42.

250 *"Good Lord!":* WWLL: *Facing War*, 479.

250 *Senator Lodge:* Tuchman, *The Zimmermann Telegram*; 161; *New York Times*, March 2, 1917.

250 *The White House and the State Department: Baltimore Sun*, March 2, 1917.

251 *The House reacted:* PWW, 41:318n1.

251 *the Senate: New York Times*, Feb. 28, 1917.

251 *the discussion began:* My account of the filibuster is based on the coverage of the *New York Times*, March 5, 1917, except where otherwise noted.

251 *Wilson's first term also expired:* PWW, 41:331; Starling and Sugrue, *Starling of the White House*, 84–85; *New York Times*, March 5, 1917.

251 *The Wilsons were back at the White House:* PWW, 41:332.

252 *"A little group of willful men":* PWW, 41:318–20.

252 *J. Fred Essary: Baltimore Sun*, March 6, 1917.

252 *The Wilsons traveled to the Capitol: New-York Tribune*, March 6, 1917.

252 *It seemed to the reporters: New York Times* and *Washington Post*, March 6, 1917.

252 *The inaugural subcommittee: Official Report of the Second Inauguration of Woodrow Wilson, 5 March 1917*, 65th Cong., 1st Sess., Senate Document 116, 117ff.

252 *Chief Justice Edward Douglass White:* Inauguration details from *The Washington Post*, March 6, 1917.

252 *but his inaugural address was a disappointment:* PWW, 41:332–35.

253 *"This is not a time":* PWW, 41:357.

253 *In the evening:* PWW, 41:341, 358.

253 *By the next morning: New York Times*, March 7, 1917, and *New-York Tribune*, March 8, 1917.

253 *La Follette was hanged in effigy: Washington Post*, March 9, 1917.

253 *Wilson regretted:* WWLL: *Facing War*, 483.

253 *he took to his bed:* PWW, 41:359, 364, 381; EBW, *My Memoir*, 130–32; WWLL: *Facing War*, 5:487–88.

254 *Woodrow clung to Edith:* PWW, 41:466, 473–74.

254 *In her diary:* EBW, *My Memoir*, 131; WWLL: *Facing War*, 5:487–88.

254 *and in 1917 he became the first to recognize:* FRUS, *1917*, 1207–11.

254 *The final blow:* RL, *War Memoirs*, 233; PWW, 41:429–30.

255 *A few hours after seeing Lansing:* John L. Heaton, *Cobb of the World* (New York: E. P. Dutton, 1924), 269–70. Cobb took no notes during the interview but years later shared his recollections of it with two associates. The words presented as verbatim quotes from Wilson come from the associates' notes. Cobb remembered that the interview took place in the wee hours of April 2, the day Wilson asked Congress for a declaration of war, but it actually occurred at three-thirty on the afternoon of March 19, a few hours after Lansing made his impassioned plea for war. (Link, *Wilson: Campaigns for Progressivism and Peace*, 399n33.)

255 *Lansing brooded all day:* RL, *War Memoirs of Robert Lansing, Secretary of State*, 234–36.

255 *The president shook hands:* Unless otherwise noted, the details come from *PWW*, 41:436–45.

257 *Next morning, on his way out: PWW*, 41:446, 448–49.

257 *"the United States and the German empire": Washington Post,* March 22, 1917.

257 *"Apparently": PWW,* 41:448–49.

257 *The cabinet saw a self-righteous version: PWW,* 41:484.

257 *"President said it offended him": PWW,* 41:541.

257 *House happened to be on hand: PWW,* 41:482–83.

258 *Wilson had often complained: PWW,* 41:506.

258 *Wilson lit into him: PWW,* 41:515.

258 *Wilson's anxiety:* Starling and Sugrue, *Starling of the White House,* 85.

258 *On Sunday morning:* EBW, *My Memoir,* 132.

258 *"it contains all": PWW,* 41:528-29.

259 *The Wilsons, accompanied by Grayson: PWW,* 41:531–32.

259 *The Capitol:* EBW, *My Memoir,* 132.

259 *He began with a review: PWW,* 41:519–27.

260 *"the finest tribute":* RL, *War Memoirs,* 242.

260 *"Mr. Wilson, you have expressed": New York Times,* April 3, 1917.

261 *"Think what it was":* JPT, *Woodrow Wilson as I Know Him,* 256. Arthur Link had doubts about Tumulty's account of the conversation (Link, *Wilson: Campaigns for Progressivism and Peace,* 427), but the next day Wilson spoke to Daniels in a similar vein. As Daniels summarized Wilson's remarks in his diary, "Told me applause in Capitol grated on him because he felt the gravity & seriousness of the situation & the necessity make applause far from his feeling." (*PWW,* 41:541.)

261 *at one o'clock in the afternoon: PWW,* 41:557–58; *WWLL: Facing War,* 516–17; EBW, *My Memoir,* 133.

262 *"When the excitement of these days is forgotten":* Sparks, ed., *A Many Colored Toga,* 57.

CHAPTER 24: *The Associate*

263 *As soon as the United States declared war:* RL, *War Memoirs,* 272.

263 *Wilson gave his consent: PWW,* 42:14; Seymour, *American Diplomacy During the World War* (Hamden, Conn.: Archon, 1964), 217.

264 *Spring Rice alerted London:* Gwynn, ed., *The Letters and Friendships of Sir Cecil Spring Rice,* 2:391–93.

264 *Arthur Balfour: PWW,* 42:123, 140.

264 *Balfour was invited: PWW,* 42:155–57. The terms of the secret treaties are outlined in Samuel Flagg Bemis, *The United States as a World Power: A Diplomatic History, 1900–1950* (New York: Henry Holt, 1950), 151–53.

265 *Balfour and House had supper with the Wilsons:* EBW, *My Memoir,* 137.

265 *(He never thought about them in bed):* Devlin, *Too Proud to Fight,* 274–76.

265 *Wilson seemed unable to relax: PWW,* 42:171–72.

265 *Wilson and Lansing knew next to nothing:* Bemis, *The United States as a World Power,* 150–51.

266 *The discussions of territorial adjustments:* Kathleen Burk, "The Diplomacy of Finance: British Financial Missions to the United States 1914–1918," *Historical Journal* 22, no. 2 (June 1979): 234.

266 *"war-weary, jangled, nervous":* WGM, *Crowded Years,* 373, 378–79, 392–95.

266 *In meetings with Secretary Daniels:* Sims, *The Victory at Sea,* 5–11.

266 *"Ships and ships and then more ships":* Cronon, ed., *The Cabinet Diaries of Josephus Daniels,* 140–44.

266 *When the British recommended:* Burk, "The Diplomacy of Finance: British Financial Missions to the United States 1914–1918," 234–35.

266 *The ships had been seized:* *New York Times,* April 7 and May 6, 1917; *Christian Science Monitor,* April 24, 1917; *Baltimore Sun,* May 9, 1917.

266 *The French delegates:* Robert D. Bruce, "America Embraces France: Marshal Joffre and the French Mission to the United States," *Journal of Military History* 66, no. 2 (April 2002): 407–41.

267 *Marshal Joseph Joffre:* Historians would question Joffre's heroism, intelligence, and devotion to his troops. See Barnett Singer, "Mon Général: The Case of Joseph Joffre," *American Scholar* 65, no. 4 (Autumn 1996): 593–99.

267 *By 1917, France had lost:* Bruce, "America Embraces France: Marshal Joffre and the French Mission to the United States," 416, 429.

267 *He decided to approach:* Ibid., 417; Elizabeth Greenhalgh, "The Viviani-Joffre Mission to the United States, April–May 1917: A Reassessment," *French Historical Studies* 35, no. 4 (Fall 2012): 644–45, 653.

267 *Joffre was acting:* Pierre Lesoeuf, "La mission du maréchal Joffre aux États-Unis au moment de leur entrée en guerre," http://www.institut-strategie.fr/ihcc _eu1gm_Lesouef.html#, accessed October 22, 2017.

267 *After meetings with the War Department:* PWW, 42:186–91.

268 *The question of sending volunteers:* Morison and Blum, eds., *Letters of Theodore Roosevelt,* 8:947–48; O'Toole, *When Trumpets Call,* 300, 305–7, 309, 310–13.

268 *A newspaper poll:* In the House, 218 members favored the bill, 186 opposed it, and 28 were undecided. In the Senate, 40 senators were in favor, 38 opposed, 18 undecided. Greenhalgh, "The Viviani-Joffre Mission to the United States, April–May 1917: A Reassessment," 650n97.

268 *Joffre agreed:* Bruce, "America Embraces France: Marshal Joffre and the French Mission to the United States," 423.

268 *The British did not object:* John Whiteclay Chambers II, *To Raise an Army: The Draft Comes to Modern America* (New York: Free Press, 1987), 146–47; Palmer, *Newton D. Baker,* 1:152–53; PWW, 42:192, 202.

268 *Wilson privately promised:* IPCH, 3:58–59; PWW, 42:191.

268 *On May 2:* Palmer, *Newton D. Baker,* 1:149–50; 168–69; Smythe, *Pershing,* 8.

269 *"you will be in command":* Ibid., 5.

269 *Pershing had been angling:* Ibid., 4; PWW, 42:225–26, 242.

269 *Pershing's chief rival: PWW,* 40:464; O'Toole, *When Trumpets Call,* 307.

269 *An expeditionary force: PWW,* 42:249–51.

269 *As Pershing told the story:* Smythe, *Pershing,* 6.

269 *In fact:* Palmer, *Newton D. Baker,* 1:170–72.

270 *Conferring with the Allies: PWW,* 42:30; *FRUS, 1918, Russia,* 1:52.

270 *The idea of sending a mission to Russia:* RL, *War Memoirs,* 331–34, *PWW,* 42:43–44, 67.

270 *McAdoo had the excellent idea: PWW,* 42:80, 152.

270 *Root received his presidential summons: New York Times,* April 10, 1917.

270 *"You have no idea":* Jessup, *Elihu Root,* 2:355–56.

271 *Vladimir Lenin:* Neiberg, *Fighting the Great War,* 215.

271 *German soldiers on the Eastern Front began fraternizing: FRUS, 1918, Russia,* 1:139–40; Jessup, *Elihu Root,* 369; Neiberg, *Fighting the Great War,* 215.

271 *A few weeks after filing their report:* Jessup, *Elihu Root,* 2:368.

272 *when he was taken to the White House:* Eisenhower, *Yanks,* 33.

CHAPTER 25: *The Right Men*

273 *A day after:* "Woodrow Wilson: Executive Order 2587A—Federal Employees Removal on Security Grounds," April 7, 1917. Online by Gerhard Peters and John T. Woolley, *The American Presidency Project.* http://www.presidency.ucsb.edu/ws/?pid=75048, accessed Oct. 18, 2017.

273 *No explanation was required:* Stephen Graubard, *Command of Office* (New York: Basic Books, 2004), 150.

273 *but 868 applicants:* Scheiber, *The Wilson Administration and Civil Liberties, 1917–1921,* 17.

274 *"If Wilson and his cabinet":* Frank Freidel, *Franklin D. Roosevelt: The Apprenticeship* (Boston: Little, Brown, 1952), 319.

274 *As commander in chief:* Arthur S. Link and John Whiteclay Chambers II, "Woodrow Wilson as Commander in Chief," in Richard H. Kohn, ed., *The United States Military Under the Constitution of the United States, 1789–1989* (New York: New York University Press, 1991), 324.

274 *"a new thing and a landmark":* Wilson, Proclamation 1370: Conscription, May 18, 1917, http://www.presidency.ucsb.edu/ws/?pid=65403, accessed Aug. 16, 2017.

274 *In the weeks leading up:* Chambers, *To Raise an Army,* 134–36; Palmer, *Newton D. Baker,* 1:184.

274 *The Senate needed:* Livermore, *Politics Is Adjourned,* 19.

275 *In a tirade: New York Times,* April 26, 1917.

275 *Some congressmen insisted:* Palmer, *Newton D. Baker,* 1:193.

275 *The most vehement opposition:* Daniel R. Beaver, *Newton D. Baker and the American War Effort, 1917–1919* (Lincoln: University of Nebraska Press, 1966), 30–31.

275 *The bill's passage:* There is a comprehensive account of the congressional fight over Roosevelt's division in Livermore, *Politics Is Adjourned,* 19–30. Dealings

between Roosevelt and Baker, complete with extensive quotations from their correspondence, appear in Palmer, *Newton D. Baker*, 1:195–206. For Wilson's reaction, see *PWW*, 42:324–26. Roosevelt's efforts to win a place for his division and the French and British reactions to the idea are chronicled in O'Toole, *When Trumpets Call*, 305–7, 310–14.

275 *Baker, fearing a reprise:* Kennedy, *Over Here*, 150–52.

275 *Not that they had a choice:* Wilson, Proclamation 1370: Conscription, May 18, 1917.

275 *The Department of Justice deputized:* Boston Globe, Chicago Tribune, New-York Tribune, San Francisco Chronicle, June 6, 1917.

276 *White planters in the South had opposed conscription:* Chad L. Williams, *Torchbearers of Democracy*, 53.

276 *On the day the Selective Service Act was signed:* PWW, 42:321.

276 *In all:* Ferrell, *Woodrow Wilson and World War I, 1917–1921*, 18; Chambers, *To Raise an Army*, 198.

276 *The job of carrying the troops:* Creel, *Rebel at Large*, 149–50; Lee A. Craig, *Josephus Daniels* (Chapel Hill: University of North Carolina Press, 2013), 367; Link, *Wilson: The New Freedom*, 122–25.

277 *At the urging of the British:* Daniels, *The Wilson Era*, 2:114–15, 121–22; *Annual Report of the Secretary of the Navy, 1918*, 17.

278 *No wartime accomplishment:* Sims, *The Victory at Sea*, 104–5, 144; Daniels, *The Wilson Era*, 2:115.

278 *Hoover spent the first weeks:* Hendrick, *The Life and Letters of Walter H. Page*, 3:215–16.

278 *"the kind of man":* EMH Diary, EMH Papers, May 3, 1917; *PWW*, 42:220.

279 *Hoover would not be a dictator:* PWW, 42:344–46; *New York Times*, June 13, 1917.

279 *Skeptics wondered:* Tom G. Hall, "Wilson and the Food Crisis: Agricultural Price Control During World War I," *Agricultural History* 47, no. 1 (Jan. 1973): 25–40.

279 *Grain reserves in Europe:* Ferrell, *Woodrow Wilson and World War I, 1917–1921*, 91.

279 *Hoover had three ideas:* PWW, 42:481–85.

279 *Edith Wilson signed on:* EBW, *My Memoir*, 136.

279 *Wilson soon came to dread their meetings:* PWW, 46:317.

279 *Yet Hoover was also confident:* Ferrell, *Woodrow Wilson and World War I, 1917–1921*, 94; Helen Zoë Veit, "We Were a Soft People," *Food, Culture and Society* 10, no. 2 (Summer 2007): 178.

280 *"the almoner of starving Belgium":* Daniels, *The Wilson Era*, 2:317; Veit, "We Were a Soft People," 170, 175.

280 *chewing his way through an entire cigar:* Steel, *Walter Lippmann and the American Century*, 123.

280 *The winter of 1917–1918:* December 29, 1917, was an especially brutal day in the Northeast. These stories appeared in the *Washington Post* and *New-York Tribune* on December 30.

280 *There was plenty of coal:* WGM, *Crowded Years,* 452–58.

280 *On December 26:* Ibid., 458–61.

280 *The blizzards: New-York Tribune,* Jan. 15, 1917; *PWW,* 46:12.

281 *But the success came: New York Times,* Feb. 17, 1918.

281 *"Broomstick preparedness":* Stout, ed., *Roosevelt in the Kansas City Star,* 10–12.

281 *Housed in unheated barracks:* Livermore, *Politics Is Adjourned,* 75.

281 *On January 10:* O'Toole, *When Trumpets Call,* 345–46; Livermore, *Politics Is Adjourned,* 79–80, 84–86.

282 *Wilson tried to dissuade Chamberlain: PWW,* 45:566–67.

282 *"The military establishment of America": PWW,* 46:49.

282 *Chamberlain confirmed: PWW,* 46:53–55.

282 *"an astonishing": PWW,* 46:55–56.

282 *The president also summoned:* Livermore, *Politics Is Adjourned,* 89.

282 *Senator William J. Stone: PWW,* 46:64n2.

282 *Lodge reminded Stone: Washington Post,* Jan. 22, 1918.

282 *Chamberlain defended himself: New York Times,* Jan. 25, 1918.

282 *The president, meanwhile: WWLL: War Leader,* 498; Starling and Sugrue, *Starling of the White House,* 103. WHU (Jan. 24–26, 1918) indicates that Wilson spent most of the next three days in his room.

283 *Chamberlain now had the upper hand: New York Times,* Jan. 26, 1918.

283 *A few days later:* Palmer, *Newton D. Baker,* 2:73–77; *Washington Post,* Jan. 29, 1918.

283 *Wilson made his legislative move: New York Times,* Feb. 7, 1918.

283 *Overman's fight: PWW,* 47:109.

283 *Once on the floor: New York Times,* April 3, 1918; *Baltimore Sun,* April 12, 1918.

283 *The impasse ended: New York Times,* April 25, 1918; *New-York Tribune,* March 13 and May 1, 1918.

283 *The Overman Act: New York Times,* April 30 and May 15, 1918; Grosvenor B. Clarkson, *Industrial America in the World War: The Strategy Behind the Line, 1917–1918* (Boston: Houghton Mifflin, 1923), 493–94.

284 *Chamberlain had convened:* Baruch, *Baruch: The Public Years,* 35–40; James Grant, *Bernard Baruch: The Adventures of a Wall Street Legend* (New York: Touchstone, 1983), 173.

284 *The two copper men: New York Times,* March 22, 1917.

284 *Wilson unchained: PWW,* 46:520–22.

284 *Baruch took over the War Industries Board:* Grant, *Bernard Baruch* 176–77.

285 *"Only the armistice":* Paul A. C. Koistinen, "The 'Industrial-Military Complex' in Historical Perspective: World War I," *Business History Review* 41, no. 4 (Winter 1967): 402.

285 *In May 1918:* O'Toole, *When Trumpets Call,* 373–74.

285 *With a team from the Department of Justice:* Pusey, *Charles Evans Hughes,* 1:375–79.

285 *William Howard Taft:* Pringle, *The Life and Times of William Howard Taft,* 2:907, 916–18.

286 *Quickest and most energetic:* WGM, *Crowded Years,* 372–77, 412.

286 *McAdoo had a well-deserved reputation:* Daniels, *The Wilson Era,* 2:38.

286 *That hurdle crossed:* WGM, *Crowded Years,* 378–83.

287 *Launched on May 2: New York Times,* May 3 and 4, 1917; *Washington Post,* May 5, 1917.

287 *McAdoo was not ready to celebrate: New York Times,* May 7, 1917; *Washington Post,* May 12, 1917.

288 *He asked Wilson to issue a proclamation: PWW,* 42:294–95.

288 *and Wilson responded: Washington Post,* June 1, 1917.

288 *Overnight:* WGM, *Crowded Years,* 385.

288 *Post offices began canceling stamps: New York Times,* May 13, 1917.

288 *Women's clubs:* WGM, *Crowded Years,* 385.

288 *The Boy Scouts of America: New York Times,* May 22, 1917.

288 *Department stores:* Ibid., May 18, 1917.

288 *The editors: Afro-American* (Baltimore), May 26, 1917.

288 *Not wanting a penny: New York Times,* May 13, 1917; *New-York Tribune,* May 18, 1917.

288 *it attracted four million investors:* WGM, *Crowded Years,* 391.

288 *By the time the second loan:* Ibid., 373–74.

288 *In all:* Ibid., 412, 414.

289 *A decade later:* John Maurice Clark, *The Costs of the World War to the American People* (New Haven: Yale University Press, 1931), 297.

289 *McAdoo became the scapegoat:* WGM, *Crowded Years,* 415–16.

CHAPTER 26: *One White-Hot Mass Instinct*

290 *The United States had been at war: PWW,* 42:55.

290 *George Creel:* Creel, *Rebel at Large,* 156.

290 *"I know I could":* Stewart Halsey Ross, *Propaganda for War* (Joshua Tree, Calif.: Progressive Press), 2009, 218–19.

291 *"expression, not suppression":* Creel, *Complete Report of the Chairman of the Committee on Public Information, 1917:1918:1919,* 1.

291 *In a preliminary statement:* Committee on Public Information, "Preliminary Statement to the Press of the United States," Washington, D.C.: U.S. Government Printing Office, 1917, 6, 13–15; Creel, *Complete Report of the Chairman of the Committee on Public Information, 1917:1918:1919,* 10–12.

291 *Like Wilson, he was certain:* Creel, *How We Advertised America,* 35.

291 *At Wilson's insistence:* Creel, *Complete Report of the Chairman of the Committee on Public Information, 1917:1918:1919,* 63–67.

291 *Creel flooded the country:* Ibid., 2, 15–19, 30; Creel, *How We Advertised America,* 137–39; Creel, *Complete Report of the Chairman of the Committee on Public Information, 1917:1918:1919,* 74–75; Schaffer, *America in the Great War,* 5.

292 *From grumbling:* Alan Axelrod, *Selling the Great War: The Making of American Propaganda* (New York: St. Martin's, 2009), xi.

292 *The CPI also produced movies:* Creel, *How We Advertised America,* 117–20, 125, 127; Creel, *Complete Report of the Chairman of the Committee on Public Information, 1917:1918:1919,* 8–10.

292 *But the president's second Flag Day address: PWW,* 42:498–504.

292 *Neither acknowledged:* Peterson and Fite, *Opponents of War, 1917–1918,* 46, 84, 127, 152–53, 196–97.

293 *Several Mennonite churches:* Gerlof D. Homan, "The Burning of the Mennonite Church, Fairview, Michigan, in 1918," *Mennonite Quarterly Review* 64 (April 1990): 99–112.

293 *The day after the speech:* Scheiber, *The Wilson Administration and Civil Liberties,1917–1921,* 40–41.

293 *Postmaster General Albert S. Burleson:* Peterson and Fite, *Opponents of War, 1917–1918,* 163–64.

293 *When the Post Office informed:* Ibid., 47–48; Zechariah Chafee, Jr., "The Milwaukee Leader Case," *Nation* 112, no. 2907 (March 23, 1921): 428–29.

293 *Protests streamed into the White House: PWW,* 44:339–40, 344.

294 *"I am afraid": PWW,* 44:396–97.

294 *Wilson retreated:* Donald Johnson, "Wilson, Burleson, and Censorship in the First World War," *Journal of Southern History* 28, no. 1 (Feb. 1962): 54–56.

294 *"Let them blow off some steam": WWLL: War Leader,* 165n1.

294 *Burleson, a master of doubletalk: PWW,* 44:389–90.

294 *After a long legal battle,* The Masses *folded:* Peterson and Fite, *Opponents of War, 1917–1918,* 96–97.

294 *In all, Burleson censored:* Peterson and Fite, *Opponents of War, 1917–1918,* 92–98.

294 *"helpless small fry":* O'Toole, *When Trumpets Call,* 362.

294 *Thomas Watt Gregory:* Evan Anders, "Thomas Watt Gregory and the Survival of His Progressive Faith," *Southwestern Historical Quarterly* 93, no. 1 (July 1989): 4.

295 *Moving as quickly as Burleson:* Geoffrey R. Stone, "Mr. Wilson's First Amendment," in Cooper, ed., *Reconsidering Woodrow Wilson,* 189–224.

295 *At the end of 1917: Annual Report of the Attorney General of the United States for the Year 1917,* 50–53.

295 *"May God have mercy on them": New York Times,* Nov. 21, 1917.

295 *The country had been scared:* Emerson Hough, *The Web: A Revelation of Patriotism* (Chicago: Reilly & Lee, 1919), 88–89; Joan M. Jensen, *The Price of Vigilance* (Chicago: Rand McNally, 1968), 293.

295 *Every day brought:* Jensen, *The Price of Vigilance,* 15–16, 21.

295 *Gregory established a War Emergency Division: Annual Report of the Attorney General of the United States for the Year 1918,* 14.

295 *Alert to the risks:* Hough, *The Web,* 12, 26, 30.

295 *The first serious complaint: PWW,* 42:441–43.

296 *"It seems to me": PWW,* 42:446.

296 *Gregory assured the president: PWW,* 42:509–10.

296 *The badges . . . were nothing alike:* PWW, 42:516.

296 *"I know of no authority":* PWW, 42:518.

296 *Investigation Bureau:* Hough, *The Web,* 495.

296 *"if I were a German spy":* PWW, 42:518n5.

296 *But there was no order:* Jensen, *The Price of Vigilance,* 148–50; Hough, *The Web,* 163–64.

297 *three million investigations:* Hough, *The Web,* 34, 48, 50.

297 *it had failed to turn up even one spy:* Ross, *Propaganda for War,* 270.

297 *In a report written at the end of the war:* Annual Report of the Attorney General of the United States for the Year 1918, 15.

297 *On July 12, 1917:* PWW, 43:156–57; *New York Times,* July 14, 1917.

297 *When the news reached the White House:* PWW, 43:156-57.

297 *Wilson deplored:* Cronon, ed., *The Cabinet Diaries of Josephus Daniels, 1913–1921,* 185.

297 *Gregory declined:* Kennedy, *Over Here,* 264.

297 *With Wilson's approval:* PWW, 44:17–18, 81.

298 *the Justice Department had piled up evidence:* The APL's role is gleefully recounted in Hough, *The Web,* 133–40.

298 *At three o'clock:* Annual Report of the Attorney General of the United States for the Year 1918, 53–54.

298 *it took the jury less than an hour:* Peterson and Fite, *Opponents of War, 1917–1918,* 240.

298 *In Tulsa:* Ibid., 172–75.

298 *Elsewhere:* Ibid., 204.

298 *Gregory could think of only one remedy:* Annual Report of the Attorney General of the United States for the Year 1918, 18.

298 *Robert Paul Prager:* Peterson and Fite, *Opponents of War, 1917–1918,* 202–4.

298 *Wilson shook his head:* PWW, 42:7–9; 48:192.

298 *"The press, from which we had the right":* Creel, *Rebel at Large,* 199.

299 *Capitalizing on the outrage:* Peterson and Fite, *Opponents of War, 1917–1918,* 212.

299 *"a condition of lawlessness":* Stone, "Mr. Wilson's First Amendment," 205.

299 *In the Senate:* Ibid., 206.

299 *The new strictures:* Peterson and Fite, *Opponents of War, 1917–1918,* 182; John Lord O'Brian, "Civil Liberty in War Time," Washington, D.C.: U.S. Government Printing Office, 1919, 17–18.

299 *Eugene V. Debs:* Ernest Freeberg, *Democracy's Prisoner: Eugene V. Debs, the Great War, and the Right to Dissent* (Cambridge: Harvard University Press, 2008), 77–79, 105–7; Eugene V. Debs, "The Canton, Ohio Speech, Anti-War Speech," *Marxists.org.,* accessed July 27, 2016, www.marxists.org/archives/debs/works/1918/canton.htm.

300 *Summing up his war against subversives:* PWW, 51:377–80; Scheiber, *The Wilson Administration and Civil Liberties, 1917–1921,* 52–53, 56; Jensen, *The Price of Vigilance,* 269; O'Brian, "Civil Liberty in War Time," 20.

300 *Wilson gave his consent:* PWW, 55:348n2.

300 *There had been a time:* PWW, 12:475.

301 *"If there should be disloyalty":* PWW, 41:526.

301 *and Gregory's Sedition Act made it worse:* O'Brian, "Civil Liberty in War Time," 18.

CHAPTER 27: *Over Here, Over There*

302 *Determined:* IPCH, 3:206, 226.

303 *Fifteen hundred miles:* Kennan, *Russia Leaves the War,* 74–75.

303 *The Allies responded:* Trask, *The AEF and Coalition Warmaking, 1917–1918,* 30–31.

303 *In Berlin, as in London and Paris:* Holger H. Herwig, *The First World War: Germany and Austria-Hungary, 1914–1918* (London: Arnold, 1997), 393–94.

303 *The danger was acute:* Trask, *The AEF and Coalition Warmaking, 1917–1918,* 36.

303 *Bliss agreed with Pershing:* Ibid., 37.

303 *When House and his delegation:* EMH Diary, EMH Papers, Dec. 3, 1917.

303 *Wilson had authorized Pershing:* PWW, 46:231–32.

303 *but Pershing refused:* PWW, 46:197.

304 *John Dos Passos:* Dos Passos, *Mr. Wilson's War,* 356–57.

304 *House understood:* IPCH, 3:281–82.

304 *"My home policy":* Clemenceau made the remark on March 18, 1918, in a speech to the Chamber of Deputies. http://www2.assemblee-nationale.fr/decouvrir-l-assemblee/histoire/grands-moments-d-eloquence/georges-clemenceau-8-mars-1918, accessed Oct. 22, 2017.

304 *The colonel decided to urge:* IPCH, 3:233, 273.

304 *But even as the colonel:* IPCH, 3:218–19.

305 *The colonel sailed home:* EMH Diary, EMH Papers, Dec. 1, 8, and 11, 1917.

305 *"I never knew a man":* PWW, 45:317–18, 323.

305 *He could not singlehandedly:* IPCH, 3:317–18.

305 *The president asked the colonel:* PWW, 45:324. There is an overview of the Inquiry's work in *IPCH,* 3:168–73. For a comprehensive treatment, see Gelfand, *The Inquiry.*

305 *House summoned the Inquiry's secretary:* Steel, *Walter Lippmann and the American Century,* 133–34, 609n8. The Inquiry's memorandum appears in *PWW,* 45:459–74.

306 *"[W]asn't it horrible?":* Sigmund Freud and William C. Bullitt, *Thomas Woodrow Wilson: A Psychological Study* (Boston: Houghton Mifflin, 1966), 200–201.

306 *Surrounded by his family:* His holiday activities are chronicled in *The Washington Post,* Dec. 23–26, 1917.

306 *The negotiations for a permanent peace between Russia and Germany:* Kennan, *Russia Leaves the War,* 219–28.

306 *The colonel reached the White House:* PWW, 45:458–59.

306 *"We actually got down to work":* PWW, 45:550–51.

306 *On Monday:* PWW, 45:555.

306 *On Tuesday:* Starling and Sugrue, *Starling of the White House,* 101.

306 *and at ten-thirty he asked his office:* PWW, 45:555.

306 *his Fourteen Points speech:* PWW, 45:534–39.

307 *The most perceptive praise:* New-York Tribune, Jan. 9, 1918.

308 *The day after the speech:* PWW, 45:549–50, 566, 577–78.

308 *As for the 177,000 American soldiers in France:* American Battle Monuments Commission, *A Guide to the American Battle Fields in Europe,* 16.

308 *In a February 3 meeting:* PWW, 46:231–32; 247–48.

308 *In a single stroke:* Neiberg, *Fighting the Great War,* 224–25.

309 *"the last card":* Herwig, *The First World War,* 392–93.

309 *"ten thousand breakers":* Palmer, *Newton D. Baker,* 2:103–4.

309 *Within forty-eight hours:* PWW, 47:131–32.

309 *At the White House:* PWW, 47:183–85.

309 *The Supreme War Council:* S. L. A. Marshall, *World War I,* 357–58.

311 *Bliss, who believed:* Smythe, *Pershing,* 101; Beaver, *Newton D. Baker and the American War Effort, 1917–1919,* 131–33.

311 *"I have come to say to you":* American Battle Monuments Commission, *A Guide to the American Battle Fields in Europe,* 17-18.

311 *Wilson agreed to send:* Palmer, *Newton D. Baker,* 2:146–48; PWW, 47:221, 229–30.

311 *The dispute:* Palmer, *Newton D. Baker,* 2:150.

311 *After consulting the Allies:* Ibid., 2:143; Smythe, *Pershing,* 96.

311 *The Allies had managed:* S. L. A. Marshall, *World War I,* 360; Smythe, *Pershing,* 102.

312 *Believing that the Germans:* Palmer, *Newton D. Baker,* 2:153; Martin Gilbert, *The First World War,* 414.

312 *Through their ambassadors:* PWW, 47:386–87, 393, 497–98.

312 *Wiseman appealed to House:* PWW, 47:433–35.

312 *A State Department official:* PWW, 47:585, 595.

312 *The AEF began to make itself felt:* Bullard, *Personalities and Reminiscences of the War,* 198–99; Trask, *The AEF and Coalition Warmaking,* 65–67; S. L. A. Marshall, *World War I,* 372–73.

312 *The fight for Cantigny:* Trask, *The AEF and the Coalition Warmaking,* 69; Eisenhower, *Yanks,* 135–36.

313 *There were 722,000 American troops:* Palmer, *Bliss, Peacemaker,* 274n3.

313 *Foch threatened:* Trask, *The AEF and Coalition Warmaking,* 74–75.

313 *"We all had the impression":* Smythe, *Pershing,* 138.

313 *"Half trained, half organized":* Churchill, *The World Crisis,* 795–96.

314 *Ludendorff believed:* Ibid., 139; Trask, *The AEF and Coalition Warmaking,* 72.

314 *By the Fourth of July:* Palmer, *Bliss, Peacemaker,* 285.

314 *Captain André Tardieu:* New York Times, July 5, 1918.

CHAPTER 28: *So Many Problems Per Diem*

315 *Wilson spent his Fourth of July:* Chicago Tribune, July 5, 1918; Creel, *How We Advertised America,* 200; Creel, *Complete Report of the Chairman of the Committee on Public Information, 1917:1918:1919,* 84; EBW, *My Memoir,* 164.

316 *Wilson spoke of the war:* PWW, 48:514–17.

316 *"work out their own salvation":* PWW, 51:350.

317 *"sweating blood":* PWW, 49:550.

317 *To Oswald Garrison Villard:* Georg Schild, *Between Ideology and Realpolitik: Woodrow Wilson and the Russian Revolution* (Westport, Conn.: Greenwood, 1995), 85.

317 *General Ludendorff concluded:* Martin Gilbert, *The First World War,* 417.

318 *Ludendorff clung:* Herwig, *The First World War,* 418–19; Görlitz, ed., *The Kaiser and His Court,* 371–74.

318 *Ludendorff would remember August 8:* Herwig, *The First World War,* 419; Strachan, *The First World War,* 310–11.

318 *By relentless, tightly coordinated fire:* Neiberg, *Fighting the Great War,* 343–44.

318 *A psychologist advised him:* Strachan, *The First World War,* 311.

318 *On August 13:* Seymour, *American Diplomacy During the World War,* 302–3; Strachan, *The First World War,* 311–12; Balfour, *The Kaiser and His Times,* 391–92.

319 *House told him (not for the first time):* PWW, 49:265–67.

320 *At a meeting of party leaders:* Seward W. Livermore, "The Sectional Issue in the 1918 Congressional Elections," *Mississippi Valley Historical Review* 25 (1948–1949): 33.

320 *In a July 3 fundraising letter:* Frank P. Woods to Dear Sir, July 3, 1918, Albert S. Burleson Papers, 21:3305.

320 *"Republican principles":* Selig Adler, "The Congressional Election of 1918," *South Atlantic Quarterly* 36 (Oct. 1937): 449–50.

320 *"These are days":* PWW, 48:162–65.

320 *Spokesmen:* New York Times, May 28, 1918.

320 *The House did not approve . . . until September:* Roy G. and Gladys C. Blakey, "The Revenue Act of 1918," *American Economic Review* 9, no. 2 (June 1919): 213–15.

320 *Lodge stayed on the sidelines:* "The Essential Terms of Peace: Speech of Hon. Henry Cabot Lodge of Massachusetts in the Senate of the United States, August 23, 1918" (Washington, D.C.: U.S. Government Printing Office, 1918).

321 *A day after Lodge delivered:* New York Times, Aug. 25, 1918.

321 *"conversion":* PWW, 51:190.

321 *"as an act of right and justice":* New York Times, Jan. 10, 1918.

321 *The resolution needed 274 votes:* Ibid., Jan. 11, 1918.

322 *The slim victory:* New-York Tribune, Jan. 12, 1918; Blum, *Joe Tumulty and the Wilson Era,* 148.

322 *When Jones introduced:* New York Times and Washington Post, Sept. 27, 1918.

322 *McAdoo telephoned the White House:* WGM, Crowded Years, 496–97.

322 *Wilson spoke at one o'clock:* PWW, 51:158–61.

323 *"No Vote Changed":* Atlanta Constitution, Oct. 1, 1918.

323 *Republicans gloated, too:* Washington Post, Oct. 2, 1918.

323 *A delegation of suffragists:* PWW, 51:189–90.

323 *The illiberal wing:* PWW, 46:436.

323 *In 1915 he outraged liberal opinion:* PWW, 47:388n2, n3.

323 *"If this is OUR country":* Edward M. Coffman. *The War to End All Wars: The American Military Experience in World War I* (Lexington: University Press of Kentucky, 1998), 69.

323 *James Weldon Johnson:* Chad L. Williams, *Torchbearers of Democracy,* 24–25.

323 *The Army had long practiced segregation:* Beaver, *Newton D. Baker and the American War Effort, 1917–1919,* 225, 228.

324 *Pressed by the NAACP:* Ferrell, *Woodrow Wilson and World War I, 1917–1921,* 212–15.

324 *In the violent summer of 1917:* Beaver, *Newton D. Baker and the American War Effort, 1917–1919,* 229; Barbeau and Henri, *The Unknown Soldiers: African-American Troops in World War I* (New York: Da Capo, 1976), 29–30.

324 *Of the sixteen additional death sentences:* PWW, 49:399–402.

324 *The ten joined fifty-three other black soldiers:* Robert V. Haynes, "Houston Riot of 1917," Texas State Historical Association, *Handbook of Texas Online,* accessed March 21, 2015.

324 *A report prepared by two black clergymen:* PWW, 48:155–61.

324 *In July, Wilson issued:* Adler, "The Congressional Election of 1918," 462–63.

324 *When Creel asked him:* PWW, 48:342, 346.

324 *On October 1:* Afro-American (Baltimore), Oct. 4, 1918.

325 *"We all have to be patient":* PWW, 51:168.

325 *On September 14:* New York Times, Sept. 7, 1918; FRUS, 1918, Supplement 1, 306–10; New York Times, Sept. 17 and 18, 1918.

325 *"Force, Force to the utmost":* PWW, 47:270.

325 *On the Fourth of July:* PWW, 48:516–17.

325 *At the end of September:* PWW, 51:127–33.

326 *It seemed to House:* New York Tribune, Sept. 30, 1918; PWW, 51:144.

326 *The Allies had accepted their first surrender:* FRUS, 1918, Supplement 1, 322.

326 *and the AEF had just recaptured:* Chicago Daily Tribune, Sept. 28, 1918.

326 *The drive was only a few days old:* Görlitz, ed., *The Kaiser and His Court,* 397.

326 *The kaiser took the news quietly:* Watson, *Ring of Steel,* 534–35.

326 *On Monday:* New-York Tribune, Oct. 1, 1918.

326 *On Tuesday:* Balfour, *The Kaiser and His Times,* 395; George P. Gooch, "Prince Max of Baden," *The Contemporary Review,* no. 132 (July 1, 1927): 446–54.

326 *On Wednesday:* Sondhaus, *World War One,* 433.

326 *On Thursday:* PWW, 51:253.

326 *Austria immediately followed:* PWW, 51:258–59.

327 *Lloyd George and Clemenceau:* FRUS, 1918, Supplement 1, 344–46.

327 *House suggested that Wilson consult them:* PWW, 51:254.

327 *"If the Germans are beaten":* PWW, 51:348.

327 *On October 8:* PWW, 51:268–69.

327 *Before Berlin made its next move:* FRUS, *1918, Supplement 1,* 353.

327 *Within hours:* PWW, 51:307–8.

327 *Geddes wrote London:* PWW, 51:325–26.

327 *Tumulty came in with a message:* PWW, 51:316–17.

327 *On Monday morning:* FRUS, *1918, Supplement 1,* 358.

328 *"I never saw him more disturbed":* PWW, 51:340–41.

328 *He and House collaborated:* PWW, 51:341–42.

328 *The Germans, having nothing else to propose, protested:* FRUS, *1918, Supplement 1,* 380–81.

328 *On October 23:* Ibid., 381–83.

328 *Roosevelt, speaking at a Liberty Loan rally:* New York Times, Oct. 13, 1918.

329 *Roosevelt stayed on the attack:* Morison and Blum, eds., *Letters of Theodore Roosevelt,* 8:1380–81.

329 *Edith was not keen:* PWW, 51:390.

329 *He shared it:* PWW, 51:389–93.

329 *"My Fellow Countrymen":* PWW, 51:381–82.

329 *"I would not send it out":* WWLL: *Armistice,* 510. See 513n1 for Baker's compilation of other White House reactions.

329 *Wilson's appeal for a Democratic Congress:* Washington Post, Oct. 26, 1918.

329 *Who was Woodrow Wilson to say . . . ?:* Washington Post, Oct. 29, 1918.

330 *"the feeling that beat him":* HCL to George Otto Trevelyan, Nov. 1918, HCL Papers.

330 *"For the political disaster":* "Choose Ye This Day," *Nation,* Nov. 16, 1918.

CHAPTER 29: *Defiance*

331 *The election results gave Wilson:* PWW, 51:639, 646–48; 53:309.

331 *He was still president:* PWW, 51:576.

331 *On November 9:* Balfour, *The Kaiser and His Times,* 405–11.

332 *As the kaiser's exit was being arranged:* PWW, 53:36–41; Eisenhower, *Yanks,* 281–82; Martin Gilbert, *The First World War,* 497–98.

332 *Among other things:* Neiberg, *Fighting the Great War,* 360–61.

332 *The White House learned:* EBW, *My Memoir,* 170.

332 *The president declared a holiday:* New-York Tribune, Nov. 12, 1918.

332 *and spent the morning:* WWLL: *War Leader,* 580.

332 *Millions of Americans:* Baltimore Sun, Boston Globe, Chicago Tribune, Los Angeles Times, New York Times, and New-York Tribune, Nov. 12, 1918.

332 *The president was cheered:* WWLL: *War Leader,* 581.

332 *"the personification of physical vigor":* New York Times, Nov. 12, 1918.

332 *After a somber recitation:* PWW, 53:35–43.

333 *The Allies' unanimous support:* Trask, *The United States in the Supreme War Council,* 165–72; Neu, *Colonel House,* 368–72.

333 *"If I do not hear from you to the contrary":* PWW, 51:568–70.

333 *Wilson agreed and directed Lansing:* FRUS, 1918, Supplement 1, 468–69.

333 *In a note to Wilson:* PWW, 51:594.

334 *"Gentlemen, I am here to say":* PWW, 47:287.

334 *Lansing begged him:* PWW, 53:65–66.

334 *From Paris, House reported:* PWW, 53:71–72; Neu, *Colonel House,* 379.

334 *Wilson took the advice:* PWW, 53:96–97, 108–9.

334 *Lloyd George, foreseeing:* Willert, *The Road to Safety,* 161.

334 *The debate on the wisdom of Wilson's decision:* PWW, 53:93–95; *New York Times,* Nov. 19, 1918.

334 *when the White House announced:* PWW, 53:243.

334 *Republicans felt insulted:* Bailey, *Wilson and the Peacemakers: Woodrow Wilson and the Lost Peace,* 97–98, 101, 104.

335 *"Republicans had said":* Cronon, ed., *The Cabinet Diaries of Josephus Daniels,* 352.

335 *After a lengthy review:* PWW, 53:274–76.

335 *Roosevelt responded:* Stout, ed., *Roosevelt in the Kansas City Star,* 272–77; *New York Times,* Dec. 4, 1918.

335 *Taft, the only sympathetic Republican:* PWW, 53:323–24n1.

335 *Wilson sailed:* PWW, 53:313–15; Gelfand, *The Inquiry,* 168; *New York Times,* Dec. 4, 1918.

336 *The Wilsons were no more hospitable:* PWW, 53:327, 343–44.

336 *Four days out:* IPCH, 4:247–49.

336 *"I am absolutely opposed to this":* PWW, 53:336–38.

336 *At one of the movie screenings:* PWW, 53:350.

336 *Wilson saw ten of the Inquiry scholars:* PWW, 53:350–51.

337 *"You are, in truth, my advisers":* Creel, *Rebel at Large,* 254.

337 *What he wanted was simple:* PWW, 53:352.

337 *Sensing:* RL to Robert A. Buck, Nov. 29, 1918, RL Papers, Library of Congress.

337 *Just after the Armistice:* FRUS, 1919, Paris Peace Conference, 1:286–87; Ephraim Koch Smith, Jr., "Robert Lansing and the Paris Peace Conference," 167.

337 *As Lansing submitted his questions:* "Memorandum on the Principle Which Should Govern the Congress of Paris, Nov. 18, 1918," Private Memoranda, RL Papers, Library of Congress.

337 *"the tendency will be to fly apart":* RL to Elihu Root, Dec. 3, 1918, RL Papers, Library of Congress.

338 *At sea he had time:* Ephraim Koch Smith, Jr., "Robert Lansing and the Paris Peace Conference," 179.

338 *Wilson had only an hour's talk with him and White:* Nevins, *Henry White,* 359.

338 *Lansing felt as frustrated as ever:* Ephraim Koch Smith, Jr., "Robert Lansing and the Paris Peace Conference," 187–88.

338 *The spell that Wilson cast over the Inquiry men wore off:* Ibid., 190; Gelfand, *The Inquiry,* 174.

338 *on an evening walk:* Creel, *Complete Report of the Chairman of the Committee on Public Information, 1917:1918:1919,* 5–6; Creel, *The War, the World and Wilson,* 163.

According to William Bullitt (*PWW*, 53:367), Wilson also confided these fears to Raymond Blaine Fosdick, who had been one of his students at Princeton. Fosdick worked for the government during the war and was invited to Paris because of his enthusiasm for the League of Nations.

CHAPTER 30: *Final Triumph*

339 *The* George Washington: *PWW,* 53:569.

339 *Thousands heard his speeches:* CTG Diary, CTG Papers, Jan. 5, 1919; Bailey, *Wilson and the Peacemakers: Woodrow Wilson and the Lost Peace,* 110–13.

340 *Watching the influx:* Dillon, *The Inside Story of the Peace Conference,* 4–6.

340 *Reporters filed innumerable:* Washington Post, Nov. 29, 1918, and Jan. 13, 1919; *PWW,* 53:398, 423, 429.

340 *"I can talk to him frankly":* Wythe Williams, *The Tiger of France* (New York: Duell, Sloan & Pearce, 1949), 186.

340 *In separate conversations: PWW,* 53:400.

341 *Clemenceau had strayed: PWW,* 53:394, 401.

341 *When Wilson decided to stay:* Lloyd George, *Memoirs of the Peace Conference,* 1:148–49.

341 *"Zeus on Mount Olympus":* Williams, *The Tiger of France,* 182–83.

341 *A few days after the chat at the Murat: PWW,* 53:456, 498.

341 *Although Wilson had not yet discovered: PWW,* 53:488.

341 *"I don't want to see":* Lawrence, *The True Story of Woodrow Wilson,* 259.

341 *He would visit the front: PWW,* 53:707–8; 54:175, 257.

341 *Stunned:* Paul Cambon, *Correspondance, 1870–1924* (Paris: Editions Bernard Grasset, 1946), 3:293.

342 *The Wilsons left Paris:* Lawrence, *The True Story of Woodrow Wilson,* 249–52; *PWW,* 53:505–6.

342 *He used his speeches: PWW,* 53:532–33, 541, 550–51.

342 *Clemenceau returned fire:* Times (London), Dec. 31, 1918; Duroselle, *Clemenceau,* 725–26.

343 *Even before meeting Clemenceau: PWW,* 53:367.

343 *Lloyd George he regarded:* Davis and Fleming, eds., *The Ambassadorial Diary of John W. Davis,* 18n36.

343 *But the Europeans were skeptical:* Tardieu, *The Truth About the Treaty,* 105; Egerton, *Great Britain and the Creation of the League of Nations,* 105–6; *PWW,* 53:652–53; Bailey, *Wilson and the Peacemakers: Woodrow Wilson and the Lost Peace,* 180.

343 *Well before the peacemaking began:* New-York Tribune and Baltimore Sun, Dec. 22, 1919; Egerton, *Great Britain and the Creation of the League of Nations,* 85; Bailey, *Wilson and the Peacemakers: Woodrow Wilson and the Lost Peace,* 184.

343 *Nor did Robert Lansing:* "Certain Phrases of the President Contain the Seeds of Trouble," Dec. 20, 1918, Confidential Memoranda, RL Papers, Princeton.

343 *There were more than two hundred such meetings:* Tardieu, *The Truth About the Treaty,* 97.

344 *The day after Lodge's speech appeared:* RL, *The Peace Negotiations,* 48–54, 62; *PWW,* 53:474–76.

344 *Lansing continued to fret:* "Self-Determination and the Dangers," Dec. 30, 1918, RL Papers, Library of Congress.

344 *General Bliss had put himself to work: PWW,* 53:402, 720–21.

344 *Colonel House, embarrassed: PWW,* 53:695.

345 *The colonel took the president:* "The President's Draft of a Covenant for a League of Nations," Jan. 11, 1919, Confidential Memoranda, RL Papers, Princeton; *FRUS, 1919, The Paris Peace Conference,* 1:319–24.

345 *Humiliated:* RL, *The Peace Negotiations,* 86–87.

345 *Worse, he admitted: PWW,* 53:695.

345 *The Paris Peace Conference flickered:* Details from Charles T. Thompson, *The Peace Conference Day by Day,* 94–96; *New York Times* and *Baltimore Sun,* Jan. 13, 1919; MacMillan, *Paris 1919,* 54; *PWW,* 54:4–5; Clive Day, "The Atmosphere and Organization of the Peace Conference" in House and Seymour, eds., *What Really Happened at Paris,* 17–18, 26.

345 *The Ten accredited: FRUS, 1919, The Paris Peace Conference,* 3:576.

346 *The Ten met:* Shotwell, *At the Paris Peace Conference,* 175.

346 *The Ten would later admit: PWW,* 54:4–6.

346 *"key to the whole settlement": WWWS,* 1:235.

346 *The European leaders had become acquainted:* Lloyd George, *Memoirs of the Peace Conference,* 1:139.

346 *One American journalist:* Heaton, *Cobb of "The World,"* 68.

346 *Lloyd George would come to like Wilson:* Lloyd George, *Memoirs of the Peace Conference,* 1:140–42.

347 *"I think one would go crazy": PWW,* 53:530.

347 *He saw Clemenceau's constant advocacy: PWW,* 54:64.

347 *As for Lloyd George: PWW,* 60:570.

348 *Wilson's opposites: PWW,* 53:456, 470; Cambon, *Correspondance, 1870–1924,* 3:307.

348 *In the first discussion of renewing the Armistice: PWW,* 54:12.

348 *But when the Ten met the next day: PWW,* 54:12, 35–37; *FRUS, 1919, The Paris Peace Conference,* 3:509–10, 525–26.

349 *On January 17:* CTG Diary, CTG Papers, Jan. 18, 1919.

349 *the plenary: Chicago Tribune, New-York Tribune,* and *New York Times,* Jan. 20, 1919.

349 *Poincaré said: FRUS, 1919, The Paris Peace Conference,* 3:163–64.

350 *"It is in yourselves":* Ibid., 3:165, 168–70.

350 *Lansing would later rank Clemenceau as the strongest:* RL, *The Big Four and Others of the Paris Peace Conference,* 10–36; RL Desk Diary, Jan. 18, 1919, RL Papers, Library of Congress.

350 *At the second plenary: FRUS, 1919, The Paris Peace Conference,* 3:177–78.

350 *"the bear-garden broke loose":* RL Desk Diary, Jan. 25, 1919, RL Papers, Library of Congress.

350 *The Belgian foreign minister asked:* FRUS, *1919, The Paris Peace Conference,* 3:182.

350 *"It is with some surprise":* Ibid., 3:186–90.

350 *Clemenceau waited out the abuse:* Ibid., 3:196–201.

351 *The presidential party set out:* EBW, *My Memoir,* 234, CTG Diary, CTG Papers, Jan. 26, 1919.

351 *Traveling back to Paris:* EBW, *My Memoir,* 235.

351 *Certainly he was exhausted:* CTG Diary, CTG Papers, Feb. 2, 1919; Creel, *Rebel at Large,* 214; Davis and Fleming, eds., *The Ambassadorial Diary of John W. Davis,* 37.

352 *"No one can put into words":* CTG Papers, Jan. 26, 1919.

352 *criticized for:* Lloyd George, *Memoirs of the Peace Conference,* 1:140.

352 *Lloyd George and Clemenceau had decided:* Davis and Fleming, eds., *The Ambassadorial Diary of John W. Davis,* 39.

352 *The commission worked late:* CTG Diary, CTG Papers, Feb. 4 and 5, 1919.

352 *Despite the high speed:* David Hunter Miller, "The Making of the League of Nations," in House and Seymour, eds., *What Really Happened at Paris,* 410; CTG Papers, Feb. 11, 1919.

352 *Wilson's notion:* Walworth, *Wilson and His Peacemakers,* 117.

352 *Thirteen of the fourteen nations:* Miller, "The Making of the League of Nations," 411.

352 *Many of the twenty-six articles:* PWW, 55:164–73.

352 *Watching from the sidelines:* RL to John W. Davis, Jan. 14, 1919, RL Papers, Princeton.

353 *"Europe is being liquidated":* J. C. Smuts, *The League of Nations: A Practical Suggestion* (London: Hodder & Stoughton, 1918), 11.

353 *mandatory powers:* Susan Pederson, *The Guardians: The League of Nations and the Crisis of Empire* (New York: Oxford University Press, 2015), 28–29; Bonsal, *Unfinished Business,* 38–39. See also MacMillan, *Paris 1919,* 98–100; Knock, *To End All Wars,* 201–3. Article XXII was Article 19 in the draft that Wilson presented to the peace conference on February 14.

353 *To Lansing, Article XXII:* RL, *The Peace Negotiations,* 149–61.

353 *Article X:* PWW, 55:167.

354 *"Do any of us really mean it?":* Walworth, *Wilson and His Peacemakers,* 116.

354 *As for the omission of freedom of the seas:* CTG Papers, Feb. 14, 1919.

354 *He asked to present it:* FRUS, *1919, The Paris Peace Conference,* 3:1023–24.

354 *Next morning:* PWW, 55:193.

355 *"Not having studied it":* RL Desk Diary, Feb. 14, 1919, RL Papers, Library of Congress.

355 *Despite the short notice:* FRUS, *1919, The Paris Peace Conference,* 3:208–9; Charles T. Thompson, *The Peace Conference Day by Day,* 197–98; PWW, 55:175–77.

355 *To Wickham Steed:* ICPH, 4:318–19.

355 *Even Lansing was impressed:* RL, *The Peace Negotiations,* 134.

356 *Lord Cecil spoke next:* FRUS, *1919, The Paris Peace Conference,* 3:215.

356 *Prime Minister Orlando:* Ibid., 3:219.

356 *Léon Bourgeois:* Ibid., 3:219.

356 *Baron Makino Nobuaki:* Ibid., 3:225.

356 *Rustem Haidar:* Ibid., 3:229.

356 *When Clemenceau had had enough:* Ibid., 3:230.

356 *"It will be sweet to go home":* EBW, *My Memoir,* 239–40.

356 *At nine o'clock:* PWW, 55:196.

CHAPTER 31: *Storm Warning*

357 *In a cable:* PWW, 55:184, 198.

358 *Picturing a Boston arrival:* PWW, 53:625–26.

358 *"The failure of the United States":* PWW, 55:224–26.

358 *Eleanor Roosevelt:* Ward, *A First-Class Temperament,* 430–31.

358 *She did not inquire:* PWW, 54:62–63.

358 *On February 24:* New-York Tribune, Feb. 25, 1919.

359 *At the city's largest auditorium:* PWW, 55:243–45.

359 *Headlines:* New York Times, Feb. 25, 1919.

359 *Lodge complained about it:* HCL to W. R. Thayer, Feb. 21, 1919, and HCL to Henry White, June 12, 1919, HCL Papers.

359 *Waiting for him was a note:* PWW, 55:262–63.

359 *Wilson declined:* PWW, 55:280.

359 *The following evening:* Chicago Tribune, Feb. 27, 1919.

359 *Lodge's notes:* HCL, *The Senate and the League of Nations,* 100; EBW, *My Memoir,* 241–42.

359 *"black with dirt":* Phyllis Lee Levin, *Edith and Woodrow,* 257.

360 *Lodge gave him high marks in goodwill:* Lodge, *The Senate and the League of Nations,* 100.

360 *Brandegee:* Stone, *The Irreconcilables,* 61–63.

360 *Years later, Edith Wilson would reveal:* EBW, *My Memoir,* 241–42.

360 *Although there is no transcript:* Knock, *To End All Wars,* 232–33.

360 *From interviews with several of the guests:* New-York Tribune, Feb. 27, 1919.

360 *A day after giving the president his say:* Ibid., Feb. 28, 1919.

360 *On February 27:* Chicago Tribune and New York Times, Feb. 27, 1919; PWW, 55:254, 408–9; Washington Post, March 3, 1919. The fight for an extra session is chronicled in Stone, *The Irreconcilables,* 64–70.

361 *With time running out:* New York Times, March 1, 1919; HCL, *The Senate and the League of Nations,* 227, 229.

361 *"Everybody hates war":* Stone, *The Irreconcilables,* 71–73.

361 *Meeting with the Democratic National Committee:* PWW, 55:312–13.

362 *Faced with a tragedy:* PWW, 55:323–24.

362 *Lodge's second move:* Garraty, *Henry Cabot Lodge,* 353–56.

362 *William Howard Taft:* Pringle, *The Life and Times of William Howard Taft,* 2:942–43.

363 *"It is a real League":* WHT to Helen Herron Taft, Feb. 15, 1919, WHT Papers.

363 *Convinced that the League was essential:* PWW, 55:328.

363 *"It is hard for me to be patient":* WHT to Robert A. Taft, Feb. 10, 1919, WHT Papers.

363 *The sight: Baltimore Sun,* March 5, 1919.

363 *Wilson, looking pale and drawn:* PWW, 55:463.

363 *(this to be true):* Cooper, *Breaking the Heart of the World,* 58.

363 *He professed to be amazed:* PWW, 55:413–21.

364 *"He never answers any argument at all":* WHT to Gus Karger, March 5, 1919, WHT Papers.

364 *He hoped that Wilson would revise:* WHT to Horace Taft, March 5, 1919, WHT Papers.

CHAPTER 32: *The Fog of Peace*

365 *The* George Washington *landed:* Edith Benham Helm, *The Captains and the Kings* (New York: G. P. Putnam's Sons, 1954), 307.

365 *Pretty as it was: WWWS,* 2:23.

366 *Colonel House:* EMH Diary, EMH Papers, March 12, 1919; *PWW,* 55:499.

366 *Edith Wilson:* EBW, *My Memoir,* 245–46.

366 *Ray Stannard Baker: WWWS,* 1:306–7.

366 *Nor had the colonel:* PWW, 55:477n1.

366 *House's cables:* PWW, 55:212–13, 233–34, 245–46, 284, 305n1, 458–59; EMH Diary, EMH Papers, March 7, 1919.

367 *Wilson immediately stopped confiding in him:* PWW, 55:488n2.

367 *For the rest of their stay in Paris:* PWW, 55:223.

367 *Lloyd George and Balfour: Washington Post,* March 3, 1919. In 1949 rue Nitot was renamed rue de l'Amiral d'Estaing.

367 *Edith's bathroom:* EBW, *My Memoir,* 247.

367 *The president's bathroom:* Helm, *The Captains and the Kings,* 307.

367 *The Wilsons' private quarters: WWWS,* 2:44; *PWW,* 60:251.

367 *"without an hour's delay":* EBW, *My Memoir,* 247.

367 *The next day Wilson issued: WWWS,* 1:311.

368 *The French immediately denied:* Egerton, *Great Britain and the Creation of the League of Nations,* 151; *Washington Post,* March 16, 1919.

368 *Wilson had it out:* Egerton, *Great Britain and the Creation of the League of Nations,* 151–52; *PWW,* 56:59.

368 *Worried about the treaty's fate:* A. J. P. Taylor, ed., *Lloyd George: A Diary by Frances Stevenson* (New York: Harper & Row, 1971), 172.

368 *Wilson seized the moment:* Pringle, *The Life and Times of William Howard Taft,* 2:944–45; *PWW,* 55:437; *Christian Science Monitor,* May 1, 1919.

368 *On several points:* Walworth, *Wilson and His Peacemakers,* 195.

368 *France was peeved:* Egerton, *Great Britain and the Creation of the League of Nations,* 163.

368 *Britain decided to support Wilson:* Ibid., 153–55; Cooper, *Breaking the Heart of the World,* 86–87.

368 *France, forced to give in:* Walworth, *Wilson and His Peacemakers,* 195–96.

369 *Cecil acknowledged:* Ibid., 119–20.

369 *The issue came to a head: PWW,* 57:259–66.

369 *Rarely consulted by Wilson:* RL, *The Big Four and Others of the Peace Conference,* 126–29.

369 *Henry White:* "Opinions of the Terms of Peace with Germany," May 19, 1919, Private Memoranda, RL Papers, Library of Congress.

370 *It was House who had proposed:* EMH Diary, EMH Papers, March 7, 1919.

370 *"race between peace and anarchy": PWW,* 56:208–9.

370 *As one historian has written:* A. Lentin, *Lloyd George, Woodrow Wilson and the Guilt of Germany* (Baton Rouge: Louisiana State University Press, 1984), 34.

370 *Clemenceau had an additional motive:* Ibid., 109.

370 *Wilson's financial advisors:* Bailey, *Wilson and the Peacemakers: Woodrow Wilson and the Lost Peace,* 239.

371 *He understood: PWW,* 56:285.

371 *At the first few meetings:* Paul Mantoux, *The Deliberations of the Council of Four (March 24–June 28, 1919),* 1:3.

371 *Lloyd George ended the impasse:* Bailey, *Wilson and the Peacemakers: Woodrow Wilson and the Lost Peace,* 247; *PWW,* 56:419, 480–82; A. Lentin, *Lloyd George, Woodrow Wilson and the Guilt of Germany,* 128–30.

371 *"I don't give a damn for logic": PWW,* 56:502.

371 *What did it matter: PWW,* 56:500n3. See also Paul Mantoux, *The Deliberations of the Council of Four (March 24–June 28, 1919),* 1:146–64.

371 *At issue:* Bailey, *Wilson and the Peacemakers: Woodrow Wilson and the Lost Peace,* 219–26; Walworth, *Wilson and His Peacemakers,* 268–69, 324–25.

373 *Lloyd George took Wilson's side:* Paul Mantoux, *The Deliberations of the Council of Four (March 24–June 28, 1919),* 1:205–8.

373 *Lloyd George had supported it:* Walworth, *Wilson and His Peacemakers,* 416.

373 *For that France wanted the Rhineland:* Bailey, *Wilson and the Peacemakers: Woodrow Wilson and the Lost Peace,* 228–29.

373 *Certain that France would not let go:* Paul Mantoux, *The Deliberations of the Council of Four (March 24–June 28, 1919),* 1:39n1, 40–41.

373 *Clemenceau was open to the idea:* Walworth, *Wilson and His Peacemakers,* 197.

374 *When Clemenceau took the proposition:* Mayer, *Politics and Diplomacy of Peacemaking,* 807; P. Mantoux, *The Deliberations of the Council of Four (March 24–June 28, 1919),* 1:318–19; 2:252.

374 *All he wanted:* Bonsal, *Suitors and Suppliants,* 216–17.

374 *As long as he could claim:* Mayer, *Politics and Diplomacy of Peacemaking,* 806–7.

375 *"Hang the Kaiser!":* Although the phrase appeared in uncountable newspaper stories, Lloyd George did not use it. Lloyd George, *Memoirs of the Peace Conference,* 1:109.

375 *The commission concluded:* Commission on the Responsibility of the Authors of the War and on Enforcement of Penalties, "Report Presented to the Preliminary Peace Conference," *American Journal of International Law* 14, no. ½ (Jan.–April 1920): 112, 115, 117, 121–22.

375 *When the Four considered the question on April 2: PWW,* 56:611–17.

375 *Making a spirited fight:* P. Mantoux, *The Deliberations of the Council of Four (March 24–June 28, 1919),* 1:119–23.

376 *"I have never seen him so irritated": PWW,* 56:540–42.

376 *Wilson also shared the thought with House: PWW,* 56:559–60.

376 *At the next morning's session: PWW,* 56:556–57, 578, 584; *PWW,* 58:615–21. Grayson diagnosed influenza. Decades later, physicians who examined the available historical evidence concluded that Wilson's symptoms were more consistent with a respiratory infection.

376 *Told that the president had a cold:* RL to Frederick M. Boyer, April 4, 1919, RL Papers, Princeton.

376 *"showing the strain of the overwork":* CTG to Alice Gertrude Gordon, March 29, 1919, CTG Papers.

377 *"Not a word":* RL to William Phillips, April 5, 1919, RL Papers, Princeton.

377 *Unable to see Wilson: PWW,* 56:577–78.

377 *The colonel ran afoul of Edith Wilson:* EBW, *My Memoir,* 250–52; Phyllis Lee Levin, *Edith and Woodrow,* 292–94. The encounter took place on April 8, a day after the offending article appeared in the *Times* of London.

377 *By Sunday, April 6: PWW,* 57:50–52.

377 *The president spent two hours: PWW,* 57:89.

377 *When the reporters called Lansing: PWW,* 57:62–65, 63n1, 65n2.

378 *"I shall never forget the utter sadness": WWWS,* 2:53–54, 59–60.

378 *The patient was well enough: PWW,* 57:98–99.

378 *When the group resumed its discussion:* Paul Mantoux, *The Deliberations of the Council of Four (March 24–June 28, 1919),* 1:187–95.

378 *For reasons that are not clear: PWW,* 57:146.

378 *Germany's former chancellor: PWW,* 61:340.

378 *and the five Great Powers asked the Dutch government: PWW,* 61:199–201.

378 *Wilhelm, his future now settled:* Balfour, *The Kaiser and His Times,* 414.

379 *As Hitler flattened:* Röhl, *The Kaiser and His Court,* 211.

379 *At last able to see an end: PWW,* 57:336.

379 *In a secret 1915 pact:* Paul Mantoux, *The Deliberations of the Council of Four (March 24–June 28, 1919),* 1:125n4.

380 *According to Colonel House:* IPCH, 4:434–35.

380 *The Italians' champion:* RL, *The Big Four and Others of the Peace Conference,* 104–5.

380 *Clemenceau and Lloyd George refused:* Paul Mantoux, *The Deliberations of the Council of Four (March 24–June 28, 1919),* 1:283–85, 369; René Albrecht-Carrié, *Italy at the Paris Peace Conference* (New York: Columbia University Press, 1938), 129–30.

380 *Orlando threatened to leave Paris:* Paul Mantoux, *The Deliberations of the Council of Four (March 24–June 28, 1919),* 1:288–89.

380 *The Big Four went round and round:* Ibid., 1:290–96.

381 *Wilson, who regarded the Italians as overemotional: PWW,* 57:575.

381 *Sonnino was in the middle of a rebuttal: PWW,* 57:526. Pershing had relayed the message to Bliss at 3:10 p.m.

381 *On hearing the official titles:* P. Mantoux, *The Deliberations of the Council of Four (March 24–June 28, 1919),* 1: 296–97; *PWW,* 57:520–21.

381 *Next Clemenceau and Lloyd George went to see Wilson: PWW,* 58:5–8.

381 *Lloyd George pronounced it fine:* Paul Mantoux, *The Deliberations of the Council of Four (March 24–June 28, 1919),* 1:308–14.

381 *he gave out his statement: New York Times,* April 25, 1919.

381 *Clemenceau wanted to know:* Paul Mantoux, *The Deliberations of the Council of Four (March 24–June 28, 1919),* 1:358–63.

382 *He left Paris: New York Times,* April 27, 1919.

382 *"Long live Fiume!": Boston Globe,* April 26, 1919.

382 *He was called out as a hypocrite: New York Times,* April 26, 1919.

382 *The British had led:* EBW, *My Memoir,* 254-55. Balfour's memorandum is reprinted in *WWWS,* 3:281–86.

382 *He was also about to crack from the strain: PWW,* 58:607–40.

382 *With sleet pelting the windows: New York Times,* April 29, 1919.

382 *Makino rose: FRUS, 1919, The Paris Peace Conference,* 3:289–91.

382 *Léon Bourgeois: FRUS, 1919, The Paris Peace Conference,* 3:294–302.

382 *As soon as the dissents ended: FRUS, 1919, The Paris Peace Conference,* 3:316–18. The Treaty of Versailles opens with the covenant of the League of Nations.

383 *American newspapers: New York Times,* April 30, 1919; *Christian Science Monitor,* May 1, 1919.

383 *Taft offered his compliments: Detroit Free Press,* May 1, 1919.

383 *Wilson barely noticed: PWW,* 58:229

383 *"The plot constantly thickens":* WW to JWS, April 28, 1919, Jessie Wilson Sayre Papers.

383 *The day that followed: New York Times,* April 30 and May 1, 1919.

383 *That night, two olive-drab trains: Manchester Guardian,* May 2, 1919; *New-York Tribune,* April 30 and May 1, 1919; Eric D. Weitz, *Weimar Germany: Promise and Tragedy* (Princeton: Princeton University Press, 2007), 34.

383 *The transaction: Boston Globe* and *New-York Tribune,* May 2, 1919.

384 *On the same day:* Paul Mantoux, *The Deliberations of the Council of Four,* 425–27.

384 *The government of the young Chinese Republic:* Jonathan Clements, *Wellington Koo* (New York: Haus Publishing, 2008), 2.

385 *Wilson resisted:* Paul Mantoux, *The Deliberations of the Council of Four (March 24–June 28, 1919),* 1:324–25.

385 *Delivered by V. K. Wellington Koo: FRUS, 1919, The Paris Peace Conference,* 3:754–57.

385 *"simply overwhelmed the Japanese":* RL, *The Peace Negotiations,* 253.

385 *"a young Chinese cat":* Clemenceau, *Grandeur and Misery of Victory,* 140.

385 *The dispute disturbed Wilson more than any other controversy: PWW*, 58:244, 248.

385 *Wilson the idealist: PWW*, 58:111; Paul Mantoux, *The Deliberations of the Council of Four (March 24–June 28, 1919)*, 1:335.

386 *The Japanese compounded Wilson's anxieties:* Paul Mantoux, *The Deliberations of the Council of Four (March 24–June 28, 1919)*, 1:322.

386 *Lansing believed*: RL, "The Japanese Claims to Kiau Chau and Shantung Admitted," May 1, 1919, Confidential Memoranda, RL Papers, Princeton.

386 *Lloyd George believed:* Paul Mantoux, *The Deliberations of the Council of Four (March 24–June 28, 1919)*, 1:378.

386 *"They are not bluffers"*: RSB, *American Chronicle*, 411.

386 *If the Japanese followed: PWW*, 58:270–71.

386 *Ultimately Wilson joined Clemenceau and Lloyd George:* RSB, *What Wilson Did at Paris*, 104–5.

386 *Refusing to be party to a secret agreement:* Paul Mantoux, *The Deliberations of the Council of Four (March 24–June 28, 1919)*, 1:407–8.

386 *"I suppose it could be called an even break": PWW*, 58:244–45.

386 *He poured his feelings:* RL to Frank Polk, May 1, 1919, RL Papers, Princeton.

386 *He also joined Bliss and White: PWW*, 58:232–34.

386 *"Frankly"*: RL, *The Peace Negotiations*, 262–63.

386 *"Japan is strong and China is weak":* Newspaper clipping from *L'Europe Nouvelle* (May 17, 1919), in RL Papers, Library of Congress, 42:935–36.

386 *Wellington Koo:* Clements, *Wellington Koo*, 3.

387 *"But I'll be a dead hero":* Bonsal, *Suitors and Suppliants*, 243–44.

387 *On May 4:* Clements, *Wellington Koo*, 88–99.

387 *Wilson's minister to China resigned: PWW*, 61:631–34.

387 *Wilson remained confident: PWW*, 58:270–71.

387 *Writing an old friend:* RL to W. C. Stebbins, May 5, 1919, RL Papers, Princeton.

CHAPTER 33: *Settling the Accounts*

389 *May 7: WWLL: New York Times* and *Manchester Guardian*, May 8, 1919.

390 *Clemenceau rose again:* FRUS, *1919, The Paris Peace Conference*, 3:415–16.

390 *The count remained in his chair:* Bailey, *Wilson and the Peacemakers: Woodrow Wilson and the Lost Peace*, 290–91.

390 *He fiddled:* Thompson, *The Peace Conference Day by Day*, 361; *Manchester Guardian*, May 8, 1919; *PWW*, 58:534.

390 *The delegation's secretary: New York Times*, May 11, 1919.

390 *another of their colleagues said:* Clifford R. Lovin, *A School for Diplomats: The Paris Peace Conference of 1919* (Lanham, Md.: University Press of America, 1997), 62.

390 *The count began straightforwardly: Washington Post*, May 11, 1919; *PWW*, 58:514–17.

391 *The prime minister stayed put:* Bailey, *Wilson and the Peacemakers: Woodrow Wilson and the Lost Peace*, 290–91; Stevenson, *Lloyd George*, 183.

391 *"stupid": PWW*, 58:529.

391 *Orlando: PWW,* 58:499.

391 *The second was the public disclosure: New York Times,* May 9 and 10, 1919; *New–York Tribune,* May 11, 1919.

391 *The last was the news: New–York Tribune,* May 9, 1919.

391 *The German envoys stayed up all night:* Lovin, *A School for Diplomats,* 63.

391 *The treaty demanded:* Bailey, *Wilson and the Peacemakers: Woodrow Wilson and the Lost Peace,* 294–95.

391 *It forced the Germans: New York Times,* May 8, 1919.

392 *Grayson noticed: PWW,* 58:535.

392 *but Benham noticed: PWW,* 58:534.

392 *While Wilson was sunning himself:* RL, *The Big Four and Others of the Peace Conference,* 133.

392 *Nor did Lansing share:* RL, *The Peace Negotiations,* 274; "The Terms of Peace to Germany," May 8, 1919, Private Memoranda, RL Papers, Library of Congress. The version in Lansing's book is milder than the one in the memorandum.

392 *Other reactions soon followed:* Both the *New York Times* (May 9, 1919) and the *New–York Tribune* (May 10 and 11, 1919) published numerous excerpts of editorial opinion in the United States and Europe.

393 *In a single editorial:* "The Madness at Versailles," *Nation* 108, no. 2811 (May 17, 1919): 778–80.

393 *The most outspoken: FRUS, 1919, The Paris Peace Conference,* 11:569–75; Will Brownell and Richard N. Billings, *So Close to Greatness: A Biography of William C. Bullitt* (New York: Macmillan, 1987), 80–96.

393 *As the German delegation labored: PWW,* 59:13n5, 28n2, 129, 274–76.

394 *On the eve of their deadline: PWW,* 59:321–22.

394 *The German reply: New York Times* and *New-York Tribune,* May 30, 1919.

394 *"We hoped for the peace of justice": FRUS, 1919, The Paris Peace Conference,* 6:795.

394 *Taking away territory and peoples:* Ibid., 6:822.

394 *The expropriation of Germany's colonies:* Ibid., 6:841.

394 *To attain peace:* Ibid., 6:796–99.

395 *Wilson passed the next afternoon in the town of Suresnes: PWW,* 59:606–10, 621.

395 *Ray Baker had wondered:* RSB, *American Chronicle,* 431.

395 *As for the enemies: New York Times* and *New-York Tribune,* June 1, 1919.

396 *He understood the necessity: PWW,* 60:373.

396 *Strained to the limit: PWW,* 59:317, 625.

396 *a "hell-peace" or a "heaven-peace": IPCH,* 4:473.

396 *General Jan Smuts: PWW,* 59:413–17, 617–18.

397 *In the end:* Walworth, *Wilson and His Peacemakers,* 417. The minutes of the four British meetings offer a look at the wide range of opinions and ideas on the treaty's probable effects on British interests. See Kenneth Bourne and D. Cameron Watt, *British Documents on Foreign Affairs: Reports and Papers from the Foreign Office Confidential Print* (Bethesda, Md.: University Publications of America, c. 1991-1997). The minutes are in Part II, "From the First to the Second World

War," Series I, M. Dockrill, ed., *The Paris Peace Conference of 1919*, 4:91–115. Churchill's comment is on p. 101.

397 *Wilson maintained the appearance:* PWW, 59:637.

397 *But by June 2:* PWW, 60:4.

397 *Lloyd George took them to the brink:* Paul Mantoux, *The Deliberations of the Council of Four (March 24–June 28, 1919)*, 2:272–73.

397 *The crisis drove Wilson:* PWW, 60:76; WWWS, 3:469–70.

397 *The financial advisors:* PWW, 60:45–50.

397 *House said little:* PWW, 59:554–55, 623–24; EMH Diary, EMH Papers, June 1, 1919.

397 *To Wilson, the essential question was:* PWW, 60:67.

398 *Lloyd George's sparring:* MacMillan, *Paris 1919*, 220.

398 *Clemenceau, asked to shorten:* IPCH, 4:473–74.

398 *The victors' reply:* FRUS, 1919, The Paris Peace Conference, 6:929–34.

399 *Brockdorff-Rantzau left for Germany:* New York Times, June 18, 1919.

399 *By June 17:* Mayer, *Politics and Diplomacy of Peacemaking*, 807–8.

399 *Against him in the cabinet:* Ibid., 792.

399 *Seven cabinet ministers:* New York Times, June 17, 1919.

399 *On June 18:* Duroselle, *Clemenceau*, 766; Thompson, *The Peace Conference Day by Day*, 397–98.

399 *On June 19:* New-York Tribune, June 20, 1919.

399 *At two o'clock in the morning:* PWW, 61:32.

399 *On June 21:* The story of the scuttling is well told in Robert Massie, *Castles of Steel* (New York: Random House, 2003), 784–88.

399 *That evening, the new chancellor:* PWW, 61:72–77.

400 *The morning of June 23:* PWW, 61:81–82.

400 *The next news:* Paul Mantoux, *The Deliberations of the Council of Four (March 24–June 28, 1919)*, 2:528, 533.

400 *Germany would sign:* Thompson, *The Peace Conference Day by Day*, 403.

400 *Clemenceau ordered Foch to stand down:* MacMillan, *Paris 1919*, 474.

400 *With the signing set:* PWW, 61:240–45, 292–93. For a succinct accounting of the fate of each of Wilson's points (the celebrated fourteen plus the eleven set forth in later addresses), see Herbert Hoover, *America's First Crusade* (New York: Charles Scribner's Sons, 1942), 66–71.

401 *The unfinished business also included Russia:* Bailey, *Wilson and the Peacemakers: Woodrow Wilson and the Lost Peace*, 311.

402 *"a closed conference":* Walter Lippmann, "The Peace Conference," *Yale Review* 8 (July 1919): 721.

402 *The treaty was signed:* Except where otherwise noted, this account is based on the coverage of the event in the *New York Times*, June 29, 1919, and "The Signing of the Treaty of Peace with Germany at Versailles on June 28th, 1919," June 28, 1919, Confidential Memoranda, RL Papers, Princeton.

403 *and four hundred members of the press:* RSB, *American Chronicle*, 454.

403 *As House approached the table:* EBW, *My Memoir,* 269.

403 *"brief, dry, and ungenerous":* Duroselle, *Clemenceau,* 767.

404 *General Smuts:* PWW, 61: 304n3. See also Anthony Lentin, *Lloyd George, Woodrow Wilson and the Guilt of Germany: An Essay in the Pre-History of Appeasement* (Baton Rouge: Louisiana State University Press, 1985), 128–30.

404 *Three days before the ceremony:* RL Diary, June 26, 1919; RL Papers, Library of Congress; *New York Times,* June 29, 1919; Jonathan Clements, *Wellington Koo* (New York: Haus Publishing, 2008), 91.

404 *President Poincaré's reception:* EBW, *My Memoir,* 269–71.

404 *Lloyd George:* EBH Diary, June 29, 1919.

404 *"I feel as though I were losing":* Thompson, *The Peace Conference Day by Day,* 421–22.

404 *House too had come:* PWW, 61:354.

404 *Also on the platform:* RL Diary, June 28, 1919, RL Papers, Library of Congress; RL to Frederick M. Boyer, June 18, 1919, RL Papers, Princeton. Lansing also discussed his worry that the Senate was determined to sabotage Wilson in "The Ferocity of the Attacks on the President in Congress," May 19, 1919, Confidential Memoranda, RL Papers, Library of Congress.

CHAPTER 34: *Stroking the Cat the Wrong Way*

407 *"Well, little girl":* EBW, *My Memoir,* 271.

407 *Grayson:* PWW, 61:354, 360, 370, 385, 397.

408 *A day later:* PWW, 61:385–88.

408 *A fourth:* Baruch, *Baruch: The Public Years,* 122.

408 *On July 8: New York Times,* July 9, 1919; PWW, 61:400–401, 404; Breckinridge Long Diary, July 8, 1919, Breckinridge Long Papers, Library of Congress.

408 *Wilson began by giving up:* PWW, 61:474–75; Cooper, *Breaking the Heart of the World,* 121.

408 *He also invited: New York Times,* July 19, 1919.

408 *And on July 10:* PWW, 61:417–24.

409 *Amendments needed it:* PWW, 62:35–40.

409 *The president's arrival:* PWW, 61:424–25; *New York Times,* July 11, 1919.

409 *Only in the final minutes:* PWW, 61:426–36.

409 *Most Republicans. . . . Most Democrats: New York World, Chicago Tribune,* and *Atlanta Constitution,* July 11, 1919.

410 *But one Democrat:* PWW, 61:445–46.

410 *(The editors):* PWW, 61:446n.

410 *On the night of June 2:* The details of the bomb at Palmer's house appeared in *The Washington Post,* June 3, 1919. The information on the Justice Department's response to radical aliens is from Stanley Coben, *A. Mitchell Palmer: Politician* (New York: Columbia University Press, 1963), 214–15, and from the *Annual*

Report of the Attorney General of the United States for the Year 1920, Washington, D.C.: U.S. Government Printing Office, 172–79.

410 *Palmer immediately added: Investigation Activities of the Department of Justice: Letter from the Attorney General* (Washington, D.C.: U.S. Government Printing Office, 1919), 13.

410 *Each of the race riots:* William Cohen, "Riots, Racism, and Hysteria: The Response of Federal Investigative Officials to the Race Riots of 1919," *Massachusetts Review* 13, no. 3 (Summer 1972): 375–76, 379.

411 *"a dangerous spirit of defiance": Investigation Activities of the Department of Justice: Letter from the Attorney General,* 187.

411 *"We are ignored":* Ibid., 171.

411 *Just before leaving Paris: PWW,* 61:351–52.

411 *Eugene V. Debs: PWW,* 61:577; 62:58–59.

411 *By early August:* United States Council of National Defense, *An Analysis of the High Cost of Living Problem* (Washington, D.C.: U.S. Government Printing Office, August 1919), 5–23.

412 *But government action: PWW,* 62:209–19.

412 *Members of both parties: St. Louis Post-Dispatch,* Aug. 9, 1919.

412 *(Wilson forwarded a few): PWW,* 62:219.

412 *On July 31:* Garraty, *Henry Cabot Lodge,* 366.

412 *some Democrats:* Houston, *Eight Years with Wilson's Cabinet,* 2:5; Creel, *The War, the World and Wilson,* 340.

412 *A poll: Literary Digest,* April 5, 1919.

412 *Lodge understood:* Garraty, *Henry Cabot Lodge,* 350.

413 *When a like-minded senator:* James E. Watson, *As I Knew Them,* 190–91, 200.

413 *Observing Wilson's hypersensitivity:* HCL, *The Senate and the League of Nations,* 215–16, 218–19, 226.

413 *Ratification required: PWW,* 61:563–65.

413 *Foes as well as friends:* See, for example, *PWW,* 61:544–47, 594.

413 *and Ambassador Jusserand assured him:* Bailey, *Wilson and the Peacemakers: Woodrow Wilson and the Great Betrayal,* 14–15.

413 *Wilson seemed to believe: PWW,* 62:92.

413 *Wilson's refusal:* Cooper, *Woodrow Wilson,* 513.

413 *some of his allies: PWW,* 62:45, 71.

413 *Tumulty and McAdoo:* Cooper, *Woodrow Wilson,* 512–14.

413 *"[H]is face": PWW,* 62:258–59.

413 *The next day Lodge attacked:* HCL, *The Senate and the League of Nations,* 380–410.

414 *A stupendous ovation: New York Times,* Aug. 13, 1919.

414 *"The greatest nationalist": PWW,* 63:33.

414 *To beat back Wilson's foes: New-York Tribune,* Aug. 14, 1919.

415 *Lodge, master of the game: PWW,* 62:275–76.

415 *Wilson granted:* Cooper, *Woodrow Wilson,* 515.

415 *"We shall not inquire":* HCL to John T. Morse, Jr., Aug. 18, 1919, HCL Papers.

415 *Sixteen of the seventeen:* PWW, 62:340–44.

415 *(Lodge and Senator Philander C. Knox):* PWW, 62:353–57.

415 *Wilson professed bafflement:* PWW, 62:340–44.

415 *For three and a half hours:* PWW, 62:355–56, 361–62.

416 *Senator William E. Borah:* PWW, 62:27–29, 363.

416 *Lodge had already stuffed the treaty:* HCL, *The Senate and the League of Nations,* 156.

416 *and on August 23:* Ibid., 162.

416 *Discussing the vote with Lansing:* PWW, 62:507.

416 *Following the fight from London:* William Starr Myers, ed., *Woodrow Wilson: Some Princeton Memories* (Princeton: Princeton University Press, 1946), 41–42.

416 *Edith Wilson and Cary Grayson:* EBW, *My Memoir,* 272, 274; JPT, *Woodrow Wilson as I Know Him,* 434–35.

416 *Tumulty drew up a schedule:* JPT, *Woodrow Wilson as I Know Him,* 438.

416 *"The president was endeavoring":* CTG, Western Trip Diary, Introduction, Sept. 1919, CTG Papers.

417 *His allies: Washington Post,* Sept. 7, 1919.

417 Constitutional Government in the United States: PWW, 62:632n14.

417 *And strange as it sounds: New York Times,* Sept. 27, 1919.

417 *The first lady and Grayson:* EBW, *My Memoir,* 274–75; PWW, 63:513.

417 *The president had not had time:* JPT, *Woodrow Wilson as I Know Him,* 439.

417 *In St. Louis:* PWW, 63:36–37, 343.

418 *He admitted the treaty's imperfections:* PWW, 63:24, 97.

418 *He conceded that the League:* PWW, 63: 101-2, 105, 359, 459, 472, 508.

418 *More than once:* PWW, 63:221–22, 243–44, 349–50, 373.

418 *After reciting:* PWW, 63:350.

418 *Arguing the case in Oregon:* PWW, 63:281.

418 *The destructive work:* PWW, 63:9.

418 *From first to last:* PWW, 63:134.

418 *The slight:* PWW, 63:235. The supporter was Vance McCormick, a progressive Democrat fighting hard for U.S. membership in the League.

418 *What were the gentlemen afraid of?:* PWW, 63:115.

418 *Had the gentlemen not read:* PWW, 63:85.

418 *The time had come:* PWW, 63:29. "Put up or shut up" became a refrain. See also 63:105, 228.

419 *Wilson seldom asked anything:* PWW, 63:294.

419 *few of his listeners: Washington Post* and *Philadelphia Public Ledger,* Sept. 7, 1919.

419 *Senators hostile:* Cooper, *Breaking the Heart of the World,* 167–68.

419 *A week after Wilson left Washington: New York Times,* Sept. 11, 1919.

419 *Sixteen of them:* See Stone, *The Irreconcilables.*

419 *Nor could they imagine:* Link, *Woodrow Wilson: Revolution, War, and Peace,* 110.

419 *authored by Lodge:* Senate Report, No. 176, 66th Cong., 1st Sess, Part 1.

419 *Talking about his handiwork:* Cooper, *Breaking the Heart of the World,* 166.

420 *At the same time:* WHT to Mr. Whiting, Sept. 12, 1919, and WHT to Horace Taft, Sept. 16, 1919, WHT Papers.

420 *William C. Bullitt:* Bullitt, *The Bullitt Mission to Russia,* 102–3.

421 *Exhausted:* CTG, *Woodrow Wilson,* 97; EBW, *My Memoir,* 280.

421 *After reading the telegram:* JPT, *Woodrow Wilson as I Know Him,* 442.

421 *Although Grayson witnessed the outburst:* PWW, 63:339n4. Grayson shared these details five years after the fact, in a conversation with Breckinridge Long, a State Department official who was a strong supporter of the League of Nations.

421 *The Senate had homed in:* PWW, 63:432–33.

421 *In Reno:* PWW, 63:428–41.

421 *In Salt Lake City:* PWW, 63:451, 453–54, 459.

421 *The next day, at Cheyenne:* EBW, *My Memoir,* 282–83; PWW, 63:467.

422 *Picking up where he had left off:* PWW, 63:469.

422 *Vowing not to surrender:* PWW, 63:480.

422 *In Denver: Baltimore Sun,* Sept. 26, 1919; PWW, 63:487.

422 *Jimmie Starling of the Secret Service put a hand on his arm:* Starling and Sugrue, *Starling of the White House,* 151–52.

422 *Telling of his visit:* PWW, 63:512–13.

423 *Soon after the train left Pueblo:* CTG, *Woodrow Wilson,* 97–98; PWW, 63:518–19.

423 *Starling, who followed them:* Starling and Sugrue, *Starling of the White House,* 152.

423 *But in the middle of the night:* EBW, *My Memoir,* 284–85.

423 *He looked at Tumulty:* JPT, *Woodrow Wilson as I Know Him,* 446–48. While the three accounts vary, the only difference worth flagging is Tumulty's description of Wilson's appearance after the stroke he had that night. Tumulty's memory was faulty; the stroke happened a week later.

423 *Just after nine o'clock: Chicago Tribune, New York Times,* and *New-York Tribune,* Sept. 27, 1919.

CHAPTER 35: *Paralyzed*

424 *The tracks:* EBW, *My Memoir,* 285–87; PWW, 63:532–33.

424 *but at 8:50 a.m.:* PWW, 63:633–35.

425 *Wilson had had a major stroke:* Ryan D. Jacobson, "President Wilson's Brain Trust: Woodrow Wilson, Francis X. Dercum, and American Neurology," *Journal of the History of the Neurosciences* 18 (2009): 67; Weinstein, *Woodrow Wilson,* 357; PWW, 63:644.

425 *Vice President Thomas Riley Marshall: Recollections of Thomas Riley Marshall: A Hoosier Salad* (Indianapolis: Bobbs-Merrill, 1925), 368; Charles M. Thomas, *Thomas Riley Marshall: Hoosier Statesman* (Oxford, Ohio: Mississippi Valley Press, 1939), 221–22.

425 *Apparently torn:* RL Diary, Oct. 2–3, 1919, RL Papers, Library of Congress.

425 *Tumulty summoned Grayson:* PWW, 63:541.

426 *Lansing raised the idea:* RL Diary, Oct. 2–4, 1919, RL Papers, Library of Congress; JPT, *Woodrow Wilson as I Know Him,* 443–45.

426 *Two days after the stroke:* PWW, 64:510.

427 *On Monday morning:* PWW, 63:555; CTG Diary, CTG Papers, Oct. 6, 1919, CTG Papers.

427 *There were many reasons not to act:* PWW, 63:561–63.

427 *Grayson told Breckinridge Long:* PWW, 63:558–59.

428 *Tumulty briefed J. Fred Essary:* Thomas, *Thomas Riley Marshall,* 206.

428 *Tumulty did not reveal:* Blum, *Joe Tumulty and the Wilson Era,* 215.

428 *Essary went to the Capitol:* Thomas, *Thomas Riley Marshall,* 207.

428 *Though the cover-up:* Ibid., 219–21.

428 *Edith Wilson's memoir:* EBW, *My Memoir,* 288–89.

429 *Writing in the 1980s:* Weinstein, *Woodrow Wilson,* 360.

429 *Many of the records:* PWW, 64:ix.

429 *About one point there is no doubt:* EBW, *My Memoir,* 288–89.

430 *On occasion Grayson also served:* RL Diary, Oct. 8 and 9, 1919, RL Papers, Library of Congress; PWW, 63:559–60, 637; Davis and Trani, *The First Cold War,* 192–93; Max Boot, *The Savage Wars of Peace: Small Wars and the Rise of American Power* (New York: Basic Books, 2002), 226–29.

430 *Minuscule as the president's role was:* PWW, 63:560–61.

430 *Though Grayson has been thrashed:* Link, "Dr. Grayson's Predicament," *Proceedings of the American Philosophical Society* 138, no. 4 (Dec. 1994): 491, 493n21.

431 *Baruch:* CPA Diary, Oct. 17, 1919, CPA Papers.

431 *The first attempt:* PWW, 63:563–64.

431 *Dercum:* Washington Post, Oct. 14, 1919.

431 *Grayson:* PWW, 63:564.

431 *Suspecting that there was more:* PWW, 63:564–65.

431 *Grayson parried:* PWW, 63:569–71.

431 *The critical downturn:* PWW, 63:572, EBW, *My Memoir,* 291–92

431 *Fortunately, several days of hot compresses:* Cooper, *Woodrow Wilson,* 534.

432 *Ike Hoover would remember:* PWW, 63:635–36.

432 *In her memoir:* EBW, *My Memoir,* 288.

432 *Bert E. Park:* PWW, 63:646.

CHAPTER 36: *Altogether an Unfortunate Mess*

433 *Congress passed a raft of bills:* Bailey, *Wilson and the Peacemakers: Woodrow Wilson and the Great Betrayal,* 142.

433 *William Howard Taft:* Washington Post, Sept. 29, 1919.

433 *Colonel House, who had stayed in Europe:* Bonsal, *Unfinished Business,* 271–80.

435 *As the vote of the treaty neared:* Baruch, *Baruch: The Public Years,* 127.

435 *So did Gilbert M. Hitchcock:* James M. Cox, *Journey Through My Year* (New York: Simon & Schuster, 1946), 104–5; *Washington Post,* July 12, 1919.

435 *Hitchcock sensed: Chicago Tribune,* Oct. 7, 1919; *PWW,* 63:44; Bailey, *Wilson and the Peacemakers: Woodrow Wilson and the Great Betrayal,*148.

436 *The senator was shocked: PWW,* 64:45n1. The date of Hitchcock's first visit with the stricken president is unknown, but a note in the diary of Senator Henry F. Ashurst (*PWW,* 63:586) indicates that it took place before October 21.

436 *(Wilson had grown it):* Weinstein, *Woodrow Wilson,* 357.

436 *In mid-November:* EBW, *My Memoir,* 296–97.

436 *A few days later, Hitchcock tried again: PWW,* 64:37–38.

436 *Two days before the vote: PWW,* 64:43–45; Garraty, *Henry Cabot Lodge,* 377–78.

437 *Perhaps inspired: PWW,* 64:50, 57.

437 *Hitchcock allowed himself: PWW,* 64:50–51.

437 *"nullification":* Cooper, *Woodrow Wilson,* 543.

438 *On November 18:* Bonsal, *Unfinished Business,* 276–77.

438 *Watching Wilson and Lodge:* Pringle, *The Life and Times of William Howard Taft,* 2:949.

438 *That evening, Hitchcock made one last effort: PWW,* 63:58–60; Bailey, *Wilson and the Peacemakers: Woodrow Wilson and the Great Betrayal,* 388–89.

439 *"Breakfasted early,"* Sparks, ed., *A Many Colored Toga,* 114.

439 *The full Senate:* Except where otherwise noted, my account of this historic day relies on Cranston, *The Killing of the Peace,* 219–33.

439 *Within minutes:* Cooper, *Breaking the Heart of the World,* 264–65.

439 *After months of senatorial speechifying:* Bailey, *Wilson and the Peacemakers: Woodrow Wilson and the Great Betrayal,*187.

439 *Ashurst was applauded but outflanked:* Stone, *The Irreconcilables,* 144.

439 *The low point: Nashville Tennessean,* Nov. 20, 1919.

440 *William E. Borah:* William Hard, "Big Bill Borah," *New Republic,* Sept. 6, 1922, 36; Marian C. McKenna, *Borah* (Ann Arbor: University of Michigan Press, 1961), 161–67; John Milton Cooper, Jr., "William E. Borah, Political Thespian," *Pacific Northwest Quarterly* 56, no. 4 (Oct. 1965): 145–53.

440 *"If the Savior": New York Times,* Feb. 1, 1919.

440 *With or without reservations: Congressional Record,* 66th Cong., 1st Sess., 8781–84.

442 *A small group of Republicans:* Alice Roosevelt Longworth, *Crowded Hours* (New York: Charles Scribner's Sons, 1935), 292.

442 *When the* Chicago Tribune's *correspondent: Chicago Tribune,* Nov. 20, 1919.

442 *The press blamed: New-York Tribune,* Nov. 20, 1919.

442 *From her exchanges with Hitchcock:* EBW, *My Memoir,* 297.

442 *Despite his banishment: PWW,* 64:88–90.

443 *He was not counseling surrender: PWW,* 64:96.

443 *House's suggestions:* Neu, *Colonel House,* 433–34.

443 *House would never again:* George and George, *Woodrow Wilson and Colonel House,* 306.

443 *Hitchcock continued to insist: PWW,* 64:70–72, 93–94.

443 *His voice was weak:* Weinstein, *Woodrow Wilson,* 369.

443 *Wilson's mind was often sharp:* Blum, *Joe Tumulty and the Wilson Era*, 312n5.

443 *The task of writing:* PWW, 64:73–87 (Tumulty's draft with Wilson's revisions); PWW, 64:106–16 (the version submitted to Congress).

444 *George Moses . . . Albert Fall:* Berg, *Wilson*, 659.

444 *The critics were immediately answered:* Wall Street Journal, Dec. 4, 1919.

444 *On December 4:* PWW, 64:123–25.

444 *William O. Jenkins:* Gilbert M. Joseph and Timothy J. Henderson, eds., *The Mexico Reader: History, Culture, Politics* (Durham: Duke University Press, 2002), 357.

444 *"a smelling expedition":* Except where otherwise noted, my account of the meeting is based on notes taken by Edith Wilson (*PWW*, 64:133–35) and Cary Grayson (*PWW*, 64:135–39).

444 *Edith, cast in the role:* EBW, *My Memoir*, 299.

445 *"I hope you consider me sincere":* Ibid., 299. John Milton Cooper, Jr., a scholar with an encyclopedic knowledge of Wilson, suspects that the retort is apocryphal, because it does not appear in notes taken at the meeting by Edith Wilson and Cary Grayson. (Cooper, *Woodrow Wilson*, 548, 661n30.) Cooper might be right. But as he occasionally says about other thinly documented remarks, "It sounds like Wilson."

445 *As if in a play:* Jenkins had been released at midnight. (*FRUS, 1919*, 2:589.)

445 *The newsmen on the portico:* PWW, 64:129–32.

445 *Believing that Wilson was more disabled:* PWW, 64:139–40.

446 *The facts that Lansing craved:* PWW, 67:611-14.

446 *"White House officials":* PWW, 64:187.

446 *On December 15:* PWW, 64:187.

447 *and Democrats who had supported:* PWW, 64:192; New-York Tribune, Dec. 21, 1919.

447 *Hitchcock's most recent exchanges:* PWW, 64:203

447 *The reply came from Edith Wilson:* PWW, 64:206.

447 *Defying Wilson's wishes:* New York Times, Dec. 21, 1919.

447 *Angered by Lodge's pettiness:* Boston Globe, Dec. 24, 1919.

CHAPTER 37: *Breaking the Heart of the World*

448 *The Wilsons had a quiet Christmas:* New York Times, Dec. 25, 1919; Washington Post, Dec. 26, 1919.

448 *The president signed a bill:* It was the Edge Act, enabling American national banks to engage in foreign banking through subsidiaries chartered by the Federal Reserve Board.

448 *A few days later:* New York Times, Dec. 29, 1919.

448 *"It would probably have been better":* PWW, 64:321, 363n1.

448 *Wilson's fight:* PWW, 64:238.

449 *On this occasion:* PWW, 64:329–30.

449 *Publicly, Henry Cabot Lodge:* Bailey, *Wilson and the Peacemakers: Woodrow Wilson and the Great Betrayal,* 229–33; Cooper, *Breaking the Heart of the World,* 309–11.

449 *Wilson's cause:* Except where otherwise noted, this section is drawn from Keynes, *The Economic Consequences of the Peace,* 38–55.

449 *In the United States:* Cooper, *Breaking the Heart of the World,* 326–27.

450 *Years later:* Baruch, *Baruch: The Public Years,* 111–12.

450 *Herbert Hoover:* Herbert Hoover, *The Ordeal of Woodrow Wilson,* 234–35, 263–64; *New York Times,* Sept. 14, 1919

451 *Senator Borah:* Stone, *The Irreconcilables,* 164–65.

451 *The other thunderbolt:* Leon E. Boothe, "A Fettered Envoy: Lord Grey's Mission to the United States, 1919–1920," *Review of Politics* 33, no. 1 (Jan. 1971): 78–94.

451 *but Lansing suspected:* EMH Diary, EMH Papers, Nov. 20, 1919; RL to John W. Davis, Jan. 1, 1920, RL Papers, Princeton; Phyllis Lee Levin, *Edith and Woodrow,* 399–404.

451 *(France was flashing):* New York Times, Dec. 8, 1919.

451 *Unable to do more:* Times (London), Jan. 31, 1920.

452 *In Washington:* PWW, 64:363–64.

452 *Unwilling:* Boothe, "A Fettered Envoy: Lord Grey's Mission to the United States, 1919–1920," 91–92; *PWW,* 64:366–67, 380.

452 *Next Wilson lit into Lansing:* PWW, 64:383.

452 *It was a peculiar query:* Daniel M. Smith, "Robert Lansing and the Wilson Interregnum, 1919–1920," *The Historian* 21, no. 2 (Feb. 1, 1959): 139–41.

452 *Before answering:* PWW, 64:385–86; 388–89.

452 *Wilson replied:* PWW, 64:404, 410, 414–15.

453 *In a talk with Edith Wilson:* RSB, *American Chronicle,* 471–72.

453 *"The poor president!":* PWW, 64:360.

454 *The new resolution of ratification:* Bailey, *Wilson and the Peacemakers: Woodrow Wilson and the Great Betrayal,* 263–64; Cooper, *Breaking the Heart of the World,* 356–59.

454 *Wilson had just made a nod:* PWW, 64:329–30.

454 *Homing in on Article X:* PWW, 65:67–71.

454 *The letter won:* Bailey, *Wilson and the Peacemakers: Woodrow Wilson and the Great Betrayal,* 267.

454 *The last chance for ratification:* Cooper, *Breaking the Heart of the World,* 366–67; Bailey, *Wilson and the Peacemakers: Woodrow Wilson and the Great Betrayal,* 267. The *Chicago Tribune* (March 20, 1920) published a list detailing the vote and broke it down by party. In favor: 28 Republicans and 21 Democrats. Against: 12 Republicans and 23 Democrats.

454 *Mourning the outcome:* New York Times, March 20, 1920.

454 *and some historians have argued:* Widenor, *Henry Cabot Lodge and the Search for an American Foreign Policy,* 328–46.

454 *Even Lodge's intimates:* Karl Schriftgiesser, *The Gentleman from Massachusetts,* (Boston: Little, Brown, 1944), 350–51.

455 *Others blamed:* See, e.g., Nevins, *Henry White,* 482–83.

455 *Senator Irvine Lenroot: Chicago Tribune,* March 20, 1920.

455 *Lodge ascribed the defeat:* HCL to J. M. Beck, March 22, 1920, HCL Papers.

456 *In the opinion:* House and Seymour, eds., *What Really Happened at Paris,* 1921, 424.

CHAPTER 38: *Best of the Second-Raters*

457 *Edith waited:* EBW, *My Memoir,* 303.

457 *"very blue":* PWW, 65:108.

457 *Wilson's fighting spirit:* PWW, 65:117–19.

457 *Wilson ignored it:* PWW, 65:123–25.

457 *Wilson was now able to walk slowly:* Starling and Sugrue, *Starling of the White House,* 156–57.

458 *Summoned: PWW,* 65:179–80.

458 *A day later the cabinet assembled:* Houston, *Eight Years with Wilson's Cabinet,* 2:70.

458 *the postmaster general:* Daniels, *The Wilson Era,* 2:461.

458 *The Senate's rejection:* Ambrosius, *Woodrow Wilson and the American Diplomatic Tradition,* 254.

458 *Taking matters into its own hands: PWW,* 65:328–29.

459 *The Republican short list:* Wesley M. Bagby, *The Road to Normalcy: The Presidential Campaign and Election of 1920* (Baltimore: Johns Hopkins University Press, 1962), 25–36.

459 *"The simple fact is":* James E. Watson, *As I Knew Them,* 226.

459 *"How can he lead":* RSB, *American Chronicle,* 485.

459 *The Democrats' early favorites:* Bagby, *The Road to Normalcy,* 63–78; Kurt Wimer, "Woodrow Wilson and a Third Nomination," *Pennsylvania History* 29, no. 2 (April 1962): 202–4.

459 *Cox struck him: PWW,* 65:435.

459 *"Dear Mac": PWW,* 67:606.

459 *As the spring wore on: PWW,* 65:382.

459 *In desperation he confided:* Blum, *Joe Tumulty and the Wilson Era,* 242–44, 320n32.

460 *Seibold's visit was staged: PWW,* 65:401–15.

460 *Seibold returned the next day: PWW,* 65:415–21.

460 *"There ain't any first-raters":* The remark, made by Senator Frank Brandegee of Connecticut, is quoted in Clinton W. Gilbert, *The Mirrors of Washington* (New York: G. P. Putnam's Sons, 1921), 5.

460 *When Seibold asked:* The Republican platform can be found in Gerhard Peters and John T. Woolley, *The American Presidency Project,* http://www.presidency.ucsb.edu/ws/?pid=29635, accessed April 17, 2017.

461 *By refusing to sideline himself: Los Angeles Times,* June 21, 1920.

461 *They could not openly disown the president: St. Louis Post-Dispatch* and *Baltimore Sun,* June 20, 1920.

461   *Reading Seibold: New-York Tribune,* June 20, 1920.

461   *The boss of Illinois: San Francisco Chronicle,* June 20, 1920.

461   *The first casualty: Baltimore Sun,* June 19, 1920; *PWW,* 65:435.

461   *Insiders understood:* Bagby, *The Road to Normalcy,* 70–71.

461   *Discussing the Democratic platform: PWW,* 65:383, 400, 435; *St. Louis Post-Dispatch,* June 20, 1920.

461   *Grayson was even more direct:* Berg, *Wilson,* 689.

462   *"the flower of his cabinet": PWW,* 65:212.

462   *New to Washington:* Wimer, "Woodrow Wilson and a Third Nomination," 208n61; *PWW,* 65:432.

462   *A dozen men: New-York Tribune,* June 19, 1920.

462   *When the convention opened: New York Times,* June 29, 1920.

462   *Colby told a reporter:* Ibid., July 1, 1920.

462   *On Friday:* Bagby, *The Road to Normalcy,* 112, 118–19.

462   *Colby's contrition: PWW,* 65:490.

462   *On Sunday: PWW,* 65:493–94.

463   *Colby folded: PWW,* 65:496.

463   *the balloting dragged on:* Bagby, *The Road to Normalcy,* 116.

463   *James M. Cox: Washington Post,* July 7, 1920, and July 16, 1957; *Chicago Tribune,* July 7, 1920; *Newsday* (New York), July 16, 1957; *San Francisco Chronicle,* July 7, 1920.

463   *"He's a fine boy": Baltimore Sun,* July 7, 1920.

463   *The boy:* Ward, *A First-Class Temperament,* 511.

463   *Wilson wired his congratulations: PWW,* 65:499–500.

463   *Watching from a distance:* Ward, *A First-Class Temperament,* 515.

464   *Wilson, clearly in low spirits: PWW,* 65:520–21.

464   *The convention had been unsettling for Wilson: PWW,* 65:481, 488.

464   *He was so depressed: PWW,* 65:512, 514.

464   *Although slow to abandon: PWW,* 65:54–55; Christine A. Lunardini and Thomas J. Knock, "Woodrow Wilson and Woman Suffrage: A New Look," *Political Science Quarterly* 95, no. 4 (Winter 1980–1981): 671.

464   *"normalcy":* Murray, *The Harding Era,* 70.

464   *Early in the campaign:* Frederick E. Schortmeier, *Rededicating America: Life and Recent Speeches of Warren G. Harding* (Indianapolis: Bobbs-Merrill,1920), 223–24.

464   *"The country was tired":* Gilbert, *The Mirrors of Washington,* 7.

464   *He reminded voters on October 3: PWW,* 66:181–83.

464   *On October 27: PWW,* 66:273–80; *Boston Globe,* Oct. 28 and 29, 1920; *Washington Post,* Oct. 28, 1920.

465   *Those who noticed: Christian Science Monitor,* Oct. 30, 1920; *PWW,* 66:289–91; *New-York Tribune,* Oct. 30, 1920.

465   *"Tomorrow the dirty job":* H. L. Mencken, *A Carnival of Buncombe: Writings on Politics,* edited by Malcolm Moos (Chicago: University of Chicago, 1984), 17–18, 32, 35.

466 *"The American people wanted a change"*: Bailey, *A Diplomatic History of the American People,* 679–80.

466 *The* Nation *observed: Nation* 111, no. 2889 (Nov. 17, 1920): 548.

466 *"Another Samson"*: EMH Diary, EMH Papers, EMH Papers, Nov. 13, 1920.

466 *Lodge privately boasted:* Garraty, *Henry Cabot Lodge,* 399.

466 *To the relief of his caretakers: PWW,* 66:306; JPT, *Woodrow Wilson as I Know Him,* 501.

466 *Stockton: PWW,* 66:319–20.

466 *When asked again to pardon Debs: PWW,* 66:25, 343n1, 515–16, 533–35; JPT, *Woodrow Wilson as I Know Him,* 504–5.

466 *Ray Stannard Baker: PWW,* 66:435, 438–42.

467 *A week later: PWW,* 66:484.

467 *A few shafts of sunlight: PWW,* 66:380–83.

467 *Wilson also managed: PWW,* 66:484–90.

468 *December also brought a Nobel Peace Prize: PWW,* 66:517.

468 *The prize carried:* Fixed at about 150,000 Swedish kronor, the prize had amounted to about $40,000 before the war, but the exchange rate in 1920 reduced Wilson's award to $29,100. *New York Times,* Dec. 7, 1920.

468 *After weighing the merits:* EBW, *My Memoir,* 308; *PWW,* 65:506.

468 *Months of searching:* EBW, *My Memoir,* 311–12; *New-York Tribune,* Dec. 18, 1920; *Washington Post,* Jan. 23 and Feb. 6, 1921.

468 *With a nudge from Grayson: PWW,* 67:vii; 137n3.

468 *Five of his Princeton chums: PWW,* 67:116–17, 148, 167–68.

468 *Wilson also imagined: PWW,* 67:107, 160–61, 190.

469 *but Grayson had walked: New York Times,* March 5, 1921.

469 *"For a moment":* Lawrence, *The True Story of Woodrow Wilson,* 307–8.

469 *Pershing, who had watched Wilson:* Smythe, *Pershing,* 273.

469 *Wilson flushed:* JPT, *Woodrow Wilson as I Know Him,* 509.

469 *But Wilson looked Lodge in the eye:* Lawrence, *The True Story of Woodrow Wilson,* 309.

CHAPTER 39: *Swimming Upstream*

471 *In the three years:* EBW, *My Memoir,* 321–22, 325, 332; *PWW,* 67:185n1; 68:398–99.

471 *To minimize the disorientation:* Ibid., 320–21.

472 *Edith's tenderness: PWW,* 67:237–38, 245–46, 256, 268–69, 284, 288–89.

472 *The press: New York World, PWW,* 67:216–29; *Baltimore Sun,* March 3, 1921; *Chicago Tribune,* March 3, 1921; *Afro-American* (Baltimore), March 11, 1921.

473 *Wilson had no intention: PWW,* 67:60, 238.

473 *The book's success:* A useful summary of *The Peace Negotiations* appears in *The New York Times,* March 25, 1921.

473 *two more memoirs: The Big Four and Others of the Peace Conference* (1921) and *War Memoirs of Robert Lansing, Secretary of State* (published posthumously in 1935).

473 *when Harding announced:* Kurt Wimer and Sarah Wimer, "The Harding Administration, the League of Nations, and the Separate Peace Treaty," *Review of Politics* 29, no. 1 (Jan. 1967): 15–16.

473 *Sir Maurice Hankey: PWW,* 67:462n2.

473 *Wilson visited the Washington offices: PWW,* 67:370–71; 68:202, 211–14, 231; EBW, *My Memoir,* 327–29.

473 *Another try at writing a book: PWW,* 68:39–42.

473 *With enormous effort: PWW,* 68:342–49n1, 393–95.

473 *"I am tired":* Irwin Hood Hoover, *Forty-Two Years at the White House,* 108.

474 *They left S Street: PWW,* 67:289.

474 *In the evening:* EBW, *My Memoir,* 324–26.

474 *Every Saturday night: PWW,* 67:308–9, 380–88; 68:404.

474 *By the end of June: PWW,* 67:360, 395–98.

474 *He relished:* Kerney, *The Political Education of Woodrow Wilson,* 485.

474 *He was also pleased: PWW,* 67:266, 334; Gene Smith, *When the Cheering Stopped,* 206.

474 *Much of the work:* Ward, *A First-Class Temperament,* 625n1.

474 *After a June visit: PWW,* 67:302, 333–34, 392.

474 *Wilson occasionally sent notes: PWW,* 67:392, 448–49, 68:36, 280.

474 *Roosevelt, unsure of his political prospects:* Ward, *A First-Class Temperament,* 563.

475 *Wilson too: PWW,* 67:311, 395.

475 *Still convinced: New York Times* and *New-York Tribune,* Sept. 27, 1921.

475 *When the treaty passed: PWW,* 67:422n4, 430.

475 *Overlooking Wilson's plot: PWW,* 67:400–402, 438–40.

475 *Everything was agreeable: PWW,* 67:445–46.

475 *who persuaded him: PWW,* 67:454n1.

475 *Armistice Day:* Details of Wilson's Armistice Day are from the *Atlanta Constitution,* Nov. 11 and 13, 1921; *New York Evening Post,* Nov. 11, 1921; *Chicago Tribune, Los Angeles Times, New York Times,* and *Washington Post,* Nov. 12, 1921; *Collier's,* Feb. 18, 1922, 14. The *World's* coverage is reprinted in *PWW,* 67:449–53.

476 *Although Wilson returned to the silence: PWW,* 67:313–401.

477 *Invited to attend: PWW,* 67:444.

477 *It was just as well: New York Times,* Nov. 13, 1921.

477 *As the presiding officer: Baltimore Sun,* Nov. 13, 1921.

477 *None would hold for the ages:* Herring, *From Colony to Superpower,* 452–56.

477 *"the Republican Versailles":* Adler, *The Uncertain Giant,* 62.

477 *In a swipe: St. Louis-Post Dispatch,* Feb. 5, 1922.

477 *But The Kansas City Post:* Quoted in the *Chicago Tribune,* Nov. 13, 1921.

477 *Wilson rejected: PWW,* 67:490, 511, 585.

478 *On January 15, 1922: PWW,* 67:521–23; *Washington Post,* Jan. 16, 1921.

478 *A journalist who knew Wilson well: PWW,* 68:594.

478 *"The Document":* PWW, 67:320n1. Among his collaborators were Bernard Baruch, Louis D. Brandeis, Frank Cobb of the *New York World*, and Bainbridge Colby.

478 *By the spring of 1922:* Blum, *Joe Tumulty and the Wilson Era*, 262–64.

479 *a letter to* The New York Times: PWW, 68:14.

479 *no one else in her memoir:* EBW, *My Memoir*, 332–39.

479 *Decades later:* Interview with Farrington R. Carpenter, Henry W. Bragdon Papers.

479 *Whiskey was hard to get:* PWW, 67:312; 68:167.

479 *As Wilson's secret pursuit:* PWW, 67:585–86.

479 *In a June talk with Homer Cummings:* PWW, 68:88–92.

480 *"Mr. Wilson was very happy":* New York Times, Nov. 12, 1911. Other details are from the *Chicago Tribune, Hartford Courant,* and *Washington Post* of the same date.

480 *when Georges Clemenceau paid him a visit:* EBW, *My Memoir*, 341; Bonsal, *Unfinished Business*, 283.

480 *Mr. Wilson's happiness evaporated:* PWW, 68:235n.

480 *Official Washington had interpreted:* Chicago Tribune, Nov. 12, 1922.

480 *Wilson complained to a friend:* PWW, 68:234-35.

480 *"political persecution":* PWW, 68:238.

480 *He told Grayson:* PWW, 68:250–52.

481 *In June 1923:* PWW, 68:375–83. My assumption that Grayson spoke to Oulahan for the article rests on the fact that a number of Oulahan's comments on Wilson's health also appear in Grayson's diary.

481 *To the evidence:* Murray, *The Harding Era*, 438–51; *Washington Post*, June 20, 1923.

482 *A few days later the Wilsons:* PWW, 68:398, 400–402; CTG to Altrude Gordon Grayson, Aug. 6, 1923, CTG Papers.

482 *She wrote her "Dearest One":* PWW, 68:408–17.

482 *Pecking away one-handed:* PWW, 68:412–13.

482 *He was astounded:* CTG to Altrude Gordon Grayson, Sept. 4, 1923, CTG Papers.

483 *Edith came home refreshed:* Phyllis Lee Levin, *Edith and Woodrow*, 488.

483 *Apparently oblivious:* PWW, 68:425–26; New-York Tribune, Sept. 19, 1923.

483 *"Physically he was a wreck":* Lloyd George, *Memoirs of the Peace Confrerence*, 1:154–55.

483 YOUR SPEECH: PWW, 68:471.

483 *In a sense:* PWW, 68:466–67; Berg, *Wilson*, 732.

484 *Deeply moved:* PWW, 68:467–71; *Washington Post* and *New-York Tribune*, Nov. 12, 1923.

484 *Wilson was dying:* PWW, 68:594.

484 *"I must get well and help":* PWW, 68:502.

484 *"The world is run by ideals":* Raymond B. Fosdick, "Before Wilson Died," *Survey* 51 (Feb. 15, 1924): 495.

484 *In January he agreed:* PWW, 68:531–32; *Chicago Tribune,* Jan. 17, 1924; *Baltimore Sun,* Jan. 18, 1924.

484 *But a few days later:* PWW, 68:535–43.

485 *At 11:20 a.m.:* PWW, 68:567.

485 *Joe Tumulty:* Blum, *Joe Tumulty and the Wilson Era,* 264; EBW, *My Memoir,* 339.

485 *Colonel House:* Neu, *Colonel House,* 456–57.

485 *When Edith learned:* PWW, 68:574.

485 *Wilson was laid out:* Berg, *Wilson,* 740–41.

485 *The cortege set off:* PWW, 68:339–40.

485 *After the brief Episcopal Ritual:* Berg, *Wilson,* 742.

EPILOGUE: *The Wilsonian Century*

487 *A few weeks:* PWW, 51:339–41, 391.

487 *Senator J. William Fulbright:* Thomas J. Knock, "Playing for a Hundred Years Hence," in G. John Ikenberry, ed., *The Crisis of American Foreign Policy: Wilsonianism in the Twenty-first Century* (Princeton: Princeton University Press, 2009), 35.

488 *Even Harding:* F. P. Walters, *A History of the League of Nations* (New York: Oxford University Press, 1952), 1:350; Ronald Allen Goldberg, *America in the Twenties* (Syracuse: Syracuse University Press, 2003), 68.

489 *But President Franklin D. Roosevelt:* Joseph Lelyveld, *His Final Battle* (New York: Alfred A. Knopf, 2016), 57–71.

489 *And when he concluded:* Strobe Talbott, *The Great Experiment* (New York: Simon & Schuster, 2008), 175, 181, 226–27.

489 *The new president, Harry S. Truman:* "Address in San Francisco at the Closing Session of the United Nations Conference," June 26, 1945, http://www.presidency.ucsb.edu/ws/?pid=12188, accessed Dec. 22, 2017.

489 *Six weeks later:* Talbott, *The Great Experiment,* 194–96.

490 *Nixon was a realist:* Henry A. Kissinger, *Diplomacy* (New York: Simon & Schuster, 1994), 704–6.

490 *In a 1969 address:* Richard Nixon, "Address to the Nation on the War in Vietnam," Nov. 3, 1969, http://www.presidency.ucsb.edu/ws/?pid=2303, accessed Dec. 22, 2017.

490 *On another occasion:* Richard Nixon, "Remarks at the Dedication of the Woodrow Wilson International Center for Scholars," Feb. 18, 1971, www.presidency.ucsb.edu/ws/index.php?pid-3313, accessed Dec. 22, 2017.

491 *Wilson's ghost:* John Judis, *The Folly of Empire* (New York: Scribner, 2004), 152–54.

491 *As Strobe Talbott:* Talbott, *The Great Experiment,* 143–44.

491 *Clinton practiced:* William J. Clinton, "Remarks on United States Foreign Policy in San Francisco," Feb. 26, 1999, http://www.presidency.ucsb.edu /ws/?pid=57170, accessed Dec. 22, 2017.

492 *"Either you are with us":* George W. Bush, "Address before a Joint Session of the Congress on the United States Response to the Terrorist Attacks of September 11," Sept. 20, 2001, http://www.presidency.ucsb.edu/ws/?pid=64731, accessed Dec. 29, 2017.

492 *"God's gift to humanity":* George W. Bush, "Address before a Joint Session of the Congress on the State of the Union," Jan. 28, 2003, http://www.presidency .ucsb.edu/ws/?pid=29645, accessed Dec. 28, 2017.

492 *"finish the job":* Tony Smith, *Why Wilson Matters* (Princeton: Princeton University Press, 2017), 245.

492 *Reflecting on the catastrophes:* Ibid., 249.

492 *Barack Obama:* Jeffrey Goldberg, "The Obama Doctrine," https://www.the atlantic.com/magazine/archive/2016/04/the-obama-doctrine/471525/, accessed Dec. 26, 2017.

493 *In its 2017 survey:* https://freedomhouse.org/report/freedom-world/freedom -world-2017, accessed Dec. 22, 2017.

Bibliography

Adler, Selig. *The Uncertain Giant*. New York: Macmillan, 1965.

Ambrosius, Lloyd E. *Wilsonian Statecraft: Theory and Practice of Liberal Internationalism During World War I*. Wilmington, Del.: SR Books, 1991.

_____. *Wilsonianism: Woodrow Wilson and His Legacy in American Foreign Relations*. New York: Palgrave Macmillan, 2002.

_____. *Woodrow Wilson and the American Diplomatic Tradition: The Treaty Fight in Perspective*. Cambridge, England: Cambridge University Press, 1987.

American Battle Monuments Commission. *A Guide to the American Battle Fields in Europe*. Washington, D.C.: U.S. Government Printing Office, 1927.

_____. *American Armies and Battlefields in Europe*. Washington, D.C.: U.S. Government Printing Office, 1938.

Axelrod, Alan. *Selling the Great War: The Making of American Propaganda*. New York: Palgrave Macmillan, 2009.

Axson, Stockton. *"Brother Woodrow": A Memoir of Woodrow Wilson*. Edited by Arthur S. Link. Princeton: Princeton University Press, 1993.

Bailey, Thomas A. *A Diplomatic History of the American People*. New York: Appleton-Century-Crofts, 1958.

_____. *Presidential Greatness: The Image and the Man from George Washington to the Present*. New York: Appleton-Century-Crofts, 1967.

_____. *Wilson and the Peacemakers*. 2 vols., *Woodrow Wilson and the Lost Peace* and *Woodrow Wilson and the Great Betrayal*. New York: Macmillan, 1947.

Baker, Newton D. *Frontiers of Freedom*. New York: George H. Doran Company, 1918.

Baker, Ray Stannard. *American Chronicle: The Autobiography of Ray Stannard Baker.* New York: Charles Scribner's Sons, 1945.

———. *What Wilson Did at Paris.* Garden City: Doubleday, Page, 1919.

———. *Woodrow Wilson and World Settlement.* 3 vols. Garden City: Doubleday, Page, 1922.

Baker, Ray Stannard. *Woodrow Wilson: Life and Letters.* Potomac edition. 8 vols.: Vol. 1, *Youth*; Vol. 2, *Princeton*; Vol. 3, *Governor, 1910–1913*; Vol. 4, *President, 1913–1914*; Vol. 5, *Neutrality, 1914–1915*; Vol. 6, *Facing War, 1915–1917*; Vol. 7, *War Leader, 1917–1918*; Vol. 8, *Armistice, March 1 to November 11, 1918.* New York: Charles Scribner's Sons, 1946.

Balfour, Michael. *The Kaiser and His Times.* New York: W. W. Norton, 1972.

Barbeau, Arthur E., and Florette Henri. *The Unknown Soldiers: African-American Troops in World War I.* New York: Da Capo, 1996.

Barnes, Harper. *Never Been a Time: The 1917 Race Riot That Sparked the Civil Rights Movement.* New York: Walker, 2008.

Baruch, Bernard M. *American Industry in the War: A Report of the War Industries Board.* New York: Prentice Hall, 1941.

———. *Baruch: My Own Story.* New York: Pocket Books, 1958.

———. *Baruch: The Public Years.* New York: Pocket Books, 1962.

Beaver, Daniel R. *Newton D. Baker and the American War Effort, 1917–1919.* Lincoln: University of Nebraska Press, 1966.

Bell, H. C. F. *Woodrow Wilson and the People.* Garden City: Doubleday, Doran, 1945.

Bernstorff, Count. *My Three Years in America.* New York: Charles Scribner's Sons, 1920.

Berg, A. Scott. *Wilson.* New York: G. P. Putnam's Sons, 2013.

Blum, John M. *Joe Tumulty and the Wilson Era.* Boston: Houghton Mifflin, 1951.

———. *Woodrow Wilson and the Politics of Morality.* Boston: Little, Brown, 1956.

Bonsal, Stephen. *Suitors and Suppliants: The Little Nations at Versailles.* New York: Prentice Hall, 1946.

———. *Unfinished Business.* Garden City: Doubleday, Doran, 1944.

Bragdon, Henry W. *Woodrow Wilson: The Academic Years.* Cambridge, Mass.: Harvard University Press, 1967.

Bryan, William Jennings. *Philadelphia: The Memoirs of William Jennings Bryan.* Edited by Mary Bryan. John C. Winston, 1925.

———. *A Tale of Two Conventions.* New York: Funk & Wagnalls, 1912.

Buehrig, Edward H., *Woodrow Wilson and the Balance of Power.* Gloucester: Peter Smith, 1968.

Buehrig, Edward H., ed. *Wilson's Foreign Policy in Perspective.* Bloomington: Indiana University Press, 1957.

Bullard, Robert Lee. *Personalities and Reminiscences of the War.* Garden City: Doubleday, Page, 1925.

Bullitt, William C. *The Bullitt Mission to Russia: Testimony Before the Committee on Foreign Relations, United States Senate.* New York: B. W. Huebsch, 1919.

Calhoun, Frederick S. *Power and Principle: Armed Intervention in Wilsonian Foreign Policy.* Kent: Kent State University Press, 1986.

_____. *Uses of Force and Wilsonian Foreign Policy.* Kent: Kent State University Press, 1993.

Capozzola, Christopher. *Uncle Sam Wants You: World War I and the Making of the Modern American Citizen.* New York: Oxford University Press, 2008.

Carr, Edward Hallett. *The Twenty Years' Crisis, 1919–1939.* New York: HarperPerennial, 2001.

Carroll, James Robert. *The Real Woodrow Wilson: An Interview with Arthur S. Link, Editor of the Wilson Papers.* Bennington, Vt.: Images from the Past, 2001.

Cecil, Hugh, and Peter H. Liddle, eds. *Facing Armageddon: The First World War Experience.* London: Leo Cooper, 1996.

Chambers, John Whiteclay, II. *To Raise an Army: The Draft Comes to Modern America.* New York: Macmillan, 1987.

Chernow, Ron. *The House of Morgan: An American Banking Dynasty and the Rise of Modern Finance.* New York: Atlantic Monthly Press, 1990.

Chickering, Roger. *Imperial Germany and the Great War, 1914–1918.* Cambridge, England: Cambridge University Press, 1998.

Churchill, Winston S. *The World Crisis, 1911–1918.* New York: Free Press, 2005.

Clarkson, Grosvenor B. *Industrial America in the World War: The Strategy Behind the Line, 1917–1918.* Boston: Houghton Mifflin, 1923.

Claude, Inis L., Jr. *Swords into Plowshares: The Problems and Progress of International Organization.* New York: Random House, 1969.

Clemenceau, Georges. *Grandeur and Misery of Victory.* New York: Harcourt, Brace, 1930.

Clements, Kendrick A. *The Presidency of Woodrow Wilson.* Lawrence: University Press of Kansas, 1992.

_____. *Woodrow Wilson, World Statesman.* Chicago: Ivan R. Dee, 1999.

Cohen, Warren I. *The American Revisionists: The Lessons of Intervention in World War I.* Chicago: University of Chicago Press, 1967.

Coletta, Paolo E. *William Jennings Bryan.* 3 vols. Lincoln: University of Nebraska Press, 1964–1970.

Cooper, John Milton, Jr. *Breaking the Heart of the World.* Cambridge, England: Cambridge University Press, 2001.

_____. *Walter Hines Page: The Southerner as American, 1855–1918.* Chapel Hill: University of North Carolina Press, 1977.

_____. *The Warrior and the Priest: Woodrow Wilson and Theodore Roosevelt.* Cambridge: Harvard University Press, 1983.

_____. *Woodrow Wilson: A Biography.* New York: Alfred A. Knopf, 2009.

Cooper, John Milton, Jr., ed. *Reconsidering Woodrow Wilson: Progressivism, Internationalism, War, and Peace.* Washington, D.C.: Woodrow Wilson Center Press, 2008.

Cranston, Alan. *The Killing of the Peace.* New York: Viking, 1960.

Creel, George. *Complete Report of the Chairman of the Committee on Public Information, 1917:1918:1919.* Washington, D.C.: U.S. Government Printing Office, 1920.

————. *How We Advertised America: The First Telling of the Amazing Story of the Committee on Public Information That Carried the Gospel of Americanism to Every Corner of the Globe*. London: Forgotten Books, 2012.

————. *Rebel at Large: Recollections of Fifty Crowded Years*. New York: G. P. Putnam's Sons, 1947.

————. *The War, the World and Wilson*. New York: Harper & Brothers, 1920.

————. *Wilson and the Issues*. New York: Century, 1916.

Cronon, E. David, ed. *The Cabinet Diaries of Josephus Daniels, 1913–1921*. Lincoln: University of Nebraska Press, 1963.

Curry, George. "Woodrow Wilson, Jan Smuts and the Versailles Settlement." *American Historical Review* 66, no. 4 (1961): 968–86.

Daniels, Jonathan. *The End of Innocence*. Philadelphia: J. B. Lippincott, 1954.

Daniels, Josephus. *The Life of Woodrow Wilson, 1856–1924*. Philadelphia: John C. Winston, 1924.

————. *The Wilson Era*. 2 vols. Chapel Hill: University of North Carolina Press, 1944–1946.

Davis, Donald E., and Eugene P. Trani. *The First Cold War: The Legacy of Woodrow Wilson in U.S.-Soviet Relations*. Columbia: University of Missouri Press, 2002.

Davis, Julia, and Dolores A. Fleming, eds. *The Ambassadorial Diary of John W. Davis*. Morgantown: West Virginia University Press, 1993.

Devlin, Patrick. *Too Proud to Fight: Woodrow Wilson's Neutrality*. New York: Oxford University Press, 1974.

Dillon, E. J. *The Inside Story of the Peace Conference*. New York: Harper & Brothers, 1920.

Doerries, Reinhard R. *Imperial Challenge: Ambassador Count Bernstorff and German-American Relations, 1908–1917*. Chapel Hill: University of North Carolina Press, 1989.

Dos Passos, John. *Mr. Wilson's War: The Story of American Participation in World War I*. New York: Doubleday, 1962.

Dumba, Konstantin Theodor. *Memoirs of a Diplomat*. Translated by Ian F. D. Morrow. Boston: Little, Brown, 1932.

Duroselle, Jean-Baptiste. *Clemenceau*. Paris: France Loisirs, 1988.

Egerton, George W. "Britain and 'The Great Betrayal': Anglo-American Relations and the Struggle for United States Ratification of the Treaty of Versailles, 1919–1920." *The Historical Journal* 21 (1978): 885–911.

————. *Great Britain and the Creation of the League of Nations*. Chapel Hill: University of North Carolina Press, 1978.

————. "The Lloyd George Government and the Creation of the League of Nations," *American Historical Review*, no. 79 , no. 2 (1974): 419–44.

Eisenhower, John S. D., with Joanne T. Eisenhower. *Yanks: The Epic Story of the American Army in World War I*. New York: Free Press, 2001.

Elliott, Margaret Axson. *My Aunt Louisa and Woodrow Wilson*. Chapel Hill: University of North Carolina Press, 1944.

Ferguson, Niall. *The Pity of War.* New York: Basic Books, 1999.

Ferrell, Robert H. *Woodrow Wilson and World War I, 1917–1921.* New York: Harper & Row, 1985.

Figes, Orlando. *A People's Tragedy: The Russian Revolution, 1891–1924.* New York: Penguin, 1996.

Fischer, Fritz. *Germany's Aims in the First World War.* New York: W. W. Norton, 1967.

Fleming, Denna Frank. *The United States and the League of Nations, 1918–1920.* New York: G. P. Putnam's Sons, 1932.

Floto, Inga. *Colonel House in Paris: A Study of American Policy at the Paris Peace Conference 1919.* Aarhus, Denmark: Universitetsforlaget I Aarhus, 1973.

Fowler, William B. *British-American Relations, 1917–1918: The Role of Sir William Wiseman.* Princeton, N.J.: Princeton University Press, 1969.

Freidel, Frank. *Franklin D. Roosevelt: The Apprenticeship.* Boston: Little, Brown, 1952.

Freud, Sigmund, and William C. Bullitt. *Thomas Woodrow Wilson: A Psychological Study.* Boston: Houghton Mifflin, 1966.

Fromkin, David. *A Peace to End All Peace: The Fall of the Ottoman Empire and the Creation of the Modern Middle East.* New York: Avon, 1989.

Gardner, Lloyd C. *Safe for Democracy: The Anglo-American Response to Revolution, 1913–1923.* New York: Oxford University Press, 1984.

Garraty, John A. *Henry Cabot Lodge.* New York: Alfred A. Knopf, 1965.

Gelfand, Lawrence E. *The Inquiry: American Preparations for Peace, 1917–1919.* Westport, Conn.: Greenwood, 1976.

George, Alexander L., and Juliette L. George. *Woodrow Wilson and Colonel House: A Personality Study.* New York: Dover, 1964.

Gerard, James W. *Face to Face with Kaiserism.* New York: George H. Doran Company, 1918.

_____. *My Four Years in Germany.* New York: Grosset & Dunlap, 1917.

Gerson, Louis L. *Woodrow Wilson and the Rebirth of Poland, 1914–1920: A Study of the Influence on American Policy of Minority Groups of Foreign Origin.* New Haven: Yale University Press, 1953.

[Gilbert, Clinton W.] *The Mirrors of Washington.* New York: G. P. Putnam's Sons, 1921.

Gilbert, Martin. *Atlas of World War I.* New York: Oxford University Press, 1994.

_____. *The First World War: A Complete History.* New York: Henry Holt, 1994.

Gilbert, Martin, ed. *Lloyd George.* Englewood Cliffs: Prentice Hall, 1968.

Görlitz, Walter, ed. *The Kaiser and His Court: The Diaries, Note Books and Letters of Admiral Georg Alexander von Müller, Chief of the Naval Cabinet, 1914–1918.* New York: Harcourt, Brace & World, 1959.

Graebner, Norman A. *Ideas and Diplomacy: Readings in the Intellectual Tradition of American Foreign Policy.* New York: Oxford University Press, 1964.

Grant, James. *Bernard Baruch: The Adventures of a Wall Street Legend.* New York: Simon & Schuster, 1976.

Grayson, Cary T. *Woodrow Wilson: An Intimate Memoir.* New York: Holt, Rinehart & Winston, 1960.

Grew, Joseph C. *Turbulent Era: A Record of Forty Years in the U.S. Diplomatic Service.* Edited by Walter Johnson. 2 vols. London: Hammond, Hammond & Co., 1953.

Grey, Edward. (Viscount Grey of Fallodon). *Twenty-five Years, 1892–1916.* 2 vols. London: Frederick A. Stokes, 1953.

Gwynn, Stephen, ed. *The Letters and Friendships of Sir Cecil Spring Rice: A Record.* 2 vols. Boston: Houghton Mifflin, 1929.

Hagedorn, Herman, ed., *The Works of Theodore Roosevelt.* 24 vols. New York: Charles Scribner's Sons, 1926.

Hale, William Bayard. *Woodrow Wilson: The Story of His Life.* Garden City: Doubleday, Page, 1912.

Haskins, Charles Homer, and Robert Howard Lord. *Some Problems of the Peace Conference.* Cambridge: Harvard University Press, 1920.

Hatch, Alden. *First Lady Extraordinary.* New York: Dodd, Mead, 1961.

Heaton, John L. *Cobb of "The World": A Leader in Liberalism.* New York: E. P. Dutton, 1924.

Heckscher, August. *Woodrow Wilson.* New York: Scribner, 1991.

Hendrick, Burton J. *The Life and Letters of Walter H. Page.* 3 vols. Garden City: Doubleday, Page, 1925.

Herring, George C. *From Colony to Superpower: U.S. Foreign Relations Since 1776.* New York: Oxford University Press, 2008.

Herwig, Holger H. *The First World War: Germany and Austria-Hungary, 1914–1918.* London: Arnold, 1997.

Hilderbrand, Robert C. *Power and the People: Executive Management of Public Opinion in Foreign Affairs, 1897–1921.* Chapel Hill: University of North Carolina Press, 1981.

Hodgson, Godfrey. *Woodrow Wilson's Right Hand: The Life of Colonel Edward M. House.* New Haven: Yale University Press, 2006.

Hoffman, Donald. *Mark Twain in Paradise: His Voyages to Bermuda.* Columbia: University of Missouri Press, 2006.

Hogan, J. Michael. *Woodrow Wilson's Western Tour: Rhetoric, Public Opinion, and the League of Nations.* College Station: Texas A&M University Press, 2006.

Hoover, Herbert. *The Ordeal of Woodrow Wilson.* New York: McGraw-Hill, 1958.

Hoover, Irwin Hood (Ike). *Forty-two Years in the White House.* Boston: Houghton Mifflin, 1934.

House, Edward Mandell, and Charles Seymour, eds. *What Really Happened at Paris; The Story of the Peace Conference, 1918–1919, by American Delegates.* New York: Charles Scribner's Sons, 1921.

Houston, David F. *Eight Years with Wilson's Cabinet.* 2 vols. Garden City: Doubleday, Page, 1926.

Jensen, Joan M. *The Price of Vigilance.* Chicago: Rand McNally, 1968.

Jessup, Philip C. *Elihu Root.* 2 vols. Hamden, Conn.: Archon, 1964.

Johnson, Claudius O. *Borah of Idaho.* New York: Longmans, Green, 1936.

Johnson, Walter, ed. *Selected Letters of William Allen White.* New York: Henry Holt, 1947.

Jusserand, Jean Jules. *Le Sentiment Américain pendant la Guerre,* Paris: Payot, 1931.

Katz, Friedrich. *The Secret War in Mexico: Europe, The United States and the Mexican Revolution.* Chicago: University of Chicago Press, 1981.

Kazin, Michael. *A Godly Hero: The Life of William Jennings Bryan.* New York: Alfred A. Knopf, 2006.

Keegan, John. *The First World War.* New York: Alfred A. Knopf, 1999.

Kennan, George F. *American Diplomacy, 1900–1950.* Chicago: University of Chicago Press, 1951.

_____. *The Decision to Intervene.* Princeton: Princeton University Press, 1958.

_____. *Russia Leaves the War.* Princeton: Princeton University Press, 1956.

Kennedy, David M. *Over Here: The First World War and American Society.* New York: Oxford University Press, 2004.

Kerney, James. *The Political Education of Woodrow Wilson.* New York: The Century Co., 1926.

Keynes, John Maynard. *The Economic Consequences of the Peace.* New York: Harcourt, Brace & Howe, 1920.

_____. *A Revision of the Treaty, Being a Sequel to the Economic Consequences of the Peace.* London: Macmillan, 1922.

Kissinger, Henry. *Diplomacy.* New York: Simon & Schuster, 1994.

Knight, Alan. *The Mexican Revolution.* 2 vols. Cambridge, England: Cambridge University Press, 1986, 1990.

Knock, Thomas J. *To End All Wars: Woodrow Wilson and the Quest for a New World Order.* Princeton: Princeton University Press, 1992.

Kohut, Thomas A. *Wilhelm II and the Germans: A Study in Leadership.* New York: Oxford University Press, 1991.

Kraig, Robert Alexander. *Woodrow Wilson and the Lost World of the Oratorical Statesman.* College Station: Texas A&M University Press, 2004.

La Follette, Belle Case, and Fola La Follette. *Robert M. La Follette.* 2 vols. New York: Macmillan, 1953.

Lane, Anne Wintermute, and Louise Herrick Wall, eds. *Letters of Franklin K. Lane.* Boston: Houghton Mifflin, 1922.

Lansing, Robert. *The Big Four and Others of the Peace Conference.* Boston: Houghton Mifflin, 1921.

_____. *The Peace Negotiations: A Personal Narrative.* Boston: Houghton Mifflin, 1921.

_____. *War Memoirs of Robert Lansing, Secretary of State.* Indianapolis: Bobbs-Merrill, 1935.

Lasswell, Harold D. *Propaganda Technique in the World War.* Mansfield, Centre, Conn.: Martino Publishing, 2013.

Lawrence, David. *The True Story of Woodrow Wilson.* New York: George H. Doran, 1924.

Le Bon, Gustave. *The World Unbalanced.* New York: Longmans, Green, 1924.

Levin, N. Gordon, Jr. *Woodrow Wilson and World Politics: America's Response to War and Revolution.* New York: Oxford University Press, 1968.

Levin, Phyllis Lee. *Edith and Woodrow: The Wilson White House.* New York: Scribner, 2001.

Lewis, David Levering. *W. E. B. Du Bois: Biography of a Race, 1868–1919.* New York: Henry Holt, 1993.

Li, Tien-Yi. *Woodrow Wilson's China Policy, 1913–1917.* New York: Twayne, 1969.

Link, Arthur S. *The Higher Realism of Woodrow Wilson and Other Essays.* Nashville: Vanderbilt University Press, 1971.

––––––. "That Cobb Interview." *Journal of American History* 72 (1985): 7–17.

––––––. *Wilson: Campaigns for Progressivism and Peace, 1916–1917.* Princeton: Princeton University Press, 1965.

––––––. *Wilson: Confusions and Crises, 1915–1916.* Princeton: Princeton University Press, 1964.

––––––. *Wilson: The New Freedom.* Princeton: Princeton University Press, 1956.

––––––. *Wilson: The Road to the White House.* Princeton: Princeton University Press, 1947.

––––––. *Wilson: The Struggle for Neutrality.* Princeton: Princeton University Press, 1960.

––––––. *Woodrow Wilson: Revolution, War, and Peace.* Arlington House, Ill.: Harlan Davidson, 1979.

Link, Arthur S., ed. *The Papers of Woodrow Wilson.* 69 vols. Princeton: Princeton University Press, 1966–1994.

––––––. *Woodrow Wilson and a Revolutionary World, 1913–1921.* Chapel Hill: University of North Carolina Press, 1982.

Livermore, Seward W. *Politics Is Adjourned: Woodrow Wilson and the War Congress, 1916–1918.* Middletown, Conn.: Wesleyan University Press, 1966.

Lloyd George, David. *Memoirs of the Peace Conference.* 2 vols. New Haven: Yale University Press, 1939.

––––––. *War Memoirs.* 8 vols. London: I. Nicholson & Watson, 1933–1936.

Lodge, Henry Cabot. *The Senate and the League of Nations.* New York: Charles Scribner's Sons, 1925.

––––––. *War Addresses, 1915–1917.* Boston: Houghton Mifflin, 1917.

MacMillan, Margaret. *Paris 1919: Six Months That Changed the World.* New York: Random House, 2001.

Magee, Malcolm D. *What the World Should Be: Woodrow Wilson and the Crafting of a Faith-Based Foreign Policy.* Waco, Tex.: Baylor University Press, 2008.

Manela, Erez. *The Wilsonian Moment: Self-Determination and the International Origins of Anticolonial Nationalism.* New York: Oxford University Press, 2007.

Mantoux, Étienne. *The Carthaginian Peace, or The Economic Consequences of Mr. Keynes.* London: Oxford University Press, 1946.

Mantoux, Paul. *The Deliberations of the Council of Four (March 24–June 28, 1919): Notes of the Official Interpreter.* Translated and edited by Arthur S. Link. Princeton, N.J.: Princeton University Press, 1992. 2 vols.

March, Peyton C. *The Nation at War.* Garden City: Doubleday, Doran, 1932.

Marshall, George C. *Memoirs of My Services in the World War, 1917–1918.* Boston: Houghton Mifflin, 1976.

Marshall, S. L. A. *World War I.* Boston: Houghton Mifflin, 1987.

Marshall, Thomas R. *Recollections of Thomas R. Marshall, Vice-President and Hoosier Philosopher: A Hoosier Salad.* Indianapolis: Bobbs-Merrill, 1925.

Maurice, Frederick. *The Last Four Months: The End of the War in the West.* New York: Cassell & Company, 1921.

May, Ernest W. *The World War and American Isolation, 1914–1917.* Cambridge: Harvard University Press, 1959.

Mayer, Arno J. *Political Origins of the New Diplomacy, 1917–1918.* New Haven: Yale University Press, 1959.

_____. *Politics and Diplomacy of Peacemaking: Containment and Counterrevolution at Versailles, 1918–1919.* New York: Vintage, 1967.

_____. *Wilson vs. Lenin: Political Origins of the New Diplomacy, 1917–1918.* Cleveland: Meridian, 1969.

Maynard, William Barksdale. *Woodrow Wilson: Princeton to the Presidency.* New Haven: Yale University Press, 2008.

McAdoo, Eleanor Wilson. *The Woodrow Wilsons.* New York: Macmillan, 1937.

McAdoo, Eleanor Wilson, ed. *The Priceless Gift: The Love Letters of Woodrow Wilson and Ellen Axson Wilson.* New York: McGraw-Hill, 1962.

McAdoo, William Gibbs. *Crowded Years: The Reminiscences of William G. McAdoo.* Boston: Houghton Mifflin, 1931.

McCombs, William. *Making Woodrow Wilson President.* Edited by Louis J. Lang. New York: Fairview, 1921.

McKenna, Marian C. *Borah.* Ann Arbor: University of Michigan Press, 1961.

Mervin, David. "Henry Cabot Lodge and the League of Nations." *Journal of American Studies* 4 (1970): 201–14.

Miller, David Hunter. *My Diary at the Conference at Paris.* 2 vols. New York: Appeal Printing Company, 1924.

Miller, Kristie. *Ellen and Edith.* Lawrence: University Press of Kansas, 2010.

Millis, Walter. *Road to War: America, 1914–1917.* Boston: Houghton Mifflin, 1935.

Morison, Elting, and John M. Blum, eds. *Letters of Theodore Roosevelt.* 8 vols. Cambridge: Harvard University Press, 1951–1954.

Morrow, John H., Jr. *The Great War: An Imperial History.* New York: Routledge, 2004.

Murray, Robert K. *The Harding Era.* Minneapolis: University of Minnesota Press, 1969.

Myers, William Starr, ed. *Woodrow Wilson: Some Princeton Memories.* Princeton: Princeton University Press, 1946.

Neiberg, Michael S. *Fighting the Great War: A Global History.* Cambridge: Harvard University Press, 2005.

Neu, Charles E. *Colonel House: A Biography of Woodrow Wilson's Silent Partner.* New York: Oxford University Press, 2015.

Nevins, Allan. *Henry White: Thirty Years of American Diplomacy*. New York: Harper & Brothers, 1930.

Nicolson, Harold. *Peacemaking 1919*. New York: Grosset & Dunlap, 1965.

Ninkovich, Frank. *The Wilsonian Century: U.S. Foreign Policy Since 1900*. Chicago: University of Chicago Press, 1999.

Nitti, Francesco. *The Wreck of Europe*. Indianapolis: Bobbs-Merrill, 1922.

Nordholt, Jan Willem Schulte. *Woodrow Wilson: A Life for World Peace*. Berkeley: University of California Press, 1991.

Notter, Harley. *The Origins of the Foreign Policy of Woodrow Wilson*. New York: Russell & Russell, 1965.

O'Brien, Francis William, ed. *Two Peacemakers in Paris: The Hoover-Wilson Post-Armistice Letters, 1918–1920*. College Station: Texas A&M University Press, 1978.

Osgood, Robert Endicott. *Ideals and Self-Interest in America's Foreign Relations: The Great Transformation of the Twentieth Century*. Chicago: University of Chicago Press, 1953.

O'Shaughnessy, Edith. *A Diplomat's Wife in Mexico*. New York: Harper & Brothers, 1916.

O'Toole, Patricia. *When Trumpets Call: Theodore Roosevelt After the White House*. New York: Simon & Schuster, 2005.

Painter, Nell Irvin. *Standing at Armageddon: The United States, 1877–1919*. New York: W. W. Norton, 1987.

Palmer, Frederick. *Bliss, Peacemaker: The Life and Letters of Tasker H. Bliss*. New York: Dodd, Mead, 1934.

———. *Newton D. Baker: America at War*. 2 vols. New York: Dodd, Mead, 1931.

Pershing, John J. *My Experiences in the World War*. 2 vols. New York: Frederick A. Stokes, 1931.

Persico, Joseph E. *Eleventh Month, Eleventh Day, Eleventh Hour: Armistice Day, 1918: World War I and Its Violent Climax*. New York: Random House, 2004.

Peterson, H. C., and Gilbert C. Fite. *Opponents of War, 1917–1918*. Seattle: University of Washington Press, 1957.

Pipes, Richard. *A Concise History of the Russian Revolution*. New York: Vintage, 1995.

Preston, Diana. *Lusitania: An Epic Tragedy*. New York: Walker, 2002.

Pringle, Henry F. *The Life and Times of William Howard Taft: A Biography*. 2 vols. Hamden, Conn.: Archon, 1964.

Pusey, Merlo J. *Charles Evans Hughes*. 2 vols. New York: Macmillan, 1951.

Quirk, Robert. *An Affair of Honor: Woodrow Wilson and the Occupation of Veracruz*. Lexington: University of Kentucky Press, 1962.

Rabban, David M. *Free Speech in Its Forgotten Years*. Cambridge, England: Cambridge University Press, 1997.

Riddell, George Allardice. *Lord Riddell's Intimate Diary of the Peace Conference and After, 1918–1923*. New York: Reynal & Hitchcock, 1934.

Röhl, John C. G. *The Kaiser and His Court: Wilhelm II and the Government of Germany*. Cambridge, England: Cambridge University Press, 1987.

Roosevelt, Elliott, ed. *F.D.R.: His Personal Letters, 1905–1928.* New York: Duell, Sloan & Pearce, 1948.

Roosevelt, Theodore, and Henry Cabot Lodge. *Selections from the Correspondence of Theodore Roosevelt and Henry Cabot Lodge, 1884–1918.* Vol. 2. New York: Charles Scribner's Sons, 1925.

Ross, Stewart Halsey. *Propaganda for War: How the United States Was Conditioned to Fight the Great War of 1914–1918.* Joshua Tree, Calif.: Progressive Press, 2009.

Salvatore, Nick. *Eugene V. Debs: Citizen and Socialist.* Urbana: University of Illinois Press, 1982.

Sammons, Jeffrey T., and John H. Morrow, Jr. *Harlem's Rattlers and the Great War: The Undaunted 369th Regiment and the African American Quest for Equality.* Lawrence: University Press of Kansas, 2014.

Saunders, Frances Wright. *Ellen Axson Wilson.* Chapel Hill: University of North Carolina Press, 1985.

Saunders, Robert M. *In Search of Woodrow Wilson: Beliefs and Behavior.* Westport, Conn.: Greenwood, 1998.

Schaffer, Ronald. *America in the Great War: The Rise of the Welfare State.* New York: Oxford University Press, 1991.

Scheiber, Harry N. *The Wilson Administration and Civil Liberties, 1917–1921.* New Orleans: Quid Pro Books, 2013.

Scott, James Brown, ed. *The Declaration of London, February 26 1909: A Collection of Official Papers and Documents Relating to the International Naval Conference Held in London December, 1908—February, 1909.* New York: Oxford University Press, 1909.

Schwabe, Klaus. *Woodrow Wilson, Revolutionary Germany, and Peacemaking, 1918–1919: Missionary Diplomacy and the Relations of Power.* Chapel Hill: University of North Carolina Press, 1985.

Seale, William. *The President's House: A History.* Washington, D.C.: White House Historical Association, 1986.

Seymour, Charles. *American Diplomacy During the World War.* Hamden, Conn.: Archon, 1964.

———. *The Intimate Papers of Colonel House.* 4 vols. Boston: Houghton Mifflin, 1926–1928.

———. *Letters from the Paris Peace Conference.* New Haven: Yale University Press, 1965.

———. *Woodrow Wilson and the World War.* Charleston, S.C.: BiblioBazaar, 2012.

The Shantung Question: A Statement of China's Claim Together with Important Documents Submitted to the Peace Conference in Paris. San Francisco: Chinese Welfare Society in America, 1919.

Shotwell, James T. *At the Paris Peace Conference.* New York: Macmillan, 1937.

Sims, William Sowden. *The Victory at Sea.* Annapolis: Naval Institute Press, 1984.

Slayden, Ellen Maury. *Washington Wife: Journal of Ellen Maury Slayden from 1897–1919.* New York: Harper & Row, 1963.

Smith, Daniel M. *The Great Departure: The United States and World War I, 1914–1920.* New York: Alfred A. Knopf, 1965.

———. "National Interest and American Intervention 1917: An Historiographical Appraisal." *Journal of American History* 52 (1965–1966): 5–24.

———. *Robert Lansing and American Neutrality, 1914–1917.* Berkeley: University of California Press, 1958.

Smith, Ephraim Koch, Jr. "Robert Lansing and the Paris Peace Conference." PhD diss., Johns Hopkins University, 1972.

Smith, Gene. *When the Cheering Stopped: The Last Years of Woodrow Wilson.* New York: Time Inc., 1964.

Smith, Norma. *Jeannette Rankin: America's Conscience.* Helena: Montana Historical Society Press, 2002.

Smythe, Donald. *Pershing: General of the Armies.* Bloomington: Indiana University Press, 1986.

Sondhaus, Lawrence. *World War One: The Global Revolution.* Cambridge, England: Cambridge University Press, 2011.

Sparks, George F., ed. *A Many Colored Toga: The Diary of Henry Fountain Ashurst.* Tucson: University of Arizona Press, 1962.

Starling, Edmund W., and Thomas Sugrue. *Starling of the White House: The Story of the Man Whose Secret Service Detail Guarded Five Presidents from Woodrow Wilson to Franklin D. Roosevelt.* New York: Simon & Schuster, 1946.

Steed, Henry Wickham. *Through Thirty Years, 1892–1922: A Personal Narrative.* 2 vols. New York: Doubleday, Page, 1924.

Steel, Ronald. *Walter Lippmann and the American Century.* Boston: Little, Brown, 1980.

Steffens, Lincoln. *Autobiography.* New York: Harcourt Brace Jovanovich, 1931.

Stoddard, H. L. *As I Knew Them: Presidents and Politics from Grant to Coolidge.* New York: Harper & Brothers, 1927.

Stone, Ralph. *The Irreconcilables: The Fight Against the League of Nations.* Lexington: University Press of Kentucky, 1970.

Stout, Ralph, ed. *Roosevelt in the Kansas City Star.* Boston: Houghton Mifflin, 1921.

Strachan, Hew. *The First World War.* New York: Pocket Books, 2006.

Strum, Philippa. *Louis D. Brandeis, Justice for the People.* Cambridge, Mass.: Harvard University Press, 1984.

Sullivan, Mark. *The Great Adventure at Washington.* Garden City: Doubleday, Page, 1922.

Tarbell, Ida M. *All in the Day's Work: An Autobiography.* Boston: G. K. Hall, 1985.

Tardieu, André. *La Paix.* Paris: Payot, 1921.

———. *The Truth About the Treaty.* Indianapolis: Bobbs-Merrill, c. 1921.

Taylor, A. J. P. *The First World War: An Illustrated History.* New York: Berkley, 1972.

———. *Lloyd George: Rise and Fall.* Cambridge, England: Cambridge University Press, 1961.

Taylor, A.J.P., ed., *Lloyd George: A Diary by Frances Stevenson.* New York: Harper & Row, 1971.

Taylor, A. J. P., ed. *Lloyd George: Twelve Essays.* New York: Atheneum, 1971.

_____. *My Darling Pussy: The Letters of Lloyd George and Frances Stevenson, 1913–1914.* Weidenfeld & Nicolson, 1975.

Thelen, David P. *Robert M. La Follette and the Insurgent Spirit.* Madison: University of Wisconsin Press, 1985.

Thompson, Charles T. *The Peace Conference Day by Day: A Presidential Peace Pilgrimage Leading to the Discovery of Europe.* New York: Brentano's, 1920.

Thompson, Charles Willis. *Presidents I've Known and Two Near Presidents.* New York: Bobbs-Merrill, 1929.

Thompson, John A. "Woodrow Wilson and World War I: A Reappraisal." *Journal of American Studies* 19 (1985): 325–48.

Towne, Ruth Warner. *Senator William J. Stone and the Politics of Compromise.* Port Washington, N.Y.: Kennikat Press, 1979.

Trachtenberg, Marc. "Versailles After Sixty Years." *Journal of Contemporary History* 17 (1982): 487-506.

Trask, David F. *The AEF and Coalition Warmaking, 1917–1918.* Lawrence: University Press of Kansas, 1993.

_____. *General Tasker Howard Bliss and the "Sessions of the World," 1919.* Philadelphia: American Philosophical Society, 1966.

_____. *The United States in the Supreme War Council.* Middletown, Conn.: Wesleyan University Press, 1961.

_____. *Victory Without Peace: American Foreign Relations in the Twentieth Century.* New York: Wiley, 1968.

Tuchman, Barbara W. *The Guns of August.* New York: Macmillan, 1962.

_____. *The Proud Tower: A Portrait of the World Before the War, 1890–1914.* New York: Bantam, 1967.

_____. *The Zimmermann Telegram.* New York: Macmillan, 1958.

Tumulty, Joseph P. *Woodrow Wilson as I Know Him.* Garden City: Doubleday, Page, 1921.

United States Department of State. *Papers Relating to the Foreign Relations of the United States.* Washington, D.C.: U.S. Government Printing Office,

_____. *Papers Relating to the Foreign Relations of the United States, 1914.*

_____. *Papers Relating to the Foreign Relations of the United States, 1914. Supplement, The World War.*

_____. *Papers Relating to the Foreign Relations of the United States. The Lansing Papers, 1914–1920. 2 vols.*

_____. *Papers Relating to the Foreign Relations of the United States, 1915.*

_____. *Papers Relating to the Foreign Relations of the United States, 1915. Supplement, The World War.*

_____. *Papers Relating to the Foreign Relations of the United States, 1916.*

_____. *Papers Relating to the Foreign Relations of the United States, 1916. Supplement, The World War.*

_____. *Papers Relating to the Foreign Relations of the United States, 1917.*

————. *Papers Relating to the Foreign Relations of the United States, 1917. Supplement 1, The World War.*

————. *Papers Relating to the Foreign Relations of the United States, 1917. Supplement 2, The World War.* 2 vols.

————. *Papers Relating to the Foreign Relations of the United States, 1918.*

————. *Papers Relating to the Foreign Relations of the United States, 1918. Russia. 3 vols.*

————. *Papers Relating to the Foreign Relations of the United States, 1918. Supplement 1, The World War. 2 vols.*

————. *Papers Relating to the Foreign Relations of the United States, 1918. Supplement 2, The World War.*

————. *Papers Relating to the Foreign Relations of the United States, 1919. 2 vols.*

————. *Papers Relating to the Foreign Relations of the United States, 1919. The Paris Peace Conference. 13 vols.*

————. *Papers Relating to the Foreign Relations of the United States, 1919. Russia.*

————. *Papers Relating to the Foreign Relations of the United States, 1920. 3 vols.*

————. *Papers Relating to the Foreign Relations of the United States, 1921.* 2 vols.

Unterberger, Betty M. "Woodrow Wilson and the Bolsheviks: The 'Acid Test' of Soviet-American Relations." *Diplomatic History* 11 (1987): 71–90.

Villard, Oswald Garrison. *Fighting Years: Memoirs of a Liberal Editor.* New York: Harcourt, Brace, 1939.

Walworth, Arthur. *Wilson and His Peacemakers: American Diplomacy at the Paris Peace Conference, 1919.* New York: W. W. Norton, 1986.

————. *Woodrow Wilson.* 2 vols. New York: Longmans, Green, 1958.

Ward, Geoffrey C. *A First-Class Temperament.* New York: Harper & Row, 1989.

Watson, Alexander. *Ring of Steel: Germany and Austria-Hungary in World War I.* New York: Basic Books, 2014.

Watson, James E. *As I Knew Them: Memoirs of James E. Watson.* Indianapolis: Bobbs-Merrill, 1936.

Weinstein, Edwin A. *Woodrow Wilson: A Medical and Psychological Biography.* Princeton: Princeton University Press, 1981.

Welsome, Eileen. *The General and the Jaguar: Pershing's Hunt for Pancho Villa: A True Story of Revolution and Revenge.* New York: Little, Brown, 2006.

White, William Allen. *The Autobiography of William Allen White.* New York: Macmillan, 1946.

————. *Masks in a Pageant.* New York: Macmillan, 1929.

————. *Woodrow Wilson: The Man, His Times and His Task.* New York: Houghton Mifflin, 1925.

Widenor, William C. *Henry Cabot Lodge and the Search for an American Foreign Policy.* Berkeley: University of California Press, 1980.

Willert, Arthur. *The Road to Safety: A Study in Anglo-American Relations.* London: D. Verschoyle, 1952.

Williams, Chad L. *Torchbearers of Democracy: African American Soldiers in the World War I Era.* Chapel Hill: University of North Carolina Press, 2010.

Williams, William Appleman. *The Tragedy of American Diplomacy*. New York: Dell, 1962.

Wilson, Edith Bolling. *My Memoir*. Indianapolis: Bobbs-Merrill, 1939.

Wilson, Henry Lane. *Diplomatic Episodes in Mexico, Belgium and Chile*. Garden City: Doubleday, Page, 1927.

Wilson, Woodrow. *Congressional Government: A Study in American Politics*. Cleveland: Meridian Books, World Publishing Company, 1956.

_____. *Constitutional Government in the United States*. New York: Columbia University Press, 1964.

_____. *Division and Reunion: 1829–1889*. New York: Collier, 1961.

_____. *When a Man Comes to Himself*. New York: Harper & Brothers, 1915.

World Almanac and Encyclopedia 1913. New York: The Press Publishing Co. (New York World), 1913.

World Almanac and Encyclopedia 1914. New York: The Press Publishing Co. (New York World), 1914.

Young, Robert J. *An American by Degrees: The Extraordinary Lives of French Ambassador Jules Jusserand*. Montreal: McGill-Queen's University Press, 2009.

Illustration Credits

14. U.S. ambassador to Great Britain Walter Hines Page (*Library of Congress*)
15. The *Lusitania* (*Library of Congress*)
16. Edith Bolling Galt (*Library of Congress*)
17. German submarine (*Library of Congress*)
18. President Wilson (*Library of Congress*)
19. Pancho Villa (*Library of Congress*)
20. Flag Day Parade (*Library of Congress*)
21. 1916 Republican nominee Charles Evans Hughes (*Library of Congress*)
22. *At right:* Johann Heinrich von Bernstorff, German ambassador to Washington, departing after Wilson severed U.S. relations with the German government (*Library of Congress*)
23. American soldiers on the Western Front (*Library of Congress*)
24. General John J. Pershing, commander of the American Expeditionary Force (*Library of Congress*)
25. Herbert Hoover, director of the U.S. Food Administration (*Library of Congress*)
26. George Creel, chairman of the Committee on Public Information (*Seeley G. Mudd Library, Princeton University*)
27. Wounded American soldiers on the Western Front (*Library of Congress*)
28. President Wilson (*Seeley G. Mudd Library, Princeton University*)
29. *From left:* Woodrow and Edith Wilson, Colonel House (*Library of Congress*)
30. The French welcome Wilson to Paris (*University of Virginia*)
31. President Wilson departing for second voyage to France (*Barry P. Fitzgerald, Estate of Edward N. Jackson*)
32. American Commission to Negotiate Peace. *From left:* House, Lansing, Wilson, White, and Bliss (*Library of Congress*)
33. Woodrow and Edith Wilson at Versailles (*University of Virginia*)
34. Wilson on his last speaking tour (*Seeley G. Mudd Library, Princeton University*)
35. Wilson on his first automobile ride after the stroke (*Library of Congress*)
36. Senator Henry Cabot Lodge (*Library of Congress*)
37. Senator Gilbert M. Hitchcock (*Library of Congress*)
38. 1920 Republican nominee Warren G. Harding (*Library of Congress*)
39. Wilson with Armistice Day crowd at his home (*Library of Congress*)

PHOTO INSERTS

Seeley G. Mudd Library, Princeton University: 1, 2, 4, 24
Library of Congress: 3, 8, 9, 10, 11, 12, 13, 14, 15, 16, 17, 18, 19, 20, 21, 23, 25, 26, 27, 28, 29, 31, 33, 34, 35, 36, 38, 39, 40, 41, 42
University of Virginia: 5, 6, 22, 32
Barry P. Fitzgerald, Estate of Edward N. Jackson: 7
Courtesy Dick Lehr: 30
Woodrow Wilson Presidential Library: 37, 43

Index

Page numbers in *italics* refer to maps. Page numbers beginning with 501 refer to endnotes.

Index

Index

About the Author

Patricia O'Toole has written biographies of Theodore Roosevelt (*When Trumpets Call*) and Henry Adams (*The Five of Hearts*, which was a finalist for the Pulitzer Prize, the National Book Critics Circle Award, and the Los Angeles Times Book Prize). Her reporting and essays have been recognized with several honors, and as a professor in the School of the Arts at Columbia University, she received a Presidential Award for Outstanding Teaching. She is a fellow of the Society of American Historians and a member of the Presidential Historical Commission at the New-York Historical Society. A native Midwesterner, she now lives in Camden, Maine.